UNITED STATES
DEPARTMENT OF AGRICULTURE

NATIONAL AGRICULTURAL STATISTICS SERVICE

AGRICULTURAL STATISTICS 2020

UNITED STATES
GOVERNMENT PRINTING OFFICE
WASHINGTON: 2020

Agricultural Statistics 2020

Agricultural Statistics, 2020 was prepared under the direction of Jackie Ross, Secretatary of the Agricultural Statistics Board, National Agricultural Statistics Service. Vincent Davis, Carolyne Foster, and Tanya Ray were responsible for coordination and technical editorial work.

The USDA and NASS invite you to explore their information via their respective web sites: **http://www.usda.gov/** and **http://www.nass.usda.gov/.**

For information on NASS products you may call the **Agricultural Statistics Hotline, 1–800–727–9540 or send e-mail to nass@nass.usda.gov.**

We gratefully acknowledge the cooperation of the contributors to this publication. Source notes below each table credit the various Government agencies which collaborated in providing information.

CONTENTS

Introduction

Agricultural Statistics is published each year to meet the diverse need for a reliable reference book on agricultural production, supplies, consumption, facilities, costs, and returns. Its tables of annual data cover a wide variety of facts in forms suited to most common use. The historical series in this volume are generally of data from 2010 and later.

Inquiries concerning more current or more detailed data, past and prospective revisions, or the statistical methodology used should be addressed directly to the agency credited with preparing the table. Most of the data were prepared or compiled in the U.S. Department of Agriculture.

Foreign agricultural trade statistics include Government as well as non-Government shipments of merchandise from the United States and Territories to foreign countries. They do not include U.S. shipments to the U.S. Armed Forces abroad for their own use or shipments between the States and U.S. Territories. The world summaries of production and trade of major farm products are prepared by the U.S. Department of Agriculture from reports of the U.S. Department of Commerce, official statistics of foreign governments, other foreign source materials, reports of U.S. Agricultural Attache and Foreign Service Officers, and the result of office research.

Statistics presented in many of the tables represent actual counts of the items covered. Most of the statistics relating to foreign trade and to Government programs, such as numbers and amounts of loans made to farmers, and amounts of loans made by the Commodity Credit Corporation, etc., are data of this type. A large number of other tables, however, contain data that are estimates made by the Department of Agriculture.

The estimates for crops, livestock, and poultry made by the U.S. Department of Agriculture are prepared mainly to give timely current State and national totals and averages. They are based on data obtained by sample surveys of farmers and of people who do business with farmers. The survey data are supplemented by information from the Censuses of Agriculture taken every five years and check data from various sources. Being estimates, they are subject to revision as more data become available from commercial or Government sources. Unless otherwise indicated, the totals for the United States shown in the various tables on area, production, numbers, price, value, supplies, and disposition are based on official Department estimates. They exclude States for which no official estimates are compiled.

DEFINITIONS

''Value of production'' as applied to crops in the various tables, is derived by multiplying production by the estimated season average price received by farmers for that portion of the commodity actually sold. In the case of fruits and vegetables, quantities not harvested because of low prices or other economic factors are not included in value of production. The word ''Value'' is used in the inventory tables on livestock and poultry to mean value of the number of head on the inventory date. It is derived by multiplying the number of head by an estimated value per head as of the date.

The word ''Year'' (alone) in a column heading means calendar year unless otherwise indicated. ''Ton'' when used in this book without qualifications means a short ton of 2,000 pounds.

WEIGHTS, MEASURES, AND CONVERSION FACTORS

The following table on weights, measures, and conversion factors covers the most important agricultural products, or the products for which such information is most frequently asked of the U.S. Department of Agriculture. It does not cover all farm products nor all containers for any one product.

The information has been assembled from State schedules of legal weights, various sources within the U.S. Department of Agriculture, and other Government agencies. For most products, particularly fruits and vegetables, there is a considerable variation in weight per unit of volume due to differences in variety or size of commodity, condition and tightness of pack, degree to which the container is heaped, etc. Effort has been made to select the most representative and fairest average for each product. For those commodities which develop considerable shrinkage, the point of origin weight or weight at harvest has been used.

The approximate or average weights as given in this table do not necessarily have official standing as a basis for packing or as grounds for settling disputes. Not all of them are recognized as legal weight. The table was prepared chiefly for use of workers in the U.S. Department of Agriculture who have need of conversion factors in statistical computations.

WEIGHTS, MEASURES, AND CONVERSION FACTORS

Commodity	Unit[1]	Approximate net weight	
		U.S.	Metric
		Pounds	*Kilograms*
Alfalfa seed	Bushel	60	27.2
Apples	.....do	48	21.8
Do	Loose pack	38–42	17.2–19.1
Do	Tray pack	40–45	18.1–20.4
Do	Cell pack	37–41	16.8–18.6
Apricots	Lug (brentwood)[2]	24	10.9
Western	4–basket crate[3]	26	11.8
Artichokes:			
Globe	Ctn, by count and loose pack	20–25	9.1–11.3
Jerusalem	Bushel	50	22.7
Asparagus	Crate (NJ)	30	13.6
Avocados	Lug[4]	12–15	5.4–6.8
Bananas	Fiber folding box[5].	40	18.1
Barley	Bushel	48	21.8
Beans:			
Lima, dry	.....do	56	25.4
Other, dry	.....do	60	27.2
	Sack	100	45.4
Lima unshelled	Bushel	28–32	12.7–14.5
Snap	.....do	28–32	12.7–14.5
Beets:			
Topped	Sack	25	11.3
Bunched	½ crate 2 dz-bchs	36–40	16.3–18.1
Berries frozen pack:			
Without sugar	50–gal. barrel	380	172
3 + 1 pack	.....do	425	193
2 + 1 pack	.....do	450	204
Blackberries	12, ½-pint basket.	6	2.7
Bluegrass seed	Bushel	14–30	6.4–13.6
Broccoli	Wirebound crate.	20–25	9.1–11.3
Broomcorn (6 bales per ton)	Bale	333	151
Broomcorn seed	Bushel	44–50	20.0–22.7
Brussels sprouts	Ctn, loose pack	25	11.3
Buckwheat	Bushel	48	21.8
Butter	Block	55,68	25,30.9
Cabbage	Open mesh bag	50	22.7
Do	Flat crate (1¾ bu)	50–60	22.7–27.2
Do	Ctn, place pack	53	24.0
Cantaloups	Crate[6]	40	18.1
Carrots	Film plastic Bags, mesh sacks & cartons holding 48 1 lb. film bags	55	24.9
Without tops	Burlap sack	74–80	33.6–36.3
Castor beans	Bushel	41	18.6
Castor oil	Gallon[7]	8	3.6
Cauliflower	W.G.A. crate	50–60	22.7–27.2
Do	Fiberboard box wrapper leaves removed film-wrapped, 2 layers	23–35	10.4–15.9
Celery	Crate[8]	60	27.2
Cherries	Lug (Campbell)[9]	16	7.3
Do	Lug	20	9.1
Clover seed	Bushel	60	27.2
Coffee	Bag	132.3	60
Corn:			
Ear, husked	Bushel[10]	70	31.8
Shelled	.....do	56	25.4
Meal	.....do	50	22.7
Oil	Gallon[7]	7.7	3.5
Syrup	.....do	11.72	5.3
Sweet	Wirebound crate	50	22.7
Do	Ctn, packed 5 oz. ears	50	22.7
Do	WDB crate, 4½–5 oz. (from FL & NJ)	42	19.1
Cotton	Bale[11], gross	500	227
Do	Bale[11], net	480	218
Cottonseed	Bushel[12]	32	14.5
Cottonseed oil	Gallon[7]	7.7	3.5
Cowpeas	Bushel	60	27.2
Cranberries	Barrel	100	45.4
Do	¼–bbl. box[13]	25	11.3
Cream, 40-percent butterfat.	Gallon	8.38	3.80
Cucumbers	Bushel	48	21.8
Dewberries	24–qt. crate	36	16.3
Eggplant	Bushel	33	15.0
Eggs, average size	Case, 30 dozen	47.0	21.3
Escarole	Bushel	25	11.3
Figs, fresh	Box single layer[14]	6	2.7
Flaxseed	Bushel	56	25.4
Flour, various	Bag	100	45.4
Do	Ctn or Crate, Bulk	30	13.6
Garlic	Ctn of 12 tubes or 12 film bag pkgs 12 cloves each	10	4.5

See footnotes on page viii.

WEIGHTS AND MEASURES—Continued

Commodity	Unit [1]	Approximate net weight	
		U.S.	Metric
		Pounds	*Kilograms*
Grapefruit:			
Florida and Texas	½–box mesh bag	40	18.1
Florida	1⅗ bu. box	85	38.6
Texas	1⅖ bu. box	80	36.3
California and Arizona	Box [15,16]	67	30.4
Grapes:			
Eastern	12–qt. basket	20	9.1
Western	Lug	28	12.7
Do	4–basket crate [17]	20	9.1
Hempseed	Bushel	44	20.0
Hickory nuts	.....do	50	22.7
Honey	Gallon	11.84	5.4
Honeydew melons	⅔ Ctn	28–32	12.7–14.5
Hops	Bale, gross	200	90.7
Horseradish roots	Bushel	35	15.9
Do	Sack	50	22.7
Hungarian millet seed	Bushel	48–50	21.8–22.7
Kale	Ctn or crate	25	11.3
Kapok seed	......do	35–40	15.9–18.1
Lard	Tierce	375	170
Lemons:			
California and Arizona	Box [18]	76	34.5
Do	Carton	38	17.2
Lentils	Bushel	60	27.2
Lettuce, iceberg	carton packed 24.	43–52	19.5–23.6
Lettuce, hot-house	24-qt. basket	10	4.5
Limes (Florida)	Box	88	39.9
Linseed oil	Gallon [7]	7.7	3.5
Malt	Bushel	34	15.4
Maple syrup	Gallon	11.02	5.0
Meadow fescue seed	Bushel	24	10.9
Milk	Gallon	8.6	3.9
Millet	Bushel	48–60	21.8–27.2
Molasses:			
edible	Gallon	11.74	5.3
inedible	......do	11.74	5.3
Mustard seed	Bushel	58–60	26.3–27.2
Oats	......do	32	14.5
Olives	Lug	25–30	11.3–13.6
Olive oil	Gallon	[7] 7.6	3.4
Onions, dry	Sack	50	22.7
Onions, green bunched	Ctn, 24-dz bchs	10–16	4.5–7.3
Oranges:			
Florida	Box	90	40.8
Texas	Box	85	38.5
California and Arizona	Box [15]	75	34.0
Do	Carton	38	17.2
Orchardgrass seed	Bushel	14	6.4
Palm oil	Gallon [7]	7.7	3.5
Parsnips	Bushel	50	22.7
Peaches	......do	48	21.8
Do	2 layer ctn or lug	22	10.0
Do	¾-Bu, Ctn/crate	38	17.2
Peanut oil	Gallon [7]	7.7	3.5
Peanuts, unshelled:			
Virginia type	Bushel	17	7.7
Runners, South-eastern	......do	21	9.5
Spanish:			
South-eastern	......do	25	11.3
South-western	......do	25	11.3
Pears:			
California	Bushel	48	21.8
Other	......do	50	22.7
Do	Std box, 4/5 bu	45–48	20.4–21.8
Do	Ctn, Tight-fill pack	36–37	16.3–16.7
Peas:			
Green, unshelled	Bushel	28–30	12.7–13.6
Dry	......do	60	27.2
Peppers, green	......do	25–30	11.3–13.6
Do	1½ bu carton	28	12.7
Perilla seed	Bushel	37–40	16.8–18.1
Pineapples	Carton	40	18.1
Plums and prunes:	Ctn & lugs	28	12.7
Do	½-bu. basket	30	13.6
Popcorn:			
On ear	Bushel [10]	70	31.8
Shelled	......do	56	25.4
Poppy seed	......do	46	20.9
Potatoes	Bushel	60	27.2
Do	Barrel	165	74.8
Do	Box	50	22.7
Do	......do	100	45.4
Quinces	Bushel	48	21.8
Rapeseed	......do	50–60	22.7–27.2
Raspberries	½-pint baskets	6	2.7
Redtop seed	Bushel	50–60	22.7–27.2
Refiners' syrup	Gallon	11.45	5.2
Rice:			
Rough	Bushel	45	20.4
Do	Bag	100	45.4
Do	Barrel	162	73.5
Milled	Pocket or bag	100	45.4
Rosin	Drum, net	520	236
Rutabagas	Bushel	56	25.4
Rye	......do	56	25.4
Sesame seed	......do	46	20.9
Shallots	Crate (4–7 doz. bunches)	20–35	9.1–15.9
Sorgo:			
Seed	Bushel	50	22.7
Syrup	Gallon	11.55	5.2
Sorghum grain [19]	Bushel	56	25.4
Soybeans	......do	60	27.2
Soybean oil	Gallon [7]	7.7	3.5
Spelt	Bushel	40	18.1
Spinach	......do	18–20	8.2–9.1
Strawberries	24-qt. crate	36	16.3
Do	12-pt. crate	9–11	4.1–5.0
Sudangrass seed	Bushel	40	18.1
Sugarcane:			
Syrup (sulfured or un-sulfured)	Gallon	11.45	5.2
Sunflower seed	Bushel	24–32	10.9–14.5
Sweet potatoes	Bushel [20]	55	24.9
Do	Crate	50	22.7
Tangerines:			
Florida	Box	95	43.1
Arizona	Box	75	34.0
California	Box	75	34.0

See footnotes on page viii.

WEIGHTS AND MEASURES—Continued

Commodity	Unit [1]	Approximate net weight U.S.	Approximate net weight Metric
		Pounds	*Kilograms*
Timothy seed	Bushel	45	20.4
Tobacco:			
Maryland	Hogshead	775	352
Flue-cured	.....do	950	431
Burley	.....do	975	442
Dark air-cured	.....do	1,150	522
Virginia fire-cured	.....do	1,350	612
Kentucky and Tennessee fire-cured	.....do	1,500	680
Cigar-leaf	Case	250–365	113–166
Do	Bale	150–175	68.0–79.4
Tomatoes	Crate	60	27.2
Do	Lug box	32	14.5
Do	2-layer flat	21	9.5
Tomatoes, hot-house	12-qt. basket	20	9.1
Tung oil	Gallon[7]	7.8	3.5
Turnips:			
Without tops	Mesh sack	50	22.7
Bunched	Crate [6]	70–80	31.8–36.3
Turpentine	Gallon	7.23	3.3
Velvetbeans (hulled)	Bushel	60	27.2
Vetch seed	.....do	60	27.2
Walnuts	Sacks	50	22.7
Water 60° F	Gallon	8.33	3.8
Watermelons	Melons of average or medium size	25	11.3
Wheat	Bushel	60	27.2
Various commodities	Short ton	2,000	907
Do	Long ton	2,240	1,016
Do	Metric ton	2,204.6	1,000

See footnotes on page viii.

To Convert From Avoirdupois Pounds

To	Multiply by
Kilograms	0.45359237
Metric tons	0.00045359237

Conversion Factors

1 Metric ton=2,204.622 pounds
1 Kilogram=2.2046 pounds
1 Acre=0.4047 hectares
1 Hectare=2.47 acres
1 Square mile=640 acres=259 hectares
1 Gallon=3.7853 liters

CONVERSION FACTORS

Commodity	Unit	Approximate equivalent
Apples	1 pound dried	7 pounds fresh; beginning 1943, 8 pounds fresh
Do	1 pound chops	5 pounds fresh
Do	1 case canned [21]	1.4 bushels fresh
Applesauce	......do [21]	1.2 bushels fresh
Apricots	1 pound dried	6 pounds fresh
Barley flour	100 pounds	4.59 bushels barley
Beans, lima	1 pound shelled	2 pounds unshelled
Beans, snap or wax	1 case canned [22]	0.008 ton fresh
Buckwheat flour	100 pounds	3.47 bushels buckwheat
Calves	1 pound live weight	0.611 pound dressed weight (1999 average)
Cattle	......do	0.607 pound dressed weight (1999 average)
Cane syrup	1 gallon	5 pounds sugar
Cherries, tart	1 case canned [21]	0.023 ton fresh
Chickens	1 pound live weight	0.72 pound ready-to-cook weight
Corn, shelled	1 bushel (56 lbs.)	2 bushels (70 pounds) of husked ear corn
Corn, sweet	1 case canned [22]	0.030 ton fresh
Cornmeal:		
Degermed	100 pounds	3.16 bushels corn, beginning 1946
Nondegermed	......do	2 bushels corn, beginning 1946
Cotton	1 pound ginned	3.26 pounds seed cotton, including trash [23]
Cottonseed meal	1 pound	2.10 pounds cottonseed
Cottonseed oil	......do	5.88 pounds cottonseed
Dairy products:		
Butter	......do	21.1 pounds milk
Cheese	......do	10 pounds milk
Condensed milk, whole	......do	2.3 pounds milk
Dry cream	......do	19 pounds milk
Dry milk, whole	......do	7.6 pounds milk
Evaporated milk, whole	......do	2.14 pounds milk
Malted milk	......do	2.6 pounds milk
Nonfat dry milk	......do	11 pounds liquid skim milk
Ice cream [24]	1 gallon	15 pounds milk
Ice cream [24] (eliminating fat from butter and concentrated milk).	......do	12 pounds milk
Eggs	1 case	47 pounds
Eggs, shell	......do	41.2 pounds frozen or liquid whole eggs
Do	......do	10.3 pounds dried whole eggs
Figs	1 pound dried	3 pounds fresh in California; 4 pounds fresh elsewhere
Flaxseed	1 bushel	About 2½ gallons oil
Grapefruit, Florida	1 case canned juice [22]	0.64 box fresh fruit
Hogs	1 pound live weight	0.737 pound dressed weight, excluding lard (1999 average)
Linseed meal	1 pound	1.51 pounds flaxseed
Linseed oil	......do	2.77 pounds flaxseed
Malt	1 bushel (34 lbs.)	1 bushel barley (48 lbs.)
Maple syrup	1 gallon	8 pounds maple sugar
Nuts:		
Almonds, imported	1 pound shelled	3⅓ pounds unshelled
Almonds, California	......do	2.22 pounds unshelled through 1949; 2 pounds thereafter
Brazil	......do	2 pounds unshelled
Cashews	......do	4.55 pounds unshelled
Chestnuts	......do	1.19 pounds unshelled
Filberts	......do	2.22 pounds unshelled through 1949; 2.5 pounds thereafter
Pecans:		
Seedling	......do	2.78 pounds unshelled
Improved	......do	2.50 pounds unshelled
Pignolias	......do	1.3 pounds unshelled
Pistachios	......do	2 pounds unshelled
Walnuts:		
Black	......do	5.88 pounds unshelled
Persian (English)	......do	2.67 pounds unshelled
Oatmeal	100 pounds	7.6 bushels oats, beginning 1943
Oranges, Florida	1 case canned juice [22]	0.53 box fresh
Peaches, California, freestone	1 pound dried	5⅓ pounds fresh through 1918; 6 pounds fresh for 1919–28; and 6½ pounds fresh from 1929 to date
Peaches, California, clingstone	......do	7½ pounds fresh
Peaches, clingstone	1 case canned [21]	1 bushel fresh
Do	......do	0.0230 ton fresh
Peanuts	1 pound shelled	1½ pounds unshelled
Pears	1 pound dried	6½ pounds fresh
Pears, Bartlett	1 case canned [22]	1.1 bushels fresh
Do	......do	0.026 ton fresh

See footnotes on page viii.

CONVERSION FACTORS—Continued

Commodity	Unit	Approximate equivalent
Peas, green	1 pound shelled	2½ pounds unshelled
Do	1 case canned[22]	0.009 ton fresh (shelled)
Prunes	1 pound dried	2.7 pounds fresh in California; 3 to 4 pounds fresh elsewhere
Raisins	1 pound	4.3 pounds fresh grapes
Rice, milled (excluding brewers)	100 pounds	152 pounds rough or unhulled rice
Rye flour	......do	2.23 bushels rye, beginning 1947
Sheep and lambs	1 pound live weight	0.504 pound dressed weight (1999 average)
Soybean meal	1 pound	1.27 pounds soybeans
Soybean oil	......do	5.49 pounds soybeans
Sugar	1 ton raw	0.9346 ton refined
Tobacco	1 pound farm-sales weight	Various weights of stemmed and unstemmed, according to aging and the type of tobacco (See circular 435, U.S. Dept. of Agr.)
Tomatoes	1 case canned[22]	0.018 ton fresh
Turkeys	1 pound live weight	0.80 pound ready-to-cook weight
Wheat flour	100 pounds	2.30 bushels wheat[25]
Wool, domestic apparel shorn	1 pound greasy	0.48 pounds scoured
Wool, domestic apparel pulled	......do	0.73 pound scoured

[1] Standard bushel used in the United States contains 2,150.42 cubic inches; the gallon, 231 cubic inches; the cranberry barrel, 5,826 cubic inches; and the standard fruit and vegetable barrel, 7,056 cubic inches. Such large-sized products as apples and potatoes sometimes are sold on the basis of a heaped bushel, which would exceed somewhat the 2,150.42 cubic inches of a bushel basket level full. This also applies to such products as sweetpotatoes, peaches, green beans, green peas, spinach, etc.

[2] Approximate inside dimensions, 4⅝ by 12½ by 16⅛ inches.

[3] Approximate inside dimensions, 4½ by 16 by 16⅛ inches.

[4] Approximate dimensions, 4½ by 13½ by 16⅛ inches.

[5] Approximate inside dimensions, 13 by 12 by 32 inches.

[6] Approximate inside dimensions, 13 by 18 by 21⅝ inches.

[7] This is the weight commonly used in trade practices, the actual weight varying according to temperature conditions.

[8] Approximate inside dimensions, 9¾ by 16 by 20 inches.

[9] Approximate inside dimensions, 4⅛ by 11½ by 14 inches.

[10] The standard weight of 70 pounds is usually recognized as being about 2 measured bushels of corn, husked, on the ear, because it required 70 pounds to yield 1 bushel, or 56 pounds, of shelled corn.

[11] For statistical purposes the bale of cotton is 500 pounds or 480 pounds net weight. Prior to Aug. 1, 1946, the net weight was estimated at 478 pounds. Actual bale weights vary considerably, and the customary average weights of bales of foreign cotton differ from that of the American square bale.

[12] This is the average weight of cottonseed, although the legal weight in some States varies from this figure of 32 pounds.

[13] Approximate inside dimensions, 9¼ by 10½ by 15 inches.

[14] Approximate inside dimensions, 1¾ by 11 by 16⅛ inches.

[15] Approximate inside dimensions, 11½ by 11½ by 24 inches.

[16] Beginning with the 1993-94 season, net weights for California Desert Valley and Arizona grapefruit were increased from 64 to 67 pounds, equal to the California other area net weight, making a 67 pound net weight apply to all of California.

[17] Approximate inside dimensions, 4¾ by 16 by 16⅛ inches.

[18] Approximate inside dimensions, 9⅞ by 13 by 25 inches.6 by 16 by 16⅛ inches.

[19] Includes both sorghum grain (kafir, milo, hegari, etc.) and sweet sorghum varieties.

[20] This average of 55 pounds indicates the usual weight of sweetpotatoes when harvested. Much weight is lost in curing or drying and the net weight when sold in terminal markets may be below 55 pounds.

[21] Case of 24 No. 2½ cans.

[22] Case of 24 No. 303 cans.

[23] Varies widely by method of harvesting.

[24] The milk equivalent of ice cream per gallon is 15 pounds. Reports from plants indicate about 81 percent of the butterfat in ice cream is from milk and cream, the remainder being from butter and concentrated milk. Thus the milk equivalent of the milk and cream in a gallon of ice cream is about 12 pounds.

[25] This is equivalent to 4.51 bushels of wheat per barrel (196 pounds) of flour and has been used in conversions, beginning July 1, 1957. Because of changes in milling processes, the following factors per barrel of flour have been used for earlier periods: 1790–1879, 5 bushels; 1880–1908, 4.75 bushels, 1909–17, 4.7 bushels; 1918 and 1919, 4.5 bushels; 1920, 4.6 bushels; 1921–44, 4.7 bushels; July 1944–Feb. 1946, 4.57 bushels; March 1946–Oct. 1946, average was about 4.31 bushels; and Nov. 1946–June 1957, 4.57 bushels.

CHAPTER I

STATISTICS OF GRAIN AND FEED

This chapter contains tables for wheat, rye, rice, corn, oats, barley, sorghum grain, and feedstuffs. Estimates are given of area, production, disposition, supply and disappearance, prices, value of production, stocks, foreign production and trade, price-support operations, animal units fed, and feed consumed by livestock and poultry.

Table 1-1.—Total grain: Supply and disappearance, United States, 2008–2016 [1]

Year [2]	Supply				Disappearance			Ending stocks
	Beginning stocks	Production	Imports	Total	Domestic use	Exports	Total disappearance	
	Million metric tons	*Million metric tons*	*Million metric tons*	*Million metric tons*	*Million metric tons*	*Million metric tons*	*Million metric tons*	*Million metric tons*
2008	54.3	400.4	7.1	461.9	314.4	81.6	396.0	65.9
2009	66.3	418.0	6.4	490.8	331.1	83.4	414.5	76.3
2010	76.3	399.6	6.0	481.9	333.1	90.8	423.9	58.0
2011	58.0	385.1	6.8	449.9	326.3	74.2	400.0	49.9
2012	49.9	355.7	11.0	416.6	318.7	53.1	371.8	44.7
2013	44.7	433.9	9.0	487.1	345.3	90.2	435.6	51.8
2014	51.5	442.4	8.5	503.4	348.8	84.6	433.3	69.7
2015	69.6	432.2	8.4	509.3	349.7	83.1	432.8	76.8
2016	76.8	475.3	7.4	560.5	365.2	98.0	463.2	96.5

[1] Aggregate data on corn, sorghum, barley, oats, wheat, rye, and rice. [2] The marketing year for corn and sorghum begins September 1; for oats, barley, wheat, and rye, June 1; and for rice, August 1.
ERS, Market and Trade Economics Division, (202) 694–5313.

Table 1-2.—Wheat: Area, yield, production, and value, United States, 2010–2019

Year	Area		Yield per harvested acre	Production	Marketing year average price per bushel received by farmers [2]	Value of production [2]
	Planted [1]	Harvested				
	1,000 acres	*1,000 acres*	*Bushels*	*1,000 bushels*	*Dollars*	*1,000 dollars*
2010	52,620	46,883	46.1	2,163,023	5.70	12,579,125
2011	54,277	45,687	43.6	1,993,111	7.24	14,269,225
2012	55,294	48,758	46.2	2,252,307	7.77	17,383,149
2013	56,236	45,332	47.1	2,134,979	6.87	14,604,442
2014	56,841	46,385	43.7	2,026,310	5.99	11,914,954
2015	54,999	47,318	43.6	2,061,939	4.89	10,018,323
2016	50,116	43,848	52.7	2,308,663	3.89	9,179,190
2017	46,052	37,555	46.4	1,740,910	4.72	8,255,119
2018	47,815	39,612	47.6	1,885,156	5.16	9,661,916
2019	45,158	37,162	51.7	1,920,139	4.55	8,882,766

[1] Includes area seeded in preceding fall for winter wheat. [2] Includes allowance for loans outstanding and purchases by the Government valued at the average loan and purchase rate, by States, where applicable.
NASS, Crops Branch, (202) 720–2127.

Table 1-3.—Wheat, by type: Area, yield, production, and value, United States, 2010–2019

Year	Area		Yield per harvested acre	Production	Marketing year average price per bushel received by farmers [2]	Value of production [2]
	Planted [1]	Harvested				
	Winter wheat					
	1,000 acres	*1,000 acres*	*Bushels*	*1,000 bushels*	*Dollars*	*1,000 dollars*
2010	36,576	31,219	46.5	1,452,313	5.37	7,835,595
2011	40,596	32,378	46.1	1,493,130	6.81	10,154,257
2012	40,897	34,609	47.1	1,630,387	7.55	12,245,482
2013	43,230	32,650	47.3	1,542,902	6.89	10,590,949
2014	42,409	32,299	42.6	1,377,216	5.92	8,036,108
2015	39,681	32,346	42.5	1,374,690	4.80	6,555,216
2016	36,149	30,235	55.3	1,672,522	3.57	6,114,353
2017	32,726	25,301	50.2	1,270,282	4.32	5,522,949
2018	32,542	24,742	47.9	1,183,939	5.08	5,985,308
2019	31,159	24,327	53.6	1,304,003	4.50	5,999,460
	Durum wheat					
	1,000 acres	*1,000 acres*	*Bushels*	*1,000 bushels*	*Dollars*	*1,000 dollars*
2010	2,503	2,462	41.2	101,482	5.98	633,469
2011	1,337	1,280	36.8	47,043	9.68	445,186
2012	2,138	2,122	38.4	81,501	8.18	682,317
2013	1,400	1,338	43.3	57,976	7.46	432,733
2014	1,407	1,346	40.2	54,056	8.81	482,417
2015	1,951	1,911	44.0	84,009	7.36	615,160
2016	2,412	2,360	44.0	103,914	6.01	608,093
2017	2,307	2,106	26.0	54,777	6.35	344,791
2018	2,073	1,974	39.5	77,985	5.33	412,749
2019	1,339	1,175	45.7	53,756	4.90	257,103
	Other spring wheat [3]					
	1,000 acres	*1,000 acres*	*Bushels*	*1,000 bushels*	*Dollars*	*1,000 dollars*
2010	13,541	13,202	46.1	609,228	6.49	4,110,061
2011	12,344	12,029	37.7	452,938	8.24	3,669,782
2012	12,259	12,027	44.9	540,419	8.24	4,455,350
2013	11,606	11,344	47.1	534,101	6.73	3,580,760
2014	13,025	12,740	46.7	595,038	5.75	3,396,429
2015	13,367	13,061	46.2	603,240	4.78	2,847,947
2016	11,555	11,253	47.3	532,227	4.56	2,456,744
2017	11,019	10,148	41.0	415,851	5.71	2,387,379
2018	13,200	12,896	48.3	623,232	5.31	3,263,859
2019	12,660	11,660	48.2	562,380	4.65	2,626,203

[1] Seeded in preceding fall for winter wheat. [2] Obtained by weighting State prices by quantity sold. [3] Includes small quantities of Durum wheat grown in other States.

NASS, Crops Branch, (202) 720–2127.

Table 1-4.—Wheat: Stocks on and off farms, United States, 2010–2019

Year beginning September	All wheat							
	On farms				Off farms [1]			
	Sept. 1	Dec. 1	Mar. 1	Jun. 1	Sept. 1	Dec. 1	Mar. 1	Jun. 1
	1,000 bushels							
2010	812,100	550,000	288,010	130,915	1,637,517	1,382,946	1,137,292	732,083
2011	633,000	405,200	217,100	112,030	1,513,669	1,257,318	982,245	630,590
2012	572,900	399,500	236,970	120,150	1,542,209	1,271,079	997,860	597,739
2013	555,000	398,400	237,530	96,995	1,314,637	1,076,451	819,435	493,288
2014	713,450	472,800	278,710	155,170	1,193,770	1,056,830	861,697	597,224
2015	650,200	503,450	319,800	197,210	1,446,889	1,242,457	1,051,862	778,393
2016	728,200	571,280	349,500	191,755	1,816,830	1,508,080	1,309,175	988,847
2017	492,500	394,180	259,310	130,475	1,774,275	1,479,335	1,236,131	968,414
2018	632,700	504,280	367,870	206,545	1,757,071	1,505,205	1,225,201	873,216
2019	734,500	519,470	338,690	231,995	1,611,025	1,321,305	1,076,724	811,847

Year beginning September	Durum wheat [2]							
	On farms				Off farms [1]			
	Sept. 1	Dec. 1	Mar. 1	Jun. 1	Sept. 1	Dec. 1	Mar. 1	Jun. 1
	1,000 bushels							
2010	71,200	46,600	35,700	22,100	28,931	21,742	20,720	13,366
2011	34,900	24,500	17,900	15,200	28,828	23,507	17,899	10,270
2012	43,600	36,700	21,400	13,600	24,842	24,306	21,088	9,450
2013	42,900	32,800	20,700	12,800	23,465	21,175	17,430	8,724
2014	38,700	23,900	16,200	10,250	19,121	20,147	21,454	15,406
2015	44,900	35,700	17,700	12,190	29,146	24,787	24,785	15,609
2016	65,500	49,200	32,400	18,350	26,386	23,719	20,584	17,953
2017	33,400	30,700	25,800	14,950	32,756	25,351	23,740	19,996
2018	51,800	46,700	40,600	26,050	38,260	36,830	33,789	28,920
2019	49,600	33,200	23,500	17,700	38,773	31,187	27,898	25,147

[1] Includes stocks at mills, elevators, warehouses, terminals, and processors. [2] Included in all wheat.
NASS, Crops Branch, (202) 720–2127.

Table 1-5.—Wheat: Supply and disappearance, by class, United States, 2015–2019 [1]

Item	Year beginning June				
	2015	2016	2017	2018	2019
	Million bushels				
All wheat:					
Stocks, June 1	752	976	1,181	1,099	1,080
Production	2,062	2,309	1,741	1,885	1,920
Supply [2]	2,927	3,402	3,079	3,119	3,105
Exports [3]	778	1,051	906	937	965
Domestic disappearance	1,174	1,171	1,075	1,102	1,096
Stocks, May 31	976	1,181	1,099	1,080	1,044
Hard red winter:					
Stocks, June 1	294	446	589	581	516
Production	830	1,082	750	662	833
Supply [2]	1,130	1,533	1,346	1,248	1,351
Exports [3]	227	453	373	332	376
Domestic disappearance	458	490	392	400	454
Stocks, May 31	446	589	581	516	521
Soft red winter:					
Stocks, June 1	154	157	215	205	158
Production	359	345	293	286	239
Supply [2]	518	510	512	495	401
Exports [3]	120	91	91	128	92
Domestic disappearance	241	204	216	209	204
Stocks, May 31	157	215	205	158	105
Hard red spring:					
Stocks, June 1	212	272	235	191	263
Production	568	491	384	587	522
Supply [2]	842	830	707	845	838
Exports [3]	254	319	229	259	268
Domestic disappearance	316	276	287	324	289
Stocks, May 31	272	235	191	263	280
Durum:					
Stocks, June 1	26	28	36	35	55
Production	84	104	55	78	54
Supply [2]	143	162	143	165	150
Exports [3]	29	25	18	22	42
Domestic disappearance	86	101	90	88	65
Stocks, May 31	28	36	35	55	43
White:					
Stocks, June 1	67	74	105	87	88
Production	221	286	259	272	272
Supply [2]	294	368	371	365	366
Exports [3]	147	163	195	197	187
Domestic disappearance	73	100	90	81	84
Stocks, May 31	74	105	87	88	95

[1] Data except production are approximations. [2] Total supply includes imports. [3] Import and exports include flour and products in wheat equivalent.

ERS, Market and Trade Economics Division, (202) 694–5285.

Table 1-6.—Wheat: Supply and disappearance, United States, 2010–2019

Year beginning June	Supply: Beginning stocks	Supply: Production	Supply: Imports [1]	Supply: Total	Disappearance: Domestic use: Food	Domestic use: Seed	Domestic use: Feed [2]	Domestic use: Total	Disappearance: Exports [1]	Disappearance: Total disappearance	Ending stocks May 31
	Million bushels										
2010	976	2,207	97	3,236	926	71	85	1,081	1,291	2,373	863
2011	863	1,993	112	2,969	941	76	159	1,176	1,051	2,227	743
2012	743	2,252	124	3,119	951	73	365	1,389	1,012	2,401	718
2013	718	2,135	172	3,025	955	76	228	1,259	1,176	2,435	590
2014	590	2,026	151	2,768	958	79	113	1,151	864	2,015	752
2015	752	2,062	113	2,927	957	67	149	1,174	778	1,951	976
2016	976	2,309	118	3,402	949	61	161	1,171	1,051	2,222	1,181
2017	1,181	1,741	158	3,079	964	63	47	1,075	906	1,981	1,099
2018	1,099	1,885	135	3,119	955	59	88	1,102	937	2,039	1,080
2019	1,080	1,920	105	3,105	962	61	73	1,096	965	2,061	1,044

[1] Imports and exports include flour and other products expressed in wheat equivalent. [2] Approximates feed and residual use and includes negligible quantities used for distilled spirits.
Totals may not add due to independent rounding.
ERS, Market and Trade Economics Division, (202) 694–5296. Data as of September 21, 2020.

Table 1-7.—All Wheat: Area, yield, and production, by State and United States, 2017–2019

State	Area planted [1] 2017	Area planted 2018	Area planted 2019	Area harvested 2017	Area harvested 2018	Area harvested 2019
	1,000 acres					
Alabama	150	160	130	100	110	85
Arizona	115	96	34	105	77	33
Arkansas	200	175	110	125	95	50
California	420	425	420	182	147	122
Colorado	2,260	2,260	2,150	2,029	1,954	2,000
Delaware	75	75	60	60	45	50
Florida [2]	20	15	(NA)	10	10	(NA)
Georgia	160	200	150	70	70	50
Idaho	1,175	1,191	1,195	1,109	1,136	1,125
Illinois	500	600	650	470	560	550
Indiana	290	310	330	240	260	260
Iowa [2]	16	16	(NA)	8	6	(NA)
Kansas	7,600	7,700	6,900	6,950	7,300	6,500
Kentucky	480	450	460	310	300	330
Louisiana [2]	20	15	(NA)	13	10	(NA)
Maryland	410	360	345	185	200	165
Michigan	480	510	540	425	470	480
Minnesota	1,170	1,621	1,450	1,135	1,575	1,400
Mississippi	45	55	45	25	30	21
Missouri	640	740	550	540	520	390
Montana	5,140	5,300	5,450	4,665	5,165	5,175
Nebraska	1,120	1,100	1,070	1,020	1,010	970
Nevada [2]	29	23	(NA)	14	8	(NA)
New Jersey	23	18	19	17	15	14
New Mexico	330	320	360	135	105	105
New York	140	110	90	125	95	66
North Carolina	450	460	290	375	370	225
North Dakota	6,680	7,735	7,505	6,260	7,635	6,620
Ohio	490	490	500	460	450	385
Oklahoma	4,500	4,400	4,200	2,900	2,500	2,750
Oregon	775	800	740	763	770	730
Pennsylvania	210	195	180	150	145	140
South Carolina	90	80	70	75	65	45
South Dakota	1,887	1,883	1,500	1,196	1,628	1,375
Tennessee	370	380	280	275	285	215
Texas	4,700	4,500	4,500	2,350	1,750	2,050
Utah	134	130	125	120	103	116
Virginia	210	230	180	145	155	105
Washington	2,195	2,220	2,260	2,140	2,165	2,205
West Virginia [2]	8	7	(NA)	4	3	(NA)
Wisconsin	210	240	195	170	200	150
Wyoming	135	130	125	105	115	110
United States	46,052	47,815	45,158	37,555	39,612	37,162

See footnote(s) at end of table.

Table 1-7.—All Wheat: Area, yield, and production, by State and United States, 2017–2019—Continued

State	Yield per harvested acre			Production		
	2017	2018	2019	2017	2018	2019
	Bushels			*1,000 bushels*		
Alabama	77.0	72.0	72.0	7,700	7,920	6,120
Arizona	100.8	102.6	104.0	10,589	7,898	3,432
Arkansas	52.0	55.0	52.0	6,500	5,225	2,600
California	68.2	81.5	59.4	12,404	11,985	7,244
Colorado	43.2	36.1	49.0	87,598	70,504	98,000
Delaware	73.0	71.0	72.0	4,380	3,195	3,600
Florida [2]	37.0	36.0	(NA)	370	360	(NA)
Georgia	47.0	54.0	56.0	3,290	3,780	2,800
Idaho	81.8	91.9	87.8	90,723	104,410	98,755
Illinois	76.0	66.0	67.0	35,720	36,960	36,850
Indiana	74.0	71.0	62.0	17,760	18,460	16,120
Iowa [2]	68.0	58.0	(NA)	544	348	(NA)
Kansas	48.0	38.0	52.0	333,600	277,400	338,000
Kentucky	77.0	66.0	76.0	23,870	19,800	25,080
Louisiana [2]	46.0	65.0	(NA)	598	650	(NA)
Maryland	71.0	63.0	75.0	13,135	12,600	12,375
Michigan	79.0	76.0	71.0	33,575	35,720	34,080
Minnesota	66.9	59.0	57.0	75,935	92,930	79,800
Mississippi	58.0	49.0	47.0	1,450	1,470	987
Missouri	68.0	59.0	63.0	36,720	30,680	24,570
Montana	27.3	38.3	42.4	127,430	197,630	219,265
Nebraska	46.0	49.0	57.0	46,920	49,490	55,290
Nevada [2]	105.7	112.5	(NA)	1,480	900	(NA)
New Jersey	64.0	62.0	66.0	1,088	930	924
New Mexico	30.0	15.0	30.0	4,050	1,575	3,150
New York	67.0	69.0	63.0	8,375	6,555	4,158
North Carolina	55.0	57.0	56.0	20,625	21,090	12,600
North Dakota	37.9	47.6	48.5	237,133	363,483	320,760
Ohio	74.0	75.0	56.0	34,040	33,750	21,560
Oklahoma	34.0	28.0	40.0	98,600	70,000	110,000
Oregon	63.0	67.0	68.0	48,069	51,590	49,640
Pennsylvania	72.0	65.0	73.0	10,800	9,425	10,220
South Carolina	49.0	54.0	48.0	3,675	3,510	2,160
South Dakota	34.8	44.4	48.0	41,678	72,294	66,055
Tennessee	70.0	65.0	67.0	19,250	18,525	14,405
Texas	29.0	32.0	34.0	68,150	56,000	69,700
Utah	52.0	52.0	54.0	6,240	5,356	6,264
Virginia	66.0	60.0	62.0	9,570	9,300	6,510
Washington	66.6	70.8	64.7	142,500	153,210	142,735
West Virginia [2]	69.0	46.0	(NA)	276	138	(NA)
Wisconsin	68.0	71.0	64.0	11,560	14,200	9,600
Wyoming	28.0	34.0	43.0	2,940	3,910	4,730
United States	46.4	47.6	51.7	1,740,910	1,885,156	1,920,139

(NA) Not available. [1] Includes area planted preceding fall. [2] Estimates discontinued in 2019.
NASS, Crops Branch, (202) 720–2127.

Table 1-8.—Wheat, by type: Area, yield, and production, by State and United States, 2017–2019

State	Area planted [1]			Area harvested		
	2017	2018	2019	2017	2018	2019
	1,000 acres					
	Winter wheat					
Alabama	150	160	130	100	110	85
Arizona [2]	25	22	(NA)	16	4	(NA)
Arkansas	200	175	110	125	95	50
California	385	380	390	155	110	100
Colorado	2,250	2,250	2,150	2,020	1,950	2,000
Delaware	75	75	60	60	45	50
Florida [2]	20	15	(NA)	10	10	(NA)
Georgia	160	200	150	70	70	50
Idaho	720	720	730	670	680	680
Illinois	500	600	650	470	560	550
Indiana	290	310	330	240	260	260
Iowa [2]	16	16	(NA)	8	6	(NA)
Kansas	7,600	7,700	6,900	6,950	7,300	6,500
Kentucky	480	450	460	310	300	330
Louisiana [2]	20	15	(NA)	13	10	(NA)
Maryland	410	360	345	185	200	165
Michigan	480	510	540	425	470	480
Minnesota [2]	10	11	(NA)	5	5	(NA)
Mississippi	45	55	45	25	30	21
Missouri	640	740	550	540	520	390
Montana	1,750	1,650	2,000	1,590	1,570	1,900
Nebraska	1,120	1,100	1,070	1,020	1,010	970
Nevada [2]	14	13	(NA)	5	5	(NA)
New Jersey	23	18	19	17	15	14
New Mexico	330	320	360	135	105	105
New York	140	110	90	125	95	66
North Carolina	450	460	290	375	370	225
North Dakota	70	85	85	35	70	70
Ohio	490	490	500	460	450	385
Oklahoma	4,500	4,400	4,200	2,900	2,500	2,750
Oregon	700	720	740	690	695	730
Pennsylvania	210	195	180	150	145	140
South Carolina	90	80	70	75	65	45
South Dakota	910	830	860	520	660	770
Tennessee	370	380	280	275	285	215
Texas	4,700	4,500	4,500	2,350	1,750	2,050
Utah	120	120	125	108	94	116
Virginia	210	230	180	145	155	105
Washington	1,700	1,700	1,750	1,650	1,650	1,700
West Virginia [2]	8	7	(NA)	4	3	(NA)
Wisconsin	210	240	195	170	200	150
Wyoming	135	130	125	105	115	110
United States	32,726	32,542	31,159	25,301	24,742	24,327
	Other spring wheat					
Colorado [2]	10	10	(NA)	9	4	(NA)
Idaho	430	400	460	415	445	440
Minnesota	1,160	1,610	1,450	1,130	1,570	1,400
Montana	2,500	2,900	2,900	2,290	2,820	2,760
Nevada [2]	15	10	(NA)	9	3	(NA)
North Dakota	5,350	6,550	6,700	5,050	6,490	5,950
Oregon [2]	75	80	(NA)	73	75	(NA)
South Dakota	970	1,050	640	670	965	605
Utah [2]	14	10	(NA)	12	9	(NA)
Washington	495	520	510	490	515	505
United States	11,019	13,200	12,660	10,148	12,896	11,660
	Durum wheat					
Arizona	90	74	34	89	73	33
California	35	45	30	27	37	22
Idaho	25	11	5	24	11	5
Montana	890	840	550	785	775	515
North Dakota	1,260	1,100	720	1,175	1,075	600
South Dakota [2]	7	3	(NA)	6	3	(NA)
United States	2,307	2,073	1,339	2,106	1,974	1,175

See footnote(s) at end of table.

Table 1-8.—Wheat, by type: Area, yield, and production, by State and United States, 2017–2019—Continued

State	Yield per harvested acre			Production		
	2017	2018	2019	2017	2018	2019
	Bushels			*1,000 bushels*		
	Winter wheat					
Alabama	77.0	72.0	72.0	7,700	7,920	6,120
Arizona [2]	100.0	40.0	(NA)	1,600	160	(NA)
Arkansas	52.0	55.0	52.0	6,500	5,225	2,600
California	64.0	77.0	50.0	9,920	8,470	5,000
Colorado	43.0	36.0	49.0	86,860	70,200	98,000
Delaware	73.0	71.0	72.0	4,380	3,195	3,600
Florida [2]	37.0	36.0	(NA)	370	360	(NA)
Georgia	47.0	54.0	56.0	3,290	3,780	2,800
Idaho	80.0	90.0	87.0	53,600	61,200	59,160
Illinois	76.0	66.0	67.0	35,720	36,960	36,850
Indiana	74.0	71.0	62.0	17,760	18,460	16,120
Iowa [2]	68.0	58.0	(NA)	544	348	(NA)
Kansas	48.0	38.0	52.0	333,600	277,400	338,000
Kentucky	77.0	66.0	76.0	23,870	19,800	25,080
Louisiana [2]	46.0	65.0	(NA)	598	650	(NA)
Maryland	71.0	63.0	75.0	13,135	12,600	12,375
Michigan	79.0	76.0	71.0	33,575	35,720	34,080
Minnesota [2]	45.0	60.0	(NA)	225	300	(NA)
Mississippi	58.0	49.0	47.0	1,450	1,470	987
Missouri	68.0	59.0	63.0	36,720	30,680	24,570
Montana	42.0	50.0	50.0	66,780	78,500	95,000
Nebraska	46.0	49.0	57.0	46,920	49,490	55,290
Nevada [2]	107.0	120.0	(NA)	535	600	(NA)
New Jersey	64.0	62.0	66.0	1,088	930	924
New Mexico	30.0	15.0	30.0	4,050	1,575	3,150
New York	67.0	69.0	63.0	8,375	6,555	4,158
North Carolina	55.0	57.0	56.0	20,625	21,090	12,600
North Dakota	37.0	43.0	53.0	1,295	3,010	3,710
Ohio	74.0	75.0	56.0	34,040	33,750	21,560
Oklahoma	34.0	28.0	40.0	98,600	70,000	110,000
Oregon	63.0	67.0	68.0	43,470	46,565	49,640
Pennsylvania	72.0	65.0	73.0	10,800	9,425	10,220
South Carolina	49.0	54.0	48.0	3,675	3,510	2,160
South Dakota	40.0	48.0	52.0	20,800	31,680	40,040
Tennessee	70.0	65.0	67.0	19,250	18,525	14,405
Texas	29.0	32.0	34.0	68,150	56,000	69,700
Utah	52.0	52.0	54.0	5,616	4,888	6,264
Virginia	66.0	60.0	62.0	9,570	9,300	6,510
Washington	73.0	76.0	70.0	120,450	125,400	119,000
West Virginia [2]	69.0	46.0	(NA)	276	138	(NA)
Wisconsin	68.0	71.0	64.0	11,560	14,200	9,600
Wyoming	28.0	34.0	43.0	2,940	3,910	4,730
United States	50.2	47.9	53.6	1,270,282	1,183,939	1,304,003
	Other spring wheat					
Colorado [2]	82.0	76.0	(NA)	738	304	(NA)
Idaho	85.0	95.0	89.0	35,275	42,275	39,160
Minnesota	67.0	59.0	57.0	75,710	92,630	79,800
Montana	21.0	34.0	37.0	48,090	95,880	102,120
Nevada [2]	105.0	100.0	(NA)	945	300	(NA)
North Dakota	41.0	49.0	49.0	207,050	318,010	291,550
Oregon [2]	63.0	67.0	(NA)	4,599	5,025	(NA)
South Dakota	31.0	42.0	43.0	20,770	40,530	26,015
Utah [2]	52.0	52.0	(NA)	624	468	(NA)
Washington	45.0	54.0	47.0	22,050	27,810	23,735
United States	41.0	48.3	48.2	415,851	623,232	562,380
	Durum wheat					
Arizona	101.0	106.0	104.0	8,989	7,738	3,432
California	92.0	95.0	102.0	2,484	3,515	2,244
Idaho	77.0	85.0	87.0	1,848	935	435
Montana	16.0	30.0	43.0	12,560	23,250	22,145
North Dakota	24.5	39.5	42.5	28,788	42,463	25,500
South Dakota [2]	18.0	28.0	(NA)	108	84	(NA)
United States	26.0	39.5	45.7	54,777	77,985	53,756

(NA) Not available. [1] Includes area planted preceding fall. [2] Estimates discontinued in 2019.
NASS, Crops Branch, (202) 720–2127.

Table 1-9.—Wheat: Support operations, United States, 2013–2019

Marketing year beginning June 1	Income support payment rates per bushel [1]	Program price levels per bushel		Put under loan		Acquired by CCC under loan program [5]	Owned by CCC at end of marketing year
		Loan [2]	Target/ Reference [3]	Quantity	Percentage of production [4]		
	Dollars	*Dollars*	*Dollars*	*Million bushels*	*Percent*	*Million bushels*	*Million bushels*
2013/2014 ...	0.52/0.00	2.94	4.17	24.7	1.2	0	0
2014/2015 ...	0.00	2.94	5.50	43.1	2.1	0	0
2015/2016 ...	0.61	2.94	5.50	80.9	3.9	0	0
2016/2017 ...	1.61	2.94	5.50	150.7	6.5	0.25	0
2017/2018 ...	0.85	2.94	5.50	44.7	2.6	0	0
2018/2019 ...	0.34	2.94	5.50	65.1	5.9	0	0
2019/2020 [6]	0.92	3.38	5.50	69.1	3.6	0	0

[1] The first entry is the direct payment rate and the second entry is the counter-cyclical payment rate for 2013/2014. For 2013/2014, producers who participated in the Average Crop Revenue (ACRE) program got a 20 percent reduction in their direct payment, not calculated in this table. For 2014/2015 and after, the entry is the price loss coverage (PLC) payment rate. Agricultural Risk Coverage (ARC) is also available, but payment rates are established at the county or farm levels. [2] For 2013/2014, producers who participated in the ACRE program got a 30 percent reduction in their loan rate, not calculated in this table. [3] Target applies to 2013/2014 and Reference applies beginning with 2014/2015. [4] Percent of production is on a grain basis. [5] Acquisitions as of September 30, 2020. [6] 2019/20 payment rate as of the July 31, 2020 NASS Agricultural Prices Report.

FPAC-BC, Commodity Analysis Branch.

Table 1-10.—Wheat: Marketing year average price and value, by State and United States, 2017–2019

State	Marketing year average price per bushel			Value of production		
	2017	2018	2019 [1]	2017	2018	2019 [1]
	Dollars			*1,000 dollars*		
Alabama	4.60	4.95	5.05	35,420	39,204	30,906
Arizona	7.06	7.01	6.55	70,822	55,038	22,480
Arkansas	4.46	4.88	4.85	28,990	25,498	12,610
California	5.42	6.39	6.10	67,730	76,413	44,338
Colorado	3.88	4.61	3.95	339,873	324,789	387,100
Delaware	4.63	4.90	4.95	20,279	15,656	17,820
Florida [2]	4.00	4.40	(NA)	1,480	1,584	(NA)
Georgia	4.10	4.80	4.90	13,489	18,144	13,720
Idaho	4.64	5.15	5.05	426,305	539,010	500,954
Illinois	4.59	4.77	4.95	163,955	176,299	182,408
Indiana	4.78	4.90	4.95	84,893	90,454	79,794
Iowa [2]	3.90	4.75	(NA)	2,122	1,653	(NA)
Kansas	4.07	4.93	4.05	1,357,752	1,367,582	1,368,900
Kentucky	4.68	5.19	5.25	111,712	102,762	131,670
Louisiana [2]	4.20	5.10	(NA)	2,512	3,315	(NA)
Maryland	4.63	4.90	4.95	60,815	61,740	105,806
Michigan	4.54	5.08	5.20	152,431	181,458	177,216
Minnesota	5.76	5.25	4.70	438,062	487,796	375,060
Mississippi	4.30	4.88	5.10	6,235	7,174	5,034
Missouri	4.47	4.84	5.15	164,138	148,491	126,536
Montana	5.34	5.24	4.05	695,891	1,041,736	1,022,114
Nebraska	4.03	4.71	3.80	189,088	233,098	210,102
Nevada [2]	4.70	5.18	(NA)	7,233	4,749	(NA)
New Jersey	4.60	4.90	4.95	5,005	4,557	4,574
New Mexico	4.20	4.75	4.50	17,010	7,481	14,175
New York	4.88	5.31	5.50	40,870	34,807	22,869
North Carolina	4.70	4.80	5.30	96,938	101,232	66,780
North Dakota	5.74	5.09	4.45	1,362,415	1,848,508	1,424,229
Ohio	4.90	5.08	5.25	166,796	171,450	113,190
Oklahoma	3.98	5.10	4.30	392,428	357,000	473,000
Oregon	5.16	5.80	5.70	245,537	298,465	282,948
Pennsylvania	5.21	5.30	5.55	56,268	49,953	56,721
South Carolina	4.20	4.70	5.25	15,435	16,497	11,340
South Dakota	5.52	5.24	4.55	233,427	378,573	298,447
Tennessee	4.60	5.24	5.45	88,550	97,071	78,507
Texas	3.89	5.17	4.40	265,104	289,520	306,680
Utah	5.20	6.00	4.95	32,448	30,998	31,007
Virginia	4.60	4.70	5.00	44,022	43,710	32,550
Washington	4.85	5.51	5.55	690,902	844,592	790,976
West Virginia [2]	4.70	4.90	(NA)	1,297	676	(NA)
Wisconsin	4.15	4.55	4.35	47,974	64,610	41,760
Wyoming	3.90	4.75	3.90	11,466	18,573	18,447
United States	4.72	5.16	4.55	8,255,119	9,661,916	8,882,766

(NA) Not available. [1] Preliminary. [2] Estimates discontinued in 2019.
NASS, Crops Branch, (202) 720–2127.

Table 1-11.—International Wheat: Area, yield, and production in specified countries, 2017/2018–2019/2020

Country	Area			Yield per hectare			Production		
	2017/2018	2018/2019	2019/2020	2017/2018	2018/2019	2019/2020	2017/2018	2018/2019	2019/2020
	1,000 hectares			*Metric tons*			*1,000 metric tons*		
European Union	26,160	25,581	26,065	5.78	5.35	5.91	151,125	136,863	154,000
China	24,508	24,268	23,730	5.48	5.42	5.63	134,334	131,430	133,590
India	30,785	29,651	29,319	3.20	3.37	3.53	98,510	99,870	103,600
Russia	27,370	26,344	27,312	3.11	2.72	2.70	85,167	71,685	73,610
United States	15,198	16,030	15,039	3.12	3.20	3.48	47,380	51,306	52,258
Canada	8,983	9,881	9,660	3.38	3.26	3.35	30,377	32,201	32,350
Ukraine	6,642	6,718	7,050	4.06	3.73	4.11	26,981	25,057	29,000
Pakistan	9,050	8,800	8,798	2.94	2.85	2.91	26,600	25,100	25,600
Argentina	5,800	6,050	6,500	3.19	3.22	3.00	18,500	19,500	19,500
Turkey	7,800	7,615	7,200	2.69	2.50	2.50	21,000	19,000	18,000
Iran	6,700	6,700	6,700	2.09	2.16	2.51	14,000	14,500	16,800
Australia	10,919	10,159	10,100	1.92	1.70	1.51	20,941	17,298	15,200
Kazakhstan	11,912	11,354	11,339	1.24	1.23	1.01	14,802	13,947	11,452
Egypt	1,320	1,320	1,370	6.40	6.40	6.40	8,450	8,450	8,770
Uzbekistan	1,446	1,400	1,400	4.80	4.29	4.86	6,941	6,000	6,800
Brazil	1,916	2,042	2,040	2.23	2.66	2.55	4,264	5,428	5,200
Afghanistan	2,104	2,000	2,300	2.04	1.80	2.17	4,281	3,600	5,000
Ethiopia	1,717	1,840	1,850	2.81	2.61	2.60	4,831	4,800	4,800
Iraq	2,200	1,700	2,400	1.82	1.77	2.00	4,000	3,000	4,800
Syria	1,100	1,100	1,600	2.00	1.82	3.00	2,200	2,000	4,800
Algeria	1,600	2,074	2,100	1.50	1.90	1.91	2,400	3,940	4,000
Morocco	3,321	2,850	2,750	2.14	2.58	1.46	7,091	7,340	4,000
Mexico	667	540	593	5.24	5.56	5.42	3,494	3,000	3,215
Belarus	718	660	750	3.65	2.75	3.83	2,620	1,815	2,875
Serbia	540	648	580	4.26	4.63	4.48	2,300	3,000	2,600
Azerbaijan	596	680	700	2.97	3.00	2.86	1,770	2,040	2,000
Nepal	770	760	760	2.31	2.35	2.35	1,780	1,786	1,786
South Africa	492	503	540	3.12	3.71	2.78	1,535	1,868	1,500
Tunisia	579	536	620	1.91	2.00	2.42	1,104	1,070	1,500
Turkmenistan	900	750	880	1.11	0.93	1.71	1,000	700	1,500
Chile	236	223	230	6.23	6.28	6.30	1,469	1,400	1,450
Bangladesh	370	320	340	3.12	3.44	3.53	1,153	1,100	1,200
Moldova	336	372	352	3.72	3.13	3.25	1,251	1,163	1,145
Paraguay	510	485	480	2.00	2.80	2.38	1,020	1,360	1,140
Japan	213	212	212	4.56	4.06	4.53	972	860	960
Tajikistan	286	300	300	3.15	2.33	2.77	900	700	830
Uruguay	186	198	230	2.37	3.68	3.30	440	728	760
Saudi Arabia	2	87	120	5.00	5.75	5.83	10	500	700
Sudan	168	200	200	2.76	2.98	3.00	463	595	600
Kyrgyzstan	250	300	280	2.40	2.05	2.11	601	616	590
Switzerland	90	90	90	6.00	6.00	6.00	540	540	540
Norway	76	58	80	5.28	2.19	5.25	401	127	420
New Zealand	41	42	45	9.88	8.81	9.11	405	370	410
Mongolia	366	342	327	0.63	1.28	1.10	231	436	360
Albania	68	75	72	4.04	4.13	4.17	275	310	300
Macedonia	73	71	80	2.74	3.39	3.75	200	241	300
Bosnia and Herzegovina	65	73	71	4.45	4.00	4.01	289	292	285
Bolivia	200	150	200	1.51	1.20	1.40	302	180	280
Peru	128	127	130	1.50	1.54	1.62	192	195	210
Kenya	86	170	125	1.92	2.12	1.60	165	360	200
Libya	165	165	165	1.21	1.21	1.21	200	200	200
Armenia	81	66	60	2.17	2.83	3.00	176	187	180
Zambia	27	22	24	7.19	5.18	6.33	194	114	152
Lebanon	39	40	41	3.33	3.25	3.42	130	130	140
Yemen	100	100	90	1.50	1.40	1.56	150	140	140
Burma	87	85	65	1.55	1.53	1.54	135	130	100
Georgia	44	43	40	2.23	2.49	2.50	98	107	100
Tanzania	102	100	100	1.00	1.00	1.00	102	100	100
Zimbabwe	44	56	25	3.59	3.57	4.00	158	200	100

FAS, Office of Global Analysis, (202) 720-6301. Prepared or estimated on the basis of official USDA production, supply, and distribution statistics from foreign governments.

Table 1-12.—Wheat and flour: United States imports, 2010–2019

Year beginning June	All wheat grain	All wheat flour [1]	All wheat products [2]	Total all wheat [3]
	1,000 bushels	*1,000 bushels* [4]	*1,000 bushels* [4]	*1,000 bushels*
2010	69,053	11,283	16,582	96,918
2011	84,382	10,666	18,068	113,116
2012	96,103	10,151	18,063	124,317
2013	141,665	11,535	19,267	172,467
2014	116,973	14,332	19,944	151,249
2015	76,433	15,822	20,470	112,725
2016	83,849	14,574	19,717	118,140
2017	120,746	16,814	20,424	157,984
2018	97,657	17,016	19,959	134,633
2019	65,345	17,095	22,569	105,009

[1] Includes meal, groats, and durum. [2] Includes bulgur, couscous, and selected categories of pasta. [3] Totals may not add due to rounding. [4] Expressed in grain-equivalent bushels.
ERS, Market and Trade Economics Division, (202) 694–5285. Data as of September 21, 2020.

Table 1-13.—Wheat: International trade, 2017/2018–2019/2020

Country	2017/2018	2018/2019	2019/2020
	1,000 metric tons	*1,000 metric tons*	*1,000 metric tons*
Principle importing countries:			
Egypt	12,407	12,347	12,500
Indonesia	10,763	10,934	11,000
Turkey	6,043	6,366	10,500
Brazil	7,021	7,020	7,500
Philippines	6,059	7,546	7,300
Algeria	8,172	7,515	6,500
Bangladesh	6,472	5,100	6,500
Japan	5,876	5,726	5,900
Mexico	5,245	4,861	5,200
Nigeria	5,162	4,585	5,100
European Union	5,824	5,762	4,800
Morocco	3,676	3,724	4,800
Korea, South	4,269	3,908	4,100
China	3,937	3,145	4,000
Yemen	3,010	3,675	3,800
Vietnam	4,709	3,149	3,500
Thailand	3,173	2,899	3,300
Saudi Arabia	3,449	2,898	3,200
Afghanistan	3,300	3,700	3,000
Uzbekistan	3,119	2,837	3,000
United States	4,301	3,674	2,858
Sudan	2,580	2,222	2,600
Iraq	4,158	3,915	2,500
Kenya	2,158	2,000	2,300
Peru	2,030	2,109	2,100
Principle exporting countries:			
Russia	41,431	35,838	35,000
United States	23,383	20,010	32,000
Canada	24,655	25,477	27,216
European Union	22,000	24,404	23,000
Ukraine	17,775	16,019	20,500
Argentina	12,730	12,188	13,500
Australia	13,849	9,006	8,000
Kazakhstan	6,194	6,350	6,800
Turkey	9,000	8,296	6,000
Pakistan	1,004	1,006	1,100
Serbia	1,147	526	1,100
China	781	1,090	900
Brazil	840	1,078	700
Moldova	230	602	600
Paraguay	650	410	600
Egypt	656	600	600
Mexico	230	538	550
India	569	496	500
Iran	1,206	1,965	500
Nigeria	400	400	400
Egypt	318	274	300
Mexico	292	293	300
India	44	325	300
Iran	277	286	280
Nigeria	257	275	275

FAS, Office of Global Analysis, (202) 720-6301. Prepared or estimated on the basis of official USDA production, supply, and distribution statistics from foreign governments.

Table 1-14.—Wheat and flour: United States exports by country of destination, 2017–2019

Country of destination	Year		
	2017	2018	2019
	Metric tons	*Metric tons*	*Metric tons*
Wheat:			
Mexico	3,698,250	2,802,765	3,547,379
Philippines	2,447,963	2,644,825	2,925,508
Japan	3,049,192	2,860,604	2,578,881
Nigeria	1,638,036	814,014	2,112,984
Korea, South	1,554,669	1,533,432	1,265,940
Taiwan	1,091,326	983,300	1,263,598
Indonesia	1,492,946	779,435	1,263,598
Egypt	180,349	120,672	827,885
Italy(*)	411,961	485,893	749,096
Yemen(*)	442,004	480,893	739,849
Thailand	735,769	696,252	669,581
Colombia	833,326	407,750	646,350
Guatemala	537,856	547,946	590,410
Algeria	840,476	307,864	565,918
Malaysia	224,883	191,605	496,407
Iraq	256,404	882,123	472,469
Peru	488,441	241,716	466,879
Ecuador	289,191	266,703	428,658
Brazil	286,837	266,462	416,427
Chile	328,770	297,856	374,240
Dominican Republic	368,341	291,581	308,326
Ethiopia(*)	321,720	218,500	304,277
Honduras	231,985	326,588	298,535
Vietnam	115,071	277,097	297,534
El Salvador	317,902	278,781	267,562
China	1,514,399	396,987	236,062
Bangladesh	308,155	449,751	225,973
Jamaica	179,086	194,670	208,377
Canada	50,751	65,126	155,127
South Africa	128,868	33,283	153,919
Rest of World	2,805,708	2,100,517	2,044,556
World Total	27,170,635	22,244,480	26,871,465
Wheat flour:			
Mexico	181,521	195,588	201,996
Canada	93,358	53,654	51,768
Djibouti	1,254	1,071	3,033
Bahamas, The	2,133	2,057	2,530
Dominican Republic	2,637	2,019	2,187
Netherlands Antilles(*)	2,166	2,157	2,178
Malaysia	1,100	1,325	2,099
Sweden	1,730	1,763	1,858
Leeward-Windward Islands(*)	839	1,015	1,144
Trinidad and Tobago	804	1,126	1,119
Panama	602	503	892
Barbados	796	763	649
China	1,204	571	593
Korea, South	1,343	276	531
United Arab Emirates	1,089	983	491
Haiti	0	0	423
Japan	744	487	417
New Zealand(*)	584	405	406
Colombia	111	340	390
Taiwan	148	182	380
Brazil	347	472	371
Guatemala	405	585	367
Turks and Caicos Islands	266	368	331
Netherlands	199	219	268
Cayman Islands	165	175	213
Micronesia	370	223	204
Jamaica	144	280	200
Venezuela	114	41	184
Palau	170	168	183
Saudi Arabia	103	146	180
Rest of World	2,463	7,502	1,915
World Total	298,906	276,464	279,498

(*) Denotes a country that is a summarization of its component countries.
FAS, Office of Global Analysis, (202) 720-6301. Prepared or estimated on the basis of official USDA production, supply, and distribution, supply, and distribution statistics from foreign governments.

Table 1-15.—Rye: Area, yield, production, disposition, and value, United States, 2010–2019

Year	Area		Yield per harvested acre	Production	Marketing year average price per bushel received by farmers [2]	Value of production [2]
	Planted [1]	Harvested				
	1,000 acres	*1,000 acres*	*Bushels*	*1,000 bushels*	*Dollars*	*1,000 dollars*
2010	1,256	270	27.7	7,480	5.18	38,767
2011	1,227	239	25.3	6,051	7.81	47,250
2012	1,271	250	26.2	6,542	7.69	50,304
2013	1,451	278	27.4	7,626	7.95	60,598
2014	1,434	258	27.9	7,189	7.74	55,639
2015	1,584	365	31.8	11,616	6.50	75,497
2016	1,891	411	32.5	13,337	5.12	68,343
2017	1,961	300	34.2	10,252	4.70	48,180
2018	2,011	273	30.9	8,432	6.27	52,870
2019	1,865	310	34.3	10,622	6.11	64,863

[1] Area planted in preceding fall. [2] 2018 data is preliminary.
NASS, Crops Branch, (202) 720–2127.

Table 1-16.—Rye: Supply and disappearance, United States, 2010–2019

Year beginning June	Supply				Disappearance							Ending stocks May 31
					Domestic use					Exports	Total disappearance [2]	
	Beginning stocks	Production	Imports	Total	Food	Seed	Industry [1]	Residual use	Total			
	1,000 bushels											
2010	932	7,480	5,552	13,964	3,300	3,000	3,000	3,714	13,014	149	13,163	801
2011	801	6,051	5,994	12,846	3,310	3,000	3,010	2,917	12,237	157	12,394	452
2012	452	6,542	8,966	15,960	3,400	3,000	3,020	5,829	15,249	310	15,559	401
2013	401	7,626	9,213	17,240	3,430	3,000	3,030	7,227	16,687	268	16,955	285
2014	285	7,189	9,320	16,794	3,460	3,000	3,040	6,465	15,965	240	16,205	589
2015	589	11,616	8,757	20,962	3,630	3,000	3,050	10,040	20,326	181	20,507	455
2016	455	13,337	6,586	20,378	3,500	6,168	4,110	5,727	19,505	175	19,680	698
2017	698	10,252	8,825	19,775	3,530	5,445	4,250	5,800	19,025	157	19,182	593
2018	593	8,432	11,964	20,989	3,550	6,982	3,890	6,000	20,422	148	20,570	419
2019	419	10,622	11,899	22,940	3,570	7,285	4,680	6,100	21,635	205	21,840	1,100

[1] Includes commercial adhesives, packaging materials, thatching, mattresses, hats, and paper. [2] Totals may not add due to independent rounding.
ERS, Market and Trade Economics Division, (202) 694–5302.

Table 1-17.—Rye: Area, yield, and production, by State and United States, 2017–2019

State	Area planted[1]			Area harvested		
	2017	2018	2019	2017	2018	2019
	1,000 acres	*1,000 acres*	*1,000 acres*	*1,000 acres*	*1,000 acres*	*1,000 acres*
Georgia	210	190	(D)	25	15	(D)
Minnesota	(D)	(D)	50	(D)	(D)	18
North Dakota	(D)	(D)	85	(D)	(D)	57
Oklahoma	260	240	260	45	50	55
Pennsylvania	(D)	(D)	100	(D)	(D)	14
Wisconsin	(D)	(D)	220	(D)	(D)	20
Other States[2]	1,491	1,581	1,150	230	208	146
United States	1,961	2,011	1,865	300	273	310

State	Yield per harvested acre			Production		
	2017	2018	2019	2017	2018	2019
	Bushels	*Bushels*	*Bushels*	*1,000 bushels*	*1,000 bushels*	*1,000 bushels*
Georgia	19.0	26.0	(D)	475	390	(D)
Minnesota	(D)	(D)	39.0	(D)	(D)	702
North Dakota	(D)	(D)	45.0	(D)	(D)	2,565
Oklahoma	24.0	22.0	27.0	1,080	1,100	1,485
Pennsylvania	(D)	(D)	26.0	(D)	(D)	364
Wisconsin	(D)	(D)	34.0	(D)	(D)	680
Other States[2]	37.8	33.4	33.1	8,697	6,942	4,826
United States	34.2	30.9	34.3	10,252	8,432	10,622

(D) Withheld to avoid disclosing data for individual operations. [1] Includes area planted preceding fall. [2] In 2017 and 2018, Other States include Illinois, Kansas, Maine, Maryland, Michigan, Minnesota, Nebraska, New Jersey, New York, North Carolina, North Dakota, Pennsylvania, South Carolina, South Dakota, Texas, Virginia, and Wisconsin. Beginning in 2019, Other States include Georgia, Illinois, Kansas, Michigan, Nebraska, New York, North Carolina, South Dakota, and Texas.
NASS, Crops Branch, (202) 720–2127.

Table 1-18.—Rye: Marketing year average price and value, by State and United States, 2017–2019

State	Marketing year average price per bushel			Value of production		
	2017	2018	2019[1]	2017	2018	2019[1]
	Dollars	*Dollars*	*Dollars*	*1,000 dollars*	*1,000 dollars*	*1,000 dollars*
Georgia	5.10	7.05	(D)	2,423	2,750	(D)
Minnesota	(D)	(D)	5.50	(D)	(D)	3,861
North Dakota	(D)	(D)	4.55	(D)	(D)	11,671
Oklahoma	5.05	7.55	8.20	5,454	8,305	12,177
Pennsylvania	(D)	(D)	5.90	(D)	(D)	2,148
Wisconsin	(D)	(D)	7.00	(D)	(D)	4,760
Other States[2]	4.63	6.02	6.27	40,303	41,815	30,246
United States	4.70	6.27	6.11	48,180	52,870	64,863

(D) Withheld to avoid disclosing data for individual operations. [1] Preliminary. [2] In 2017 and 2018, Other States include Illinois, Kansas, Maine, Maryland, Michigan, Minnesota, Nebraska, New Jersey, New York, North Carolina, North Dakota, Pennsylvania, South Carolina, South Dakota, Texas, Virginia, and Wisconsin. Beginning in 2019, Other States include Georgia, Illinois, Kansas, Michigan, Nebraska, New York, North Carolina, South Dakota, and Texas.
NASS, Crops Branch, (202) 720-2127.

Table 1-19.—International Rye: Area, yield, and production in specified countries, 2017/2018–2019/2020

Country	Area			Yield			Production		
	2017/2018	2018/2019	2019/2020	2017/2018	2018/2019	2019/2020	2017/2018	2018/2019	2019/2020
	1,000 hectares			*Metric tons per hectare*			*1,000 metric tons*		
European Union	1,931	1,920	2,070	3.84	3.23	3.84	7,405	6,208	7,950
Russia	1,171	957	823	2.17	2.00	1.73	2,540	1,914	1,424
Belarus	256	252	200	2.62	2.00	3.25	670	503	650
Ukraine	172	149	110	2.97	2.66	3.09	510	396	340
Canada	101	79	100	3.39	2.99	3.30	342	236	330
Turkey	101	110	110	3.17	2.91	2.91	320	320	320
United States	121	110	125	2.15	1.95	2.16	260	214	270
Argentina	45	49	56	1.91	1.78	2.14	86	87	120
Norway	9	3	9	5.56	3.00	5.56	50	9	50
Australia	40	44	44	0.75	0.68	0.68	30	30	30
Kazakhstan	31	22	23	1.26	1.05	1.00	39	23	23
Bosnia and Herzegovina	3	4	4	3.67	2.75	3.50	11	11	14
Switzerland	2	2	2	5.50	5.50	5.50	11	11	11
Serbia	4	4	4	2.50	2.50	2.50	10	10	10
Macedonia	4	4	4	2.00	2.25	2.00	8	9	8
Brazil	4	4	4	1.50	2.00	1.75	6	8	7
Chile	1	1	1	5.00	5.00	5.00	5	5	5
Albania	1	1	1	3.00	3.00	3.00	3	3	3
South Africa	20	20	20	0.15	0.15	0.15	3	3	3

FAS, Office of Global Analysis, (202) 720-6301. Prepared or estimated on the basis of official USDA production, supply, and distribution, supply, and distribution statistics from foreign governments.

Table 1-20.—Rye: [1] International trade, 2017/2018–2019/2020 [2]

Country	2017/2018	2018/2019	2019/2020
	1,000 metric tons	*1,000 metric tons*	*1,000 metric tons*
Principle exporting countries:			
European Union	81	195	200
Canada	193	144	150
Ukraine	38	88	30
Russia	71	283	25
United States	4	4	5
Principle importing countries:			
United States	224	304	305
European Union	61	298	25
Israel	21	15	20
Japan	21	23	20
Belarus	15	21	10
Korea, South	3	3	5
Norway	4	18	5
Canada	1	2	2
Switzerland	2	2	2
Bosnia and Herzegovina	1	1	1
Ukraine	0	2	1

[1] Flour and products reported in terms of grain equivalent. [2] Year beginning July 1.
FAS, Office of Global Analysis, (202) 720-6301. Prepared or estimated on the basis of official USDA production, supply, and distribution statics from foreign governments.

Table 1-21.—Rice, rough: Area, yield, production, and value, United States, 2010–2019

Year	Area planted	Area harvested	Yield per acre	Production	Marketing year average price per cwt. received by farmers	Value of production
	1,000 acres	*1,000 acres*	*Pounds*	*1,000 cwt*	*Dollars*	*1,000 dollars*
2010	3,636	3,615	6,725	243,104	12.70	3,183,213
2011	2,689	2,617	7,067	184,941	14.50	2,737,423
2012	2,700	2,679	7,463	199,939	15.10	3,067,365
2013	2,490	2,463	7,694	189,500	16.30	3,175,107
2014	2,954	2,933	7,576	222,215	13.40	3,075,618
2015	2,625	2,584	7,472	193,080	12.20	2,421,111
2016	3,150	3,097	7,237	224,145	10.40	2,384,690
2017	2,463	2,374	7,507	178,228	12.90	2,360,439
2018	2,946	2,910	7,692	223,833	12.60	2,903,041
2019	2,540	2,472	7,471	184,675	13.00	2,459,035

NASS, Crops Branch, (202) 720–2127.

Table 1-22.—Rice, rough: Stocks on and off farms, United States, 2010–2019

Year beginning previous December	On farms			Off farms [1]		
	Dec. 1	Mar. 1	Aug. 1	Dec. 1	Mar. 1	Aug. 1
	1,000 cwt					
2010	51,880	23,465	1,200	104,726	80,516	29,176
2011	63,617	33,895	3,772	109,869	86,720	37,917
2012	41,180	23,825	910	105,689	82,666	35,052
2013	39,385	18,430	640	108,650	85,839	29,880
2014	36,935	14,995	305	96,636	73,959	26,299
2015	47,865	25,810	1,480	110,061	86,658	41,293
2016	43,245	18,255	3,762	101,804	90,507	34,983
2017	48,595	21,600	4,693	111,734	85,969	34,077
2018	31,570	12,565	1,902	88,104	70,831	21,962
2019	40,115	23,305	6,663	98,602	80,515	31,927

[1] Stocks at mills and in attached warehouses, in warehouses not attached to mills, and in ports or in transit.
NASS, Crops Branch, (202) 720–2127.

Table 1-23.—Rice, by length of grain: Harvest, yield, and production, United States, 2010–2019

Year	Area harvested			Yield per acre			Production		
	Long grain	Medium grain	Short grain	Long grain	Medium grain	Short grain	Long grain	Medium grain	Short grain
	1,000 acres	*1,000 acres*	*1,000 acres*	*Pounds*	*Pounds*	*Pounds*	*1,000 cwt*	*1,000 cwt*	*1,000 cwt*
2010	2,826	746	43	6,486	7,660	6,195	183,296	57,144	2,664
2011	1,739	834	44	6,691	7,861	6,880	116,352	65,562	3,027
2012	1,979	643	57	7,291	8,059	6,737	144,280	51,819	3,840
2013	1,762	654	47	7,464	8,385	6,685	131,896	54,840	3,142
2014	2,196	700	37	7,407	8,175	6,292	162,665	57,222	2,328
2015	1,848	698	38	7,219	8,162	7,121	133,401	56,973	2,706
2016	2,403	651	43	6,927	8,377	7,319	166,465	54,533	3,147
2017	1,748	587	39	7,314	8,155	6,438	127,850	47,867	2,511
2018	2,176	693	41	7,517	8,274	7,112	163,578	57,339	2,916
2019	1,730	708	34	7,261	8,004	7,047	125,610	56,669	2,396

NASS, Crops Branch, (202) 720-2127.

Table 1-24.—Rice, rough, by length of grain: Stocks in all positions, United States, 2010–2019

Year beginning previous December	Dec. 1	Mar. 1	Jun. 1	Aug. 1	Oct. 1 [1]
	1,000 cwt				
	Long grain				
2010	103,430	67,910	37,041	19,532	(2)
2011	123,521	86,864	54,636	32,847	(2)
2012	93,027	68,469	37,552	22,034	(2)
2013	99,111	69,313	(NA)	19,439	(2)
2014	84,738	56,125	31,622	14,010	(2)
2015	106,786	71,243	42,295	23,917	(2)
2016	91,814	66,307	36,305	19,801	(2)
2017	106,700	71,636	47,199	28,198	(2)
2018	81,250	57,863	31,903	17,431	(2)
2019	95,679	71,492	46,335	29,146	(2)
	Medium grain				
2010	49,264	33,395	18,344	9,527	3,053
2011	46,853	31,548	15,327	7,870	1,366
2012	50,935	35,978	20,272	12,983	1,870
2013	45,349	32,558	(NA)	10,057	2,029
2014	45,497	30,491	17,294	11,631	6,691
2015	48,483	39,505	27,988	18,169	7,892
2016	50,582	40,718	26,960	18,347	3,732
2017	50,547	33,644	17,612	9,878	3,180
2018	35,376	23,512	11,901	5,561	546
2019	40,000	30,178	15,829	8,564	1,660
	Short grain				
2010	3,912	2,676	2,023	1,317	(2)
2011	3,112	2,203	1,410	972	(2)
2012	2,907	2,044	1,282	945	(2)
2013	3,575	2,398	(NA)	1,024	(2)
2014	3,336	2,348	1,435	963	(2)
2015	2,657	1,720	1,057	687	(2)
2016	2,653	1,737	999	597	(2)
2017	3,082	2,289	1,533	694	(2)
2018	3,048	2,021	1,246	872	(2)
2019	3,038	2,150	1,377	880	(2)

(NA) Not available. [1] California only. [2] Not published to avoid disclosing individual reports.
NASS, Crops Branch, (202) 720–2127.

Table 1-25.—Rough and milled rice (rough equivalent): Supply and disappearance, United States, 2009–2018 [1]

Year beginning August	Supply				Disappearance					Ending stocks July 31
	Beginning stocks	Production	Imports	Total	Food, industrial, & residual [2]	Seed	Total	Exports	Total disappearance	
	Million cwt									
2009	30.4	219.9	19.0	269.3	121.3	3.1	124.4	108.4	232.8	36.5
2010	36.5	243.1	18.3	297.9	134.5	2.4	136.9	112.6	249.5	48.5
2011	48.5	184.9	19.4	252.8	108.4	2.4	110.8	100.9	211.7	41.1
2012	41.1	199.9	21.1	262.1	116.9	2.2	119.0	106.6	225.7	36.4
2013	36.4	189.5	23.1	249.0	121.5	2.4	123.9	93.3	217.2	31.8
2014	31.8	222.2	24.6	278.7	131.8	2.1	133.9	96.3	230.2	48.5
2015	48.5	193.1	24.1	265.7	109.8	2.5	112.3	107.0	219.3	46.5
2016	46.5	224.1	23.5	294.1	131.3	2.0	133.2	114.8	248.0	46.0
2017	46.0	178.2	26.9	251.2	132.5	2.3	134.8	87.0	221.8	29.4
2018 [3]	29.4	224.2	29.0	282.6	(NA)	(NA)	135.0	98.0	233.0	49.6

(NA) Not available. [1] Consolidated supply and disappearance of rough and milled rice. Milled rice data converted to a rough basis using annually derived extraction rates as factors. [2] The residual includes unaccounted losses in transporting, processing, and marketing. [3] Projected as of March 8, 2019.
ERS, Market and Trade Economics Division, (202) 694–5292. Sources: USDA, ERS using data from USDA, National Agricultural Statistics Service, *Quick Stats* and USDA, World Agricultural Outlook Board, *World Agricultural Supply and Demand Estimates* report.

Table 1-26.—Rice, by length of grain: Area, yield, and production, by State and United States, 2017–2019

State	Area harvested			Yield per acre			Production		
	2017	2018	2019	2017	2018	2019	2017	2018	2019
	Long grain								
	1,000 acres	*1,000 acres*	*1,000 acres*	*Pounds*	*Pounds*	*Pounds*	*1,000 cwt*	*1,000 cwt*	*1,000 cwt*
Arkansas	955	1,240	935	7,510	7,550	7,550	71,721	93,620	70,593
California	7	11	10	7,400	6,000	7,300	518	660	730
Louisiana	366	392	361	6,720	7,160	6,380	24,595	28,067	23,032
Mississippi	114	139	111	7,400	7,350	7,350	8,436	10,217	8,159
Missouri	151	211	166	7,460	7,760	7,360	11,265	16,374	12,218
Texas	155	183	147	7,300	8,000	7,400	11,315	14,640	10,878
United States	1,748	2,176	1,730	7,314	7,517	7,261	127,850	163,578	125,610
	Medium grain								
	1,000 acres	*1,000 acres*	*1,000 acres*	*Pounds*	*Pounds*	*Pounds*	*1,000 cwt*	*1,000 cwt*	*1,000 cwt*
Arkansas	148	181	190	7,340	7,330	7,160	10,863	13,267	13,604
California	398	453	453	8,620	8,810	8,580	34,308	39,909	38,867
Louisiana	29	44	53	6,580	6,880	6,370	1,908	3,027	3,376
Mississippi	-	-	2	(X)	(X)	7,150	-	-	143
Missouri	9	9	7	7,060	7,950	7,550	635	716	529
Texas	3	6	3	5,100	7,000	5,000	153	420	150
United States	587	693	708	8,155	8,274	8,004	47,867	57,339	56,669
	Short grain [1]								
	1,000 acres	*1,000 acres*	*1,000 acres*	*Pounds*	*Pounds*	*Pounds*	*1,000 cwt*	*1,000 cwt*	*1,000 cwt*
Arkansas	1	1	1	6,000	6,000	6,000	60	60	60
Calfornia	38	40	33	6,450	7,140	7,080	2,451	2,856	2,336
United States	39	41	34	6,438	7,112	7,047	2,511	2,916	2,396

- Represents zero.
(X) Not applicable.
[1] Sweet rice acreage included with short grain.
NASS, Crops Branch, (202) 720–2127.

Table 1-27.—Rice: Area, yield, and production, by State and United States, 2017–2019

State	Area planted			Area harvested		
	2017	2018	2019	2017	2018	2019
	1,000 acres	*1,000 acres*	*1,000 acres*	*1,000 acres*	*1,000 acres*	*1,000 acres*
Arkansas	1,161	1,441	1,156	1,104	1,422	1,126
California	445	506	498	443	504	496
Louisiana	400	440	425	395	436	414
Mississippi	115	140	117	114	139	113
Missouri	169	224	187	160	220	173
Texas	173	195	157	158	189	150
United States	2,463	2,946	2,540	2,374	2,910	2,472

State	Yield per harvested acre			Production		
	2017	2018	2019	2017	2018	2019
	Pounds	*Pounds*	*Pounds*	*1,000 cwt*	*1,000 cwt*	*1,000 cwt*
Arkansas	7,490	7,520	7,480	82,644	106,947	84,257
California	8,410	8,620	8,450	37.277	43,425	41,933
Louisiana	6,710	7,130	6,380	26,503	31,094	26,408
Mississippi	7,400	7,350	7,350	8,436	10,217	8,302
Missouri	7,440	7,770	7,370	11,900	17,090	12,747
Texas	7,260	7,970	7,350	11,468	15,060	11,028
United States	7,507	7,692	7,471	178,228	223,833	184,675

NASS, Crops Branch, (202) 720–2127.

Table 1-28.—Rice: Marketing year average price and value, by State and United States, 2017–2019

State	Marketing year average price per cwt.			Value of production		
	2017	2018	2019 [1]	2017	2018	2019 [1]
	Dollars	*Dollars*	*Dollars*	*1,000 dollars*	*1,000 dollars*	*1,000 dollars*
Arkansas	11.10	10.70	11.70	917,348	1,148,378	985,807
California	20.30	21.30	18.50	756,723	924,953	775,761
Louisiana	11.70	11.20	11.70	310,085	348,253	308,974
Mississippi	11.50	10.80	11.50	97,014	110,344	95,473
Missouri	12.00	10.70	12.00	142,800	182,863	152,964
Texas	11.90	12.50	12.70	136,469	188,250	140,056
United States	12.90	12.60	13.00	2,360,439	2,903,041	2,459,035

[1] Preliminary.
NASS, Crops Branch, (202) 720–2127.

Table 1-29.—Rice, milled, by length of grain: Stocks in all positions, United States, 2010–2019

Year beginning previous December	Whole kernels (head rice)				
	Dec. 1	Mar. 1	Jun. 1	Aug. 1	Oct.. 1 [1]
	Long grain				
	1,000 cwt	*1,000 cwt*	*1,000 cwt*	*1,000 cwt*	*1,000 cwt*
2010	2,022	2,370	2,043	2,511	(2)
2011	2,665	3,038	3,291	1,924	(2)
2012	2,699	1,856	1,906	1,550	1
2013	2,574	3,144	(NA)	1,704	(2)
2014	3,348	2,379	(3)	1,556	(2)
2015	2,308	1,952	2,523	1,792	(2)
2016	2,716	2,616	3,463	2,022	(2)
2017	2,453	2,659	2,056	1,969	(2)
2018	2,307	1,717	2,633	2,028	(2)
2019	2,037	1,657	2,451	2,422	(2)
	Medium grain				
	1,000 cwt	*1,000 cwt*	*1,000 cwt*	*1,000 cwt*	*1,000 cwt*
2010	1,496	1,472	1,188	799	454
2011	1,743	1,803	981	845	[illegible]
2012	1,406	935	1,041	496	281
2013	1,638	772	(NA)	726	(2)
2014	1,285	1,584	1,601	472	603
2015	1,694	1,139	1,662	878	1,430
2016	1,279	1,459	1,030	1,324	389
2017	1,017	971	1,292	609	388
2018	1,220	1,317	909	801	(2)
2019	988	1,057	748	466	281
	Short grain				
	1,000 cwt	*1,000 cwt*	*1,000 cwt*	*1,000 cwt*	*1,000 cwt*
2010	73	74	47	60	(2)
2011	97	62	53	45	(2)
2012	199	49	60	38	69
2013	99	64	(NA)	61	28
2014	58	48	(2)	47	(2)
2015	51	59	54	37	(2)
2016	75	62	41	40	(2)
2017	65	75	101	45	(2)
2018	62	62	56	43	(2)
2019	78	48	42	52	(2)

See footnote(s) at end of table.

Table 1-29.—Rice, milled, by length of grain: Stocks in all positions, United States, 2010–2019—Continued

Year beginning previous December	Broken kernels				
	Dec. 1	Mar. 1	Jun. 1	Aug. 1	Oct. 1[1]
	Second heads				
	1,000 cwt	*1,000 cwt*	*1,000 cwt*	*1,000 cwt*	*1,000 cwt*
2010	1,374	707	961	670	(2)
2011	888	634	817	992	(2)
2012	1,037	1,021	778	870	(2)
2013	1,231	1,225	(NA)	1,104	(2)
2014	1,243	1,064	1,159	797	(2)
2015	727	1,663	1,227	1,120	(2)
2016	1,385	1,550	1,634	1,436	(2)
2017	1,777	1,924	1,222	1,588	(2)
2018	1,968	1,559	887	566	(2)
2019	676	1,046	665	701	(2)
	Screenings[3]				
	1,000 cwt	*1,000 cwt*	*1,000 cwt*	*1,000 cwt*	*1,000 cwt*
2010	52	20	34	93	
2011	110	91	153	75	
2012	192	82	145	51	
2013	136	271	(NA)	153	
2014	96	118	72	92	
2015	118	115	153	88	
2016	56	61	70	33	
2017	82	81	76	84	
2018	107	118	205	138	
2019	12	136	123	217	
	Brewers				
	1,000 cwt	*1,000 cwt*	*1,000 cwt*	*1,000 cwt*	*1,000 cwt*
2010	662	252	247	247	(2)
2011	799	647	673	786	(2)
2012	710	551	532	573	(2)
2013	1,241	1,189	(NA)	384	(2)
2014	575	651	589	747	(2)
2015	748	941	1,153	141	(2)
2016	734	387	678	551	(2)
2017	401	510	650	798	(2)
2018	1,038	687	364	285	(2)
2019	170	223	707	525	(2)

(NA) Not available. [1] California only; included in Second heads. [2] Not published to avoid disclosing individual operations. [3] Screenings included in Second heads in California.

NASS, Crops Branch, (202) 720–2127.

Table 1-30.—Rice, rough: Support operations, United States, 2016–2019

Marketing year beginning August 1	Price loss coverage payment rates per cwt	Program price levels per cwt		Put under loan		Acquired by CCC under loan program [1]	Owned by CCC at end of marketing year
		Loan	Reference	Quantity	Percentage of production		
	Dollars	*Dollars*	*Dollars*	*Million cwt*	*Percent*	*1,000 cwt*	*1,000 cwt*
Long grain							
2016/2017	4.36	6.50	14.00	30.24	18.16	0	0
2017/2018	2.50	6.50	14.00	17.07	13.35	0	0
2018/2019	3.20	6.50	14.00	21.11	12.88	0	0
2019/2020 [2]	2.00	7.00	14.00	16.53	13.16	0	0
Medium grain [3]							
2016/2017	3.90	6.50	14.00	16.74	29.02	0	0
2017/2018	2.30	6.50	14.00	12.19	24.20	0	0
2018/2019	1.70	6.50	14.00	15.19	25.21	0	0
2019/2020 [2]	2.30	7.00	14.00	18.02	30.49	0	0
Temperate Japonica [4]							
2016/2017	2.00	6.50	16.10	16.40	35.09	0	0
2017/2018	0.00	6.50	16.10	10.98	29.86	0	0
2018/2019	0.00	6.50	16.10	12.95	30.29	0	0
2019/2020 [2]	0.00	7.00	17.30	14.38	34.91	0	0

[1] Acquisitions as of September 30, 2020. [2] Payment rate as of the July 31, 2020 NASS Agricultural Prices Report. [3] Medium Grain includes all short grain rice and medium grain rice for the marketing assistance loan program. The quantity under loan for 2014/2015 includes the medium and short grain rice in California. The medium and short grain rice in California is also shown in the Temperate Japonica section below. [4] Temperate Japonica Rice is medium and short grain rice in California starting with the 2014/2015 crop. Prior to the 2014/2015 crop, temperate japonica rice was classified as medium grain rice for program purposes.
FPAC-BC, Commodity Analysis Branch, (202) 690-0734.

Table 1-31.—Rice: United States exports (milled basis), by country of destination, 2017–2019 [1]

Country of destination	Year		
	2017	2018	2019
	Metric tons	*Metric tons*	*Metric tons*
Mexico	924,842	756,638	851,271
Haiti	530,530	412,253	451,253
Japan	302,873	274,054	339,480
Canada	222,000	240,358	251,726
Korea, South	152,693	111,325	162,159
Honduras	140,912	106,100	159,044
Iraq	33,472	156,906	154,048
Colombia	118,927	147,059	147,357
Nicaragua	6,697	10,675	132,034
Saudi Arabia	119,821	94,255	117,331
Guatemala	113,077	121,320	111,791
Jordan	140,970	80,921	93,337
El Salvador	66,328	78,712	76,544
Costa Rica	72,176	73,582	74,719
Taiwan	51,620	46,887	64,550
Libya	72,502	75,610	56,973
Venezuela	239,062	42,218	53,776
Panama	49,386	23,925	51,317
Dominican Republic	41,245	20,176	22,816
Guinea	37,137	4,588	21,929
Israel(*)	14,661	10,376	19,865
Benin	27,791	11,753	18,090
Cote d'Ivoire	4,171	19,003	11,875
Vietnam	375	180	11,249
Australia(*)	11,985	10,020	9,969
Togo	30	625	9,446
Liberia	20,231	9,279	8,683
Hong Kong	18,240	6,212	7,985
United Kingdom	30,070	25,341	7,622
Bahamas, The	7,643	7,362	7,546
Rest of World	263,847	136,639	130,219
World Total	3,842,612	3,204,392	3,636,401

(*) Denotes a country that is a summarization of its component countries. [1] Year beginning Jan 1.
FAS, Grain and Feed Division, (202) 720–6219. www.fas.usda.gov/grain/default.html.

Table 1-32.—International Rice, milled: Area, yield, and production in specified countries, 2017/2018–2019/2020

Country	Area			Yield per hectare			Production		
	2017/2018	2018/2019	2019/2020	2017/2018	2018/2019	2019/2020	2017/2018	2018/2019	2019/2020
	1,000 hectares			*Metric tons*			*1,000 metric tons*		
China	30,747	30,189	29,690	6.92	7.03	7.06	148,873	148,490	146,730
India	43,774	43,800	44,000	3.86	3.99	4.02	112,760	116,480	118,000
Indonesia	12,250	12,100	12,000	4.76	4.78	4.79	37,000	36,700	36,500
Bangladesh	11,272	11,770	11,830	4.35	4.45	4.55	32,650	34,909	35,850
Vietnam	7,645	7,615	7,665	5.79	5.83	5.91	27,657	27,767	28,300
Thailand	10,756	10,830	10,000	2.90	2.85	2.80	20,577	20,340	18,500
Burma	7,100	7,100	7,100	2.91	2.90	2.93	13,200	13,175	13,300
Philippines	4,844	4,741	4,700	4.01	3.93	4.05	12,235	11,732	12,000
Japan	1,557	1,550	1,545	6.87	6.79	6.94	7,787	7,657	7,800
Pakistan	2,800	2,880	2,900	4.02	3.80	3.88	7,500	7,300	7,500
Brazil	1,973	1,700	1,680	6.12	6.18	6.25	8,204	7,140	7,140
United States	961	1,178	1,000	8.41	8.62	8.38	5,659	7,107	5,864
Cambodia	3,184	3,240	3,190	2.86	2.91	2.92	5,554	5,742	5,688
Nigeria	3,600	3,600	3,600	2.08	2.11	2.16	4,725	4,788	4,900
Egypt	762	462	760	8.18	8.78	8.20	4,300	2,800	4,300
Korea, South	755	738	730	7.02	6.99	6.84	3,972	3,868	3,744
Nepal	1,490	1,500	1,500	3.34	3.73	3.53	3,310	3,730	3,530
Sri Lanka	769	975	900	4.30	4.72	4.44	2,248	3,131	2,720
Madagascar	1,425	1,500	1,500	2.18	2.67	2.80	1,984	2,560	2,688
Peru	422	438	425	7.20	7.99	7.53	2,097	2,415	2,208
Laos	964	856	985	3.29	3.12	3.30	2,000	1,680	2,050
Tanzania	1,170	1,200	1,200	2.46	2.58	2.58	1,896	2,046	2,046

FAS, Office of Global Analysis, (202) 720-6301. Prepared or estimated on the basis of official USDA production, supply, and distribution, supply, and and distribution statistics from foreign governments.

Table 1-33.—Rice, milled equivalent: International trade, 2017/2018–2019/2020

Country	2017/2018	2018/2019	2019/2020
	1,000 metric tons		
Principle exporting countries:			
India	12,041	10,420	12,500
Thailand	11,056	7,562	9,800
Vietnam	6,590	6,581	6,500
Pakistan	4,011	4,500	4,000
China	1,364	2,770	2,858
United States	2,764	2,971	2,800
Burma	2,750	2,500	2,600
Cambodia	1,300	1,350	1,300
Uruguay	756	800	785
Brazil	1,152	830	650
Paraguay	653	689	650
Guyana	455	414	414
Argentina	426	370	330
European Union	349	302	300
Russia	139	153	150
South Africa	112	112	125
Kazakhstan	95	88	100
Cote d'Ivoire	80	100	100
Egypt	50	20	95
Guinea	80	100	90
Principle importing countries:			
Philippines	1,300	3,600	2,600
China	5,500	3,000	2,400
European Union	2,007	2,150	2,200
Nigeria	2,000	1,900	1,500
Saudi Arabia	1,290	1,425	1,450
Cote d'Ivoire	1,370	1,350	1,350
Iraq	1,130	1,200	1,200
Brazil	562	900	1,100
Iran	1,200	1,200	1,100
Senegal	1,100	1,100	1,050
South Africa	1,074	1,010	1,050
United States	874	920	1,032
Indonesia	2,350	600	1,000
Malaysia	800	1,000	1,000
Ghana	780	900	950
United Arab Emirates	775	850	925
Mexico	813	744	785
Nepal	670	630	750
Japan	686	631	685
Kenya	575	625	675

FAS, Office of Global Analysis, (202) 720-6301. Prepared or estimated on the basis of official USDA production, supply, and distribution statistics from foreign governments.

Table 1-34.—Food grains: Average price, selected markets and grades, 2010–2019[1]

Calendar year[2]	Kansas City: Wheat, No. 1 Hard Winter, Ordinary Protein (rail)	Kansas City: Wheat, No. 1 Hard Winter, 13% protein (rail)	Kansas City: Wheat, No. 2 Soft Red Winter (rail)	Minneapolis (rail): Wheat, No. 1 Hard Amber Durum (milling) (rail)	Minneapolis (rail): Wheat, No. 1 Dark Northern Spring (rail), 14% protein	Minneapolis (rail): Rye, No. 2, 20 day delivery (truck)	Portland Wheat No. 1 Soft White	St. Louis Wheat, No. 2 Soft Red Winter (truck)
	Dollars per bushel							
2010	5.90	6.58	6.03	8.75	7.79	4.58	5.45	5.36
2011	8.44	9.17	7.87	....	11.36	....	7.08	7.49
2012	8.47	8.96	7.25	....	9.69	....	7.74	7.56
2013	7.22	8.60	6.67	(NA)	8.08	(NA)	7.67	6.97
2014	7.89	7.95	5.72	(NA)	8.73	5.75	7.09	6.45
2015	6.05	6.16	4.43	(NA)	7.00	5.75	5.88	4.81
2016	4.80	5.50	3.35	(NA)	6.60	4.48	4.95	4.32
2017	5.03	6.25	3.98	(NA)	7.18	4.07	4.99	4.36
2018	6.22	6.67	6.19	(NA)	7.12	5.38	5.88	(NA)
2019	5.62	6.10	4.79	(NA)	6.56	7.12	5.91	5.14

Calendar year[2]	Chicago Wheat, No. 2 Soft Red Winter (rail)	Denver Wheat, No. 1 Hard Winter (truck red)	S.W. Louisiana Milled Rice: Medium	S.W. Louisiana Milled Rice: Long	Arkansas Milled Rice: Medium	Arkansas Milled Rice: Long	Texas Milled Rice: Long
	Dollars per bushel		Dollars per cwt				
2010	5.36	5.00	30.80	23.12	29.68	23.91	26.46
2011	6.83	7.36	33.47	26.20	34.99	27.10	29.25
2012	7.44	7.44	28.89	25.77	27.91	26.18	27.18
2013	6.84	7.27	30.56	28.48	28.68	28.52	29.61
2014	5.89	6.38	30.76	27.04	31.30	27.62	29.15
2015	5.08	4.77	27.88	23.30	27.41	23.35	25.31
2016	4.31	3.35	27.39	22.65	22.92	23.01	23.92
2017	4.22	3.45	22.88	22.88	23.75	22.52	23.07
2018	4.88	4.52	29.43	22.54	27.41	27.41	26.37
2019	4.91	4.21	31.50	22.84	30.93	24.52	26.34

(NA) Not available. [1] Simple average of daily prices. [2] For wheat and rye, crop year begins in June. For rice, crop year begins in August.
AMS, Livestock and Grain Market News branch, (202) 720–6231.

Table 1-35.—Corn: Area, yield, production, and value, United States, 2010–2019

Year	Area planted, all purposes	Corn for grain: Area harvested	Corn for grain: Yield per harvested acre	Corn for grain: Production	Corn for grain: Marketing year average price per bushel	Corn for grain: Value of production	Corn for silage: Area harvested	Corn for silage: Yield per harvested acre	Corn for silage: Production
	1,000 acres	1,000 acres	Bushels	1,000 bushels	Dollars	1,000 dollars	1,000 acres	Tons	1,000 tons
2010	88,192	81,446	152.6	12,425,330	5.18	64,529,628	5,567	19.3	107,314
2011	91,936	83,879	146.8	12,313,956	6.22	76,651,242	5,935	18.4	109,091
2012	97,291	87,365	123.1	10,755,111	6.89	74,155,299	7,419	15.7	116,148
2013	95,365	87,451	158.1	13,828,964	4.46	61,927,548	6,281	18.8	118,296
2014	90,597	83,136	171.0	14,215,532	3.70	52,951,760	6,371	20.1	128,048
2015	88,019	80,753	168.4	13,601,964	3.61	49,339,261	6,237	20.4	127,311
2016	94,004	86,748	174.6	15,148,038	3.36	51,304,297	6,206	20.3	126,020
2017	90,167	82,733	176.6	14,609,407	3.36	49,567,854	6,385	20.0	127,434
2018	88,871	81,276	176.4	14,340,369	3.61	52,102,404	6,120	19.9	121,564
2019	89,700	81,482	168.0	13,691,561	3.85	52,911,254	6,587	20.2	132,807

NASS, Crops Branch, (202) 720–2127.

Table 1-36.—Corn: Area, yield, and production, by State and United States, 2017–2019

State	Area planted for all purposes			Area harvested for grain		
	2017	2018	2019	2017	2018	2019
	1,000 acres					
Alabama	250	255	320	235	245	305
Arizona	65	80	90	32	20	37
Arkansas	620	660	770	595	645	725
California	430	430	460	80	65	60
Colorado	1,460	1,460	1,550	1,300	1,190	1,300
Connecticut	24	23	23	(NA)	(NA)	(NA)
Delaware	180	170	185	171	166	180
Florida	75	95	90	37	62	54
Georgia	290	325	395	245	285	350
Idaho	340	350	385	115	125	148
Illinois	11,200	11,000	10,500	10,950	10,800	10,200
Indiana	5,350	5,300	5,000	5,200	5,120	4,820
Iowa	13,300	13,200	13,500	12,900	12,750	13,050
Kansas	5,500	5,450	6,400	5,200	4,980	6,020
Kentucky	1,320	1,330	1,550	1,220	1,220	1,450
Louisiana	620	500	460	550	490	450
Maine	31	30	29	(NA)	(NA)	(NA)
Maryland	480	440	510	420	380	460
Massachusetts	15	14	14	(NA)	(NA)	(NA)
Michigan	2,250	2,250	2,000	1,890	1,890	1,610
Minnesota	8,050	7,900	7,800	7,630	7,460	7,260
Mississippi	520	480	660	500	460	620
Missouri	3,400	3,500	3,200	3,250	3,330	2,990
Montana	115	115	115	65	68	60
Nebraska	9,550	9,600	10,100	9,300	9,300	9,810
Nevada	12	13	15	(NA)	(NA)	(NA)
New Hampshire	14	13	12	(NA)	(NA)	(NA)
New Jersey	77	70	77	70	60	68
New Mexico	125	135	145	43	35	46
New York	1,000	1,070	1,020	485	615	545
North Carolina	890	910	990	840	830	930
North Dakota	3,420	3,150	3,500	3,230	2,930	3,230
Ohio	3,400	3,500	2,800	3,150	3,300	2,570
Oklahoma	350	310	370	305	270	330
Oregon	85	75	80	44	40	48
Pennsylvania	1,400	1,350	1,350	950	920	950
Rhode Island	2	2	2	(NA)	(NA)	(NA)
South Carolina	350	340	380	325	310	350
South Dakota	5,700	5,300	4,530	5,080	4,860	3,910
Tennessee	750	720	970	710	670	910
Texas	2,450	2,200	2,500	2,240	1,750	2,150
Utah	80	70	85	20	22	26
Vermont	82	85	81	(NA)	(NA)	(NA)
Virginia	500	485	540	340	325	380
Washington	170	165	170	80	85	90
West Virginia	50	46	52	33	33	38
Wisconsin	3,900	3,900	3,800	2,930	3,170	2,680
Wyoming	95	95	95	63	70	67
United States	90,167	88,871	89,700	82,733	81,276	81,482

See footnote(s) at end of table.

Table 1-36.—Corn: Area, yield, and production, by State and United States, 2017–2019—Continued

State	Corn for grain					
	Yield per harvested acre			Production		
	2017	2018	2019	2017	2018	2019
	1,000 acres					
Alabama	167.0	156.0	147.0	39,245	38,220	44,835
Arizona	195.0	220.0	231.0	6,240	4,400	8,547
Arkansas	183.0	181.0	175.0	108,885	116,745	126,875
California	167.0	173.0	168.0	13,360	11,245	10,080
Colorado	143.0	130.0	123.0	185,900	154,700	159,900
Connecticut	(NA)	(NA)	(NA)	(NA)	(NA)	(NA)
Delaware	189.0	145.0	161.0	32,319	24,070	28,980
Florida	161.0	157.0	161.0	5,957	9,734	8,694
Georgia	176.0	176.0	160.0	43,120	50,160	56,000
Idaho	203.0	213.0	205.0	23,345	26,625	30,340
Illinois	201.0	210.0	181.0	2,200,950	2,268,000	1,846,200
Indiana	180.0	189.0	169.0	936,000	967,680	814,580
Iowa	202.0	196.0	198.0	2,605,800	2,499,000	2,583,900
Kansas	132.0	129.0	133.0	686,400	642,420	800,660
Kentucky	178.0	175.0	169.0	217,160	213,500	245,050
Louisiana	184.0	173.0	165.0	90,160	77,850	89,925
Maine	(NA)	(NA)	(NA)	(NA)	(NA)	(NA)
Maryland	172.0	146.0	161.0	72,240	55,480	74,060
Massachusetts	(NA)	(NA)	(NA)	(NA)	(NA)	(NA)
Michigan	159.0	153.0	149.0	300,510	289,170	239,890
Minnesota	194.0	182.0	174.0	1,480,220	1,357,720	1,263,240
Mississippi	189.0	185.0	174.0	94,500	85,100	107,880
Missouri	170.0	140.0	155.0	552,500	466,200	463,450
Montana	70.0	85.0	95.0	4,550	5,780	5,700
Nebraska	181.0	192.0	182.0	1,683,300	1,785,600	1,785,420
Nevada	(NA)	(NA)	(NA)	(NA)	(NA)	(NA)
New Hampshire	(NA)	(NA)	(NA)	(NA)	(NA)	(NA)
New Jersey	167.0	141.0	155.0	11,690	8,460	10,540
New Mexico	134.0	187.0	135.0	5,762	6,545	6,210
New York	161.0	159.0	158.0	78,085	97,785	86,110
North Carolina	142.0	113.0	111.0	119,280	93,790	103,230
North Dakota	139.0	153.0	141.0	448,070	448,290	455,430
Ohio	177.0	187.0	164.0	557,550	617,100	421,400
Oklahoma	126.0	134.0	137.0	38,430	36,180	45,210
Oregon	212.0	195.0	237.0	9,328	7,800	11,376
Pennsylvania	161.0	140.0	153.0	148,120	124,600	162,180
Rhode Island	(NA)	(NA)	(NA)	(NA)	(NA)	(NA)
South Carolina	136.0	127.0	106.0	44,200	39,370	37,100
South Dakota	145.0	160.0	145.0	736,600	777,600	566,950
Tennessee	171.0	168.0	177.0	121,410	112,560	161,070
Texas	140.0	108.0	133.0	313,600	189,000	285,950
Utah	176.0	182.0	143.0	3,520	4,004	3,718
Vermont	(NA)	(NA)	(NA)	(NA)	(NA)	(NA)
Virginia	140.0	146.0	144.0	47,600	47,450	54,720
Washington	225.0	220.0	237.0	18,000	18,700	21,330
West Virginia	152.0	152.0	165.0	5,016	5,016	6,270
Wisconsin	174.0	172.0	168.0	509,820	545,240	450,240
Wyoming	155.0	164.0	123.0	9,765	11,480	8,241
United States	176.6	176.4	168.0	14,609,407	14,340,369	13,691,561

(NA) Not available.
NASS, Crops Branch, (202) 720–2127.

Table 1-37.—Corn: Supply and disappearance, United States, 2009–2018

Year beginning September 1	Supply: Beginning stocks	Supply: Production	Supply: Imports	Supply: Total [1]	Disappearance: Domestic use: Food, alcohol, and industrial	Disappearance: Domestic use: Seed	Disappearance: Domestic use: Feed and residual	Disappearance: Exports	Disappearance: Total disappearance	Ending stocks Aug. 31
	Million bushels									
2009	1,673	13,067	8	14,749	5,939	27.8	5,096	1,979	13,041	1,708
2010	1,708	12,425	28	14,161	6,403	29.6	4,770	1,831	13,033	1,128
2011	1,128	12,314	29	13,471	6,400	31.0	4,512	1,539	12,482	989
2012	989	10,755	160	11,904	6,013	31.0	4,309	730	11,083	821
2013	821	13,831	36	14,688	6,501	29.7	5,004	1,921	13,456	1,232
2014	1,232	14,217	32	15,481	6,566	29.3	5,287	1,867	13,750	1,731
2015	1,731	13,602	68	15,401	6,617	30.6	5,118	1,899	13,664	1,737
2016	1,737	15,148	57	16,942	6,856	29.3	5,470	2,294	14,649	2,293
2017	2,293	14,609	36	16,939	7,027	29.6	5,304	2,438	14,798	2,140
2018	2,140	14,430	28	16,509	6,764	29.1	5,429	2,066	14,288	2,221

Latest data may be preliminary or projected. [1] Total may not add due to rounding.
ERS, Market and Trade Economics Division, (202) 694–5313. Source: USDA, World Agricultural Outlook Board, World Agricultural Supply and Demand Estimates and supporting materials.

Table 1-38.—Corn: Stocks on and off farms, United States, 2010–2019

Year beginning previous December	On farms: Dec. 1	On farms: Mar. 1	On farms: Jun. 1	On farms: Sep. 1 [2]	Off farms [1]: Dec. 1	Off farms [1]: Mar. 1	Off farms [1]: Jun. 1	Off farms [1]: Sep. 1 [2]
	1,000 bushels							
2010	7,405,000	4,548,000	2,131,400	485,100	3,497,460	3,145,787	2,178,671	1,222,687
2011	6,302,000	3,384,000	1,681,500	314,950	3,754,769	3,139,228	1,988,832	812,695
2012	6,175,000	3,192,000	1,482,000	313,700	3,471,823	2,831,356	1,666,204	675,327
2013	4,586,000	2,669,200	1,260,100	275,000	3,446,732	2,730,726	1,506,144	546,185
2014	6,380,000	3,860,500	1,863,200	462,000	4,072,532	3,147,623	1,988,516	769,904
2015	7,087,000	4,380,000	2,275,000	593,000	4,124,380	3,369,806	2,177,988	1,138,164
2016	6,829,000	4,335,000	2,471,400	627,400	4,406,178	3,487,233	2,239,679	1,109,658
2017	7,611,000	4,908,000	2,841,400	787,000	4,772,471	3,713,992	2,387,682	1,506,303
2018	7,739,000	5,002,000	2,750,000	620,000	4,827,501	3,890,126	2,554,704	1,520,335
2019	7,451,000	5,131,000	2,949,600	814,100	4,485,798	3,482,206	2,252,636	1,406,649

[1] Includes stocks at mills, elevators, warehouses, terminals, and processors. [2] Old crop only.
NASS, Crops Branch, (202) 720–2127.

Table 1-39.—Corn: Utilization for silage, by State and United States, 2017–2019

State	Silage								
	Area harvested			Yield per acre			Production		
	2017	2018	2019	2017	2018	2019	2017	2018	2019
	1,000 acres	*1,000 acres*	*1,000 acres*	*Tons*	*Tons*	*Tons*	*1,000 tons*	*1,000 tons*	*1,000 tons*
Alabama	7	5	7	17.0	16.0	13.0	119	80	91
Arizona	32	58	50	31.0	29.0	29.0	992	1,682	1,450
Arkansas	2	3	7	19.0	21.0	16.0	38	63	112
California	345	360	395	26.5	26.5	27.5	9,143	9,900	10,665
Colorado	130	190	175	25.5	22.0	24.0	3,315	4,180	4,200
Connecticut	20	20	21	19.5	19.0	21.0	390	380	441
Delaware	7	3	4	19.5	24.0	23.0	137	72	92
Florida	35	30	35	19.0	21.0	20.0	665	630	700
Georgia	35	30	25	16.0	21.0	22.0	560	630	550
Idaho	220	220	235	30.0	30.0	28.0	6,600	6,600	6,580
Illinois	190	100	170	17.0	20.0	20.0	3,230	2,000	3,400
Indiana	110	100	110	21.0	21.0	20.0	2,310	2,100	2,200
Iowa	330	270	360	21.0	20.5	22.0	6,930	5,535	7,920
Kansas	250	390	250	21.5	13.5	17.5	5,375	5,265	4,375
Kentucky	85	90	80	20.0	21.0	21.0	1,700	1,890	1,680
Louisiana	1	2	3	20.0	20.0	19.0	20	40	57
Maine	27	27	26	18.0	20.0	19.0	486	540	494
Maryland	50	45	40	20.5	19.0	22.0	1,025	855	880
Massachusetts	12	12	11	19.0	20.0	20.0	228	240	220
Michigan	340	340	340	18.5	17.5	18.5	6,290	5,950	6,290
Minnesota	360	340	460	21.5	22.0	19.0	7,740	7,480	8,740
Mississippi	7	7	7	18.0	15.0	15.0	126	105	105
Missouri	70	100	70	15.0	13.0	16.0	1,050	1,300	1,120
Montana	25	37	50	20.0	20.0	23.0	500	740	1,150
Nebraska	210	220	200	19.5	21.0	23.0	4,095	4,620	4,600
Nevada	10	7	12	24.0	26.0	25.0	240	182	300
New Hampshire	13	12	11	20.0	21.0	20.0	260	252	220
New Jersey	6	6	7	19.5	19.0	22.0	117	114	154
New Mexico	80	95	90	25.0	22.0	20.0	2,000	2,090	1,800
New York	495	445	445	18.0	19.0	18.0	8,910	8,455	8,010
North Carolina	40	50	50	18.0	18.0	16.0	720	800	900
North Dakota	160	170	140	10.0	15.0	19.5	1,600	2,550	2,730
Ohio	210	160	170	20.0	20.0	19.0	4,200	3,200	3,230
Oklahoma	20	20	20	20.0	11.0	13.0	400	220	260
Oregon	40	34	35	24.0	23.0	24.0	960	782	840
Pennsylvania	420	390	380	21.5	19.0	20.0	9,030	7,410	7,600
Rhode Island	2	2	2	18.0	21.0	20.0	36	42	40
South Carolina	16	19	13	18.0	14.0	14.0	288	266	182
South Dakota	510	360	340	12.5	16.5	17.5	6,375	5,940	5,950
Tennessee	30	38	40	22.0	19.0	20.0	660	722	800
Texas	150	270	280	22.0	16.0	20.0	3,300	4,320	5,600
Utah	56	45	55	25.0	23.0	24.0	1,400	1,035	1,320
Vermont	76	79	77	16.5	19.0	18.0	1,254	1,501	1,386
Virginia	135	135	135	18.0	19.0	19.0	2,430	2,565	2,565
Washington	90	80	80	27.0	26.0	23.0	2,430	2,080	1,840
West Virginia	16	11	12	20.0	19.0	20.0	320	209	240
Wisconsin	880	670	1,040	19.0	20.0	17.5	16,720	13,400	18,200
Wyoming	30	23	22	24.0	24.0	24.0	720	552	528
United States	6,385	6,120	6,587	20.0	19.9	20.2	127,434	121,564	132,807

NASS, Crops Branch, (202) 720–2127.

Table 1-40.—Corn for grain: Marketing year average price and value, by State and United States, 2017–2019

State	Marketing year average price per bushel			Value of production		
	2017	2018	2019 [1]	2017	2018	2019 [1]
	Dollars	*Dollars*	*Dollars*	*1,000 dollars*	*1,000 dollars*	*1,000 dollars*
Alabama	4.04	4.11	4.20	158,550	157,084	188,307
Arizona	4.55	4.96	5.30	28,392	21,842	45,299
Arkansas	3.64	3.80	3.90	396,341	443,631	494,813
California	4.20	4.40	4.55	56,112	49,478	45,864
Colorado	3.37	3.70	3.95	626,483	572,390	631,605
Delaware	4.02	4.11	4.30	129,922	98,928	124,614
Florida	4.47	4.47	4.50	26,628	43,511	39,123
Georgia	4.33	4.35	4.50	186,710	218,196	252,000
Idaho	4.21	4.42	4.50	98,282	117,683	136,530
Illinois	3.41	3.62	3.85	7,505,240	8,210,160	7,107,870
Indiana	3.56	3.78	4.10	3,332,160	3,657,830	3,339,778
Iowa	3.31	3.59	3.80	8,625,198	8,971,410	9,818,820
Kansas	3.20	3.28	3.60	2,251,392	2,299,864	2,962,442
Kentucky	3.69	3.84	4.10	801,320	819,840	1,004,705
Louisiana	3.72	3.86	3.95	335,395	300,501	355,204
Maryland	4.02	4.11	4.30	290,405	228,023	318,458
Michigan	3.46	3.72	4.00	1,039,765	1,075,712	959,560
Minnesota	3.18	3.47	3.65	4,707,100	4,711,288	4,610,826
Mississippi	3.68	3.80	4.00	347,760	323,380	431,520
Missouri	3.41	3.68	3.90	1,884,025	1,715,616	1,807,455
Montana	3.41	3.79	3.50	15,516	21,906	23,940
Nebraska	3.35	3.58	3.80	5,639,055	6,392,448	6,784,596
New Jersey	3.75	3.90	4.30	43,838	32,994	45,322
New Mexico	3.90	4.30	4.40	22,472	28,144	27,342
New York	4.07	4.16	4.27	317,806	406,786	367,690
North Carolina	4.24	4.39	4.45	505,747	411,738	459,374
North Dakota	3.04	3.32	3.55	1,364,869	1,488,323	1,616,777
Ohio	3.61	3.74	4.20	2,012,756	2,307,954	1,770,216
Oklahoma	3.59	3.86	4.10	137,964	139,655	185,361
Oregon	3.78	4.13	4.45	35,260	32,214	50,623
Pennsylvania	3.87	4.22	4.40	573,224	525,812	713,592
South Carolina	4.40	4.50	4.65	194,480	177,165	172,515
South Dakota	3.09	3.38	3.70	2,276,094	2,628,288	2,097,715
Tennessee	3.55	3.76	3.95	431,006	423,226	636,227
Texas	3.70	4.13	4.30	1,160,320	780,570	1,229,585
Utah	3.96	4.31	4.40	13,939	17,257	16,359
Virginia	3.96	4.06	4.15	188,496	192,647	227,088
Washington	4.05	4.11	4.15	72,900	76,857	88,520
West Virginia	3.95	4.08	4.15	19,813	20,465	26,021
Wisconsin	3.30	3.52	3.70	1,682,406	1,919,245	1,665,888
Wyoming	3.35	3.69	3.85	32,713	42,361	31,728
United States	3.36	3.61	3.85	49,567,854	52,102,404	52,911,254

[1] Preliminary.
NASS, Crops Branch, (202) 720–2127.

Table 1-41.—International Corn: Area, yield, and production in specified countries, 2017/2018–2019/2020

Country	Area			Yield per hectare			Production		
	2017/ 2018	2018/ 2019	2019/ 2020	2017/ 2018	2018/ 2019	2016/ 2017	2017/ 2018	2018/ 2019	2019/ 2020
	1,000 hectares			*Metric tons*			*1,000 metric tons*		
United States	33,481	32,891	32,975	11.08	11.08	10.55	371,096	364,262	347,782
China	42,399	42,129	41,280	6.11	6.11	6.32	259,071	257,330	260,770
Brazil	16,600	17,500	18,100	4.94	5.77	5.58	82,000	101,000	101,000
European Union	8,258	8,241	8,700	7.51	7.82	7.47	62,007	64,440	65,000
Argentina	5,200	6,100	6,200	6.15	8.36	8.07	32,000	51,000	50,000
Ukraine	4,433	4,567	5,000	5.44	7.84	7.16	24,115	35,805	35,800
India	9,380	9,275	9,300	3.07	2.99	3.07	28,753	27,715	28,500
Mexico	7,322	7,200	6,800	3.77	3.83	3.68	27,569	27,600	25,000
South Africa	2,634	2,597	3,000	4.98	4.55	5.33	13,104	11,824	16,000
Russia	2,694	2,373	2,504	4.90	4.81	5.70	13,201	11,415	14,275
Canada	1,406	1,431	1,450	10.03	9.70	9.24	14,095	13,885	13,400
Indonesia	3,650	3,700	3,900	3.26	3.24	3.26	11,900	12,000	12,700
Nigeria	6,540	6,500	6,500	1.59	1.69	1.69	10,420	11,000	11,000
Ethiopia	2,230	2,300	2,300	3.77	3.63	3.65	8,400	8,350	8,400
Philippines	2,604	2,480	2,550	3.11	3.07	3.18	8,084	7,608	8,100
Serbia	1,000	900	950	4.00	7.78	7.11	4,000	7,000	6,750
Egypt	800	850	800	8.00	8.00	8.00	6,400	6,800	6,400
Tanzania	4,200	4,200	4,200	1.59	1.49	1.48	6,681	6,273	6,200
Pakistan	1,230	1,320	1,330	4.64	4.62	4.59	5,701	6,100	6,100
Turkey	530	530	520	10.00	10.76	11.54	5,300	5,700	6,000

FAS, Office of Global Analysis, (202) 720-6301. Prepared or estimated on the basis of offical USDA production, supply, and distribution statistics from foreign governments.

Table 1-42.—Corn: International trade, 2017/2018–2019/2020

Country	2017/2018	2018/2019	2019/2020
		Metric tons	
Principle exporting countries:			
United States	61,916	52,457	43,817
Argentina	24,154	39,749	36,000
Brazil	22,473	37,000	33,500
Ukraine	18,036	30,321	32,000
Russia	5,532	2,770	4,700
Serbia	1,749	3,629	2,900
European Union	2,009	1,170	2,500
Paraguay	819	2,836	2,200
Canada	1,739	2,800	2,000
Burma	1,400	1,500	1,400
South Africa	1,936	1,797	900
Mexico	958	718	700
Cambodia	600	500	500
India	500	500	500
Moldova	1,089	419	400
Vietnam	460	581	400
Laos	200	200	200
Zambia	50	100	200
Indonesia	1,200	600	100
Thailand	400	100	100
Principle importing countries:			
European Union	18,465	25,209	21,000
Mexico	16,129	16,658	17,500
Japan	15,668	16,047	16,000
Vietnam	8,600	10,200	11,500
Korea, South	10,018	10,856	10,800
Iran	8,900	9,000	10,000
Egypt	9,464	9,367	9,900
China	3,456	4,483	7,000
Colombia	5,201	6,048	6,200
Algeria	4,184	4,521	4,500
Taiwan	4,410	4,508	4,300
Malaysia	3,645	3,674	4,000
Peru	3,402	3,694	4,000
Saudi Arabia	3,983	3,662	4,000
Morocco	2,558	2,341	3,000
Turkey	2,719	2,876	3,000
Chile	2,132	2,300	2,600
Israel	1,861	1,611	2,000
Canada	1,669	2,633	1,500
Dominican Republic	1,329	1,536	1,500

FAS, Office of Global Analysis, (202) 720-6301. Prepared or estimated on the basis of official USDA production, supply, and distribution statistics from foreign governments.

Table 1-43.—Corn: Support operations, United States, 2013–2019

Marketing year beginning September 1	Income support payment rates per bushel[1]	Program price levels per bushel		Put under loan		Acquired by CCC under loan program[5]	Owned by CCC at end of marketing year
		Loan[2]	Target/ reference[3]	Quantity	Percentage of production[4]		
	Dollars	*Dollars*	*Dollars*	*Million bushels*	*Percent*	*Million bushels*	*Million bushels*
2013/2014	0.28/0.00	1.95	2.63	460	3.3	0	0
2014/2015	0.00	1.95	3.70	574	4.0	0	0
2015/2016	0.09	1.95	3.70	746	5.5	0	0
2016/2017	0.34	1.95	3.70	880	5.8	0	0
2017/2018	0.35	1.95	3.70	980	6.7	0	0
2018/2019	0.10	1.95	3.70	919	6.4	0	0
2019/2020	0.00	2.20	3.70	805	5.9	0	0

[1] The first entry is the direct payment rate and the second entry is the counter-cyclical payment rate for 2004/2005-2013/2014. For 2009/2010-2013/2014, producers who participated in the Average Crop Revenue (ACRE) program got a 20 percent reduction in their direct payment, not calculated in this table. For 2014/2015 and after, the entry is the price loss coverage (PLC) payment rate. For 2017/2018, projected PLC payment rate is based on March 2018 WASDE MY price. Agricultural Risk Coverage (ARC) is also available, but payment rates are established at the county or farm levels. [2] For 2009/2010-2013/2014, producers who participated in the ACRE program got a 30 percent reduction in their loan rate, not calculated in this table. [3] Target applies to 2003/2004-2013/2014 and Reference applies beginning with 2014/2015. [4] Percent of production is on a grain basis. [5] Acquisitions as of January 31, 2020.
FPAC-BC, Commodity Analysis Branch.

Table 1-44.—Corn: United States exports, specified by country of destination, 2017–2019[1]

Country of destination	2017	2018	2019
	Metric tons		
Mexico	14,698,071	16,698,898	14,305,372
Japan	12,378,239	15,267,093	10,461,561
Colombia	4,798,510	5,511,589	3,911,611
Canada	837,742	1,971,476	2,104,913
Korea, South	4,000,781	7,264,399	1,880,096
Taiwan	2,256,756	3,208,807	1,182,447
Peru	3,216,248	3,074,252	1,029,891
Guatemala	859,355	1,149,313	1,001,003
Costa Rica	835,332	850,465	847,215
Honduras	489,966	617,583	674,390
Saudi Arabia	1,599,150	1,724,045	623,485
El Salvador	456,031	601,587	587,544
Panama	475,507	507,012	503,289
Dominican Republic	562,416	939,054	368,859
China	811,069	290,173	309,474
Nicaragua	257,712	338,400	287,332
Jamaica	295,841	277,224	253,266
New Zealand(*)	521	46,531	126,597
Israel(*)	107,459	814,810	84,791
Trinidad and Tobago	80,752	91,781	80,079
Philippines	56,060	167,333	78,843
Vietnam	541	1,908,658	65,266
Morocco	575,272	820,957	61,752
Cuba	230,863	116,599	57,999
Haiti	36,594	17,832	47,579
Guyana	34,735	44,549	41,076
Venezuela	336,081	509,994	34,898
Hong Kong	32,103	34,105	34,322
Barbados	29,655	36,042	29,536
Ecuador	838,625	4,254	27,601
Rest of World	2,358,569	4,844,101	81,577
World Total	52,746,556	69,748,916	41,305,372

[1] Data Source: U.S. Census Bureau trade data. Excludes seed, popcorn.
FAS, Office of Global Analysis, (202) 720-6301.

Table 1-45.—Oats: Area, yield, production, and value, United States, 2010–2019

Year	Area		Yield per harvested acre	Production	Marketing year average price per bushel received by farmers	Value of production
	Planted [1]	Harvested				
	1,000 acres	*1,000 acres*	*Bushels*	*1,000 bushels*	*Dollars*	*1,000 dollars*
2010	3,113	1,267	64.6	81,856	2.52	218,536
2011	2,349	875	57.3	50,126	3.49	175,523
2012	2,700	1,005	61.2	61,486	3.89	243,018
2013	2,980	1,009	64.1	64,642	3.75	239,643
2014	2,753	1,035	67.9	70,232	3.21	241,472
2015	3,088	1,275	70.2	89,455	2.12	214,415
2016	2,829	979	66.0	64,628	2.06	153,824
2017	2,589	804	61.7	49,585	2.59	139,635
2018	2,746	865	64.9	56,130	2.66	167,640
2019 [2]	2.810	826	64.3	53,148	2.95	162,711

[1] Relates to the total area of oats sown for all purposes, including oats sown in the preceding fall.
[2] Price and value are preliminary.
NASS, Crops Branch, (202) 720–2127.

Table 1-46.—Oats: Stocks on and off farms, United States, 2010–2019

Year beginning September	On farms				Off farms [1]			
	Sep. 1	Dec. 1	Mar. 1	Jun. 1	Sep. 1	Dec. 1	Mar. 1	Jun. 1
2010	45,850	34,100	26,950	14,580	70,722	66,911	59,361	53,049
2011	30,300	24,600	19,550	11,070	47,391	54,244	55,044	43,869
2012	34,100	26,100	18,900	11,380	50,872	47,051	33,726	24,957
2013	37,150	25,650	19,800	9,710	26,339	22,394	15,323	15,029
2014	41,400	31,300	20,810	15,120	32,910	35,670	38,609	38,625
2015	47,800	36,750	26,800	18,350	46,066	45,981	48,429	38,452
2016	37,400	30,430	22,320	13,540	41,190	45,058	40,885	36,790
2017	33,950	23,300	17,240	11,410	38,039	43,166	37,699	29,606
2018	39,200	25,410	18,050	10,500	35,573	41,864	32,232	27,314
2019	37,900	24,770	16,970	10,070	22,153	29,139	30,722	26,738

[1] Includes stocks at mills, elevators, warehouses, terminals, and processors.
NASS, Crops Branch, (202) 720–2127.

Table 1-47.—Oats: Supply and disappearance, United States, 2009–2018

Year beginning June 1	Supply				Disappearance					Ending stocks May 31 [1]
					Domestic use					
	Beginning stocks	Production	Imports	Total	Food, alcohol, and industrial	Seed	Feed and residual	Exports	Total disappearance	
	Million bushels									
2009	84	91	95	270	66	8	113	2	190	80
2010	80	82	85	247	67	7	103	3	180	68
2011	68	50	94	212	69	7	78	2	157	55
2012	55	61	93	209	68	8	96	1	173	36
2013	36	65	97	198	66	7	98	2	173	25
2014	25	70	109	204	69	8	71	2	150	54
2015	54	89	86	229	69	7	93	2	172	57
2016	57	65	90	212	70	6	82	3	161	50
2017	50	50	89	189	71	7	68	2	148	41
2018	41	56	87	184	71	7	66	2	146	38

[1] Privately held: Includes quantity under loan and farmer-owned reserve.
Latest data may be preliminary or projected. Totals may not add due to rounding.
ERS, Market and Trade Economics Division, (202) 694–5313. Source: USDA, World Agricultural Outlook Board, World Agricultural Supply and Demand Estimates and supporting materials.

Table 1-48.—Oats: Area, yield, and production, by State and United States, 2017–2019

State	Area planted [1]			Area harvested		
	2017	2018	2019	2017	2018	2019
	1,000 acres					
Alabama	40	40	(NA)	10	15	(NA)
Arkansas	11	10	5	8	7	3
California	110	110	75	10	6	2
Colorado	50	95	(NA)	9	7	(NA)
Georgia	50	60	70	15	15	15
Idaho	50	40	60	10	10	12
Illinois	35	40	70	20	25	10
Iowa	115	135	215	42	33	69
Kansas	100	120	120	25	18	18
Maine	22	21	22	21	19	19
Michigan	55	75	70	40	50	25
Minnesota	170	180	240	95	105	100
Missouri	30	35	50	13	16	6
Montana	70	70	70	18	23	24
Nebraska	110	125	120	35	22	18
New York	55	69	56	35	43	39
North Carolina	35	30	22	10	11	7
North Dakota	295	300	355	80	105	115
Ohio	60	55	75	20	30	25
Oklahoma	45	50	100	16	10	25
Oregon	25	20	20	10	5	9
Pennsylvania	70	65	85	40	35	50
South Carolina	20	19	(NA)	8	7	(NA)
South Dakota	290	290	245	60	95	75
Texas	455	450	400	60	50	40
Washington	16	17	(NA)	4	4	(NA)
Wisconsin	180	200	265	85	90	120
Wyoming	25	25	(NA)	5	9	(NA)
United States	2,589	2,746	2,810	804	865	826

State	Yield per harvested acre			Production		
	2017	2018	2019	2017	2018	2019
	Bushels			*1,000 bushels*		
Alabama	60.0	63.0	(NA)	600	945	(NA)
Arkansas	85.0	75.0	70.0	680	525	210
California	65.0	70.0	60.0	650	420	120
Colorado	65.0	50.0	(NA)	585	350	(NA)
Georgia	49.0	71.0	55.0	735	1,065	825
Idaho	71.0	84.0	92.0	710	840	1,104
Illinois	79.0	83.0	65.0	1,580	2,075	650
Iowa	77.0	63.0	58.0	3,234	2,079	4,002
Kansas	54.0	49.0	64.0	1,350	882	1,152
Maine	67.0	67.0	76.0	1,407	1,273	1,444
Michigan	54.0	63.0	57.0	2,160	3,150	1,425
Minnesota	75.0	59.0	62.0	7,125	6,195	6,200
Missouri	65.0	45.0	47.0	845	720	282
Montana	47.0	43.0	55.0	846	989	1,320
Nebraska	49.0	69.0	63.0	1,715	1,518	1,134
New York	55.0	54.0	60.0	1,925	2,322	2,340
North Carolina	66.0	66.0	71.0	660	726	497
North Dakota	58.0	82.0	86.0	4,640	8,610	9,890
Ohio	70.0	65.0	46.0	1,400	1,950	1,150
Oklahoma	42.0	48.0	50.0	672	480	1,250
Oregon	83.0	99.0	97.0	830	495	873
Pennsylvania	58.0	46.0	53.0	2,320	1,610	2,650
South Carolina	51.0	62.0	(NA)	408	434	(NA)
South Dakota	70.0	82.0	82.0	4,200	7,790	6,150
Texas	45.0	50.0	50.0	2,700	2,500	2,000
Washington	42.0	46.0	(NA)	168	184	(NA)
Wisconsin	59.0	61.0	54.0	5,015	5,490	6,480
Wyoming	85.0	57.0	(NA)	425	513	(NA)
United States	61.7	64.9	64.3	49,585	56,130	53,148

(NA) Not available. [1] Relates to the total area of oats sown for all purposes, including oats sown in the preceding fall.
NASS, Crops Branch, (202) 720–2127.

Table 1-49.—Oats: Support operations, United States, 2013–2019

Marketing Year beginning June 1	Income support payment rates per bushel [1]	Program price levels per bushel		Put under loan		Acquired by CCC under loan program [5]	Owned by CCC at end of marketing year
		Loan [2]	Target/ reference [3]	Quantity	Percentage of production [4]		
	Dollars	*Dollars*	*Dollars*	*Million bushels*	*Percent*	*Million bushels*	*Million bushels*
2013/2014	0.02/0.00	1.39	1.79	0.3	0.5	0	0
2014/2015	0.00	1.39	2.40	0.5	0.7	0	0
2015/2016	0.28	1.39	2.40	1.1	1.3	0	0
2016/2017	0.34	1.39	2.40	0.8	1.2	0	0
2017/2018	0.00	1.39	2.40	0.4	0.8	0	0
2018/2019	0.00	1.39	2.40	0.4	0.7	0	0
2019/2020	0.00	2.00	2.40	1.1	2.1	0	0

[1] The first entry is the direct payment rate and the second entry is the counter-cyclical payment rate for 2004/2005-2013/2014. For 2009/2010-2013/2014, producers who participated in the Average Crop Revenue (ACRE) program got a 20 percent reduction in their direct payment, not calculated in this table. For 2014/2015 and after, the entry is the price loss coverage (PLC) payment rate. Agricultural Risk Coverage (ARC) is also available, but payment rates are established at the county or farm levels. [2] For 2009/2010-2013/2014, producers who participated in the ACRE program got a 30 percent reduction in their loan rate, not calculated in this table. [3] Target applies to 2003/2004-2013/2014 and Reference applies beginning with 2014/2015. [4] Percent of production is on a grain basis. [5] Acquisitions as of January 31, 2020.
FPAC-BC, Commodity Analysis Branch.

Table 1-50.—Oats: Marketing year average price and value of production, by State and United States, 2017–2019

State	Marketing year average price per bushel			Value of production		
	2017	2018	2019 [1]	2017	2018	2019 [1]
	Dollars	*Dollars*	*Dollars*	*1,000 dollars*	*1,000 dollars*	*1,000 dollars*
Alabama	4.05	4.50	(NA)	2,430	4,253	(NA)
Arkansas	2.80	2.75	2.80	1,904	1,444	588
California	2.90	(D)	3.00	1,885	(D)	360
Colorado	3.20	3.66	(NA)	1,872	1,281	(NA)
Georgia	3.67	4.15	4.10	2,697	4,420	3,383
Idaho	2.73	2.80	2.65	1,938	2,352	2,926
Illinois	3.39	3.12	4.10	5,356	6,474	2,665
Iowa	2.54	2.93	3.50	8,214	6,091	14,007
Kansas	2.93	3.32	3.15	3,956	2,928	3,629
Maine	2.80	2.80	3.40	3,940	3,564	4,910
Michigan	2.91	3.31	3.50	6,286	10,427	4,988
Minnesota	2.15	2.49	2.70	15,319	15,426	16,740
Missouri	3.25	3.00	3.70	2,746	2,160	1,043
Montana	2.00	2.71	2.75	2,420	2,680	3,630
Nebraska	2.62	2.85	3.00	4,493	4,326	3,402
New York	2.20	2.92	2.40	4,235	6,780	5,616
North Carolina	2.60	3.10	3.10	1,716	2,251	1,541
North Dakota	2.55	2.41	2.50	11,832	20,750	24,725
Ohio	3.51	3.76	3.70	4,914	7,332	4,255
Oklahoma	3.02	2.75	2.30	2,029	1,320	2,875
Oregon	2.65	(D)	3.20	2,200	(D)	2,794
Pennsylvania	3.57	4.02	4.25	8,282	6,472	11,263
South Carolina	3.64	3.95	(NA)	1,485	1,714	(NA)
South Dakota	2.45	2.67	2.90	10,290	20,799	17,835
Texas	4.28	4.82	4.40	11,556	12,050	8,800
Washington	2.26	2.18	(NA)	380	401	(NA)
Wisconsin	2.78	2.77	3.20	13,942	15,207	20,736
Wyoming	3.10	3.60	(NA)	1,318	1,847	(NA)
Other States	(X)	3.16	(X)	-	2,891	-
United States	2.59	2.66	2.95	139,635	167,640	162,711

(D) Withheld to avoid disclosing data for individual. (NA) Not available. (X) Not applicable. [1] Preliminary.
NASS, Crops Branch, (202) 720–2127.

Table 1-51.—International Oats: Area, yield, and production in specified countries, 2017/2018–2019/2020

Country	Area			Yield per hectare			Production		
	2017/ 2018	2018/ 2019	2019/ 2020	2017/ 2018	2018/ 2019	2019/ 2020	2017/ 2018	2018/ 2019	2019/ 2020
	1,000 hectares			*Metric tons*			*1,000 metric tons*		
European Union	2,666	2,711	2,552	3.02	2.85	3.10	8,058	7,715	7,920
Russia	2,780	2,725	2,429	1.96	1.73	1.82	5,448	4,715	4,420
Canada	1,052	1,005	1,160	3.55	3.42	3.59	3,733	3,436	4,160
Australia	874	680	675	1.40	1.31	1.39	1,227	888	935
Brazil	340	376	381	1.87	2.11	2.17	634	795	825
United States	325	350	334	2.22	2.33	2.31	720	815	771
China	475	500	525	1.16	1.15	1.19	550	575	625
Belarus	150	151	150	3.33	2.27	3.00	500	342	450
Chile	108	75	80	5.31	5.13	5.50	573	385	440
Ukraine	208	198	180	2.31	2.14	2.39	481	423	430
Argentina	220	238	143	2.24	2.40	2.31	492	572	330
Norway	68	69	70	4.16	2.09	4.29	283	144	300
Kazakhstan	213	235	243	1.34	1.43	1.10	285	336	267
Turkey	113	100	100	2.21	2.30	2.30	250	230	230
Algeria	85	85	85	1.29	1.29	1.29	110	110	110
Mexico	44	50	50	1.64	2.06	1.80	72	103	90
Serbia	30	30	30	2.17	2.17	2.17	65	65	65
Bosnia and Herzegovina	11	14	14	2.73	2.79	3.00	30	39	42
Morocco	30	45	45	1.17	1.40	0.89	35	63	40
South Africa	15	20	25	1.53	1.65	1.60	23	33	40
New Zealand	6	5	6	5.83	5.00	5.50	35	25	33
Albania	15	13	14	2.27	2.08	2.14	34	27	30
Uruguay	19	26	14	1.68	2.04	1.86	32	53	26

FAS, Office of Global Analysis, (202) 720-6301. Prepared or estimated on the basis of official USDA production, supply, and distribution, supply, and and distribution statistics from foreign governments.

Table 1-52. Oats: International trade, 2017/2018–2019/2020

Country	2017/2018	2018/2019	2019/2020
	1,000 metric tons		
Principle exporting countries:			
Canada	1,631	1,734	1,800
Australia	550	240	250
European Union	186	106	125
Russia	28	122	110
Chile	38	38	40
United States	35	25	29
Kazakhstan	10	29	20
Ukraine	9	8	10
Argentina	0	0	5
Brazil	4	6	5
Serbia	1	1	2
Principle importing countries:			
United States	1,537	1,493	1,637
China	389	224	200
Mexico	129	151	100
Japan	44	46	50
Switzerland	51	54	50
South Africa	39	23	40
Ecuador	41	30	30
Norway	16	92	30
Korea, South	46	31	25
Algeria	7	1	20
India	19	21	20
Belarus	2	26	10
Canada	14	11	10
Bosnia and Herzegovina	6	3	5
Colombia	1	5	5
European Union	4	14	5
Turkey	0	0	5
Uruguay	6	5	5
Serbia	1	1	3
Morocco	2	2	2
Ukraine	0	3	1
Kazakhstan	0	1	0

FAS, Office of Global Analysis, (202) 720-6301. Prepared or estimated on the basis of official USDA production, supply, and distribution statistics from foreign governments.

Table 1-53.—Barley: Area, yield, production, and value, United States, 2010–2019

Year	Area		Yield per harvested acre	Production	Marketing year average price per bushel received by farmers	Value of production
	Planted [1]	Harvested				
	1,000 acres	*1,000 acres*	*Bushels*	*1,000 bushels*	*Dollars*	*1,000 dollars*
2010	2,872	2,465	73.1	180,241	3.86	691,573
2011	2,564	2,241	69.1	154,788	5.35	808,741
2012	3,660	3,274	66.9	218,990	6.43	1,371,381
2013	3,528	3,040	71.3	216,745	6.06	1,265,798
2014	3,031	2,497	72.7	181,542	5.30	914,955
2015	3,583	3,158	69.1	218,187	5.52	1,149,831
2016	3,059	2,565	77.9	199,914	4.96	949,876
2017	2,486	1,962	73.0	143,258	4.47	624,184
2018	2,548	1,982	77.5	153,527	4.62	697,598
2019	2,721	2,182	77.7	169,566	4.60	761,152

[1] Barley sown for all purposes, including barley sown in the preceding fall.
NASS, Crops Branch, (202) 720–2127.

Table 1-54.—Barley: Stocks on and off farms, United States, 2010–2019

Year beginning September	On farms				Off farms [1]			
	Sep. 1	Dec. 1	Mar. 1	June 1	Sep. 1	Dec. 1	Mar. 1	June 1
	1,000 bushels							
2010	125,070	91,660	67,370	40,440	98,818	88,720	89,985	75,059
2011	93,050	55,320	57,700	26,040	82,007	82,999	80,424	63,311
2012	112,550	72,580	26,480	9,670	85,226	85,473	67,248	50,317
2013	105,620	81,340	35,180	15,840	90,470	88,063	81,897	64,557
2014	97,820	74,510	43,830	19,110	81,997	81,625	77,734	63,145
2015	135,840	96,670	41,990	20,940	83,132	83,738	76,247	57,639
2016	130,600	99,100	57,910	27,740	99,737	93,429	79,832	74,370
2017	90,400	74,340	56,490	27,050	89,283	84,528	88,211	79,314
2018	91,350	72,070	48,540	26,420	83,456	80,561	81,491	68,061
2019	116,720	87,630	46,180	22,870	73,112	69,756	75,216	63,653

[1] Includes stocks at mills, elevators, warehouses, terminals, and processors.
NASS, Crops Branch, (202) 720–2127.

Table 1-55.—Barley: Supply and disappearance, United States, 2009–2018

Year beginning June 1	Supply				Disappearance					Ending stocks May 31
					Domestic use					
	Beginning stocks	Production	Imports	Total	Food, alcohol, and industrial	Seed	Feed and residual	Exports	Total disappearance	Total [1]
	Million bushels									
2009	89	227	17	332	159	5	47	6	216	115
2010	115	180	9	305	154	5	50	8	216	89
2011	89	155	16	260	149	6	37	9	200	60
2012	60	219	23	302	141	6	66	9	222	80
2013	80	217	19	316	148	5	66	14	234	82
2014	82	182	24	287	154	6	34	14	209	79
2015	79	218	19	315	153	5	44	11	213	102
2016	102	200	10	312	158	4	39	4	205	106
2017	106	143	9	259	153	4	2	5	164	94
2018	94	154	6	254	143	5	15	5	167	87

[1] Privately held: Includes quantity under loan and farmer-owned reserve.
Includes quantity under loan and farmer–owned reserve. Latest data may be preliminary or projected. Totals may not add due to independent rounding.
ERS, Market and Trade Economics Division, (202) 694–5313.

Table 1-56.—Barley: Area, yield, and production, by State and United States, 2017–2019

State	Area planted[1]			Area harvested		
	2017	2018	2019	2017	2018	2019
	1,000 acres	*1,000 acres*	*1,000 acres*	*1,000 acres*	*1,000 acres*	*1,000 acres*
Alaska[2]	(X)	5	6	(X)	4	5
Arizona	20	14	17	17	11	14
California	75	65	60	29	26	43
Colorado	70	60	54	68	53	52
Delaware	32	25	21	18	14	14
Idaho	530	550	540	510	530	520
Kansas[3]	(NA)	17	14	(NA)	6	4
Maine[3]	(NA)	17	16	(NA)	16	15
Maryland	50	45	32	27	24	17
Michigan[3]	(NA)	20	11	(NA)	5	8
Minnesota	80	80	70	68	67	55
Montana	770	790	920	565	600	740
New York[3]	(NA)	10	10	(NA)	8	4
North Carolina[3]	(NA)	11	11	(NA)	8	6
North Dakota	520	470	580	400	385	445
Oregon	47	43	40	38	26	31
Pennsylvania	60	45	35	45	33	25
South Dakota[3]	(NA)	48	37	(NA)	13	9
Utah	25	21	17	18	16	10
Virginia	30	30	30	11	9	7
Washington	95	85	95	85	67	84
Wisconsin[3]	(NA)	25	24	(NA)	10	8
Wyoming	82	72	81	63	51	66
United States[4]	2,486	2,548	2,721	1,962	1,982	2,182

State	Yield per harvested acre			Production		
	2017	2018	2019	2017	2018	2019
	Bushels	*Bushels*	*Bushels*	*1,000 bushels*	*1,000 bushels*	*1,000 bushels*
Alaska[2]	(X)	43.0	38.0	(X)	172	190
Arizona	131.0	100.0	126.0	2,227	1,100	1,764
California	50.0	69.0	66.0	1,450	1,794	2,838
Colorado	132.0	145.0	138.0	8,976	7,685	7,176
Delaware	85.0	78.0	80.0	1,530	1,092	1,120
Idaho	95.0	101.0	104.0	48,450	53,530	54,080
Kansas[3]	(NA)	31.0	33.0	(NA)	186	132
Maine[3]	(NA)	73.0	82.0	(NA)	1,168	1,230
Maryland	76.0	70.0	85.0	2,052	1,680	1,445
Michigan[3]	(NA)	43.0	44.0	(NA)	215	352
Minnesota	76.0	76.0	67.0	5,168	5,092	3,685
Montana	51.0	56.0	59.0	28,815	33,600	43,660
New York[3]	(NA)	58.0	52.0	(NA)	464	208
North Carolina[3]	(NA)	80.0	66.0	(NA)	640	396
North Dakota	65.0	74.0	72.0	26,000	28,490	32,040
Oregon	62.0	53.0	78.0	2,356	1,378	2,418
Pennsylvania	70.0	63.0	70.0	3,150	2,079	1,750
South Dakota[3]	(NA)	55.0	43.0	(NA)	715	387
Utah	75.0	86.0	93.0	1,350	1,376	930
Virginia	73.0	70.0	65.0	803	630	455
Washington	53.0	73.0	70.0	4,505	4,891	5,880
Wisconsin[3]	(NA)	45.0	46.0	(NA)	450	368
Wyoming	102.0	100.0	107.0	6,426	5,100	7,062
United States[4]	73.0	77.5	77.7	143,258	153,527	169,566

(NA) Not available. (X) Not applicable. [1] Includes area planted in the preceding fall. [2] Alaska data previously included in a separate table for Alaska. [3] Estimates began in 2018. [4] Beginning in 2018, United States total includes data for Alaska.
NASS, Crops Branch, (202) 720–2127.

Table 1-57.—Barley: Marketing year average price and value, by State and United States, 2017–2019

State	Marketing year average price per bushel			Value of production		
	2017	2018	2019[1]	2017	2018	2019[1]
	Dollars	*Dollars*	*Dollars*	*1,000 dollars*	*1,000 dollars*	*1,000 dollars*
Alaska[2]	(X)	5.20	5.20	(X)	894	988
Arizona	3.91	3.84	4.20	8,708	4,224	7,409
California	4.82	4.84	4.60	6,989	8,683	13,055
Colorado	4.60	4.55	4.55	41,290	34,967	32,651
Delaware	2.90	2.60	3.10	4,437	2,839	3,472
Idaho	4.75	5.03	4.90	230,138	269,256	264,992
Kansas[3]	(NA)	3.20	3.30	(NA)	595	436
Maine[3]	(NA)	2.90	3.05	(NA)	3,387	3,752
Maryland	2.90	2.60	3.10	5,951	4,368	4,480
Michigan[3]	(NA)	2.45	3.00	(NA)	527	1,056
Minnesota	4.33	4.22	4.40	22,377	21,488	16,214
Montana	4.34	4.62	4.40	125,057	155,232	192,104
New York[3]	(NA)	2.90	3.85	(NA)	1,346	801
North Carolina[3]	(NA)	2.70	3.25	(NA)	1,728	1,287
North Dakota	4.31	4.24	4.15	112,060	120,798	132,966
Oregon	2.99	3.28	3.90	7,044	4,520	9,430
Pennsylvania	3.10	2.90	3.90	9,765	6,029	6,825
South Dakota[3]	(NA)	3.65	3.85	(NA)	2,610	1,490
Utah	3.08	3.69	3.80	4,158	5.077	3,534
Virginia	2.60	2.60	3.00	2,088	1,638	1,365
Washington	3.09	4.40	4.55	13,920	21,520	26,754
Wisconsin[3]	(NA)	4.00	5.00	(NA)	1,800	1,840
Wyoming	4.70	4.72	4.85	30,202	24,072	34,251
United States	4.47	4.62	4.60	624,184	697,598	761,152

(NA) Not available. (X) Not applicable. [1] Preliminary. [2] Alaska data previously included in a separate table for Alaska. [3] Estimates began in 2018. [4] Beginning in 2018, United States total includes data for Alaska.
NASS, Crops Branch, (202) 720–2127.

Table 1-58.—Barley: Support operations, United States, 2013–2019

Marketing year beginning June 1	Income support payment rates per bushel[1]	Program price levels per bushel		Put under loan		Acquired by CCC under loan program[5]	Owned by CCC at end of marketing year
		Loan[2]	Target/ reference[3]	Quantity	Percentage of production[4]		
	Dollars	*Dollars*	*Dollars*	*Million bushels*	*Percent*	*Million bushels*	*Million bushels*
2013/2014	0.24/0.00	1.95	2.63	4.2	1.0	0	0
2014/2015	0.00	1.95	4.95	3.9	2.1	0	0
2015/2016	0.00	1.95	4.95	8.3	3.8	0	0
2016/2017	0.00	1.95	4.95	9.3	4.6	0	0
2017/2018	0.50	1.95	4.95	4.5	3.1	0	0
2018/2019	0.33	1.95	4.95	5.1	3.3	0	0
2019/2020	0.35	2.50	4.95	6.1	3.6	0	0

[1] The first entry is the direct payment rate and the second entry is the counter-cyclical payment rate for 2004/2005-2013/2014. For 2009/2010-2013/2014, producers who participated in the Average Crop Revenue (ACRE) program got a 20 percent reduction in their direct payment, not calculated in this table. For 2014/2015 and after, the entry is the price loss coverage payment rate. Agricultural Risk Coverage (ARC) is also available, but payment rates are established at the county or farm levels. [2] For 2009/2010-2013/2014, producers who participated in the ACRE program got a 30 percent reduction in their loan rate, not calculated in this table. [3] Target applies to 2003/2004-2013/2014 and Reference applies beginning with 2014/2015. [4] Percent of production is on a grain basis. [5] Acquisitions as of January 31, 2020.
FPAC-BC, Commodity Analysis Branch.

Table 1-59.—International Barley: Area, yield, and production in specified countries, 2017/2018–2019/2020

Country	Area			Yield per hectare			Production		
	2017/2018	2018/2019	2019/2020	2017/2018	2018/2019	2019/2020	2017/2018	2018/2019	2019/2020
	1,000 hectares			*Metric tons*			*1,000 metric tons*		
European Union	12,095	12,278	12,380	4.85	4.56	5.07	58,654	55,947	62,750
Russia	7,714	7,784	8,403	2.62	2.15	2.37	20,211	16,737	19,939
Canada	2,114	2,395	2,700	3.73	3.50	3.85	7,891	8,380	10,400
Ukraine	2,652	2,569	2,700	3.28	2.96	3.52	8,695	7,604	9,500
Australia	4,124	3,719	3,950	2.24	2.24	2.23	9,254	8,310	8,800
Turkey	3,400	3,600	3,800	1.88	1.94	2.08	6,400	7,000	7,900
Kazakhstan	2,069	2,516	2,977	1.60	1.58	1.29	3,305	3,971	3,830
Argentina	935	1,200	1,000	4.00	4.22	3.80	3,740	5,060	3,800
United States	794	802	883	3.93	4.17	4.18	3,119	3,343	3,692
Iran	1,600	1,550	1,700	1.94	1.81	2.12	3,100	2,800	3,600
Ethiopia	955	1,000	1,000	2.13	2.20	2.30	2,032	2,200	2,300
Algeria	763	1,026	1,025	1.27	1.90	2.00	968	1,950	2,050
Syria	800	800	1,500	0.97	0.50	1.33	777	400	2,000
India	656	661	696	2.66	2.69	2.35	1,747	1,781	1,633
Iraq	775	600	1,200	1.26	1.30	1.33	975	780	1,600
Belarus	452	429	400	3.14	2.20	3.50	1,420	944	1,400
Morocco	1,893	1,597	1,450	1.30	1.82	0.83	2,466	2,910	1,200
Mexico	358	353	360	2.81	2.82	2.81	1,005	996	1,010
China	330	263	260	3.29	3.64	3.46	1,085	957	900
Azerbaijan	319	337	320	2.48	2.72	2.72	792	916	870

FAS, Office of Global Analysis, (202) 720-6301. Prepared or estimated on the basis of official USDA production, supply, and distribution statistics from foreign governments.

Table 1-60.—Barley: International trade, 2017/2018–2019/2020

Country	2017/2018	2018/2019	2019/2020
	1,000 metric tons		
Principle importing countries:			
Saudi Arabia	8,000	6,500	7,500
China	8,144	5,181	6,500
Iran	3,200	3,100	3,000
Japan	1,253	1,158	1,200
Morocco	429	204	1,000
Jordan	773	916	900
Brazil	547	656	700
Turkey	753	279	700
Libya	438	888	650
European Union	451	127	600
Tunisia	604	639	500
Kuwait	521	474	400
United Arab Emirates	263	476	400
Colombia	324	341	350
Israel	234	236	300
Thailand	147	206	300
India	211	135	250
Algeria	522	323	200
Egypt	21	78	200
Lebanon	197	191	200
Mexico	5	1	200
Belarus	49	197	175
United States	199	128	174
Principle exporting countries:			
European Union	5,667	5,899	5,000
Russia	2,951	5,884	4,800
Australia	9,190	5,725	4,600
Ukraine	5,354	4,289	3,800
Argentina	2,556	2,500	3,100
Canada	1,546	2,021	2,200
Kazakhstan	682	1,347	1,800
United States	95	111	109
Turkey	14	0	100
Uruguay	114	5	100
Serbia	26	53	85
Moldova	117	127	70
India	1	1	7
Belarus	16	0	0
Azerbaijan	7	0	0

FAS, Office of Global Analysis, (202) 720-6301. Prepared or estimated on the basis of official USDA production, supply, and distribution statistics from foreign governments.

Table 1-61.—Grains and grain products: Food availability, United States, 2009–2018

Year [1]	Wheat			Rye		Rice (milled)	
	Total [2]	Per capita availability		Total [2]	Per capita availability of rye flour	Total [4]	Per capita availability
		Flour [3]	Non-milled product				
	Million bushels	*Pounds*	*Pounds*	*Million bushels*	*Pounds*	*Million cwt.*	*Pounds*
2009	920	134.7	2.3	3.3	0.5	62.6	20.4
2010	928	134.8	2.3	3.3	0.5	63.1	20.4
2011	925	132.5	2.3	3.3	0.5	(NA)	(NA)
2012	952	134.3	2.3	3.4	0.5	(NA)	(NA)
2013	945	135.0	2.3	3.4	0.5	(NA)	(NA)
2014		134.7		3.5	0.5	(NA)	(NA)
2015		133.0		3.6	0.5	(NA)	(NA)
2016		131.7		3.7	0.5	(NA)	(NA)
2017		131.8		3.8	0.5	(NA)	(NA)
2018		132.1		3.6	0.5	(NA)	(NA)

Year [1]	Corn					Oats		Barley	
	Total [5]	Per capita availability of food products				Total [6]	Per capita availability of food products	Total [7]	Per capita availability of food products [8]
		Flour and meal	Hominy and grits	Food Starch	Total				
	Million bushels	*Pounds*	*Pounds*	*Pounds*	*Pounds*	*Million bushels*	*Pounds*	*Million bushels*	*Pounds*
2009	986	19.3	9.3	4.4	33.0	66.2	4.7	6.9	0.7
2010	973	19.3	9.3	4.5	33.1	67.2	4.7	6.8	0.7
2011	989	19.9	9.6	4.6	34.1	68.8	4.8	6.8	0.7
2012	980	19.8	9.5	4.6	33.9	68.1	4.7	6.5	0.6
2013	958	19.8	9.5	4.6	33.9	66.2	4.5	7.5	0.7
2014		19.9	9.5	4.6	34.0	66.4	4.5	7.7	0.7
2015		19.9	9.5	4.6	34.0	68.0	4.6	8.0	0.8
2016		20.0	9.5	4.7	34.2	69.0	4.6	9.0	0.8
2017		21.0	9.5	4.7	35.2	72.0	4.8	9.5	0.9
2018		21.0	9.5	4.7	35.2	72.6	4.8	9.7	0.9

Estimates of corn syrup and sugar are unofficial estimates; industry data were not reported after April 1968.

Annual data and per capita estimates for rice are unavailable beyond 2010 due to a large and unexplained decline in the implied total domestic and residual use estimate.

(NA) Not available. [1] Data are in marketing year; for corn, September 1-August 31; for oats and barley, June 1-May 31; and rice, August 1-July 31. Wheat, rye, syrup, and sugar are in calendar year. [2] Excludes quantities used in alcoholic beverages. [3] Includes white, whole wheat, and semolina flour. [4] Does not include shipments to U.S. territories. Excludes rice used in alcoholic beverages. Includes imports and rice used in processed foods and pet foods. [5] Includes an allowance for the quantity used as hominy and grits. This series is not adjusted for trade. [6] Oats used in oatmeal, prepared breakfast foods, infant foods, and food products. [7] Malt for food, breakfast food uses, pearl barley, and flour. [8] Malt equivalent of barley food products.

ERS, Market & Trade Economics Division, (202) 694-5290. All figures are estimates based on data from private industry sources, the U.S. Department of Commerce, the Internal Revenue Service, and other Government agencies.

Table 1-62.—Sorghum: Area, yield, production, and value, United States, 2010–2019

Year	Area planted for all purposes [1]	Sorghum for grain [2]					Sorghum for silage		
		Area harvested	Yield per harvested acre	Production	Marketing year average price per cwt [3]	Value of production [3]	Area harvested	Yield per harvested acre	Production
	1,000 acres	*1,000 acres*	*Bushels*	*1,000 bushels*	*Dollars*	*1,000 dollars*	*1,000 acres*	*Tons*	*1,000 tons*
2010 ..	5,369	4,806	71.9	345,464	8.96	1,616,773	272	12.5	3,412
2011 ..	5,451	3,945	54.0	212,993	10.70	1,259,635	226	10.4	2,353
2012 ..	6,259	4,995	49.6	247,742	11.30	1,606,237	353	11.9	4,196
2013 ..	8,076	6,585	59.6	392,331	7.64	1,716,927	380	14.3	5,420
2014 ..	7,138	6,401	67.6	432,575	7.20	1,721,330	315	13.1	4,123
2015 ..	8,459	7,851	76.0	596,751	5.91	2,064,638	306	14.6	4,475
2016 ..	6,690	6,163	77.9	480,261	4.98	1,352,438	298	14.0	4,171
2017 ..	5,629	5,044	71.7	361,871	5.75	1,168,526	282	13.4	3,772
2018 ..	5,690	5,061	72.1	364,986	5.82	1,180,847	264	12.6	3,326
2019 ..	5,265	4,675	73.0	341,460	6.00	1,151,709	339	11.9	4,019

[1] Grain and sweet sorghum for all uses, including syrup. [2] Includes both grain sorghum for grain, and sweet sorghum for grain or seed. [3] Based on the reported price of grain sorghum.
NASS, Crops Branch, (202) 720–2127.

Table 1-63.—Sorghum grain: Stocks on and off farms, United States, 2010–2019

Year beginning previous Dec.	On farms				Off farms [1]			
	Dec. 1	Mar. 1	Jun. 1	Sep. 1	Dec. 1	Mar. 1	Jun. 1	Sep. 1
	1,000 bushels	*1,000 bushels*	*1,000 bushels*	*1,000 bushels*	*1,000 bushels*	*1,000 bushels*	*1,000 bushels*	*1,000 bushels*
2010	48,000	23,680	10,700	4,500	202,759	151,873	77,162	36,740
2011	30,500	13,020	3,140	2,030	207,168	158,027	76,894	25,420
2012	27,850	12,800	4,120	1,160	123,101	95,266	54,405	21,792
2013	17,600	10,850	2,710	602	122,247	80,685	38,398	14,551
2014	32,950	15,950	4,500	1,945	198,466	159,784	87,924	32,087
2015	30,500	9,000	2,960	1,895	192,094	110,856	31,329	16,514
2016	51,500	25,000	9,700	3,755	271,035	176,584	80,654	32,877
2017	43,000	21,250	8,620	4,280	266,079	159,495	76,088	29,179
2018	33,800	13,250	5,220	3,355	193,692	127,006	60,113	31,499
2019 [2]	44,200	24,990	9,470	3,210	214,580	167,736	107,962	60,451

[1] Includes stocks at mills, elevators, warehouses, terminals, and processors. [2] Preliminary.
NASS, Crops Branch, (202) 720–2127.

Table 1-64.—Sorghum: Supply and disappearance, United States, 2009–2018

Year beginning September 1	Supply			Disappearance					Ending stocks Aug. 31 [1]
				Domestic use					
	Beginning stocks	Production	Total	Food, alcohol, and industrial	Seed	Feed and residual	Exports	Total disappearance	
	Million bushels								
2009	55	382	436	89	1	141	164	395	41
2010	41	345	387	84	1	123	152	359	27
2011	27	213	241	84	1	69	63	218	23
2012	23	248	280	94	1	93	76	265	15
2013	15	392	408	69	1	93	211	374	34
2014	34	433	467	14	1	82	352	449	18
2015	18	597	620	136	1	104	342	583	37
2016	37	480	519	114	1	133	238	485	33
2017	33	362	397	60	1	102	200	362	35
2018	35	365	400	105	1	138	93	336	64

[1] Includes quantity under loan and farmer–owned reserve.
Latest data may be preliminary or projected. Totals may not add due to independent rounding.
ERS, Market and Trade Economics Division, (202) 694–5313. Source: USDA, World Agricultural Outlook Board, World Agricultural Supply and Demand Estimates and supporting materials.l

Table 1-65.—Sorghum: Area, yield, and production, by State and United States, 2017–2019

State	Area planted for all purposes			Sorghum for grain		
				Area harvested		
	2017	2018	2019	2017	2018	2019
	1,000 acres	*1,000 acres*	*1,000 acres*	*1,000 acres*	*1,000 acres*	*1,000 acres*
Arkansas	9	12	(NA)	7	10	(NA)
Colorado	410	355	365	360	325	310
Georgia	21	25	(NA)	12	15	(NA)
Illinois	17	18	(NA)	15	16	(NA)
Kansas	2,600	2,800	2,600	2,450	2,650	2,400
Louisiana	15	8	(NA)	13	6	(NA)
Mississippi	5	4	(NA)	4	3	(NA)
Missouri	30	30	(NA)	23	21	(NA)
Nebraska	180	230	200	130	170	130
New Mexico	85	80	(NA)	48	47	(NA)
North Carolina	22	18	(NA)	17	8	(NA)
Oklahoma	315	300	300	295	240	260
South Dakota	270	260	250	170	200	175
Texas	1,650	1,550	1,550	1,500	1,350	1,400
United States	5,629	5,690	5,265	5,044	5,061	4,675

State	Yield per harvested acre			Production		
	2016	2017	2018	2016	2017	2018
	Bushels	*Bushels*	*Bushels*	*1,000 bushels*	*1,000 bushels*	*1,000 bushels*
Arkansas	78.0	77.0	(NA)	546	770	(NA)
Colorado	52.0	53.0	41.0	18,720	17,225	12,710
Georgia	54.0	53.0	(NA)	648	795	(NA)
Illinois	83.0	111.0	(NA)	1,245	1,776	(NA)
Kansas	82.0	88.0	85.0	200,900	233,200	204,000
Louisiana	91.0	84.0	(NA)	1,183	504	(NA)
Mississippi	72.0	90.0	(NA)	288	270	(NA)
Missouri	107.0	100.0	(NA)	2,461	2,100	(NA)
Nebraska	89.0	94.0	93.0	11,570	15,980	12,090
New Mexico	35.0	38.0	(NA)	1,680	1,786	(NA)
North Carolina	55.0	60.0	(NA)	935	480	(NA)
Oklahoma	53.0	50.0	51.0	15,635	12,000	13,260
South Dakota	68.0	80.0	80.0	11,560	16,000	14,000
Texas	63.0	46.0	61.0	94,500	62,100	85,400
United States	71.7	72.1	73.0	361,871	364,986	341,460

(NA) Not available.
NASS, Crops Branch, (202) 720–2127.

Table 1-66.—Sorghum silage: Area harvested, yield, and production, by State and United States, 2017–2019

State	Silage								
	Area harvested			Yield per acre			Production		
	2017	2018	2019	2017	2018	2018	2017	2018	2019
	1,000 acres	*1,000 acres*	*1,000 acres*	*Tons*	*Tons*	*Tons*	*1,000 tons*	*1,000 tons*	*1,000 tons*
Arkansas	1	1	(NA)	16.0	18.0	(NA)	16	18	(NA)
Colorado	25	8	18	15.0	14.0	17.0	375	112	306
Georgia	8	8	(NA)	13.0	11.0	(NA)	104	88	(NA)
Illinois	1	1	(NA)	12.0	14.0	(NA)	12	14	(NA)
Kansas	85	60	95	13.0	15.0	11.0	1,105	900	1,045
Louisiana	1	1	(NA)	12.0	12.0	(NA)	12	12	(NA)
Mississippi	1	1	(NA)	8.0	10.0	(NA)	8	10	(NA)
Missouri	5	7	(NA)	19.0	12.0	(NA)	95	84	(NA)
Nebraska	20	20	60	11.0	11.0	10.0	220	220	600
New Mexico	17	18	(NA)	11.0	11.0	(NA)	187	198	(NA)
North Carolina	4	7	(NA)	10.0	10.0	(NA)	40	70	(NA)
Oklahoma	12	12	16	18.0	5.0	10.0	216	60	160
South Dakota	37	40	65	11.0	12.5	13.0	407	500	845
Texas	65	80	85	15.0	13.0	12.5	975	1,040	1,063
United States	282	264	339	13.4	12.6	11.9	3,772	3,326	4,019

(NA) Not available.
NASS, Crops Branch, (202) 720–2127.

Table 1-67.—Sorghum grain: Marketing year average price and value of production, by State and United States, 2017–2019

State	Marketing year average price per cwt			Value of production		
	2017	2018	2019 [1]	2017	2018	2019 [1]
	Dollars	*Dollars*	*Dollars*	*1,000 dollars*	*1,000 dollars*	*1,000 dollars*
Arkansas	5.66	(D)	(NA)	1,731	(D)	(NA)
Colorado	5.45	4.93	4.70	57,133	47,555	33,453
Georgia	7.96	7.40	(NA)	2,889	3,294	(NA)
Illinois	6.37	6.14	(NA)	4,441	6,107	(NA)
Kansas	5.58	5.59	5.85	627,772	730,009	668,304
Louisiana	6.19	6.10	(NA)	4,101	1,722	(NA)
Mississippi	5.72	(D)	(NA)	923	(D)	(NA)
Missouri	5.60	6.40	(NA)	7,718	7,526	(NA)
Nebraska	5.15	5.45	5.85	33,368	48,771	39,607
New Mexico	6.12	6.98	(NA)	5,758	6,981	(NA)
North Carolina	6.50	6.60	(NA)	3,403	1,774	(NA)
Oklahoma	5.64	5.95	6.15	49,382	39,984	45,667
South Dakota	5.64	5.86	5.95	36,511	52,506	46,648
Texas	6.30	6.64	6.65	333,396	230,913	318,030
Other States [2]	(X)	6.36	(X)	-	3,705	-
United States	5.75	5.82	6.00	1,168,526	1,180,847	1,151,709

(D) Withheld to avoid disclosing data for individual operations. (NA) Not available. (X) Not applicable. [1] Preliminary. [2] Includes data withheld above.
NASS, Crops Branch, (202) 720–2127.

Table 1-68.—Sorghum grain: Support operations, United States, 2013–2019

Marketing year beginning September 1	Income support payment rates per cwt [1]	Program price levels per cwt		Put under support		Acquired by CCC under loan program [5]	Owned by CCC at end of marketing year
		Loan [2]	Target/ reference [3]	Quantity	Percentage of production [4]		
	Dollars	*Dollars*	*Dollars*	*Million cwt*	*Percent*	*Millions cwt*	*Million cwt*
2013/2014	0.63/0.00	3.48	4.70	0.3	0.1	0	0
2014/2015	0.00	3.48	7.05	0.4	0.2	0	0
2015/2016	0.64	3.48	7.05	1.4	0.4	0	0
2016/2017	1.16	3.48	7.05	1.9	0.7	0	0
2017/2018	0.73	3.48	7.05	1.3	0.6	0	0
2018/2019	1.25	3.48	7.05	1.2	0.6	0	0
2019/2020	1.10	3.93	7.05	1.6	0.8	0	0

[1] The first entry is the direct payment rate and the second entry is the counter-cyclical payment rate for 2004/2005-2013/2014. For 2009/2010-2013/2014, producers who participated in the Average Crop Revenue (ACRE) program got a 20 percent reduction in their direct payment, not calculated in this table. For 2014/2015 and after, the entry is the price loss coverage (PLC) payment rate. For 2017/2018, projected PLC payment rate is based on March 2018 WASDE MY price. Agricultural Risk Coverage (ARC) is also available, but payment rates are established at the county or farm levels. [2] For 2009/2010-2013/2014, producers who participate in the ACRE program get a 30 percent reduction in their loan rate, not calculated in this table. [3] Target applies to 2003/2004-2013/2014 and Reference applies beginning with 2014/2015. [4] Percent of production is on a grain basis. [5] Acquisitions as of January 31, 2020.
FPAC-BC, Commodity Analysis Branch.

Table 1-69.—International Sorghum: Area, yield, and production in specified countries, 2017/2018–2019/2020

Country	Area			Yield per hectare			Production		
	2017/ 2018	2018/ 2019	2019/ 2020	2017/ 2018	2018/ 2019	2019/ 2020	2017/ 2018	2018/ 2019	2019/ 2020
	1,000 hectares			*Metric tons*			*1,000 metric tons*		
United States	2,041	2,048	1,892	4.50	4.53	4.58	9,192	9,271	8,673
Nigeria	5,820	5,800	5,900	1.19	1.17	1.17	6,939	6,800	6,900
Ethiopia	1,900	1,900	1,900	2.72	2.71	2.74	5,170	5,150	5,200
Mexico	1,350	1,350	1,350	3.37	3.48	3.33	4,545	4,700	4,500
Sudan	5,024	3,919	4,600	0.96	0.89	0.96	4,803	3,475	4,400
India	5,412	7,000	7,000	0.69	0.71	0.57	3,743	4,953	4,000
China	506	720	750	4.87	4.79	4.80	2,465	3,450	3,600
Argentina	700	630	575	4.29	3.97	4.35	3,000	2,500	2,500
Brazil	782	732	730	2.73	2.97	2.88	2,136	2,177	2,100
Niger	3,821	3,700	3,700	0.51	0.57	0.51	1,945	2,100	1,900
Burkina	1,667	1,800	1,800	0.82	1.07	1.00	1,366	1,930	1,800
Mali	1,386	1,500	1,500	1.03	0.98	0.87	1,424	1,470	1,300
Cameroon	852	850	850	1.59	1.41	1.41	1,352	1,200	1,200
Australia	1,147	1,100	1,100	0.83	0.90	0.86	946	988	950
Chad	388	285	335	2.64	2.74	2.60	1,023	780	871
Tanzania	124	135	157	5.32	5.46	5.22	660	737	820
Bolivia	783	800	800	0.96	0.84	1.00	755	672	800
Egypt	140	140	140	5.36	5.36	5.36	750	750	750
European Union	600	600	600	1.11	1.08	1.17	667	650	700
South Sudan	462	496	250	2.72	2.58	1.60	1,257	1,278	400

FAS, Office of Global Analysis, (202) 720-6301. Prepared or estimated on the basis of official USDA production, supply, and distribution statistics from foreign governments.

Table 1-70.—Sorghum: International trade, 2017/2018–2019/2020

Country	2017/2018	2018/2019	2019/2020
		1,000 metric tons	
Principle exporting countries:			
United States	5,089	2,351	3,429
Argentina	36	196	200
Nigeria	100	100	100
Ukraine	123	93	100
Ethiopia	75	75	75
India	125	51	50
Australia	456	110	40
China	43	49	40
Kenya	129	41	30
Bolivia	21	18	20
Paraguay	4	15	15
Brazil	1	33	5
Burkina	5	5	5
South Africa	6	5	5
Sudan	100	50	5
Tanzania	5	5	5
Uganda	5	5	5
European Union	2	7	2
Thailand	5	1	2
Principle importing countries:			
China	4,436	652	1,300
Mexico	98	596	700
Japan	594	452	500
European Union	420	759	200
Sudan	150	160	200
Kenya	119	129	150
South Sudan	148	26	150
Chile	76	40	100
Colombia	56	0	50
Somalia	80	85	50
South Africa	48	60	50
Taiwan	64	70	50
Uganda	35	35	40
Eritrea	30	60	30
Botswana	4	1	25
Cameroon	15	25	25
Chad	25	25	25
Niger	25	25	25
Pakistan	63	27	25
Israel	29	36	20
Philippines	21	36	20
Rwanda	20	20	20

FAS, Office of Global Analysis, (202) 720-6301. Prepared or estimated on the basis of official USDA production, supply, and distribution statistics from foreign governments.

Table 1-71.—International Mixed grain: Area, yield, and production in specified countries, 2017/2018–2019/2020

Country	Area			Yield per hectare			Production		
	2017/ 2018	2018/ 2019	2019/ 2020	2017/ 2018	2018/ 2019	2019/ 2020	2017/ 2018	2018/ 2019	2019/ 2020
	1,000 hectares			*Metric tons*			*1,000 metric tons*		
Bangladesh	35	35	35	0.71	0.71	0.71	25	25	25
Canada	66	90	95	2.76	2.96	2.79	182	266	265
European Union	3,900	3,872	4,016	3.93	3.39	3.64	15,320	13,138	14,600
Switzerland	10	10	10	6.00	6.00	6.00	60	60	60
Turkey	1	1	1	1.00	1.00	1.00	1	1	1

FAS, Office of Global Analysis, (202) 720-6301. Prepared or estimated on the basis of official USDA production, supply, and distribution statistics from foreign governments.

Table 1-72.—Commercial feeds: Disappearance for feed, United States, 2007–2018

Year beginning October	Oilseed cake and meal						
	Soybean	Cottonseed	Linseed	Peanut [1]	Sunflower	Canola	Total
	1,000 Short tons						
2009	30,640	767	210	91	415	1,984	33,109
2010	30,301	1,079	208	112	281	2,968	33,354
2011	31,552	982	194	109	197	3,753	34,491
2012	28,999	1,012	199	123	241	4,260	31,913
2013	29,514	811	153	130	268	4,750	31,862
2014	32,277	794	212	141	224	4,891	35,038
2015	33,118	638	196	144	288	4,975	35,520
2016	33,420	687	190	177	293	5,011	41,290
2017	36,971	708	166	....	261	4,616	....
2018	35,952	750	173	....	270	4,842	....

Year beginning October	Animal protein				Mill products [3]					Total commercial feeds
	Tankage and meat meal	Fish meal	Dried milk [2]	Total	Wheat millfeeds	Gluten feed and meal [4]	Rice millfeeds	Alfalfa meal	Total	
	1,000 Short tons									
2007	2,367	197	356	2,920	6,863	4,560	580	225	12,228	54,148
2008	2,302	182	364	2,848	6,514	5,166	547	225	12,453	51,065
2009	2,260	178	338	2,775	6,445	5,203	574	225	12,447	50,316
2010	2,027	298	436	2,762	6,204	5,034	608	225	12,070	51,156
2011	(NA)	198	463	2,857	6,404	5,772	535	225	12,936	54,038
2012	(NA)	198	368	2,728	6,345	5,707	531	225	12,808	51,709
2013	(NA)	198	219	2,545	6,345	5,651	447	225	12,669	51,827
2014	(NA)	198	248	2,608	6,603	5,837	845	225	13,510	56,048
2015	2,594	198	248	3,041	6,513	5,921	235	225	12,894	56,434
2016	2,933	198	248	3,379	9,101	5,864	579	225	15,768	60,438

This data has not been updated, but contains the most recent data available. [1] Year beginning August 1. [2] Includes dried skim milk, and whey for feed, but does not include any milk products fed on farms. [3] Other mill products that are not listed include screenings, hominy, and oats feed etc., for which no statistics are available. [4] Adjusted for export data.

ERS, Market and Trade Economics Division, (202) 694–5313.

Table 1-73.—High-protein feeds: Quantity for feeding, high-protein animal units, quantity per animal unit, and prices, United States, 2007–2016

Year beginning October	Quantity for feeding [1]						High-protein animal units	Quantity per animal unit	High protein feed prices
	Oilseed meal			Animal protein	Grain protein [3]	Total			
	Soybean meal	Other oilseed meals [2]	Total						
	1,000 tons	*1,000 tons*	*1,000 tons*	*1,000 tons*	*1,000 tons*	*1,000 tons*	*Million units*	*Pounds*	*Index numbers 1992=100*
2007	36,555	2,945	39,500	3,207	2,715	45,422	71	1,271	173
2008	33,827	2,282	36,109	3,113	3,076	42,298	71	1,193	171
2009	33,703	2,262	35,965	3,049	3,098	42,112	70	1,195	153
2010	33,331	2,814	36,145	2,950	2,998	42,093	69	1,214	177
2011	34,695	2,721	37,416	3,037	3,437	43,890	68	1,290	203
2012	31,899	2,689	34,587	2,965	3,398	40,951	68	1,212	239
2013	32,466	2,166	34,632	2,879	3,365	40,877	67	1,225	250
2014	35,506	2,546	38,052	2,929	3,476	44,456	67	1,319	191
2015	36,430	2,211	38,641	3,450	3,526	45,616	69	1,313	166
2016	36,630	2,686	39,316	3,858	3,492	46,665	71	1,316	159

This data has not been updated, but contains the most recent data available. [1] In terms of 44 percent protein soybean meal equivalent. [2] Includes cottonseed, linseed, peanut meal, and sunflower meal. [3] Beginning 1974, adjusted for exports of corn gluten feed and meal.
ERS, Market and Trade Economics Division, (202) 694–5313.

Table 1-74.—Feed concentrates: Fed to livestock and poultry, 2007–2016

Year beginning October	Feed grains				Wheat [2]	Rye [2]	By-product feeds [3]	Total concentrates	Grain consuming animal units	Concentrates fed per grain-consuming animal unit
	Corn [1]	Sorghum [1]	Oats [2] and barley [2]	Total						
	Million tons	*Million tons*	*Million tons*	*Million tons*	*Million tons*	*Million tons*	*Million tons*	*Million tons*	*Millions*	*Tons*
2007	163.9	4.6	3.2	171.7	4.9	0.1	62.0	238.8	92.7	2.58
2008	143.6	6.6	3.2	153.4	3.4	0.1	58.2	215.1	91.7	2.35
2009	142.7	3.9	3.0	140.6	0.2	0.1	67.3	210.1	92.4	2.27
2010	133.6	3.4	2.7	139.7	2.1	0.1	57.7	196.6	92.9	2.15
2011	126.3	1.9	3.0	131.3	10.8	0.1	57.7	202.9	93.1	2.18
2012	120.6	2.6	3.6	126.9	11.6	0.1	57.6	196.7	92.3	2.13
2013	140.1	2.6	3.1	145.7	1.8	0.1	57.7	206.3	90.5	2.28
2014	148.0	2.3	2.5	152.8	4.7	0.1	63.3	220.9	92.4	2.39
2015	143.2	3.0	2.7	148.9	3.5	0.1	63.6	216.1	94.2	2.29
2016	153.0	3.6	2.4	159.0	2.2	0.1	68.0	229.3	95.8	2.39

This data has not been updated, but contains the most recent data available. [1] Marketing year beginning September 1. [2] Marketing year beginning June 1. [3] Oilseed meals, animal protein feeds, mill byproducts, and mineral supplements.
ERS, Market and Trade Economics Division, (202) 694–5313.

Table 1-75.—Feed: Consumed per head and per unit of production, by class of livestock or poultry, with quantity expressed in equivalent feeding value of corn, 2007–2016

Year beginning October	Dairy cattle			Beef cattle				Sheep and lambs	
	Milk cows		Other dairy cattle per head	Cattle on feed per head Jan. 1 [1]	Other beef cattle per head	All beef cattle per head	Cattle and calves per 100 pounds produced [2]	Per head	Per 100 pounds produced [3]
	Per head	Per 100 pounds milk produced							
	Pounds	*Pounds*	*Pounds*	*Pounds*	*Pounds*	*Pounds*	*Pounds*	*Pounds*	*Pounds*
2007	12,949	65	6,526	9,114	5,307	5,993	1,261	1,271	1,718
2008	12,265	60	6,473	8,854	5,283	5,895	1,214	1,263	1,741
2009	12,303	59	6,425	8,942	5,269	5,896	1,227	1,260	1,680
2010	12,013	57	6,378	8,403	5,253	5,815	1,183	1,254	1,695
2011	12,030	57	6,369	8,056	5,263	5,782	1,145	1,261	1,669
2012	11,918	57	6,364	7,830	5,255	5,717	1,137	1,261	1,659
2013	12,143	56	6,434	8,677	5,314	5,891	1,143	1,269	1,631
2014	12,345	56	6,453	8,912	5,292	5,919	1,183	1,265	1,649
2015	12,224	55	6,399	8,577	5,280	5,838	1,173	1,260	1,649
2016	12,408	55	6,905	9,398	5,282	5,958	1,180	1,265	1,624

Year beginning October	Poultry								Hogs per 100 pounds produced	Horses and mules two years and over per head
	Hens and pullets		Chickens raised		Broilers produced		Turkeys raised			
	Per head Jan. 1	Per 100 eggs	Per head	Per 100 pounds live weight	Per head	Per 100 pounds produced	Per head	Per 100 pounds produced		
	Pounds	*Pounds*	*Pounds*	*Pounds*	*Pounds*	*Pounds*	*Pounds*	*Pounds*	*Pounds*	*Pounds*
2007	136	47	28	1,045	11	197	86	313	574	3,832
2008	126	44	27	1,017	10	175	84	270	496	3,735
2009	119	43	26	1,077	10	180	85	293	487	3,707
2010	113	40	24	1,037	9	162	82	285	487	3,650
2011	119	42	25	1,019	10	163	79	272	486	3,663
2012	117	41	25	1,049	9	160	78	252	447	3,641
2013	119	40	26	1,156	9	165	82	255	471	3,674
2014	115	41	30	1,321	10	173	89	287	516	3,723
2015	106	43	28	1,255	10	164	85	290	483	3,695
2016	115	43	28	1,316	10	170	87	284	498	3,728

This data has not been updated, but contains the most recent data available. [1] Feed consumed by all cattle divided by the number on feed January 1. [2] Feed for all cattle, except milk cows, divided by the net live-weight production of cattle and calves. It includes the growth on dairy heifers and calves as well as all beef cattle. [3] Including wool produced.
ERS, Market and Trade Economics Division, (202) 694–5313.

Table 1-76.—Feed: Consumed by livestock and poultry, by type of feed, with quantity expressed in equivalent feeding value of corn, 2007–2016

Year beginning October	Concentrates	Harvested roughage	Pasture	Total
	Million tons	*Million tons*	*Million tons*	*Million tons*
2007	239	80	163	482
2008	215	83	158	456
2009	210	83	156	450
2010	200	81	155	435
2011	203	76	155	434
2012	197	75	155	427
2013	206	78	149	433
2014	221	82	148	450
2015	216	81	155	452
2016	229	81	160	470

This data has not been updated, but contains the most recent data available.
ERS, Market and Trade Economics Division, (202) 694–5313.

Table 1-77.—Animal units fed: Grain-consuming, roughage-consuming, and grain-and-roughage-consuming, United States, 2007–2016 [1]

Year beginning October	Grain-consuming [2]	Roughage-consuming [3]	Grain and roughage-consuming [4]
	1,000 units	*1,000 units*	*1,000 units*
2007	95,118	71,479	80,042
2008	92,702	70,887	78,782
2009	91,687	70,452	78,111
2010	92,411	69,352	77,720
2011	93,104	68,023	77,192
2012	92,311	67,593	76,617
2013	90,502	66,758	75,347
2014	92,433	67,413	76,532
2015	94,187	69,498	85,126
2016	95,771	70,917	80,814

This data has not been updated, but contains the most recent data available. [1] Index series based on average feeding rates for years 1969–71. In calculations for the feeding years 1969 to date, cattle numbers used are the new categories shown in the Livestock and Poultry Inventory, published by NASS, USDA. [2] Livestock and poultry numbers weighted by all concentrates consumed. [3] Livestock and poultry numbers weighted by all roughage (including pasture) consumed. [4] Livestock and poultry numbers weighted by all feed (including pasture) fed to livestock.
ERS, Market and Trade Economics Division, (202) 694–5313.

Table 1-78.—Feed grains: Average price, selected markets and grades, 2010–2019 [1]

Calendar year	Kansas City			Minneapolis		
	Corn, No. 2 Yellow (truck)	Corn, No. 2 White (rail)	Sorghum, No. 2 Yellow (truck)	Corn, No. 2 Yellow	Barley, No. 3 or Better malting	Oats, No. 2 White
	Dollars per bushel					
2010	4.08	4.27	6.94	3.65	4.70	2.74
2011	6.81	7.11	11.73	6.58	6.96	3.72
2012	7.17	7.29	11.81	6.87	7.06	3.67
2013	6.28	6.35	10.40	5.97	6.35	3.90
2014	4.07	4.30	7.30	3.83	6.23	4.02
2015	3.76	3.82	6.97	3.45	6.23	2.84
2016	3.49	3.93	5.59	3.18	(NA)	2.57
2017	3.43	3.62	5.61	3.19	4.70	3.43
2018	3.57	3.73	5.87	3.21	2.74	2.96
2019	3.85	4.00	6.28	3.55	2.79	3.17

Calendar year	Omaha: Corn, No. 2 Yellow (truck)	Chicago: Corn, No. 2 Yellow	Texas High Plains: Sorghum, No. 2 Yellow	Memphis Corn, No 2 Yellow	St. Louis: Corn, No. 2 Yellow (truck)
	Dollars per bushel		*Dollars per cwt*		
2010	4.03	4.16	7.81	4.25	4.26
2011	6.72	6.78	12.64	6.85	7.08
2012	7.06	0.00	13.15	6.95	7.08
2013	6.23	5.81	10.51	6.07	6.25
2014	3.99	4.03	7.26	4.33	4.84
2015	3.66	3.68	6.72	3.87	3.87
2016	3.34	3.61	5.53	3.67	3.70
2017	3.29	3.44	5.85	(NA)	3.62
2018	3.49	3.50	5.85	(NA)	3.73

[1] Simple average of daily prices.
AMS, Livestock and Grain Market News Branch, (202) 720–6231.

Table 1-79.—Feedstuffs: Average price per ton bulk, in wholesale lots, at leading markets, 2010–2019

Year beginning October	Soybean meal	Cottonseed meal		Linseed meal	Meat meal	Fish meal	Wheat bran	Wheat middlings
	48% protein	41% protein	41% protein	34% protein	50% protein	60% protein	Kansas City	Minneapolis
	Decatur	Kansas City	Memphis	Minneapolis	Kansas City	Gulf Coast		
	Dollars per ton							
2010	313.47	249.72	212.57	210.80	299.05	1,265.78	94.62	94.44
2011	333.73	310.43	275.43	242.60	342.84	1,198.89	176.20	172.74
2012	439.77	336.79	303.37	282.67	391.49	1,168.09	175.06	192.91
2013	464.61	430.80	333.42	(NA)	467.00	(NA)	129.57	182.40
2014	478.26	410.64	369.30	(NA)	456.61	1,466.28	119.45	117.43
2015	341.20	333.31	291.97	(NA)	328.33	1,531.77	98.42	93.66
2016	328.64	290.99	247.63	(NA)	275.20	1,386.72	75.10	73.51
2017	307.57	246.30	209.00	(NA)	254.17	1,291.67	75.47	69.59
2018	334.68	307.24	264.85	(NA)	270.39	(NA)	141.88	(NA)
2019	300.28	271.81	224.58	(NA)	233.60	(NA)	125.95	92.46

Year beginning October	Wheat shorts or middlings	Wheat millrun	Gluten feed	Hominy feed	Distillers' dried grains	Alfalfa meal	
			21% protein			Dehydrated, 17% protein	Sun-cured
	Kansas City	Portland	Illinois Points	Midwest	Lawrenceburg	Kansas City	Kansas City
	Dollars per ton						
2010	94.62	124.06	....	115.61	122.77	210.36	178.16
2011	176.20	187.71	....	206.85	202.42	254.72	243.29
2012	174.78	219.71	....	....	200.00	347.23	....
2013	129.99	228.57	166.35	202.42	236.07	339.28	275.70
2014	119.41	191.60	165.00	124.84	172.22	324.74	267.10
2015	98.42	170.20	98.28	103.53	164.40	283.53	206.99
2016	75.10	144.76	90.72	92.12	148.60	253.90	185.82
2017	74.08	131.65	(NA)	95.20	(NA)	227.37	190.02
2018	102.72	143.33	(NA)	(NA)	80.00	247.07	231.43
2019	90.70	162.26	106.27	106.30	(NA)	306.44	(NA)

(NA) Not available.
AMS, Livestock and Grain Market News Branch, (202) 720–6231.

Table 1-80.—International Millet: Area, yield, and production in specified countries, 2017/2018–2019/2020

Country	Area			Yield per hectare			Production		
	2017/2018	2018/2019	2019/2020	2017/2018	2018/2019	2019/2020	2017/2018	2018/2019	2019/2020
	1,000 hectares			*Metric tons*			*1,000 metric tons*		
India	9,221	8,146	8,000	1.26	1.26	1.36	11,640	10,236	10,900
Niger	6,999	7,000	7,000	0.54	0.55	0.54	3,790	3,847	3,800
China	861	870	900	2.96	2.53	2.56	2,548	2,200	2,300
Nigeria	2,212	2,000	2,000	0.68	1.06	1.00	1,500	2,119	2,000
Mali	2,156	2,000	2,000	0.69	0.92	0.73	1,493	1,840	1,450
Burkina	1,223	1,200	1,200	0.68	0.99	0.92	828	1,189	1,100
Ethiopia	464	450	450	2.32	2.22	2.44	1,078	1,000	1,100
Sudan	2,142	3,000	2,500	0.45	0.67	0.40	954	2,000	1,000
Senegal	850	850	850	1.03	1.06	1.00	875	897	850
Chad	1,165	1,100	1,100	0.57	0.69	0.64	660	756	700
Russia	235	187	350	1.34	1.16	1.25	315	217	437
Tanzania	333	350	350	1.17	0.90	1.00	389	316	350
Pakistan	489	476	470	0.69	0.65	0.64	335	307	300
Nepal	260	260	260	0.96	0.96	0.96	250	250	250
Burma	240	240	240	1.00	1.00	1.00	240	240	240
Uganda	151	175	175	1.42	1.45	1.37	214	253	240
Guinea	194	200	200	1.09	1.07	1.00	211	214	200
Ghana	167	160	160	1.00	1.09	1.09	167	175	175
Ukraine	58	55	90	1.50	1.47	1.89	87	81	170
Cameroon	72	72	72	1.39	1.39	1.39	100	100	100

FAS, Office of Global Analysis, (202) 720-6301. Prepared or estimated on the basis of official USDA production, supply, and distribution statistics from foreign governments.

Table 1-81.—Proso millet: Area, yield, production, and value, United States, 2010–2019

Year	Area		Yield per harvested acre	Production	Marketing year average price per bushel received by farmers	Value of production
	Planted	Harvested				
	1,000 acres	*1,000 acres*	*Bushels*	*1,000 dollars*	*Dollars*	*1,000 dollars*
2010	390	363	31.8	11,535	4.54	52,419
2011	370	338	27.1	9,149	6.01	54,974
2012	335	205	15.0	3,075	15.10	46,548
2013	720	638	28.9	18,436	4.61	84,915
2014	505	430	31.4	13,483	3.35	45,104
2015	445	418	33.9	14,159	2.93	41,547
2016	443	413	30.4	12,558	2.87	36,065
2017	478	403	36.9	14,889	3.32	49,444
2018	443	390	29.7	11,595	5.22	60,566
2019	506	465	35.7	16,608	4.99	82,907

NASS, Crops Branch, (202) 720–2127.

Table 1-82.—Proso millet: Area, yield, and production, by State and United States, 2017–2019

State	Area planted			Area harvested		
	2017	2018	2019	2017	2018	2019
	1,000 acres	*1,000 acres*	*1,000 acres*	*1,000 acres*	*1,000 acres*	*1,000 acres*
Colorado	320	300	340	290	270	320
Nebraska	105	95	115	86	81	106
South Dakota	53	48	51	27	39	39
United States	478	443	506	403	390	465
State	**Yield per acre**			**Production**		
	2017	2018	2019	2017	2018	2019
	Bushels	*Bushels*	*Bushels*	*1,000 bushels*	*1,000 bushels*	*1,000 bushels*
Colorado	38.5	28.0	37.0	11,165	7,560	11,840
Nebraska	32.0	32.0	31.0	2,752	2,592	3,286
South Dakota	36.0	37.0	38.0	972	1,443	1,482
United States	36.9	29.7	35.7	[illegible]	11,595	16,608

NASS, Crops Branch, (202) 720–2127.

Table 1-83.—Proso millet: Marketing year average price and value, by State and United States, 2017–2019

State	Marketing year average price per bushel			Value of production		
	2017	2018	2019	2017	2018	2019
	Dollars	*Dollars*	*Dollars*	*1,000 dollars*	*1,000 dollars*	*1,000 dollars*
Colorado	3.32	5.42	5.20	37,068	40,975	61,568
Nebraska	3.13	5.07	4.69	8,614	13,141	15,411
South Dakota	3.87	4.47	4.00	3,762	6,450	5,928
United States	3.32	5.22	4.99	36,065	60,566	82,907

NASS, Crops Branch, (202) 720–2127.

CHAPTER II

STATISTICS OF COTTON, TOBACCO, SUGAR CROPS, AND HONEY

In addition to tables on cotton, tobacco, sugar, and honey, this chapter includes tables on fibers other than cotton and syrups. Cottonseed data, however, are in the following chapter on oilseeds, fats, and oils.

Table 2-1.—Cotton: Area, yield, production, market year average price, and value, United States, 2010–2019

Year	Area		Yield per harvested acre	Production	Marketing year average price per pound received by farmers [2]	Value of production [2]
	Planted	Harvested				
	1,000 acres	*1,000 acres*	*Pounds*	*1,000 bales* [1]	*Dollars*	*1,000 dollars*
2010	10,974.2	10,698.7	812	18,101.8	0.846	7,346,868
2011	14,735.4	9,460.9	790	15,573.2	0.935	6,985,976
2012	12,264.4	9,321.8	892	17,313.8	0.757	6,291,813
2013	10,407.0	7,359.4	822	12,909.2	0.838	5,191,505
2014	11,148.4	9,351.8	838	16,319.4	0.657	5,147,241
2015	8,580.5	8,074.9	766	12,888.0	0.645	3,988,978
2016	10,073.5	9,507.8	867	17,160.0	0.705	5,813,774
2017	12,717.5	11,100.4	905	20,922.5	0.719	7,222,535
2018	14,100.3	10,205.8	864	18,367.0	0.723	6,375,167
2019	13,737.8	11,804.5	817	20,102.0	0.623	6,012,662

[1]Value based on 480-pound net weight bale. [2]Based on marketings and monthly prices received from August1, 2019 - December 31, 2019.
NASS, Crops Branch, (202) 720–2127.

Table 2-2.—Cotton: Marketing year average price per pound, and value, by State and United States, 2017–2019

State	Marketing year average price per pound			Value of production [1]		
	2017	2018	2019 [2]	2017	2018	2019 [2]
	Dollars	*Dollars*	*Dollars*	*1,000 dollars*	*1,000 dollars*	*1,000 dollars*
Upland:						
Alabama	0.729	0.730	0.640	282,735	311,155	331,776
Arizona	0.727	0.680	0.659	169,246	142,637	150,252
Arkansas	0.710	0.708	0.616	366,019	385,039	413,952
California	(D)	(D)	0.527	(D)	(D)	46,798
Florida	0.729	0.709	0.577	54,238	35,053	52,022
Georgia	0.760	0.741	0.635	801,000	695,354	807,720
Kansas	(D)	0.600	0.609	(D)	98,208	84,773
Louisiana	0.715	0.755	0.669	138,653	152,208	186,250
Mississippi	0.738	0.751	0.597	478,578	527,022	458,496
Missouri	0.747	0.712	0.579	268,920	314,761	283,478
New Mexico	0.507	(D)	0.535	27,500	(D)	33,384
North Carolina	0.709	0.748	0.596	252,177	252,040	303,245
Oklahoma	0.712	0.653	0.597	348,595	213,766	183,398
South Carolina	0.726	0.747	0.589	164,134	150,595	141,360
Tennessee	0.680	0.696	0.609	238,925	257,242	280,627
Texas	0.663	0.679	0.589	2,950,085	2,232,552	1,809,408
Virginia	0.699	0.718	0.609	64,420	62,380	64,310
Other States [3]	0.734	0.702	(X)	152,146	101,433	-
United States	0.686	0.703	0.603	6,757,371	5,931,451	5,631,849
American-Pima:						
Arizona	(D)	(D)	(D)	(D)	(D)	(D)
California	(D)	(D)	(D)	(D)	(D)	(D)
New Mexico	(D)	(D)	(D)	(D)	(D)	(D)
Texas	(D)	(D)	(D)	(D)	(D)	(D)
Other States [3]	1.390	1.150	1.099	465,164	443,716	380,813
United States	1.390	1.150	1.099	465,164	443,716	380,813
All:						
United States	0.719	0.723	0.623	7,222,535	6,375,167	6,012,662

(D) Withheld to avoid disclosing data for individual operations. [1]Value based on 480-pound net weight bale. [2]Based on marketings and monthly prices received from August 1, 2019-December 31, 2019. [3]Includes data withheld above.
NASS, Crops Branch, (202) 720–2127.

Table 2-3.—Cotton: Area, yield, production, and type by State and United States, 2017–2019

State	Area planted			Area harvested		
	2017	2018	2019	2017	2018	2019
	1,000 acres	*1,000 acres*	*1,000 acres*	*1,000 acres*	*1,000 acres*	*1,000 acres*
Upland:						
Alabama	435.0	510.0	540.0	430.0	497.0	535.0
Arizona	160.0	160.0	160.0	159.0	159.0	158.0
Arkansas	445.0	485.0	620.0	438.0	480.0	610.0
California	88.0	48.0	55.0	87.0	47.0	54.0
Florida	99.0	117.0	112.0	98.0	93.0	111.0
Georgia	1,280.0	1,430.0	1,400.0	1,270.0	1,305.0	1,390.0
Kansas	93.0	165.0	175.0	90.0	152.0	153.0
Louisiana	220.0	195.0	280.0	217.0	189.0	270.0
Mississippi	630.0	620.0	710.0	625.0	615.0	700.0
Missouri	305.0	325.0	380.0	297.0	322.0	368.0
New Mexico	66.0	77.0	63.0	46.0	56.0	47.0
North Carolina	375.0	430.0	510.0	367.0	415.0	500.0
Oklahoma	590.0	780.0	640.0	555.0	550.0	480.0
South Carolina	250.0	300.0	300.0	248.0	275.0	297.0
Tennessee	345.0	360.0	410.0	340.0	355.0	405.0
Texas	7,000.0	7,750.0	7,050.0	5,500.0	4,350.0	5,400.0
Virginia	84.0	98.0	103.0	83.0	97.0	102.0
United States	12,465.0	13,850.0	13,508.0	10,850.0	9,957.0	11,580.0
American Pima:						
Arizona	15.0	14.5	7.5	15.0	14.5	7.5
California	216.0	211.0	205.0	215.0	210.0	202.0
New Mexico	7.5	6.8	5.3	7.4	6.8	5.0
Texas	14.0	18.0	12.0	13.0	17.5	10.0
United States	252.5	250.3	229.8	250.4	248.8	224.5
All:						
United States	12,717.5	14,100.3	13,737.8	11,100.4	10,205.8	11,804.5

State	Yield per harvested acre			Production [1]		
	2017	2018	2019	2017	2018	2019
	Pounds	*Pounds*	*Pounds*	*1,000 bales* [2]	*1,000 bales* [2]	*1,000 bales* [2]
Upland:						
Alabama	902	858	969	808.0	888.0	1,080.0
Arizona	1,464	1,319	1,443	485.0	437.0	475.0
Arkansas	1,177	1,133	1,102	1,074.0	1,133.0	1,400.0
California	1,297	1,910	1,644	235.0	187.0	185.0
Florida	759	532	822	155.0	103.0	190.0
Georgia	841	719	915	2,225.0	1,955.0	2,650.0
Kansas	1,051	1,077	910	197.0	341.0	290.0
Louisiana	894	1,067	1,031	404.0	420.0	580.0
Mississippi	1,038	1,141	1,097	1,351.0	1,462.0	1,600.0
Missouri	1,212	1,373	1,330	750.0	921.0	1,020.0
New Mexico	1,179	977	1,328	113.0	114.0	130.0
North Carolina	969	812	1,018	741.0	702.0	1,060.0
Oklahoma	882	595	640	1,020.0	682.0	640.0
South Carolina	912	733	808	471.0	420.0	500.0
Tennessee	1,033	1,041	1,138	732.0	770.0	960.0
Texas	809	756	569	9,270.0	6,850.0	6,400.0
Virginia	1,110	896	1,035	192.0	181.0	220.0
United States	895	847	803	20,223.0	17,566.0	19,380.0
American Pima:						
Arizona	966	943	896	30.2	28.5	14.0
California	1,407	1,662	1,616	620.0	727.0	680.0
New Mexico	863	812	864	13.3	11.5	9.0
Texas	960	933	912	26.0	34.0	19.0
United States	1,341	1,545	1,544	699.5	801.0	722.0
All:						
United States	905	864	817	20,922.5	18,367.0	20,102.0

[1] Production ginned and to be ginned. [2] 480-pound net weight bales.
NASS, Crops Branch, (202) 720–2127.

Table 2-4.—Cotton, American Upland: Support operations, United States, 2013–2019

Marketing Year beginning August 1	Income support payment rates per pound [1]	Program price levels per pound		Put under Loan		Acquired by CCC under loan program [4]	Owned by CCC at end of marketing year
		Loan [2]	Target/ Reference [3]	Quantity	Percentage of production		
	Cents	*Cents*	*Cents*	*1,000 bales*	*Percent*	*1,000 bales*	*1,000 bales*
2013/2014	6.67/0	52.00	71.25	3,981	32.4	0	0
2014/2015	(NA)	52.00	(NA)	7,625	48.4	0	0
2015/2016	(NA)	52.00	(NA)	6,758	54.3	0	0
2016/2017	(NA)	52.00	(NA)	9,373	56.4	0	0
2017/2018	(NA)	49.49	(NA)	9,597	46.7	0.1	0
2018/2019	2.17	52.00	36.70	8,250	47.0	73	0
2019/2020 [5]	6.14	52.00	36.70	11,787	61.3	0	0

(NA) Not available. [1] The first entry is the direct payment rate and the second entry is the counter-cyclical payment rate for 2004/2005-2013/2014. For 2009/2010-2013/2014, producers who participate in the Average Crop Revenue (ACRE) program get a 20 percent reduction in their direct payment, not calculated in this table. The Agricultural Act of 2014 excludes upland cotton as a covered commodity for the Agricultural Risk Coverage and Price Loss Coverage Programs. The Bipartisan Budget Act of 2018 amended the Agricultural Act of 2014 to make seed cotton a covered commodity for the Agriculture Risk Coverage and Price Loss Coverage Programs effective with the 2018 crop year. The Agriculture Improvement Act of 2018 continued seed cotton as a covered commodity for the Agriculture Risk Coverage and Price Loss Coverage Programs. Beginning with 2018, the income support payment rate is the Price Loss Coverage payment rate for seed cotton. [2] For 2009/2010-2013/2014, producers who participate in the ACRE program get a 30 percent reduction in their loan rate, not calculated in this table. [3] Target applies to 2003/2004-2013/2014 and Reference applies beginning with 2014. Beginning with 2018, Reference Price is for seed cotton. Beginning with 2019, value represents Effective Reference Price for seed cotton. [4] Aquisitions as of September 30, 2020. [5] Payment rate as of the July 31, 2020 NASS Agricultural Prices Report.
FPAC-BC, Commodity Analysis Branch.

Table 2-5.—International Cotton: Area, yield, and production in specified countries, 2017/2018–2019/2020

Country	Area			Yield			Production		
	2017/ 2018	2018/ 2019	2019/ 2020	2017/ 2018	2018/ 2019	2019/ 2020	2017/ 2018	2018/ 2019	2019/ 2020
	1,000 hectares			*Kilograms per hectare*			*1,000 480 lb. bales*		
India	12,600	12,600	13,000	501	446	494	29,000	25,800	29,500
China	3,400	3,500	3,450	1,761	1,726	1,720	27,500	27,750	27,250
United States	4,492	4,130	4,777	1,014	968	902	20,923	18,367	19,800
Brazil	1,175	1,640	1,700	1,708	1,726	1,665	9,220	13,000	13,000
Pakistan	2,700	2,300	2,500	661	719	575	8,200	7,600	6,600
Uzbekistan ...	1,250	1,100	1,010	672	648	754	3,860	3,275	3,500
Turkey	470	520	560	1,853	1,549	1,322	4,000	3,700	3,400
Greece	230	245	280	1,157	1,253	1,283	1,222	1,410	1,650
Mexico	210	243	225	1,617	1,555	1,519	1,560	1,735	1,570
Benin	530	650	675	468	469	468	1,140	1,400	1,450
Mali	705	725	735	432	381	400	1,400	1,270	1,350
Argentina	320	380	360	558	642	605	820	1,120	1,000
Burkina	850	630	575	307	294	379	1,200	850	1,000
Cote d'Ivoire	327	392	426	536	520	512	805	937	1,000
Turkmenistan	545	545	545	535	364	399	1,340	910	1,000
Burma	249	240	240	634	635	635	725	700	700
Australia	530	380	60	1,972	1,261	2,449	4,800	2,200	675
Cameroon	225	250	260	484	523	540	500	600	645
Sudan	180	180	200	575	605	653	475	500	600
Tajikistan	185	180	180	671	502	689	570	415	570
Tanzania	350	420	450	143	194	242	230	375	500
Azerbaijan	130	130	140	569	653	700	340	390	450
Kazakhstan ..	125	128	125	523	587	644	300	345	370
Egypt	91	141	100	718	772	762	300	500	350
Chad	120	60	250	181	145	283	100	40	325
Spain	63	65	65	1,016	1,005	1,005	294	300	300
Iran	85	80	80	640	748	748	250	275	275
Togo	160	180	185	299	308	312	220	255	265
Ethiopia	60	77	80	639	687	680	176	243	250
Nigeria	270	270	270	190	190	190	235	235	235

FAS, Office of Global Analysis, (202) 720–6301. Prepared or estimated on the basis of official USDA production, supply, and distribution statistics from foreign governments.

Table 2-6.—Cotton: United States exports by country of destination, 2017–2019

Country of destination	Year		
	2017	2018	2019
	Metric tons	*Metric tons*	*Metric tons*
Cotton linters:			
Japan	11,088	6,629	3,258
China	6,473	5,515	3,146
Vietnam	9	134	773
Germany(*)	1,123	980	662
Thailand	0	619	460
Malaysia	0	0	278
United Kingdom	35	19	43
Costa Rica	6	0	36
Turkey	31	23	34
Canada	45	71	31
Chile	31	19	29
Guatemala	4	31	25
Sweden	10	27	24
Mexico	0	0	22
Colombia	0	0	21
Nigeria	3	0	19
South Africa	0	12	17
Australia(*)	0	0	17
Netherlands	5	0	11
Dominican Republic	0	0	1
Spain	1,760	229	0
Argentina	100	41	0
France(*)	151	32	0
Brazil	47	27	0
Korea, South	76	18	0
Trinidad and Tobago	8	17	0
Italy(*)	0	13	0
United Arab Emirates	4	11	0
Singapore	0	6	0
Libya	0	6	0
Rest of World	81	3	0
World Total	21,088	14,480	8,907
Cotton <1:			
Vietnam	15,417	31,740	79,517
Indonesia	12,510	29,613	23,347
Thailand	6,196	17,821	16,521
Taiwan	8,383	17,391	15,145
Turkey	12,198	19,355	13,257
Pakistan	949	5,948	13,134
China	15,386	26,059	10,937
Japan	3,043	6,637	8,222
Korea, South	681	4,843	8,217
Bangladesh	635	2,919	6,138
India	571	7,613	3,353
Malaysia	415	1,035	2,445
Mexico	1,028	1,139	1,204
Hong Kong	7	66	952
Colombia	2	1	901
Ecuador	0	0	647
Oman	0	0	555
British Indian Ocean Territory	0	0	351
Guatemala	119	551	238
Italy(*)	431	327	23
Peru	0	20	21
Portugal	0	31	6
Dominican Republic	93	23	6
Jordan	5	0	5
Venezuela	0	0	4
Israel(*)	0	0	4
Spain	0	0	2
Paraguay	0	0	1
Honduras	0	0	1
Brazil	19	0	1
Rest of World	1,590	919	0
World Total	79,676	174,053	205,154

See footnote(s) at end of table.

Table 2-6.—Cotton: United States exports by country of destination, 2017–2019—Continued

Country of destination	Year		
	2017	2018	2019
	Metric tons		
Cotton >1 <1 1/8:			
Vietnam	322,337	348,245	320,042
Mexico	195,692	176,629	145,610
Turkey	116,639	157,895	120,106
Bangladesh	30,798	65,779	98,497
Indonesia	91,705	112,260	84,546
Pakistan	53,161	99,618	70,106
China	103,464	88,241	55,229
India	15,475	19,633	49,425
Thailand	46,598	48,507	37,962
Taiwan	26,514	32,660	35,413
Guatemala	31,766	38,031	29,106
Malaysia	15,024	26,394	25,692
El Salvador	10,855	13,809	14,668
Colombia	12,304	15,845	10,843
Korea, South	15,716	20,335	10,170
Japan	12,488	10,117	9,965
Peru	10,620	16,766	5,435
Egypt	295	803	4,691
Ecuador	3,745	8,466	3,753
Philippines	8,015	6,097	3,425
Portugal	2,485	2,480	2,429
Honduras	392	319	2,029
Bahrain	764	800	1,528
Italy(*)	137	1,906	1,081
Hong Kong	0	2	1,051
Oman	0	0	405
Netherlands	48	63	300
Belgium-Luxembourg(*)	304	277	156
Austria	0	0	97
Nicaragua	0	616	80
Rest of World	13,692	5,254	437
World Total	1,141,032	1,317,845	1,144,277
Pima >= 1 3/8:			
India	34,327	36,931	40,782
China	28,410	38,823	33,377
Vietnam	4,649	7,378	12,178
Pakistan	2,717	5,457	10,338
Turkey	548	2,362	6,964
Peru	3,946	6,236	5,652
Thailand	2,097	2,851	2,768
Bangladesh	1,109	1,972	2,724
Austria	785	982	2,242
El Salvador	41	40	2,011
Egypt	1,920	3,282	1,738
Indonesia	3,210	2,053	1,355
Malaysia	296	137	1,051
Venezuela	0	496	1,000
Bahrain	0	178	850
Japan	3,084	1,417	791
Germany(*)	39	861	789
Taiwan	455	1,383	744
Italy(*)	78	84	330
Ethiopia(*)	0	0	294
Korea, South	483	0	196
United Kingdom	67	248	152
Honduras	0	0	139
Greece	0	0	116
Brazil	0	271	104
Guatemala	39	0	99
Colombia	134	39	97
Slovenia	0	0	80
Mexico	306	19	58
Portugal	0	1	40
Rest of World	7	9	0
World Total	88,747	113,510	129,061

See footnote(s) at and of table.

Table 2-6.—Cotton: United States exports by country of destination, 2017–2019—Continued

Country of destination	Year		
	2017	2018	2019
	Metric tons	*Metric tons*	*Metric tons*
Cotton Other > 1 1/8:			
Vietnam	284,136	367,884	448,940
Pakistan	114,925	233,734	276,534
China	379,305	332,112	275,435
Turkey	280,913	210,148	252,415
India	159,555	91,222	239,341
Indonesia	177,783	193,063	135,594
Bangladesh	119,566	131,511	115,961
Korea, South	125,903	93,778	77,369
Thailand	63,088	76,714	64,705
Malaysia	32,463	34,739	36,916
Taiwan	46,805	54,689	35,716
Peru	34,051	30,962	35,450
Guatemala	9,382	15,412	20,598
Mexico	28,226	13,964	12,988
Egypt	14,808	22,520	10,724
Costa Rica	7,423	9,281	8,573
Ecuador	11,118	7,376	7,232
Japan	8,490	6,312	7,043
Honduras	2,476	4,199	5,066
Philippines	4,510	6,243	3,616
Colombia	8,666	6,390	2,017
Algeria	0	675	1,770
Nicaragua	717	1,259	1,765
El Salvador	2,269	2,653	1,094
Tunisia	799	459	1,058
Portugal	504	122	957
Dominican Republic	185	176	874
Bahrain	2,624	2,217	834
Italy(*)	1,631	799	613
Hong Kong	124	420	529
Rest of World	20,482	19,394	2,676
World Total	1,942,927	1,970,423	2,084,403

(*) Denotes a country that is a summarization of its component countries.
Users should use cautious interpretation on quantity reports using mixed units of measure. Quantity line items will only include statistics on the units of measure that are equal to, or are able to be converted to, the assigned unit of measure of the grouped commodities.
FAS, Office of Global Analysis, (202) 720–6301.

Table 2-7.—Cotton, excluding linters: United States exports and imports, 2017–2019

Area/Partners of Destination	Year beginning August		
	2017	2018	2019
	Metric tons		
Exports:			
Vietnam	643,745	729,216	834,027
Turkey	423,336	412,162	360,243
China	502,957	571,651	355,623
Pakistan	187,406	317,087	320,653
India	240,827	160,850	291,434
Indonesia	321,331	345,488	225,843
Bangladesh	139,819	194,854	186,186
Mexico	219,210	206,572	172,874
Thailand	125,633	144,903	122,579
Korea, South	130,162	131,949	97,703
Taiwan	91,823	101,354	93,808
Malaysia	44,972	53,681	65,320
Guatemala	42,725	46,786	53,688
Peru	42,486	52,186	50,294
Japan	26,387	26,467	21,982
Egypt	20,919	24,647	18,686
El Salvador	13,901	14,549	15,831
Colombia	17,878	24,895	15,798
Ecuador	14,076	15,829	13,199
Philippines	14,125	12,418	10,054
Costa Rica	8,618	8,482	8,772
Honduras	2,950	4,141	5,382
Algeria	0	0	3,208
Bahrain	4,330	3,154	2,797
Portugal	2,989	2,482	2,668
Austria	785	1,736	2,334
Nicaragua	449	1,938	2,149
Italy(*)	1,894	3,096	2,054
Hong Kong	123	494	1,484
Switzerland(*)	908	992	1,382
Rest of World	47,421	24,994	7,114
World Total	3,334,183	3,639,054	3,365,168

Country of origin	Year beginning August		
	2017	2018	2019
	Metric tons		
Imports:			
Germany(*)	17	38	12
Spain	0	0	6
Korea, South	0	0	6
Turkey	1	0	1
Tanzania	0	0	1
China	0	4	0
Japan	0	0	0
Mexico	0	0	0
Peru	0	0	0
Italy(*)	0	0	0
Brazil	0	1	0
Canada	0	0	0
Denmark(*)	0	0	0
Egypt	140	100	0
France(*)	1	0	0
Hong Kong	0	0	0
India	818	7	0
Kazakhstan	35	0	0
Morocco	0	1	0
Pakistan	0	0	0
Taiwan	1	0	0
World Total	1,013	150	26

(*) Denotes a country that is a summarization of its component countries.
All zeroes for a data item may show that statistics exist in the other import type.
Users should use cautious interpretation on quantity reports using mixed units of measure. Quantity line items will only include statistics on the units of measure that are equal to, or are able to be converted to, the assigned unit of measure of the grouped commodities.
FAS, Office of Global Analysis, (202) 720-6301. Data Source: USDA FAS Global Agricultural Trade System (GATS)-BICO-HS10.

Table 2-8.—Cotton: International trade, 2017/2018–2019/2020[1]

Country	2017/2018	2018/2019	2019/2020
		1,000 480 lb. bales	
Principle exporting countries:			
United States	16,279	14,763	16,500
Brazil	4,174	6,018	8,800
India	5,182	3,511	3,600
Greece	1,076	1,355	1,500
Benin	1,000	1,400	1,400
Australia	3,915	3,632	1,300
Mali	1,300	1,350	1,300
Cote d'Ivoire	620	895	1,000
Burkina	1,225	940	900
Cameroon	400	575	600
Argentina	168	545	500
Sudan	350	425	500
Malaysia	152	313	450
Mexico	350	500	425
Tajikistan	505	350	425
Azerbaijan	162	384	350
Turkey	325	482	350
Kazakhstan	250	275	300
Spain	239	322	300
Uzbekistan	1,000	750	300
Egypt	220	350	250
Tanzania	90	200	250
Togo	200	225	250
Turkmenistan	625	150	250
Chad	250	100	200
Zambia	117	156	200
Principle importing countries:			
China	5,710	9,640	8,250
Bangladesh	7,600	7,200	7,300
Vietnam	7,000	6,900	6,800
Turkey	4,024	3,499	4,300
Pakistan	3,400	2,850	4,200
Indonesia	3,517	3,051	3,000
India	1,677	1,800	2,300
Malaysia	739	744	1,000
Thailand	1,149	1,075	950
Mexico	925	850	800
Korea, South	904	781	600
Taiwan	632	592	525
Egypt	550	520	500
Iran	325	300	300
Japan	262	230	250
Peru	242	214	250
El Salvador	156	177	180
Portugal	184	174	170
Italy	171	159	160
Guatemala	118	148	150
Mauritius	115	120	120
Russia	200	150	100

[1] Marketing year beginning August 1.
FAS, Office of Global Analysis, (202) 720–6301. Prepared or estimated on the basis of official USDA production, supply, and distribution statistics from foreign governments.

Table 2-9.—Sugarbeets: Area, yield, production, and value, United States, 2010–2019 [1]

Year	Area		Yield per harvested acre	Production	Marketing year average price per ton received by farmers	Value of production
	Planted	Harvested				
	1,000 acres	*1,000 acres*	*tons*	*1,000 tons*		*1,000 dollars*
2010	1,171.9	1,156.1	27.7	32,034	66.90	2,142,162
2011	1,232.8	1,213.2	23.8	28,896	69.40	2,004,116
2012	1,230.1	1,204.1	29.3	35,224	66.40	2,338,789
2013	1,198.0	1,154.0	28.4	32,789	46.60	1,526,821
2014	1,162.5	1,146.3	27.3	31,285	46.00	1,440,068
2015	1,159.8	1,145.4	30.9	35,371	47.20	1,669,310
2016	1,163.4	1,126.4	32.8	36,920	35.70	1,318,267
2017	1,131.4	1,113.8	31.7	35,317	41.20	1,456,165
2018	1,113.1	1,096.4	30.4	33,282	35.50	1,177,992
2019	1,132.0	979.3	29.2	28,600	38.40	1,099,574

[1] Relates to year of intended harvest for fall planted beets in central California and to year of planting for overwintered beets in central and southern California.
NASS, Crops Branch, (202) 720–2127.

Table 2-10.—Sugarbeets: Area, yield, and production, by State and United States, 2017–2019

State	Area planted			Area harvested			Yield per harvested acre			Production		
	2017	2018	2019	2017	2018	2019	2017	2018	2019	2017	2018	2019
	1,000 acres	*1,000 acres*	*1,000 acres*	*1,000 acres*	*1,000 acres*	*1,000 acres*	*Tons*	*Tons*	*Tons*	*1,000 tons*	*1,000 tons*	*1,000 tons*
California [1]	25.0	24.6	24.5	24.4	24.6	24.5	43.7	48.8	44.1	1,066	1,200	1,080
Colorado	29.4	26.3	25.1	29.0	25.5	24.4	35.7	32.6	30.7	1,035	831	749
Idaho	167.0	163.0	171.0	166.0	163.0	165.0	39.2	40.5	39.0	6,507	6,602	6,435
Michigan	144.0	150.0	146.0	143.0	148.0	145.0	25.2	29.1	28.6	3,604	4,307	4,147
Minnesota	420.0	415.0	424.0	409.0	408.0	336.0	30.6	25.7	25.0	12,515	10,486	8,400
Montana	42.9	43.5	41.8	42.7	42.4	36.5	32.7	31.1	31.6	1,396	1,319	1,153
Nebraska	46.1	45.5	44.0	45.2	44.1	42.1	31.8	31.9	25.4	1,437	1,407	1,069
North Dakota	214.0	202.0	212.0	212.0	199.0	170.0	30.4	28.8	26.0	6,445	5,731	4,420
Oregon	9.1	9.3	10.0	9.1	9.3	9.8	36.7	39.4	38.5	334	366	377
Washington [2]	1.8	1.8	2.0	1.8	1.8	2.0	48.2	48.2	45.4	87	87	91
Wyoming	32.1	32.1	31.6	31.6	30.7	24.7	28.2	30.8	28.3	891	946	679
United States	1,131.4	1,113.1	1,132.0	1,113.8	1,096.4	979.3	31.7	30.4	29.2	35,317	33,282	28,600

[1] Relates to year of intended harvest for fall planted beets in central California and to year of planting for overwintered beets in central and southern California.
NASS, Crops Branch, (202) 720–2127.

Table 2-11.—Sugarbeets: Production and value, by State and United States, 2017–2018

State	Production		Marketing year average price per ton received by farmers		Value of production	
	2017	2018	2017	2018	2017	2018
	1,000 tons	*1,000 tons*	*Dollars*	*Dollars*	*1,000 dollars*	*1,000 dollars*
California [1]	1,066	1,200	47.70	47.70	50,848	52,088
Colorado	1,035	831	31.60	29.20	32,706	24,265
Idaho	6,507	6,602	40.20	46.00	261,581	303,692
Michigan	3,604	4,307	38.30	35.10	138,033	150,158
Minnesota	12,515	10,486	42.50	27.50	531,888	288,365
Montana	1,396	1,319	41.30	41.40	57,655	54,607
Nebraska	1,437	1,407	33.70	30.00	48,427	42,210
North Dakota	6,445	5,731	44.20	35.60	284,869	204,024
Oregon	334	366	40.20	46.00	13,427	16,836
Washington [2]	87	87	40.20	46.00	3,497	4,002
Wyoming	891	946	37.30	39.90	33,234	37,745
United States	35,317	33,282	41.20	35.50	1,456,165	1,177,992

[1] Relates to year of intended harvest for fall planted beets in central California and to year of planting for overwintered beets in central and southern California.
NASS, Crops Branch, (202) 720–2127.

Table 2-12.—Sugarcane for sugar and seed: Area, yield, production, and value, United States, 2010–2019

Year	Area harvested			Yield per acre [1]			Production [1]		
	For sugar	For seed	Total	For sugar	For seed	For sugar and seed	For sugar	For seed	Total
	1,000 acres	*1,000 acres*	*1,000 acres*	*Tons*	*Tons*	*Tons*	*1,000 tons*	*1,000 tons*	*1,000 tons*
2010	825.3	52.2	877.5	31.1	32.5	31.2	25,663	1,697	27,360
2011	827.1	45.5	872.6	33.5	32.7	33.5	27,738	1,486	29,224
2012	854.9	47.5	902.4	35.7	36.4	35.7	30,500	1,727	32,227
2013	859.6	51.2	910.8	33.8	33.9	33.8	29,023	1,521	30,761
2014	823.7	44.8	868.5	35.1	34.1	35.0	28,895	1,529	30,424
2015	831.1	43.6	874.7	36.8	35.9	36.7	30,535	1,567	32,122
2016	853.2	49.9	903.1	35.6	35.0	35.6	30,371	1,747	32,118
2017	851.5	52.6	904.1	36.6	39.1	36.8	31,182	2,056	33,238
2018	859.6	40.1	899.7	38.3	40.1	38.4	32,934	1,608	34,542
2019	870.3	42.9	913.2	34.8	38.5	35.0	30,287	1,650	31,937

Year	Marketing year average price per ton received by farmers	Value of production	
		Of cane used for sugar	Of cane used for sugar and seed [2]
	Dollars	*1,000 dollars*	*1,000 dollars*
2010	41.70	1,069,537	1,140,636
2011	47.20	1,308,951	1,379,498
2012	41.90	1,276,631	1,348,361
2013	31.40	910,377	962,807
2014	34.70	1,002,138	1,054,657
2015	31.20	953,328	1,000,620
2016	32.60	990,209	966,757
2017	31.00	966,757	1,025,524
2018	33.40	1,100,218	1,154,907
2019	37.80	1,144,859	1,207,893

[1] Net tons. [2] Price per ton of cane for sugar used in evaluating value of production for seed.
NASS, Crops Branch, (202) 720–2127.

Table 2-13.—Sugarcane for sugar and seed: Production and value, by State and United States, 2017–2018

State	Sugarcane for sugar						Sugar and seed: Value of production [1]	
	Production [2]		Price per ton		Value of production			
	2017	2018	2017	2018	2017	2018	2017	2018
	1,000 tons	*1,000 tons*	*Dollars*	*Dollars*	*1,000 dollars*	*1,000 dollars*	*1,000 dollars*	*1,000 dollars*
Florida	16,237	16,555	37.90	31.10	615.382	514,861	642,102	536,662
Louisiana	13,455	15,003	23.90	37.20	321,575	558,112	352,382	590,030
Texas	1,490	1,376	20.00	19.80	29,800	27,245	31,040	28,215
United States	31,182	32,934	31.00	33.40	966,757	1,100,218	1,025,524	1,154,907

[1] Price per ton of cane for sugar used in evaluating value of production for seed. [2] Net tons.
NASS, Crops Branch, (202) 720–2127.

Table 2-14.—Sugarcane for sugar and seed: Area, yield, and production, by State and United States, 2017–2019

State	Area harvested			Yield per acre [1]			Cane production [1]		
	2017	2018	2019	2017	2018	2019	2017	2018	2019
For sugar:	*1,000 acres*	*1,000 acres*	*1,000 acres*	*Tons*	*Tons*	*Tons*	*1,000 tons*	*1,000 tons*	*1,000 tons*
Florida	397	397	397	40.9	41.7	42.8	16,237	16,555	16,992
Louisiana	414	425	442	32.5	35.3	27.7	13,455	15,003	12,243
Texas	40.5	37.6	31.3	36.8	36.6	33.6	1,490	1,376	1,052
United States	851.5	859.6	870.3	36.6	38.3	34.8	31,182	32,934	30,287
For seed:									
Florida	15.7	15.3	13.7	44.9	45.8	47.6	705	701	652
Louisiana	35.6	23.5	27.0	36.2	36.5	34.0	1,289	858	918
Texas	1.3	1.3	2.2	48.0	37.9	36.5	62	49	80
United States	52.6	40.1	42.9	39.1	40.1	38.5	2,056	1,608	1,650
For sugar and seed:									
Florida	412.7	412.3	410.7	41.1	41.9	43.0	16,942	17,256	17,644
Louisiana	449.6	448.5	469.0	32.8	35.4	28.1	14,744	15,861	13,161
Texas	41.8	38.9	33.5	37.1	36.6	33.8	1,552	1,425	1,132
United States	904.1	899.7	913.2	36.8	38.4	35.0	33,238	34,542	31,937

[1] Net tons.
NASS, Crops Branch, (202) 720–2127.

Table 2-15.—Sugar, cane (raw value [1]): Refiners' raw stocks, receipts, meltings, continental United States, 2010–2019

Year	Jan. 1 stocks	Receipts [2]	Meltings
	1,000 tons		
2010	346	5,754	5,843
2011	257	5,776	5,534
2012	498	5,880	5,805
2013	574	5,956	5,938
2014	592	6,099	6,135
2015	556	6,310	6,552
2016	322	6,473	6,434
2017	362	6,272	6,096
2018	538	6,328	6,339
2019	528	6,487	6,450

[1] Raw value is the equivalent in terms of 96° sugar. [2] Receipts include refiners' total offshore raw sugar receipts in continental U.S. ports, whether entered through the customs or held pending availability of quota and raw cane sugar produced from sugarcane in the continental United States.
FPAC-BC, Commodity Analysis Branch, (202) 690 0734.

Table 2-16.—Sugar, cane and beet: Domestic marketings, by source of supply, continental United States, 2017–2019

Area of supply	2017	2018	2019
	1,000 tons		
Domestic areas			
Mainland (beet)	5,529	5,096	5,045
Mainland and Hawaii (cane)	3,843	3,937	4,018
Total domestic areas	9,371	9,033	9,063

FPAC-BC, Commodity Analysis Branch, (202) 690-0734.

Table 2-17.—Sugar, cane and beet (refined): Stocks, production, and food use deliveries, continental United States, 2010–2019

Item and year	Cane refiners	Sugarbeet processors	Importers of direct consumption sugar	Mainland cane processors[1]	Total
	1,000 short tons, raw value				
Stocks as of Jan. 1[2]					
2010	484	1,456	0	8	1,947
2011	466	1,691	0	4	2,161
2012	315	1,597	0	6	1,918
2013	388	2,013	0	3	2,404
2014	572	1,603	0	5	2,180
2015	351	1,589	0	4	1,944
2016	413	1,889	0	4	2,307
2017	325	2,029	0	0	2,354
2018	316	1,716	0	0	2,032
2019	288	1,889	0	0	2,177
Sugar Production					
2010	5,833	4,758	0	23	10,615
2011	5,476	4,561	0	19	10,056
2012	5,841	5,070	0	16	10,927
2013	5,883	4,881	0	17	10,781
2014	6,106	4,895	0	10	11,012
2015	6,528	4,878	0	42	11,448
2016	6,419	4,990	0	82	11,491
2017	6,084	5,198	0	0	11,282
2018	6,303	5,322	0	0	11,625
2019	6,366	4,668	0	0	11,034
Food and Beverage Deliveries[3]					
2010	5,615	4,514	904	20	11,054
2011	5,554	4,552	995	17	11,118
2012	5,630	4,633	977	18	11,257
2013	5,834	4,777	949	15	11,575
2014	6,058	4,875	796	11	11,740
2015	6,274	4,614	1,034	11	11,933
2016	6,373	4,809	921	12	12,115
2017	5,976	5,425	682	0	12,083
2018	6,219	5,121	705	0	12,045
2019	6,317	5,099	644	0	12,060

[1] Sugar for human consumption only. [2] Stocks include sugar in bond and in Customs custody and control. [3] Consists of all refined sugar.
FPAC-BC, Commodity Analysis Branch, (202) 690-0734.

Table 2-18.—Sugar (raw and refined): Average price per pound at specified markets, 2010–2019

Year	Cane sugar		Refined beet: Mid-west markets, U.S. wholesale	Retail price, granulated: United States
	Raw, 96 centrifugal			
	Intercontinental contract No. 11, nearby futures, world price	Duty fee paid, New York, U.S. price		
	Cents	*Cents*	*Cents*	*Cents*
2010	22.49	35.97	53.23	62.86
2011	27.22	38.12	56.22	68.30
2012	21.69	28.90	43.38	69.41
2013	17.46	20.46	27.22	64.32
2014	16.34	24.15	32.86	60.90
2015	13.14	24.88	33.88	65.36
2016	18.13	27.65	29.65	64.19
2017	15.81	27.92	31.33	64.76
2018	12.25	25.37	35.54	61.63
2019	12.36	26.16	36.14	59.01

ERS, Market and Trade Economics Division, (202) 694–5247. Compiled from the following sources: (New York) Coffee, Sugar & Cocoa Exchange; the U.S. Department of Labor, Bureau of Labor Statistics; Milling and Baking News, New York Board of Trade; Intercontinental Exchange,.

Table 2-19.—Sugar, centrifugal: International trade, 2017/2018–2019/2020

Country	2017/2018	2018/2019	2019/2020
	1,000 metric tons, raw value		
Principle exporting countries:			
Brazil	28,200	19,600	18,620
Thailand	10,907	9,300	10,500
India	2,236	4,700	5,000
Australia	3,600	3,800	3,500
Guatemala	1,881	1,999	2,019
Mexico	1,146	2,337	1,693
South Africa	768	1,041	1,600
European Union	3,920	1,800	1,500
Eswatini	519	680	760
Colombia	732	720	750
Algeria	610	651	671
Cuba	553	592	610
Russia	621	315	605
Pakistan	1,600	600	500
Morocco	380	450	470
El Salvador	449	451	465
United Arab Emirates	458	430	430
Belarus	393	400	420
Nicaragua	388	421	420
Mauritius	390	347	360
Principle importing countries:			
Indonesia	4,298	5,362	4,500
China	4,350	4,100	4,000
United States	2,972	2,816	2,866
Bangladesh	2,654	2,455	2,480
Algeria	2,349	2,217	2,170
Malaysia	2,002	2,125	2,050
European Union	1,341	1,900	2,000
Nigeria	1,870	1,870	1,890
Korea, South	1,864	1,996	1,860
Saudi Arabia	1,486	1,528	1,600
India	2,071	1,300	1,500
United Arab Emirates	2,804	1,573	1,330
Canada	1,243	1,285	1,325
Japan	1,240	1,187	1,196
Iraq	1,340	1,154	1,175
Morocco	1,128	1,058	1,142
Venezuela	1,030	1,000	1,000
Iran	237	851	851
Egypt	990	860	830
Sudan	827	805	825

FAS, Office of Global Analysis, (202) 720–6301. Prepared or estimated on the basis of official USDA production, supply, and distribution statistics from foreign governments.

Table 2-20.—U.S. Sugar (raw value): Supply and use, includes Puerto Rico, 2009/10–2018/19

Fiscal Year	Beginning stocks	Production	Imports	Exports	Total deliveries, domestic use
	1,000 short tons				
2009/10	1,534	7,963	3,320	211	11,152
2010/11	1,498	7,831	3,738	248	11,422
2011/12	1,378	8,488	3,632	269	11,313
2012/13	1,979	8,981	3,224	274	11,776
2013/14	2,158	8,462	3,742	306	12,246
2014/15	1,810	8,656	3,553	185	12,019
2015/16	1,815	8,989	3,341	74	12,051
2016/17	2,054	8,970	3,244	95	12,258
2017/18	1,876	9,293	3,277	170	12,185
2018/19	2,008	8,948	2,875	35	12,270

ERS, Market and Trade Economics Division, (202) 694–5247. Source: ERS Sugar and Sweetener Outlook

Table 2-21.—Honey: United States exports for consumption, by country of destination, 2017–2019

Country	2017	2018	2019
	Metric tons	*Metric tons*	*Metric tons*
Philippines	747	812	672
Canada	647	739	635
Korea, South	787	507	583
Japan	208	538	571
Kuwait	487	150	407
Yemen(*)	59	72	180
China	316	120	155
United Arab Emirates	125	157	135
India	0	59	130
Panama	51	66	99
Trinidad and Tobago	21	20	70
Barbados	57	48	64
Vietnam	198	511	56
Hong Kong	27	41	45
Bahamas, The	102	76	44
Netherlands Antilles(*)	31	31	42
Bahrain	43	51	40
Taiwan	10	6	34
Bermuda	38	37	24
Singapore	93	19	23
Nicaragua	0	0	20
Pakistan(*)	31	25	16
United Kingdom	1	5	14
Cambodia	3	14	12
Austria	0	11	11
Germany(*)	3	0	11
Costa Rica	2	4	10
Netherlands	0	0	8
Romania)	0	0	8
Cayman Islands	7	5	7
Rest of World	383	287	45
World Total	4,478	4,407	4,169

(*) Denotes a country that is a summarization of its component countries.
FAS, Office of Global Analysis, (202) 720-6301. Data Source: U.S. Census Bureau Trade Data, as of March 10, 2020.

Table 2-22.—Honey: Number of colonies, yield, production, stocks, price, and value, United States, 2010–2019[1]

State	Honey producing colonies[2]	Yield per colony	Production[3]	Stocks Dec 15[4]	Average price per pound[5]	Value of production
	1,000	*Pounds*	*1,000 pounds*	*1,000 pounds*	*Cents*	*1,000 dollars*
2010	2,692	65.6	176,462	45,018	161.9	285,692
2011	2,491	59.6	148,357	36,761	176.5	261,850
2012	2,539	56.0	142,296	31,829	199.2	283,454
2013	2,641	56.6	149,550	38,175	214	320,037
2014	2,741	65.1	178,310	41,207	217	386,933
2015	2,661	58.9	156,705	42,205	208	325,946
2016	2,780	58.4	162,246	41,314	212	343,962
2017	2,684	55.5	149,025	30,671	220	327,855
2018	2,828	54.5	154,008	29,303	221	340,358
2019	2,812	55.8	156,922	41,022	197	309,136

[1] For producers with 5 or more colonies that also qualify as a farm. Colonies which produced honey in more than one State were counted in each State. [2] Honey producing colonies are the maximum number of colonies from which honey was taken during the year. It is possible to take honey from colonies which did not survive the entire year. [3] Due to rounding, total colonies multiplied by total yield may not exactly equal production. [4] Stocks held by producers. [5] Average price per pound based on expanded sales.

NASS, Livestock Branch, (202) 720–3570.

Table 2-23.—Honey: Number of colonies, yield, production, stocks, price and value, by State and United States, 2018[1]

State	Honey producing colonies[2]	Yield per colony	Production	Stocks Dec 15[3]	Average price per pound[4]	Value of production[5]
	1,000	*Pounds*	*1,000 pounds*	*1,000 pounds*	*Cents*	*1,000 dollars*
Alabama	6	45	270	14	372	1,004
Arizona	24	38	912	109	301	2,745
Arkansas	28	50	1,400	84	188	2,632
California	335	41	13,735	3,022	211	28,981
Colorado	31	48	1,488	283	205	3,050
Florida	215	49	10,535	737	240	25,284
Georgia	98	34	3,332	200	276	9,196
Hawaii	17	103	1,751	18	192	3,362
Idaho	96	31	2,976	655	196	5,833
Illinois	11	41	451	108	483	2,178
Indiana	7	46	322	106	358	1,153
Iowa	38	49	1,862	1,005	240	4,469
Kansas	5	73	365	95	310	1,132
Kentucky	4	41	164	34	543	891
Louisiana	45	83	3,735	261	191	7,134
Maine	12	32	384	92	298	1,144
Michigan	97	44	4,268	768	249	10,627
Minnesota	119	61	7,259	1,161	194	14,082
Mississippi	20	87	1,740	70	207	3,602
Missouri	9	45	405	36	283	1,146
Montana	160	92	14,720	3,680	190	27,968
Nebraska	40	59	2,360	850	201	4,744
New Jersey	13	31	403	165	747	3.010
New York	56	48	2,688	833	324	8,709
North Carolina ...	10	33	330	63	576	1,901
North Dakota	550	72	39,600	4,752	187	74,052
Ohio	14	73	1,022	491	372	3,802
Oregon	93	35	3,255	1,009	236	7,682
Pennsylvania	19	44	836	309	389	3,252
South Carolina ...	16	48	768	15	317	2,435
South Dakota	255	47	11,985	5,154	191	22,891
Tennessee	7	46	322	84	411	1,323
Texas	132	56	7,392	1,035	212	15,671
Utah	26	41	1,066	75	210	2,239
Vermont	7	48	336	94	376	1,263
Virginia	4	40	160	35	724	1,158
Washington	77	43	3,311	563	215	7,119
West Virginia	6	37	222	38	433	961
Wisconsin	51	45	2,295	711	295	6,770
Wyoming	39	56	2,184	175	191	4,171
Other States[6 7]	36	39	1,399	314	602	8,422
United States[7 8]	2,828	54.5	154,008	29,303	221	340,358

[1] For producers with 5 or more colonies that also qualify as a farm. Colonies which produced honey in more than one State were counted in each State. [2] Honey producing colonies are the maximum number of colonies from which honey was taken during the year. It is possible to take honey from colonies which did not survive the entire year. [3] Stocks held by producers. [4] Average price per pound based on expanded sales. [5] Value of production is equal to production multiplied by average price per pound. [6] Alaska, Connecticut, Delaware, Maryland, Massachusetts, Nevada, New Hampshire, New Mexico, Oklahoma, and Rhode Island not published separately to avoid disclosing data for individual operations. [7] Due to rounding, total colonies multiplied by total yield may not exactly equal production. [8] United States value of production will not equal summation of States.

NASS, Livestock Branch, (202) 720–3570.

Table 2-24.—Honey: Number of colonies, yield, production, stocks, price and value, by State and United States, 2019[1]

State	Honey producing colonies[2]	Yield per colony	Production	Stocks Dec 15[3]	Average price per pound[4]	Value of production[5]
COM008	*1,000*	*Pounds*	*1,000 pounds*	*1,000 pounds*	*Cents*	*1,000 dollars*
Alabama	7	42	294	44	320	941
Arizona	23	46	1,058	201	197	2,084
Arkansas	20	55	1,100	176	153	1,683
California	335	48	16,080	3,216	156	25,085
Colorado	33	46	1,472	500	214	3,150
Florida	205	45	9,225	830	248	22,878
Georgia	102	33	3,366	370	261	8,785
Hawaii	16	80	1,280	51	128	1,638
Idaho	92	32	2,944	677	167	4,916
Illinois	11	39	429	116	431	1,849
Indiana	9	55	495	198	395	1,955
Iowa	38	55	2,090	1,170	224	4,682
Kansas	7	79	553	171	295	1,631
Kentucky	6	41	246	44	450	1,107
Louisiana	54	72	3,888	428	204	7,932
Maine	15	35	525	110	292	1,533
Michigan	94	50	4,700	1,363	236	11,092
Minnesota	118	59	6,962	3,063	163	11,348
Mississippi	22	80	1,760	141	185	3,256
Missouri	10	43	430	73	332	1,428
Montana	173	86	14,878	5,802	148	22,019
Nebraska	39	52	2,028	223	146	2,961
New Jersey	15	28	420	155	333	1,399
New York	59	58	3,422	1,027	449	15,365
North Carolina	14	42	588	118	406	2,387
North Dakota	520	65	33,800	6,422	140	47,320
Ohio	15	67	1,005	442	342	3,437
Oregon	87	32	2,784	1,141	207	5,763
Pennsylvania	19	50	950	409	424	4,028
South Carolina	16	47	752	45	501	3,768
South Dakota	270	72	19,440	7,582	153	29,743
Tennessee	8	57	456	91	465	2,120
Texas	126	60	7,560	1,814	230	17,388
Utah	22	29	638	89	206	1,314
Vermont	6	48	288	84	434	1,250
Virginia	5	39	195	49	751	1,464
Washington	81	35	2,835	1,191	212	6,010
West Virginia	6	37	222	47	450	999
Wisconsin	46	47	2,162	692	299	6,464
Wyoming	39	56	2,184	306	135	2,948
Other States[6 7]	30	47	1,418	351	591	8,380
United States[7 8]	2,812	55.8	156,922	41,022	197	309,136

[1] For producers with 5 or more colonies that also qualify as a farm. Colonies which produced honey in more than one State were counted in each State. [2] Honey producing colonies are the maximum number of colonies from which honey was taken during the year. It is possible to take honey from colonies which did not survive the entire year. [3] Stocks held by producers. [4] Average price per pound based on expanded sales. [5] Value of production is equal to production multiplied by average price per pound. [6] Alaska, Connecticut, Delaware, Maryland, Massachusetts, Nevada, New Hampshire, New Mexico, Oklahoma, and Rhode Island not published separately to avoid disclosing data for individual operations. [7] Due to rounding, total colonies multiplied by total yield may not exactly equal production. [8] United States value of production will not equal summation of States.

NASS, Livestock Branch, (202) 720–3570.

Table 2-25.—U.S. per capita caloric sweeteners estimated deliveries for domestic food and beverage use, by calendar year 2009–2018 [1] [2]

Calendar year	U.S. population [3] (July 1)	Refined sugar [4]	HFCS	Corn Sweeteners: Glucose syrup	Corn Sweeteners: Dextrose	Corn Sweeteners: Total	Pure honey	Edible syrups	Total caloric sweeteners
	Millions	Pounds, dry basis							
2009	307.2	63.4	49.7	13.0	2.7	65.3	0.9	0.6	130.3
2010	309.3	66.0	48.4	12.6	2.9	64.0	1.0	0.7	131.7
2011	311.6	66.0	46.7	12.2	2.9	61.8	1.1	0.7	129.6
2012	313.9	66.7	45.8	12.5	2.7	61.0	1.1	0.7	129.5
2013	316.1	68.0	43.8	12.0	2.6	58.4	1.2	0.7	128.3
2014	318.4	68.2	43.4	12.2	3.0	58.6	1.3	0.8	128.9
2015	320.7	69.1	42.6	12.3	3.0	57.8	1.3	0.9	129.0
2016	323.1	69.5	41.4	12.4	2.7	56.5	1.3	0.7	128.0
2017	325.1	69.1	40.5	13.1	3.0	56.5	1.4	0.7	127.7
2018	327.2	68.5	37.6	13.1	3.0	53.7	1.4	0.7	124.4

[1] Per capita deliveries of sweeteners by U.S. processors and refiners and direct-consumption imports to food manufacturers, retailers, and other end users represent the per capita supply of caloric sweeteners. The data exclude deliveries to manufacturers of alcoholic beverages. Actual human intake of caloric sweeteners is lower because of uneaten food, spoilage, and other losses. See Table 51 of the Sugar and Sweeteners Yearbook series for estimated intake of sugar. [2] Totals may not add due to rounding. [3] Source: U.S. Census Bureau. [4] Based on U.S. sugar deliveries for domestic food and beverage use.
ERS, Market and Trade Economics Division (202) 694–5247. Source: ERS Sugars and Sweeteners Outlook.

Table 2-26.—Tobacco: Area, yield, production, price, and value, United States, 2010–2019

Year	Area harvested	Yield per acre	Production	Marketing year average price per pound received by farmers	Value of production
	Acres	Pounds	1,000 pounds	Dollars	1,000 dollars
2010	337,500	2,128	718,190	1.782	1,279,920
2011	325,040	1,841	598,252	1.857	1,110,737
2012	336,245	2,268	762,709	2.027	1,557,604
2013	356,250	2,033	724,266	2.181	1,579,823
2014	378,480	2,316	876,689	2.094	1,835,663
2015	328,850	2,188	719,563	2.006	1,443,320
2016	319,660	1,967	628,720	2.007	1,262,087
2017	321,470	2,209	710,161	2.058	1,461,855
2018	291,430	1,830	533,241	2.051	1,093,418
2019	227,120	2,060	467,956	2.009	946,252

Table 2-27.—Tobacco: Area, yield, and production, by State and United States, 2017–2019

State	Area harvested 2017	Area harvested 2018	Area harvested 2019	Yield per harvested acre 2017	Yield per harvested acre 2018	Yield per harvested acre 2019	Production 2017	Production 2018	Production 2019
	Acres	Acres	Acres	Pounds	Pounds	Pounds	1,000 pounds	1,000 pounds	1,000 pounds
Georgia	12,500	12,500	9,000	2,100	1,900	2,100	26,250	23,750	18,900
Kentucky	80,500	68,100	57,400	2,277	1,973	2,150	183,300	134,370	123,390
North Carolina	163,900	152,750	117,400	2,197	1,649	1,999	360,040	251,925	234,700
Pennsylvania ...	8,100	7,800	5,700	2,344	2,231	2,509	18,990	17,400	14,300
South Carolina	12,000	12,300	8,300	2,100	1,800	1,900	25,200	22,140	15,770
Tennessee	21,100	15,700	13,300	2,038	2,523	2,292	43,000	39,610	30,490
Virginia	23,370	22,280	16,020	2,284	1,977	1,898	53,381	44,046	30,406
United States ...	321,470	291,430	227,120	2,209	1,830	2,060	710,161	533,241	467,956

CHAPTER III

STATISTICS OF OILSEEDS, FATS, AND OILS

This chapter includes information on cottonseed, flaxseed, olive oil, peanuts, soybeans, and fats and oils. Most butter statistics are included in the chapter on dairy and poultry statistics. Lard data are mostly in the chapter on livestock.

Table 3-1.—Cottonseed: All cotton harvested area and cottonseed production, farm disposition, marketing year average price per ton received by farmers, and value, United States, 2010–2019

Year	Harvested area of all cotton	Cottonseed				
		Production	Farm disposition		Marketing year average price [2]	Value of production
			Sales to oil mills	Other [1]		
	1,000 acres	*1,000 tons*	*1,000 tons*	*1,000 tons*	*Dollars*	*1,000 dollars*
2010	10,698.7	6,096.1	3,252.9	2,843.2	161.00	988,656
2011	9,460.9	5,370.0	2,695.0	2,675.0	260.00	1,413,343
2012	9,321.8	5,666.0	2,985.0	2,681.0	252.00	1,456,245
2013	7,539.4	4,203.0	2,070.0	2,133.0	246.00	1,054,003
2014	9,351.8	5,125.0	2,459.0	2,666.0	194.00	1,015,607
2015	8,074.9	4,043.0	1,916.0	2,127.0	227.00	932,894
2016	9,507.8	5,369.0	2,921.0	2,448.0	195.00	1,055,924
2017	11,100.4	6,422.0	3,059.0	3,363.0	142.00	911,925
2018	10,205.8	5,631.0	2,435.0	3,196.0	155.00	878,254
2019	11,804.5	5,945.0	2,575.0	3,370.0	159.00	1,021,832

[1] Includes planting seed, feed, exports, inter-farm sales, shrinkage, losses, and other uses. [2] 2018 based on monthly prices received from August 1, 2018 - December 31, 2018.
NASS, Crops Branch, (202) 720–2127.

Table 3-2.—Cottonseed: Production and farm disposition, by State and United States, 2018 and 2019

State	Production		Farm disposition				Seed for planting [1]	
	2018	2019	Sales to oil mills		Other [2]		2018	2019
			2018	2019	2018	2019		
	1,000 tons	*1,000 tons*	*1,000 tons*	*1,000 tons*	*1,000 tons*	*1,000 tons*	*1,000 tons*	*1,000 tons*
Alabama	254.0	267.0	43.0	46.0	211.0	221.0	3.1	3.0
Arizona	156.0	136.0	3.0	....	153.0	136.0	1.1	1.0
Arkansas	366.0	472.0	268.0	280.0	98.0	192.0	3.7	3.7
California	342.0	290.0	62.0	69.0	280.0	221.0	2.0	1.8
Florida	27.0	57.0	26.0	39.0	1.0	18.0	0.5	0.6
Georgia	546.0	778.0	202.0	296.0	344.0	482.0	6.5	6.2
Kansas	106.0	85.0	....	....	106.0	85.0	0.9	1.1
Louisiana	135.0	192.0	107.0	121.0	28.0	71.0	1.6	1.4
Mississippi	451.0	503.0	240.0	265.0	211.0	238.0	4.4	4.3
Missouri	310.0	253.0	150.0	117.0	160.0	136.0	2.1	2.2
New Mexico	42.0	26.0	....	....	42.0	26.0	0.5	0.5
North Carolina	224.0	308.0	10.0	4.0	214.0	304.0	3.1	3.3
Oklahoma	197.0	191.0	124.0	132.0	73.0	59.0	4.0	3.7
South Carolina	117.0	116.0	30.0	41.0	87.0	75.0	1.5	1.5
Tennessee	219.0	301.0	175.0	255.0	44.0	46.0	2.3	2.3
Texas	2,088.0	1,902.0	995.0	910.0	1,093.0	992.0	41.6	39.3
Virginia	51.0	68.0	....	....	51.0	68.0	0.6	0.6
United States	5,631.0	5,945.0	2,435.0	2,575.0	3,196.0	3,370.0	79.5	76.5

[1] Included in "other" farm disposition. Seed for planting is produced in crop year shown, but used in the following year. [2] Includes planting seed, feed, exports, inter-farm sales, shrinkage, losses, and other uses.
NASS, Crops Branch, (202) 720–2127.

Table 3-3.—Cottonseed: Marketing year average price per ton and value of production, by State and United States, crop of 2017–2019

State	Marketing year average price per ton			Value of production		
	2017	2018	2019 [1]	2017	2018	2019 [1]
	Dollars	*Dollars*	*Dollars*	*1,000 dollars*	*1,000 dollars*	*1,000 dollars*
Alabama	118.00	118.00	119.00	24,072	29,972	37,485
Arizona	183.00	214.00	242.00	31,293	33,384	40,172
Arkansas	152.00	152.00	175.00	53,352	55,632	79,975
California	226.00	260.00	305.00	72,998	88,920	98,820
Florida	100.00	110.00	120.00	4,400	2,970	6,360
Georgia	116.00	113.00	115.00	74,008	61,698	86,365
Kansas	170.00	175.00	170.00	9,860	18,550	15,300
Louisiana	160.00	148.00	157.00	20,320	19,980	29,045
Mississippi	156.00	157.00	163.00	67,392	70,807	82,641
Missouri	152.00	153.00	169.00	38,760	47,430	58,812
New Mexico	164.00	200.00	210.00	6,560	8,400	9,660
North Carolina	118.00	127.00	142.00	25,606	28,448	45,156
Oklahoma	116.00	140.00	152.00	34,104	27,580	29,032
South Carolina	133.00	123.00	124.00	16,685	14,391	18,352
Tennessee	137.00	143.00	157.00	31,510	31,317	46,629
Texas	138.00	159.00	167.00	393,576	331,992	329,658
Virginia	121.00	133.00	135.00	6,292	6,783	8,370
United States	142.00	155.00	159.00	911,925	878,254	1,021,832

[1] Based on monthly prices received from August 1, 2019 - December 31, 2019.
NASS, Crops Branch, (202) 720–2127.

Table 3-4.—Cottonseed: Crushings, output of products and product prices, United States, 2009–2018

Year beginning August	Quantity crushed	Cottonseed products and prices			
		Oil		Cake and meal	
		Quantity	Price [1]	Quantity	Price [2]
	1,000 tons	*Million pounds*	*Cents per pound*	*1,000 tons*	*Dollars per ton*
2009	1,901	617	40.27	883	220.90
2010	2,563	835	54.50	1,163	273.84
2011	2,400	755	53.22	1,090	275.13
2012	2,500	800	48.60	1,125	331.52
2013	2,000	630	60.66	900	377.51
2014	1,900	610	45.74	855	304.27
2015	1,500	465	45.87	705	261.19
2016	1,769	542	40.92	805	208.61
2017	1,854	561	31.87	845	260.88
2018	1,900	590	33.0-36.0	855	225-265

[1] Tanks, f.o.b. Valley Points. [2] 41 percent protein, solvent, Memphis.
ERS, Field Crops Branch, (202) 694–5300. Compiled from annual reports of the U.S. Department of Commerce.

Table 3-5.—International meal, cottonseed: Production in specified countries, 2017/2018–2019/2020

Country	2017/2018	2018/2019	2019/2020
	1,000 metric tons		
India	4,301	3,975	4,535
China	4,116	4,093	4,038
Brazil	1,310	1,875	1,900
Pakistan	1,465	1,395	1,350
United States	766	678	726
Turkey	710	732	605
Uzbekistan	651	558	600
Benin	145	166	173
Mali	167	172	162
European Union	130	135	158
Turkmenistan	205	144	153
Australia	386	300	145
Burma	141	134	131
Burkina	116	97	104
Cameroon	84	88	95

FAS, Office of Global Analysis, (202) 720-6301. Prepared or estimated on the basis of official USDA production, supply, and distribution statistics from foreign governments.

Table 3-6.—Cottonseed and Cottonseed oil: United States exports by country of destination, 2017–2019

Country of destination	2017	2018	2019
	Metric tons	*Metric tons*	*Metric tons*
Cottonseed:			
Korea, South	123,769	131,012	118,194
Saudi Arabia	77,740	82,694	65,686
Japan	53,872	63,478	58,636
Mexico	120,085	95,329	36,400
Morocco	4,228	6,194	6,077
United Arab Emirates	6,784	11,270	3,068
Oman	1,292	1,145	2,865
Canada	2,477	3,366	2,865
Qatar	1,259	4,872	1,991
Taiwan	258	325	1,675
Jordan	1,740	1,576	1,483
China	0	2,330	985
Malaysia	0	0	579
United Kingdom	0	744	168
Colombia	8	6	86
Hong Kong	0	0	8
Guatemala	0	1	1
Bangladesh	519	824	0
Costa Rica	19	0	0
Indonesia	988	894	0
Italy(*)	686	745	0
Lebanon	302	639	0
Panama	0	1	0
Philippines	0	420	0
Spain	49	0	0
Trinidad and Tobago	1	5	0
Vietnam	0	50	0
World Total	396,075	407,919	300,768
Cottonseed oil:			
Mexico	22,013	17,089	21,069
Australia(*)	4,347	7,782	9,964
Canada	5,141	6,304	3,990
Libya	0	0	1,805
Malaysia	7,350	8,080	1,304
Japan	591	1,101	1,242
Korea, South	0	43	110
Vietnam	0	0	101
India	261	1,857	84
Thailand	59	108	31
Brazil	32	65	28
Portugal	133	71	15
Belgium-Luxembourg(*)	0	56	13
Turkey	29	20	9
Germany(*)	0	1	6
United Kingdom	0	9	5
China	0	0	5
Peru	0	0	3
Colombia	0	1	3
El Salvador	0	0	2
Chile	0	29	1
United Arab Emirates	24	0	0
Argentina	8	38	0
Bahamas, The	2	5	0
Belize	5	0	0
Costa Rica	0	2	0
Egypt	0	3,150	0
Guatemala	207	0	0
Honduras	48	0	0
Hungary	0	26	0
Rest of World	1,519	1,485	0
World Total	41,770	47,319	39,791

(*) Denotes a country that is a summarization of its component countries.
FAS, Office of Global Analysis, (202) 720-6301. Data Source: U.S. Census Bureau Trade Data

Table 3-7.—International oilseed, cottonseed: Area and production in specified countries, 2017/2018–2019/2020

Country	Area			Production		
	2017/2018	2018/2019	2019/2020	2017/2018	2018/2019	2019/2020
	1,000 hectares			*1,000 metric tons*		
India	12,600	12,600	13,000	12,312	10,953	12,524
China	3,400	3,500	3,450	10,800	10,875	10,679
United States	4,492	4,130	4,777	5,826	5,108	5,654
Brazil	1,175	1,640	1,700	3,019	4,254	4,254
Pakistan	2,700	2,300	2,500	3,552	3,292	2,900
Uzbekistan	1,250	1,100	1,010	1,512	1,283	1,374
Turkey	470	520	560	1,300	1,350	1,110
European Union	295	312	347	487	550	627
Mexico	210	243	225	530	593	533
Benin	530	650	675	376	463	479
Turkmenistan	545	545	545	525	356	391
Mali	705	725	735	396	359	382
Argentina	320	380	360	277	414	370
Cameroon	225	250	260	250	300	322
Sudan	180	180	200	243	255	308
Burma	249	240	240	310	295	289
Burkina	850	630	575	331	235	276
Cote d'Ivoire	327	392	425	215	250	267
Tajikistan	185	180	180	180	162	223
Tanzania	350	420	450	101	163	219
Australia	530	380	60	1,442	661	202
Azerbaijan	130	130	140	133	152	176
Uganda	109	81	89	150	141	149
Kazakhstan	125	128	125	117	135	145
Chad	120	60	250	40	16	130
Togo	160	180	185	100	116	121
Egypt	91	141	100	91	152	106
Nigeria	270	270	270	102	102	102

FAS, Office of Global Analysis, (202) 720–6301. Prepared or estimated on the basis of official USDA production, supply, and distribution statistics from foreign governments.

Table 3-8.—International oil, cottonseed: Production in specified countries, 2017/2018–2019/2020 [1]

Country	2017/2018	2018/2019	2019/2020
	1,000 metric tons		
India	1,325	1,225	1,400
China	1,382	1,374	1,356
Brazil	440	632	640
Pakistan	488	465	450
United States	255	207	234
Uzbekistan	230	197	212
Turkey	232	240	198
Benin	48	56	58
Turkmenistan	77	54	57
Mali	56	58	54
European Union	44	45	53
Australia	133	104	50
Burma	50	48	47
Burkina	36	30	32
Cameroon	28	30	32
Tanzania	13	21	26
Tajikistan	21	22	25
Kazakhstan	18	22	23
Sudan	18	21	23
Uganda	22	22	23
Chad	6	2	20
Korea, South	20	20	20
Egypt	14	23	16
Nigeria	16	16	16
Argentina	20	15	15

[1] Year beginning July 1.
FAS, Office of Global Analysis, (202) 720–6301. Prepared or estimated on the basis of official USDA production, supply, and distribution statistics from foreign governments.

Table 3-9.—Flaxseed: Area, yield, production, disposition, and value, United States, 2010–2019

Year	Area planted	Area harvested	Yield per harvested acre	Production	Marketing year average price per bushel received by farmers	Value of production
	1,000 acres	*1,000 acres*	*Bushels*	*1,000 bushels*	*Dollars*	*1,000 dollars*
2010	421	418	21.7	9,056	12.20	110,251
2011	178	173	16.1	2,791	13.90	38,570
2012	349	336	17.3	5,798	13.80	79,919
2013	181	172	19.5	3,356	13.80	46,325
2014	311	302	21.1	6,368	11.80	75,077
2015	463	456	22.1	10,095	8.95	90,561
2016	374	366	23.7	8,656	8.00	69,352
2017	303	272	14.1	3,842	9.53	36,340
2018	208	198	22.6	4,466	9.89	43,533
2019	374	319	20.0	6,395	8.85	56,062

NASS, Crops Branch, (202) 720–2127.

Table 3-10.—Flaxseed: Area, yield, and production, by State and United States, 2017–2019

State	Area planted			Area harvested		
	2017	2018	2019	2018	2017	2019
	1,000 acres	*1,000 acres*	*1,000 acres*	*1,000 acres*	*1,000 acres*	*1,000 acres*
Montana	52	39	99	38	37	89
North Dakota	245	165	275	229	158	230
South Dakota [1] ...	6	4	(NA)	5	3	(NA)
United States	303	208	374	272	198	319
State	**Yield per harvested acre**			**Production**		
	2017	2018	2019	2017	2018	2019
	Bushels	*Bushels*	*Bushels*	*1,000 bushels*	*1,000 bushels*	*1,000 bushels*
Montana	9.0	17.0	15.0	342	629	1,335
North Dakota	15.0	24.0	22.0	3,435	3,792	5,060
South Dakota [1] ...	13.0	15.0	(NA)	65	45	(NA)
United States	14.1	22.6	20.0	3,842	4,466	6,395

(NA) Not available. [1] Estimates discontinued in 2019.
NASS, Crops Branch, (202) 720–2127.

Table 3-11.—Flaxseed: Marketing year average price and value of production, by State and United States, 2017–2019

State	Marketing year average price per bushel			Value of production		
	2017	2018	2019	2017	2018	2019
	Dollars	*Dollars*	*Dollars*	*1,000 dollars*	*1,000 dollars*	*1,000 dollars*
Montana	8.73	8.89	8.45	2,986	5,592	11,281
North Dakota	9.53	9.89	8.85	32,736	37,503	44,781
South Dakota [1]	9.50	9.73	(NA)	618	438	(NA)
United States	9.53	9.89	8.85	36,340	43,533	56,062

(NA) Not available. [1] Estimates discontinued in 2019.
NASS, Crops Branch, (202) 720–2127.

Table 3-12.—Flaxseed: Support operations, United States, 2012–2018

Marketin year beginning June 1	Income support payment rates per bushels [1]	Program price levels per bushel		Put under loan		Acquired by CCC under loan program [4]	Owned by CCC at end of marketing year
		Loan [2]	Target/ Reference [3]	Quantity	Percentage of production		
	Dollars	*Dollars*	*Dollars*	*1,000 bushels*	*Percent*	*1,000 bushels*	*1,000 bushels*
2012/2013	0.45/0.00	5.65	7.10	26.8	0.5	0	0
2013/2014	0.45/0.00	5.65	7.10	10.7	0.3	0	0
2014/2015	0.00	5.65	11.28	37.5	0.6	0	0
2015/2016	2.33	5.65	11.28	269.6	2.7	0	0
2016/2017	3.28	5.65	11.28	236.1	2.7	0	0
2017/2018	1.75	5.65	11.28	76.8	1.9	0	0
2018/2019	1.47	5.65	11.28	81.4	1.8	0	0

[1] The first entry is the direct payment rate and the second entry is the counter-cyclical payment rate for 2004/2005-2013/2014. For 2009/2010-2013/2014, producers who participated in the Average Crop Revenue (ACRE) program got a 20 percent reduction in their direct payment, not calculated in this table. For 2014/2015 and after, the entry is the price loss coverage payment rate. For 2017/2018, projected PLC payment rate is based on March 2018 WASDE MY price. Agricultural Risk Coverage (ARC) is also available, but payment rates are established at the county or farm levels. [2] For 2009/2010-2013/2014, producers who participated in the ACRE program get a 30 percent reduction in their loan rate, not calculated in this table. [3] Target applies to 2003/2004-2013/2014 and Reference applies beginning with 2014/2015. [4] Acquisitions as of September 30, 2019.
FPAC-BC, Commodity Analysis Branch.

Table 3-13.—Flaxseed: Supply and disappearance, United States, 2009–2018

Year beginning June	Supply				Disappearance			
	Stocks June 1	Production	Imports	Total	Total used for seed	Exports	Crushings [1]	Total domestic disappearance [2]
	1,000 bushels	*1,000 bushels*	*1,000 bushels*	*1,000 bushels*	*1,000 bushels*	*1,000 bushels*	*1,000 bushels*	*1,000 bushels*
2009	2,552	7,423	6,283	16,258	341	1,752	12,000	14,701
2010	1,557	9,056	6,040	16,653	144	2,130	11,635	14,483
2011	2,170	2,791	8,286	13,247	279	654	10,500	12,127
2012	1,120	5,798	6,928	13,846	147	1,020	11,000	12,922
2013	924	3,356	6,759	11,039	252	599	8,700	10,276
2014	763	6,368	7,464	14,595	375	528	11,850	13,787
2015	808	10,095	4,481	15,339	303	870	10,700	12,425
2016	2,914	8,656	3,091	14,661	245	1,332	10,500	12,491
2017	2,170	3,842	5,125	11,137	168	480	9,000	10,337
2018 [3]	1,629	4,466	5,524	11,619	162	335	9,300	10,819

[1] From domestic and imported seed. [2] Total supply minus exports and stocks June 1 of following year. [3] Forecast.
ERS, Field Crops Branch, (202) 694–5300.

Table 3-14.—Flaxseed and linseed oil and meal: Average price Minneapolis, 2009–2018

Year	Average price received by farmers per bushel	Minneapolis	
		Oil, per pound [1]	Linseed meal, per ton [2]
	Dollars	*Cents*	*Dollars*
2009	8.15	86.52	217.24
2010	12.20	67.49	223.23
2011	13.90	(NA)	238.35
2012	13.80	(NA)	320.13
2013	13.80	(NA)	359.42
2014	11.80	(NA)	263.90
2015	8.95	(NA)	234.78
2016	8.00	(NA)	313.17
2017	9.53	(NA)	236.92
2018 [3]	9.25-10.25	(NA)	195-235

(NA) Not available. [1] Raw oil in tank cars. [2] Bulk carlots, 34 percent protein. [3] Forecast.
ERS, Field Crops Branch, (202) 694–5300.

Table 3-15.—Flaxseed crushed; production, imports, and exports of linseed oil, cake, and meal; and June 1 stocks of oil, United States, 2009–2018

Year beginning June	Total flaxseed crushed	Linseed oil			Linseed cake and meal		
		Stocks June 1	Production	Exports	Production	Imports for consumption	Exports
	1,000 bushels	*Million pounds*	*Million pounds*	*Million pounds*	*1,000 tons*	*1,000 tons*	*1,000 tons*
2009	12,000	73	234	103	216	3	10
2010	11,635	37	227	101	209	7	7
2011	10,500	38	205	89	189	8	3
2012	11,000	35	215	94	198	6	5
2013	8,700	35	170	58	157	1	6
2014	11,850	35	231	52	213	3	4
2015	10,700	35	209	17	193	7	4
2016	10,500	35	205	15	189	6	5
2017	9,000	35	176	14	162	7	3
2018 [1]	9,300	35	181	23	167	10	4

[1] Forecast.
ERS, Field Crops Branch, (202) 694–5300.

Table 3-16.—Peanuts: Area, yield, production, disposition, marketing year average price per pound received by farmers, and value, United States, 2010–2019

Year	Area planted	Peanuts for nuts				
		Area harvested	Yield per acre	Production [1]	Marketing year average price [2]	Value of production
	1,000 acres	*1,000 acres*	*Pounds*	*1,000 pounds*	*Cents*	*1,000 dollars*
2010	1,288.0	1,255.0	3,312	4,156,840	21.0	938,611
2011	1,140.6	1,080.6	3,386	3,658,590	25.0	1,168,587
2012	1,638.0	1,604.0	4,211	6,753,880	34.0	2,026,326
2013	1,067.0	1,043.0	4,001	4,173,170	27.0	1,055,095
2014	1,353.5	1,322.5	3,923	5,188,665	23.0	1,158,251
2015	1,625.0	1,560.9	3,845	6,001,357	21.3	1,160,560
2016	1,671.0	1,536.0	3,634	5,581,570	19.7	1,088,165
2017	1,871.6	1,775.6	4,007	7,115,410	22.9	1,634,017
2018	1,425.5	1,373.5	4,001	5,495,935	21.5	1,169,953
2019	1,427.7	1,391.7	3,949	5,496,087	20.1	1,129,584

[1] Estimates comprised of quota and non-quota peanuts. [2] Based on marketings and monthly prices received from August 1, 2019 - December 31, 2019.
NASS, Crops Branch, (202) 720–2127.

Table 3-17.—Peanuts, farmer stock: Stocks, production, and quantity milled, United States, 2010–2019

Year beginning August	Stocks Aug. 1 [1]	Production harvested for nuts [1]	Imports	Total supply	Milled [1 2]
	1,000 pounds				
2010	991,394	4,156,840	163	5,148,397	3,976,460
2011	769,016	3,658,590	1,299	4,428,905	3,949,494
2012	272,838	6,753,880	3,117	7,029,835	4,979,182
2013	1,924,996	4,173,170	174	6,098,340	4,955,484
2014	1,059,524	5,188,665	11	6,248,200	4,775,454
2015	1,445,310	6,001,357	287	7,446,954	4,998,028
2016	1,051,096	5,581,570	574	6,633,240	4,699,164
2017	732,966	7,115,410	0	7,848,376	4,448,304
2018	1,916,798	5,495,935	4,232	7,416,965	4,498,876
2019	1,627,938	5,466,487	3	7,094,428	4,472,126

[1] Net weight basis. [2] Includes peanuts milled for seed.
NASS, Crops Branch, (202) 720–2127, ERS, and Foreign trade from the Bureau of the Census.

Table 3-18.—Peanuts: Crushings, and oil and meal stocks, production, and foreign trade, United States, 2010–2019

Year beginning August	Peanuts crushed (shelled basis)	Peanut oil				Peanut cake and meal	
		Stocks Aug. 1 [1]	Production of crude	Imports	Exports [2]	Stocks Aug. 1 [3]	Production
	1,000 pounds						
2010	441,017	6,888	190,110	60,012	15,933	7,045	250,043
2011	453,835	6,836	188,479	28,290	15,646	9,959	250,037
2012	493,835	2,478	210,702	10,359	12,598	10,446	270,328
2013	497,272	(NA)	209,808	55,265	8,940	(NA)	268,554
2014	506,677	(NA)	214,041	30,174	18,840	(NA)	278,380
2015	531,770	2,667	226,219	93,314	10,253	3,197	291,193
2016	659,966	4,868	283,689	40,445	11,908	5,460	357,751
2017	528,750	10,646	231,748	71,354	10,943	8,750	282,346
2018	486,398	9,250	219,334	58,844	9,399	4,552	255,683
2019	580,628	10,181	254,109	3,338	26,843	4,721	304,718

(NA) Not available. [1] Crude plus refined. [2] Reported as edible peanut oil and crude peanut oil; in this tabulation added without converting. [3] Holding at producing mills only.
NASS, Crops Branch, (202) 720–2127, ERS, and Foreign trade from the Bureau of the Census.

Table 3-19.—Cleaned peanuts (roasting stock): Supply and disposition, United States, 2010–2019

Year beginning August	Supply				Disposition		
	Stocks Aug. 1	Production	Imports	Total	Exports	Domestic disappearance	
						Total	Per capita
	1,000 pounds	*1,000 pounds*	*1,000 pounds*	*1,000 pounds*	*1,000 pounds*	*1,000 pounds*	*Pounds*
2010	52,929	268,956	163	322,048	78,693	184,385	0.60
2011	58,970	226,481	1,299	286,750	66,819	179,965	0.58
2012	39,966	323,731	3,117	366,814	194,821	100,098	0.32
2013	71,895	323,607	174	395,676	143,921	178,602	0.56
2014	73,153	248,170	11	321,334	168,504	112,495	0.35
2015	40,335	251,484	287	292,106	418,066	(157,559)	(0.49)
2016	31,599	230,537	574	262,710	183,379	46,853	0.14
2017	32,478	225,475	0	257,953	159,366	43,054	0.13
2018	55,533	188,223	4,232	247,988	140,540	64,814	0.20
2019	42,633	194,835	3	237,471	550,735	(350,601)	(1.06)

NASS, Crops Branch, (202) 720–2127, ERS, and Foreign trade from the Bureau of the Census.

Table 3-20.—Shelled peanuts (all grades): Supply, exports, and quantity crushed, United States, 2010–2019

Year beginning August	Supply						Exports	Crushed
	Stocks Aug. 1		Production		Imports	Total		
	Edible	Oil stock	Edible	Oil stock				
	1,000 pounds	*1,000 pounds*	*1,000 pounds*	*1,000 pounds*	*1,000 pounds*	*1,000 pounds*	*1,000 pounds*	*1,000 pounds*
2010	554,295	35,498	2,450,639	357,130	46,031	3,443,593	395,554	441,017
2011	473,878	43,380	2,399,004	345,505	203,836	3,465,753	352,994	453,835
2012	466,310	52,883	3,125,786	351,284	90,472	4,086,735	741,109	493,205
2013	547,965	33,883	3,098,392	373,008	65,709	4,118,957	708,391	497,272
2014	519,824	25,364	2,997,078	391,728	69,278	4,003,272	675,930	506,677
2015	431,674	31,012	3,141,099	442,650	66,951	4,113,386	839,203	531,770
2016	467,139	65,350	2,944,760	448,377	114,730	4,040,356	852,040	659,966
2017	482,010	26,372	2,853,147	358,282	127,903	3,847,714	810,578	528,750
2018	535,730	24,232	2,932,229	368,168	84,172	3,944,531	785,928	486,398
2019	540,802	23,498	2,908,778	405,622	79,280	3,957,980	786,790	580,628

NASS, Crops Branch, (202) 720–2127, ERS, and Foreign trade from the U.S. Bureau of the Census.

Table 3-21.—Peanuts: Shelled (raw basis) by types, used in primary products and apparent disappearance of peanuts, United States, 2010–2019

Type and year beginning August	Edible grades used in products					Apparent disappearance [2]
	Peanut butter [1]	Peanut snack	Peanut candy	Other products	Total	
	1,000 pounds	*1,000 pounds*	*1,000 pounds*	*1,000 pounds*	*1,000 pounds*	*1,000 pounds*
Virginia and Valencia:						
2010	(D)	62,708	16,070	(D)	211,194	....
2011	(D)	78,333	17,856	(D)	203,958	....
2012	82,981	83,722	17,731	8,452	192,888	....
2013	86,759	85,298	17,109	13,373	202,536	....
2014	102,340	91,909	12,079	26,440	232,768	....
2015	108,156	89,766	14,319	26,258	238,494	....
2016	118,109	92,331	13,427	23,606	247,473	....
2017	129,823	84,479	15,455	28,998	258,754	....
2018	120,939	81,418	15,589	18,753	236,696	....
2019	140,527	94,614	9,145	19,836	264,121	....
Runner:						
2010	1,076,521	319,529	365,260	13,036	1,774,346	....
2011	1,091,541	303,631	360,797	14,840	1,770,809	....
2012	1,143,108	309,860	347,428	12,195	1,812,591	....
2013	1,128,206	337,934	(D)	(D)	1,844,490	....
2014	1,196,277	329,930	348,367	26,737	1,901,311	....
2015	1,186,810	408,726	346,831	35,128	1,977,495	....
2016	1,215,212	370,766	379,549	33,156	1,998,683	....
2017	1,179,186	434,139	346,985	66,943	2,027,254	....
2018	1,213,018	380,165	349,081	93,897	2,036,161	....
2019	1,259,768	(D)	372,153	(D)	2,084,164	....
Spanish:						
2010	(D)	12,940	14,122	(D)	35,207	....
2011	(D)	8,104	16,025	(D)	27,390	....
2012	(D)	6,847	16,755	(D)	25,389	....
2013	(D)	6,564	15,996	(D)	(D)	....
2014	(D)	6,638	15,410	(D)	27,188	....
2015	(D)	7,200	16,355	(D)	28,225	....
2016	(D)	7,195	14,725	(D)	26,801	....
2017	(D)	6,227	17,064	(D)	28,851	....
2018	8,480	(D)	16,266	(D)	30,840	....
2019	9,969	(D)	14,349	(D)	30,622	....
All types:						
2010	1,213,229	395,177	395,452	16,890	2,020,748	2,880,304
2011	1,197,748	390,068	394,678	19,661	2,002,155	2,742,724
2012	1,227,859	400,429	381,914	20,664	2,030,866	3,417,047
2013	1,218,170	429,796	395,726	29,103	2,072,795	3,508,060
2014	1,303,755	428,477	375,856	53,179	2,161,267	3,471,308
2015	1,299,634	505,692	377,505	61,388	2,244,219	3,513,946
2016	1,338,195	470,292	407,701	56,769	2,272,957	3,417,244
2017	1,314,567	524,845	379,504	95,943	2,843,609	3,159,849
2018	1,342,437	467,676	380,936	112,651	2,790,098	3,296,059
2019	1,410,264	481,430	395,647	91,567	2,959,536	3,339,239

(D) Data withheld to avoid disclosure of individual operations. [1] Excludes peanut butter made by manufacturers for own use in candy. Includes peanut butter used in spreads, sandwiches, and cookies. [2] Apparent disappearance represents stocks beginning of year plus production, minus stocks at end of year. Includes edible grades and oilstocks.
NASS, Crops Branch, (202) 720–2127, and ERS.

Table 3-22.—Peanuts: Area, yield, and production, by State and United States, 2017–2019

State	Area planted			Peanuts for nuts: Area harvested		
	2017	2018	2019	2017	2018	2019
	1,000 acres					
Alabama	195.0	165.0	160.0	193.0	161.0	158.0
Arkansas	30.0	26.0	34.0	29.0	23.0	33.0
Florida	195.0	155.0	165.0	185.0	143.0	155.0
Georgia	835.0	665.0	670.0	825.0	655.0	660.0
Mississippi	44.0	25.0	20.0	43.0	24.0	19.0
New Mexico	7.6	5.5	4.7	7.6	5.5	4.7
North Carolina	119.0	102.0	104.0	117.0	98.0	102.0
Oklahoma	22.0	16.0	15.0	21.0	15.0	14.0
South Carolina	122.0	87.0	65.0	118.0	80.0	62.0
Texas	275.0	155.0	165.0	210.0	145.0	160.0
Virginia	27.0	24.0	25.0	27.0	24.0	24.0
United States	1,871.6	1,425.5	1,427.7	1,775.6	1,373.5	1,391.7

State	Peanuts for nuts: Yield per harvested acre			Peanuts for nuts: Production		
	2017	2018	2019	2017	2018	2019
	Pounds			1,000 pounds		
Alabama	3,650	3,550	3,350	704,450	571,550	529,300
Arkansas	5,300	4,900	5,200	153,700	112,700	171,600
Florida	3,450	3,950	3,800	638,250	564,850	589,000
Georgia	4,330	4,390	4,200	3,572,250	2,875,450	2,772,000
Mississippi	4,000	3,900	4,000	172,000	93,600	76,000
New Mexico	3,500	2,850	3,210	26,600	15,675	15,087
North Carolina	4,100	3,870	4,350	479,700	379,260	443,700
Oklahoma	3,780	3,070	4,100	79,380	46,050	57,400
South Carolina	4,000	3,400	3,800	472,000	272,000	235,600
Texas	3,320	3,200	3,100	697,200	464,000	496,000
Virginia	4,550	4,200	4,600	122,850	100,800	110,400
United States	4,007	4,001	3,949	7,115,410	5,495,935	5,496,087

NASS, Crops Branch, (202) 720–2127.

Table 3-23.—Peanuts: Marketing year average price, and value of production, by State and United States, 2017–2019

State	Marketing year average price per pound			Value of production		
	2017	2018	2019 [1]	2017	2018	2019
	Dollars			1,000 dollars		
Alabama	0.221	0.208	0.185	155,683	114,566	97,921
Arkansas	0.212	0.190	0.198	32,277	21,850	33,977
Florida	0.229	0.207	0.202	146,159	104,328	118,978
Georgia	0.221	0.205	0.192	789,467	592,963	532,224
Mississippi	0.206	0.202	0.186	35,432	19,392	14,136
New Mexico	0.289	0.292	0.282	7,687	4,818	4,255
North Carolina	0.237	0.230	0.223	113,689	87,906	98,945
Oklahoma	0.250	0.234	0.235	19,845	10,881	13,489
South Carolina	0.224	0.217	0.198	105,728	59,384	46,649
Texas	0.286	0.275	0.292	199,399	131,588	144,832
Virginia	0.239	0.221	0.219	28,651	22,277	24,178
United States	0.229	0.215	0.201	1,634,017	1,169,953	1,129,584

[1] Based on monthly prices received from August 1, 2019 - December 31, 2019.
NASS, Crops Branch, (202) 720–2127.

Table 3-24.—Peanuts, farmer's stock: Support operations, United States, 2012–2018

Marketing year beginning August 1	Income support payment rates per short ton [1]	Program price levels per short ton		Put under support		Acquired by CCC under loan program	Owned by CCC at end of marketing year
		Loan [2]	Target/ Reference [3]	Quantity	Percentage of production		
	Dollars	*Dollars*	*Dollars*	*1,000 short tons*	*Percent*	*1,000 short tons*	*1,000 short tons*
2012/2013	36.00/0.00	355.00	495.00	2,640	78.2	55.9	0.0
2013/2014	36.00/0.00	355.00	495.00	1,452	69.6	6.1	2.5
2014/2015	95.00	355.00	535.00	2,123	81.8	173.2	6.8
2015/2016	149.00	355.00	535.00	2,233	74.4	0.0	0.0
2016/2017	141.00	355.00	535.00	2,270	79.9	39.1	0.0
2017/2018	77.00	355.00	535.00	2,735	75.6	121.7	0.0
2018/2019	105.00	355.00	535.00	2,340	85.7	90.8	0.0

[1] The first entry is the direct payment rate and the second entry is the counter-cyclical payment rate for 2004/2005-2013/2014. The 2014 Act eliminated direct payments and replaced the counter-cyclical rate with a new reference price. For 2009/2010-2013/2014, producers who participated in the Average Crop Revenue (ACRE) program got a 20 percent reduction in their direct payment, not calculated in this table. For 2014/2015 and after, the entry is the price loss coverage payment rate. For 2017/2018, projected PLC payment rate is based on March 2018 WASDE MY price. Agricultural Risk Coverage (ARC) is also available, but payment rates are established at the county or farm levels. [2] For 2009/2010-2013/2014, producers who participate in the ACRE program get a 30 percent reduction in their loan rate, not calculated in this table. [3] Target applies to 2003/2004-2013/2014 and Reference applies beginning with 2014/2015. [4] Acquisitions as of September 30, 2019.

FPAC-BC, Commodity Analysis Branch.

Table 3-25.—International oilseed, peanut: Area and production in specified countries, 2017/2018–2019/2020

Country	Area			Production		
	2017/2018	2018/2019	2019/2020	2017/2018	2018/2019	2019/2020
	1,000 hectares			*1,000 metric tons*		
China	4,608	4,620	4,600	17,092	17,333	17,500
India	4,888	4,990	4,700	6,650	4,720	6,200
Nigeria	2,820	2,820	2,800	4,248	4,422	3,500
United States	719	556	563	3,228	2,493	2,493
Sudan	2,215	3,065	2,300	1,648	2,884	1,800
Burma	989	1,034	885	1,572	1,583	1,375
Argentina	382	326	320	867	1,419	1,255
Senegal	1,254	1,250	1,200	1,412	1,450	1,100
Tanzania	1,000	1,000	1,000	1,100	1,100	1,100
Indonesia	580	570	550	1,075	1,025	990
Chad	768	770	770	870	890	850
Guinea	670	680	680	696	770	750
Cameroon	430	430	430	600	600	600
Brazil	139	147	155	516	435	550
Niger	922	925	900	462	592	500
Vietnam	190	190	190	450	458	469

FAS, Office of Global Analysis, (202) 720–6301. Prepared or estimated on the basis of official USDA production, supply, and distribution statistics from foreign governments.

Table 3-26.—International meal, peanut: Production in specified countries, 2017/2018–2019/2020

Country	2017/2018	2018/2019	2019/2020
	1,000 metric tons		
China	3,580	3,660	3,680
India	1,555	1,385	1,510
Burma	325	325	325
Sudan	259	268	272
Nigeria	245	245	245
Tanzania	170	170	170
United States	128	116	132
Argentina	117	117	130
Senegal	76	90	108
Burkina	90	90	96
Chad	84	84	84
Brazil	73	62	70
Cameroon	57	57	57
Niger	54	54	54
Congo (Kinshasa)	50	50	50

FAS, Office of Global Analysis, (202) 720–6301. Prepared or estimated on the basis of official USDA production, supply, and distribution statistics from foreign governments.

Table 3-27.—Soybeans: Area, yield, production, and value, United States, 2010–2019

Year	Area planted	Soybeans for beans				
		Area harvested	Yield per acre	Production	Marketing year average price per bushel received by farmers [1]	Value of production [1]
	1,000 acres	*1,000 acres*	*Bushels*	*1,000 bushels*	*Dollars*	*1,000 dollars*
2010	77,404	76,610	43.5	3,331,306	11.30	37,571,277
2011	75,046	73,776	42.0	3,097,179	12.50	38,542,177
2012	77,198	76,144	40.0	3,042,044	14.40	43,723,144
2013	76,820	76,233	44.0	3,357,004	13.00	43,570,161
2014	83,296	82,611	47.5	3,928,070	10.10	39,484,465
2015	82,660	81,742	48.0	3,926,779	8.95	35,195,882
2016	83,453	82,706	51.9	4,296,496	9.47	40,694,573
2017	90,162	89,542	49.3	4,411,633	9.33	41,308,740
2018	89,167	87,594	50.6	4,428,150	8.48	36,819,008
2019	76,100	75,021	47.4	3,558,281	8.75	31,202,680

[1] Based on marketings and monthly prices received from August 1, 2019 - December 31, 2019.
NASS, Crops Branch, (202) 720–2127.

Table 3-28.—Soybeans: Stocks on and off farms, United States, 2009–2018

Year beginning previous December	On farms				Off farms [1]			
	Dec. 1	Mar. 1	June 1	Sep. 1 [2]	Dec. 1	Mar. 1	June 1	Sep. 1 [2]
	1,000 bushels	*1,000 bushels*	*1,000 bushels*	*1,000 bushels*	*1,000 bushels*	*1,000 bushels*	*1,000 bushels*	*1,000 bushels*
2009	1,229,500	656,500	226,300	35,100	1,109,050	645,289	369,859	103,098
2010	1,091,000	609,200	232,600	35,400	1,187,084	660,868	338,523	115,485
2011	1,139,000	505,000	217,700	48,500	1,230,885	743,800	401,583	166,513
2012	910,000	555,000	179,000	38,250	1,056,161	819,488	488,465	131,120
2013	955,000	456,700	171,100	39,550	1,198,621	541,320	263,564	101,007
2014	1,218,000	381,900	109,100	21,325	1,300,744	611,928	295,945	70,666
2015	1,308,500	609,200	246,300	49,700	1,405,577	717,300	380,768	140,910
2016	1,335,000	727,500	281,300	41,560	1,564,056	803,406	590,481	155,169
2017	1,485,000	668,500	332,500	87,900	1,675,679	1,070,433	633,356	213,695
2018	1,935,000	855,000	377,000	101,000	1,810,824	1,254,303	842,329	337,105

[1] Includes stocks at mills, elevators, warehouses, terminals, and processors. [2] Old crop only.
NASS, Crops Branch, (202) 720–2127.

Table 3-29.—Soybeans, soybean meal, and oil: Average price at specified markets, 2009–2018

Year [1]	Soybeans per bushel: No. 1 Yellow Chicago	Soybean oil per pound crude, tanks, f.o.b. Decatur	Soybean meal per short ton: 48 percent protein Decatur
	Dollars	*Cents*	*Dollars*
2009	9.91	35.95	311.27
2010	13.14	53.20	345.52
2011	13.49	51.90	393.53
2012	14.86	47.13	468.11
2013	13.51	38.23	489.94
2014	9.84	31.60	368.49
2015	9.54	29.86	324.56
2016	9.77	32.55	316.88
2017	9.53	30.04	345.02
2018 [2]	8.89	28.5-31.5	295-335

[1] Year beginning September for soybeans and October for oil and meal. [2] Forecast.
ERS, Field Crops Branch, (202) 694–5300.

Table 3-30.—Soybeans: Supply and disappearance, United States, 2008–2017

Year beginning September	Supply				
	Stocks by position			Production	Total [1]
	On-Farm, Sep 1	Terminal market, interior mill, elevator, and warehouse	Beginning, Sep-Nov		
	1,000 bushels	*1,000 bushels*	*1,000 bushels*	*1,000 bushels*	*1,000 bushels*
2008	47,000	158,034	205,034	2,967,007	3,185,304
2009	35,100	103,098	138,198	3,360,931	3,513,717
2010	35,400	115,485	150,885	3,331,306	3,496,640
2011	48,500	166,513	215,013	3,097,179	3,328,324
2012	38,250	131,120	169,370	3,042,044	3,251,930
2013	39,550	101,007	140,557	3,357,004	3,569,338
2014	21,325	70,666	91,991	3,928,070	4,053,306
2015	49,700	140,910	190,610	3,926,779	4,140,930
2016	41,560	155,169	196,729	4,296,496	4,515,506
2017	87,900	213,695	301,595	4,411,633	4,735,050

Year beginning September	Disappearance			
	Crushed [2]	Seed, feed and residual	Exports	Total
	1,000 bushels	*1,000 bushels*	*1,000 bushels*	*1,000 bushels*
2008	1,661,922	105,890	1,279,294	3,047,106
2009	1,751,686	112,098	1,499,048	3,362,832
2010	1,648,043	128,607	1,504,978	3,281,627
2011	1,703,019	90,684	1,365,251	3,158,954
2012	1,688,903	94,944	1,327,526	3,111,373
2013	1,733,888	104,900	1,638,559	3,477,347
2014	1,873,494	146,779	1,842,423	3,862,696
2015	1,886,237	115,325	1,942,639	3,944,201
2016	1,901,198	146,296	2,166,417	4,213,911
2017	2,054,932	551,017	2,129,101	4,735,050

[1] Includes imports. [2] Reported by the U.S. Department of Commerce.
ERS, Field Crops Branch, (202) 694–5300.

Table 3-31.—Soybeans: Support operations, United States, 2013–2019

Marketing year beginning September 1	Income support payment rates per bushels [1]	Program price levels per bushel		Put under loan		Acquired by CCC under loan program [4]	Owned by CCC at end of marketing year
		Loan [2]	Target/ Reference [3]	Quantity	Percentage of production		
	Dollars	*Dollars*	*Dollars*	*Million bushels*	*Percent*	*Million bushels*	*Million bushels*
2013/2014	0.44/0.00	5.00	6.00	49	1.5	0	0
2014/2015	0.00	5.00	8.40	80	2.0	0	0
2015/2016	0.00	5.00	8.40	124	3.2	0	0
2016/2017	0.00	5.00	8.40	105	2.4	0	0
2017/2018	0.00	5.00	8.40	145	3.3	0	0
2018/2019	0.00	5.00	8.40	218	4.8	0	0
2019/2020	0.00	6.20	8.40	142	4.0	0	0

[1] The first entry is the direct payment rate and the second entry is the counter-cyclical payment rate for 2004/2005-2013/2014. For 2009/2010-2013/2014, producers who participated in the Average Crop Revenue (ACRE) program got a 20 percent reduction in their direct payment, not calculated in this table. For 2014/2015 and after, the entry is the price loss coverage (PLC) payment rate. For 2017/2018, projected PLC payment rate is based on March 2018 WASDE MY price. Agricultural Risk Coverage (ARC) is also available, but payment rates are established at the county or farm levels. [2] For 2009/2010-2013/2014, producers who participated in the ACRE program got a 30 percent reduction in their loan rate, not calculated in this table. [3] Target applies to 2003/2004-2013/2014 and Reference applies beginning with 2014/2015. [4] Acquisitions as of September 30, 2019.
FPAC-BC, Commodity Analysis Branch.

Table 3-32.—Soybeans for beans: Area, yield, and production, by State and United States, 2017–2019

State	Area planted			Area harvested		
	2017	2018	2019	2017	2018	2019
	1,000 acres	*1,000 acres*	*1,000 acres*	*1,000 acres*	*1,000 acres*	*1,000 acres*
Alabama	350	345	265	345	335	260
Arkansas	3,530	3,270	2,650	3,500	3,210	2,610
Delaware	160	170	155	158	168	153
Florida [1]	15	18	(NA)	14	12	(NA)
Georgia	155	145	100	150	130	93
Illinois	10,600	10,800	9,950	10,550	10,500	9,860
Indiana	5,950	6,000	5,400	5,940	5,960	5,360
Iowa	10,000	9,950	9,200	9,940	9,830	9,120
Kansas	5,150	4,750	4,550	5,110	4,690	4,490
Kentucky	1,950	1,950	1,700	1,940	1,930	1,690
Louisiana	1,270	1,340	890	1,250	1,190	860
Maryland	500	530	480	495	515	475
Michigan	2,280	2,330	1,760	2,270	2,310	1,730
Minnesota	8,150	7,750	6,850	8,090	7,650	6,770
Mississippi	2,190	2,230	1,660	2,170	2,190	1,630
Missouri	5,950	5,850	5,100	5,910	5,780	5,010
Nebraska	5,700	5,650	4,900	5,670	5,590	4,840
New Jersey	100	110	95	99	107	92
New York	270	335	235	265	325	225
North Carolina	1,700	1,650	1,540	1,690	1,570	1,520
North Dakota	7,100	6,900	5,600	7,050	6,840	5,450
Ohio	5,100	5,050	4,300	5,090	5,020	4,270
Oklahoma	655	640	465	640	600	440
Pennsylvania	610	640	620	605	630	610
South Carolina	400	390	335	390	330	320
South Dakota	5,650	5,650	3,500	5,610	5,580	3,440
Tennessee	1,690	1,700	1,400	1,660	1,670	1,370
Texas	210	175	80	185	135	73
Virginia	600	600	570	590	590	560
West Virginia [1]	27	29	(NA)	26	27	(NA)
Wisconsin	2,150	2,220	1,750	2,140	2,180	1,700
United States	90,162	89,167	76,100	89,542	87,594	75,021

State	Yield per harvested acre			Production		
	2017	2018	2019	2017	2018	2019
	Bushels	*Bushels*	*Bushels*	*1,000 bushels*	*1,000 bushels*	*1,000 bushels*
Alabama	46.0	40.0	36.0	15,870	13,400	9,360
Arkansas	51.0	50.5	49.0	178,500	162,105	127,890
Delaware	51.0	41.5	47.0	8,058	6,972	7,191
Florida [1]	34.0	37.0	(NA)	476	444	(NA)
Georgia	42.0	39.5	29.0	6,300	5,135	2,697
Illinois	58.0	63.5	54.0	611,900	666,750	532,440
Indiana	54.0	57.5	51.0	320,760	342,700	273,360
Iowa	57.0	56.0	55.0	566,580	550,480	501,600
Kansas	37.5	43.0	41.5	191,625	201,670	186,335
Kentucky	53.0	51.0	46.0	102,820	98,430	77,740
Louisiana	54.0	51.5	48.0	67,500	61,285	41,280
Maryland	51.0	47.5	44.0	25,245	24,463	20,900
Michigan	42.5	47.5	41.0	96,475	109,725	70,930
Minnesota	47.5	49.0	44.0	384,275	374,850	297,880
Mississippi	53.0	54.0	50.0	115,010	118,260	81,500
Missouri	49.5	44.5	46.0	292,545	257,210	230,460
Nebraska	57.5	58.0	58.5	326,025	324,220	283,140
New Jersey	45.0	39.5	37.0	4,455	4,227	3,404
New York	45.0	52.0	48.0	11,925	16,900	10,800
North Carolina	40.0	33.0	35.0	67,600	51,810	53,200
North Dakota	34.5	35.0	32.0	243,225	239,400	174,400
Ohio	49.5	56.0	49.0	251,955	281,120	209,230
Oklahoma	29.0	28.0	29.0	18,560	16,800	12,760
Pennsylvania	48.0	44.5	49.0	29,040	28,035	29,890
South Carolina	38.0	29.0	26.0	14,820	9,570	8,320
South Dakota	43.0	45.0	42.5	241,230	251,100	146,200
Tennessee	50.0	45.5	47.0	83,000	75,985	64,390
Texas	37.0	31.5	28.0	6,845	4,253	2,044
Virginia	44.0	42.0	34.0	25,960	24,780	19,040
West Virginia [1]	54.0	53.0	(NA)	1,404	1,431	(NA)
Wisconsin	47.5	48.0	47.0	101,650	104,640	79,900
United States	49.3	50.6	47.4	4,411,633	4,428,150	3,558,281

(NA) Not available. [1] Estimates discontinued in 2019.
NASS, Crops Branch, (202) 720–2127.

Table 3-33.—Soybeans: Crushings, and oil and meal stocks, production, and foreign trade, United States, 2008–2017

Year beginning October	Soybeans crushed	Soybean oil			Soybean cake and meal		
		Stocks Oct. 1	Production	Exports	Stocks Oct. 1	Production	Exports
	1,000 bushels	*Million pounds*	*Million pounds*	*Million pounds*	*1,000 tons*	*1,000 tons*	*1,000 tons*
2008	1,661,922	2,485	18,745	2,193	294	39,102	8,497
2009	1,751,686	2,861	19,615	3,359	235	41,707	11,159
2010	1,648,043	3,406	18,888	3,233	302	39,251	9,081
2011	1,703,019	2,675	19,740	1,464	350	41,036	9,750
2012	1,688,903	2,590	19,820	2,163	300	39,875	11,146
2013	1,733,888	1,655	20,130	1,877	275	40,685	11,578
2014	1,873,494	1,165	21,399	2,014	250	45,062	13,107
2015	1,886,237	1,855	21,950	2,243	260	44,672	11,954
2016	1,901,198	1,687	22,123	2,556	264	44,787	11,580
2017 [1]	2,054,932	1,711	23,772	2,447	401	49,226	12,400

[1] Forecast.
ERS, Field Crops Branch, (202) 694–5300. Data from the U.S. Department of Commerce.

Table 3-34.—Soybeans for beans: Marketing year average price and value, by State and United States, 2017–2019

State	Marketing year average price per bushel			Value of production		
	2017	2018	2019 [1]	2017	2018	2019 [1]
	Dollars	*Dollars*	*Dollars*	*1,000 dollars*	*1,000 dollars*	*1,000 dollars*
Alabama	9.43	8.50	9.25	149,654	113,900	86,580
Arkansas	9.77	8.81	9.00	1,743,945	1,428,145	1,151,010
Delaware	9.19	8.25	8.30	74,053	57,519	59,685
Florida [2]	8.85	8.10	(NA)	4,213	3,596	(NA)
Georgia	9.62	7.90	9.00	60,606	40,567	24,273
Illinois	9.60	8.74	9.15	5,874,240	5,827,395	4,871,826
Indiana	9.61	8.73	9.10	3,082,504	2,991,771	2,487,576
Iowa	9.25	8.46	8.65	5,240,865	4,657,061	4,338,840
Kansas	9.00	7.93	8.40	1,724,625	1,599,243	1,565,214
Kentucky	9.70	8.79	9.10	997,354	865,200	707,434
Louisiana	9.67	8.95	8.75	652,725	548,501	361,200
Maryland	9.20	8.12	8.30	232,254	198,640	173,470
Michigan	9.39	8.53	8.90	905,900	935,954	631,277
Minnesota	9.17	8.40	8.60	3,523,802	3,148,740	2,561,768
Mississippi	9.74	8.85	8.90	1,120,197	1,046,601	725,350
Missouri	9.48	8.56	8.90	2,773,327	2,201,718	2,051,094
Nebraska	9.08	8.20	8.40	2,960,307	1,920,604	2,378,376
New Jersey	9.30	7.98	8.60	41,432	33,731	29,274
New York	9.26	8.20	8.30	110,426	137,760	89,640
North Carolina	9.50	8.66	8.80	642,200	448,675	468,160
North Dakota	8.88	7.98	8.10	2,159,838	1,910,412	1,412,640
Ohio	9.62	8.69	9.15	2,423,807	2,442,933	1,914,455
Oklahoma	9.10	7.89	8.40	168,896	132,552	107,184
Pennsylvania	9.34	8.42	8.45	271,234	236,055	252,571
South Carolina	9.52	9.10	9.15	141,086	87,087	76,128
South Dakota	8.94	7.97	8.40	2,156,596	2,001,267	1,228,080
Tennessee	9.70	8.75	9.05	805,100	664,869	582,730
Texas	8.90	7.59	7.90	60,921	32,280	16,148
Virginia	9.40	8.30	8.80	244,024	205,674	167,552
West Virginia [2]	9.40	8.50	(NA)	13,198	12,164	(NA)
Wisconsin	9.34	8.49	8.55	949,411	888,394	683,145
United States	9.33	8.48	8.75	41,308,740	36,819,008	31,202,680

(NA) Not available. [1] Preliminary. [2] Estimates discontinued in 2019.
NASS, Crops Branch, (202) 720–2127.

Table 3-35.—International oilseed, soybean: Area and production in specified countries, 2017/2018–2019/2020

Country	Area			Production		
	2017/2018	2018/2019	2019/2020	2017/2018	2018/2019	2019/2020
	1,000 hectares			*1,000 Metric tons*		
Brazil	35,150	35,900	36,900	122,000	117,000	126,000
United States	36,236	35,448	30,360	120,065	120,515	96,841
Argentina	16,300	16,600	17,000	37,800	55,300	54,000
China	8,245	8,413	9,300	15,283	15,967	18,100
Paraguay	3,380	3,700	3,540	10,478	8,850	9,900
India	10,400	11,330	11,250	8,350	10,930	9,300
Canada	2,935	2,540	2,300	7,717	7,267	6,000
Russia	2,568	2,739	2,776	3,621	4,027	4,359
Ukraine	2,020	1,875	1,600	3,985	4,831	3,700
Bolivia	1,315	1,400	1,400	2,819	2,700	2,800
European Union	926	926	910	2,540	2,664	2,600
Uruguay	1,098	965	950	1,334	2,828	2,200
South Africa	787	730	800	1,540	1,170	1,450
Nigeria	1,000	1,000	1,000	994	1,054	1,100
Serbia	200	220	220	460	625	600
Indonesia	420	410	400	540	520	510
Zambia	225	192	196	351	303	281
Japan	150	147	150	249	213	253
Mexico	263	191	150	433	335	235
Korea, North	150	150	150	223	225	225
Iran	83	70	70	200	160	170
Burma	143	150	150	149	160	160
Bangladesh	82	82	82	156	156	156
Turkey	24	25	27	90	95	105
Ethiopia	39	42	40	84	120	100

FAS, Office of Global Analysis, (202) 720–6301. Prepared or estimated on the basis of official USDA production, supply, and distribution statistics from foreign governments.

Table 3-36.—Soybeans: United States exports by country of destination, 2017–2019

Country of destination	2017	2018	2019
	Metric tons		
China	31,688,893	8,235,317	22,575,940
Mexico	3,883,102	4,814,461	5,145,404
Egypt	1,010,074	3,186,587	2,789,926
Japan	2,299,038	2,268,969	2,451,291
Indonesia	2,392,357	2,636,629	2,420,711
Netherlands	2,045,877	3,482,933	2,381,757
Taiwan	1,447,092	2,261,542	1,845,002
Spain	607,995	1,737,344	1,588,837
Thailand	1,193,359	1,600,245	1,428,287
Bangladesh	1,049,387	1,192,983	1,136,758
Pakistan	1,138,302	1,733,277	1,130,977
Korea, South	676,902	837,727	1,065,807
Vietnam	742,000	1,254,697	802,931
Malaysia	437,202	590,357	642,980
Colombia	554,157	708,737	637,641
Canada	385,971	776,012	519,799
Portugal	123,156	538,550	407,969
Italy(*)	75,523	879,428	405,958
Germany(*)	1,314,686	1,203,633	400,558
Peru	109,471	261,751	308,614
United Kingdom	100	326,895	289,920
Costa Rica	296,126	297,643	271,070
Saudi Arabia	224,694	338,066	259,149
Tunisia	221,094	451,168	218,864
Argentina	256	1,986,162	203,017
Israel(*)	79,454	118,187	140,329
Nepal	0	5,861	139,047
Philippines	234,239	167,119	136,657
France(*)	64,900	182,732	133,745
Lebanon	0	75,242	78,364
Rest of World	965,978	2,045,364	329,833
World Total	55,261,450	46,195,618	52,287,140

(*) Denotes a country that is a summarization of its component countries.
FAS, Office of Global Analysis, (202) 720–6301. Data Source: U.S. Census Bureau Trade Data.

Table 3-37.—Soybean oil: United States exports by country of destination, 2017–2019

Country of destination	2017	2018	2019
	Metric tons		
Korea, South	264,506	281,161	356,797
Mexico	241,240	149,136	134,293
Dominican Republic	176,792	142,728	128,614
Colombia	52,752	75,474	84,871
Peru	89,426	128,416	75,516
Guatemala	33,489	27,013	32,628
Venezuela	23,052	21,825	19,819
Jamaica	12,200	17,200	15,029
Canada	2	93,051	11,964
Mozambique	8,407	7,565	11,859
Nicaragua	12,402	48,857	11,428
Morocco	7,137	10,867	9,995
Trinidad and Tobago	10,030	11,518	9,704
Senegal	15,293	15,737	8,434
Pakistan	4,121	5,772	6,815
Panama	2,685	3,589	6,446
Cuba	3,922	4,399	4,271
El Salvador	3,558	4,391	4,083
Costa Rica	6,583	7,779	3,018
United Arab Emirates	1,224	2,064	2,424
Honduras	2,732	2,543	2,418
Malaysia	1,933	1,894	2,201
Saudi Arabia	129	327	1,755
Japan	2,030	2,146	1,646
Bahamas, The	474	865	1,625
Kuwait	979	1,761	1,545
Lebanon	0	24	968
Jordan	372	668	840
China	422	401	590
Qatar	30,332	888	482
Rest of World	62,380	38,677	3,416
World Total	1,070,602	1,108,733	955,492

Users should use cautious interpretation on quantity reports using mixed units of measure. Quantity line items will only include statistics on the units of measure that are equal to, or are able to be converted to, the assigned unit of measure of the grouped commodities.
FAS, Office of Global Analysis, (202) 720–6301. Data Source: U.S. Census Bureau Trade Data.

Table 3-38.—Soybean cake and meal: United States exports by country of destination, 2017–2019

Country of destination	2017	2018	2019
	Metric tons		
Philippines	2,041,069	2,156,732	2,136,990
Mexico	1,630,154	1,781,852	1,783,591
Colombia	973,684	1,229,025	1,257,328
Canada	916,203	998,377	977,677
Ecuador	184,928	320,420	549,545
Dominican Republic	489,358	491,461	544,332
Vietnam	192,398	762,580	537,417
Guatemala	367,103	430,002	463,249
Japan	250,131	330,619	340,274
Morocco	215,372	553,234	328,033
Honduras	238,532	273,006	291,041
El Salvador	192,725	217,846	290,729
Burma	91,088	153,197	269,240
Sri Lanka	152,975	169,787	216,864
Panama	200,093	218,113	201,016
Peru	254,811	217,228	170,091
Venezuela	301,804	182,796	150,332
Israel(*)	146,714	53,657	146,821
Thailand	366,966	344,341	142,710
Nicaragua	104,700	107,284	134,451
Poland	160	54,036	127,155
Jamaica	116,497	126,079	115,197
Italy(*)	2,029	125,119	106,126
Costa Rica	63,374	108,712	105,559
Cuba	27,005	0	90,391
United Kingdom	3,575	56,333	85,947
Spain	114,261	354,736	69,964
Korea, South	6,767	20,717	63,471
Belgium-Luxembourg(*)	54,600	55,079	57,759
Slovenia	0	0	50,455
Rest of World	979,339	1,124,450	568,964
World Total	10,678,413	13,016,818	12,372,721

(*) Denotes a country that is a summarization of its component countries. Users should use cautious interpretation on quantity reports using mixed units of measure. Quantity line items will only include statistics on the units of measure that are equal to, or are able to be converted to, the assigned unit of measure of the grouped commodities.
FAS, Office of Global Analysis, (202) 720–6301. Data Source: U.S. Census Bureau Trade Data.

Table 3-39.—International oil, soybean: Production in specified countries, 2017/2018–2019/2020

Country	2017/2018	2018/2019	2019/2020
	1,000 metric tons		
China	16,128	15,232	15,411
United States	10,783	10,976	11,018
Argentina	7,236	7,910	8,500
Brazil	8,485	8,150	8,400
European Union	2,841	2,945	3,021
India	1,386	1,730	1,495
Mexico	937	1,100	1,110
Russia	824	834	881
Paraguay	733	700	739
Egypt	582	620	656
Japan	468	468	474
Bolivia	425	470	470
Taiwan	383	401	420
Pakistan	375	375	410
Thailand	251	359	410
Bangladesh	222	293	370
Canada	355	396	360
Iran	486	288	324
Turkey	250	250	259
South Africa	220	220	238

FAS, Office of Global Analysis, (202) 720–6301. Prepared or estimated on the basis of official USDA production, supply, and distribution statistics from foreign governments.

Table 3-40.—International trade: Meal, soybean in specified countries, 2017/2018–2019/2020

Country	2017/2018	2018/2019	2019/2020
	1,000 metric tons		
Principle exporting countries:			
Argentina	26,265	28,832	30,000
Brazil	16,032	15,973	15,400
United States	12,715	12,296	11,975
Paraguay	2,625	2,333	2,550
Bolivia	1,651	1,725	1,750
India	1,863	2,200	1,450
China	1,198	932	975
Ukraine	365	777	700
Russia	403	371	400
Canada	357	425	325
European Union	395	374	300
Belarus	105	204	245
Norway	182	182	182
Vietnam	120	100	110
South Africa	91	85	85
Korea, South	41	60	65
Turkey	31	62	55
Nigeria	49	50	60
Malaysia	57	52	45
Serbia	38	30	35
Principle importing countries:			
European Union	18,354	18,699	18,700
Vietnam	4,850	5,400	5,450
Indonesia	4,486	4,575	4,750
Thailand	3,191	2,889	3,225
Philippines	2,625	2,900	2,850
Iran	1,514	2,700	2,100
Mexico	1,818	1,932	1,980
Korea, South	1,846	1,900	1,925
Japan	1,728	1,625	1,675
Colombia	1,373	1,425	1,500
Algeria	1,500	1,350	1,450
Malaysia	1,609	1,578	1,400
Peru	1,353	1,345	1,375
Ecuador	1,145	1,150	1,170
Australia	923	1,050	1,100
Canada	1,022	1,018	1,050
Chile	824	967	1,000
Saudi Arabia	922	915	925
Turkey	557	724	850
Morocco	602	615	650

FAS, Office of Global Analysis, (202) 720–6301. Prepared or estimated on the basis of official USDA production, supply, and distribution statistics from foreign governments.

Table 3-41.—International trade: Oil, soybean in specified countries, 2017/2018–2019/2020

Country	2017/2018	2018/2019	2019/2020
	1,000 metric tons		
Principle exporting countries:			
Argentina	4,164	5,261	5,800
Brazil	1,511	1,079	1,000
United States	1,108	881	953
European Union	902	788	850
Paraguay	702	654	710
Russia	568	564	620
Bolivia	380	350	370
Ukraine	192	334	240
Canada	157	169	165
China	211	197	150
Malaysia	124	123	125
Thailand	70	80	90
Turkey	58	85	90
Norway	62	67	66
South Africa	55	55	55
Serbia	43	66	50
Saudi Arabia	33	33	33
Egypt	25	25	25
Vietnam	40	25	25
Taiwan	7	17	19
Principle importing countries:			
India	2,984	3,100	3,500
China	481	783	1,100
Algeria	720	760	770
Bangladesh	859	1,038	700
Morocco	502	536	545
Peru	503	500	525
Colombia	355	375	390
European Union	284	416	375
Korea, South	276	300	295
United States	152	180	204
Venezuela	226	210	200
Dominican Republic	165	180	190
South Africa	150	175	185
Mexico	195	142	170
Iran	213	135	165
Egypt	227	83	150
Chile	67	100	115
Ecuador	105	110	110
Malaysia	88	100	110
Tunisia	95	106	108
Cuba	97	97	100
Korea, North	90	100	100
Pakistan	104	90	100

FAS, Office of Global Analysis, (202) 720–6301. Prepared or estimated on the basis of official USDA production, supply, and distribution statistics from foreign governments.

Table 3-42.—International trade: Oil, soybean local in specified countries, 2017/2018–2019/2020

Country	2017/2018	2018/2019	2019/2020
	1,000 metric tons		
Principle exporting countries:			
Argentina	4,567	5,400	5,900
Brazil	1,410	1,008	1,000
Principle importing countries:			
Brazil	41	35	30

FAS, Office of Global Analysis, (202) 720–6301. Prepared or estimated on the basis of official USDA production, supply, and distribution statistics from foreign governments.

Table 3-43.—International trade: Oilseed, soybean in specified countries, 2017/2018–2019/2020

Country	2017/2018	2018/2019	2019/2020
	1,000 metric tons		
Principle exporting countries:			
Brazil	76,136	74,594	77,000
United States	58,071	47,564	49,668
Argentina	2,132	9,104	8,200
Paraguay	6,029	4,901	5,900
Canada	4,925	5,258	4,700
Ukraine	2,757	2,531	2,450
Uruguay	1,250	2,750	2,130
Russia	892	797	950
European Union	276	179	250
India	217	178	150
Serbia	28	143	150
China	134	116	125
Ethiopia	93	95	80
Malaysia	17	30	35
Nigeria	28	30	30
Turkey	20	25	25
Bolivia	7	10	10
Chile	7	8	8
South Africa	34	5	5
Uganda	5	5	5
Principle importing countries:			
China	94,095	82,540	88,000
European Union	14,584	15,004	15,200
Mexico	4,873	5,908	6,000
Argentina	4,703	6,408	3,900
Egypt	3,550	3,350	3,700
Thailand	2,482	3,155	3,400
Japan	3,256	3,300	3,350
Indonesia	2,483	2,725	2,950
Taiwan	2,666	2,730	2,850
Turkey	2,777	2,600	2,800
Pakistan	2,300	1,719	2,200
Russia	2,237	2,066	2,200
Bangladesh	1,179	1,733	1,900
Iran	2,559	2,000	1,850
Vietnam	1,824	1,800	1,850
Korea, South	1,256	1,365	1,450
Canada	487	1,172	900
Malaysia	690	770	825
Tunisia	683	670	710
Saudi Arabia	590	585	640

FAS, Office of Global Analysis, (202) 720–6301. Prepared or estimated on the basis of official USDA production, supply, and distribution statistics from foreign governments.

Table 3-44.—International trade: Oilseed, Soybeans local in specified countries, 2017/2018–2019/2020

Country	2017/2018	2018/2019	2019/2020
	1,000 metric tons		
Principle exporting countries:			
Brazil	83,729	73,234	77,000
Argentina	3,841	10,310	8,000
Principle importing countries:			
Argentina	7,256	3,850	3,900
Brazil	185	145	150

FAS, Office of Global Analysis, (202) 720–6301. Prepared or estimated on the basis of official USDA production, supply, and distribution statistics from foreign governments.

Table 3-45.—Sunflower, all: Area, yield, production, and value, United States, 2010–2019

Year	Area planted	Area harvested	Yield per harvested acre	Production	Price per cwt	Value of production
	1,000 acres	*1,000 acres*	*Pounds*	*1,000 pounds*	*Dollars*	*1,000 dollars*
2010	1,951.5	1,873.8	1,460	2,735,570	23.30	633,778
2011	1,543.0	1,457.8	1,398	2,038,275	29.10	589,282
2012	1,920.0	1,840.0	1,487	2,736,060	25.40	699,970
2013	1,575.5	1,464.6	1,380	2,021,765	21.40	443,296
2014	1,565.3	1,505.1	1,470	2,212,350	21.70	496,469
2015	1,860.1	1,800.4	1,625	2,925,030	19.60	574,481
2016	1,596.6	1,532.0	1,731	2,651,635	17.40	464,015
2017	1,403.0	1,333.8	1,603	2,137,750	17.20	375,077
2018	1,301.0	1,217.4	1,731	2,107,045	17.40	370,466
2019	1,350.6	1,244.5	1,562	1,943,435	17.80	358,408

NASS, Crops Branch, (202) 720–2127.

Table 3-46.—Sunflower, oil varieties: Area, yield, production, and value, United States, 2010–2019

Year	Area planted	Area harvested	Yield per harvested acre	Production	Price per cwt.	Value of production
	1,000 acres	*1,000 acres*	*Pounds*	*1,000 pounds*	*Dollars*	*1,000 dollars*
2010	1,463.0	1,422.5	1,458	2,074,500	22.60	457,135
2011	1,289.5	1,233.4	1,397	1,722,675	28.00	480,412
2012	1,658.0	1,589.8	1,484	2,359,775	24.40	580,404
2013	1,279.0	1,200.9	1,363	1,637,205	19.30	322,605
2014	1,174.0	1,134.5	1,461	1,657,390	19.30	322,163
2015	1,550.5	1,510.0	1,579	2,383,870	18.20	434,795
2016	1,418.0	1,368.5	1,731	2,369,015	16.90	403,850
2017	1,216.0	1,168.0	1,582	1,847,525	16.90	312,065
2018	1,164.0	1,094.0	1,725	1,887,260	16.70	320,867
2019	1,197.0	1,118.0	1,562	1,746,350	17.40	310,179

NASS, Crops Branch, (202) 720–2127.

Table 3-47.—Sunflower, non-oil varieties: Area, yield, production, and value, United States, 2010–2019

Year	Area planted	Area harvested	Yield per harvested acre	Production	Price per cwt.	Value of production
	1,000 acres	*1,000 acres*	*Pounds*	*1,000 pounds*	*Dollars*	*1,000 dollars*
2010	488.5	451.3	1,465	661,070	26.60	176,643
2011	253.5	224.4	1,406	315,600	33.80	108,870
2012	262.0	250.2	1,504	376,285	29.60	119,566
2013	296.5	263.7	1,458	384,560	31.30	120,691
2014	391.3	370.6	1,497	554,960	31.50	174,306
2015	309.6	290.4	1,863	541,160	26.60	139,686
2016	178.6	163.5	1,729	282,620	21.20	60,165
2017	187.0	165.8	1,750	290,225	21.00	63,012
2018	137.0	123.4	1,781	219,785	22.80	49,579
2019	153.6	126.5	1,558	197,085	22.40	48,229

NASS, Crops Branch, (202) 720–2127.

Table 3-48.—Sunflower, all: Area, yield, production, and value, by type, State and United States, 2018–2019

Type and State	Area planted		Area harvested		Yield per harvested acre	
	2018	2019	2018	2019	2018	2019
Oil:	*1,000 acres*	*1,000 acres*	*1,000 acres*	*1,000 acres*	*Pounds*	*Pounds*
California	58.0	49.0	57.0	49.0	1,300	1,400
Colorado	58.0	47.0	49.0	44.0	1,100	1,000
Kansas	43.0	37.0	41.0	32.0	1,500	1,400
Minnesota	45.0	53.0	44.0	51.0	2,250	1,850
Nebraska	25.0	28.0	24.0	26.0	1,420	1,300
North Dakota	395.0	470.0	380.0	430.0	1,750	1,500
South Dakota	520.0	485.0	480.0	460.0	1,830	1,700
Texas	20.0	28.00	19.0	26.0	1,120	1,300
United States	1,164.0	1,197.0	1,094	1,118.0	1,726	1,562
Non-oil:						
California	2.0	1.6	2.0	1.6	1,200	1,300
Colorado	8.0	12.0	7.0	11.0	1,150	1,400
Kansas	10.0	8.0	8.5	7.3	1,500	1,250
Minnesota	7.5	5.0	6.9	4.6	2,150	1,800
Nebraska	12.0	9.0	9.5	8.5	1,400	1,300
North Dakota	41.0	65.0	40.0	58.0	1,860	1,650
South Dakota	51.0	48.0	45.0	31.0	1,950	1,600
Texas	5.5	5.0	4.5	4.5	1,400	1,300
United States	137.0	153.6	123.4	126.5	1,781	1,562
Total:						
California	60.0	50.6	59.0	50.6	1,297	1,397
Colorado	66.0	59.0	56.0	55.0	1,106	1,080
Kansas	53.0	45.0	49.5	39.3	1,500	1,372
Minnesota	52.5	58.0	50.9	55.6	2,236	1,846
Nebraska	37.0	37.0	33.5	34.5	1,414	1,300
North Dakota	436.0	535.0	420.0	488.0	1,760	1,518
South Dakota	571.0	533.0	525.0	491.0	1,840	1,694
Texas	25.5	33.0	23.5	30.5	1,174	1,300
United States	1,301.0	1,350.6	1,217.4	1,244.5	1,731	1,562

Type and State	Production		Marketing year average price per cwt		Value of production	
	2018	2019	2018	2019[1]	2018	2019[1]
Oil:	*1,000 lbs*	*1,000 lbs*	*Dollars*	*Dollars*	*1,000 dollars*	*1,000 dollars*
California	74,100	68,600	(D)	27.10	(D)	18,591
Colorado	53,900	44,000	(D)	18.40	(D)	8,096
Kansas	61,500	44,800	(D)	(D)	(D)	(D)
Minnesota	99,000	94,350	(D)	(D)	(D)	(D)
Nebraska	34,080	33,800	15.50	17.00	5,282	5,746
North Dakota	665,000	645,000	17.10	17.60	110,715	112,875
South Dakota	878,400	782,000	(D)	(D)	(D)	(D)
Texas	21,280	33,800	18.00	18.00	3,830	6,084
Other States[2]	....	....	17.00	17.20	198,940	158,787
United States	1,887,260	1,746,350	16.70	17.40	320,867	310,179
Non-oil:						
California	2,400	2,080	(D)	24.20	(D)	503
Colorado	8,050	15,400	(D)	20.80	(D)	3,203
Kansas	12,750	9,125	(D)	(D)	(D)	(D)
Minnesota	14,835	8,280	(D)	(D)	(D)	(D)
Nebraska	13,300	11,050	25.60	21.00	3,405	2,321
North Dakota	74,400	95,700	23.40	23.90	17,410	22,872
South Dakota	87,750	49,600	(D)	(D)	(D)	(D)
Texas	6,300	5,850	24.00	20.00	1,512	1,170
Other States[2]	....	....	21.70	27.10	27,252	18,160
United States	219,785	197,085	22.80	22.40	49,579	48,229
Total:						
California	76,500	70,680	25.00	27.00	19,101	19,094
Colorado	61,950	59,400	17.30	19.00	10,692	11,299
Kansas	74,250	53,925	17.60	17.90	13,235	9,651
Minnesota	113,835	102,630	18.40	18.90	21,272	19,526
Nebraska	47,380	44,850	18.30	18.00	8,687	8,067
North Dakota	739,400	740,700	18.10	18.30	131,125	135,747
South Dakota	966,150	831,600	16.50	17.20	160,992	147,770
Texas	27,580	39,650	19.40	18.30	5,342	7,254
United States	2,107,045	1,943,435	17.40	17.80	370,446	358,408

(D) Withheld to avoid disclosing data for individual operations. [1] Preliminary. [2] Includes data withheld above.
NASS, Crops Branch, (202) 720–2127.

Table 3-49.—International Oilseed, sunflowerseed: Area and production in specified countries, 2017/2018–2019/2020

Country	Area			Production		
	2017/2018	2018/2019	2019/2020	2017/2018	2018/2019	2019/2020
	1,000 hectares			*1,000 metric tons*		
Ukraine	6,800	6,500	6,200	13,700	15,000	16,000
Russia	7,146	7,944	8,363	10,362	12,710	15,305
European Union	4,394	4,122	4,350	10,128	9,513	9,750
Argentina	1,678	1,876	1,590	3,538	3,825	3,400
China	1,171	921	1,250	3,149	2,494	3,250
Turkey	700	715	730	1,550	1,800	1,750
Kazakhstan	883	850	815	903	848	918
United States	540	493	504	970	956	882
Moldova	385	364	356	804	789	806
South Africa	602	515	610	862	680	750
Serbia	220	220	220	540	680	660
Burma	600	600	600	390	390	390
India	284	281	225	230	172	170
Pakistan	80	120	140	90	144	145
Brazil	96	65	80	142	111	120
Uruguay	50	56	60	78	90	100
Bolivia	109	115	120	121	80	90
Canada	26	27	29	58	57	63
Paraguay	41	31	30	65	49	51
Iran	40	40	40	43	43	43

FAS, Office of Global Analysis, (202) 720–6301. Prepared or estimated on the basis of official USDA production, supply, and distribution statistics from foreign governments.

Table 3-50—Sunflowerseed: United States exports by country of destination, 2017–2019

Country	2017	2018	2019
	Metric tons		
Spain	19,785	19,790	16,450
Canada	17,168	14,218	15,474
Mexico	22,803	14,053	11,472
Israel(*)	2,491	3,462	1,945
Korea, South	1,818	1,484	1,170
Romania	684	794	1,078
Greece	1,559	1,492	1,039
Turkey	2,561	1,430	755
Egypt	2,210	539	655
Poland	0	419	499
Ukraine	0	201	492
Japan	1,068	526	483
Indonesia	0	14	339
Colombia	466	492	279
Germany(*)	577	361	257
Chile	84	116	112
Jordan	1,472	490	100
Singapore	90	91	91
Argentina	354	44	81
Morocco	1,205	660	80
Malaysia	123	69	68
Kuwait	164	256	32
India	0	0	28
Philippines	24	27	26
Lebanon	287	18	20
Netherlands	0	0	20
Hong Kong	5	0	15
Guatemala	6	3	13
Jamaica	8	0	9
Italy(*)	0	20	6
Rest of World	1,695	1,450	23
World Total	78,704	762,518	53,111

(*) Denotes a country that is a summarization of its component countries.
FAS, Office of Global Analysis, (202) 720–6301. Data Source: U.S. Census Bureau Trade Data.

Table 3-51.—Sunflowerseed oil: United States exports by country of destination, 2017–2019

Country	2017	2018	2019
	Metric tons		
Canada	17,580	20,694	21,671
Mexico	5,419	16,209	16,349
Malaysia	60	2,322	6,420
Germany(*)	2	6	4,569
Korea, South	179	257	1,162
Vietnam	475	1,507	1,105
Japan	2,606	901	864
Philippines	0	18	695
Australia(*)	47	1,471	658
Taiwan	1,028	624	532
Argentina	0	39	466
Honduras	626	732	326
India	5	45	198
Singapore	28	13	153
Mali	0	0	120
Italy(*)	310	62	100
Indonesia	59	11	91
China	364	35	84
Peru	6	18	52
Colombia	2,694	14	49
New Zealand(*)	0	13	43
United Kingdom	13	0	38
Netherlands	176	224	36
Thailand	14	44	31
Turkey	0	0	19
Brazil	27	8	8
Hong Kong	18	6	6
Portugal	0	0	6
Uruguay	919	6	6
United Arab Emirates	0	0	4
Rest of World	618	496	7
World Total	33,272	45,773	55,869

(*) Denotes a country that is a summarization of its component countries.
FAS, Office of Global Analysis, (202) 720–6301.

Table 3-52.—International oil, sunflowerseed: Production in specified countries, 2017/2018–2019/2020

Country	2017/2018	2018/2019	2019/2020
	1,000 metric tons		
Ukraine	5,913	6,364	6,772
Russia	4,192	4,875	5,660
European Union	3,760	3,718	3,676
Argentina	1,385	1,425	1,350
Turkey	892	1,022	979
China	645	466	717
South Africa	352	293	335
Serbia	212	212	233
United States	197	201	187
Kazakhstan	213	138	169
Burma	131	131	131
Moldova	83	83	87
India	103	63	62
Pakistan	44	48	60
Iran	66	48	54
Brazil	57	49	51
Uruguay	31	36	40
Bolivia	52	34	39
Bosnia and Herzegovina	40	38	38
Egypt	37	37	35
Georgia	23	23	23
Belarus	10	22	20
Paraguay	23	18	18
Mexico	14	14	15
Morocco	17	10	13
Australia	10	13	8
Israel	8	8	8
Guatemala	7	7	7
Switzerland	7	7	7
Macedonia	6	4	5
Chile	3	3	3

FAS, Office of Global Analysis, (202) 720–6301. Prepared or estimated on the basis of official USDA production, supply, and distribution statistics from foreign governments.

Table 3-53.—Mint oil: Production and value, by State and United States, 2017–2019

State	Production			Price per pound			Value of production		
	2017	2018	2019	2017	2018	2019[1]	2017	2018	2019[1]
	1,000 pounds	*1,000 pounds*	*1,000 pounds*	*Dollars*	*Dollars*	*Dollars*	*1,000 dollars*	*1,000 dollars*	*1,000 dollars*
Peppermint:									
California[2]	123	136	(NA)	22.80	(D)	(NA)	2,804	(D)	(NA)
Idaho	1,890	1,785	2,040	17.60	18.90	18.60	33,264	33,737	37,944
Indiana	383	350	307	21.50	21.50	22.30	8,235	7,525	6,846
Oregon	1,710	1,615	1,805	19.40	21.10	19.70	33,174	34,077	35,559
Washington	1,440	1,320	1,300	16.50	19.40	19.30	23,760	25,608	25,090
Wisconsin[2]	204	171	(NA)	18.50	(D)	(NA)	3,774	(D)	(NA)
Other States[3]	....	....	....	(X)	18.10	(X)	....	5,542	....
United States	5,750	5,377	5,452	18.30	19.80	19.30	105,011	106,489	105,439
Spearmint:									
Idaho	(D)	(D)	154	(D)	(D)	(D)	(D)	2,170	(D)
Indiana	167	216	281	17.00	(D)	(D)	2,839	(D)	(D)
Michigan[2]	(D)	(D)	(NA)	(D)	(D)	(NA)	(D)	(D)	(NA)
Oregon	263	313	313	19.50	17.40	15.90	5,129	5,446	4,977
Washington	2,100	1,748	1,665	15.60	16.70	17.40	32,832	29,229	28,995
Native	1,320	1,264	(D)	16.60	16.50	(D)	21,912	20,856	(D)
Scotch	780	484	(D)	14.00	17.30	(D)	10,920	8,373	(D)
Other States[3]	266	294	....	17.10	16.70	15.60	4,536	6,333	6,793
United States	2,796	2,571	2,413	16.20	16.80	16.90	45,336	43,178	40,765

(D) Withheld to avoid disclosing data for individual operations. (NA) Not available. (X) Not applicable. [1] Preliminary. [2] Estimates discontinued in 2019. [3] Includes data withheld above.
NASS, Crops Branch, (202) 720–2127.

Table 3-54.—Peppermint oil: Area, yield, production, and value, United States, 2010–2019

Year	Area harvested	Yield per harvested acre	Production	Price per pound	Value of production
	1,000 acres	*Pounds*	*1,000 pounds*	*Dollars*	*1,000 dollars*
2010	72.8	89	6,495	20.30	131,805
2011	75.5	89	6,700	23.10	154,626
2012	75.7	87	6,549	24.10	158,121
2013	70.0	90	6,273	23.80	149,557
2014	65.0	91	5,887	22.90	134,775
2015	64.9	91	5,876	21.80	127,956
2016	64.5	91	5,843	20.90	121,923
2017	60.8	95	5,750	18.30	105,011
2018	58.5	92	5,377	19.80	106,489
2019	52.4	104	5,452	19.30	105,439

NASS, Crops Branch (202), 720–2127.

Table 3-55.—Spearmint oil: Area, yield, production, and value, United States, 2010–2019

Year	Area harvested	Yield per harvested acre	Production	Price per pound	Value of production
	1,000 acres	*Pounds*	*1,000 pounds*	*Dollars*	*1,000 dollars*
2010	18.6	125	2,318	16.20	37,553
2011	17.3	132	2,286	18.60	42,438
2012	20.0	119	2,386	19.50	46,521
2013	24.5	119	2,926	19.10	55,829
2014	24.4	114	2,784	19.80	54,977
2015	25.8	114	2,930	18.30	53,664
2016	24.5	131	3,208	17.30	55,378
2017	22.3	125	2,796	16.20	45,336
2018	20.8	124	2,571	16.80	43,178
2019	18.5	130	2,413	16.90	40,765

NASS, Crops Branch, (202) 720–2127.

Table 3-56.—International oil, olive: Production in specified countries, 2017/2018–2019/2020

Country	2017/2018	2018/2019	2019/2020
	1,000 metric tons		
European Union	2,220	2,400	2,100
Tunisia	280	120	250
Turkey	263	183	250
Morocco	140	200	170
Syria	100	100	140
Algeria	83	76	80
Argentina	44	26	40
Jordan	25	24	24
Lebanon	17	24	20
Saudi Arabia	5	10	20
Libya	18	16	18
Australia	22	20	17
Chile	17	18	16
United States	16	16	16
Israel	15	15	14
China	5	4	4

FAS, Office of Global Analysis, (202) 720–6301. Prepared or estimated on the basis of official USDA production, supply, and distribution statistics from foreign governments.

Table 3-58.—Fats and oils: Wholesale price per pound, 2013–2017 [1]

Item and market	2013	2014	2015	2016	2017
	Cents	*Cents*	*Cents*	*Cents*	*Cents*
Coconut oil, crude, tanks, f.o.b. New York	44.26	60.21	52.27	69.12	80.36
Corn oil, crude, tank cars, f.o.b. Decatur	43.13	38.36	38.24	29.24	36.78
Cottonseed oil, crude, tank cars, f.o.b. Valley	46.60	60.33	47.01	45.81	38.53
Palm oil, U.S. ports, refined	41.13	39.86	32.10	34.39	35.67
Canola oil, Midwest	52.81	42.46	36.70	36.44	38.65
Soybean oil, crude, tank cars, f.o.b. Decatur	44.98	36.83	30.20	31.58	32.06
Sunflower oil, crude, Minneapolis	62.79	59.77	38.03	55.27	53.40
Tallow, edible, number 1 delivered Chicago	42.52	38.91	28.42	32.96	34.43

[1] All prices are calendar year average.
ERS, Market and Trade Economics Division, Field Crops Branch, (202) 694–5300. Compiled from the Chemical Marketing Reporter, Milling and Baking News, and the Agricultural Marketing Service.

CHAPTER IV

STATISTICS OF VEGETABLES AND MELONS

This chapter contains statistics on potatoes, sweet potatoes, and commercial vegetables and melons.

For potatoes and sweet potatoes, the estimates of area, production, value, and farm disposition pertain to the total crop and include quantities produced both for sale and for use on farms where grown. Potato statistics are shown on a within-year seasonal grouping of winter, spring, summer, and fall crops, by States. Some States have production in more than one seasonal group.

Commercial vegetables for fresh market include 26 principal vegetable and melon crops in the major producing States. These estimates relate to crops which are grown primarily for sale and do not include vegetables and melons produced in farm and non-farm gardens. The bulk of the production of the principal vegetable and melon crops is for consumption in the fresh state. The commercial estimates of these crops include local market production from areas near consuming centers as well as production from well recognized commercial areas which specialize in producing supplies for shipment to distant markets. For fresh market vegetables and melons, value per unit and total value are on an f.o.b. basis.

For processing vegetables, the estimates of area, production, and value for each of 10 crops relate to production used by commercial canners, freezers, and other processors, except dehydrators. These estimates include raw products grown by processors themselves and those grown under contract or purchased on the open market. This production and the actual area harvested are not duplicated in the fresh market estimates for the same commodities. The production of those vegetables used for processing for which regular processing estimates are not made is included in the fresh market estimates. The processed segment of production for asparagus, broccoli, and cauliflower, combined with fresh market production during the year, is published separately at the end of the season. For processed vegetables, value per unit and total value are at processing plant door.

Beginning in 2016, acreage and yield estimates for fresh market and processing utilizations were discontinued. Total production and utilized production are estimated for each crop. Harvested not sold estimates were added to the estimating program. This is defined as the difference between total production and total utilized production.

Table 4-1.—Vegetables, principal: Fresh Market and Processing, Area Harvested, Production, and Value, by State and United States, 2017–2019

State	Area harvested			Total production		
	2017	2018	2019	2017	2018	2019
	Acres	*Acres*	*Acres*	*1,000 cwt*	*1,000 cwt*	*1,000 cwt*
Alabama	5,400	5,900	(NA)	756.0	619.5	(NA)
Arizona	127,000	(D)	123,900	35,019.0	(D)	35,018
California	1,039,900	985,800	972,400	437,802.4	464,180.6	451,426.0
Colorado	(D)	(D)	2,700	(D)	(D)	1,147.5
Delaware	(D)	(D)	(NA)	(D)	(D)	(NA)
Florida	172,700	172,800	170,700	38,117.5	34,121.0	34,509.9
Georgia	91,900	95,400	92,900	21,770.6	17,731.3	21,289.0
Idaho	16,400	12,300	10,900	9,491.5	7,827.0	8,938.0
Illinois	46,100	38,850	38,100	9,204.2	7,980.0	7,464.8
Indiana	27,800	28,000	11,100	9,018.2	10,219.2	3,543.0
Maryland	(D)	(D)	(NA)	(D)	(D)	(NA)
Michigan	107,500	101,900	87,200	19,181.6	16,683.2	12,419.1
Minnesota	165,100	160,600	154,300	21,166.5	17,454.8	15,647.4
Mississippi	-	-	27,500	-	-	4,262.5
Missouri	3,000	(D)	(NA)	705.0	(D)	(NA)
New Jersey	28,800	28,500	10,600	4,197.4	3,533.3	1,630.0
New Mexico	14,700	15,000	15,300	6,082.0	5,611.0	5,254.5
New York	90,100	89,200	86,300	15,265.9	12,763.8	13,413.6
North Carolina	37,300	36,500	126,300	7,458.6	6,614.5	24,732.0
Ohio	21,300	21,500	3,500	4,732.5	4,913.0	437.5
Oregon	(D)	(D)	79,000	(D)	(D)	23,908.0
Pennsylvania	27,650	25,500	13,500	2,731.1	1,957.3	1,151.1
South Carolina	(D)	10,300	4,500	(D)	2,501.4	1,440.0
Tennessee	11,300	12,700	(NA)	1,786.9	1,626.6	(NA)
Texas	67,600	62,000	50,100	14,692.5	15,926.3	13,477.2
Virginia	6,000	7,500	5,600	1,418.8	1,491.7	924.0
Washington	154,300	144,100	140,300	43,145.8	40,206.3	37,515.2
Wisconsin	(D)	(D)	155,900	(D)	(D)	19,787.5
Other States [1]	310,630	430,750	-	59,577.1	89,653.4	-
United States	2,572,480	2,485,100	2,382,600	763,321.1	763,615.2	739,335.8

State	Utilized production			Value of utilized production		
	2017	2018	2019	2017	2018	2019
	1,000 cwt	*1,000 cwt*	*1,000 cwt*	*1,000 dollars*	*1,000 dollars*	*1,000 dollars*
Alabama	756.0	615.2	(NA)	16,659	15,379	(NA)
Arizona	35,019.0	(D)	35,018.0	1,635,572	(D)	2,167,239
California	432,410.5	461,897.6	499,755.6	8,561,502	7,327,501	7,864,286
Colorado	(D)	(D)	1,109.6	(D)	(D)	18,531
Delaware	(D)	(D)	(NA)	(D)	(D)	(NA)
Florida	37,647.7	33,363.7	34,291.9	1,078,197	1,121,981	1,223,430
Georgia	21,376.3	17,702.3	20,825.6	476,744	452,589	517,659
Idaho	9,390.5	7,808.6	8,893.3	85,740	60,831	65,815
Illinois	9,069.0	7,949.0	7,458.2	43,077	39,577	44,205
Indiana	9,017.2	10,206.6	3,539.3	96,292	97,104	52,276
Maryland	(D)	(D)	(NA)	(D)	(D)	(NA)
Michigan	19,166.0	16,633.1	12,352.7	301,363	273,314	213,547
Minnesota	21,027.4	17,430.1	15,477.7	110,856	116,288	76,579
Mississippi	-	-	4,262.5	-	-	75,021
Missouri	702.2	(D)	(NA)	8,445	(D)	(NA)
New Jersey	4,188.9	3,262.7	1,593.0	162,394	138,376	82,520
New Mexico	6,082.0	5,611.0	5,254.5	129,043	133,357	152,628
New York	14,782.0	12,528.2	13,108.7	246,805	209,911	233,112
North Carolina	7,351.4	6,506.4	24,611.4	170,273	145,025	425,943
Ohio	4,707.5	4,899.0	434.0	94,499	103,562	9,911
Oregon	(D)	(D)	23,712.9	(D)	(D)	192,879
Pennsylvania	2,678.5	1,905.7	1,136.0	76,175	59,224	25,389
South Carolina	(D)	2,495.3	1,402.6	(D)	68,470	16,022
Tennessee	1,759.2	1,584.1	(NA)	76,431	66,984	(NA)
Texas	14,456.0	15,803.7	13,294.1	283,237	298,047	192,710
Virginia	1,413.9	1,439.2	903.7	54,146	43,653	16,427
Washington	41,868.9	39,330.3	36,759.8	368,660	351,475	362,740
Wisconsin	(D)	(D)	19,711.1	(D)	(D)	128,310
Other States [1]	59,496.2	89,342.7	-	591,782	1,747,898	-
United States	754,366.3	758,314.5	734,906.6	14,667,892	12,869,883	14,157,179

(D) Withheld to avoid disclosing data for individual operations. (NA) Not available. [1] Includes data withheld above.
NASS, Crops Branch, (202) 720–2127.

Table 4-2.— Artichokes for fresh market and processing: Area, yield, production, value, and total value, United States, 2010-2019

Year	Area harvested	Yield per acre	Utilized Production	Value	
				Per cwt	Total
	Acres	*Cwt*	*1,000 cwt*	*Dollars*	*1,000 dollars*
2010	7,200	120	864	50.20	43,373
2011	7,400	135	999	51.10	51,049
2012	7,300	145	1,059	54.30	57,504
2013	7,100	135	959	61.00	58,499
2014	7,300	130	949	57.60	54,662
2015	6,800	135	918	87.80	80,600
2016	6,800	145	986	78.80	77,697
2017	7,200	130.0	936.0	70.00	65,520
2018	6,900	145.0	1,000.5	63.00	63,032
2019	7,200	125.0	1,008.0	78.00	78,624

Note: Beginning in 2016, Acreage and Yield estimates for fresh market and processing utilizations were discontinued. Total Production and Utilized Production are estimated for each crop. Harvested Not Sold estimates were added to the estimating program. This is defined as the difference between Total Production and Total Utilized Production. Table 4-2, 2016-2018 includes utilized production.
NASS, Crops Branch, (202) 720–2127.

Table 4-3.—Asparagus for Fresh Market and Processing: Area planted and harvested, yield, production, price and value - State and United States, 2017–2019

State	Area planted			Area harvested		
	2017	2018	2019	2017	2018	2019
	Acres	*Acres*	*Acres*	*Acres*	*Acres*	*Acres*
California	8,300	6,200	5,300	8,000	6,000	5,200
Michigan	12,000	10,000	10,000	11,300	9,500	9,400
New Jersey	2,200	2,200	2,100	2,100	2,100	2,000
Washington	5,100	4,500	4,500	4,900	4,100	4,100
United States	27,600	22,900	21,900	26,300	26,300	20,700
State	**Yield per acre**			**Utilized Production**		
	2017	2018	2019	2017	2018	2019
	Cwt	*Cwt*	*Cwt*	*1,000 cwt*	*1,000 cwt*	*1,000 cwt*
California	25.0	30.0	35.0	198.0	178.2	182.0
Michigan	27.0	28.0	30.0	305.1	266.0	270.0
New Jersey	34.0	33.0	32.0	71.4	69.3	63.7
Washington	54.0	65.0	55.0	264.6	261.2	216.5
United States	32.0	36.0	36.4	839.1	774.7	735.7
State	**Price per cwt**			**Value of Production**		
	2017	2018	2019	2017	2018	2019
	Dollars	*Dollars*	*Dollars*	*1,000 dollars*	*1,000 dollars*	*1,000 dollars*
California	175.00	149.00	202.00	34,650	26,552	36,764
Michigan	85.70	87.50	93.60	26,136	23,275	25,607
New Jersey	183.00	167.00	256.00	13,054	11,562	16,302
Washington	101.40	100.00	98.10	26,832	26,195	21,242
United States	120.00	113.00	136.00	100,672	87,584	99,915

NASS, Crops Branch, (202) 720–2127.

Table 4-4.—Asparagus for Fresh Market and Processing: Production, price and value by utilization - States and United States, 2017–2019

Utilization and State	Utilized Production		
	2017	2018	2019
	1,000 cwt	*1,000 cwt*	*1,000 cwt*
Fresh market			
California	198.0	178.2	182.0
Michigan	144.0	133.0	141.0
New Jersey	(D)	(D)	(D)
Washington	(D)	(D)	(D)
Other States [1]	311.0	306.4	257.0
United States	653.0	617.6	580.0
	Tons	*Tons*	*Tons*
Processing			
California	-	-	-
Michigan	8,055	6,650	6,627
New Jersey	(D)	(D)	(D)
Washington	(D)	(D)	(D)
Other States [1]	1,252	1,202	1,160
United States	9,307	7,852	7,787

Utilization and State	Price per unit		
	2017	2018	2019
	Dollars per cwt	*Dollars per cwt*	*Dollars per cwt*
Fresh market			
California	175.00	149.00	202.00
Michigan	92.00	95.00	105.00
New Jersey	(D)	(D)	(D)
Washington	(D)	(D)	(D)
Other States [1]	123.00	117.00	139.00
United States	132.00	122.00	151.00
	Dollars per ton	*Dollars per ton*	*Dollars per ton*
Processing			
California	(X)	(X)	(X)
Michigan	1,600.00	1,600.00	1,630.00
New Jersey	(D)	(D)	(D)
Washington	(D)	(D)	(D)
Other States [1]	1,350.00	1,470.00	1,500.00
United States	1,570.00	1,580.00	1,610.00

Utilization and State	Value of utilized production		
	2016	2017	2018
	1,000 dollars	*1,000 dollars*	*1,000 dollars*
Fresh market			
California	34,650	26,552	36,764
Michigan	13,248	12,635	14,805
New Jersey	(D)	(D)	(D)
Washington	(D)	(D)	(D)
Other States [3]	38,201	35,988	35,801
United States	86,099	75,175	87,370
	1,000 dollars	*1,000 dollars*	*1,000 dollars*
Processing			
California [1]	-	-	-
Michigan	12,888	10,640	10,802
New Jersey [2]	(D)	(D)	(D)
Washington	(D)	(D)	(D)
Other States [3]	1,685	1,769	1,743
United States	14,573	12,409	12,545

(D) Withheld to avoid disclosing data for individual operations. (X) Not applicable. [1] Includes data withheld above.
NASS, Crops Branch, (202) 720–2127.

Table 4-5.—Snap Beans for Fresh Market and Processing: Area Harvested, Production, and Value - States and United States, 2017–2019

State	Area harvested			Total production		
	2017	2018	2019	2017	2018	2019
	Acres	*Acres*	*Acres*	*1,000 cwt*	*1,000 cwt*	*1,000 cwt*
California	7,600	7,900	7,500	798.0	908.5	712.5
Delaware	2,200	1,700	(NA)	132.0	102.0	(NA)
Florida	27,500	27,600	26,200	1,595.0	1,575.0	1,755.4
Georgia	10,600	11,900	10,200	646.6	559.3	612.0
Illinois	7,500	8,800	11,700	600.0	800.8	865.8
Indiana	2,400	2,600	(NA)	187.2	187.2	(NA)
Maryland	3,000	3,000	(NA)	222.0	180.0	(NA)
Michigan	17,800	18,200	17,600	1,780.0	1,365.0	1,601.6
Minnesota	4,700	2,800	3,400	493.5	215.6	323.0
New Jersey	2,600	2,700	(NA)	101.4	118.8	(NA)
New York	24,000	26,300	30,200	1,752.0	2,104.0	2,144.2
North Carolina	5,000	4,800	(NA)	185.0	216.0	(NA)
Oregon	11,900	11,500	12,200	1,547.0	1,437.5	1,830.0
Pennsylvania	7,200	7,400	7,200	482.4	436.6	489.6
Tennessee	6,300	7,100	(NA)	384.3	269.8	(NA)
Texas	6,700	2,800	(NA)	402.0	196.0	(NA)
Washington	2,600	3,200	(NA)	205.4	246.4	(NA)
Wisconsin	62,500	63,500	63,500	6,562.5	6,350.0	6,223.0
United States	212,100	213,800	189,700	18,076.3	17,073.5	16,557.1

State	Utilized production			Value of utilized production		
	2017	2018	2019	2017	2018	2019
	1,000 cwt	*1,000 cwt*	*1,000 cwt*	*1,000 dollars*	*1,000 dollars*	*1,000 dollars*
California	796.4	908.5	712.5	55,532	69,008	47,766
Delaware	132.0	102.0	(NA)	2,522	2,385	(NA)
Florida	1,572.7	1,373.1	1,755.4	81,453	58,702	68,866
Georgia	646.6	559.3	612.0	20,124	28,025	27,647
Illinois	600.0	800.8	865.8	3,750	9,294	11,588
Indiana	187.2	187.2	(NA)	2,893	3,123	(NA)
Maryland	222.0	100.0	(NA)	4,264	3,456	(NA)
Michigan	1,778.2	1,365.0	1,600.0	25,898	21,520	25,611
Minnesota	488.6	215.4	322.7	3,153	4,714	6,675
New Jersey	101.4	117.6	(NA)	4,539	5,986	(NA)
New York	1,748.5	2,104.0	2,129.2	35,881	34,023	38,259
North Carolina	184.3	214.3	(NA)	6,704	8,020	(NA)
Oregon	1,547.0	1,437.5	1,830.0	27,429	23,596	26,202
Pennsylvania	482.4	435.3	489.1	10,220	8,057	8,612
Tennessee	382.4	265.5	(NA)	12,580	10,544	(NA)
Texas	402.0	196.0	(NA)	[illegible]	5,723	(NA)
Washington	205.4	246.4	(NA)	8,770	7,856	(NA)
Wisconsin	6,562.5	6,337.3	6,223.0	40,115	47,877	42,254
United States	18,039.6	17,045.2	16,539.7	349,445	351,909	303,480

(NA) Not available.
NASS, Crops Branch, (202) 720–2127.

Table 4-6.—Broccoli, fresh market and processing: Area, yield, production, value per hundredweight and per ton, and total value, United States, 2013-2019[1]

Year	Total crop: Area harvested	Yield per acre	Production	Value[2]: Per cwt	Value[2]: Total
	Acres	*Cwt*	*1,000 cwt*	*Dollars*	*1,000 dollars*
2013	131,500	162.0	21,360.0	42.80	913,520
2014	126,400	163.0	20,600.0	40.00	824,961
2015	124,400	176.0	21,888.0	48.40	1,058,770
2016	131,300	171.0	22,466.0	37.70	846,595
2017	128,600	158.5	20,384.0	45.40	925,716
2018	113,900	151.7	17,273.0	42.80	738,527
2019	111,600	156.3	17,439.5	50.00	872,629

Year	Fresh market: Utilized Production	Value[2]: Per cwt	Value[2]: Total	Processing: Utilized Production	Value[3]: Per ton	Value[3]: Total
	1,000 cwt	*Dollars*	*1,000 dollars*	*Tons*	*Dollars*	*1,000 dollars*
2013	20,664.0	43.20	893,336	34,800	580.00	20,184
2014	19,910.0	40.70	809,608	34,500	445.00	15,353
2015	21,104.0	49.10	1,035,211	39,200	601.00	23,559
2016	21,548.0	38.20	824,103	45,903	490.00	22,492
2017	19,908.0	46.00	916,482	23,800	388.00	9,234
2018	16,778.1	43.10	722,789	24,746	636.00	15,738
2019	16,641.9	51.30	853,088	39,880	490.00	19,541

[1] Sprouting broccoli only. Does not include broccoli rabe nor heading (cauliflower) broccoli. [2] Price and value at point of first sale. [3] Price and value at processing plant door.
NASS, Crops Branch, (202) 720–2127.

Table 4-7.—Broccoli: Area, production, and value, by State and United States, 2017–2019[1]

State	Area harvested 2017	2018	2019	Utilized production 2017	2018	2019
	Acres			*1,000 cwt*		
Arizona	9,600	10,900	11,900	1,344.0	1,308.0	1,478.5
California	119,000	103,000	99,700	19,040.0	15,965.0	15,952.0
United States	128,600	113,900	111,600	20,384.0	17,273.0	17,439.5

State	Price per cwt 2017	2018	2019	Value of utilized production 2017	2018	2019
	Dollars			*1,000 dollars*		
Arizona	56.20	45.20	45.20	75,533	59,122	86,275
California	44.70	42.60	42.60	850,183	679,405	786,354
United States	45.40	42.80	50.00	925,716	738,527	872,629

Utilization and State	Utilized production 2017	2018	2019	Price per unit 2017	2018	2019	Value of utilized production 2017	2018	2019
	1,000 cwt			*Dollars per cwt*			*1,000 dollars*		
Fresh Market									
Arizona	1,344.0	1,308.0	1,478.5	56.20	45.20	58.00	75,533	59,122	86,275
California	18,564.0	15,470.1	15,154.4	45.30	42.90	50.60	840,949	663,667	766,813
United States	19,908.0	16,778.1	16,641.9	46.00	43.10	51.30	916,482	722,789	853,088
	Tons			*Dollars per ton*			*1,000 dollars*		
Processing									
Arizona	....	....	....	(X)	(X)	(X)	....	....	....
California	23,800	24,746	24,746	388.00	636.00	490.00	9,234	15,738	19,541
United States	23,800	24,746	24,746	388.00	636.00	490.00	9,234	15,738	19,541

(X) Not applicable. [1] Sprouting broccoli only. Does not include broccoli rabe nor heading (cauliflower) broccoli.
NASS, Crops Branch, (202) 720–2127.

Table 4-8.—Cabbage for fresh market and processing: Area Harvested, production, and value, by State and United States, 2017–2019

State	Area harvested			Total production		
	2017	2018	2019	2017	2018	2019
	Acres			*1,000 cwt*		
Arizona	3,300	3,300	(D)	1,666.5	1,650.0	(D)
California	14,500	14,200	14,500	5,510.0	4,828.0	5,945.0
Florida	8,600	8,900	8,200	3,096.0	3,204.0	2,952.0
Georgia	3,800	2,900	4,800	1,596.0	1,160.0	1,920.0
Michigan	3,900	3,700	4,500	1,326.0	1,295.0	1,530.0
New York	12,700	10,100	11,700	5,270.5	3,939.0	4,446.0
North Carolina	2,700	2,800	(NA)	756.0	644.0	(NA)
Texas	6,000	5,000	(D)	1,800.0	1,350.0	(D)
Wisconsin	5,100	3,300	5,000	2,805.0	1,336.5	1,325.0
Other States	-	-	10,400	-	-	3,588.0
United States	60,600	54,200	59,100	23,826.0	19,406.5	21,706.0

State	Utilized production			Value of utilized production		
	2017	2018	2019	2017	2018	2019
	1,000 cwt			*1,000 dollars*		
Arizona	1,666.5	1,650.0	(D)	29,164	33,495	(D)
California	5,510.0	4,828.0	5,945.0	158,625	181,533	212,237
Florida	3,065.0	3,172.0	2,922.5	47,508	62,806	58,394
Georgia	1,596.0	1,160.0	1,887.4	20,583	14,845	30,723
Michigan	1,326.0	1,295.0	1,526.9	14,619	14,327	18,684
New York	5,270.5	3,820.8	4,423.8	74,434	52,862	82,430
North Carolina	756.0	606.0	(NA)	11,416	10,120	(NA)
Texas	1,800.0	1,350.0	(D)	32,040	27,405	(D)
Wisconsin	2,805.0	1,336.5	1,325.0	42,918	10,698	15,598
Other States	-	-	3,588.0	-	-	100,854
United States	23,795.0	19,218.3	21,618.6	431,307	408,091	518,920

State	Utilized production			Price per unit			Value of utilized production		
	2017	2018	2019	2017	2018	2019	2017	2018	2019
	1,000 cwt			*Dollars per cwt*			*1,000 dollars*		
Fresh Market									
Arizona	(D)	(D)	(D)	(D)	(D)	(D)	(D)	(D)	(D)
California	(D)	4,828.0	(D)	(D)	37.60	(D)	(D)	181,533	(D)
Florida	3,065.0	3,172.0	(D)	15.50	10.80	(D)	47,508	[illegible]	(D)
Georgia	(D)	(D)	(D)	(D)	(D)	(D)	(D)	(D)	(D)
Michigan	(D)	686.4	608.9	(D)	14.00	19.00	(D)	9,610	11,569
New York	4,653.9	3,663.3	(D)	15.00	14.00	(D)	69,809	51,286	(D)
North Carolina	756.0	606.0	(NA)	15.10	16.70	(NA)	11,416	10,120	(NA)
Texas	1,800.0	1,350.0	(D)	17.80	20.30	(D)	32,040	27,405	(D)
Wisconsin	(D)	(D)	(D)	(D)	(D)	(D)	(D)	(D)	(D)
Other States [1]	9,490.0	2,991.3	18,321.2	24.20	17.90	26.10	229,705	53,572	483,426
United States	19,764.9	17,297.0	18,930.1	19.80	22.90	26.10	390,558	396,332	494,995
	Tons			*Dollars per ton*			*1,000 dollars*		
Processing									
Arizona	(D)	(D)	(D)	(D)	(D)	(D)	(D)	(D)	(D)
California	(D)	-	(D)	(D)	(X)	(D)	(D)	-	(D)
Florida	-	-	(D)	(X)	(X)	(D)	-	-	(D)
Georgia	(D)	(D)	(D)	(D)	(D)	(D)	(D)	(D)	(D)
Michigan	(D)	30,433	45,900	(D)	155.00	155.00	(D)	4,717	7,115
New York	30,832	7,878	(D)	150.00	200.00	(D)	4,625	1,576	(D)
North Carolina	-	-	(NA)	(X)	(X)	(NA)	-	-	(NA)
Texas	-	-	(D)	(X)	(X)	(D)	-	-	(D)
Wisconsin	(D)	(D)	(D)	(D)	(D)	(D)	(D)	(D)	(D)
Other States [1]	170,681	57,761	88,524	212.00	94.60	190.00	36,124	5,466	16,810
United States	201,513	96,072	134,424	202.00	122.00	178.00	40,749	11,759	23.925

(D) Withheld to avoid disclosing data for individual operations. (NA) Not available. [1] Includes data withheld above.
NASS, Crops Branch, (202) 720–2127.

Table 4-9.—Cantaloupes for fresh market: Area Harvested, production, and value, by State and United States, 2017–2019

State	Area harvested			Yield per acre		
	2017	2018	2019	2017	2018	2019
	Acres			*1,000 cwt*		
Arizona	15,700	16,300	14,000	225.0	230.0	225.0
California	34,300	31,500	32,800	275.0	265.0	250.0
Florida	2,200	(D)	2,300	260.0	(D)	210.0
Georgia	4,500	(D)	4,000	140.0	(D)	220.0
Indiana	1,500	1,700	(NA)	230.0	225.0	(NA)
North Carolina	1,200	1,200	(NA)	205.0	255.0	(NA)
Pennsylvania	950	900	(NA)	145.0	120.0	(NA)
South Carolina	900	(D)	(NA)	310.0	(D)	(NA)
Texas	2,000	2,000	(NA)	110.0	110.0	(NA)
Other States [1]	-	7,100	-	(X)	210.0	(X)
United States	63,250	60,700	53,100	243.4	240.6	239.4

State	Total production			Utilized production		
	2017	2018	2019	2017	2018	2019
	1,000 cwt			*1,000 dollars*		
Arizona	3,532.5	3,749.5	3,150.0	3,532.5	3,749.0	3,150.0
California	9,432.5	8,347.5	8,200.0	9,432.5	8,347.5	8,200.0
Florida	572.0	(D)	483.0	572.0	(D)	481.0
Georgia	630.0	(D)	880.0	630.0	(D)	874.7
Indiana	345.0	382.5	(NA)	345.0	382.5	(NA)
North Carolina	246.0	306.0	(NA)	246.0	302.9	(NA)
Pennsylvania	137.8	108.0	(NA)	135.0	106.9	(NA)
South Carolina	279.0	(D)	(NA)	279.0	(D)	(NA)
Texas	220.0	220.0	(NA)	220.0	220.0	(NA)
Other States [1]	-	1,494.0	-	....	1,494.0	-
United States	15,394.8	14,607.0	12,713.0	15,392.0	14,602.8	12,705.8

State	Price per cwt			Value of utilized production		
	2017	2018	2019	2017	2018	2019
	Dollars			*1,000 dollars*		
Arizona	23.90	23.20	25.60	84,427	86,977	80,640
California	16.50	22.50	23.50	155,636	187,819	192,700
Florida	18.00	(D)	17.00	10,296	(D)	8,179
Georgia	24.60	(D)	25.00	15,498	(D)	21,868
Indiana	24.00	22.50	(NA)	8,280	8,606	(NA)
North Carolina	26.00	15.00	(NA)	6,396	4,544	(NA)
Pennsylvania	32.90	38.80	(NA)	4,442	4,148	(NA)
South Carolina	20.50	(D)	(NA)	5,720	(D)	(NA)
Texas	24.00	23.00	(NA)	5,280	5,060	(NA)
Other States [1]	(X)	23.00	(X)	-	34,388	-
United States	19.20	22.70	23.90	295,975	331,542	303,387

(D) Withheld to avoid disclosing data for individual operations. (NA) Not available. (X) Not applicable. [1] Includes data withheld above.

NASS, Crops Branch, (202) 720–2127.

Table 4-10.—Carrot for fresh market and processing: Area Harvested, production, and value, by State and United States, 2017–2019

State	Area harvested 2017	Area harvested 2018	Area harvested 2019	Total production 2017	Total production 2018	Total production 2019
	Acres			*1,000 cwt*		
California	58,500	64,300	69,900	21,645.0	38,580.0	43,338.0
Michigan	4,000	4,000	(NA)	1,480.0	1,520.0	(NA)
Texas	1,900	1,600	(NA)	456.0	400.0	(NA)
Washington	7,000	5,900	6,400	4,900.0	3,658.0	4,864.0
Wisconsin	4,500	4,000	3,300	2,520.0	1,720.0	1,600.5
United States	75,900	79,800	79,600	31,001.0	45,878.0	49,802.5

State	Utilized production 2017	Utilized production 2018	Utilized production 2019	Value of utilized production 2017	Value of utilized production 2018	Value of utilized production 2019
	1,000 cwt			*1,000 dollars*		
California	21,645.0	38,464.3	43,338.0	635,624	687,631	827,126
Michigan	1,480.0	1,520.0	(NA)	14,948	14,456	(NA)
Texas	456.0	400.0	(NA)	4,771	3,785	(NA)
Washington	4,900.0	3,658.0	4,864.0	31,966	19,982	29,415
Wisconsin	2,515.0	1,714.8	1,600.5	8,820	7,092	6,977
United States	30,996.0	45,757.1	49,802.5	696,129	732,946	863,518

Utilization and State	Utilized production 2017	Utilized production 2018	Utilized production 2019	Price per unit 2017	Price per unit 2018	Price per unit 2019	Value of utilized production 2017	Value of utilized production 2018	Value of utilized production 2019
	1,000 cwt			*Dollars per cwt*			*1,000 dollars*		
Fresh Market									
California	(D)	(D)	(D)	(D)	(D)	(D)	(D)	(D)	(D)
Michigan	(D)	410.4	(NA)	(D)	19.00	(NA)	(D)	7,798	(NA)
Texas	(D)	(D)	(NA)	(D)	(D)	(NA)	(D)	(D)	(NA)
Washington	(D)	(D)	170.2	(D)	(D)	57.00	(D)	(D)	9,701
Wisconsin	2.5	3.4	(D)	110.00	138.00	(D)	278	469	(D)
Other States [1]	20,854.0	36,201.8	40,305.9	30.10	18.40	19.60	628,564	664,918	790,090
United States	20,856.5	36,615.6	40,476.1	30.20	18.40	19.80	628,842	673,185	799,791
	Tons			*Dollars per ton*			*1,000 dollars*		
Processing									
California	(D)	(D)	(D)	(D)	(D)	(D)	(D)	(D)	(D)
Michigan	(D)	55,480	(NA)	(D)	120.00	(NA)	(D)	6,658	(NA)
Texas	(D)	(D)	(NA)	(D)	(D)	(NA)	(D)	(D)	(NA)
Washington	(D)	(D)	234,688	(D)	(D)	84.00	(D)	(D)	19,714
Wisconsin	125,622	85,570	(D)	68.00	77.40	(D)	8,542	6,623	(D)
Other States [1]	381,351	316,023	231,628	154.00	147.00	190.00	58,745	46,480	44,013
United States	506,973	457,073	466,316	133.00	131.00	137.00	67,287	59,761	63,727

(D) Withheld to avoid disclosing data for individual operations. (NA) Not available. [1] Includes data withheld above.
NASS, Crops Branch, (202) 720–2127.

Table 4-11.—Cauliflower for fresh market and processing: Area harvested, yield, production, and value, United States, 2010-2019 [1]

Year	Area for harvest	Yield per acre	Production	Value [2]	
				Per cwt.	Total [3]
	Acres	*1,000 cwt*	*cwt*	*Dollars*	*1,000 dollars*
2010	38,460	184.0	7,087.0	41.70	295,186
2011	36,430	183.0	6,649.0	46.00	305,539
2012	36,070	185.0	6,690.0	35.80	239,203
2013	36,830	181.0	6,662.0	44.30	295,450
2014	35,070	181.0	6,361.0	49.80	316,937
2015	37,210	176.0	6,559.0	61.30	401,747
2016	41,900	178.1	7,461.0	55.70	415,761
2017	45,800	198.1	9,074.5	45.90	415,737
2018	44,900	211.6	9,501.0	45.80	434,491
2019	45,500	221.2	10,063.0	46.30	465,879

Note: Beginning in 2016, acreage and yield estimates for fresh market and processing utilizations were discontinued. Only total acreage and total yield will be published beginning in 2016. Total production and utilized production are estimated for each crop. Harvested not sold estimates were added to the estimating program. This is defined as the difference between total production and total utilized production.

[1] Includes heading (cauliflower) broccoli. [2] Price and value at point of first sale. [3] Beginning in 2016, value of utilized production.

NASS, Crops Branch, (202) 720–2127.

Table 4-12.—Cauliflower for fresh market and processing: Area harvested, production, and value, by State and United States, 2017–2019

State	Area harvested			Total Production		
	2017	2018	2019	2017	2018	2019
	Acres			*1,000 cwt*		
Arizona	5,700	6,100	6,700	1,054.5	1,159.0	1,139.0
California	40,100	38,800	38,800	8,020.0	8,342.0	8,924.0
United States	45,800	44,900	45,500	9,074.5	9,501.0	10,063.0

State	Utilized production			Value of total production		
	2017	2018	2019	2017	2018	2019
	1,000 cwt			*1,000 dollars*		
Arizona	1,054.5	1,159.0	1,139.0	86,153	79,739	99,549
California	7,995.9	8,333.7	8,915.1	329,584	354,752	366,330
United States	9,050.4	9,492.7	10,054.1	415,737	434,491	465,879

Utilization and State	Utilized production			Price per unit			Value of utilized production		
	2017	2018	2019	2017	2018	2019	2017	2018	2019
	1,000 cwt			*Dollars per cwt*			*1,000 dollars*		
Fresh Market									
Arizona	1,054.5	(D)	(D)	81.70	(D)	(D)	86,153	(D)	(D)
California	7,635.0	(D)	(D)	42.00	(D)	(D)	320,670	(D)	(D)
Other States [1]	-	9,309.1	10,045.2	(X)	46.00	46.30	-	428,563	465,594
United States	8,689.5	9,309.1	10,045.2	46.80	46.00	46.30	406,823	428,563	465,594
	Tons			*Dollars per ton*			*1,000 dollars*		
Processing									
Arizona	-	(D)	(D)	(X)	(D)	(D)	-	(D)	(D)
California	18,045	(D)	(D)	494.00	(D)	(D)	8,914	(D)	(D)
Other States [1]	-	9,176	446	(X)	646.00	639.00	-	5,928	285
United States	18,045	9,176	446	494.00	646.00	639.00	8,914	5,928	285

(D) Withheld to avoid disclosing data for individual operations. (X) Not applicable. [1] Includes data withheld above.

NASS, Crops Branch, (202) 720–2127.

Table 4-13.—Celery for fresh market and processing: Area harvested, yield, production, price, and value, United States, 2012–2019[1]

Year	Area harvested	Yield per acre	Production	Value[2] Per cwt	Value[2] Total
	Acres	*Cwt*	*1,000 cwt*	*Dollars*	*1,000 dollars*
2013	28,800	625.0	18,003	25.40	457,765
2014	28,900	636.0	18,393	17.10	314,134
2015	27,700	618.0	17,110	24.80	424,664
2016	33,100	534.0	17,676	18.10	319,321
2017	31,800	505.9	16,089	20.10	322,047
2018	30,200	580.0	17,516	25.00	436,818
2019	28,100	560.0	15,736	30.20	474,711

Note: Beginning in 2016, acreage and yield estimates for fresh market and processing utilizations were discontinued. Only total acreage and total yield will be published beginning in 2016. Total production and utilized production are estimated for each crop. Harvested Not Sold estimates were added to the estimating program. This is defined as the difference between total production and total utilized production.

[1] Mostly for fresh market use, but includes quantities used for processing. [2] Price and value at point of first sale.

NASS, Crops Branch, (202) 720–2127.

Table 4-14.—Celery for fresh market and processing: Area harvested, production, price, and value, by State and United States, 2017–2019

State	Area harvested 2017	Area harvested 2018	Area harvested 2019	Total Production 2017	Total Production 2018	Total Production 2019
	Acres			*1,000 cwt*		
California	29,700	28,300	28,100	14,850.0	16,414.0	15,736.0
Michigan	2,100	1,900	(NA)	1,239.0	1,102.0	(NA)
United States	31,800	30,200	28,100	16,089.0	17,516.0	15,736.0

State	Utilized production 2017	Utilized production 2018	Utilized production 2019	Value of total production 2017	Value of total production 2018	Value of total production 2019
	1,000 cwt			*1,000 dollars*		
California	14,805.5	16,397.6	15,720.3	305,411	417,347	474,711
Michigan	1,239.0	1,102.0	(NA)	16,636	19,471	(NA)
United States	16,044.5	17,499.6	15,720.3	322,047	436,818	474,711

Utilization and State	Utilized production 2017	Utilized production 2018	Utilized production 2019	Price per unit 2017	Price per unit 2018	Price per unit 2019	Value of utilized production 2017	Value of utilized production 2018	Value of utilized production 2019
	1,000 cwt			*Dollars per cwt*			*1,000 dollars*		
Fresh Market									
California	(D)	(D)	(D)	(D)	(D)	(D)	(D)	(D)	(D)
Michigan	(D)	(D)	(NA)	(D)	(D)	(NA)	(D)	(D)	(NA)
Other States[1]	15,381.8	16,272.7	(D)	20.50	25.90	(D)	315,484	421,967	(D)
United States	15,381.8	16,272.7	(D)	20.50	25.90	(D)	315,484	421,967	(D)
	Tons			*Dollars per ton*			*1,000 dollars*		
Processing									
California	(D)	(D)	(D)	(D)	(D)	(D)	(D)	(D)	(D)
Michigan	(D)	(D)	(NA)	(D)	(D)	(NA)	(D)	(D)	(NA)
Other States[1]	33,136	61,344	(D)	198.00	242.00	(D)	6,563	14,954	(D)
United States	33,136	61,344	(D)	198.00	242.00	(D)	6,563	14,954	(D)

(D) Withheld to avoid disclosing data for individual operations. (NA) Not available. [1] Includes data withheld above.

NASS, Crops Branch, (202) 720–2127.

Table 4-15.—Sweet corn for fresh market and processing: Area harvested, production, price, and value, by State and United States, 2017–2019

State	Area harvested			Total Production		
	2017	2018	2019	2017	2018	2019
	Acres			*1,000 cwt*		
California	33,500	33,800	33,600	6,365.0	6,084.0	6,048.0
Delaware	10,800	11,200	(NA)	1,512.0	1,512.0	(NA)
Florida	39,000	39,700	41,000	5,460.0	4,764.0	4,715.0
Georgia	25,100	29,000	26,900	4,016.0	4,350.0	3,228.0
Idaho	3,900	3,900	(NA)	429.0	351.0	(NA)
Illinois	14,200	14,600	15,500	1,917.0	1,825.0	2,402.5
Indiana	3,900	4,100	(NA)	351.0	389.5	(NA)
Maryland	7,100	8,100	(NA)	887.5	972.0	(NA)
Michigan	9,100	9,100	(NA)	910.0	837.2	(NA)
Minnesota	112,600	110,600	99,100	18,579.0	15,484.0	13,874.0
New Jersey	6,300	6,400	(NA)	611.1	556.8	(NA)
New York	25,700	26,600	26,500	3,341.0	2,793.0	3,445.0
Ohio	9,000	9,100	(NA)	810.0	864.5	(NA)
Oregon	23,900	28,900	23,700	4,541.0	5,924.5	4,858.5
Pennsylvania	11,600	10,600	(NA)	742.4	604.2	(NA)
Washington	74,000	72,000	75,000	15,540.0	16,560.0	15,750.0
Wisconsin	54,900	56,400	49,400	9,662.4	9,588.0	8,645.0
United States	464,600	474,100	390,700	75,674.4	73,459.7	62,966.0

State	Utilized production			Value of total production		
	2017	2018	2019	2017	2018	2019
	1,000 cwt			*1,000 dollars*		
California	6,365.0	6,084.0	6,048.0	196,042	175,828	172,368
Delaware	1,512.0	1,512.0	(NA)	19,439	16,633	(NA)
Florida	5,460.0	4,764.0	4,696.1	158,340	142,920	140,883
Georgia	3,935.7	4,345.7	3,050.5	98,393	111,684	75,042
Idaho	427.7	347.5	(NA)	11,548	12,163	(NA)
Illinois	1,917.0	1,825.0	2,400.1	11,792	13,763	15,532
Indiana	351.0	389.5	(NA)	9,126	8,959	(NA)
Maryland	883.1	972.0	(NA)	11,647	13,994	(NA)
Michigan	910.0	837.2	(NA)	20,930	19,256	(NA)
Minnesota	18,467.5	15,468.5	13,707.5	79,361	81,899	50,431
New Jersey	607.4	542.9	(NA)	18,334	13,868	(NA)
New York	3,307.6	2,765.1	3,431.2	31,992	36,257	40,422
Ohio	801.1	864.5	(NA)	20,829	23,342	(NA)
Oregon	4,541.0	5,924.5	4,839.1	36,283	44,492	38,103
Pennsylvania	737.2	590.9	(NA)	28,488	24,745	(NA)
Washington	15,493.4	16,560.0	15,750.0	94,772	84,080	85,806
Wisconsin	9,652.7	9,588.0	8,575.8	44,863	40,181	33,470
United States	75,369.4	73,381.3	62,498.3	892,179	864,064	652,057

See footnote(s) at end of table.

Table 4-15.—Sweet corn for fresh market and processing: Area harvested, production, price, and value, by State and United States, 2017–2019—Continued

Utilization and State	Utilized production			Price per unit			Value of utilized production		
	2017	2018	2019	2017	2018	2019	2017	2018	2019
	1,000 cwt			*Dollars per cwt*			*1,000 dollars*		
Fresh Market									
California	6,365.0	6,084.0	6,048.0	30.80	28.90	28.50	196,042	175,828	172,368
Delaware	423.4	362.9	(NA)	31.00	30.00	(NA)	13,125	10,887	(NA)
Florida	5,460.0	4,764.0	4,696.1	29.00	30.00	30.00	158,340	142,920	140,883
Georgia	3,935.7	4,345.7	3,050.5	25.00	25.70	24.60	98,393	111,684	75,042
Idaho	(D)	347.5	(NA)	(D)	35.00	(NA)	(D)	12,163	(NA)
Illinois	210.9	310.3	235.4	25.90	27.00	31.50	5,462	8,378	7,415
Indiana	351.0	389.5	(NA)	26.00	23.00	(NA)	9,126	8,959	(NA)
Maryland	353.2	335.3	(NA)	26.00	33.00	(NA)	9,183	11,065	(NA)
Michigan	910.0	837.2	(NA)	23.00	23.00	(NA)	20,930	19,256	(NA)
Minnesota	668.8	588.4	263.6	33.50	46.00	24.80	22,405	27,066	6,537
New Jersey	509.7	(D)	(NA)	35.00	(D)	(NA)	17,840	(D)	(NA)
New York	795.2	1,027.8	809.6	28.70	28.60	37.30	22,822	29,395	30,198
Ohio	801.1	864.5	(NA)	26.00	27.00	(NA)	20,829	23,342	(NA)
Oregon	454.1	521.4	685.0	29.50	27.30	25.00	13,396	14,234	17,125
Pennsylvania	(D)	(D)	(NA)	(D)	(D)	(NA)	(D)	(D)	(NA)
Washington	808.1	447.1	630.0	35.50	43.90	34.20	28,688	19,628	21,546
Wisconsin	405.8	326.0	354.4	30.80	26.80	21.60	12,499	8,737	7,655
Other States [1] ...	1,161.2	996.8	....	34.50	38.00	(X)	40,008	37,910	....
United States	23,613.2	22,548.4	16,772.6	29.20	29.30	28.50	689,088	661,452	478,769

Utilization and State	Utilized production			Price per unit			Value of utilized production		
	2017	2018	2019	2017	2018	2019	2017	2018	2019
	Tons			*Dollars per ton*			*1,000 dollars*		
Processing									
California	....	....	....	(X)	(X)	(X)	....	....	....
Delaware	54,432	57,456	(NA)	116.00	100.00	(NA)	6,314	5,746	(NA)
Florida	....	....	....	(X)	(X)	(X)	....	....	....
Georgia	....	....	....	(X)	(X)	(X)	....	....	....
Idaho	(D)	....	(NA)	(D)	(X)	(NA)	(D)	....	(NA)
Illinois	85,307	75,738	108,233	74.20	71.10	75.00	6,330	5,385	8,117
Indiana	....	....	(NA)	(X)	(X)	(NA)	....	....	(NA)
Maryland	26,492	31,833	(NA)	93.00	92.00	(NA)	2,464	2,920	(NA)
Michigan	....	....	(NA)	(X)	(X)	(NA)	....	....	(NA)
Minnesota	889,934	744,006	672,195	64.00	73.70	65.30	56,956	54,833	43,894
New Jersey	4,889	(D)	(NA)	101.00	(D)	(NA)	494	(D)	(NA)
New York	125,622	86,862	131,082	73.00	79.00	78.00	9,170	6,862	10,224
Ohio	....	....	(NA)	(X)	(X)	(NA)	....	....	(NA)
Oregon	204,345	270,157	207,701	112.00	112.00	101.00	22,887	30,258	20,978
Pennsylvania	(D)	(D)	(NA)	(D)	(D)	(NA)	(D)	(D)	(NA)
Washington	734,265	805,644	756,000	90.00	80.00	85.00	66,084	64,452	61,260
Wisconsin	462,316	463,100	411,070	70.00	67.00	62.80	32,364	31,444	25,815
Other States [1] ...	186	6,850	....	151.00	103.00	(X)	28	703	....
United States	2,587,818	2,541,646	2,286,281	78.50	79.70	75.80	203,091	202,612	173,288

(D) Withheld to avoid disclosing data for individual operations. (NA) Not available. (X) Not applicable. [1] Includes data withheld above.

NASS, Crops Branch, (202) 720–2127

Table 4-16.—Cucumbers for fresh market and processing: Area harvested, production, price, and value, by State and United States, 2017–2019

State	Area harvested			Total Production		
	2017	2018	2019	2017	2018	2019
	Acres			*1,000 cwt*		
Alabama	5,400	5,900	(NA)	756.0	619.5	(NA)
California	8,200	8,100	6,800	1,435.0	1,660.5	1,088.0
Delaware	(D)	(D)	(NA)	(D)	(D)	(NA)
Florida	25,900	24,900	23,000	5,309.5	4,233.0	3,450.0
Georgia	9,500	9,400	9,100	1,662.5	1,410.0	1,820.0
Michigan	37,500	34,400	39,600	5,625.0	4,128.0	5,940.0
New Jersey	2,900	2,600	(NA)	464.0	244.4	(NA)
North Carolina	10,500	9,600	11,400	1,680.0	1,488.0	1,653.0
Ohio	2,000	1,900	(NA)	340.0	294.5	(NA)
South Carolina	(D)	(D)	(NA)	(D)	(D)	(NA)
Texas	6,100	4,900	(D)	610.0	475.3	(D)
Wisconsin	5,900	5,100	(D)	737.5	612.0	(D)
Other States [1]	3,300	4,100	10,900	293.3	285.2	993.7
United States	117,200	110,900	100,800	18,912.8	15,450.4	14,944.7

State	Utilized production			Value of utilized production		
	2017	2018	2019	2017	2018	2019
	1,000 cwt			*1,000 dollars*		
Alabama	756.0	615.2	(NA)	16,659	15,379	(NA)
California	1,435.0	1,660.5	1,088.0	35,485	33,781	30,133
Delaware	(D)	(D)	(NA)	(D)	(D)	(NA)
Florida	5,309.5	4,233.0	3,443.1	137,601	118,524	89,277
Georgia	1,662.5	1,410.0	1,801.8	43,853	35,212	46,172
Michigan	5,625.0	4,123.9	5,928.1	79,739	55,418	70,560
New Jersey	463.1	240.7	(NA)	16,431	7,028	(NA)
North Carolina	1,664.9	1,482.0	1,653.0	28,699	25,582	25,478
Ohio	332.2	294.5	(NA)	5,376	4,983	(NA)
South Carolina	(D)	(D)	(NA)	(D)	(D)	(NA)
Texas	610.0	475.3	(D)	11,590	8,746	(D)
Wisconsin	736.0	603.4	(D)	11,531	12,913	(D)
Other States [1]	292.8	282.3	991.6	5,049	5,433	17,174
United States	18,887.0	15,420.8	14,905.6	392,013	322,999	278,794

Utilization and State	Utilized production			Price per unit			Value of utilized production		
	2017	2018	2019	2017	2018	2019	2017	2018	2019
	1,000 cwt			*Dollars per cwt*			*1,000 dollars*		
Fresh Market									
Alabama	(D)	(D)	(NA)	(D)	(D)	(NA)	(D)	(D)	(NA)
California	(D)	513.1	400.4	(D)	45.60	59.20	(D)	23,397	23,704
Delaware	(D)	(D)	(NA)	(D)	(D)	(NA)	(D)	(D)	(NA)
Florida	1,391.1	(D)	(D)	29.20	(D)	(D)	40,620	(D)	(D)
Georgia	(D)	(D)	(D)	(D)	(D)	(D)	(D)	(D)	(D)
Michigan	871.9	1,060.9	1,098.9	27.40	21.20	22.90	23,890	22,491	25,165
New Jersey	(D)	240.7	(NA)	(D)	29.20	(NA)	(D)	7,028	(NA)
North Carolina	445.2	626.4	271.1	22.00	22.40	16.50	9,794	14,031	4,473
Ohio	72.4	88.4	(NA)	32.10	27.80	(NA)	2,324	2,458	(NA)
South Carolina	(D)	(D)	(NA)	(D)	(D)	(NA)	(D)	(D)	(NA)
Texas	122.0	95.1	(D)	25.00	24.00	(D)	3,050	2,282	(D)
Wisconsin	(D)	(D)	(D)	(D)	(D)	(D)	(D)	(D)	(D)
Other States [1]	2,126.1	2,970.9	2,829.5	32.10	29.80	28.90	68,209	88,433	81,855
United States	5,028.7	5,595.5	4,599.9	29.40	28.60	29.40	147,887	160,120	135,197

See footnote(s) at end of table.

Table 4-16.—Cucumbers for fresh market and processing: Area harvested, production, price, and value, by State and United States, 2017–2019—Continued

Utilization and State	Utilized production			Price per unit			Value of utilized production		
	2017	2018	2019	2017	2018	2019	2017	2018	2019
	Tons			*Dollars per ton*			*1,000 dollars*		
Processing									
Alabama	(D)	(D)	(NA)	(D)	(D)	(NA)	(D)	(D)	(NA)
California	(D)	57,370	34,381	(D)	353.00	187.00	(D)	10,384	6,429
Delaware	(D)	(D)	(NA)	(D)	(D)	(NA)	(D)	(D)	(NA)
Florida	195,921	(D)	(D)	495.00	(D)	(D)	96,981	(D)	(D)
Georgia	(D)	(D)	(D)	(D)	(D)	(D)	(D)	(D)	(D)
Michigan	237,656	153,149	241,461	235.00	215.00	188.00	55,849	32,927	45,395
New Jersey	(D)	-	(NA)	(D)	(X)	(NA)	(D)	-	(NA)
North Carolina ..	60,984	42,780	69,095	310.00	270.00	304.00	18,905	11,551	21,005
Ohio	12,988	10,308	(NA)	235.00	245.00	(NA)	3,052	2,525	(NA)
South Carolina ..	(D)	(D)	(NA)	(D)	(D)	(NA)	(D)	(D)	(NA)
Texas	24,400	19,012	(D)	350.00	340.00	(D)	8,540	6,464	(D)
Wisconsin	(D)	(D)	(D)	(D)	(D)	(D)	(D)	(D)	(D)
Other States [1] ...	160,961	208,649	170,352	378.00	475.00	415.00	60,799	99,028	70,768
United States	692,910	491,268	515,289	313.00	352.00	279.00	244,126	162,879	143,597

(D) Withheld to avoid disclosing data for individual operations. (NA) Not available. (X) Not applicable. [1] Includes data withheld above.
NASS, Crops Branch, (202) 720–2127.

Table 4-17.—Garlic for fresh market and processing: Area harvested, production, price, and value, by State and United States, 2017–2019

State	Area harvested			Total Production		
	2017	2018	2019	2017	2018	2019
	Acres			*1,000 cwt*		
California	33,000	29,900	27,000	5,115.0	5,232.5	4,185.0
United States	33,000	29,900	27,000	5,115.0	5,232.5	4,185.0

State	Utilized production			Value of utilized production		
	2017	2018	2019	2017	2018	2019
	1,000 cwt			*1,000 dollars*		
California	5,115.0	5,232.5	4,185.0	390,021	412,587	327,277
United States	5,115.0	5,232.5	4,185.0	390,021	412,587	327,277

Utilization and State	Utilized production			Price per unit			Value of utilized production		
	2017	2018	2019	2017	2018	2019	2017	2018	2019
	1,000 cwt			*Dollars per cwt*			*1,000 dollars*		
Fresh Market									
California	1,754.4	1,831.4	1,464.8	184.00	190.00	190.00	322,810	347,966	278,312
United States	1,754.4	1,831.4	1,464.8	184.00	190.00	190.00	322,810	347,966	278,312
	Tons			*Dollars per ton*			*1,000 dollars*		
Processing									
California	168,028	170,056	136,013	400.00	380.00	360.00	67,211	64,621	48,965
United States	168,028	170,056	136,013	400.00	380.00	360.00	67,211	64,621	48,965

NASS, Crops Branch, (202) 720–2127.

Table 4-18.—Honeydew for fresh market: Area harvested, production, price, and value, by State and United States, 2017–2019

State	Area harvested			Yield per acre		
	2017	2018	2019	2017	2018	2019
	Acres			*Cwt*		
California	11,600	12,400	11,100	290.0	310.0	255.0
United States	11,600	12,400	11,100	290.0	310.0	255.0

State	Total production			Utilized production		
	2017	2018	2019	2017	2018	2019
	1,000 cwt			*1,000 cwt*		
California	3,364.0	3,844.0	2,830.5	3,364.0	3,844.0	2,830.5
United States	3,364.0	3,844.0	2,830.5	3,364.0	3,844.0	2,830.5

State	Price			Value of utilized production		
	2017	2018	2019	2017	2018	2019
	Dollars per cwt			*1,000 dollars*		
California	28.00	19.60	20.90	94,192	75,342	59,157
United States	28.00	19.60	20.90	94,192	75,342	59,157

NASS, Crops Branch, (202) 720–2127.

Table 4-19.—Head lettuce for fresh market: Area harvested, production, price, and value, by State and United States, 2017–2019

State	Area harvested			Yield per acre		
	2017	2018	2019	2017	2018	2019
	Acres			*Cwt*		
Arizona	39,200	38,600	37,300	315.0	310.0	335.0
California	101,500	81,700	77,200	365.0	350.0	375.0
United States	140,700	120,300	114,500	351.1	337.2	362.0

State	Total production			Utilized production		
	2017	2018	2019	2017	2018	2019
	1,000 cwt			*1,000 cwt*		
Arizona	12,348.0	11,966.0	12,495.5	12,348.0	11,966.0	12,495.5
California	37,047.5	28,595.0	28,950.0	37,047.5	28,595.0	28,950.0
United States	49,395.5	40,561.0	41,445.5	49,395.5	40,561.0	41,445.5

State	Price			Value of utilized production		
	2017	2018	2019	2017	2018	2019
	Dollars per cwt			*1,000 dollars*		
Arizona	45.90	37.90	86.90	566,773	453,511	1,085,859
California	32.60	26.80	30.20	1,207,749	766,346	874,290
United States	35.90	30.10	47.30	1,774,522	1,219,857	1,960,149

NASS, Crops Branch, (202) 720–2127.

Table 4-20.—Leaf lettuce for fresh market: Area harvested, production, price, and value, by State and United States, 2017–2019

State	Area harvested			Yield per acre		
	2017	2018	2019	2017	2018	2019
	Acres			*Cwt*		
Arizona	9,400	9,700	9,800	225.0	240.0	230.0
California	57,800	56,000	47,500	200.0	150.0	215.0
United States	67,200	65,700	57,300	203.5	163.3	217.6
State	**Total production**			**Utilized production**		
	2017	2018	2019	2017	2018	2019
	1,000 cwt			*1,000 cwt*		
Arizona	2,115.0	2,328.0	2,254.0	2,115.0	2,328.0	2,254.0
California	11,560.0	8,400.0	10,212.5	11,560.0	8,400.0	10,212.5
United States	13,675.0	10,728.0	12,466.5	13,675.0	10,728.0	12,466.5
State	**Price**			**Value of utilized production**		
	2017	2018	2019	2017	2018	2019
	Dollars per cwt			*1,000 dollars*		
Arizona	65.40	44.70	102.70	138,321	104,062	231,711
California	60.10	53.80	41.00	694,756	451,920	418,713
United States	60.90	51.80	52.20	833,077	555,982	650,424

NASS, Crops Branch, (202) 720–2127.

Table 4-21.—Romaine lettuce for fresh market: Area harvested, production, price, and value, by State and United States, 2017–2019

State	Area harvested			Yield per acre		
	2017	2018	2019	2017	2018	2019
	Acres			*Cwt*		
Arizona	27,200	26,900	23,900	340.0	330.0	330.0
California	90,200	72,700	64,000	300.0	280.0	305.0
United States	117,400	99,600	87,900	309.3	293.5	311.8
State	**Total production**			**Utilized production**		
	2017	2018	2019	2017	2018	2019
	1,000 cwt			*1,000 cwt*		
Arizona	9,248.0	8,877.0	7,887.0	9,248.0	8,877.0	7,887.0
California	27,060.0	20,356.0	19,520.0	27,060.0	20,152.4	19,324.8
United States	36,308.0	29,233.0	27,407.0	36,308.0	29,029.4	27,211.8
State	**Price**			**Value of utilized production**		
	2017	2018	2019	2017	2018	2019
	Dollars per cwt			*1,000 dollars*		
Arizona	55.50	37.50	44.30	513,264	332,888	349,394
California	41.20	28.20	27.50	1,114,872	568,298	531,432
United States	44.80	31.00	32.40	1,628,136	901,186	880,826

NASS, Crops Branch, (202) 720–2127.

Table 4-22.—Onions for fresh market and processing: Area harvested, production, price, and value, by State and United States, 2017–2019

State	Area harvested			Total Production		
	2017	2018	2019	2017	2018	2019
	Acres			*1,000 cwt*		
California	44,800	41,000	43,500	21,056.0	18,450.0	18,270.0
Colorado	3,600	2,600	2,500	1,656.0	1,170.0	1,147.5
Georgia	10,800	10,800	9,500	3,780.0	2,808.0	3,040.0
Idaho	12,500	8,400	10,900	9,062.5	7,476.0	8,938.0
New Mexico	7,100	7,100	6,600	4,828.0	4,189.0	3,993.0
New York	6,900	7,500	7,000	3,036.0	2,250.0	2,240.0
Oregon	24,500	19,300	20,300	16,163.5	15,494.0	14,921.0
Malheur County	13,700	11,800	12,500	9,521.5	9,794.0	9,500.0
All other counties	10,800	7,500	7,800	6,642.0	5,700.0	5,421.0
Texas	11,500	11,000	9,000	2,990.0	3,300.0	3,015.0
Washington	29,800	21,900	19,900	19,817.0	17,301.0	14,328.0
United States	151,500	129,600	129,400	82,389.0	72,438.0	69,892.5

State	Utilized production			Value of utilized production		
	2017	2018	2019	2017	2018	2019
	1,000 cwt			*1,000 dollars*		
California	21,056.0	18,154.9	18,270.0	291,568	240,220	294,676
Colorado	1,656.0	1,170.0	1,109.6	39,413	27,261	18,531
Georgia	3,685.5	2,794.0	2,973.1	128,301	110,519	144,181
Idaho	8,962.8	7,461.1	8,893.3	74,192	48,668	65,815
New Mexico	4,828.0	4,189.0	3,993.0	84,490	79,591	102,620
New York	2,620.1	2,196.0	2,047.4	50,682	42,752	36,140
Oregon	16,154.0	15,288.3	14,778.5	138,036	100,339	108,409
Malheur County	9,512.0	9,588.3	9,357.5	73,841	60,439	60,292
All other counties	6,642.0	5,700.0	5,421.0	64,195	39,900	48,117
Texas	2,990.0	3,234.0	2,954.7	73,913	61,380	51,038
Washington	18,608.2	16,436.0	13,625.9	161,495	176,211	180,576
United States	80,560.6	70,923.3	68,645.5	1,042,090	886,941	1,001,986

Utilization and State	Utilized production			Price per unit			Value of utilized production		
	2017	2018	2019	2017	2018	2019	2017	2018	2019
	1,000 cwt			*Dollars per cwt*			*1,000 dollars*		
Fresh Market									
California	15,328.8	8,542.4	9,719.6	14.50	19.40	23.50	222,268	165,723	228,411
Colorado	1,656.0	(D)	(D)	23.80	(D)	(D)	39,413	(D)	(D)
Georgia	(D)	(D)	(D)	(D)	(D)	(D)	(D)	(D)	(D)
Idaho	7,023.4	5,308.0	(D)	9.10	7.10	(D)	63,913	37,687	(D)
New Mexico	4,828.0	4,189.0	3,993.0	17.50	19.00	25.70	84,490	79,591	102,620
New York	2,529.0	(D)	1,953.3	19.50	(D)	17.90	49,316	(D)	34,964
Oregon	9,585.2	(D)	9,195.1	8.69	(D)	6.62	83,323	(D)	60,895
Malheur County	(D)	(D)	(D)	(D)	(D)	(D)	(D)	(D)	(D)
All other counties	(D)	(D)	(D)	(D)	(D)	(D)	(D)	(D)	(D)
Texas	(D)	(D)	(D)	(D)	(D)	(D)	(D)	(D)	(D)
Washington	(D)	11,764.7	(D)	(D)	12.00	(D)	(D)	141,176	(D)
Other States [1]	19,435.6	18,628.8	22,981.9	16.70	16.10	17.80	324,905	300,467	408,978
United States	60,386.0	48,432.9	47,842.9	14.40	15.00	17.50	867,628	724,644	835,868

See footnote(s) at end of table.

Table 4-22.—Onions for fresh market and processing: Area harvested, production, price, and value, by State and United States, 2017–2019—Continued

Utilization and State	Utilized production 2017	Utilized production 2018	Utilized production 2019	Price per unit 2017	Price per unit 2018	Price per unit 2019	Value of utilized production 2017	Value of utilized production 2018	Value of utilized production 2019
	Tons			*Dollars per ton*			*1,000 dollars*		
Processing									
California	286,362	480,623	427,518	242.00	155.00	155.00	69,300	74,497	66,265
Colorado	....	(D)	(D)	(X)	(D)	(D)	....	(D)	(D)
Georgia	(D)	(D)	(D)	(D)	(D)	(D)	(D)	(D)	(D)
Idaho	96,969	107,654	(D)	106.00	102.00	(D)	10,279	10,981	(D)
New Mexico	....	....	....	(X)	(X)	(X)	....	....	....
New York	4,554	(D)	4,704	300.00	(D)	250.00	1,366	(D)	1,176
Oregon	328,440	(D)	279,171	167.00	(D)	170.00	54,713	(D)	47,514
Malheur County	(D)	(D)	(D)	(D)	(D)	(D)	(D)	(D)	(D)
All other counties	(D)	(D)	(D)	(D)	(D)	(D)	(D)	(D)	(D)
Texas	(D)	(D)	(D)	(D)	(D)	(D)	(D)	(D)	(D)
Washington	(D)	233,564	(D)	(D)	150.00	(D)	(D)	35,035	(D)
Other States [1]	292,404	302,675	328,741	133.00	138.00	156.00	38,804	41,784	51,163
United States	1,008,729	1,124,516	1,040,134	173.00	144.00	160.00	174,462	162,297	166,118

(D) Withheld to avoid disclosing data for individual operations. (X) Not applicable. [1] Includes data withheld above.
NASS, Crops Branch, (202) 720–2127.

Table 4-23.—Green Peas for fresh market and processing: Area harvested, production, price, and value, by State and United States, 2017–2019

State	Area harvested 2017	Area harvested 2018	Area harvested 2019	Total Production 2017	Total Production 2018	Total Production 2019
	Acres			*1,000 cwt*		
Illinois	5,600	4,000	(NA)	207.2	168.0	(NA)
Minnesota	46,000	45,800	51,800	1,932.0	1,328.2	1,450.4
New York	8,900	6,700	(NA)	364.9	247.9	(NA)
Oregon	20,000	18,900	17,500	700.0	567.0	595.0
Washington	31,200	32,400	32,300	1,840.8	1,782.0	1,905.7
Wisconsin	22,500	23,300	26,500	967.5	978.6	1,086.5
United States	134,200	131,100	128,100	6,012.4	5,071.7	5,037.6

State	Utilized production 2017	Utilized production 2018	Utilized production 2019	Value of utilized production 2017	Value of utilized production 2018	Value of utilized production 2019
	1,000 cwt			*1,000 dollars*		
Illinois	207.2	168.0	(NA)	2,223	2,477	(NA)
Minnesota	1,932.0	1,326.9	1,447.5	24,651	17,306	19,473
New York	364.9	247.9	(NA)	6,760	3,351	(NA)
Oregon	700.0	567.0	595.0	8,706	7,190	6,896
Washington	1,840.8	1,780.2	1,903.8	28,772	22,700	30,157
Wisconsin	967.5	978.6	1,086.5	14,363	11,811	11,272
United States	6,012.4	5,068.6	5,032.8	85,475	64,901	67,798

Utilization and State	Utilized production 2017	Utilized production 2018	Utilized production 2019	Price per unit 2017	Price per unit 2018	Price per unit 2019	Value of utilized production 2017	Value of utilized production 2018	Value of utilized production 2019
	1,000 cwt			*Dollars per cwt*			*1,000 dollars*		
Fresh Market									
Illinois	(D)	(D)	(NA)	(D)	(D)	(NA)	(D)	(D)	(NA)
Minnesota	1.9	(D)	(D)	73.10	(D)	(D)	139	(D)	(D)
New York	20.1	5.5	(NA)	115.00	89.00	(NA)	2,312	490	(NA)
Oregon	(D)	(D)	(D)	(D)	(D)	(D)	(D)	(D)	(D)
Washington	(D)	(D)	(D)	(D)	(D)	(D)	(D)	(D)	(D)
Wisconsin	12.6	1.0	1.1	329.00	275.00	281.00	4,145	275	309
Other States [1]	66.1	3.9	25.0	75.60	173.00	185.00	4,999	675	4,618
United States	100.7	10.4	26.1	138.00	115.00	189.00	11,595	1,440	4,927

See footnote(s) at end of table.

Table 4-23.—Green Peas for fresh market and processing: Area harvested, production, price, and value, by State and United States, 2017–2019—Continued

Utilization and State	Utilized production			Price per unit			Value of utilized production		
	2017	2018	2019	2017	2018	2019	2017	2018	2019
	Tons			*Dollars per ton*			*1,000 dollars*		
Processing									
Illinois	(D)	(D)	(NA)	(D)	(D)	(NA)	(D)	(D)	(NA)
Minnesota	96,503	(D)	(D)	254.00	(D)	(D)	24,512	(D)	(D)
New York	17,242	12,122	(NA)	258.00	236.00	(NA)	4,448	2,861	(NA)
Oregon	(D)	(D)	(D)	(D)	(D)	(D)	(D)	(D)	(D)
Washington	(D)	(D)	(D)	(D)	(D)	(D)	(D)	(D)	(D)
Wisconsin	47,746	48,881	54,271	214.00	236.00	202.00	10,218	11,536	10,963
Other States [1]	134,093	191,913	196,068	259.00	256.00	265.00	34,702	49,064	51,908
United States	295,584	252,916	250,339	250.00	251.00	251.00	73,880	63,461	62,871

(D) Withheld to avoid disclosing data for individual operations. (NA) Not available. [1] Includes data withheld above.
NASS, Crops Branch, (202) 720–2127.

Table 4-24.—Bell peppers for fresh market and processing: Area harvested, production, price, and value, by State and United States, 2017–2019

State	Area harvested			Total Production		
	2017	2018	2019	2017	2018	2019
	Acres			*1,000 cwt*		
California	15,900	13,500	15,000	6,678.0	6,075.0	5,400.0
Florida	12,000	11,900	11,800	4,020.0	3,570.0	3,481.0
Georgia	3,400	3,200	3,600	986.0	848.0	1,116.0
Michigan	2,200	2,000	2,100	561.0	480.0	535.0
New Jersey	3,400	3,400	3,500	952.0	935.0	1,050.0
New York	900	1,400	(NA)	103.5	154.0	(NA)
North Carolina	2,100	2,000	2,300	567.0	400.0	552.0
Ohio	1,300	1,400	(NA)	292.5	280.0	(NA)
Pennsylvania	1,000	900	(NA)	230.0	153.0	(NA)
United States	42,200	39,700	38,300	14,390.0	12,895.0	12,134.5

State	Utilized production			Value of utilized production		
	2017	2018	2019	2017	2018	2019
	1,000 cwt			*1,000 dollars*		
California	6,504.4	6,075.0	5,400.0	282,452	210,007	181,400
Florida	4,020.0	3,570.0	3,481.0	188,940	180,642	234,968
Georgia	986.0	848.0	1,104.8	43,581	40,110	54,467
Michigan	561.0	480.0	531.8	15,318	18,220	19,674
New Jersey	951.0	929.4	1,042.7	39,381	39,726	45,854
New York	97.3	154.0	(NA)	5,196	8,455	(NA)
North Carolina	567.0	376.0	529.9	25,487	15,685	21,297
Ohio	292.5	280.0	(NA)	11,700	12,040	(NA)
Pennsylvania	213.9	151.8	(NA)	13,522	8,422	(NA)
United States	14,193.1	12,864.2	12,090.2	625,577	533,307	557,660

Utilization and State	Utilized production			Price per unit			Value of utilized production		
	2017	2018	2019	2017	2018	2019	2017	2018	2019
	1,000 cwt			*Dollars per cwt*			*1,000 dollars*		
Fresh Market									
California	4,480.9	4,835.7	2,970.0	54.50	39.20	50.40	244,209	189,559	149,688
Florida	4,020.0	3,570.0	3,481.0	47.00	50.60	67.50	188,940	180,642	234,968
Georgia	986.0	848.0	1,104.8	44.20	47.30	49.30	43,581	40,110	54,467
Michigan	(D)	(D)	(D)	(D)	(D)	(D)	(D)	(D)	(D)
New Jersey	(D)	865.8	924.0	(D)	44.80	47.50	(D)	38,788	43,890
New York	97.3	154.0	(NA)	53.40	54.90	(NA)	5,196	8,455	(NA)
North Carolina	(D)	(D)	(D)	(D)	(D)	(D)	(D)	(D)	(D)
Ohio	(D)	280.0	(NA)	(D)	43.00	(NA)	(D)	12,040	(NA)
Pennsylvania	(D)	(D)	(NA)	(D)	(D)	(NA)	(D)	(D)	(NA)
Other States [1]	2,419.7	981.1	1,023.7	42.40	42.30	39.00	102,575	41,468	39,930
United States	12,003.9	11,534.6	9,503.5	48.70	44.30	55.00	584,501	511,062	522,943

See footnote(s) at end of table.

Table 4-24.—Bell peppers for fresh market and processing: Area harvested, production, price, and value, by State and United States, 2017–2019—Continued

Utilization and State	Utilized production			Price per unit			Value of utilized production		
	2017	2018	2019	2017	2018	2019	2017	2018	2019
	Tons			*Dollars per ton*			*1,000 dollars*		
Processing									
California	101,172	61,965	121,500	378.00	330.00	261.00	38,243	20,448	31,712
Florida	....	....	....	(X)	(X)	(X)	....	....	....
Georgia	....	....	....	(X)	(X)	(X)	....	....	....
Michigan	(D)	(D)	(D)	(D)	(D)	(D)	(D)	(D)	(D)
New Jersey	(D)	3,179	5,933	(D)	295.00	331.00	(D)	938	1,964
New York	....	....	(NA)	(X)	(X)	(NA)	....	....	(NA)
North Carolina	(D)	(D)	(D)	(D)	(D)	(D)	(D)	(D)	(D)
Ohio	(D)	....	(NA)	(D)	(X)	(NA)	(D)	....	(NA)
Pennsylvania	(D)	(D)	(NA)	(D)	(D)	(NA)	(D)	(D)	(NA)
Other States [1]	8,293	1,336	1,899	342.00	643.00	548.00	2,833	859	1,041
United States	109,465	66,480	129,332	375.00	335.00	268.00	41,076	22,245	34,717

(D) Withheld to avoid disclosing data for individual operations. (NA) Not available. (X) Not applicable. [1] Includes data withheld above.
NASS, Crops Branch, (202) 720–2127.

Table 4-25.—Chili peppers for fresh market and processing: Area harvested, production, price, and value, by State and United States, 2017–2019

State	Area harvested			Total Production		
	2017	2018	2019	2017	2018	2019
	Acres			*1,000 cwt*		
Arizona	1,200	1,100	(NA)	78.0	66.0	(NA)
California	4,800	2,700	1,500	1,872.0	1,039.5	382.5
New Mexico	7,600	7,900	8,700	1,254.0	1,422.0	1,261.5
Texas	2,400	2,500	(NA)	132.0	137.5	(NA)
United States	16,000	14,200	10,200	3,336.0	2,665.0	1,644.0

State	Utilized production			Value of utilized production		
	2017	2018	2019	2017	2018	2019
	1,000 cwt			*1,000 dollars*		
Arizona	78.0	66.0	(NA)	2,039	2,660	(NA)
California	1,872.0	1,039.5	382.1	58,874	29,468	13,703
New Mexico	1,254.0	1,422.0	1,261.5	44,553	53,766	50,008
Texas	132.0	137.5	(NA)	8,096	8,873	(NA)
United States	3,336.0	2,665.0	1,643.6	113,562	94,767	63,711

Utilization and State	Utilized production			Price per unit			Value of utilized production		
	2017	2018	2019	2017	2018	2019	2017	2018	2019
	1,000 cwt			*Dollars per cwt*			*1,000 dollars*		
Fresh Market									
Arizona	(D)	(D)	(NA)	(D)	(D)	(NA)	(D)	(D)	(NA)
California	280.8	187.1	187.0	44.20	43.60	48.50	12,411	8,158	9,070
New Mexico	263.3	270.2	227.1	30.00	37.00	38.00	7,899	9,997	8,630
Texas	(D)	(D)	(NA)	(D)	(D)	(NA)	(D)	(D)	(NA)
Other States [1]	55.9	94.5	....	53.10	64.80	(X)	2,968	6,128	....
United States	600.0	551.8	414.1	38.80	44.00	42.70	23,278	24,283	17,700
	Tons			*Dollars per ton*			*1,000 dollars*		
Processing									
Arizona	(D)	(D)	(NA)	(D)	(D)	(NA)	(D)	(D)	(NA)
California	79,560	42,620	9,754	584.00	500.00	475.00	46,463	21,310	4,633
New Mexico	49,533	57,591	51,722	740.00	760.00	800.00	36,654	43,769	41,378
Texas	(D)	(D)	(NA)	(D)	(D)	(NA)	(D)	(D)	(NA)
Other States [1]	7,704	5,448	....	930.00	992.00	(X)	7,167	5,405	....
United States	136,797	105,659	61,476	660.00	667.00	748.00	90,284	70,484	46,011

(D) Withheld to avoid disclosing data for individual operations. (NA) Not available. (X) Not applicable. [1] Includes data withheld above.
NASS, Crops Branch, (202) 720–2127.

Table 4-26.—Potatoes: Area, yield, production, season average price, and value, United States, 2009–2018

Year	Area planted	Area harvested	Yield per harvested acre	Production	Season average price per cwt received by farmers	Value of production
	1,000 acres	*1,000 acres*	*Cwt*	*1,000 cwt*	*Dollars*	*1,000 dollars*
2009	1,071.2	1,044.0	414	432,601	8.25	3,557,574
2010	1,026.7	1,008.9	401	404,549	9.20	3,724,821
2011	1,100.7	1,078.5	399	430,037	9.41	4,044,869
2012	1,154.8	1,138.5	408	464,970	8.63	4,017,245
2013	1,063.9	1,050.9	414	434,652	9.75	4,237,284
2014	1,062.6	1,051.1	421	442,170	8.88	3,928,211
2015	1,066.1	1,054.4	418	441,205	8.76	3,865,538
2016	1,056.7	1,037.7	434	450,324	9.08	4,090,689
2017	1,052.6	1,044.5	432	450,921	9.17	4,133,073
2018	1,026.5	1,014.8	443	450,020	8.90	4,006,340

NASS, Crops Branch, (202) 720–2127.

Table 4-27.—Potatoes: Area harvested, yield, and production by seasonal group, by State and United States, 2016–2018

Season and State	Area harvested			Yield			Production		
	2016	2017	2018	2016	2017	2018	2016	2017	2018
	1,000 acres	*1,000 acres*	*1,000 acres*	*Cwt*	*Cwt*	*Cwt*	*1,000 cwt*	*1,000 cwt*	*1,000 cwt*
Spring:									
California	30.4	33.5	31.0	390	435	395	11,856	14,573	12,245
Florida	22.9	28.7	20.8	235	250	265	5,382	7,175	5,512
United States	53.3	62.2	51.8	323	350	343	17,238	21,748	17,757
Summer:									
Illinois	7.4	8.1	7.6	380	410	375	2,812	3,321	2,850
Kansas	4.2	4.1	3.3	300	380	430	1,260	1,558	1,419
Maryland	(D)	2.5	2.0	(D)	365	255	(D)	913	510
Missouri	7.9	8.5	7.4	305	285	225	2,410	2,423	1,665
New Jersey	(D)	2.0	2.0	(D)	300	265	(D)	600	530
North Carolina	13.6	15.1	12.2	220)	230	190	2,992	3,473	2,318
Texas	21.0	22.8	17.5	395	390	425	8,295	8,892	7,438
Virginia	4.1	4.5	4.4	290	265	235	1,189	1,193	1,034
Other States [1]	4.6	....	....	313	....	....	1,440	....	....
United States	62.8	67.6	56.4	325	331	315	20,398	22,373	17,764
Fall:									
Alaska [2]	(X)	(X)	0.5	(X)	(X)	280	(X)	(X)	140
California	7.9	8.2	7.3	445	405	440	3,516	3,321	3,212
Colorado	57.1	55.6	55.0	389	382	395	22,236	21,220	21,722
San Luis Valley	51.5	51.5	51.6	385	375	390	19,828	19,313	20,124
All other areas	5.6	4.1	3.4	430	465	470	2,408	1,907	1,598
Idaho	324.0	310.0	315.0	430	435	450	139,320	134,850	141,750
Maine	46.5	47.5	48.5	325	320	310	15,113	15,200	15,035
Michigan	47.0	49.5	48.0	370	370	380	17,390	18,315	18,240
Minnesota	43.0	45.5	43.5	400	405	430	17,200	18,428	18,705
Montana	11.0	11.1	11.1	335	340	350	3,685	3,774	3,885
Nebraska	16.4	19.0	19.3	450	475	480	7,380	9,025	9,264
New York	14.8	14.4	13.4	240	280	290	3,552	4,032	3,886
North Dakota	72.0	74.0	73.0	300	330	325	21,600	24,420	23,725
Oregon	44.9	45.9	45.0	590	550	600	26,491	25,245	27,000
Washington	169.0	164.0	160.0	625	605	630	105,625	99,220	100,800
Wisconsin	68.0	70.0	67.0	435	425	405	29,580	29,750	27,135
United States [3]	921.6	914.7	906.6	448	445	457	412,688	406,800	414,499
All Potatoes:									
United States [3]	1,037.7	1,044.5	1,014.8	434	432	443	450,324	450,921	450,020

(D) Withheld to avoid disclosing data for individual operations. (X) Not applicable. [1] Includes data withheld above. [2] Previously included in Alaska table. [3] Beginning in 2018, United States total includes data for Alaska.
NASS, Crops Branch, (202) 720–2127.

Table 4-28.—Fall potatoes: Stocks held by growers, local dealers, and processors [1] - 13 Fall States: 2017 and 2018 [1]

State	Current year	Following year		
	Dec. 1, 2017	Feb. 1, 2018	Apr. 1, 2018	June 1, 2018
	1,000 cwt			
California	2,600	1,800	1,100	(D)
Colorado	15,300	11,400	7,200	2,800
Idaho	96,000	75,000	52,000	27,000
Maine	11,500	8,500	5,000	1,700
Michigan	11,000	6,900	3,800	(D)
Minnesota	13,600	10,400	7,200	3,900
Montana	3,500	3,400	2,800	240
Nebraska	5,400	3,900	2,100	(D)
New York	2,300	1,300	800	300
North Dakota	20,600	15,300	9,600	4,000
Oregon	19,800	13,300	8,300	3,500
Washington	57,000	45,000	29,000	13,000
Wisconsin	19,300	14,400	9,900	5,300
Other States [2]				2,000
United States	277,900	210,600	138,800	63,740
Klamath Basin [3]	5,000	3,300	1,800	(D)

State	Current year	Following year		
	Dec. 1, 2018	Feb. 1, 2019	Apr. 1, 2019	June 1, 2019
	1,000 cwt			
California	2,200	(D)	900	(D)
Colorado	15,600	11,600	7,600	3,000
Idaho	101,000	79,000	57,000	34,000
Maine	10,900	7,800	4,700	1,500
Michigan	10,500	6,700	3,400	300
Minnesota	12,800	9,700	6,700	4,200
Montana	3,700	3,600	3,100	70
Nebraska	5,000	3,700	2,300	(D)
New York	2,000	(D)	800	400
North Dakota	17,000	11,700	6,000	2,800
Oregon	21,100	14,500	9,800	3,900
Washington	57,500	46,000	29,500	14,800
Wisconsin	20,000	15,700	12,000	4,700
Other States [2]		2,800		700
United States	279,300	212,800	144,700	70,370
Klamath Basin [3]	5,100	(D)	1,700	(D)

(D) Withheld to avoid disclosing data for individual operations. [1] Stocks are defined as the quantity (whether sold or not) remaining in storage for all purposes and uses, including seed potatoes that are not yet moved, and shrinkage, waste, and other losses that occur after the date of each estimate. [2] Includes data withheld above. [3] Includes potato stocks in California and Klamath County, Oregon.
NASS, Crops Branch, (202) 720–2127.

Table 4-29.—Fall potatoes: Production and total stocks held by growers and local dealers, 13 Major States, 2009–2018

Crop year	Production	Total stocks			
		Dec. 1	Following year		
			Feb. 1	Apr. 1	June 1
	1,000 cwt	1,000 cwt	1,000 cwt	1,000 cwt	1,000 cwt
2009	383,962	265,800	203,500	128,700	55,120
2010	357,467	240,200	180,300	111,000	41,320
2011	382,318	253,000	187,500	115,650	43,340
2012	410,367	271,500	204,600	(NA)	(NA)
2013	386,824	(NA)	(NA)	119,050	46,885
2014	396,798	265,700	200,800	128,700	56,335
2015	404,701	262,700	198,100	125,700	51,280
2016	450,324	275,800	213,000	142,600	67,570
2017	450,921	277,900	210,600	138,800	63,740
2018	450,020	279,300	212,800	144,700	70,370

(NA) Not available.
NASS, Crops Branch, (202) 720–2127.

Table 4-30.—Potatoes: Production, seed used, and disposition, United States, 2009–2018

Year	Production	Total used for seed	Used on farms where produced		Sold
			For seed, feed, and household use	Shrinkage and loss	
	1,000 cwt				
2009	432,601	24,027	4,535	29,135	398,931
2010	404,549	25,100	4,227	24,996	375,326
2011	430,037	26,527	4,146	27,789	398,102
2012	464,970	25,656	4,850	28,505	431,615
2013	434,652	25,249	4,323	26,211	404,118
2014	442,170	26,259	4,192	26,762	411,216
2015	441,205	25,715	4,631	26,509	410,065
2016	450,324	26,167	4,437	26,883	419,004
2017	450,921	24,673	4,410	25,139	421,372
2018	450,020	24,973	4,047	25,526	420,447

NASS, Crops Branch, (202) 720–2127.

Table 4-31.—Potatoes: Utilization and processing, Program States, 2017 and 2018

Utilization items	2017	2018
	1,000 cwt	*1,000 cwt*
Sales		
Table stock	109,824	106,462
Processing	284,411	289,209
Other sales		
Livestock feed	1,913	697
Seed	25,224	24,079
Other Sales Total	27,137	24,776
Total sales	421,372	420,447
Non-sales		
Seed used on farms where grown	3,526	3,491
Household use and used for feed on farms where grown	884	556
Shrinkage and loss	25,139	25,526
Total non-sales	29,549	29,573
Total production	450,921	450,020
Processing - United States	**2016**	**2017**
	1,000 cwt	*1,000 cwt*
Processing		
Chips and shoestring	58,751	62,700
All Dehydrated (including starch and flour)	45,761	49,066
Frozen french fries	155,798	162,640
Other frozen products	13,803	15,956
Canned potatoes	1,152	1,113
Other canned products (hash, stews, soups)	703	758
Other (including fresh pack, potato salad, vodka, etc)	6,160	5,550
Total	282,128	297,783

NASS, Crops Branch, (202) 720–2127.

Table 4-32.—Potatoes: Production, seed use, and farm disposition, by seasonal groups, by States and United States, 2017 crop[1]

Season and State	Production	Total used for seed	Used on farms where produced		Sold
			For seed, feed, and household use	Shrinkage and loss	
	1,000 cwt				
Spring					
California	14,573	776	227	291	14,055
Florida	7,175	684	17	145	7,013
United States	21,748	1,460	244	436	21,068
Summer					
Illinois	3,321	127	....	33	3,288
Kansas	1,558	114	....	....	1,558
Maryland	913	(D)	(D)	(D)	(D)
Missouri	2,423	183	....	....	2,423
New Jersey	600	(D)	(D)	(D)	(D)
North Carolina	3,473	294	1	1	3,471
Texas	8,892	420	22	....	8,870
Virginia	1,193	93	....	4	1,189
Other States[2]	....	84	1	1	1,511
United States	22,373	1,315	24	39	22,310
Fall					
California	3,321	203	....	13	3,308
Colorado	21,220	1,383	981	1,550	18,689
Idaho	134,850	7,529	808	8,300	125,742
Maine	15,200	1,092	221	879	14,100
Michigan	18,315	1,344	379	623	17,313
Minnesota	18,428	880	86	1,071	17,271
Montana	3,774	264	275	189	3,310
Nebraska	9,025	546	259	640	8,126
New York	4,032	375	56	236	3,740
North Dakota	24,420	1,517	200	1,500	22,720
Oregon	25,245	882	271	1,575	23,399
Washington	99,220	4,208	263	6,040	92,917
Wisconsin	29,750	1,675	343	2,048	27,359
United States	406,800	21,898	4,142	24,664	377,994
All potatoes					
United States	450,921	24,673	4,4104	25,139	421,372

(D) Withheld to avoid disclosing data for individual operations. [1] Totals may not add due to rounding. [2] Includes data withheld above.

NASS, Crops Branch, (202) 720–2127.

Table 4-33.—Potatoes: Production, seed use, and farm disposition, by seasonal groups, by States and United States, 2018 crop[1]

Season and State	Production	Total used for seed	Used on farms where produced		Sold
			For seed, feed, and household use	Shrinkage and loss	
	1,000 cwt				
Spring					
California	12,245	748	4	495	11,746
Florida	5,512	564	1	82	5,429
United States	17,757	1,312	5	577	17,175
Summer					
Illinois	2,850	214		20	2,830
Kansas	1,419	92			1,419
Maryland	510	48	1	1	508
Missouri	1,665	163		210	1,455
New Jersey	530	33		1	529
North Carolina	2,318	391			2,318
Texas	7,438	401	28	25	7,385
Virginia	1,034	119			1,034
United States	17,764	1,461	29	257	17,478
Fall					
California	3,212	195		62	3,150
Colorado	21,722	1,350	945	1,616	19,161
Idaho	141,750	7,592	795	8,700	132,255
Maine	15,035	1,100	252	783	14,000
Michigan	18,240	1,400	373	680	17,187
Minnesota	18,705	738	67	1,028	17,610
Montana	3,885	289	202	190	3,493
Nebraska	9,264	566	217	825	8,222
New York	3,886	343	45	181	3,660
North Dakota	23,725	1,548	150	2,000	21,575
Oregon	27,000	1,148	341	1,680	24,979
Washington	100,800	4,241	258	5,800	94,742
Wisconsin	27,135	1,680	344	1,136	25,655
United States	414,499	22,200	4,013	24,692	385,794
All potatoes					
United States	450,020	24,973	4,047	25,526	420,447

[1] United States and totals may not add due to rounding.
NASS, Crops Branch, (202) 720–2127.

Table 4-34.—Potatoes, fresh & seed: United States exports by country of destination and imports by country of origin, 2017–2019

Country	2017	2018	2019
	Metric tons		
Imports			
Canada	501,679	486,399	412,260
Colombia	50	40	35
Ghana	9	0	23
China	0	4	15
Ecuador	30	32	14
Togo	0	0	4
Peru	1	3	1
Costa Rica	0	3	0
Netherlands	24	0	0
World Total	501,794	486,481	412,351
Exports			
Canada	265,211	207,226	278,047
Mexico	93,206	113,027	100,529
Japan	39,876	33,914	32,348
Taiwan	42,883	30,443	32,172
Philippines	22,271	12,090	20,150
Korea, South	20,974	22,639	14,229
Malaysia	12,355	9,725	13,769
Dominican Republic	6,230	8,207	8,609
Honduras	10,175	10,227	8,604
Thailand	3,057	5,630	7,447
Singapore	5,489	4,892	5,116
Hong Kong	3,648	3,346	4,293
Guatemala	3,032	2,411	3,892
Bahamas, The	1,531	1,495	2,316
Costa Rica	1,270	1,021	2,198
Vietnam	221	1,557	1,527
Leeward-Windward Islands(*)	1,212	1,741	1,459
Panama	3,139	2,981	1,398
Cayman Islands	743	968	968
Nicaragua	809	963	781
French Pacific Islands(*)	262	449	757
Trinidad and Tobago	807	601	703
United Arab Emirates	558	653	633
El Salvador	618	406	593
Netherlands Antilles(*)	285	389	517
Turks and Caicos Islands	171	275	475
Kuwait	81	70	361
Barbados	196	185	298
Chile	142	183	290
Bermuda	262	302	271
Rest of World	5,614	3,040	1,432
World Total	546,324	481,056	546,210

(*) Denotes a country that is a summarization of its component countries.
FAS, Office of Global Analysis, (202) 720-6301.

Table 4-35.—Potatoes (fresh market): Foreign trade, United States, 2009–2018[1]

Year beginning July	Imports for consumption	Domestic exports
	1,000 cwt.	1,000 cwt.
2009/2010	9,050	8,183
2010/2011	10,384	9,294
2011/2012	9,041	9,348
2012/2013	7,375	10,467
2013/2014	10,833	10,001
2014/2015	8,514	9,369
2015/2016	10,103	10,135
2016/2017	11,265	11,306
2017/2018	10,852	10,865
2018/2019	....	....

[1] Includes seed.
ERS, (202) 694–5253. Based on data from U.S. Department of Commerce, U.S. Census Bureau.

Table 4-36.—Pumpkins for fresh market and processing: Area harvested, production, price, and value, by State and United States, 2017–2019[1]

State	Area harvested			Total Production		
	2017	2018	2019	2017	2018	2019
	Acres			*1,000 cwt*		
California	4,400	4,900	4,700	1,452.0	1,347.5	1,198.5
Illinois	17,400	11,000	10,900	6,438.0	5,170.0	4,196.5
Indiana	6,000	5,500	5,000	960.0	1,265.0	1,225.0
Michigan	4,900	5,400	5,400	759.5	1,026.0	810.0
Minnesota	1,800	1,400	(NA)	162.0	427.0	(NA)
New Jersey	2,100	1,700	(NA)	199.5	110.5	(NA)
New York	5,600	5,700	5,700	588.0	467.4	410.4
North Carolina	2,700	2,300	3,100	567.0	253.0	713.0
Ohio	3,500	3,700	3,500	595.0	666.0	437.5
Oregon	2,500	2,500	1,900	450.0	675.0	598.5
Pennsylvania	6,900	5,700	6,300	1,138.5	655.5	661.5
Tennessee	1,400	1,600	(NA)	124.6	116.8	(NA)
Texas	4,500	4,900	(D)	877.5	1,617.0	(D)
Virginia	3,200	5,200	5,600	720.0	1,066.0	924.0
Washington	2,600	2,400	2,600	468.0	300.0	442.0
Wisconsin	2,800	3,700	(D)	420.0	244.2	(D)
Other States	....	....	6,500	....	....	1,834.0
United States	72,300	67,600	61,200	15,919.6	15,406.9	13,450.9

State	Utilized production			Value of utilized production		
	2017	2018	2019	2017	2018	2019
	1,000 cwt			*1,000 dollars*		
California	1,450.5	1,339.4	1,191.3	20,742	27,592	22,754
Illinois	6,302.8	5,139.0	4,192.3	24,421	13,751	17,085
Indiana	959.0	1,252.4	1,221.3	18,457	16,971	16,982
Michigan	758.0	1,010.6	806.8	8,314	14,947	12,909
Minnesota	139.3	419.3	(NA)	3,691	12,369	(NA)
New Jersey	198.1	108.8	(NA)	6,101	4,178	(NA)
New York	570.4	435.1	380.4	11,123	8,037	8,635
North Carolina	560.8	250.5	703.0	10,437	6,609	10,991
Ohio	586.7	652.0	434.4	7,968	11,024	9,911
Oregon	427.5	645.3	568.6	6,514	9,781	5,147
Pennsylvania	1,110.0	620.8	646.9	19,503	13,852	16,777
Tennessee	111.6	103.4	(NA)	2,132	2,264	(NA)
Texas	864.3	1,615.4	(D)	23,163	24,069	(D)
Virginia	718.6	1,024.4	903.7	10,348	15,366	16,427
Washington	446.5	296.1	399.6	12,604	11,844	15,544
Wisconsin	396.5	214.7	(D)	11,023	2,791	(D)
Other States	....	....	1,772.8	....	....	27,028
United States	15,600.6	15,127.2	13,221.1	196,541	195,445	180,190

See footnote(s) at end of table.

Table 4-36.—Pumpkins for fresh market: Area harvested, production, price, and value, by State and United States, 2017–2019 [1]—Continued

Utilization and State	Utilized production			Price per unit			Value of utilized production		
	2017	2018	2019	2017	2018	2019	2017	2018	2019
	1,000 cwt			*Dollars per cwt*			*1,000 dollars*		
Fresh Market									
California	1,450.5	1,339.4	1,191.3	14.30	20.60	19.10	20,742	27,592	22,754
Illinois	(D)	325.7	537.2	(D)	16.80	18.40	(D)	5,472	9,884
Indiana	(D)	(D)	(D)	(D)	(D)	(D)	(D)	(D)	(D)
Michigan	(D)	(D)	806.8	(D)	(D)	16.00	(D)	(D)	12,909
Minnesota	139.3	419.3	(NA)	26.50	29.50	(NA)	3,691	12,369	(NA)
New Jersey	198.1	108.8	(NA)	30.80	38.40	(NA)	6,101	4,178	(NA)
New York	570.4	(D)	380.4	19.50	(D)	22.70	11,123	(D)	8,635
North Carolina	(D)	(D)	(D)	(D)	(D)	(D)	(D)	(D)	(D)
Ohio	(D)	(D)	(D)	(D)	(D)	(D)	(D)	(D)	(D)
Oregon	(D)	276.1	139.5	(D)	25.80	20.90	(D)	7,123	2,916
Pennsylvania	(D)	(D)	(D)	(D)	(D)	(D)	(D)	(D)	(D)
Tennessee	111.6	103.4	(NA)	19.10	21.90	(NA)	2,132	2,264	(NA)
Texas	864.3	1,615.4	(D)	26.80	14.90	(D)	23,163	24,069	(D)
Virginia	718.6	1,024.4	(D)	14.40	15.00	(D)	10,348	15,366	(D)
Washington	(D)	296.1	399.6	(D)	40.00	38.90	(D)	11,844	15,544
Wisconsin	396.5	214.7	(D)	27.80	13.00	(D)	11,023	2,791	(D)
Other States [1]	5,234.5	4,154.9	5,615.7	18.10	17.00	17.30	94,540	70,771	97,424
United States	9,683.8	9,878.2	9,070.5	18.90	18.60	18.70	182,863	183,839	170,066
	Tons			*Dollars per ton*			*1,000 dollars*		
Processing									
California	....	....	....	(X)	(X)	(X)	....	....	....
Illinois	(D)	240,664	182,758	(D)	34.40	39.40	(D)	8,279	7,201
Indiana	(D)	(D)	(D)	(D)	(D)	(D)	(D)	(D)	(D)
Michigan	(D)	(D)	....	(D)	(D)	(X)	(D)	(D)	....
Minnesota	....	....	(NA)	(X)	(X)	(NA)	....	....	(NA)
New Jersey	....	....	(NA)	(X)	(X)	(NA)	....	....	(NA)
New York	....	(D)	....	(X)	(D)	(X)	....	(D)	....
North Carolina	(D)	(D)	(D)	(D)	(D)	(D)	(D)	(D)	(D)
Ohio	(D)	(D)	(D)	(D)	(D)	(D)	(D)	(D)	(D)
Oregon	(D)	18,461	21,456	(D)	144.00	104.00	(D)	2,658	2,231
Pennsylvania	(D)	(D)	(D)	(D)	(D)	(D)	(D)	(D)	(D)
Tennessee	....	....	(NA)	(X)	(X)	(NA)	....	....	(NA)
Texas	....	....	(D)	(X)	(X)	(D)	....	....	(D)
Virginia	....	....	(D)	(X)	(X)	(D)	....	....	(D)
Washington	(D)	....	....	(D)	(X)	(X)	(D)	....	....
Wisconsin	....	....	(D)	(X)	(X)	(D)	....	....	(D)
Other States [1]	295,841	3,325	3,324	46.20	201.00	208.00	13,678	669	692
United States	295,841	262,450	207,538	46.20	44.20	48.80	13,678	11,606	10,124

(D) Withheld to avoid disclosing data for individual operations. (NA) Not available. (X) Not applicable. [1] Includes data withheld above.

NASS, Crops Branch, (202) 720–2127.

Table 4-37.—Spinach for fresh market and processing: Area Harvested, production, price, and value, by State and United States, 2017–2019

State	Area harvested 2017	Area harvested 2018	Area harvested 2019	Utilized production 2017	Utilized production 2018	Utilized production 2019
	Acres			*1,000 cwt*		
Arizona	12,200	11,100	(D)	1,830.0	1,887.0	(D)
California	46,400	44,200	50,100	5,104.0	5,525.0	7,014.0
Colorado	(D)	(D)	(NA)	(D)	(D)	(NA)
Maryland	(D)	(D)	(NA)	(D)	(D)	(NA)
New Jersey	2,100	2,000	1,900	315.0	230.0	228.0
Texas	2,800	2,800	(D)	672.0	322.0	(D)
Other States [1]	1,230	1,350	13,800	169.6	138.5	2,364.0
United States	64,730	61,450	65,800	8,090.6	8,102.5	9,606.0

State	Price per cwt 2017	Price per cwt 2018	Price per cwt 2019	Value of utilized production 2017	Value of utilized production 2018	Value of utilized production 2019
	Dollars			*1,000 dollars*		
Arizona	53.30	44.40	(D)	97,539	83,783	(D)
California	67.20	57.30	55.40	342,809	316,699	388,741
Colorado	(D)	(D)	(NA)	(D)	(D)	(NA)
Maryland	(D)	(D)	(NA)	(D)	(D)	(NA)
New Jersey	28.70	22.70	29.20	9,039	5,230	6,658
Texas	28.80	19.10	(D)	19,369	6,138	(D)
Other States [1]	12.40	27.60	55.60	2,104	3,821	131,371
United States	58.20	49.90	54.80	470,860	415,671	526,770

State	Utilized production 2017	Utilized production 2018	Utilized production 2019	Price per unit 2017	Price per unit 2018	Price per unit 2019	Value of utilized production 2017	Value of utilized production 2018	Value of utilized production 2019
	1,000 cwt			*Dollars per cwt*			*1,000 dollars*		
Fresh Market									
Arizona	1,830.0	1,887.0	(D)	53.30	44.40	(D)	97,539	83,783	(D)
California	(D)	(D)	6,284.5	(D)	(D)	60.00	(D)	(D)	377,070
Colorado	(D)	(D)	(NA)	(D)	(D)	(NA)	(D)	(D)	(NA)
Maryland	(D)	(D)	(NA)	(D)	(D)	(NA)	(D)	(D)	(NA)
New Jersey	(D)	(D)	(D)	(D)	(D)	(D)	(D)	(D)	(D)
Texas	463.7	132.0	(D)	39.30	38.80	(D)	18,223	5,122	(D)
Other States [1]	4,339.9	4,724.4	2,420.4	78.50	66.10	56.60	340,801	312,356	137,111
United States	6,633.6	6,743.4	8,704.9	68.80	59.50	59.10	456,563	401,261	514,181
	Tons			*Dollars per ton*			*1,000 dollars*		
Processing									
Arizona	....	....	(D)	(X)	(X)	(X)	....	....	(D)
California	(D)	(D)	36,473	(D)	(D)	320.00	(D)	(D)	11,671
Colorado	(D)	(D)	(NA)	(D)	(D)	(NA)	(D)	(D)	(NA)
Maryland	(D)	(D)	(NA)	(D)	(D)	(NA)	(D)	(D)	(NA)
New Jersey	(D)	(D)	(D)	(D)	(D)	(D)	(D)	(D)	(D)
Texas	10,416	9,499	(D)	110.00	107.00	(D)	1,146	1,016	(D)
Other States [1]	62,434	58,457	8,580	211.00	229.00	107.00	13,151	13,394	918
United States	72,850	67,956	45,053	196.00	212.00	279.00	14,297	14,410	12,589

(D) Withheld to avoid disclosing data for individual operations. (NA) Not available. (X) Not applicable. [1] Includes data withheld above.
NASS, Crops Branch, (202) 720–2127.

Table 4-38.—Squash for fresh market and processing: Area Harvested, production, price, and value, by State and United States, 2017–2019

State	Area harvested			Total production		
	2017	2018	2019	2017	2018	2019
	Acres			*1,000 cwt*		
California	7,700	6,700	7,300	1,309.0	1,038.5	1,460.0
Florida	7,500	(D)	7,700	975.0	(D)	808.5
Georgia	3,300	(D)	3,700	511.5	(D)	444.0
Michigan	9,200	8,700	8,600	2,116.0	1,914.0	1,720.0
New Jersey	3,300	3,500	3,200	363.0	325.5	288.0
New York	5,400	4,900	5,200	810.0	808.5	728.0
North Carolina	2,800	3,500	4,400	271.6	612.5	572.0
Oregon	5,000	4,300	3,400	1,500.0	1,333.0	1,105.0
Texas	1,700	1,500	(NA)	153.0	88.5	(NA)
Other States [1]	....	11,700	....	....	1,272.0	....
United States	45,900	44,800	43,500	8,009.1	7,392.5	7,125.5

State	Utilized production			Value of utilized production		
	2017	2018	2019	2017	2018	2019
	1,000 cwt			*1,000 dollars*		
California	1,288.1	968.9	1,455.6	45,022	30,973	58,339
Florida	970.1	(D)	808.5	39,095	(D)	35,412
Georgia	506.4	(D)	424.0	22,180	(D)	16,343
Michigan	2,116.0	1,883.4	1,685.6	42,838	37,072	40,502
New Jersey	362.6	307.3	258.6	16,313	8,387	13,706
New York	802.7	805.3	696.7	30,737	24,174	27,226
North Carolina	271.1	611.3	561.7	12,313	18,306	20,311
Oregon	1,500.0	1,333.0	1,101.7	17,369	13,194	8,122
Texas	153.0	88.2	(NA)	9,746	3,481	(NA)
Other States [1]	....	1,252.9	....	....	57,335	....
United States	7,970.0	7,250.3	6,992.4	235,613	192,922	219,961

State	Utilized production			Price per unit			Value of utilized production		
	2017	2018	2019	2017	2018	2019	2017	2018	2019
	1,000 cwt			*Dollars per cwt*			*1,000 dollars*		
Fresh Market									
California	(D)	884.8	(D)	(D)	33.20	(D)	(D)	29,375	(D)
Florida	970.1	(D)	808.5	40.30	(D)	43.80	39,095	(D)	35,412
Georgia	506.4	(D)	(D)	43.80	(D)	(D)	22,180	(D)	(D)
Michigan	1,299.2	1,225.0	1,186.8	28.10	26.50	31.50	36,508	32,463	37,384
New Jersey	(D)	(D)	258.6	(D)	(D)	53.00	(D)	(D)	13,706
New York	(D)	(D)	587.5	(D)	(D)	41.50	(D)	(D)	24,381
North Carolina	(D)	(D)	(D)	(D)	(D)	(D)	(D)	(D)	(D)
Oregon	217.5	122.6	82.9	43.00	46.90	35.30	9,353	5,750	2,926
Texas	153.0	(D)	(NA)	63.70	(D)	(NA)	9,746	(D)	(NA)
Other States [1]	2,598.4	2,883.8	2,220.6	39.40	37.30	41.20	102,251	107,629	91,405
United States	5,744.6	5,116.2	5,144.9	38.10	34.20	39.90	219,133	175,217	205,214
	Tons			*Dollars per ton*			*1,000 dollars*		
Processing									
California	(D)	4,206	(D)	(D)	380.00	(D)	(D)	1,598	(D)
Florida	....	(D)	....	(X)	(D)	(X)	....	(D)	....
Georgia	....	(D)	(D)	(X)	(D)	(D)	....	(D)	(D)
Michigan	40,839	32,921	24,940	155.00	140.00	125.00	6,330	4,609	3,118
New Jersey	(D)	(D)	....	(D)	(D)	(X)	(D)	(D)	....
New York	(D)	(D)	5,460	(D)	(D)	521.00	(D)	(D)	2,845
North Carolina	(D)	(D)	(D)	(D)	(D)	(D)	(D)	(D)	(D)
Oregon	64,125	60,518	50,941	125.00	123.00	102.00	8,016	7,444	5,196
Texas	....	(D)	(NA)	(X)	(D)	(NA)	....	(D)	(NA)
Other States [1]	6,304	9,057	11,305	339.00	448.00	325.00	2,134	4,054	3,588
United States	111,268	106,702	92,376	148.00	166.00	160.00	16,480	17,705	14,747

(D) Withheld to avoid disclosing data for individual operations. (NA) Not available. (X) Not applicable. [1] Includes data withheld above.

NASS, Crops Branch, (202) 720–2127.

Table 4-39.—Sweet Potatoes: Area, yield, production, season average price per hundredweight received by farmers, and value, United States, 2010–2019

Year	Area harvested	Yield per acre	Production	Market year average price [1]	Value of production
	1,000 acres	*Cwt*	*1,000 cwt*	*Dollars*	*1,000 dollars*
2010	116.9	204.0	23,845.0	19.80	472,218
2011	129.7	208.0	26,964.0	18.80	505,938
2012	126.6	209.0	26,482.0	17.40	461,861
2013	113.2	219.0	24,785.0	24.10	597,217
2014	135.2	219.0	29,584.0	23.90	706,916
2015	153.1	203.0	31,016.0	21.80	675,583
2016	163.3	193.0	31,546.0	20.70	651,514
2017	159.3	224.0	35,646.0	18.40	657,021
2018	144.4	190.0	27,378.0	23.20	634,228
2019	146.7	217.9	31,972.5	18.50	588,125

[1] Obtained by weighting State prices by production.
NASS, Crops Branch, (202) 720–2127.

Table 4-40 .—Sweet Potatoes: Area harvested, production, season average price, and value, by State and United States, 2017–2019

State	Area harvested			Production		
	2017	2018	2019	2017	2018	2019
	1,000 Acres			*1,000 cwt*		
Arkansas	(D)	4.8	(NA)	(D)	1,056.0	(NA)
California	21.0	21.0	21.5	6,510.0	7,770.0	8,170.0
Florida	(D)	5.8	(NA)	(D)	812.0	(NA)
Louisiana	9.5	8.3	(NA)	2,185.0	2,200.0	(NA)
Mississippi	29.0	26.0	27.5	4,930.0	4,550.0	4,262.5
North Carolina	89.5	78.5	97.7	19,690.0	10,990.0	19,540.0
Other States [2]	10.3			2,331.0		
United States	159.3	144.4	146.7	35,646.0	27,378.0	31,972.5

State	Price per cwt			Value of production		
	2017	2018	2019 [1]	2017	2018	2019 [1]
	Dollars			*1,000 dollars*		
Arkansas	(D)	23.20	(NA)	(D)	24,499	(NA)
California	23.70	23.60	23.30	154,287	183,372	189,236
Florida	(D)	47.90	(NA)	(D)	38,895	(NA)
Louisiana	19.90	20.00	(NA)	43,482	44,000	(NA)
Mississippi	18.50	18.00	17.60	91,205	81,900	75,021
North Carolina	15.30	23.80	16.60	301,257	261,562	323,868
Other States [2]	28.60	(X)	(X)	66,790		
United States	18.40	23.20	18.50	657,021	634,228	588,125

(D) Withheld to avoid disclosing data for individual operations. (NA) Not available. (X) Not applicable. [1] Preliminary. [2] Includes data withheld above.
NASS, Crops Branch, (202) 720–2127.

Table 4-41.—Tomatoes for fresh market and processing: Area Harvested, production, and value, by State and United States, 2017–2019

State	Area harvested			Total production		
	2017	2018	2019	2017	2018	2019
	Acres			*1,000 cwt*		
California	247,700	260,600	247,700	221,691.5	255,388.0	231,599.5
Florida	28,000	27,000	26,000	8,400.0	7,560.0	7,800.0
Indiana	7,800	7,600	(NA)	4,602.0	4,940.0	(NA)
Michigan	5,500	5,000	(NA)	3,080.0	2,750.0	(NA)
New Jersey	4,000	4,100	(NA)	1,120.0	943.0	(NA)
North Carolina	3,200	3,000	(NA)	1,056.0	870.0	(NA)
Ohio	5,500	5,400	(NA)	2,695.0	2,808.0	(NA)
South Carolina	2,800	3,200	(NA)	1,036.0	1,152.0	(NA)
Tennessee	3,600	4,000	(NA)	1,278.0	1,240.0	(NA)
Virginia	2,400	2,000	(NA)	696.0	420.0	(NA)
United States	310,500	321,900	273,700	245,654.5	278,071.0	239,399.5

State	Utilized production			Value of utilized production		
	2017	2018	2019	2017	2018	2019
	1,000 cwt			*1,000 dollars*		
California	216,592.6	253,855.7	230,209.9	1,075,824	1,197,642	1,174,395
Florida	7,988.4	6,917.4	7,729.8	262,020	344,131	425,912
Indiana	4,602.0	4,940.0	(NA)	30,519	31,530	(NA)
Michigan	3,067.7	2,750.0	(NA)	35,987	35,352	(NA)
New Jersey	1,118.9	716.7	(NA)	39,202	42,411	(NA)
North Carolina	999.0	863.9	(NA)	46,116	33,845	(NA)
Ohio	2,695.0	2,808.0	(NA)	48,626	52,173	(NA)
South Carolina	1,033.9	1,150.8	(NA)	34,429	44,881	(NA)
Tennessee	1,265.2	1,215.2	(NA)	61,719	54,176	(NA)
Virginia	692.5	409.1	(NA)	43,518	27,774	(NA)
United States	240,055.2	275,626.8	237,939.7	1,677,960	1,863,915	1,600,307

State	Utilized production			Price per unit			Value of utilized production		
	2017	2018	2019	2017	2018	2019	2017	2018	2019
	1,000 cwt			*Dollars per cwt*			*1,000 dollars*		
Fresh Market									
California	7,315.8	8,172.4	6,484.8	31.20	27.80	43.10	228,253	227,193	279,495
Florida	7,988.4	(D)	7,729.8	32.80	(D)	55.10	262,020	(D)	425,912
Indiana	32.2	49.4	(NA)	75.00	69.00	(NA)	2,415	3,409	(NA)
Michigan	406.6	495.0	(NA)	54.80	47.50	(NA)	22,282	23,513	(NA)
New Jersey	689.9	510.2	(NA)	53.90	80.90	(NA)	37,186	41,275	(NA)
North Carolina	(D)	(D)	(NA)	(D)	(D)	(NA)	(D)	(D)	(NA)
Ohio	649.5	561.6	(NA)	56.60	69.90	(NA)	36,762	39,256	(NA)
South Carolina	1,033.9	1,150.8	(NA)	33.30	39.00	(NA)	34,429	44,881	(NA)
Tennessee	(D)	(D)	(NA)	(D)	(D)	(NA)	(D)	(D)	(NA)
Virginia	(D)	(D)	(NA)	(D)	(D)	(NA)	(D)	(D)	(NA)
Other States [1]	2,853.4	8,683.1	....	52.10	50.00	(X)	148,744	442,090	....
United States	20,969.7	19,622.5	14,214.6	36.80	41.60	49.60	772,091	821,617	705,407
	Tons			*Dollars per ton*			*1,000 dollars*		
Processing									
California	10,463,839	12,284,163	11,186,256	81.00	79.00	80.00	847,571	970,449	894,900
Florida	....	(D)	....	(X)	(D)	(X)	....	(D)	....
Indiana	228,489	244,530	(NA)	123.00	115.00	(NA)	28,104	28,121	(NA)
Michigan	133,056	112,750	(NA)	103.00	105.00	(NA)	13,705	11,839	(NA)
New Jersey	21,448	10,326	(NA)	94.00	110.00	(NA)	2,016	1,136	(NA)
North Carolina	(D)	(D)	(NA)	(D)	(D)	(NA)	(D)	(D)	(NA)
Ohio	102,275	112,320	(NA)	116.00	115.00	(NA)	11,864	12,917	(NA)
South Carolina	....	....	(NA)	(X)	(X)	(NA)	....	....	(NA)
Tennessee	(D)	(D)	(NA)	(D)	(D)	(NA)	(D)	(D)	(NA)
Virginia	(D)	(D)	(NA)	(D)	(D)	(NA)	(D)	(D)	(NA)
Other States [1]	5,160	28,566	....	506.00	624.00	(X)	2,609	17,836	....
United States	10,954,267	12,792,655	11,186,256	82.70	81.50	80.00	905,869	1,042,298	894,900

(D) Withheld to avoid disclosing data for individual operations. (NA) Not available. (X) Not applicable. [1] Includes data withheld above.

NASS, Crops Branch, (202) 720–2127.

Table 4-42.—Watermelon for fresh market and processing: Area harvested, production, and value, by State and United States, 2017–2019

State	Area harvested			Total production		
	2017	2018	2019	2017	2018	2019
	Acres			*1,000 cwt*		
Arizona	3,500	(D)	5,000	1,802.5	(D)	2,525.0
California	10,600	11,900	10,200	6,201.0	6,426.0	5,100.0
Delaware	3,900	3,800	(NA)	1,092.0	1,026.0	(NA)
Florida	22,000	22,500	24,500	8,690.0	8,100.0	9,056.0
Georgia	20,900	20,600	21,100	7,942.0	5,356.0	8,229.0
Indiana	6,200	6,500	6,100	2,573.0	3,055.0	2,318.0
Maryland	3,700	3,500	(NA)	1,110.0	1,050.0	(NA)
Missouri	3,000	(D)	(NA)	705.0	(D)	(NA)
North Carolina	7,100	7,300	7,400	2,130.0	1,825.0	1,702.0
South Carolina	4,900	4,300	4,500	2,156.0	989.0	1,440.0
Texas	22,000	23,000	23,000	6,380.0	7,820.0	6,670.0
Other States	....	8,000	....	....	3,698.0	....
United States	107,800	112,000	101,800	40,781.5	39,345.5	37,049.0

State	Utilized production			Value of utilized production		
	2017	2018	2019	2017	2018	2019
	1,000 cwt			*1,000 dollars*		
Arizona	1,802.5	(D)	2,525.0	42,359	(D)	34,593
California	6,176.2	6,393.9	5,100.0	117,348	116,369	105,060
Delaware	1,092.0	1,026.0	(NA)	8,736	11,286	(NA)
Florida	8,690.0	8,043.3	8,974.4	152,944	160,866	161,539
Georgia	7,727.6	5,345.3	8,097.3	84,231	76,438	101,216
Indiana	2,573.0	3,055.0	2,318.0	27,017	27,915	35,294
Maryland	1,110.0	1,039.5	(NA)	12,321	10,395	(NA)
Missouri	702.2	(D)	(NA)	8,445	(D)	(NA)
North Carolina	2,102.3	1,799.5	1,702.0	22,705	22,314	23,998
South Carolina	2,153.8	987.0	1,402.6	26,276	17,174	16,022
Texas	6,156.7	7,765.3	6,603.3	91,651	143,387	83,202
Other States	....	3,694.0	....	....	77,291	....
United States	40,286.3	39,148.8	36,722.6	594,033	663,435	560,924

State	Utilized production			Price per unit			Value of utilized production		
	2017	2018	2019	2017	2018	2019	2017	2018	2019
	1,000 cwt			*Dollars per cwt*			*1,000 dollars*		
Fresh Market									
Arizona	1,802.5	(D)	2,525.0	23.50	(D)	13.70	42,359	(D)	34,593
California	6,176.2	6,393.9	5,100.0	19.00	18.20	20.60	117,348	116,369	105,060
Delaware	1,092.0	1,026.0	(NA)	8.00	11.00	(NA)	8,736	11,286	(NA)
Florida	8,690.0	8,043.3	8,974.4	17.60	20.00	18.00	152,944	160,866	161,539
Georgia	7,727.6	5,345.3	8,097.3	10.90	14.30	12.50	84,231	76,438	101,216
Indiana	2,573.0	(D)	(D)	10.50	(D)	(D)	27,017	(D)	(D)
Maryland	1,110.0	1,039.5	(NA)	11.10	10.00	(NA)	12,321	10,395	(NA)
Missouri	(D)	(D)	(NA)	(D)	(D)	(NA)	(D)	(D)	(NA)
North Carolina	2,102.3	1,799.5	1,702.0	10.80	12.40	14.10	22,705	22,314	23,998
South Carolina	2,153.8	987.0	(D)	12.20	17.40	(D)	26,276	17,174	(D)
Texas	(D)	(D)	6,603.3	(D)	(D)	12.60	(D)	(D)	83,202
Other States [1]	6,606.0	14,345.9	3,664.2	15.10	17.20	14.00	99,782	247,360	51,132
United States	40,033.4	38,980.4	36,666.2	14.80	17.00	15.30	593,719	662,202	560,740
	Tons			*Dollars per ton*			*1,000 dollars*		
Processing									
Arizona	....	(D)	....	(X)	(D)	(X)	....	(D)	....
California	....	....	....	(X)	(X)	(X)	....	....	....
Delaware	....	....	(NA)	(X)	(X)	(NA)	....	....	(NA)
Florida	....	....	....	(X)	(X)	(X)	....	....	....
Georgia	....	....	....	(X)	(X)	(X)	....	....	....
Indiana	....	(D)	(D)	(X)	(D)	(D)	....	(D)	(D)
Maryland	....	....	(NA)	(X)	(X)	(NA)	....	....	(NA)
Missouri	(D)	(D)	(NA)	(D)	(D)	(NA)	(D)	(D)	(NA)
North Carolina	....	....	....	(X)	(X)	(X)	....	....	....
South Carolina	....	....	(D)	(X)	(X)	(D)	....	....	(D)
Texas	(D)	(D)	....	(D)	(D)	(X)	(D)	(D)	....
Other States [1]	12,646	8,420	2,815	24.80	146.00	146.00	314	1,233	184
United States	12,646	8,420	2,815	24.80	146.00	146.00	64	1,233	184

(D) Withheld to avoid disclosing data for individual operations. (NA) Not available. (X) Not applicable. [1] Includes data withheld above.
NASS, Crops Branch, (202) 720–2127.

Table 4-43.—Vegetables and melons, fresh: Total reported domestic rail, truck, and air shipments, 2019

Commodity	Jan.	Feb.	Mar.	Apr.	May	June	July
Vegetables:				*1,000 cwt*			
Artichokes	51	72	67	79	55	58	71
Artichokes-organic	2	3	2	1	3	4	3
Asparagus	...	...	...	17	112	123	11
Beans	182	176	232	229	224	120	43
Beans-organic	...	1	...	...	...	...	...
Beets	6	6	8	9	6	3	4
Beets-organic	...	...	...	1	3	3	3
Broccoli	557	435	518	549	506	570	466
Broccoli-organic	36	39	56	54	46	50	50
Brussels sprouts	59	19	26	33	27	41	76
Cabbage	928	784	1,062	602	472	261	300
Cabbage-organic	11	18	17	7	7	8	10
Carrots	627	624	670	651	694	568	578
Carrots-organic	251	226	228	223	231	209	201
Cauliflower	494	375	496	435	468	419	362
Cauliflower-organic	14	16	32	37	46	41	32
Celery	1,340	1,014	1,078	997	1,016	1,162	1,097
Celery-organic	63	51	66	98	81	95	104
Chinese cabbage	34	32	45	45	52	70	49
Corn, sweet	394	360	597	1,179	2,072	1,995	525
Corn, sweet-organic	...	...	...	...	...	...	...
Cucumbers	35	1	126	336	366	397	297
Cucumbers-organic	...	...	2	...	...	...	...
Eggplant	50	40	81	128	77	139	16
Eggplant-organic	1	1	1	1	...	...	...
Endive	16	16	13	11	3	2	2
Escarole	21	23	18	16	6	3	3
Greens	170	144	240	222	197	165	89
Greens-organic	15	16	25	23	10	8	8
Lettuce, iceberg	2,069	1,819	2,300	2,359	2,409	2,000	2,140
Lettuce, iceberg-organic	10	9	16	26	19	15	25
Lettuce, other	337	320	358	273	224	179	195
Lettuce, other-organic	6	7	9	8	3	5	4
Lettuce, romaine	1,928	1,543	2,061	1,888	1,738	1,500	1,575
Lettuce, romaine-organic	92	84	137	153	114	103	113
Lettuce processed	752	688	715	509	142	125	...

Commodity	Aug.	Sep.	Oct.	Nov.	Dec.	Total
Artichokes	67	52	61	48	29	710
Artichokes-organic	2	3	2	1	2	28
Asparagus	...	...	...	...	...	263
Beans	62	71	106	162	141	1,748
Beans-organic	...	...	...	...	...	1
Beets	4	5	6	6	4	67
Beets-organic	3	4	4	3	...	24
Broccoli	448	377	415	501	507	5,849
Broccoli-organic	49	36	36	33	46	531
Brussels sprouts	103	95	97	124	85	785
Cabbage	473	497	516	461	841	7,197
Cabbage-organic	6	4	5	66	19	178
Carrots	590	535	592	534	573	7,236
Carrots-organic	229	213	240	240	218	2,709
Cauliflower	411	364	367	435	477	5,103
Cauliflower-organic	48	26	27	24	27	370
Celery	1,058	1,013	1,208	1,631	1,329	13,943
Celery-organic	115	111	126	99	69	1,078
Chinese cabbage	53	50	68	43	35	576
Corn, sweet	420	283	337	366	178	8,706
Corn, sweet-organic	...	...	...	...	1	1
Cucumbers	474	389	326	287	137	3,171
Cucumbers-organic	...	...	1	3	1	7
Eggplant	27	46	77	88	63	832
Eggplant-organic	...	...	...	...	2	6
Endive	2	2	2	8	5	82
Escarole	3	3	4	11	12	123
Greens	109	95	145	417	302	2,295
Greens-organic	7	6	9	10	11	148
Lettuce, iceberg	2,248	2,040	1,936	1,697	2,042	25,059
Lettuce, iceberg-organic	20	17	18	84	117	376
Lettuce, other	202	185	217	262	371	3,123
Lettuce, other-organic	3	3	3	7	6	64
Lettuce, romaine	1,577	1,451	1,515	1,439	1,739	19,954
Lettuce, romaine-organic	141	132	128	117	104	1,418
Lettuce processed	141	124	149	801	792	4,938

See footnote(s) at end of table.

Table 4-43.—Vegetables and melons, fresh: Total reported domestic rail, truck, and air shipments, 2019—Continued

Commodity	Jan.	Feb.	Mar.	Apr.	May	June	July
Vegetables:				*1,000 cwt*			
Onions, dry	4,631	3,492	3,632	4,034	4,358	3,890	3,877
Onions, dry-organic	2	1	2	6	16	13	13
Onions, green	9	6	19	24	25	31	26
Onions, green-organic	...	...	...	1	2	2	2
Onions processed	458	487	559	418	539	573	303
Parsley	43	41	36	45	44	37	45
Parsley-organic	1	1	1	1	1	2	2
Peppers, bell	247	251	383	529	740	885	665
Peppers, bell-organic	3	2	3	3	...	8	14
Peppers, other	30	41	73	72	31	32	14
Peppers, other-organic	...	...	1	...	...	...	...
Potatoes, table	7,694	6,433	7,615	7,254	7,230	7,458	7,432
Potatoes, table-organic	145	138	143	110	118	149	113
Potatoes, chipper	3,922	4,031	4,794	3,825	3,863	5,799	5,378
Potatoes, chipper-organic	...	...	...	1	...	...	...
Potatoes, seed	265	203	4,173	7,416	2,007	112	10
Radishes	68	63	71	81	63	52	55
Spinach	199	202	210	104	52	42	53
Spinach-organic	47	48	67	22	1	2	3
Squash	117	142	215	212	237	119	132
Squash-organic	5	5	6	5	2	...	...
Sweet potatoes	720	738	843	702	655	622	462
Sweet potatoes-organic	5	7	7	5	6	4	16
Tomatoes	933	799	843	1,076	1,166	763	1,120
Tomatoes, greenhouse	...	...	90	79	119	113	129
Toms, Grape Type	...	...	106	112	115	143	122
Toms, Grape Type-greenhouse	23	21	33	24	22	20	19
Toms, Cherry	...	...	26	30	23	27	24
Toms, Plum Type	...	...	...	...	5	106	245
Toms, Plum Type-greenhouse	90	79	119	113	129	140	132
Total	30,208	26,193	35,372	37,503	32,998	31,585	28,858

Commodity	Aug.	Sep.	Oct.	Nov.	Dec.	Total
Onions, dry	4,001	3,369	3,827	4,152	3,955	47,218
Onions, dry-organic	2	1	1	1	...	58
Onions, green	29	28	31	33	22	283
Onions, green-organic	2	1	2	1	...	13
Onions processed	325	402	431	493	403	5,391
Parsley	47	43	45	49	39	514
Parsley-organic	2	1	2	1	2	17
Peppers, bell	659	677	636	699	395	6,766
Peppers, bell-organic	...	...	...	1	3	37
Peppers, other	10	...	26	56	26	411
Peppers, other-organic	...	...	...	...	...	1
Potatoes, table	7,092	6,841	7,010	8,275	7,077	87,411
Potatoes, table-organic	87	66	100	124	126	1,419
Potatoes, chipper	4,980	4,258	4,038	4,578	4,063	53,529
Potatoes, chipper-organic	...	3	...	...	...	4
Potatoes, seed	1	62	25	42	72	14,388
Radishes	58	55	52	58	82	758
Spinach	50	49	50	85	153	1,249
Spinach-organic	4	2	7	34	50	287
Squash	161	117	114	147	158	1,871
Squash-organic	...	...	1	5	8	37
Sweet potatoes	461	479	656	1,057	651	8,046
Sweet potatoes-organic	3	5	7	7	7	79
Tomatoes	1,025	1,020	1,014	1,178	778	90
Tomatoes, greenhouse	140	132	109	73	89	108
Toms, Grape Type	103	60	41	44	84	107
Toms, Grape Type-greenhouse	20	9	8	19	18	236
Toms, Cherry	13	9	9	9	16	27
Toms, Plum Type	209	127	59	...	...	751
Toms, Plum Type-greenhouse	109	73	89	108	81	1,262
Total	28,688	26,121	27,133	31,337	28,643	351,067

See footnote(s) at end of table.

Table 4-43.—Vegetables and melons, fresh: Total reported domestic rail, truck, and air shipments, 2019–Continued

Commodity	Jan.	Feb.	Mar.	Apr.	May	June	July
Melons:				1,000 cwt			
Cantaloupe	....	....	....	13	914	2,404	2,241
Cantaloupe-organic	....	....	....	....	7	78	67
Honeydews	....	....	....	....	49	432	685
Honeydews-organic	....	....	....	....	3	30	19
Mixed & misc. melons	....	....	....	....	7	46	113
Mixed & misc. melons-organic	....	....	....	....	1	15	5
Watermelon, seeded	....	....	1	150	472	484	390
Watermelon, seeded-organic	....	....	....	....	....	3	6
Watermelon, seedless	....	....	14	1,261	6,369	10,347	8,084
Watermelon, seedless-organic	....	....	....	....	12	118	144
Total	....	....	15	1,424	7,834	13,957	11,754

Commodity	Aug.	Sep.	Oct.	Nov.	Dec.	Total
Cantaloupe	2,317	1,558	926	228	....	10,601
Cantaloupe-organic	52	18	....	....	....	222
Honeydews	696	567	225	89	....	2,773
Honeydews-organic	22	9	....	....	....	83
Mixed & misc. melons	72	17	....	....	....	255
Mixed & misc. melons-organic	7	2	....	....	....	30
Watermelon, seeded	323	87	4	....	....	1,911
Watermelon, seeded-organic	2	....	....	....	....	11
Watermelon, seedless	6,733	2,832	254	11	....	35,905
Watermelon, seedless-organic	204	30	....	....	....	508
Total	10,428	5,120	1,439	328	....	52,299

AMS, Fresh Fruit and Vegetable Specialty Crops, Market News Division, (202) 205–9690.

Table 4-44.—Commercially produced vegetables: Per capita utilization, United States, 2009–2018

Year	Farm weight equivalent						
	Total fresh and processed	Fresh [2]	Processed				
			Total	Canning	Freezing	Potatoes	Others [1]
	Pounds	Pounds	Pounds	Pounds	Pounds	Pounds	Pounds
2009	349.0	141.3	207.7	98.8	21.4	76.7	10.8
2010	352.0	144.9	207.1	97.7	20.9	77.1	11.4
2011	342.2	142.2	200.3	89.6	22.0	76.4	12.3
2012	350.5	144.8	205.7	91.1	22.3	80.3	12.0
2013	341.1	141.2	199.9	90.3	19.6	79.0	11.0
2014	346.8	142.6	204.2	92.1	19.9	79.5	12.7
2015	337.2	141.9	195.3	80.6	20.5	81.3	12.9
2016	351.3	155.9	195.4	86.0	20.2	76.5	12.7
2017	357.3	157.4	199.9	83.3	21.4	83.0	12.2
2018	351.8	144.8	207.0	90.0	22.9	82.7	11.4

Year	Percentage of annual total					
	Fresh [2]	Processed				
		Total	Canning	Freezing	Potatoes	Others [1]
	Percent	Percent	Percent	Percent	Percent	Percent
2009	40.5	59.5	28.3	6.1	22.0	3.1
2010	41.2	58.8	27.7	6.0	21.9	3.2
2011	41.5	58.5	26.2	6.4	22.3	3.6
2012	41.3	58.7	26.0	6.4	22.9	3.4
2013	41.4	58.6	26.5	5.7	23.2	3.2
2014	41.1	58.9	26.6	5.7	22.9	3.7
2015	42.1	57.9	24.0	6.1	24.1	3.8
2016	42.3	57.7	25.5	6.0	22.4	3.8
2017	40.7	59.3	26.7	5.9	23.1	3.5
2018	....	....	....	....	....	....

[1] Others include mushrooms, sweet potatoes, and onions for dehydrating market. [2] See table 4-45 for items included under Fresh category. Excludes melons.
ERS, Market and Trade Economics Division, (202) 694–5326.

Table 4-45.—Vegetables, fresh: Per capita civilian availability (farm-weight basis), United States, 2009–2018 [1]

Year	Asparagus	Snap beans	Broccoli	Cabbage	Carrots	Cauliflower
	Pounds	*Pounds*	*Pounds*	*Pounds*	*Pounds*	*Pounds*
2009	1.3	1.7	6.2	7.3	7.4	1.7
2010	1.4	1.9	6.0	7.5	7.8	1.3
2011	1.4	1.7	6.0	6.6	7.5	1.2
2012	1.4	1.6	6.3	6.3	8.0	1.2
2013	1.4	1.6	6.9	6.9	8.0	1.3
2014	1.7	1.5	6.7	6.7	8.5	1.3
2015	1.5	1.6	7.4	6.3	8.8	1.6
2016	1.6	1.7	7.5	5.9	7.8	1.7
2017	1.6	1.6	7.1	6.2	7.4	2.4
2018	1.8	1.7	5.9	5.7	8.5	2.4

Year	Celery	Sweet Corn	Cucumbers	Head lettuce	Leaf/ romaine	Garlic
	Pounds	*Pounds*	*Pounds*	*Pounds*	*Pounds*	*Pounds*
2009	6.2	9.2	6.8	16.1	10.0	2.4
2010	6.1	9.3	6.7	15.9	12.0	2.3
2011	6.0	8.2	6.4	15.8	11.7	2.3
2012	6.0	8.7	7.1	16.0	11.9	2.3
2013	5.5	8.9	7.3	14.1	11.4	2.3
2014	5.5	7.7	7.4	14.5	10.8	2.2
2015	5.1	8.6	7.6	13.6	11.9	2.4
2016	5.0	7.1	8.1	16.9	14.5	3.0
2017	4.7	7.2	7.4	15.3	15.1	3.0
2018	5.0	6.7	8.0	12.3	12.3	2.5

Year	Onions	Bell peppers	Spinach	Tomatoes [2]	Others [3]	Total vegetables [4]
	Pounds	*Pounds*	*Pounds*	*Pounds*	*Pounds*	*Pounds*
2009	19.6	9.8	2.0	19.6	18.4	141.3
2010	19.6	10.3	1.7	20.6	18.4	144.9
2011	19.1	10.6	1.8	21.0	18.8	142.2
2012	19.3	10.8	1.6	20.8	19.3	144.8
2013	18.5	10.0	1.6	20.3	18.8	141.2
2014	18.4	10.7	1.7	20.6	20.5	142.6
2015	18.3	10.7	1.7	20.6	18.3	141.9
2016	22.8	11.1	2.0	20.3	24.0	155.9
2017	25.1	11.3	1.9	20.5	24.6	157.4
2018	20.4	11.2	1.9	20.6	22.2	144.8

[1] Fresh vegetable consumption computed for total commercial production for fresh market. Does not include production for home use. Consumption obtained by dividing the total apparent consumption by total July 1 population as reported by the Bureau of the Census. All data for calendar year. [2] After 1996, includes an ERS estimate of domestically produced hothouse tomatoes. Hothouse imports included in all years. [3] Includes artichokes, brussels sprouts, eggplant, endive/escarole, garlic, radishes, green limas, squash, spinach, okra, pumpkins, kale, collards, turnip greens, and mustard greens. [4] Excludes melons, mushrooms, potatoes, and sweet potatoes.

ERS, Market and Trade Economics Division, (202) 694–5326.

Table 4-46.—Vegetables, canning: Per capita availability (farm weight), United States, 2009–2018

Year	Cabbage	Asparagus	Snap beans	Carrots	Green peas
	Pounds	*Pounds*	*Pounds*	*Pounds*	*Pounds*
2009	0.9	0.2	3.6	0.9	1.3
2010	1.0	0.1	3.7	0.8	1.1
2011	1.0	0.1	3.2	0.8	0.8
2012	1.2	0.1	2.9	0.8	0.8
2013	1.0	0.1	2.9	0.8	0.9
2014	1.0	0.1	2.8	0.7	0.7
2015	0.9	0.1	3.0	0.7	0.8
2016	1.0	0.1	3.2	1.1	0.8
2017	1.3	0.1	3.1	1.1	0.7
2018	0.8	0.1	2.9	0.9	0.6

Year	Tomatoes	Sweet corn	Pickling Cucumbers	Other [1]	Total
	Pounds	*Pounds*	*Pounds*	*Pounds*	*Pounds*
2009	70.3	7.6	5.1	2.3	98.8
2010	71.3	6.9	3.8	2.5	97.7
2011	65.8	5.8	2.8	2.6	89.6
2012	66.6	5.9	3.0	2.7	91.1
2013	66.0	5.8	3.2	2.7	90.3
2014	67.4	5.8	3.9	2.6	92.1
2015	56.3	5.3	3.4	2.9	80.6
2016	61.2	5.0	3.0	3.0	86.0
2017	57.9	5.0	3.7	2.9	83.3
2018	65.6	5.2	3.3	3.4	90.0

[1] Includes beets, green limas (1992-2014), spinach, and miscellaneous imports (1990-2014).
ERS, Market and Trade Economics Division, (202) 694–5326.

Table 4-47.—Vegetables, freezing: Per capita utilization (farm weight basis), United States, 2009–2018

Year	Asparagus	Snap beans	Carrots	Peas	Broccoli
	Pounds	*Pounds*	*Pounds*	*Pounds*	*Pounds*
2009	0.1	1.9	1.5	1.7	2.5
2010	0.1	2.0	1.5	1.5	2.5
2011	0.1	1.5	1.6	1.6	2.7
2012	0.1	1.9	1.2	1.9	2.6
2013	0.1	2.1	1.7	1.5	2.5
2014	0.1	1.8	1.2	1.6	2.6
2015	0.1	1.9	1.4	1.5	2.6
2016	0.2	2.0	1.9	1.0	2.6
2017	0.1	1.9	2.4	1.3	2.4
2018	0.1	1.9	2.2	1.3	2.5

Year	Cauliflower	Sweet Corn	Other [1]	Total vegetables excluding potatoes
	Pounds	*Pounds*	*Pounds*	*Pounds*
2009	0.4	9.1	4.3	21.4
2010	0.4	8.6	4.5	20.9
2011	0.4	9.8	4.3	22.0
2012	0.3	9.8	4.5	22.3
2013	0.3	7.0	4.3	19.6
2014	0.4	7.7	4.6	19.9
2015	0.3	8.0	4.7	20.5
2016	0.4	7.5	4.6	20.2
2017	0.5	8.0	4.7	21.4
2018	0.6	7.9	4.4	22.9

[1] Includes green lima beans, spinach, and miscellaneous freezing vegetables.
ERS, Market and Trade Economics Division, (202) 694–5326.

Table 4-48.—Frozen Vegetables and potato products: Cold storage holdings, United States, 2018 and 2019

End of the month	Asparagus		Green beans, french cut		Green beans, Lima		Green beans, regular cut	
	2018	2019	2018	2019	2018	2019	2018	2019
	1,000 pounds							
January	9,690	7,694	14,738	12,622	49,217	34,443	172,503	143,960
February	8,119	7,136	13,923	12,025	45,506	29,861	155,853	130,780
March	6,989	6,419	13,402	11,534	42,315	26,059	128,304	117,427
April	6,036	5,714	12,230	11,471	37,826	18,879	109,337	110,140
May	7,767	5,807	10,651	10,112	36,335	17,010	93,324	87,598
June	10,855	7,220	11,184	9,879	33,421	14,441	81,164	82,556
July	10,971	7,297	12,886	16,571	29,161	29,161	115,005	125,225
August	10,120	6,454	14,413	21,160	33,072	33,072	172,836	163,225
September	9,358	6,372	15,847	20,285	44,301	44,301	202,123	203,481
October	8,933	6,344	15,328	19,950	47,691	47,691	190,921	185,412
November	8,364	6,257	13,793	17,143	42,601	42,601	173,687	173,403
December	8,106	6,002	13,747	14,887	38,647	38,647	152,495	155,713

End of the month	Broccoli, chopped & cut		Broccoli, spears		Brussels sprouts		Carrots, diced	
	2018	2019	2018	2019	2018	2019	2018	2019
	1,000 pounds							
January	30,206	36,913	25,814	26,337	21,121	15,728	128,815	120,219
February	31,302	39,476	29,513	28,628	20,636	13,164	121,470	116,148
March	33,530	37,688	31,806	34,710	20,900	12,916	114,872	109,514
April	36,759	35,876	34,494	40,829	20,736	13,341	108,053	105,619
May	35,108	32,798	38,616	39,849	19,317	12,501	98,881	110,909
June	34,532	32,061	45,339	43,927	17,361	12,774	84,708	100,442
July	38,981	36,520	44,166	45,936	17,102	12,930	65,564	84,444
August	41,735	43,555	44,250	48,278	15,536	12,823	53,967	72,505
September	43,080	45,550	37,705	47,694	13,257	12,237	48,927	62,579
October	41,796	39,750	35,174	46,109	13,410	12,982	86,070	113,935
November	39,422	37,303	30,802	43,369	13,940	12,505	129,184	171,712
December	37,761	34,048	26,691	41,991	15,680	13,254	125,994	173,673

End of the month	Carrots, other		Cauliflower		Sweet corn, cut		Sweet corn, cob	
	2018	2019	2018	2019	2018	2019	2018	2019
	1,000 pounds							
January	149,233	100,107	34,901	28,000	446,194	433,018	231,840	242,621
February	136,166	93,262	36,257	26,134	403,945	394,400	207,582	226,032
March	125,914	87,761	35,212	24,059	356,223	351,796	176,477	202,924
April	119,288	77,125	32,896	23,981	312,151	295,948	142,645	169,151
May	104,184	73,787	30,354	18,478	276,599	259,917	107,713	149,776
June	94,449	64,844	25,340	18,926	240,908	240,636	79,134	137,539
July	87,118	57,293	24,701	19,682	257,797	250,720	105,145	137,583
August	84,641	53,727	24,088	18,565	443,885	461,516	208,224	246,139
September	96,342	67,712	23,258	19,684	558,378	662,567	276,776	332,852
October	105,654	86,019	30,422	21,973	592,617	674,400	307,075	345,723
November	113,794	105,246	28,645	23,324	530,696	637,174	288,300	307,982
December	110,822	98,720	29,760	24,382	475,712	567,306	269,689	275,612

End of the month	Greens, southern		Okra		Onions, other		Onion rings	
	2018	2019	2018	2019	2018	2019	2018	2019
	1,000 pounds							
January	13,243	11,889	20,870	37,915	53,999	52,133	14,859	17,588
February	12,661	11,164	16,743	31,855	56,916	53,274	16,629	18,362
March	11,268	10,351	14,666	21,396	60,604	59,335	17,190	15,731
April	10,534	9,976	13,443	16,652	62,211	66,088	18,696	16,500
May	9,144	10,514	12,632	17,388	60,049	73,692	18,698	16,229
June	10,996	12,907	30,181	28,658	60,160	72,312	17,976	15,146
July	12,352	15,254	41,318	43,014	58,276	64,400	16,534	12,880
August	13,146	15,149	50,058	56,509	60,197	66,956	16,117	11,357
September	12,725	14,477	54,779	58,883	55,390	64,243	16,875	12,238
October	13,195	14,583	55,093	57,568	47,346	55,543	17,056	11,825
November	12,778	13,272	48,631	52,782	48,431	52,817	16,801	15,724
December	12,174	10,908	44,156	48,906	51,663	51,024	17,160	14,918

See footnote(s) at end of table.

Table 4-48.—Frozen Vegetables and potato products: Cold storage holdings, United States, 2018 and 2019—Continued

End of the month	Blackeye peas		Green peas		Peas & carrots mixed		Spinach	
	2018	2019	2018	2019	2018	2019	2018	2019
	1,000 pounds							
January	1,606	1,497	247,040	188,769	7,454	7,826	51,346	30,847
February	1,655	1,394	223,679	174,792	8,135	7,391	50,691	28,965
March	1,512	1,712	198,966	147,662	7,410	8,001	50,882	33,114
April	1,357	1,495	190,125	132,510	8,083	7,954	51,731	34,603
May	1,407	1,373	177,152	121,763	7,758	8,436	57,378	38,555
June	1,293	1,413	284,008	233,194	6,754	9,098	57,896	41,009
July	2,089	1,615	341,193	385,001	7,424	9,953	52,689	39,444
August	2,009	1,655	319,549	352,447	7,605	9,545	44,851	34,753
September	2,000	1,930	303,905	309,511	6,947	8,515	40,251	30,952
October	2,037	1,904	268,892	277,596	7,457	8,423	38,782	32,030
November	1,790	1,332	244,288	250,797	6,928	8,567	35,439	32,739
December	1,479	1,227	207,808	212,684	7,262	9,058	30,994	33,492

End of the month	Squash		Vegetables, mixed		Vegetables, other		Total frozen vegetables	
	2018	2019	2018	2019	2018	2019	2018	2019
	1,000 pounds							
January	65,820	55,342	59,410	52,405	563,016	535,862	2,412,935	2,193,735
February	59,535	55,155	60,105	54,958	504,878	510,354	2,221,899	2,064,710
March	54,323	52,618	53,310	53,253	461,985	476,131	2,018,060	1,902,111
April	50,724	48,370	52,886	55,753	406,018	440,646	1,838,259	1,738,621
May	48,427	43,275	54,013	48,189	376,945	377,702	1,682,452	1,575,658
June	44,881	40,456	56,417	47,214	377,555	355,236	1,706,512	1,621,888
July	44,933	37,843	60,139	52,260	422,205	354,953	1,867,749	1,821,909
August	46,032	45,421	66,995	50,131	502,853	384,582	2,276,179	2,191,605
September	48,877	46,079	63,700	47,185	569,778	423,955	2,544,579	2,530,067
October	61,029	55,609	60,301	50,241	623,597	458,115	2,669,876	2,615,705
November	60,200	58,825	56,423	41,737	606,165	455,499	2,548,102	2,555,201
December	60,482	56,884	53,845	41,323	582,039	435,111	2,374,166	2,354,632

End of the month	Frozen potatoes					
	French fries		Other frozen potatoes		Total frozen potatoes	
	2018	2019	2018	2019	2018	2019
	1,000 pounds					
January	1,001,232	1,030,263	257,077	234,970	1,258,300	1,265,233
February	997,602	1,052,280	267,617	246,684	1,265,219	1,298,964
March	964,870	1,038,225	260,942	253,586	1,225,812	1,291,811
April	938,695	969,089	254,107	242,123	1,192,802	1,211,212
May	889,808	932,737	266,879	240,164	1,156,687	1,172,901
June	941,336	945,264	270,621	239,233	1,211,957	1,184,497
July	859,456	907,021	237,286	227,235	1,096,742	1,134,256
August	898,725	935,993	242,029	226,265	1,140,754	1,162,258
September	932,954	921,903	252,068	238,779	1,185,022	1,160,682
October	1,002,221	942,518	248,025	228,186	1,250,246	1,170,704
November	962,841	954,826	235,592	226,101	1,198,433	1,180,927
December	944,230	948,850	230,329	207,080	1,174,559	1,155,930

NASS, Livestock Branch, (202) 720–3570.

CHAPTER V

STATISTICS OF FRUITS, TREE NUTS, AND HORTICULTURAL SPECIALTIES

For most fruits, production is estimated at two levels—total and utilized. Total production is the quantity of fruit harvested plus quantities which would have been acceptable for fresh market or processing but were not harvested or utilized because of economic and other reasons. Utilized production is the amount sold plus the quantities used on farms where grown and quantities held in storage. The difference between total and utilized production is the quantity of marketable fruit not harvested and fruit harvested but not sold or utilized because of economic and other reasons. Production relates to the crop produced on all farms, except for apples and strawberries. In accordance with Congressional enactment, the Department's estimates of apple production since 1938 have related only to commercial production. The estimates for strawberries cover production on area grown primarily for sale. Statistics on utilization of fruit by commercial processors refer to first utilization, not necessarily final utilization. For example, frozen fruit includes fruit which may later be used for preserves.

The price shown for each crop is a marketing year average price for all methods of sales. Prices for most fresh fruit are the average prices producers received at the point of first sale, commonly referred to as the "average price as sold." Since the point of first sale is not the same for all producers, prices for the various methods of sale are weighted by the proportionate quantity sold. For example, if in a given State part of the fruit crop is sold f.o.b. packed by growers, part sold as bulk fruit at the packinghouse door, and some sold retail at roadside stands, the fresh fruit average price as sold is a weighted average of the average price for each method of sale.

The annual estimates are checked and adjusted at the end of each marketing season on the basis of shipment and processing records from transportation agencies, processors, cooperative marketing associations, and other industry organizations. The estimates are reviewed (and revised if necessary) at 5-year intervals, when the Census of Agriculture data become available. The Department's available statistics are limited to the major tree fruits and nuts and to grapes, cranberries, and strawberries, and exclude some States where census data indicate production is of only minor importance.

Table 5-1.—Fruits and planted nuts: Bearing area, United States, 2009–2018

Year	Citrus fruits [1]	Major deciduous fruits [2]	Miscellaneous Noncitrus [3]	Nuts [4]	Total
	Acres				
2009	844,800	1,739,670	306,280	1,159,700	4,050,450
2010	825,200	1,750,300	309,995	1,206,000	4,091,495
2011	809,200	1,744,240	315,510	1,261,500	4,130,450
2012	801,800	1,734,600	260,710	1,316,000	4,113,110
2013	791,200	1,757,980	347,950	1,409,000	4,306,130
2014	777,700	1,742,290	368,955	1,487,000	4,375,945
2015	764,900	1,729,230	371,150	1,533,000	4,398,280
2016	737,800	1,693,970	367,460	1,971,200	4,770,430
2017	709,800	1,680,250	351,680	2,076,800	4,818,530
2018	697,900	1,551,800	329,460	2,174,800	4,753,960

[1] Grapefruit, lemons, oranges, tangelos, and tangerines. [2] Commercial apples, apricots, cherries, grapes, nectarines, peaches, pears, plums, and prunes. [3] Avocados, bananas, berries, coffee, cranberries, dates, figs, guavas, kiwifruit, olives, papayas, and strawberries. [4] Almonds, hazelnuts, macadamia nuts, pistachios, and walnuts. Bearing acreage estimates for pecans began in 2016.

NASS, Crops Branch, (202) 720–2127.

Table 5-2.—Fruits: Total production in tons, United States, 2009–2018 [1]

Year	Apples, commercial crop [2]	Pears	Grapes (fresh basis)	Sweet cherries	Tart cherries	Apricots
	Tons					
2009	4,843,850	957,220	7,267,890	442,870	179,600	68,720
2010	4,641,050	813,600	7,432,120	313,220	95,200	66,380
2011	4,719,800	965,720	7,408,740	334,415	115,900	66,650
2012	4,496,150	851,240	7,530,883	424,000	42,600	60,800
2013	5,261,700	877,130	8,631,790	332,090	147,100	61,035
2014	5,931,550	831,610	7,883,830	363,640	152,100	64,928
2015	5,051,250	816,520	7,621,150	335,480	126,250	45,657
2016	5,747,500	738,770	7,697,030	350,240	164,650	64,050
2017	5,776,850	737,450	7,383,850	437,550	129,750	45,650
2018	5,128,500	805,500	7,596,000	344,400	149,150	39,550

Year	Figs [3] (CA) (fresh basis)	Plums (CA)	Prunes (dry basis) (CA)	Olives (CA)	Strawberries	Avocados [4]
	Tons					
2009	43,750	112,000	166,000	46,300	1,400,650	298,520
2010	40,910	142,000	130,000	206,000	1,426,000	174,330
2011	38,660	160,000	137,000	71,200	1,450,800	262,950
2012	35,200	115,000	138,000	160,000	1,526,000	(NA)
2013	33,000	100,600	85,000	166,000	1,523,500	182,920
2014	33,400	104,000	108,000	95,000	1,511,850	172,940
2015	31,700	92,500	112,000	179,000	1,532,750	228,990
2016	32,700	108,800	54,000	164,900	1,480,345	138,050
2017	31,200	117,900	105,000	192,300	1,360,400	187,680
2018	(NA)	100,000	90,200	53,600	1,428,895	185,770

Year	Nectarines	Oranges [5]	Tangerines and Mandarins [5 6]	Grapefruit [5]	Lemons [5]	Tangelos [5 7] (FL)
	Tons					
2009	219,800	9,128,000	443,000	1,304,000	912,000	52,000
2010	233,200	8,243,000	596,000	1,238,000	882,000	41,000
2011	225,200	8,905,000	657,000	1,264,000	920,000	52,000
2012	188,900	8,982,000	644,000	1,153,000	850,000	52,000
2013	162,100	8,268,000	682,000	1,204,000	912,000	45,000
2014	187,300	6,768,000	732,000	1,047,000	824,000	40,000
2015	159,500	6,353,000	863,000	910,000	904,000	30,000
2016	151,350	6,088,000	935,000	803,000	904,000	18,000
2017	141,850	5,088,000	1,029,000	698,000	882,000	(NA)
2018	120,500	3,875,000	804,000	509,000	888,000	(NA)

Year	Bananas [3]	Kiwifruit (CA)	Dates	Papayas (HI) [8]	Peaches	Cranberries
	Tons					
2009	9,250	25,600	23,700	15,750	1,103,520	345,650
2010	8,900	32,700	29,000	15,050	1,149,430	340,410
2011	8,700	37,700	33,300	14,300	1,071,270	385,685
2012	(NA)	29,600	31,100	(NA)	968,070	402,250
2013	7,250	27,600	30,500	12,100	905,371	447,870
2014	6,000	28,500	33,400	11,750	852,799	420,000
2015	4,530	20,900	39,000	12,600	844,780	428,150
2016	2,775	28,300	37,340	9,875	791,940	481,370
2017	3,305	33,600	43,320	11,125	700,770	419,703
2018	(NA)	37,800	41,050	5,145	651,500	446,300

(NA) Not available. [1] For some crops in certain years, production includes some quantities unharvested for economic reasons or excess cullage fruit. [2] Estimates of the commercial crop refer to production in orchards of 100 or more bearing-age trees. [3] Estimates discontinued in 2018. [4] Year of bloom. [5] Year harvest was complete. [6] Beginning in 2015, tangerine and mandarin estimates are discontinued for Arizona. [7] Beginning in 2016, tangelos are included in tangerines and mandarins. [8] Utilized production.

NASS, Crops Branch, (202) 720–2127.

Table 5-3.—Apples, commercial crop: Production and season average price per pound, by State and United States, 2016–2018

State	Total production			Utilized production			Price per pound for crop of—		
	2016	2017	2018	2016	2017	2018	2016	2017	2018
	Million pounds						*Dollars*		
California	255.0	230.0	250.0	250.0	225.0	245.0	0.207	0.333	0.290
Connecticut [1]	12.9	29.5	(NA)	12.5	29.3	(NA)	0.973	0.679	(NA)
Idaho [1]	55.2	47.4	(NA)	55.0	45.0	(NA)	0.175	0.181	(NA)
Illinois [1]	18.7	22.4	(NA)	18.1	21.4	(NA)	0.872	0.647	(NA)
Maine [1]	33.9	39.2	(NA)	33.7	37.5	(NA)	0.484	0.439	(NA)
Maryland [1]	40.6	48.4	(NA)	40.5	48.0	(NA)	0.262	0.193	(NA)
Massachusetts [1]	31.0	49.6	(NA)	30.4	48.5	(NA)	0.444	0.382	(NA)
Michigan	1,275.0	900.0	1,050.0	1,273.0	899.0	1,049.0	0.255	0.303	0.281
Minnesota [1]	21.5	25.7	(NA)	20.9	24.2	(NA)	0.816	0.864	(NA)
New Jersey [1]	31.9	38.5	(NA)	31.0	37.0	(NA)	1.080	0.943	(NA)
New York	1,250.0	1,350.0	1,395.0	1,240.0	1,330.0	1,376.8	0.279	0.269	0.191
North Carolina [1] ..	114.0	104.0	(NA)	113.0	102.0	(NA)	0.238	0.247	(NA)
Ohio [1]	41.9	58.9	(NA)	41.4	58.4	(NA)	0.523	0.474	(NA)
Oregon	195.4	175.2	170.0	195.0	175.0	169.0	0.307	0.221	0.327
Pennsylvania	467.0	528.0	488.0	464.0	526.0	484.1	0.192	0.223	0.222
Vermont [1]	30.0	30.9	(NA)	29.8	30.7	(NA)	0.685	0.742	(NA)
Virginia	180.0	225.0	204.0	178.0	224.0	201.9	0.201	0.217	0.185
Washington	7,320.0	7,500.0	6,700.0	6,900.0	7,200.0	6,365.0	0.341	0.338	0.343
West Virginia [1]	80.0	102.0	(NA)	79.8	101.0	(NA)	0.185	0.179	(NA)
Wisconsin [1]	41.0	49.0	(NA)	39.5	47.9	(NA)	0.552	0.549	(NA)
United States	11,495.0	11,553.7	10,257.0	11,045.6	11,209.9	9,890.8	0.316	0.321	0.305

-Represents zero. (NA) Not available. [1] Estimates discontinued in 2018.
NASS, Crops Branch, (202) 720–2127.

Table 5-4.—Apples: Production and value, United States, 2009–2018

Year	Apples, commercial crop			
	Total production	Utilized production	Marketing year average price [1]	Value
	Million pounds	*Million pounds*	*Cents per pound*	*1,000 dollars*
2009	9,687.7	9,435.6	23.1	2,182,003
2010	9,282.1	9,205.0	25.1	2,310,982
2011	9,439.6	9,328.8	30.3	2,830,784
2012	8,992.3	8,926.5	37.1	3,314,996
2013	10,523.4	10,131.7	30.2	3,147,435
2014	11,863.1	11,269.9	25.6	2,886,900
2015	10,102.5	10,022.9	33.6	3,365,665
2016	11,495.0	11,045.6	31.6	3,492,607
2017	11,553.7	11,209.9	32.1	3,601,447
2018	10,257.0	9,890.8	30.5	3,013,713

[1] Fresh fruit prices are equivalent packinghouse-door returns for California, Michigan, New York, Pennsylvania, and Washington; prices at point of first sale for other States. Processing prices are equivalent at processing plant door.
NASS, Crops Branch, (202) 720–2127.

Table 5-5.—International Apples, fresh: Production, 2016/2017–2018/2019

Country	2016/2017	2017/2018	2018/2019
	metric tons		
China	40,393,000	41,390,000	31,000,000
European Union	12,722,620	10,013,600	14,008,570
United States	5,010,201	5,084,727	5,048,000
Turkey	2,900,000	2,750,000	3,000,000
Iran	2,799,200	2,799,200	2,799,200
India	2,258,000	1,920,000	2,300,000
Russia	1,509,148	1,359,580	1,503,100
Chile	1,310,000	1,330,000	1,264,000
Ukraine	1,099,200	1,099,200	1,099,200
Brazil	1,049,300	1,049,300	1,049,300
South Africa	902,130	790,000	840,000
Japan	765,000	765,000	765,000
Mexico	716,930	714,149	660,000
Argentina	560,000	560,000	590,000
New Zealand	523,000	575,500	561,000
Belarus	509,300	509,300	509,300
Canada	408,404	345,568	395,300
Serbia	328,400	328,400	328,400
Australia	308,300	308,300	308,300
Azerbaijan	254,300	254,300	254,300
Kazakhstan	188,100	188,100	188,100
Kyrgyzstan	135,600	135,600	135,600
Uruguay	37,700	37,700	37,700
Guatemala	26,500	26,500	26,500
Norway	12,400	12,400	12,400
Colombia	2,300	2,300	2,300
Taiwan	1,483	1,451	1,500
World Total	76,730,516	74,350,175	68,687,070

FAS, Office of Global Analysis, (202) 720-6301. Prepared or estimated on the basis of official USDA production, supply, and distribution statistics from foreign governments.

Table 5-6.—Apples, commercial crop: Production and utilization, United States, 2009–2018

Crop of—	Total production	Utilized production	Utilization				
			Fresh	Processed (fresh basis)			
				Canned	Dried	Frozen	Juice, cider & other [1]
	Million pounds						
2009	9,687.7	9,435.6	6,296.4	1,158.2	161.2	236.2	1,583.6
2010	9,282.1	9,205.0	6,248.8	1,088.3	175.5	206.0	1,486.4
2011	9,439.6	9,328.8	6,312.9	1,123.7	183.5	190.5	1,517.8
2012	8,992.3	8,926.5	6,594.9	748.9	223.0	66.6	1,292.8
2013	10,523.4	10,431.7	6,918.7	1,311.2	161.0	249.3	1,791.0
2014	11,863.1	11,269.9	7,909.0	1,161.5	171.0	250.5	1,767.8
2015	10,102.5	10,022.9	6,928.1	1,121.1	179.0	187.5	1,527.5
2016	11,495.0	11,045.6	7,745.1	1,211.1	339.2	137.5	1,478.6
2017	11,553.7	11,209.9	7,815.8	1,161.9	370.0	119.0	1,574.8
2018	10,257.0	9,890.8	6,865.1	(NA)	(NA)	(NA)	(NA)

[1] Includes vinegar, wine, and slices for pie making.
NASS, Crops Branch, (202) 720–2127.

Table 5-7.—Apples, commercial crop: Production and utilization, by State and United States, crop of 2017 and 2018

State	Total production	Utilized production	Utilization: Fresh	Processed (fresh basis): Canned	Dried	Frozen	Juice, cider & other [1]
	2017						
	Million pounds						
California	230.0	225.0	(D)	....	....	....	....
Connecticut	29.5	29.3	25.9	....	....	....	....
Idaho	47.4	45.0	24.6	....	....	....	....
Illinois	22.4	21.4	(D)	....	....	....	....
Maine	39.2	37.5	27.5	....	....	....	....
Maryland	48.4	48.0	16.4	....	....	....	....
Massachusetts	49.6	48.5	31.0	....	....	....	....
Michigan	900.0	899.0	490.0	210.0	....	....	75.0
Minnesota	25.7	24.2	22.0	....	....	....	....
New Jersey	38.5	37.0	28.0	....	....	....	....
New York	1,350.0	1,330.0	735.0	252.0	....	....	284.0
North Carolina	104.0	102.0	52.0	....	....	....	....
Ohio	58.9	58.4	48.5	....	....	....	....
Oregon	175.2	175.0	148.0	....	....	....	....
Pennsylvania	528.0	526.0	236.0	220.0	....	....	38.0
Vermont	30.9	30.7	24.3	....	....	....	....
Virginia	225.0	224.0	91.0	....	....	....	....
Washington	7,500.0	7,200.0	5,650.0	(D)	....	....	(D)
West Virginia	102.0	101.0	36.0	....	....	....	....
Wisconsin	49.0	47.9	37.0	....	....	....	....
Other States [2]	....	....	92.6	479.9	....	....	997.8
United States	11,553.7	11,209.9	7,815.8	1,161.9	370.0	123.0	1,574.8

State	Total production	Utilized production	Fresh
	2018		
	Million pounds		
California	250.0	245.0	(D)
Connecticut [3]	(NA)	(NA)	(NA)
Idaho [3]	(NA)	(NA)	(NA)
Illinois [3]	(NA)	(NA)	(NA)
Maine [3]	(NA)	(NA)	(NA)
Maryland [3]	(NA)	(NA)	(NA)
Massachusetts [3]	(NA)	(NA)	(NA)
Michigan	1,050.0	1,049.0	545.0
Minnesota [3]	(NA)	(NA)	(NA)
New Jersey [3]	(NA)	(NA)	(NA)
New York	1,395.0	1,376.8	747.7
North Carolina [3]	(NA)	(NA)	(NA)
Ohio [3]	(NA)	(NA)	(NA)
Oregon	170.0	169.0	(D)
Pennsylvania	488.0	484.1	233.8
Vermont [3]	(NA)	(NA)	(NA)
Virginia	204.0	201.9	83.6
Washington	6,700.0	6,365.0	5,025.0
West Virginia [3]	(NA)	(NA)	(NA)
Wisconsin [3]	(NA)	(NA)	(NA)
Other States [2]	-	-	230.0
United States	10,257.0	9,890.8	6,865.1

(D) Data withheld to avoid disclosing data for individual operations. [1] Includes vinegar, wine, and slices for pie making. [2] Includes data withheld above and/or data for States not listed in this table. [3] Estimates discontinued in 2018.
NASS, Crops Branch, (202) 720–2127.

Table 5-8.—Fruits, fresh: United States exports by country of destination, 2017–2019

Country	2017	2018	2019
	Metric tons		
Fresh fruits, deciduous:			
Mexico	428,149	462,730	424,824
Canada	348,683	351,058	340,211
Taiwan	94,584	81,088	116,561
Vietnam	35,747	53,087	70,978
India	105,352	153,411	58,616
Hong Kong	76,718	58,102	49,181
Indonesia	44,102	35,029	39,723
Korea, South	32,244	40,267	31,808
Thailand	20,002	21,799	26,791
Dominican Republic	22,705	24,990	26,011
China	50,874	31,984	25,653
Japan	21,222	23,297	24,454
Philippines	24,977	23,201	24,402
Australia(*)	18,754	20,729	20,702
Saudi Arabia	22,961	20,927	20,204
Guatemala	15,843	16,892	18,407
United Arab Emirates	35,014	24,802	17,150
Singapore	12,042	13,075	12,712
Colombia	16,794	13,381	11,728
El Salvador	10,384	11,630	11,223
Malaysia	14,856	18,989	11,178
Israel(*)	8,999	14,478	10,870
Honduras	10,741	9,322	10,713
New Zealand(*)	8,482	9,864	9,779
Costa Rica	12,103	12,511	8,768
Peru	6,490	4,718	7,040
Ecuador	6,203	6,100	6,987
Panama	8,239	7,317	6,126
Trinidad and Tobago	4,939	4,832	4,952
Chile	3,210	3,815	3,990
Rest of World	46,368	40,839	35,359
World Total	1,567,780	1,614,262	1,487,102

(*) Denotes a country that is a summarization of its component countries. All zeroes for a data item may show that statistics exist in the other import type. Consumption or General. Users should use cautious interpretation on Quantity reports using mixed units of measure. Quantity line items will only include statistics on the units of measure that are equal to, or are able to be converted to, the assigned unit of measure of the grouped commodities.

FAS, Office of Global Analysis, (202) 720-6301. Data Source: U.S. Census Bureau Trade Data.

Table 5-9.—Apples: Foreign trade, United States, 2009–2018[1]

Year beginning October	Imports, fresh and dried, in terms of fresh	Domestic exports	
		Fresh	Dried, in terms of fresh[1]
	Metric tons	*Metric tons*	*Metric tons*
2009	225,717	748,054	22,127
2010	184,475	817,906	26,802
2011	219,305	856,819	28,492
2012	243,093	908,751	22,282
2013	243,875	848,671	23,741
2014	209,498	1,057,853	26,092
2015	233,564	746,893	27,894
2016	220,426	880,568	25,397
2017	181,452	996,498	18,652
2018	193,182	744,453	13,172

[1] Dried converted to terms of fresh apples on following basis; 1 pound dried is equivalent to 8 pounds fresh. No re-exports reported.
ERS, Crops Branch, (816) 926–6007.

Table 5-10.—Apricots: Production and value, United States, 2009–2018

Year	Total production	Utilized production	Market year average price per ton	Value
	Tons	*Tons*	*Dollars*	*1,000 dollars*
2009	68,720	68,690	654.00	44,912
2010	66,380	66,350	722.00	47,876
2011	66,650	66,620	616.00	41,056
2012	60,800	60,770	673.00	40,879
2013	61,035	61,028	737.00	44,987
2014	64,928	64,918	818.00	53,096
2015	45,657	45,507	1,010.00	45,889
2016	64,050	63,950	898.00	57,402
2017	45,650	45,500	979.00	44,556
2018	39,550	39,370	1,230.00	48,465

NASS, Crops Branch, (202) 720–2127.

Table 5-11.—Apricots: Production and marketing year average price per ton, by State and United States, 2016–2018

Utate	Total production			Utilized production			Price for crop of—		
	2016	2017	2018	2016	2017	2018	2016	2017	2018
	Tons	*Tons*	*Tons*	*Tons*	*Tons*	*Tons*	*Dollars*	*Dollars*	*Dollars*
California	56,000	37,000	31,700	55,950	36,900	31,570	875.00	945.00	1,210.00
Washington	8,050	8,650	7,850	8,000	8,600	7,800	1,060.00	1,130.00	1,330.00
United States	64,050	45,650	39,550	63,950	45,500	39,370	898.00	979.00	1,230.00

NASS, Crops Branch, (202) 720–2127.

Table 5-12.—Apricots: Production and utilization, United States, 2009–2018

Crop of—	Total production	Utilized production	Utilization of quantities sold		
			Fresh	Processed [1]	
				Canned	Dried (fresh basis)
	Tons	*Tons*	*Tons*	*Tons*	*Tons*
2009	68,720	68,690	25,170	23,120	9,000
2010	66,380	66,350	23,510	20,340	10,000
2011	66,650	66,620	23,990	17,230	12,000
2012	60,800	60,770	23,130	16,640	9,500
2013	61,035	61,028	25,228	14,550	10,000
2014	64,928	64,918	25,812	17,550	9,500
2015	45,657	45,507	19,104	9,000	9,000
2016	64,050	63,950	28,500	13,350	11,000
2017	45,650	45,500	22,300	8,400	(D)
2018	39,550	39,370	23,870	(NA)	(NA)

(D) Withheld to avoid disclosure of individual operations. (NA) Not available. [1] California only. Estimates discontinued in 2018.
NASS, Crops Branch, (202) 720–2127.

Table 5-13.—Apricots: Production and utilization, by State and United States, crop of 2018

State	Total production	Utilized production	Utilization	
			Fresh	Processed
	Tons			
California	31,700	31,570	(D)	(D)
Washington	7,850	7,800	(D)	(D)
Other States [1]			23,870	15,500
United States	39,550	39,370	23,870	15,500

(D) Withheld to avoid disclosure of individual operations. [1] Includes data withheld above.
NASS, Crops Branch, (202) 720–2127.

Table 5-14.—Apricots: Foreign trade, United States, 2009–2018

Year beginning October	Domestic exports				
	Fresh	Canned [1]	Dried [1]	Dried, in fruit salad [2]	Total, in terms of fresh [3]
	Metric tons	*Metric tons*	*Metric tons*	*Metric tons*	*Metric tons*
2009	5,555	1,308	1,011	389	11,691
2010	5,646	1,389	708	470	10,283
2011	7,459	660	634	519	11,191
2012	7,774	646	533	547	10,978
2013	6,859	755	473	504	9,831
2014	5,402	621	370	409	7,749
2015	7,249	508	668	214	11,045
2016	7,775	718	894	163	12,887
2017	4,458	666	749	88	8,784
2018	5,010	560	859	106	9,827

[1] Net processed weight. [2] Dried apricots are 12⅓ percent of total dried fruit for salad. [3] Dried fruit converted to unprocessed dry weight by dividing by 1.07. Unprocessed dry weight converted to terms of fresh fruit on the basis that 1 pound dried equals 5.5 pounds fresh. Canned apricots converted to terms of fresh on the basis that 1 pound canned equals 0.717 pounds fresh.
ERS, Crops Branch, (816) 926–6007.

Table 5-15.—Avocados: Foreign trade, United States, 2009–2018

Year beginning October	Imports
	Metric tons
2009	365,146
2010	385,434
2011	475,630
2012	565,127
2013	699,388
2014	832,841
2015	874,209
2016	877,043
2017	1,017,273
2018	1,083,948

ERS, Crops Branch, (816) 926–5255.

Table 5-16.—Avocados: Total production, marketing year average price per ton, and value of utilized production, by State and United States, 2009/2010 to 2018/2019

Season	California			Florida		
	Production	Price per ton	Value	Production	Price per ton	Value
	Tons	*Dollars*	*1,000 dollars*	*Tons*	*Dollars*	*1,000 dollars*
2009/2010	274,800	1,510.00	414,948	23,200	600.00	13,920
2010/2011	151,500	3,040.00	460,560	22,500	800.00	18,000
2011/2012	231,500	1,650.00	381,975	31,100	756.00	23,512
2012/2013	(NA)	(NA)	(NA)	(NA)	(NA)	(NA)
2013/2014	149,000	2,240.00	333,760	33,400	796.00	26,586
2014/2015	140,000	2,170.00	303,800	32,500	656.00	21,320
2015/2016	201,000	2,050.00	412,050	27,300	745.00	20,339
2016/2017	113,000	3,140.00	351,240	24,100	798.00	19,080
2017/2018	170,000	2,260.00	382,460	16,900	477.00	8,014
2018/2019	171,000	2,270.00	383,485	13,900	1,120.00	15,278

Season	Hawaii			United States		
	Production	Price per ton	Value	Production	Price per ton	Value
	Tons	*Dollars*	*1,000 dollars*	*Tons*	*Dollars*	*1,000 dollars*
2009/2010	520	1,380.00	718	298,520	1,440.00	429,586
2010/2011	330	1,540.00	508	174,330	2,750.00	479,068
2011/2012	350	1,600.00	560	262,950	1,540.00	406,047
2012/2013	(NA)	(NA)	(NA)	(NA)	(NA)	(NA)
2013/2014	520	2,000.00	1,040	182,920	1,980.00	361,386
2014/2015	440	2,860.00	1,258	172,940	1,890.00	326,378
2015/2016	690	2,310.00	1,481	228,990	1,900.00	433,870
2016/2017	950	2,150.00	1,934	138,050	2,720.00	372,254
2017/2018	780	2,080.00	1,538	187,680	2,100.00	392,012
2018/2019	870	2,040.00	1,591	185,770	2,180.00	400,354

(NA) Not available.
NASS, Crops Branch, (202) 720–2127.

Table 5-17.—Bananas: Bearing acreage, yield, utilized production, marketing year average price, and value, Hawaii, 2008–2017 [1]

Year	Bearing acreage	Yield per acre	Utilized Production	Price per pound	Value
	Acres	*1,000 pounds*	*1,000 pounds*	*Cents*	*1,000 dollars*
2008	1,100	15.8	17,400	46.0	8,004
2009	1,100	16.8	18,500	55.0	10,175
2010	1,100	16.2	17,800	60.0	10,680
2011	1,000	17.4	17,400	65.0	11,310
2012	(NA)	(NA)	(NA)	(NA)	(NA)
2013	1,250	11.6	14,500	90.0	13,050
2014	1,210	9.9	12,000	82.0	9,840
2015	1,150	8.0	9,060	91.2	8,265
2016	1,050	5.3	5,550	101.0	5,592
2017	950	7.0	6,610	91.2	6,028

(NA) Not available. [1] Estimates discontinued in 2018.
NASS, Crops Branch, (202) 720–2127.

Table 5-18.—Kiwifruit: Area, yield, utilized production, marketing year average price, and value, California, 2009–2018

Year	Bearing acreage	Yield [1]	Utilized Production	Price per ton	Value
	Acres	*Tons*	*Tons*	*Dollars*	*1,000 dollars*
2009	4,200	6.10	24,900	847	21,084
2010	4,200	7.79	32,500	768	24,961
2011	4,000	8.98	36,700	775	28,439
2012	3,700	8.00	27,100	1,020	27,508
2013	3,800	7.26	26,900	1,110	29,812
2014	3,700	7.70	27,900	1,190	33,333
2015	3,500	5.97	20,900	1,470	30,723
2016	3,900	7.26	28,300	1,570	44,431
2017	3,600	9.33	33,200	1,050	34,860
2018	3,900	9.70	37,800	870	32,886

[1] Yield based on total production.
NASS, Crops Branch, (202) 720-2127.

Table 5-19.—Cherries: Foreign trade, United States, 2009–2018

Year beginning October	Imports		Domestic exports	
	Fresh	Dried and preserved	Fresh	Canned
	Metric tons	*Metric tons*	*Metric tons*	*Metric tons*
2009	13,601	5,036	58,737	13,758
2010	23,126	5,076	71,542	13,544
2011	17,250	6,289	101,073	16,127
2012	10,362	6,350	66,937	14,491
2013	12,033	6,614	87,626	17,761
2014	16,096	10,517	74,707	19,035
2015	11,463	8,067	75,952	17,465
2016	12,422	8,125	111,772	17,107
2017	14,509	9,194	86,648	18,805
2018	10,005	9,472	84,318	12,836

ERS, Crops Branch, (816) 926–6007.

Table 5-20.—Sweet cherries: Production and value, United States, 2009–2018

Year	Total production	Utilized production	Marketing year average price per ton [1]	Value
	Tons	*Tons*	*Dollars*	*1,000 dollars*
2009	442,870	385,625	1,330.00	513,330
2010	313,220	307,630	2,330.00	715,684
2011	334,415	330,290	2,530.00	834,585
2012	424,000	418,415	2,020.00	843,313
2013	332,090	295,950	2,610.00	771,798
2014	363,640	358,910	2,140.00	766,551
2015	335,480	333,886	2,250.00	751,122
2016	350,240	343,090	2,250.00	773,021
2017	437,550	433,020	2,060.00	891,652
2018	344,400	342,070	1,860.00	637,700

[1] Fresh fruit prices are equivalent packinghouse-door returns for Western States, and the average price as sold for other States. Quantities processed are priced at the equivalent processing plant door level.
NASS, Crops Branch, (202) 720–2127.

Table 5-21.—Tart cherries: Production and value, United States, 2009–2018

Year	Total production	Utilized production	Marketing year average price per pound [1]	Value
	Million pounds	*Million pounds*	*Dollars*	*1,000 dollars*
2009	359.2	320.8	0.192	61,628
2010	190.4	183.2	0.222	40,741
2011	231.8	230.3	0.300	69,072
2012	85.2	85.0	0.594	50,520
2013	294.2	291.1	0.359	104,395
2014	304.2	300.6	0.355	106,810
2015	252.5	251.1	0.347	87,037
2016	329.3	318.7	0.274	87,335
2017	259.5	254.1	0.224	56,868
2018	214.4	288.8	0.196	56,635

[1] Fresh fruit prices are equivalent packinghouse-door returns for Western States, and the average price as sold for other States. Quantities processed are priced at the equivalent processing plant door level.
NASS, Crops Branch, (202) 720–2127.

Table 5-22.—Sweet cherries: Production and season average price, by State and United States, 2016–2018

State	Total production			Utilized production			Price [1]		
	2016	2017	2018	2016	2017	2018	2016	2017	2018
	Tons	*Tons*	*Tons*	*Tons*	*Tons*	*Tons*	*Dollars per ton*	*Dollars per ton*	*Dollars per ton*
California	55,000	97,800	44,800	52,500	95,000	44,170	3,510.00	3,480.00	3,180.00
Michigan [2]	22,610	21,300	(NA)	22,510	21,020	(NA)	808.00	765.00	(NA)
Oregon	62,080	55,900	54,600	59,080	55,400	54,100	1,340.00	1,270.00	1,310.00
Washington	210,550	262,550	245,000	209,000	261,600	243,800	2,350.00	1,810.00	1,750.00
United States	350,240	437,550	344,400	343,090	433,020	342,070	2,250.00	2,060.00	1,860.00

(NA) Not available. [1] Fresh fruit prices are equivalent packinghouse-door returns for California, Oregon, and Washington, and the average price as sold for other States. Quantities processed are priced at the equivalent processing plant door level. [2] Estimates discontinued in 2018.
NASS, Crops Branch, (202) 720–2127.

Table 5-23.—Tart cherries: Production and season average price, by State and United States, 2016–2018

State	Total production			Utilized production			Price [1]		
	2016	2017	2018	2016	2017	2018	2016	2017	2018
	Million pounds	*Million pounds*	*Million pounds*	*Million pounds*	*Million pounds*	*Million pounds*	*Dollars per Lb.*	*Dollars per Lb.*	*Dollars per Lb.*
Michigan	227.0	189.2	201.0	224.7	188.0	198.2	0.239	0.211	0.191
New York	7.9	8.0	(D)	7.9	7.7	(D)	0.304	0.316	(D)
Utah	52.8	26.0	45.0	49.6	25.0	41.0	0.353	0.304	0.222
Washington	28.0	25.0	(D)	23.0	24.0	(D)	0.415	0.210	(D)
Wisconsin	13.6	11.3	10.9	13.5	9.4	10.0	0.302	0.224	0.193
Other States	....	....	41.4	....	....	39.6	(X)	(X)	0.194
United States	329.3	259.5	298.3	318.7	254.1	288.8	0.274	0.224	0.196

(D) Withheld to avoid disclosing data for individual operations. (X) Not applicable. [1] Fresh fruit prices are equivalent packinghouse-door returns for Oregon and Washington, and the average price as sold for other States. Quantities processed are priced at the equivalent processing plant door level.
NASS, Crops Branch, (202) 720–2127.

Table 5-24.—Sweet cherries: Production and utilization, by State and United States, crop of 2018[1]

State	Total production	Utilized production	Utilization		
			Fresh[1]	Processed[2]	
				Canned	Brined
	Tons				
California	44,800	44,170	35,660	....	....
Michigan[2]	(NA)	(NA)	(NA)	....	....
Oregon	54,600	54,100	41,000	....	(NA)
Washington	245,000	243,800	214,400	(NA)	(NA)
United States	344,400	343,090	291,060	(NA)	(NA)

- Represents zero. (NA) Not available. [1] Includes "Home use." [2] Estimates discontinued in 2018.
NASS, Crops Branch, (202) 720–2127.

Table 5-25.—Tart cherries: Production and utilization, by State and United States, crop of 2018[1]

State	Total production	Utilized production	Utilization		
			Fresh[1]	Processed	
				Canned[2]	Frozen[2]
	Million pounds				
Michigan	201.0	198.2	0.2	(NA)	(NA)
New York	(D)	(D)	(D)	....	....
Utah	45.0	41.0	....	....	....
Washington	(D)	(D)	(D)	....	....
Wisconsin	10.9	10.0	0.3	....	....
Other States[3]	41.4	39.6	0.3	(NA)	(NA)
United States	298.3	288.8	0.8	(NA)	(NA)

(D) Withheld to avoid disclosing data for individual operations. (NA) Not available. [1] Includes "Home use." [2] Estimates discontinued in 2018. [3] Includes data withheld above and/or data for States not listed in this table.
NASS, Crops Branch, (202) 720–2127.

Table 5-26.—Sweet cherries: Production and utilization, United States, 2009–2018

Crop of—	Total production	Utilized production	Utilization of quantities sold		
			Fresh [1]	Processed	
				Other [2]	Brined
	Tons				
2009	442,870	385,625	296,750	29,053	51,571
2010	313,220	307,630	244,340	21,905	38,234
2011	334,415	330,290	258,920	25,495	39,625
2012	424,000	418,415	332,555	35,795	47,065
2013	332,090	295,950	217,950	28,535	44,945
2014	363,640	358,910	268,010	40,360	47,041
2015	335,480	333,886	250,806		43,090
2016	350,240	343,090	257,860		51,600
2017	437,550	433,020	348,920		51,850
2018	344,400	342,070	291,060		

[1] Includes "Home use." [2] Includes canned utilization and other processed utilizations from all States.
NASS, Crops Branch, (202) 720–2127.

Table 5-27.—Tart cherries: Production and utilization, United States, 2009–2018

Crop of—	Total production	Utilized production	Utilization of quantities sold		
			Fresh [1]	Processed	
				Other [2]	Frozen
	Million pounds				
2009	359.2	320.8	1.3	35.3	232.0
2010	190.4	183.2	0.8	21.2	125.9
2011	231.8	230.3	0.5	37.3	154.1
2012	85.2	85.0	0.4	18.3	59.8
2013	294.2	291.1	1.2	92.4	158.4
2014	304.2	300.6	1.9	63.3	198.9
2015	252.5	251.1	1.2		175.4
2016	329.3	318.7	0.6		240.6
2017	259.5	254.1	0.8		169.8
2018	298.3	288.8	0.8		

[1] Includes "Home use." [2] Includes canned utilization and other processed utilizations from all states.
NASS, Crops Branch, (202) 720–2127.

Table 5-28.—Citrus fruit: Utilized production and value, United States, for season of 2009/2010 to 2018/2019

Season [1]	Production	Marketing year average returns per box [2]	Value	Quantities processed
	Oranges [3]			
	1,000 boxes	*Dollars*	*1,000 dollars*	*1,000 boxes*
2009/2010	192,835	10.24	1,997,188	137,628
2010/2011	204,949	10.90	2,230,412	148,237
2011/2012	206,119	12.70	2,621,620	149,972
2012/2013	189,893	10.85	2,073,638	134,799
2013/2014	155,977	14.29	2,254,303	109,376
2014/2015	146,602	13.29	1,963,353	102,388
2015/2016	141,891	13.55	1,927,270	91,791
2016/2017	118,520	16.30	1,943,678	74,437
2017/2018	91,130	19.82	1,830,445	50,081
2018/2019	124,050	13.76	1,704,399	83,115
	Grapefruit			
2009/2010	30,400	9.65	291,424	13,231
2010/2011	30,360	9.29	283,597	14,276
2011/2012	27,650	10.08	279,033	13,121
2012/2013	28,950	8.87	256,524	14,340
2013/2014	25,200	9.60	241,686	12,389
2014/2015	21,950	9.85	216,258	9,755
2015/2016	19,400	13.09	254,318	8,794
2016/2017	16,960	15.12	256,917	7,123
2017/2018	12,480	16.71	207,970	5,136
2018/2019	13,810	15.04	206,541	6,889
	Lemons			
2009/2010	23,200	17.04	395,339	10,482
2010/2011	23,000	16.80	386,514	7,987
2011/2012	21,250	21.12	448,698	4,869
2012/2013	22,800	17.56	400,295	7,394
2013/2014	20,600	31.13	641,259	4,840
2014/2015	22,600	30.83	696,835	7,302
2015/2016	22,600	33.41	755,080	5,224
2016/2017	22,050	34.62	763,446	4,535
2017/2018	22,200	32.24	715,761	5,195
2018/2019	24,150	28.39	685,708	6,538
	Tangerines and Mandarins [4]			
2009/2010	14,700	18.30	274,519	3,204
2010/2011	15,550	20.87	330,503	3,260
2011/2012	15,290	22.34	349,167	3,029
2012/2013	18,440	25.00	426,101	2,785
2013/2014	17,750	31.05	557,357	2,869
2014/2015	21,135	22.13	468,083	5,614
2015/2016	23,115	21.23	490,217	7,657
2016/2017	25,420	22.35	568,084	8,366
2017/2018	19,950	28.86	575,976	4,664
2018/2019	26,990	28.01	757,189	6,647

[1] The crop year begins with the bloom of the first year shown and ends with completion of harvest the following year. [2] Equivalent packing-house door returns. [3] Includes small quantities of tangerines in Texas and Temples in Florida. [4] Arizona and California tangelos and tangors included. Beginning in 2016/2017, Florida includes tangelos.
NASS, Crops Branch, (202) 720–2127.

Table 5-29.—Citrus fruit: Utilized production and marketing year average returns per box, by State, 2017/2018 and 2018/2019 [1]

Crop and State	Utilized production		Market year average price [2]	
	2017/2018	2018/2019	2017/2018	2018/2019
	1,000 boxes [3]	*1,000 boxes [3]*	*Dollars*	*Dollars*
Oranges				
Early, midseason, and Navel varieties:				
California	35,900	40,800	25.36	14.23
Florida	18,950	30,400	13.70	12.40
Texas	1,530	2,210	17.37	8.95
Total	56,380	73,410	20.92	13.26
Valencia:				
California	8,300	9,000	22.00	9.99
Florida	26,100	41,350	22.85	18.25
Texas	350	290	25.60	16.60
Total	34,750	50,640	18.14	14.44
All oranges:				
California	44,200	49,800	24.73	13.46
Florida	45,050	71,750	15.58	14.07
Texas	1,880	2,500	18.90	9.84
United States	91,130	124,050	19.82	13.76
Grapefruit				
California	3,800	3,200	18.34	17.49
Florida, all	3,880	4,510	18.87	18.93
Red	3,180	3,740	19.32	18.92
White [4]	700	770	16.81	18.98
Texas	4,800	6,100	13.56	10.69
United States	12,480	13,810	16.71	15.04
Lemons				
Arizona	1,000	1,350	34.20	30.89
California	21,200	22,800	32.15	28.25
United States	22,200	24,150	32.24	28.29
Tangerines and Mandarins				
California [5]	19,200	26,000	28.96	28.29
Florida	750	990	26.60	21.84
United States	19,950	26,990	28.86	28.01

[1] The crop year begins with the bloom of the first year shown and ends with completion of harvest the following year. [2] Equivalent packinghouse-door returns. [3] Net lbs. per box: oranges—California, 80; Florida, 90; and Texas, 85; grapefruit—California, 80, Florida, 95; Florida, 85; Texas, 80; lemons—80; tangerines and mandarins—California, 80. [4] Includes seedy grapefruit. [5] Includes tangelos and tangors.

NASS, Crops Branch, (202) 720–2127.

Table 5-30.—International Citrus, fresh: Production in specified countries, 2017/2018-2019/2020

Country	Production		
	2017/2018	2018/2019	2019/2020
	1,000 metric tons		
Grapefruit:			
China	4,800	4,900	4,930
United States	462	512	582
Mexico	418	456	468
South Africa	403	390	420
Turkey	260	250	300
Israel	144	139	155
European Union	107	108	89
Japan	26	26	26
Lemons/limes:			
Mexico	2,311	2,401	2,422
Argentina	1,770	1,800	1,600
European Union	1,472	1,684	1,470
Turkey	1,000	1,100	1,000
United States	806	876	740
South Africa	446	498	530
Israel	65	68	75
Japan	50	42	51
Morocco	36	45	40
United Arab Emirates	5	5	5
Oranges:			
Brazil	15,953	19,380	15,100
China	7,300	7,200	7,300
European Union	6,270	6,505	5,840
United States	3,560	4,833	4,898
Mexico	4,737	4,389	4,417
Egypt	3,120	3,600	3,000
Turkey	1,905	1,900	1,800
South Africa	1,586	1,500	1,560
Morocco	1,021	1,183	815
Vietnam	770	770	770
Argentina	750	800	720
Australia	525	510	500
Costa Rica	315	295	310
Guatemala	180	180	180
Israel	76	68	76
Iraq	75	75	75
Mozambique	68	68	68
Bangladesh	21	21	21
Malaysia	13	13	13
Japan	6	6	6
Tangerines/mandarins:			
China	21,200	22,000	23,000
European Union	2,913	3,213	2,643
Turkey	1,550	1,650	1,500
Japan	968	904	952
Morocco	1,185	1,375	910
United States	729	986	844
Korea, South	577	608	645
South Africa	356	390	420
Argentina	350	450	390
Israel	162	198	200
Thailand	135	135	135
Philippines	13	13	13

FAS, Office of Global Analysis, (202) 720-6301. Prepared or estimated on the basis of official USDA production, supply, and distribution statistics from foreign governments.

Table 5-31.—Fresh fruits, citrus: United States exports by country of destination, 2017–2019

Country of destination	2017	2018	2019
	Metric tons		
Canada	185,034	162,503	166,742
Korea, South	226,947	163,937	155,299
Japan	125,874	110,944	119,065
Hong Kong	95,831	94,244	81,899
Mexico	21,637	25,460	39,323
China	46,975	42,197	24,719
Australia(*)	18,498	16,387	19,935
Taiwan	19,466	9,091	16,222
Singapore	11,343	10,123	9,916
Malaysia	10,110	9,388	9,514
New Zealand(*)	9,964	10,018	8,979
France(*)	10,566	6,935	8,909
Netherlands	7,858	9,856	6,816
Chile	6,876	6,918	5,867
Philippines	5,737	3,790	3,961
Peru	2,735	2,394	2,599
Indonesia	2,593	1,371	2,185
Ecuador	1,311	891	1,766
Bahamas, The	1,518	1,564	1,707
Dominican Republic	761	1,411	1,584
Belgium-Luxembourg(*)	2,895	1,071	1,170
Thailand	1,729	1,537	1,034
Guatemala	838	984	960
United Kingdom	1,159	833	832
Vietnam	133	113	729
Panama	577	595	641
Barbados	544	577	555
Cayman Islands	353	299	540
Other Pacific Islands, NEC(*)	119	281	517
French Pacific Islands(*)	331	474	356
Rest of World	4,466	2,914	2,318
World Total	824,779	699,097	696,656

(*) Denotes a country that is a summarization of its component countries. Users should use cautious interpretation on quantity reports using mixed units of measure. Quantity line items will only include statistics on the units of measure that are equal to, or are able to be converted to, the assigned unit of measure of the grouped commodities.
FAS, Office of Global Analysis,(202) 720–6301. Data Source: U.S. Census Bureau Trade Data.

Table 5-32.—Fresh citrus fruits: Foreign trade, United States, 2009–2018

Year[1]	Oranges		Grapefruit		Lemons		Limes		Tangerines	
	Imports	Domestic exports	Imports	Domestic exports	Imports	Domestic exports	Imports	Domestic exports	Imports	Domestic exports
	Metric tons	*Metric tons*	*Metric tons*	*Metric tons*	*Metric tons*	*Metric tons*	*Metric tons*	*Metric tons*	*Metric tons*	*Metric tons*
2009	101,180	665,157	11,370	245,696	40,848	91,445	362,317	2,317	7,748	18,195
2010	92,159	752,613	7,103	225,836	56,278	97,275	352,956	2,550	6,101	30,419
2011	131,519	694,530	2,869	207,537	50,939	92,081	423,350	3,434	4,202	22,786
2012	130,812	679,660	11,862	182,725	38,152	104,031	438,830	4,389	3,614	23,529
2013	156,261	507,665	13,777	146,673	56,996	122,420	438,273	4,569	2,573	17,628
2014	152,211	523,345	9,291	140,729	85,519	109,663	499,221	3,954	4,565	18,713
2015	166,074	655,187	21,931	123,458	83,851	107,338	542,152	4,433	7,882	12,837
2016	172,345	613,808	26,845	108,030	110,252	106,831	602,749	4,846	2,250	12,916
2017	219,023	511,675	10,216	57,647	110,827	88,565	605,356	5,342	3,550	11,749
2018	195,781	476,937	15,206	57,395	135,860	89,978	643,428	6,860	4,003	11,531

[1] Year beginning October for all commodities.
ERS, Crops Branch, (816) 926–6007.

Table 5-33.—Concentrated citrus juices: Annual packs, Florida, 2009–2018

Season beginning December	Frozen concentrated juice[1]		
	Orange[2]	Grapefruit[2]	Tangerine
	1,000 gallons	*1,000 gallons*	*1,000 gallons*
2009	82,260	7,904	740
2010	82,106	9,297	1,374
2011	106,432	9,059	1,083
2012	76,132	7,437	928
2013	35,655	5,745	825
2014	28,878	4,504	1,046
2015	22,269	3,275	276
2016	17,916	2,187	....
2017	9,948	600	....
2018	21,012	696	....

[1] Net pack. [2] Frozen orange juice reported in 42.0° Brix; Grapefruit 40.0° Brix. Includes concentrated juice for manufacture.
ERS, Crops Branch, (816) 926–6007.

Table 5-34.—Dates: Area, yield, total production, marketing year average price per ton, and value, California, 2009–2018

Year	Bearing acreage	Yield per acre	Production	Price per ton	Value
	Acres	*Tons*	*Tons*	*Dollars*	*1,000 dollars*
2009	6,700	3.54	23,700	1,180	27,966
2010	7,700	3.77	29,000	1,270	36,830
2011	8,400	3.96	33,300	1,320	43,956
2012	8,800	3.53	31,100	1,340	41,674
2013	8,200	3.72	30,500	1,220	37,210
2014	10,000	3.34	33,400	1,510	50,434
2015	10,200	3.82	39,000	1,560	60,840
2016	12,300	3.04	37,340	2,020	75,156
2017	13,400	3.23	43,320	3,510	150,959
2018	13,100	3.13	41,050	3,800	152,175

NASS, Crops Branch, (202) 720–2127.

Table 5-35.—Dates: Foreign trade, United States, 2009–2018

Year beginning October	Imports
	Metric tons
2009	12,094
2010	20,113
2011	22,875
2012	23,945
2013	28,974
2014	32,189
2015	27,939
2016	21,900
2017	35,823
2018	27,930

ERS, Crops Branch, (816) 927–6007.

Table 5-36.—Cranberries: Area, yield, production, season average price per barrel, value and quantities processed, United States, 2009–2018[1]

Year	Area harvested	Yield per acre[2]	Total production[3]	Utilized production	Price[4]	Value	Quantities processed[5]
	Acres	*Barrels*[6]	*Barrels*[6]	*Barrels*[6]	*Dollars*	*1,000 dollars*	*Barrels*[6]
2009	38,500	179.6	6,913,000	6,913,000	44.20	305,669	6,580,000
2010	38,500	176.8	6,808,200	6,808,200	43.90	299,123	6,589,000
2011	38,500	200.4	7,713,700	7,713,700	44.80	345,561	7,473,200
2012	40,300	199.6	8,045,000	8,045,000	47.90	385,506	7,791,000
2013	42,000	211.4	8,957,400	8,880,700	32.40	287,322	8,559,300
2014	40,600	202.9	8,400,000	8,236,000	30.90	254,412	7,968,000
2015	40,900	206.7	8,563,000	8,455,000	31.00	261,853	8,004,800
2016	41,500	230.0	9,627,400	9,544,000	30.60	292,292	9,083,900
2017	39,900	209.1	8,394,050	8,343,150	30.20	252,088	8,010,250
2018	39,300	227.1	8,926,000	8,846,560	25.10	222,440	8,578,900

[1] Estimates relate to Massachusetts, New Jersey, Oregon, Washington, and Wisconsin. [2] Derived from utilized production. [3] Differences between utilized and total production are quantities unharvested for economic reasons or excess cullage and/or set-aside production under provisions of the Cranberry Marketing Order. [4] Average price of utilized production. Equivalent returns at first delivery point, screened basis of utilized production. [5] Mainly for canning. [6] Barrels of 100 pounds.

NASS, Crops Branch, (202) 720–2127.

Table 5-37.—Cranberries: Area, yield, production, and season average price per barrel, by State and United States, 2016–2018

State	Area harvested			Yield per acre[1]		
	2016	2017	2018	2016	2017	2018
	Acres	*Acres*	*Acres*	*Bbl.*	*Bbl.*	*Bbl.*
Massachusetts	12,900	12,300	12,700	174.3	154.0	180.4
New Jersey	3,100	2,700	3,100	208.4	178.8	165.3
Oregon	2,800	2,800	2,800	140.7	173.0	206.7
Washington[2]	1,600	1,500	(NA)	109.4	98.4	(NA)
Wisconsin	21,100	20,600	20,700	288.2	259.5	267.8
United States	41,500	39,900	39,300	230.0	209.1	227.1
State	**Total production**			**Price per barrel[3]**		
	2016	2017	2018	2016	2017	2018
	Bbl.	*Bbl.*	*Bbl.*	*Dollars*	*Dollars*	*Dollars*
Massachusetts	2,268,000	1,911,400	2,290,000	30.70	31.50	22.30
New Jersey	653,000	473,300	512,000	43.10	36.60	31.10
Oregon	401,000	489,700	579,000	26.50	26.40	24.30
Washington[2]	175,400	147,650	(NA)	44.20	42.50	(NA)
Wisconsin	6,130,000	5,372,000	5,545,000	29.20	29.20	25.90
United States	9,627,400	8,394,050	8,926,000	30.60	30.20	25.10

[1] 2016 and 2017 yield is based upon utilized production. 2018 yield is based upon total production. [2] Estimates discontinued in 2018. [3] Average price of utilized production. Equivalent returns at first delivery point, screened basis of utilized production.
NASS, Crops Branch, (202) 720–2127.

Table 5-38.—Figs: Total production, marketing year average price per ton, and value, California, 2008–2017[1]

Year	Dried				Total		
	Production (dry basis)			Price per ton	Production	Price per ton	Value
	Total	Standard	Substandard				
	Tons	*1,000 tons*	*Tons*	*Dollars*	*Tons*	*Dollars*	*1,000 dollars*
2008	13,100	11,800	1,300	1,200	43,300	599	25,954
2009	13,300	12,000	1,300	1,540	43,750	695	30,422
2010	12,320	10,000	1,420	1,220	40,910	542	22,185
2011	11,560	10,140	1,420	1,230	38,660	526	20,336
2012	10,400	9,600	800	1,350	35,200	555	19,520
2013	9,300	8,600	700	1,500	33,000	610	20,143
2014	9,470	8,840	630	1,640	33,400	719	23,998
2015	8,940	8,320	620	1,760	31,700	799	25,333
2016	9,260	8,720	540	1,870	32,700	911	29,779
2017	9,100	8,570	530	1,490	31,200	916	28,568

[1] Estimates discontinued in 2018.
NASS, Crops Branch, (202) 720–2127.

Table 5-39.—Figs, dried: Foreign trade, United States, 2009–2018

Year beginning October	Imports for consumption	Domestic exports
	Metric tons	*Metric tons*
2009	4,035	5,795
2010	4,042	5,065
2011	4,236	5,449
2012	5,816	4,895
2013	10,294	4,537
2014	7,137	4,670
2015	11,821	3,964
2016	9,983	4,295
2017	12,427	3,353
2018	10,917	2,654

ERS, Crops Branch, (816) 926–6007.

Table 5-40.—Grapes: Production, price, and value, United States, 2009–2018

Year	Grapes			
	Production (fresh basis)		Market year average price per ton [1]	Value
	Total	Utilized		
	Tons	*Tons*	*Dollars*	*1,000 dollars*
2009	7,267,890	7,240,310	566.00	4,101,600
2010	7,432,120	7,429,490	542.00	4,023,967
2011	7,408,740	7,401,370	576.00	4,262,945
2012	7,530,883	7,524,443	752.00	5,661,096
2013	8,631,790	8,620,810	712.00	6,135,301
2014	7,883,830	7,871,580	740.00	5,822,250
2015	7,621,150	7,621,080	776.00	5,914,468
2016	7,697,030	7,694,900	818.00	6,294,150
2017	7,383,850	7,383,160	881.00	6,507,849
2018	7,596,000	7,596,000	871.00	6,615,121

[1] Fresh fruit prices are equivalent packinghouse-door returns for California and Washington, and the average price as sold for other States. Quantities processed are priced at the equivalent processing plant door level.
NASS, Crops Branch, (202) 720–2127.

Table 5-41.—Grapes: Production and marketing year average price per ton, by State and United States, 2016–2018

State	Total production			Utilized production		
	2016	2017	2018	2016	2017	2018
	Tons	*Tons*	*Tons*	*Tons*	*Tons*	*Tons*
California	6,752,000	6,507,000	7,130,000	6,752,000	6,507,000	7,130,000
Raisin [1]	1,570,000	1,301,000	1,545,000	1,570,000	1,301,000	1,545,000
Table [1]	1,150,000	1,190,000	1,300,000	1,150,000	1,190,000	1,300,000
Wine	4,032,000	4,016,000	4,285,000	4,032,000	4,016,000	4,285,000
Michigan [2]	93,400	63,600	(NA)	93,400	63,500	(NA)
Missouri [2]	5,330	6,130	(NA)	5,330	6,100	(NA)
New York [2]	171,000	187,000	(NA)	171,000	187,000	(NA)
North Carolina [2]	4,900	7,210	(NA)	4,900	7,200	(NA)
Ohio [2]	5,500	4,640	(NA)	5,470	4,600	(NA)
Oregon [2]	67,000	77,000	(NA)	67,000	77,000	(NA)
Pennsylvania [2]	85,800	91,700	(NA)	83,800	91,300	(NA)
Texas [2]	13,600	11,760	(NA)	13,500	11,660	(NA)
Virginia [2]	8,500	8,810	(NA)	8,500	8,800	(NA)
Washington	490,000	419,000	466,000	490,000	419,000	466,000
Juice	220,000	190,000	205,000	220,000	190,000	205,000
Wine	270,000	229,000	261,000	270,000	229,000	261,000
United States	7,697,030	7,383,850	7,596,000	7,694,900	7,383,160	7,596,000

State	Price per ton [3]		
	2016	2017	2018
	Dollars	*Dollars*	*Dollars*
California	832.00	899.00	877.00
Raisin [1]	277.00	414.00	424.00
Table [1]	1,340.00	1,330.00	978.00
Wine	905.00	927.00	1,010.00
Michigan [2]	312.00	379.00	(NA)
Missouri [2]	934.00	702.00	(NA)
New York [2]	373.00	369.00	(NA)
North Carolina [2]	895.00	734.00	(NA)
Ohio [2]	554.00	644.00	(NA)
Oregon [2]	2,140.00	2,230.00	(NA)
Pennsylvania [2]	324.00	281.00	(NA)
Texas [2]	1,530.00	1,620.00	(NA)
Virginia [2]	1,980.00	2,170.00	(NA)
Washington	735.00	761.00	774.00
Juice	213.00	220.00	220.00
Wine	1,160.00	1,210.00	1,210.00
United States	818.00	881.00	871.00

(NA) Not available. [1] Fresh equivalent of dried and not dried. [2] Estimates discontinued in 2018. [3] Fresh fruit prices are equivalent packinghouse-door returns for California and Washington, and the average price as sold for other States. Quantities processed are priced at the equivalent processing plant door level.
NASS, Crops Branch, (202) 720–2127.

Table 5-42.—Grapes: Production and utilization, United States, 2009–2018

Crop of—	Total production [1]	Utilized production	Utilization of quantities sold				
			Fresh	Processed			
				Canned	Dried (fresh basis)	Crushed for wine	Crushed for juice, etc. [2]
	Tons						
2009	7,267,890	7,240,310	898,940	20,000	1,510,000	4,373,070	438,300
2010	7,432,120	7,429,490	953,290	25,000	1,777,000	4,270,300	403,900
2011	7,408,740	7,401,370	944,740	25,000	1,807,000	4,154,530	470,100
2012	7,530,883	7,524,443	963,483	20,000	1,488,000	4,706,470	346,490
2013	8,631,790	8,620,810	1,116,940	22,000	1,909,000	5,067,610	504,160
2014	7,883,830	7,871,580	1,053,040	21,000	1,721,000	4,526,020	549,920
2015	7,621,150	7,621,080	1,043,970	22,000	1,864,000	4,254,330	435,780
2016	7,697,030	7,694,900	1,039,950	19,000	1,478,000	4,667,830	488,420
2017	7,383,850	7,383,160	1,030,310	16,000	1,221,000	4,662,950	451,900
2018	7,596,000	7,596,000	1,098,900	(NA)	(NA)	(NA)	(NA)

[1] Total production includes utilized production plus production not harvested and harvested not sold. [2] Mostly juice, but includes some quantities used for jam, jelly, etc.
NASS, Crops Branch, (202) 720–2127.

Table 5-43.—Grapes: Production and utilization, by State and United States, crop of 2018

State	Total production	Utilized production	Utilization	
			Fresh	Processed
	Tons			
California	7,130,000	7,130,000	1,098,900	6,031,100
Raisin	1,545,000	1,545,000	10,800	1,534,200
Table	1,300,000	1,300,000	1,088,100	211,900
Wine	4,285,000	4,285,000		4,285,000
Michigan [1]	(NA)	(NA)	(NA)	(NA)
Missouri [1]	(NA)	(NA)	(NA)	(NA)
New York [1]	(NA)	(NA)	(NA)	(NA)
North Carolina [1]	(NA)	(NA)	(NA)	(NA)
Ohio [1]	(NA)	(NA)	(NA)	(NA)
Oregon [1]	(NA)	(NA)	(NA)	(NA)
Pennsylvania [1]	(NA)	(NA)	(NA)	(NA)
Texas [1]	(NA)	(NA)	(NA)	(NA)
Virginia [1]	(NA)	(NA)	(NA)	(NA)
Washington	466,000	466,000		466,000
Juice	205,000	205,000		205,000
Wine	261,000	261,000		261,000
United States	7,596,000	7,596,000	1,098,900	6,497,100

(NA) Not available. [1] Estimates discontinued in 2018.
NASS, Crops Branch, (202) 720–2127.

Table 5-44.—Grapes and raisins: Foreign trade, United States, 2009–2018

Year beginning October	Grapes		Raisins [1]	
	Imports, fresh	Domestic exports, fresh	Imports for consumption	Domestic exports
	Metric tons			
2009	602,273	284,092	24,289	173,049
2010	557,397	334,609	18,813	154,541
2011	557,310	378,504	19,336	142,997
2012	566,038	366,088	17,102	131,980
2013	500,977	421,560	14,904	174,024
2014	554,674	366,143	20,588	132,274
2015	532,383	329,973	25,421	124,775
2016	625,371	330,190	14,753	136,454
2017	580,062	333,931	46,411	104,550
2018	643,553	370,511	29,380	84,051

[1] Raisins converted to sweatbox or production basis by multiplying by 1.08.
ERS, Crops Branch, (816) 926–6007.

Table 5-45.—Nectarines: Total Production, utilization, and value, United States, 2009–2018

Year	Total Production	Utilization		Marketing year average price per ton	Value
		Fresh	Processed (fresh basis)		
	Tons	*Tons*	*Tons*	*Dollars*	*1,000 dollars*
2009	219,800	219,800	(NA)	631.00	138,611
2010	233,200	233,200	(NA)	553.00	129,075
2011	225,200	225,200	(NA)	582.00	130,973
2012	188,900	188,900	(NA)	767.00	144,906
2013	162,100	148,300	13,800	772.00	125,113
2014	187,300	170,000	9,300	866.00	162,221
2015	159,500	150,600	6,600	910.00	143,061
2016	151,350	145,600	5,600	885.00	133,791
2017	141,850	135,200	5,600	911.00	128,255
2018	120,500	(D)	(D)	874.00	104,626

(D) Withheld to avoid disclosing data for individual operations. (NA) Not available
NASS, Crops Branch, (202) 720–2127.

Table 5-46.—Olives: Total production, marketing year average price, value, and processed utilization, California, 2009–2018

Year	Total Production	Marketing year average price per ton	Value	Processed utilization			
				Crushed for oil	Canned	Limited	Undersized
	Tons	*Dollars*	*1,000 dollars*	*Tons*	*Tons*	*Tons*	*Tons*
2009	46,300	696	32,209	20,000	24,500	1,500	300
2010	206,000	664	136,796	36,000	125,000	37,000	8,000
2011	71,200	733	52,168	42,000	26,500	2,200	500
2012	160,000	813	130,038	74,000	78,500	6,400	1,100
2013	166,000	813	134,881	75,000	78,800	10,500	1,700
2014	95,000	774	73,559	45,000	30,500	5,900	900
2015	179,000	894	160,043	101,000	60,000	14,600	3,400
2016	164,900	860	141,761	97,700	54,000	11,100	2,000
2017	192,300	974	186,649	101,000	70,000	17,300	3,400
2018	53,600	766	40,523	35,500	14,920	2,060	420

NASS, Crops Branch, (202) 720–2127.

Table 5-47.—Olives and olive oil: Foreign trade, United States, 2009–2018

Year beginning October	Imports			
	Olives		Olive oil	
	In brine	Dried	Edible	Inedible
	Metric tons			
2009	137,533	184	268,069	114
2010	117,915	206	290,226	258
2011	118,614	145	314,937	788
2012	119,035	131	296,029	379
2013	118,734	202	311,142	351
2014	119,442	130	310,110	163
2015	127,273	48	330,323	153
2016	121,988	47	315,493	156
2017	121,041	75	321,496	215
2018	141,063	123	319,443	196

ERS, Crops Branch, (816) 926–6007.

Table 5-48.—Papayas: Area, utilized production, utilization, marketing year average price, and value, Hawaii, 2009–2018

Year	Area harvested	Utilized production	Utilization		Price per pound	Value
			Fresh	Processed		
	Acres	*1,000 pounds*	*1,000 pounds*	*1,000 pounds*	*Cents*	*dollars*
2009	1,325	31,500	30,300	1,200	45.0	14,186
2010	1,350	30,100	29,200	900	37.0	11,123
2011	1,300	28,600	27,700	900	34.0	9,722
2012	(NA)	(NA)	(NA)	(NA)	(NA)	(NA)
2013	700	24,200	23,000	1,200	34.4	8,316
2014	900	23,500	23,000	500	48.0	11,285
2015	900	25,200	(D)	(D)	41.9	10,570
2016	700	19,750	(D)	(D)	49.2	9,713
2017	1,100	22,250	(D)	(D)	42.2	9,400
2018	800	10,290	7,000	3,290	55.4	5,702

(D) Withheld to avoid disclosing data for individual operations. (NA) Not available.
NASS, Crops Branch, (202) 720–2127.

Table 5-49.—Peaches: Production and value, United States, 2009–2018

Year	Total production	Utilized production	Marketing year average price [1]	Value
	1,000 tons	*1,000 tons*	*Dollars per ton*	*1,000 dollars*
2009	1,103,520	1,082,420	548	593,387
2010	1,149,430	1,129,770	547	617,459
2011	1,071,270	1,042,340	563	587,228
2012	968,070	955,890	647	618,369
2013	905,371	890,181	618	550,243
2014	852,799	837,907	750	628,846
2015	844,780	823,005	732	602,214
2016	791,940	775,230	803	622,624
2017	700,770	694,220	864	599,862
2018	651,500	638,020	801	511,226

[1] Fresh fruit prices are equivalent packinghouse-door returns for California and Washington except equivalent returns for bulk fruit at the first delivery point for California Clingstone, and the average price as sold for other States. Quantities processed are priced at the equivalent processing plant door level.
NASS, Crops Branch, (202) 720–2127.

Table 5-50.—Peaches: Production and utilization, United States, 2009–2018

Year	Total production [1]	Utilized production	Utilization of quantities sold					
			Fresh [2]	Processed (fresh basis)				
				Canned [3]	Dried	Frozen [3]	Other [4]	
	Tons							
2009	1,103,520	1,082,420	502,920	463,740	7,100	92,000	16,850	
2010	1,149,430	1,129,770	566,400	428,470	12,700	104,400	17,800	
2011	1,071,270	1,042,340	531,050	387,190	4,600	100,600	18,900	
2012	968,070	955,890	480,750	364,640	9,800	90,210	10,490	
2013	905,371	890,181	398,470	369,751	4,200	103,740	14,020	
2014	852,799	837,907	393,200	330,220	4,200	95,290	14,497	
2015	844,780	823,005	355,335	339,530	(NA)	108,400	(NA)	
2016	791,940	775,230	333,350	322,350	(NA)	100,320	(NA)	
2017	700,770	694,220	314,600	301,460	(NA)	62,500	(NA)	
2018	651,500	638,020	279,790	(NA)	(NA)	(NA)	(NA)	

[1] Includes harvested not sold and unharvested production for California Clingstone peaches. [2] Includes "Home use." [3] Estimated discontinued in 2018. [4] Used for jams, preserves, pickles, wine, brandy, baby food, etc. Includes small quantities frozen for some years.
NASS, Crops Branch, (202) 720–2127.

Table 5-51.—Peaches: Foreign trade, United States, 2009–2018

Year beginning October	Domestic exports				
	Fresh	Canned	Canned, in fruit salad [1]	Dried, in fruit salad [2][3]	Total, in terms of fresh [4]
	Metric tons	*Metric tons*	*Metric tons*	*Metric tons*	*Metric tons*
2009	103,038	16,914	11,701	662	135,329
2010	103,523	25,636	15,568	801	149,175
2011	95,798	28,295	17,605	884	146,609
2012	102,140	25,526	21,811	931	154,648
2013	80,241	20,847	20,144	859	126,004
2014	84,680	18,007	20,098	696	126,653
2015	77,769	10,689	18,698	364	109,179
2016	54,845	7,378	19,441	278	83,207
2017	63,966	9,451	20,470	150	94,720
2018	73,555	5,848	19,602	181	100,012

[1] Canned peaches are 40 percent of total canned fruit for salad. [2] Net processed weight. [3] Dried peaches are 21 percent of total dried fruit for salad. [4] Dried fruit converted to unprocessed dry weight by dividing by 1.08. Unprocessed dry weight converted to terms of fresh fruit on the basis that 1 pound dried equals 6.0 pounds fresh. Canned peaches converted to terms of fresh on basis that 1 pound canned equals about 1 pound fresh.
ERS, Crops Branch, (816) 926–6007.

Table 5-52.—Peaches: Production and season average price, by State and United States, 2016–2018

State	Total production			Utilized production			Price per ton [1]		
	2016	2017	2018	2016	2017	2018	2016	2017	2018
	Tons	*Tons*	*Tons*	*Tons*	*Tons*	*Tons*	*Dollars*	*Dollars*	*Dollars*
Alabama [2]	3,300	1,500	(NA)	3,270	1,500	(NA)	1,390.00	2,750.00	(NA)
California	569,000	553,000	479,000	569,000	550,000	475,870	616.00	701.00	639.00
Clingstone	322,000	297,000	259,000	322,000	296,000	256,950	518.00	474.00	480.00
Freestone	247,000	256,000	220,000	247,000	254,000	218,920	743.00	966.00	826.00
Colorado	13,730	10,750	15,000	13,260	10,160	14,550	2,040.00	2,070.00	1,930.00
Georgia	43,300	10,000	26,000	39,500	9,600	23,400	1,070.00	1,820.00	1,020.00
Idaho [2]	7,770	5,220	(NA)	7,720	5,120	(NA)	900.00	1,290.00	(NA)
Illinois [2]	5,420	6,030	(NA)	5,370	5,880	(NA)	2,570.00	1,460.00	(NA)
Maryland [2]	2,550	4,060	(NA)	2,430	4,000	(NA)	1,280.00	1,320.00	(NA)
Michigan	11,000	9,600	12,000	10,900	9,500	11,940	885.00	1,140.00	1,060.00
Missouri [2]	2,570	2,230	(NA)	2,540	2,230	(NA)	1,740.00	2,340.00	(NA)
New Jersey	18,470	24,580	23,000	18,400	24,570	23,000	1,430.00	1,560.00	1,780.00
New York [2]	2,420	4,810	(NA)	2,410	4,720	(NA)	1,380.00	1,720.00	(NA)
North Carolina [2]	2,700	1,740	(NA)	2,700	1,740	(NA)	1,290.00	1,540.00	(NA)
Ohio [2]	1,570	4,730	(NA)	1,530	4,680	(NA)	1,750.00	1,720.00	(NA)
Pennsylvania	16,000	21,400	17,400	15,800	21,000	16,970	1,210.00	1,180.00	1,220.00
South Carolina	63,300	11,000	65,800	52,800	10,400	59,220	1,290.00	1,700.00	1,210.00
Texas [2]	4,400	2,700	(NA)	4,200	2,500	(NA)	2,200.00	2,500.00	(NA)
Utah [2]	5,160	3,400	(NA)	4,250	3,370	(NA)	1,640.00	1,460.00	(NA)
Virginia [2]	3,250	4,650	(NA)	3,250	3,950	(NA)	1,340.00	1,450.00	(NA)
Washington	12,530	12,770	13,300	12,400	12,700	13,070	1,090.00	963.00	696.00
West Virginia [2]	3,500	6,600	(NA)	3,500	6,600	(NA)	1,090.00	940.00	(NA)
United States	791,940	700,770	651,500	775,230	694,220	638,020	803.00	864.00	801.00

(NA) Not available. [1] Fresh fruit prices are equivalent packing house-door returns for California and Washington except equivalent returns for bulk fruit at the first delivery point for California Clingstone, and the average price as sold for other States. Quantities processed are priced at the equivalent processing plant door level. [2] Estimates discontinued in 2018.
NASS, Crops Branch, (202) 720–2127.

Table 5-53.—Peaches: Production and utilization, by State and United States, crop of 2018

State	Total production	Utilized production [1]	Utilization	
			Fresh [2]	Processed (fresh basis)
	Tons			
California	479,000	475,870	134,000	341,870
Clingstone	259,000	256,950	-	256,950
Freestone	220,000	218,920	134,000	84,920
Colorado	15,000	14,550	(D)	(D)
Georgia	26,000	23,400	23,400	-
Michigan	12,000	11,940	(D)	(D)
New Jersey	23,000	23,000	(D)	(D)
Pennsylvania	17,400	16,970	13,940	3,030
South Carolina	65,800	59,220	(D)	(D)
Washington	13,300	13,070	(D)	(D)
Other States [3]	(NA)	(NA)	108,450	13,330
United States	651,500	638,020	279,790	358,230

- Represents zero. (D) Withheld to avoid disclosing data for individual operations. (NA) Not available. [1] Difference between total and utilized production is harvested not sold and unharvested production. [2] Includes "Home use." [3] Includes data withheld above.
NASS, Crops Branch, (202) 720–2127.

Table 5-54.—Pears: Foreign trade, United States, 2009–2018

Year beginning October	Imports for consumption, fresh	Domestic exports				
		Fresh [1]	Canned	Dried, in fruit salad [1 2]	Canned, in fruit salad [3]	Total, in terms of fresh fruit [4]
	Metric tons	*Metric tons*	*Metric tons*	*Metric tons*	*Metric tons*	*Metric tons*
2009	62,808	159,677	7,112	525	10,238	180,342
2010	77,992	154,025	7,958	635	13,622	179,615
2011	64,000	197,633	8,681	702	15,404	226,146
2012	79,034	186,855	7,535	739	19,084	218,137
2013	81,586	200,928	6,283	682	17,626	229,139
2014	89,741	174,774	4,425	553	17,586	200,271
2015	79,523	148,454	5,824	289	16,361	172,464
2016	74,356	123,088	7,473	220	17,011	148,963
2017	79,887	120,757	7,428	119	17,911	146,848
2018	74,332	148,829	3,412	114	17,152	170,301

[1] Net processed weight. [2] Dried pears are 16⅔ percent of total dried fruit for salad. [3] Canned pears are 35 percent of total canned fruit for salad. [4] Dried converted to unprocessed dry weight by dividing by 1.03. Unprocessed dry weight converted to terms of fresh on the basis that 1 pound dried equals about 6.5 pounds fresh. Canned converted to terms of fresh on basis that 1 pound of canned equals about 1 pound fresh.
ERS, Crops Branch, (816) 926-6007.

Table 5-55.—Pears: Production and value, United States 2009–2018

Year	Total production	Utilized production	Marketing year average price [1]	Value
	Tons	*Tons*	*Dollars per ton*	*1,000 dollars*
2009	957,220	955,820	372.00	355,662
2010	813,600	813,400	476.00	386,955
2011	965,720	965,110	380.00	366,552
2012	851,240	851,130	509.00	432,988
2013	877,130	876,520	491.00	430,660
2014	831,610	831,250	562.00	467,194
2015	816,520	803,130	615.00	494,190
2016	738,770	735,870	660.00	485,763
2017	737,450	731,350	710.00	519,290
2018	805,500	800,260	536.00	428,940

[1] Fresh fruit prices are equivalent packinghouse-door returns for California, Oregon, and Washington, and the average price as sold for other States. Quantities processed are priced at the equivalent processing plant door level.
NASS, Crops Branch, (202) 720–2127.

Table 5-56.—Pears: Production and season average price per ton, by State and United States, 2016–2018

State and Variety	Total production			Utilized production			Price per ton [1]		
	2016	2017	2018	2016	2017	2018	2016	2017	2018
	Tons	*Tons*	*Tons*	*Tons*	*Tons*	*Tons*	*Dollars*	*Dollars*	*Dollars*
California	175,000	195,000	161,500	175,000	192,000	161,000	548.00	501.00	480.00
Bartlett [2]	141,000	162,000	(NA)	141,000	160,000	(NA)	500.00	420.00	(NA)
Other [2]	34,000	33,000	(NA)	34,000	32,000	(NA)	748.00	905.00	(NA)
Oregon	214,910	226,050	246,000	214,010	224,950	245,260	720.00	785.00	575.00
Bartlett [2]	53,660	53,850	(NA)	52,860	52,850	(NA)	635.00	776.00	(NA)
Other [2]	161,250	172,200	(NA)	161,150	172,100	(NA)	748.00	788.00	(NA)
Washington	348,860	316,400	398,000	346,860	314,400	394,000	680.00	784.00	535.00
Bartlett [2]	147,660	125,400	(NA)	146,660	124,400	(NA)	582.00	838.00	(NA)
Other [2]	201,200	191,000	(NA)	200,200	190,000	(NA)	752.00	748.00	(NA)
United States	738,770	737,450	805,500	735,870	731,350	800,260	660.00	710.00	536.00

(NA) Not available. [1] Fresh fruit prices are equivalent packinghouse-door returns for California, Oregon, and Washington, and the average price as sold for other States. Quantities processed are priced at the equivalent processing plant door level. [2] Estimates discontinued in 2018.
NASS, Crops Branch, (202) 720–2127.

Table 5-57.—Pears: Production and utilization, by State and United States, crop of 2018

State and variety	Total production	Utilized production	Utilization	
			Fresh [1]	Processed
	Tons			
California	161,500	161,000	54,100	106,900
Bartlett [2]	(NA)	(NA)	(NA)	(NA)
Other [2]	(NA)	(NA)	(NA)	(NA)
Oregon	246,000	245,260	209,100	36,160
Bartlett [2]	(NA)	(NA)	(NA)	(NA)
Other [2]	(NA)	(NA)	(NA)	(NA)
Washington	398,000	394,000	294,500	99,500
Bartlett [2]	(NA)	(NA)	(NA)	(NA)
Other [2]	(NA)	(NA)	(NA)	(NA)
United States [3]	805,500	800,260	557,700	242,560

(NA) Not available. [1] Includes "Home use." [2] Estimates discontinued in 2018. [3] Mostly canned, but includes small quantities dried, juiced, and other uses.
NASS, Crops Branch, (202) 720–2127.

Table 5-58.—Pears: Production and utilization, United States, 2009–2018

Crop of—	Total production	Utilized production	Utilization of quantities sold—Fresh [1]
	Tons		
2009	957,220	955,820	603,800
2010	813,600	813,400	531,430
2011	965,720	965,110	643,710
2012	851,240	851,130	551,820
2013	877,130	876,520	584,730
2014	831,610	831,250	550,080
2015	816,520	803,130	514,780
2016	738,770	735,870	505,000
2017	737,450	731,350	486,150
2018	805,500	800,260	557,700

[1] Includes "Home use."
NASS, Crops Branch, (202) 720–2127.

Table 5-59.—Plums: Production, value, and utilization, California, 2009–2018

Season	Total production	Utilized production	Marketing year average price per ton	Value
	Tons	*Tons*	*Dollars*	*1,000 dollars*
2009	112,000	112,000	514	57,568
2010	142,000	142,000	555	78,810
2011	160,000	160,000	402	64,320
2012	115,000	115,000	695	79,940
2013	100,600	98,600	665	65,527
2014	104,000	104,000	912	94,842
2015	92,500	91,500	996	91,125
2016	108,800	107,800	811	87,460
2017	117,900	114,900	1,000	114,897
2018	100,000	99,000	935	92,570

NASS, Crops Branch, (202) 720–2127.

Table 5-60.—Prunes (dried basis): Production, price and value, California, 2009–2018

Season	Total production	Utilized production	Marketing year average price per ton	Value
	Tons	*Tons*	*Dollars*	*1,000 dollars*
2009	166,000	166,000	1,230.00	204,180
2010	130,000	130,000	1,350.00	175,500
2011	137,000	137,000	1,310.00	179,470
2012	138,000	138,000	1,330.00	183,540
2013	85,000	85,000	2,000.00	170,000
2014	108,000	108,000	2,470.00	266,760
2015	112,000	110,000	2,050.00	225,500
2016	54,000	54,000	2,180.00	117,720
2017	105,000	105,000	1,980.00	207,900
2018	90,200	90,200	2,160.00	194,832

NASS, Crops Branch, (202) 720–2127.

Table 5-61.—Prunes: Foreign trade, United States, 2009–2018

Year beginning October	Imports				Domestic exports			
	Fresh prunes and plums	Otherwise prepared or preserved	Dried prunes [1]	Total, in terms of fresh [2]	Fresh prunes and plums	Dried prunes [1]	Dried, in fruit salad [1 3]	Total, in terms of fresh [2]
	Metric tons							
2009	27,226	805	620	29,559	47,213	65,070	1,355	219,664
2010	29,768	831	497	31,805	59,653	69,110	1,639	243,328
2011	24,105	822	565	26,311	56,788	67,529	1,810	236,801
2012	30,417	680	1,159	34,036	52,426	68,642	1,906	235,579
2013	13,625	821	6,844	32,129	41,741	48,498	1,759	172,216
2014	25,259	798	11,514	55,869	36,506	48,026	1,426	164,891
2015	26,533	985	19,183	77,221	29,660	38,342	746	131,139
2016	22,631	1,094	15,069	62,733	25,533	33,159	569	113,095
2017	22,432	1,038	9,737	48,644	31,026	37,281	307	128,611
2018	26,661	991	3,700	34,157	29,129	31,973	371	113,100

[1] Net processed weight. [2] Exports and imports of dried prunes converted to unprocessed dry weight by dividing by 1.04. Unprocessed dry weight converted to terms of fresh fruit on the basis that 1 pound dried equals 2.7 pounds fresh. "Otherwise prepared or preserved" converted to terms of fresh fruit on the basis that 1 pound equals 0.899 pound fresh. [3] Dried prunes in salad estimated at 43 percent of total dried fruit for salad.
ERS, Crops Branch, (816) 926–6007.

Table 5-62.—Strawberries, commercial crop: Production and value per hundredweight, by State and United States, 2016–2018

Utilization, season, and State	Utilized Production			Value per unit		
	2016	2017	2018	2016	2017	2018
	1,000 cwt	1,000 cwt	1,000 cwt	Dollars per cwt	Dollars per cwt	Dollars per cwt
Fresh market:						
California	20,829.7	18,996.1	20,285.7	123.00	123.00	104.00
Florida	1,947.5	(D)	2,450.0	166.00	(D)	115.00
New York	50.4	(D)	(D)	235.00	(D)	(D)
North Carolina	132.0	126.0	125.0	187.00	168.00	171.00
Oregon	34.9	32.8	(D)	108.00	195.00	(D)
Washington	29.3	(D)	(D)	205.00	(D)	(D)
Other States[1]	....	2,217.1	58.1	(X)	143.00	211.00
United States	23,023.8	21,372.0	22,918.8	127.00	125.00	106.00
Processing:						
California	6,265.2	5,553.8	5,464.5	45.90	35.00	42.20
Florida	....	(D)	....	(X)	(D)	(X)
New York	....	(D)	(D)	(X)	(D)	(D)
North Carolina	....	2.7	....	(X)	51.90	(X)
Oregon	197.9	167.4	(D)	83.00	93.50	(D)
Washington	91.7	(D)	(D)	88.00	(D)	(D)
Other States[1]	....	78.8	167.6	(X)	69.10	88.30
United States	6,554.8	5,802.7	5,632.1	47.60	37.20	43.60

(D) Withheld to avoid disclosing data for individual operations. (X) Not applicable. [1] Includes data withheld above.
NASS, Crops Branch, (202) 720–2127.

Table 5-63.—Strawberries, commercial crop: Area, yield, production, value per hundred weight, and total value, United States, 2009–2018

Year	Area for harvest	Yield per acre	Total production	Value[2]	
				Per cwt	Total
	Acres	*Cwt*	*1,000 cwt*	*Dollars per cwt*	*1,000 dollars*
2009 ...	58,080	482	28,013	76.00	2,129,585
2010 ...	56,890	501	28,520	79.30	2,260,733
2011 ...	57,250	507	29,016	82.40	2,391,406
2012 ...	58,310	523	30,520	80.40	2,453,039
2013 ...	60,410	504	30,470	85.60	2,609,038
2014 ...	59,895	505	30,237	93.30	2,821,854
2015 ...	58,010	528	30,655	73.00	2,239,301
2016 ...	53,760	550.7	29,606.9	110.00	3,243,711
2017 ...	53,200	511.4	27,208.0	107.00	2,895,813
2018 ...	49,220	580.6	28,577.9	93.50	2,670,523

Year	Fresh market[1]			Processing		
	Production	Value[2]		Production	Value[2]	
		Per cwt	Total		Per cwt	Total
	1,000 cwt	*Dollars per cwt*	*1,000 dollars*	*1,000 cwt*	*Dollars per cwt*	*1,000 dollars*
2009 ...	22,880	86.10	1,970,920	5,133	30.90	158,665
2010 ...	23,196	90.80	2,105,492	5,324	29.20	155,241
2011 ...	23,324	94.00	2,193,379	5,692	34.80	198,027
2012 ...	24,552	91.80	2,253,854	5,968	33.40	199,185
2013 ...	25,085	96.50	2,421,370	5,385	34.90	187,668
2014 ...	24,543	105.00	2,579,425	5,694	42.60	242,429
2015 ...	24,372	79.90	1,946,121	6,283	46.70	293,180
2016 ...	23,023.8	127.00	2,931,642	6,554.8	47.60	312,069
2017 ...	21,372.0	125.00	2,680,189	5,802.7	37.20	215,624
2018 ...	22,918.8	106.00	2,425,126	5,632.1	43.60	245,397

[1] Fresh market price and value at point of first sale. Processing price and value at processing plant door. [2] Mostly for fresh market, but includes some quantities used for processing in States for which processing estimates are not prepared.
NASS, Crops Branch, (202) 720–2127.

Table 5-64.—Strawberries, commercial crop: Area harvested, production, value per hundred weight, by State and United States, 2016–2018[1]

Season and State	Area harvested			Total production			Value per unit		
	2016	2017	2018	2016	2017	2018	2016	2017	2018
	Acres			*1,000 cwt*			*Dollars per cwt*		
California	38,200	38,100	35,800	27,122.0	24,574.5	25,776.0	105.00	103.00	90.90
Florida	9,500	9,500	9,800	1,947.5	2,137.5	2,450.0	166.00	140.00	115.00
New York	1,260	1,200	700	50.4	46.8	30.8	235.00	229.00	204.00
North Carolina	1,100	1,000	1,000	132.0	135.0	125.0	187.00	166.00	171.00
Oregon	2,400	2,200	1,100	232.8	200.2	110.0	86.70	110.00	107.00
Washington ...	1,300	1,200	820	122.2	114.0	86.1	116.00	107.00	107.00
United States	53,760	53,200	49,220	29,606.9	27,208.0	28,577.9	110.00	107.00	93.50

(NA) Not available. [1] Includes quantities used for fresh market and processing.
NASS, Crops Branch, (202) 720–2127.

Table 5-65.—Fruits, noncitrus: Production, utilization, and value, United States, 2009–2018 [1]

Year	Utilized production	Fresh [2]	Processed						Value of utilized production
			Canned	Dried	Juice	Frozen	Wine	Other	
	1,000 tons	*1,000 tons*	*1,000 tons*	*1,000 tons*	*1,000 tons*	*1,000 tons*	*1,000 tons*	*1,000 tons*	*1,000 dollars*
2009	18,069	7,562	1,394	2,148	1,235	742	4,373	269	11,811,298
2010	17,879	7,458	1,386	2,318	1,103	706	4,270	298	12,367,607
2011	18,147	7,702	1,301	2,399	1,153	737	4,154	316	13,910,375
2012	17,635	7,443	1,100	2,091	1,213	707	4,707	374	15,611,441
2013	19,433	7,718	1,373	2,321	1,630	827	5,068	497	16,220,440
2014	19,151	8,267	1,208	2,194	1,617	857	4,526	483	16,410,049
2015	18,334	7,702	1,252	2,323	1,391	881	4,255	530	16,602,493
2016	18,690	8,042	1,234	1,858	1,519	890	4,668	479	17,865,364
2017	18,455	8,107	1,188	1,754	1,477	731	4,665	531	18,589,066
2018 [3]	(NA)	(NA)	(NA)	(NA)	(NA)	(NA)	(NA)	(NA)	(NA)

(NA) Not available. [1] Includes the following crops: Apples, apricots, avocados, bananas, berries, cherries, cranberries, dates, figs, grapes, guavas, kiwifruit, nectarines, olives, papayas, peaches, pears, pineapples, plums, prunes, and strawberries. [2] Includes local and roadside sales. [3] Estimates discontinued.
NASS, Crops Branch, (202) 720–2127.

Table 5-66.—Fruits, fresh: Total reported domestic rail, truck, and air shipments, 2018

Commodity	Jan.	Feb.	Mar.	Apr.	May	Jun.	Jul.
Citrus:				*1,000 cwt*			
Grapefruit	812	599	448	609	417	407	308
Grapefruit-organic	19	19	20	27	27	27	18
Lemons	616	616	1,780	1,716	1,724	1,716	927
Lemons-organic	104	104	320	81	81	81	12
Oranges	5,794	5,558	5,614	4,328	4,310	3,358	659
Oranges-organic	111	111	111	56	56	56	51
Tangelos	385	354	346	38	38	38	.....
Tangelos-organic	5	5	5	.....	.....	.....	.....
Tangerines	2,174	2,155	2,144	806	806	806	.....
Tangerines-organic	25	25	25	9	9	9	.....
Temples	2	8	3	.....	.....	.....	.....
Total	10,047	9,554	10,816	7,670	7,468	6,498	1,975

Commodity	Aug.	Sep.	Oct.	Nov.	Dec.	Total
				1,000 cwt		
Grapefruit	309	309	291	614	814	5,937
Grapefruit-organic	18	18	15	18	15	241
Lemons	922	916	1,370	1,379	1,393	15,075
Lemons-organic	12	12	65	65	65	1,002
Oranges	621	637	2,649	2,957	3,074	39,559
Oranges-organic	51	51	78	78	78	888
Tangelos	.....	.....	3	5	18	1,225
Tangelos-organic	.....	.....	3	3	1	22
Tangerines	.....	3	96	98	139	9,227
Tangerines-organic	.....	.....	.....	.....	2	104
Temples	.....	.....	.....	.....	.....	13
Total	1,933	1,946	4,570	5,217	5,599	73,293

See footnote(s) at end of table.

Table 5-66.—Fruits, fresh: Total reported domestic rail, truck, and air shipments, 2018—Continued

Commodity	Jan.	Feb.	Mar.	Apr.	May	Jun.	Jul.
Noncitrus:	1,000 cwt						
Apples	5,243	5,297	6,557	5,136	4,899	4,397	3,006
Apples-organic	571	558	702	543	482	348	166
Apricots					5	31	56
Apricots-organic						2	7
Avocados	55	151	304	613	655	818	506
Blueberries		1	14	201	295	517	468
Blueberries-organic	7	10	18	35	58	43	65
Cherries						451	2,141
Cherries-organic					2	70	72
Cranberries							
Cranberries-organic							
Grapes	134	2			154	465	1,595
Grapes-organic							
Kiwifruit	90	94	105	44			
Kiwifruit-organic							
Nectarines					81	303	313
Peaches					203	655	868
Peaches-organic							5
Pears	773	697	763	546	441	387	248
Pears-organic	72	61	33	12	4	3	
Persimmons							
Plums					1	50	115
Pomegranates							
Prunes							1
Raspberries	27	20	15	21	71	151	189
Raspberries-organic	12	9	4	4	12	31	49
Strawberries	727	1,268	1,062	1,917	3,039	2,501	2,075
Strawberries-organic	30	44	37	97	300	286	278
Total	7,741	8,212	9,614	9,169	10,702	11,509	12,223

Commodity	Aug.	Sep.	Oct.	Nov.	Dec.	Total
Noncitrus:	1,000 cwt					
Apples	3,546	5,151	4,626	4,775	5,509	58,142
Apples-organic	191	523	482	520	637	5,723
Apricots	4					96
Apricots-organic						9
Avocados	359	330	166	41	22	4,020
Blueberries	238	81				1,815
Blueberries-organic	35	18	2		1	292
Cherries	2,795	496	6			5,889
Cherries-organic	7					151
Cranberries		19	39	126	35	219
Cranberries-organic			1	1		2
Grapes	3,440	3,680	3,745	3,152	1,595	17,959
Grapes-organic	2					2
Kiwifruit			27	66	79	505
Kiwifruit-organic				9		9
Nectarines	218	184	19			1,118
Peaches	835	769	351	32		3,713
Peaches-organic	31	36				72
Pears	508	874	972	1,035	1,263	8,507
Pears-organic	34	98	97	98	96	608
Persimmons			4	12	11	27
Plums	58	86	16	1		327
Pomegranates		7	189	144	44	384
Prunes	16	5				22
Raspberries	155	155	117	51	24	996
Raspberries-organic	43	38	22	13	12	249
Strawberries	1,830	1,541	1,414	718	449	18,541
Strawberries-organic	272	221	154	68	33	1,820
Total	14,617	14,312	12,449	10,862	9,810	131,217

AMS, Fruit and Vegetable Programs, Market News Division, (202) 205–9690.

Table 5-67.—Fruits, dried: Production (dry basis), California, 2009–2018

Year	Apricots	Figs [1]	Peaches [2]	Prunes	Grapes [3]
	Tons				
2009	1,090	13,300	850	166,000	335,500
2010	1,400	12,320	2,010	130,000	394,800
2011	1,810	11,560	470	137,000	384,300
2012	1,210	10,400	1,230	138,000	345,900
2013	1,080	9,300	420	85,000	406,100
2014	1,500	9,470	610	108,000	366,200
2015	1,050	8,940	880	110,000	388,500
2016	1,280	9,260	(NA)	54,000	335,900
2017	(D)	9,100	(NA)	105,000	271,300
2018 [4]	(NA)	(NA)	(NA)	(NA)	(NA)

(NA) Not available. [1] Standard and substandard. [2] Freestone only. Discontinued in 2015. [3] Raisin and table type. [4] Estimates discontinued in 2018.
NASS, Crops Branch, (202) 720–2127.

Table 5-68.—International Raisins: Production in specified countries, 2016/2017–2018/2019

Country	2016/2017	2017/2018	2018/2019
	Metric tons		
Turkey	310,000	306,000	280,000
United States	304,723	241,402	263,000
China	165,000	180,000	190,000
Iran	170,000	110,000	150,000
South Africa	62,300	70,500	73,000
Uzbekistan	71,000	65,000	70,000
Chile	53,700	57,000	60,000
Argentina	31,000	41,000	42,000
Afghanistan	26,000	36,500	38,000
Australia	18,000	20,000	20,000
Other	19,000	22,000	19,000

FAS, Office of Global Analysis, (202) 720-6301. Prepared or estimated on the basis of official USDA production, supply, and distribution statistics from foreign governments.

Table 5-69.—Fruits: Per capita consumption, United States, 2009–2018 [1]

Year	Fruits used fresh		Canned fruits [4]	Juice [5]	Frozen fruit [6]	Dried fruits [7]
	Citrus fruit [2]	Noncitrus fruits [3]				
	Pounds	*Pounds*	*Pounds*	*Gallons*	*Pounds*	*Pounds*
2009	20.7	77.4	13.6	7.1	5.1	2.1
2010	21.6	80.9	13.1	7.2	5.7	2.3
2011	22.8	82.4	12.1	6.1	5.3	2.3
2012	23.5	85.1	11.5	6.4	5.0	2.3
2013	23.9	87.9	13.0	6.2	5.3	2.4
2014	23.3	90.7	11.8	5.9	6.5	2.3
2015	22.7	89.7	12.4	5.8	6.5	2.4
2016	24.1	91.3	11.7	5.6	5.3	2.4
2017	23.8	92.9	11.4	5.4	6.1	2.3
2018	24.0	91.2	10.1	5.2	6.0	1.0

[1] Fresh citrus fruits, canned fruit, and fruit juices are on a crop-year basis. Dried fruits are on a pack-year basis. The per capita consumption was obtained by dividing the total consumption by total population. [2] Oranges and temples, tangerines and tangelos, lemons, limes, and grapefruit. [3] Apples, apricots, avocados, bananas, cherries, cranberries, grapes, kiwifruit, mangoes, peaches and nectarines, pears, pineapples, papayas, plums and prunes, and strawberries. [4] Apples, apricots, cherries, olives, peaches, pears, pineapples, and plums and prunes. [5] Orange, grapefruit, lemon, lime, apple, grape, pineapple, prune, and cranberry. [6] Blackberries, blueberries, raspberries, strawberries, other berries, apples, apricots, cherries, and peaches. [7] Apples, apricots, dates, figs, peaches, pears, prunes, and raisins. Dried data in terms of processed weight.
ERS, Crops Branch, (816) 926–6007.

Table 5-70.—Fruit: Exports, 2016–2018

Country	2016	2017	2018
	Metric tons		
Fruit, processed:			
Canada	81,103	77,039	76,946
China	19,958	43,280	26,182
Netherlands	35,738	33,160	22,349
Mexico	20,691	26,442	22,223
Korea, South	7,398	7,926	7,454
Japan	7,271	6,168	6,450
Australia(*)	5,580	4,972	5,351
United Kingdom	3,376	4,538	4,670
Hong Kong	2,191	2,374	4,140
Poland	2,766	3,498	3,461
Taiwan	3,790	4,120	3,239
Germany(*)	1,302	1,314	2,591
India	2,158	2,629	2,579
Israel(*)	4,479	3,869	2,541
Indonesia	1,585	1,662	2,347
Malaysia	1,929	2,120	2,268
Switzerland(*)	682	230	2,265
Russia	1,186	1,661	2,071
Thailand	3,035	3,040	1,958
Vietnam	1,066	1,819	1,634
Singapore	1,323	1,954	1,525
New Zealand(*)	1,920	1,415	1,308
Colombia	1,110	1,073	1,244
Belgium-Luxembourg(*)	3,149	3,749	1,210
Philippines	1,283	1,383	1,157
Turkey	1,826	2,228	1,021
Panama	795	841	955
France(*)	415	1,825	848
Italy(*)	1,264	879	810
Greece	898	709	747
Rest of World	9,856	8,727	8,007
World Total	231,120	256,641	221,553
Fruit, prepared, misc:			
Canada	75,277	77,340	72,441
Mexico	8,079	10,638	9,679
Netherlands	507	347	8,569
China	7,497	5,832	3,862
Japan	3,347	2,634	3,023
Australia(*)	5,958	1,538	1,876
Korea, South	9,018	2,916	1,858
Hong Kong	3,784	6,258	1,382
Philippines	1,056	939	1,242
Saudi Arabia	5,999	1,248	1,218
Panama	981	1,081	1,005
Dominican Republic	863	555	1,000
Germany(*)	278	251	954
Malaysia	880	605	731
Taiwan	1,230	614	708
Bahamas, The	471	779	679
Thailand	1,230	671	674
Singapore	795	601	610
Turkey	113	36	583
United Arab Emirates	923	794	578
Trinidad and Tobago	567	301	568
Israel(*)	398	295	472
Costa Rica	548	660	465
United Kingdom	748	963	414
Netherlands Antilles(*)	534	238	370
Indonesia	643	250	360
Chile	793	626	333
Jordan	227	268	314
Vietnam	4,081	85	310
France(*)	540	1,415	302
Rest of World	9,417	6,068	3,885
World Total	146,780	126,845	120,463

(*) Denotes a country that is a summarization of its component countries. All zeroes for a data item may show that statistics exist in the other import type. Consumption or General. Users should use cautious interpretation on Quantity reports using mixed units of measure. Quantity line items will only include statistics on the units of measure that are equal to, or are able to be converted to, the assigned unit of measure of the grouped commodities.

FAS, Office of Global Analysis, (202) 720-6301. Data Source: Department of Commerce, U.S. Census Bureau, Foreign Trade Statistics.

Table 5-71.—International Fruits, fresh: Production in specified countries, 2016/2017-2018/2019

Country	Production		
	2016/2017	2017/2018	2018/2019
	Metric tons		
Apples:			
China	40,393,000	41,390,000	31,000,000
European Union	12,722,620	10,013,600	14,008,570
United States	5,010,201	5,084,727	5,048,000
Turkey	2,900,000	2,750,000	3,000,000
Iran	2,799,200	2,799,200	2,799,200
India	2,258,000	1,920,000	2,300,000
Russia	1,509,148	1,359,580	1,503,100
Chile	1,310,000	1,330,000	1,264,000
Ukraine	1,099,200	1,099,200	1,099,200
Brazil	1,049,300	1,049,300	1,049,300
South Africa	902,130	790,000	840,000
Japan	765,000	765,000	765,000
Mexico	716,930	714,149	660,000
Argentina	560,000	560,000	590,000
New Zealand	523,000	575,500	561,000
Belarus	509,300	509,300	509,300
Canada	408,404	345,568	395,300
Serbia	328,400	328,400	328,400
Australia	308,300	308,300	308,300
Azerbaijan	254,300	254,300	254,300
Kazakhstan	188,100	188,100	188,100
Kyrgyzstan	135,600	135,600	135,600
Uruguay	37,700	37,700	37,700
Guatemala	26,500	26,500	26,500
Norway	12,400	12,400	12,400
Colombia	2,300	2,300	2,300
Taiwan	1,483	1,451	1,500
Cherries, sweet and sour:			
European Union	734,199	607,288	793,058
Turkey	525,000	520,000	590,000
United States	455,806	508,087	443,633
China	330,000	380,000	340,000
Russia	276,500	276,500	276,500
Ukraine	219,800	219,800	219,800
Chile	116,000	206,741	210,000
Uzbekistan	150,000	150,000	150,000
Serbia	98,000	98,000	98,000
Syria	69,200	69,200	69,200
Azerbaijan	44,700	44,700	44,700
Belarus	42,800	42,800	42,800
Canada	20,400	20,400	20,400
Japan	19,800	19,100	18,500
Australia	10,000	16,000	18,000
Argentina	7,100	7,100	7,100
Kyrgyzstan	4,500	4,500	4,500
Peaches & nectarines:			
China	14,200,000	14,300,000	13,500,000
European Union	3,777,707	4,086,458	3,582,400
United States	858,850	768,295	734,000
Turkey	510,000	505,000	600,000
Argentina	248,100	248,100	248,100
Uzbekistan	220,000	226,000	226,000
Brazil	192,000	192,000	192,000
South Africa	180,000	180,000	180,000
Mexico	176,900	176,900	176,900
Chile	149,234	159,285	151,000
Japan	127,300	124,900	122,000
Australia	90,000	92,000	94,000
Russia	36,200	36,200	36,200
Canada	23,200	23,200	23,200
Taiwan	22,430	23,254	23,000
Ukraine	18,000	18,000	18,000
Kazakhstan	1,400	1,400	1,400
Switzerland	200	200	200

See footnote(s) at end of table.

Table 5-71.—International Fruits, fresh: Production in specified countries, 2016/2017-2018/2019—Continued

Country	Production		
	2016/2017	2017/2018	2018/2019
	Metric tons		
Pears, fresh:			
China	15,960,000	16,410,000	13,100,000
European Union	2,340,171	2,386,396	2,524,958
United States	667,570	663,470	666,605
Argentina	540,000	580,000	600,000
Turkey	440,000	420,000	450,000
South Africa	431,535	408,146	410,000
India	340,000	280,000	340,000
Japan	278,100	278,100	278,100
Chile	290,000	262,000	252,000
Korea, South	238,014	265,757	214,000
Russia	236,482	205,920	211,100
Taiwan	140,000	140,000	140,000
Australia	105,000	105,000	105,000
Switzerland	43,900	43,900	43,900
Belarus	30,800	30,800	30,800
Mexico	26,952	27,930	27,800
Brazil	14,900	14,900	14,900
New Zealand	11,876	13,812	12,000
Canada	8,285	9,676	8,700

FAS, Office of Global Analysis, (202) 720-6301. Prepared or estimated on the basis of official USDA production, supply, and distribution statistics from foreign governments.

Table 5-72.—All tree nuts: Supply and utilization, United States, 2009/2010–2018/2019

Market year[1]	Beginning stocks	Marketable production[2]	Imports	Total supply	Exports	Ending stocks	Domestic consumption	
							Total	Per capita Pounds
	—Million pounds (shelled)—							
2009/2010	542.6	2,113.3	468.9	3,124.8	1,546.4	422.1	1,156.3	3.74
2010/2011	422.1	2,482.2	485.1	3,389.4	1,786.1	407.4	1,195.9	3.85
2011/2012	407.4	2,787.2	449.2	3,643.9	1,977.1	480.2	1,186.6	3.79
2012/2013	480.2	2,762.3	515.6	3,753.1	1,979.6	462.1	1,316.5	4.17
2013/2014	462.1	2,806.7	582.1	3,758.1	2,075.2	505.5	1,270.1	4.00
2014/2015	505.5	2,738.4	666.9	3,910.9	2,025.2	585.2	1,300.5	4.07
2015/2016	585.2	2,665.8	668.1	3,919.1	2,035.2	575.5	1,308.4	4.06
2016/2017	575.5	3,328.2	697.2	4,601.0	2,381.8	647.4	1,571.9	4.85
2017/2018	647.4	3,187.4	738.8	4,573.6	2,395.2	536.1	1,642.3	5.03
2018/2019	536.1	3,468.5	720.2	4,724.8	2,485.6	536.6	1,702.6	5.19

[1] Marketing season begins July 1 for hazelnuts and macadamias; August 1 for almonds and walnuts; September 1 for pistachios; and October 1 for pecans. [2] Utilized production (NASS data) minus inedibles and noncommercial useage.
ERS, Crops Branch, (816) 926–6007.

Table 5-73.—International Nuts, Almonds: Production in specified countries, 2017/2018–2019/2020

Country	2017/2018	2018/2019	2019/2020
	Metric tons		
United States	1,029,650	1,034,190	997,900
European Union	109,500	123,800	121,000
Australia	76,000	92,000	95,000
China	43,000	43,000	45,000
Turkey	15,000	16,000	15,000
Chile	9,500	11,000	11,500
India	4,000	4,500	4,500

FAS, Office of Global Analysis, (202) 720-6301. Prepared or estimated on the basis of official USDA production, supply, and distribution statistics from foreign governments.

Table 5-74.—Almonds (shelled basis): Bearing acreage, yield, production, price, and value, California, 2009–2018 [1]

Year	Bearing Acreage	Yield per acre [2]	Utilized production	Price per pound	Value
	Acres	Pounds	1,000 pounds	Dollars	1,000 dollars
2009	750,000	1,960	1,410,000	1.65	2,293,500
2010	770,000	2,220	1,640,000	1.79	2,903,380
2011	800,000	2,540	2,030,000	1.99	4,007,860
2012	820,000	2,310	1,890,000	2.58	4,816,860
2013	880,000	2,280	2,010,000	3.21	6,384,690
2014	930,000	2,010	1,870,000	4.00	7,388,000
2015	950,000	2,000	1,900,000	3.13	5,868,750
2016	970,000	2,210	2,140,000	2.39	5,052,460
2017	1,030,000	2,200	2,270,000	2.53	5,603,950
2018	1,090,000	2,090	2,280,000	2.44	5,468,040

[1] Price and value are based on edible portion of the crop only. Production includes inedible quantities of no value as follows (million pounds): 2009-20.0; 2010-18.0; 2011-16.0; 2012-23.0; 2013-21.0; 2014-23.0; 2015-25.0; 2016-26.0; 2017-55.0; 2018-39.0. [2] Yield is based on utilized production.
NASS, Crops Branch, (202) 720–2127.

Table 5-75.—Almonds (shelled basis): Foreign trade, United States, 2009–2018 [1]

Year beginning October	Imports	Domestic exports
	Metric tons	Metric tons
2009	776	462,276
2010	2,301	527,228
2011	5,729	615,275
2012	15,653	579,553
2013	14,724	581,398
2014	10,026	546,116
2015	9,501	562,036
2016	7,638	640,175
2017	10,306	667,221
2018	11,637	685,856

[1] Imports of unshelled nuts converted to shelled basis at ratio of 1.67 to 1. Exports of unshelled nuts converted to shelled basis at ratio of 1.67 to 1.0.
ERS, Crops Branch, (816) 926–6007.

Table 5-76.—Hazelnuts (in-shell basis): Bearing acreage, yield, production, price, and value, Oregon, 2009–2018

Year	Bearing Acreage	Yield per acre	Utilized production	Price per ton	Value
	Acres	Tons	Tons	Dollars	*1,000 dollars*
2009	28,700	1.64	47,000	1,690	79,430
2010	29,000	1.00	28,000	2,410	67,480
2011	28,500	1.00	38,500	2,330	89,705
2012	29,000	1.22	35,500	1,830	64,965
2013	30,000	1.50	45,000	2,680	120,600
2014	30,000	1.20	36,000	3,600	129,600
2015	34,000	0.91	31,000	2,800	86,800
2016	37,000	1.19	44,000	2,700	118,800
2017	40,000	0.80	32,000	2,300	73,600
2018	44,000	1.16	51,000	1,620	91,800

NASS, Crops Branch, (202) 720–2127.

Table 5-77.—Hazelnuts (shelled basis): Foreign trade, United States, 2009–2018 [1]

Year beginning October	Imports	Domestic exports
	Metric tons	*Metric tons*
2009	2,533	13,917
2010	4,417	7,691
2011	3,118	10,031
2012	5,392	11,243
2013	4,747	14,862
2014	1,761	20,309
2015	2,748	8,766
2016	3,333	11,634
2017	5,443	8,850
2018	5,646	9,956

[1] Imports of unshelled nuts converted to shelled basis at ratio of 2.22 to 1. Exports of unshelled nuts converted to shelled basis at ratio of 2.50 to 1.
ERS, Crops Branch, (816) 926–6007.

Table 5-78.—Macadamia nuts (in-shell basis): Bearing acreage, yield, production, price, and value, Hawaii, 2009–2018

Year	Bearing Acreage	Yield per acre	Utilized production	Price per pound	Value
	Acres	Pounds	*1,000 pounds*	*Cents*	*1,000 dollars*
2009	15,000	2,800	42,000	70.0	29,400
2010	15,000	2,670	40,000	75.0	30,000
2011	15,000	3,270	49,000	78.0	38,220
2012	15,000	2,930	44,000	80.0	35,200
2013	16,000	2,560	41,000	87.0	35,670
2014	16,000	2,880	46,000	87.0	40,020
2015	16,000	2,940	47,000	97.0	45,590
2016	16,500	2,550	42,000	100.0	42,000
2017	17,000	2,880	49,000	110.0	53,900
2018	16,900	2,090	35,300	119.0	42,007

NASS, Crops Branch, (202) 720–2127.

Table 5-79.—Pecans (in-shell basis): Production, price per pound, and value, United States, 2009–2018

Year	Improved varieties [1]			Native and seedling			All pecans		
	Utilized production	Price per pound	Value	Utilized production	Price per pound	Value	Utilized production	Price per pound	Value
	1,000 pounds	*Dollars*	*1,000 dollars*	*1,000 pounds*	*Dollars*	*1,000 dollars*	*1,000 pounds*	*Dollars*	*1,000 dollars*
2009	249,720	1.530	381,550	52,300	0.934	48,838	302,020	1.430	430,388
2010	232,560	2.490	578,149	61,180	1.580	96,679	293,740	2.300	674,828
2011	227,030	2.590	587,064	42,670	1.610	68,825	269,700	2.430	655,889
2012	247,100	1.730	427,473	55,200	0.879	48,518	302,300	1.570	475,991
2013	220,000	1.900	417,758	46,330	0.920	42,632	266,330	1.730	460,390
2014	227,410	2.120	482,323	36,740	0.933	34,268	264,150	1.960	516,591
2015	225,180	2.310	520,529	29,110	1.360	39,687	254,290	2.200	560,216
2016	249,970	2.660	663,746	18,800	1.760	33,060	268,770	2.590	696,806
2017	278,600	2.400	667,858	26,250	1.580	41,360	304,850	2.330	709,218
2018	228,470	1.790	408,807	14,460	1.140	16,524	242,930	1.751	425,331

[1] Budded, grafted or topworked varieties.
NASS, Crops Branch, (202) 720–2127.

Table 5-80.—Pecans (in-shell basis): Production and marketing year average price per pound, by State and United States, 2016–2018

Item and State	Utilized production			Price per pound		
	2016	2017	2018	2016	2017	2018
	1,000 pounds	*1,000 pounds*	*1,000 pounds*	*Dollars*	*Dollars*	*Dollars*
Improved Varieties [1]						
Alabama	1,900	1,600	1,490	2.130	2.030	1.500
Arizona	24,800	28,000	27,900	2.710	2.500	1.870
California	5,770	5,000	3,700	2.540	2.300	2.000
Georgia	109,000	107,000	70,000	2.500	2.400	1.620
Louisiana	1,500	3,000	2,510	1.950	2.000	1.250
New Mexico	72,000	92,000	91,100	2.960	2.400	1.900
Oklahoma	3,000	3,000	2,970	2.670	2.100	2.250
Texas	32,000	39,000	28,800	2.540	2.390	1.760
United States	249,970	278,600	228,470	2.66	2.400	1.790
Native and Seedling						
Alabama	300	250	110	1.400	1.520	1.119
Louisiana	2,500	5,000	3,520	1.300	1.250	0.800
Oklahoma	9,000	11,000	6,030	1.850	1.630	1.360
Texas	7,000	10,000	4,800	1.820	1.680	1.120
United States	18,800	26,250	14,460	1.760	1.580	1.140
All Pecans						
Alabama	2,200	1,850	1,600	2.030	1.960	1.480
Arizona	24,800	28,000	27,900	2.710	2.500	1.870
California	5,770	5,000	3,700	2.540	2.300	2.000
Georgia	109,000	107,000	70,000	2.500	2.400	1.620
Louisiana	4,000	8,000	6,030	1.540	1.530	0.990
New Mexico	72,000	92,000	91,100	2.960	2.400	1.900
Oklahoma	12,000	14,000	9,000	2.060	1.730	1.650
Texas	39,000	49,000	33,600	2.410	2.250	1.670
United States	268,770	304,850	242,930	2.590	2.330	1.751

[1] Budded, grafted or topworked varieties.
NASS, Crops Branch, (202) 720–2127.

Table 5-81.—Pecans (shelled basis): Foreign trade, United States, 2009–2018 [1]

Year beginning October	Imports	Domestic exports
	Metric tons	*Metric tons*
2009	33,735	30,607
2010	35,906	25,531
2011	30,449	31,141
2012	33,525	37,873
2013	39,000	33,098
2014	43,736	40,727
2015	46,612	35,721
2016	52,830	42,987
2017	58,230	47,689
2018	70,118	41,660

[1] Imports of unshelled nuts converted to shelled basis at ratio of 2.50 to 1. Exports of unshelled nuts converted to shelled basis at ratio of 2.50 to 1.
ERS, Crops Branch, (816) 926–6007.

Table 5-82.—Pistachios (in-shell basis): Bearing acreage, yield, production, price, and value, California, 2009–2018

Year	Bearing Acreage	Yield per acre	Utilized production	Price per pound	Value
	Acres	Pounds	1,000 pounds	*Dollars*	*1,000 dollars*
2009	126,000	2,820	355,000	1.67	592,850
2010	137,000	3,810	522,000	2.00	1,158,840
2011	153,000	2,900	444,000	2.00	879,120
2012	182,000	3,030	551,000	2.61	1,438,110
2013	203,000	2,320	470,000	3.48	1,635,600
2014	221,000	2,330	514,000	3.57	1,834,980
2015	233,000	1,160	270,000	3.29	888,300
2016	239,000	3,750	896,500	1.68	1,506,120
2017	250,000	2,400	600,300	1.69	1,014,507
2018	264,000	3,740	987,000	2.65	2,615,550

NASS, Crops Branch, (202) 720–2127.

Table 5-83.—Walnuts, English (in-shell basis): Bearing acreage, yield, production, price, and value, California, 2009–2018

Year	Bearing Acreage	Yield per acre [1]	Utilized production	Price per ton	Value
	Acres	*Tons*	*Tons*	*Dollars*	*1,000 dollars*
2009	240,000	1.82	437,000	1,710	747,270
2010	255,000	1.98	504,000	2,040	1,028,160
2011	265,000	1.74	461,000	2,900	1,336,900
2012	270,000	1.84	497,000	3,030	1,505,910
2013	280,000	1.76	492,000	3,710	1,825,320
2014	290,000	1.97	571,000	3,340	1,907,140
2015	300,000	2.02	606,000	1,670	1,012,020
2016	315,000	2.19	689,000	1,850	1,274,650
2017	335,000	1.88	630,000	2,490	1,568,700
2018	350,000	1.93	676,000	1,300	878,800

[1]Yield is based on utilized production.
NASS, Crops Branch, (202) 720–2127.

Table 5-84.—Walnuts (shelled basis): Foreign trade, United States, 2009–2018 [1]

Year beginning October	Imports	Domestic exports
	Metric tons	*Metric tons*
2009	1,529	101,865
2010	186	133,868
2011	2,442	117,031
2012	3,957	133,049
2013	5,266	134,379
2014	9,780	158,186
2015	5,319	188,467
2016	6,495	191,336
2017	5,618	176,115
2018	1,334	182,933

[1]Imports of unshelled nuts converted to shelled basis at ratio of 2.50 to 1. Exports of unshelled nuts converted to shelled basis at ratio of 2.50 to 1.
ERS, Crops Branch, (816) 926–6007.

Table 5-85.—Coffee, green: International trade, 2016/2017-2018/2019

Country of origin	2016/2017	2017/2018	2018/2019
	1,000 60-Kg bags		
Principle exporting countries:			
Brazil	33,081	0,450	39,720
Vietnam	27,550	7,900	27,200
Colombia	13,755	2,725	13,400
Indonesia	8,174	,010	6,150
Honduras	7,175	,225	6,700
India	6,158	,148	5,540
Peru	4,025	,185	4,260
Ethiopia	3,853	,893	3,980
Uganda	4,600	,500	4,600
Mexico	2,865	,220	3,220
Guatemala	3,330	,465	3,405
Malaysia	2,940	,050	3,100
Nicaragua	2,450	,520	2,415
European Union	1,905	,130	2,400
China	1,829	,885	1,770
Cote d'Ivoire	990	,150	1,615
Switzerland	1,150	,225	1,300
Tanzania	1,030	,030	1,230
Costa Rica	1,120	,210	1,110
Principle importing countries:			
European Union	46,050	47,430	49,000
United States	26,480	24,790	26,600
Japan	8,030	7,720	8,500
Philippines	6,420	6,100	6,200
Canada	4,550	4,750	4,720
Russia	4,740	4,465	4,450
China	3,534	2,705	2,750
Korea South	2,725	2,645	2,700
Switzerland	2,600	2,750	2,700
Algeria	2,205	2,300	2,340
Australia	1,730	1,875	1,875
Malaysia	1,510	1,550	1,800
Mexico	1,565	1,546	1,670
India	1,386	1,472	1,341
Ukraine	960	1,095	1,280
Morocco	660	825	1,020
Indonesia	743	1,751	1,676
Vietnam	1,000	1,060	1,160
Turkey	960	875	1,080
Argentina	754	775	780

FAS, Office of Global Analysis, (202) 720-6301. Prepared or estimated on the basis of official USDA production, supply, and distribution statistics from foreign governments. Data Source: Department of Commerce, U.S. Census Bureau, Foreign Trade Statistics.

Table 5-86.—Coffee: Area, yield, production, marketing year average price, and value, Hawaii, 2009/2010–2018/2019 [1]

Year	Area Harvested	Yield per acre	Utilized production	Price per pound	Value
	Acres	*Pounds*	*1,000 pounds*	*Dollars*	*1,000 dollars*
2009/2010	7,200	1,210	8,700	3.60	31,320
2010/2011	7,500	1,170	8,800	3.25	33,440
2011/2012	7,700	990	7,600	4.15	31,540
2012/2013	7,900	890	7,000	5.90	41,300
2013/2014	8,200	1,020	8,400	6.20	52,080
2014/2015	7,800	4,720	36,408	1.72	62,622
2015/2016	6,900	4,600	30,137	1.55	46,712
2016/2017	7,000	4,180	28,571	1.71	48,856
2017/2018	7,200	3,530	24,592	1.78	43,774
2018/2019	7,100	3,845	26,400	1.90	50,160

[1] For 2009/2010 season thru 2013/2014 season, all data in a parchment basis. Beginning with the 2014/2015 season, all data is for a cherry basis.
NASS, Crops Branch, (202) 720–2127.

Table 5-87.—Coffee and tea: U.S. Imports, Area/Partners of Origin, 2016-2018

Country	2016	2017	2018
	Metric tons		
Coffee and coffee products:			
Brazil	402,269	373,064	380,798
Colombia	315,207	346,040	342,045
Vietnam	269,684	237,187	213,499
Guatemala	60,673	76,914	82,787
Mexico	61,805	78,279	81,945
Nicaragua	70,810	80,083	72,856
Honduras	75,342	85,389	67,616
Peru	66,706	63,870	63,111
Indonesia	72,715	74,798	58,141
Canada	49,838	50,635	50,900
Costa Rica	38,862	29,520	36,201
Germany(*)	38,594	37,016	36,043
Ethiopia(*)	17,497	26,350	25,472
Uganda	8,954	12,075	15,003
El Salvador	13,027	16,362	14,869
Papua New Guinea	14,317	11,721	13,332
Italy(*)	10,563	11,512	11,671
China	10,618	10,830	9,008
Switzerland(*)	6,565	6,599	8,044
Kenya	6,435	9,012	6,685
Rwanda	4,220	4,197	5,742
Tanzania	4,740	4,968	5,600
India	4,150	5,962	5,154
Venezuela	0	0	4,274
Spain	1,487	1,709	2,735
Belgium-Luxembourg(*)	1,373	984	1,904
Malaysia	1,498	1,584	1,612
Korea, South	1,466	1,306	1,582
Burundi	1,430	1,314	1,580
Rest of World	19,287	15,791	12,824
World Total	1,650,131	1,675,071	1,633,032
Tea, including herbal tea:			
Argentina	54,061	52,918	49,990
Canada	54,586	53,532	48,994
China	23,762	20,612	21,186
India	17,265	16,859	14,610
Vietnam	6,096	6,897	6,602
Sri Lanka	5,635	5,458	6,149
Malawi	9,224	7,458	5,671
Germany(*)	6,582	4,517	4,939
Nigeria	833	1,490	4,668
Indonesia	4,084	3,639	3,358
Kenya	5,630	5,779	3,133
Mexico	3,892	3,616	3,094
Zimbabwe	1,498	1,867	2,439
Taiwan	1,631	1,800	2,233
Japan	1,975	1,878	1,990
Chile	2,326	2,101	1,816
Thailand	1,116	1,299	1,588
United Kingdom	1,335	1,059	1,299
Brazil	1,233	929	734
Korea, South	747	433	716
Egypt	580	565	686
Pakistan	534	590	674
Poland	583	474	627
Ecuador	574	620	584
Hong Kong	450	610	523
South Africa	293	344	471
Ireland	336	297	336
Bulgaria	260	211	300
Morocco	334	182	295
Rest of World	4,363	4,053	3,473
World Total	211,814	202,089	193,178

(*) Denotes a country that is a summarization of its component countries. All zeroes for a data item may show that statistics exist in the other import type. Consumption or General. Users should use cautious interpretation on Quantity reports using mixed units of measure. Quantity line items will only include statistics on the units of measure that are equal to, or are able to be converted to, the assigned unit of measure of the grouped commodities.
FAS, Office of Global Analysis, (202) 720-6301. Data Source: U.S. Census Bureau Trade Data.

Table 5-88.—Specialty mushrooms: Number of growers, total production, volume of sales, price per pound, and value of sales, United States: 2016/2017-2018/2019

Year and variety	Growers [1]	Total Production [2]	All sales		
			Volume of sales [3]	Price per pound [4]	Value of sales
	Number	*1,000 pounds*	*1,000 pounds*	*Dollars*	*1,000 dollars*
2016/2017					
Shiitake	185	11,025	10,806	3.91	42,301
Oyster	128	11,394	11,087	3.12	34,542
Other	59	5,223	4,869	5.43	26,463
United States	232	27,652	26,762	3.86	103,306
2017/2018					
Shiitake	185	10,429	10,112	4.44	44,883
Oyster	116	11,268	10,842	3.13	33,890
Other	64	5,690	5,050	5.33	26,923
United States	229	27,387	26,004	4.06	105,696
2018/2019 [5]					
Shiitake	(NA)	6,987	6,727	3.21	21,563
Oyster	(NA)	9,164	8,847	3.09	27,314
Other	(NA)	3,968	3,904	4.59	17,922
United States	(NA)	20,119	19,478	3.43	66,799

(NA) Not available. [1] Growers counted only once for United States total if growing more than one specialty type mushroom. Growers growing Agaricus and specialty mushrooms are included. Estimates discontinued in 2018-2019. [2] Total production includes all fresh market and processing sales plus amount harvested but not sold (shrinkage, cullage, dumped, etc.). [3] Virtually all specialty mushroom sales are for fresh market. [4] Prices for mushrooms are the average prices producers receive at the point of first sale, commonly referred to as the average price as sold. For example, if in a given State, part of the fresh mushrooms are sold F.O.B. packed by growers, part are sold bulk to brokers or repackers, and some are sold retail at roadside stands, the mushroom average price as sold is a weighted average of the average price for each method of sale. [5] Beginning in 2018-2019, includes California, Florida, Illinois, Maryland, Oklahoma, Pennsylvania, Tennessee, and Texas.
NASS, Crops Branch, (202) 720–2127.

Table 5-89.—Agaricus mushrooms: Area, volume of sales, marketing year average price, and value of sales, United States: 2009-2018 [1]

Year	Area in production Total fillings	Volume of sales	Price per pound	Value of sales		
				Total	Fresh market	Processing
	1,000 sq. ft.	*1,000 pounds*	*Dollars*	*1,000 dollars*	*1,000 dollars*	*1,000 dollars*
2009/2010	129,268	777,064	1.140	884,390	821,472	62,918
2010/2011	134,266	845,951	1.140	964,192	887,839	76,353
2011/2012	139,331	881,857	1.180	1,039,159	969,847	69,312
2012/2013	139,846	869,625	1.190	1,038,541	969,278	69,263
2013/2014	134,685	882,075	1.190	1,049,972	971,521	78,451
2014/2015	143,292	907,191	1.230	1,118,371	1,054,652	63,719
2015/2016	142,147	919,012	1.200	1,098,745	1,035,106	63,639
2016/2017	143,497	906,593	1.240	1,122,821	1,060,281	62,540
2017/2018	140,563	891,231	1.270	1,127,886	1,070,316	57,570
2018/2019 [2]	119,701	827,013	1.290	1,064,765	1,020,440	44,325

[1] Marketing year begins July 1 and ends June 30 the following year. [2] Beginning in 2018-2019, includes California, Florida, Illinois, Maryland, Oklahoma, Pennsylvania, Tennessee, and Texas.
NASS, Crops Branch, (202) 720–2127.

Table 5-90.—Cut flowers: Sales and wholesale value for operations with $100,000+ sales, Surveyed States, 2007–2018

Year	Quantity sold	Wholesale price	Value of sales at whole-sale [1]	Quantity sold	Wholesale price	Value of sales at whole-sale [1]	Quantity sold	Wholesale price	Value of sales at whole-sale [1]
	Alstromeria			Carnations, standard			Chrysanthemums pompon		
	1,000 stems	*Cents per stem*	*1,000 dollars*	*1,000 stems*	*Cents per stem*	*1,000 dollars*	*1,000 bunches*	*Cents per bunch*	*1,000 dollars*
2007 ...	9,879	20.8	2,057	3,328	18.8	626	18,059	0.76	13,810
2008 ...	10,774	17.9	1,927	3,343	17.0	567	10,058	1.34	13,428
2009 ...	8,800	18.5	1,629	2,837	16.9	480	7,920	1.43	11,298
2010 ...	9,868	16.7	1,650	1,893	16.7	317	8,347	1.40	11,705
2011 ...	8,764	19.1	1,676	1,441	16.2	233	7,823	1.41	11,048
2012 ...	10,964	21.0	2,307	715	23.4	167	9,167	1.43	13,115
2013 ...	10,164	20.7	2,104	624	24.5	153	9,009	1.53	13,816
2014 ...	8,890	19.1	1,702	797	30.6	244	6,677	1.73	11,518
2015 ...	7,747	19.6	1,517	896	30.5	273	7,777	1.48	11,524
2018 ...	(NA)	(NA)	(NA)	(NA)	(NA)	(NA)	6,880	1.52	10,459
	Delphinium & Larkspur			Gerbera Daisies			Gladioli		
	1,000 stems	*Cents per stem*	*1,000 dollars*	*1,000 stems*	*Cents per stem*	*1,000 dollars*	*1,000 spikes*	*Cents per spike*	*1,000 dollars*
2007 ...	32,158	24.4	7,842	117,403	30.6	35,939	85,471	27.0	23,081
2008 ...	31,221	24.0	7,505	120,836	29.8	35,976	76,850	25.9	19,935
2009 ...	22,373	27.1	6,071	106,805	30.9	33,027	94,951	24.1	22,880
2010 ...	27,173	26.5	7,193	107,678	30.4	32,737	89,672	25.4	22,801
2011 ...	19,639	30.5	5,981	113,655	28.5	32,385	60,167	27.1	16,299
2012 ...	19,448	37.4	7,265	107,899	30.6	33,067	60,747	25.3	15,349
2013 ...	16,929	38.6	6,542	98,535	31.0	30,552	59,435	34.1	20,244
2014 ...	17,091	35.3	6,030	105,028	31.4	32,987	61,724	32.7	20,193
2015 ...	12,671	41.0	5,199	106,680	30.4	32,423	60,778	32.3	19,608
2018 ...	(NA)	(NA)	(NA)	90,999	35.1	31,930	61,647	32.7	20,175
	Iris			Lilies, all			Lisianthus		
	1,000 stems	*Cents per stem*	*1,000 dollars*	*1,000 stems*	*Cents per stem*	*1,000 dollars*	*1,000 stems*	*Cents per stem*	*1,000 dollars*
2007 ...	90,890	22.4	20,349	111,185	67.4	74,954	13,956	38.2	5,338
2008 ...	92,404	22.1	20,462	116,797	67.3	78,609	15,180	35.6	5,406
2009 ...	64,114	24.3	15,550	101,339	63.5	64,392	8,689	38.3	3,327
2010 ...	57,576	25.2	14,518	93,373	65.5	61,165	7,650	38.8	2,966
2011 ...	62,414	26.1	16,303	141,337	56.5	79,798	7,502	42.1	3,160
2012 ...	55,025	24.5	13,477	99,743	66.7	66,553	9,846	43.1	4,240
2013 ...	54,635	24.4	13,356	87,094	68.4	59,558	9,216	45.2	4,167
2014 ...	45,682	26.4	12,078	79,432	77.6	61,661	8,484	45.2	3,839
2015 ...	43,787	26.4	11,554	82,551	75.4	62,235	9,010	45.0	4,055
2018 ...	36,466	27.7	10,107	72,435	102.6	74,321	(NA)	(NA)	(NA)
	Orchids, all			Roses, all			Snapdragons		
	1,000 blooms	*Cents per bloom*	*1,000 dollars*	*1,000 stems*	*Cents per stem*	*1,000 dollars*	*1,000 spikes*	*Cents per spike*	*1,000 dollars*
2007 ...	11,209	99.5	11,150	67,701	41.5	28,110	41,887	29.1	12,202
2008 ...	7,882	98.2	7,737	57,999	38.8	22,481	42,696	27.6	11,790
2009 ...	7,637	185.1	14,133	42,031	42.0	17,662	37,473	27.0	10,118
2010 ...	7,852	99.8	7,834	39,497	42.9	16,950	31,475	27.1	8,524
2011 ...	7,166	83.0	5,949	37,004	48.4	17,912	34,777	25.1	8,744
2012 ...	6,498	90.9	5,909	32,736	49.4	16,184	35,061	29.7	10,396
2013 ...	5,846	163.6	9,564	28,626	56.3	16,105	42,013	25.4	10,652
2014 ...	6,737	245.6	16,546	30,555	56.2	17,178	41,467	24.8	10,274
2015 ...	4,682	170.5	7,983	27,812	61.3	17,039	43,863	29.5	12,933
2018 ...	3,628	169.4	6,146	29,774	64.4	19,168	28,218	26.1	7,368

Year	Tulips			Other cut flowers
	1,000 stems	*Cents per stem*	*1,000 dollars*	*1,000 dollars*
2007 ...	157,992	35.9	56,719	133,017
2008 ...	170,854	37.6	64,285	126,990
2009 ...	150,228	38.1	57,185	103,687
2010 ...	155,667	36.6	56,900	129,466
2011 ...	169,219	35.3	59,788	99,824
2012 ...	161,802	37.2	60,172	171,159
2013 ...	161,926	36.8	59,535	116,509
2014 ...	160,990	35.5	57,198	112,006
2015 ...	167,378	34.6	57,840	130,135
2018 ...	173,247	38.4	66,489	112,778

(NA) Not available. [1] Equivalent wholesale value of all sales.
NASS, Crops Branch, (202) 720–2127.

Table 5-91.—Cut Cultivated Greens: Sales and wholesale value for operations with $100,000+ sales, Surveyed States, 2007–2018

Year	Leatherleaf Ferns			Other cut cultivated greens
	Quantity sold	Wholesale price	Value of sales at wholesale [1]	Value of sales at wholesale [1]
	1,000 bunches	*Dollars per bunch*	*1,000 dollars*	*1,000 dollars*
2007	39,437	1.00	39,543	58,527
2008	34,761	0.98	33,924	57,824
2009	31,800	0.94	29,942	43,993
2010	28,474	1.03	29,312	47,713
2011	26,277	0.97	25,499	46,537
2012	32,063	0.99	31,706	43,811
2013	32,209	1.02	32,779	42,706
2014	32,385	0.99	32,209	40,974
2015	33,319	1.02	33,853	46,573
2018	29,650	1.35	40,115	61,882

[1] Equivalent wholesale value of all sales.
NASS, Crops Branch, (202) 720–2127.

Table 5-92.—Foliage Plants for Indoor or Patio Use: Sales and Wholesale value for operations with $100,000+ sales, Surveyed States, 2007–2018

Year	Foliage, Hanging Baskets			Foliage, Pots
	Quantity Sold	Wholesale price	Value of sales at wholesale	Value of sales at wholesale
	1,000 baskets	*Dollars per basket*	*1,000 dollars*	*1,000 dollars*
2007	14,118	4.66	65,857	589,545
2008	11,003	4.90	53,949	456,362
2009	12,072	5.29	63,881	493,148
2010	14,530	5.39	78,247	507,882
2011	14,483	5.42	78,438	534,943
2012	10,323	6.12	63,158	576,770
2013	11,493	5.92	67,996	544,562
2014	10,199	6.19	63,103	559,779
2015	11,556	5.85	67,562	646,127
2018	13,071	6.26	81,785	571,294

NASS, Crops Branch, (202) 720–2127.

Table 5-93.— Potted Flowering Plants for Indoor or Patio Use: Sales and wholesale value for operations with $100,000+ sales, Surveyed States, 2007–2018

Year	Quantity sold		Wholesale price		Value of sales at wholesale [1]
	Less than 5 inches	5 inches or more	Less than 5 inches	5 inches or more	
	African violets [2]				
	1,000 pots	*1,000 pots*	*Dollars per pot*	*Dollars*	*1,000 dollars*
2007	4,357	430	1.37	1.95	6,809
2008	2,946	9	1.35	3.34	3,993
2009	2,313	38	1.49	3.48	3,580
2010	2,727	23	1.31	1.88	3,614
2011	2,582	51	1.25	3.84	3,414
2012	2,632	27	1.55	2.38	4,150
2013	2,572	33	1.47	2.53	3,870
2014	2,595	9	1.55	4.13	4,063
2015	2,641	8	1.56	3.85	4,161
2018	(NA)	(NA)	(NA)	(NA)	(NA)
	Florist azaleas [2]				
	1,000 pots	*1,000 pots*	*Dollars per pot*	*Dollars per pot*	*1,000 dollars*
2007	1,514	5,081	2.34	4.90	28,435
2008	1,095	7,188	2.24	4.65	35,897
2009	2,345	5,214	2.30	4.92	31,044
2010	1,348	3,289	2.59	5.67	22,138
2011	1,266	3,012	2.32	6.01	21,022
2012	1,129	3,544	2.68	5.28	21,734
2013	1,109	3,313	2.48	5.05	19,471
2014	22	4,063	4.25	4.65	18,977
2015	103	3,587	5.26	4.96	18,343
2018	(NA)	(NA)	(NA)	(NA)	(NA)
	Florist chrysanthemums				
	1,000 pots	*1,000 pots*	*Dollars per pot*	*Dollars*	*1,000 dollars*
2007	1,810	11,363	1.65	3.15	38,777
2008	1,927	9,902	1.57	3.21	34,762
2009	1,314	6,181	1.90	3.61	24,842
2010	2,225	4,526	1.82	3.97	22,029
2011	1,351	5,210	2.43	3.54	21,720
2012	1,654	4,400	2.00	4.14	21,535
2013	613	5,343	2.82	3.99	23,045
2014	1,239	4,673	3.02	3.96	22,238
2015	457	4,119	2.02	3.83	16,699
2018	2,185	5,495	1.84	4.55	28,999
	Easter lilies				
	1,000 pots	*1,000 pots*	*Dollars per pot*	*Dollars per pot*	*1,000 dollars*
2007	....	6,546	....	4.05	26,512
2008	31	5,824	4.05	4.33	25,335
2009	93	6,196	3.16	4.38	27,405
2010	147	5,891	3.29	4.29	25,764
2011	99	5,094	2.73	4.35	22,436
2012	37	5,011	3.48	4.36	21,958
2013	295	5,901	2.80	4.23	25,758
2014	785	5,099	3.90	4.59	26,460
2015	155	5,370	2.54	4.45	24,317
2018	1,098	4,935	4.58	4.54	27,453
	Potted Orchids				
	1,000 pots	*1,000 pots*	*Dollars per pot*	*Dollars per pot*	*1,000 dollars*
2007	10,661	6,655	6.95	9.89	139,960
2008	10,689	5,415	7.16	9.23	126,509
2009	12,503	7,135	7.36	9.70	161,208
2010	13,395	7,933	7.10	9.71	172,196
2011	15,415	8,520	6.78	10.19	191,306
2012	15,915	12,389	7.01	9.62	230,695
2013	18,934	12,750	7.34	8.83	251,559
2014	19,085	14,474	7.65	8.80	273,481
2015	19,393	16,983	7.25	8.70	288,284
2018	20,546	14,142	7.59	9.71	293,399

See footnote(s) at end of table.

Table 5-93.—Potted flowering for indoor or patio use: Sales and wholesale value for operations with $100,000+ sales, Surveyed States, 2007–2018—Continued

Year	Quantity sold		Wholesale price		Value of sales at wholesale [1]
	Less than 5 inches	5 inches or more	Less than 5 inches	5 inches or more	
	Poinsettias				
	1,000 pots	*1,000 pots*	*Dollars per pot*	*Dollars per pot*	*1,000 dollars*
2007	7,130	31,901	2.07	4.60	161,409
2008	6,373	28,922	2.07	4.82	152,611
2009	6,679	28,649	2.13	4.69	148,579
2010	7,710	26,942	2.02	4.65	140,841
2011	7,470	27,259	1.84	4.60	139,274
2012	6,620	27,301	2.12	4.77	144,309
2013	6,610	26,797	2.06	4.82	142,805
2014	6,338	27,263	2.15	4.77	143,715
2015	6,509	25,459	2.14	4.94	139,710
2018	8,479	25,720	2.22	5.05	148,760
	Potted florist roses				
	1,000 pots	*1,000 pots*	*Dollars per pot*	*Dollars*	*1,000 dollars*
2007	6,834	2,364	1.94	5.16	25,425
2008	7,252	1,064	2.74	5.34	25,569
2009	6,924	1,031	2.57	5.14	23,115
2010	5,599	2,167	2.50	5.83	26,669
2011	5,183	2,550	2.16	4.87	23,619
2012	5,729	2,828	2.18	5.74	28,741
2013	5,976	2,750	2.40	6.14	31,214
2014	7,751	934	3.26	6.41	31,282
2015	6,341	1,784	2.42	5.25	24,696
2018	8,353	2,478	1.91	4.88	28,069
	Potted spring flowering bulbs				
	1,000 pots	*1,000 pots*	*Dollars per pot*	*Dollars*	*1,000 dollars*
2007	10,073	8,624	1.91	3.66	50,861
2008	13,317	10,958	1.69	3.56	61,532
2009	4,689	11,204	1.74	3.43	46,662
2010	9,766	12,382	1.46	3.52	57,903
2011	8,162	11,637	1.52	3.54	53,638
2012	5,095	11,434	1.74	3.63	50,376
2013	4,623	11,013	1.96	3.77	50,614
2014	5,018	10,791	1.78	3.86	50,561
2015	5,548	16,865	2.19	3.38	69,115
2018	6,347	16,502	2.42	3.27	69,376
	Other flowering				
	1,000 pots	*1,000 pots*	*Dollars per pot*	*Dollars per pot*	*1,000 dollars*
2007	27,176	36,862	2.09	4.51	223,111
2008	22,529	31,482	2.10	4.91	201,962
2009	19,531	29,173	2.13	4.62	176,570
2010	17,162	25,695	2.71	5.00	175,006
2011	24,663	21,896	1.88	5.36	163,903
2012	22,670	25,625	2.57	5.99	211,766
2013	24,868	26,835	2.67	5.87	223,931
2014	25,569	32,190	2.70	5.29	239,162
2015	23,575	29,889	1.93	5.99	224,335
2018	31,310	40,991	2.48	4.95	280,698

(NA) Not available. [1] Equivalent wholesale value of all sales except for potted foliage which is value of sales less cost of plant material purchased from other growers for growing on. [2] Estimates discontinued in 2018.
NASS, Crops Branch, (202) 720–2127.

Table 5-94.—Annual Bedding and Garden Hanging Baskets: Sales and wholesale value for operations with $100,000+ sales, Surveyed States, 2007–2018

Year	Quantity sold	Wholesale price	Value of sales at wholesale [1]	Quantity sold	Wholesale price	Value of sales at wholesale [1]
	Begonias			Geraniums from vegetative cuttings		
	1,000 baskets	*Dollars*	*1,000 dollars*	*1,000 baskets*	*Dollars*	*1,000 dollars*
2007	1,701	5.76	9,796	3,296	6.87	22,640
2008	1,707	5.80	9,899	3,056	7.32	22,366
2009	1,531	5.84	8,944	3,564	7.44	26,523
2010	1,650	5.96	9,839	3,753	7.10	26,659
2011	1,622	5.99	9,723	3,561	7.13	25,390
2012	1,823	5.94	10,830	3,280	7.49	24,562
2013	2,016	6.33	12,770	3,126	7.39	23,113
2014	1,849	6.00	11,089	3,320	7.56	25,089
2015	1,960	6.25	12,250	3,310	7.43	24,586
2018	1,954	7.38	14,424	4,005	7.63	30,561
	Geraniums from seeds [2]			Impatiens, Other		
	1,000 baskets	*Dollars*	*1,000 dollars*	*1,000 baskets*	*Dollars*	*1,000 dollars*
2007	316	5.63	1,778	2,597	5.22	13,548
2008	267	6.05	1,616	2,375	5.29	12,561
2009	455	5.95	2,708	2,098	5.79	12,146
2010	286	7.01	2,005	2,534	5.63	14,260
2011	337	6.61	2,227	2,385	5.72	13,639
2012	475	6.56	3,115	2,479	5.44	13,494
2013	415	7.28	3,020	2,065	5.33	11,015
2014	460	7.46	3,432	2,021	5.32	10,750
2015	438	7.39	3,237	2,098	5.45	11,432
2018	(NA)	(NA)	(NA)	2,124	5.44	11,560
	New Guinea Impatiens			Marigolds		
	1,000 baskets	*Dollars*	*1,000 dollars*	*1,000 baskets*	*Dollars*	*1,000 dollars*
2007	2,987	6.96	20,797	184	6.08	1,118
2008	2,668	7.23	19,280	202	6.30	1,272
2009	2,556	7.09	18,122	55	6.33	348
2010	2,615	7.11	18,581	83	6.01	499
2011	2,456	7.14	17,526	77	5.77	444
2012	2,380	7.32	17,420	87	4.92	428
2013	2,254	7.37	16,613	117	4.38	513
2014	2,294	7.31	16,764	137	5.88	805
2015	2,388	7.39	17,637	139	5.99	833
2018	2,123	7.51	15,936	192	5.10	979
	Pansies/Violas			Petunias		
	1,000 baskets	*Dollars*	*1,000 dollars*	*1,000 baskets*	*Dollars*	*1,000 dollars*
2007	694	5.02	3,485	4,011	5.99	24,017
2008	695	5.20	3,612	3,969	5.98	23,752
2009	1,077	5.43	5,848	4,186	6.38	26,711
2010	911	5.59	5,091	5,066	6.16	31,225
2011	941	5.83	5,483	5,047	6.29	31,767
2012	1,096	5.75	6,299	5,028	6.21	31,240
2013	1,085	5.62	6,096	4,986	6.11	30,459
2014	1,182	5.92	7,002	5,557	6.28	34,906
2015	1,111	6.23	6,920	5,294	6.27	33,196
2018	1,077	6.51	7,006	6,154	5.97	36,712

Year	Other flowering hanging baskets and foliar		
	1,000 baskets	*Dollars*	*1,000 dollars*
2007	15,153	6.95	105,330
2008	14,718	6.92	101,856
2009	14,451	7.36	106,323
2010	13,483	7.67	103,399
2011	12,759	7.56	96,500
2012	14,865	7.33	109,030
2013	14,797	7.73	114,409
2014	13,259	8.23	109,117
2015	15,269	7.67	117,065
2018	15,269	8.20	124,587

(NA) Not available. [1] Equivalent wholesale value of all sales. [2] Estimates discontinued in 2018.
NASS, Crops Branch, (202) 720–2127.

Table 5-95.—Annual bedding garden plants flats: Sales and wholesale value for operations with $100,000+ sales, Surveyed States, 2007–2018

Year	Quantity sold	Wholesale price	Value of sales at wholesale [1]	Quantity sold	Wholesale price	Value of sales at wholesale [1]
	Begonias			Geraniums from vegetative cuttings		
	1,000 flats	*Dollars*	*1,000 dollars*	*1,000 flats*	*Dollars*	*1,000 dollars*
2007	4,094	8.17	33,444	417	12.32	5,138
2008	4,360	8.49	36,999	396	12.57	4,979
2009	4,055	8.75	35,490	353	15.09	5,326
2010	4,218	8.13	34,313	306	13.12	4,015
2011	3,983	7.97	31,738	264	14.08	3,716
2012	3,865	8.56	33,005	237	13.57	3,215
2013	3,758	8.15	30,640	325	11.65	3,785
2014	3,970	8.62	34,208	252	14.03	3,535
2015	3,819	8.33	31,813	248	12.83	3,182
2018	4,240	8.53	36,182	556	13.72	7,626
	Geraniums from seeds [2]			Impatients, other		
	1,000 flats	*Dollars*	*1,000 dollars*	*1,000 flats*	*Dollars*	*1,000 dollars*
2007	380	11.54	4,387	8,915	8.11	72,320
2008	384	11.00	4,223	8,547	8.52	72,815
2009	424	9.23	3,915	7,973	8.67	69,093
2010	465	10.29	4,784	8,641	8.24	71,160
2011	332	10.62	3,526	8,353	7.96	66,519
2012	394	9.81	3,866	6,852	9.08	62,230
2013	475	7.51	3,565	5,055	8.17	41,300
2014	372	9.26	3,445	4,775	8.38	40,034
2015	425	8.07	3,431	4,404	8.78	38,647
2018	(NA)	(NA)	(NA)	4,896	8.45	41,357
	New Guinea Impatiens			Marigolds		
	1,000 flats	*Dollars*	*1,000 dollars*	*1,000 flats*	*Dollars*	*1,000 dollars*
2007	243	11.09	2,696	3,694	8.39	31,001
2008	218	11.55	2,518	3,933	8.69	34,190
2009	290	10.77	3,124	3,976	8.98	35,713
2010	276	9.69	2,675	4,100	8.89	36,444
2011	190	10.56	2,006	3,884	8.45	32,807
2012	226	9.86	2,229	3,436	8.49	29,188
2013	335	10.01	3,355	3,488	8.24	28,733
2014	625	9.84	6,148	3,671	8.36	30,706
2015	368	9.76	3,592	3,587	8.20	29,425
2018	547	9.93	5,432	3,495	9.24	32,282
	Pansies/Violas			Petunias		
	1,000 flats	*Dollars*	*1,000 dollars*	*1,000 flats*	*Dollars*	*1,000 dollars*
2007	8,047	8.33	67,050	7,023	8.52	59,808
2008	8,169	8.82	72,036	7,402	8.80	65,129
2009	7,430	9.15	67,957	7,006	9.32	65,317
2010	7,538	8.88	66,916	7,448	8.92	66,404
2011	7,200	8.66	62,936	7,227	8.56	61,891
2012	7,343	9.02	66,245	6,667	8.64	57,618
2013	6,369	8.94	56,926	6,581	8.36	55,034
2014	7,272	8.45	61,441	6,896	9.11	62,822
2015	6,297	8.91	56,113	6,448	8.76	56,509
2018	5,269	9.72	51,195	5,751	9.62	55,348
	Other flowering and foliar plants			Vegetable type plants		
	1,000 flats	*Dollars*	*1,000 dollars*	*1,000 flats*	*Dollars*	*1,000 dollars*
2007	21,350	8.70	185,788	4,135	9.39	38,822
2008	19,441	9.00	175,027	4,545	10.25	46,573
2009	16,331	9.45	154,342	5,025	10.53	52,911
2010	17,898	9.40	168,261	4,862	10.20	49,603
2011	17,836	9.50	169,484	5,102	10.53	53,740
2012	16,934	9.10	154,089	6,297	9.64	60,714
2013	16,275	8.71	141,740	4,998	10.18	50,858
2014	14,788	9.38	138,683	4,861	10.82	52,616
2015	14,811	8.87	131,358	5,453	10.60	57,808
2018	14,488	10.00	144,925	7,330	11.73	86,013

(NA) Not available. [1] Equivalent wholesale value of all sales. [2] Estimates discontinued in 2018.
NASS, Crops Branch, (202) 720–2127.

Table 5-96.—Potted annual bedding and garden plants: Sales and wholesale value for operations with $100,000+ sales, Surveyed States, 2007–2018

Year	Quantity sold: Less than 5 inches	Quantity sold: 5 inches or more	Wholesale price: Less than 5 inches	Wholesale price: 5 inches or more	Value of sales at wholesale [1]
	Begonias				
	1,000 pots	*1,000 pots*	*Dollars*	*Dollars*	*1,000 dollars*
2007	16,748	3,683	0.84	2.06	21,645
2008	16,481	4,296	0.91	2.17	24,293
2009	17,821	3,272	0.86	2.34	22,907
2010	14,709	3,163	0.92	2.22	20,617
2011	14,763	3,374	0.91	2.24	20,973
2012	15,837	3,323	0.91	2.40	22,340
2013	18,296	4,118	0.94	2.58	27,922
2014	16,901	3,619	1.02	2.48	26,248
2015	16,853	4,757	1.05	2.82	31,023
2018	16,923	5,958	1.03	2.91	34,772
	Geraniums from cuttings				
	1,000 pots	*1,000 pots*	*Dollars*	*Dollars*	*1,000 dollars*
2007	22,785	13,253	1.66	3.35	82,364
2008	23,094	13,050	1.76	3.35	84,300
2009	22,985	14,209	1.79	3.18	86,303
2010	23,339	13,431	1.81	3.54	89,770
2011	21,156	12,844	1.85	3.57	85,031
2012	21,563	13,560	1.85	3.38	85,842
2013	20,429	11,554	1.88	3.62	80,293
2014	21,093	11,119	1.93	3.70	81,970
2015	19,821	11,724	1.92	3.66	80,989
2018	20,587	11,701	1.82	3.77	81,641
	Geraniums from seed [2]				
	1,000 pots	*1,000 pots*	*Dollars*	*Dollars*	*1,000 dollars*
2007	28,897	343	0.83	2.86	25,071
2008	25,114	367	0.87	3.31	23,186
2009	24,622	495	0.92	2.78	23,923
2010	18,748	1,248	1.03	4.67	25,097
2011	23,673	1,648	0.93	5.20	30,680
2012	16,449	728	0.88	3.42	16,988
2013	17,825	393	1.12	3.49	21,604
2014	17,230	340	1.11	4.06	20,552
2015	13,336	1,119	1.00	3.58	17,297
2018	(NA)	(NA)	(NA)	(NA)	(NA)
	Other impatiens				
	1,000 pots	*1,000 pots*	*Dollars*	*Dollars*	*1,000 dollars*
2007	19,575	5,575	0.81	1.69	25,267
2008	20,606	4,973	0.78	1.91	25,663
2009	21,923	5,075	0.76	1.87	26,065
2010	21,955	4,033	0.77	2.43	26,702
2011	20,480	4,220	0.77	2.25	25,334
2012	13,941	4,834	0.82	2.11	21,678
2013	8,825	3,629	0.94	1.90	15,245
2014	7,115	3,776	0.95	1.88	13,880
2015	6,754	3,614	1.00	2.25	14,911
2018	7,786	2,104	1.38	2.78	16,608
	New guinea impatiens				
	1,000 pots	*1,000 pots*	*Dollars*	*Dollars*	*1,000 dollars*
2007	11,885	4,735	1.58	2.83	32,180
2008	12,630	4,283	1.57	3.18	33,459
2009	12,439	3,834	1.59	3.25	32,177
2010	10,919	3,961	1.50	3.28	29,376
2011	9,794	3,658	1.59	3.44	28,130
2012	11,640	4,236	1.47	3.27	30,956
2013	13,325	4,045	1.51	3.46	34,105
2014	12,971	4,160	1.59	3.39	34,762
2015	12,864	4,024	1.52	3.63	34,158
2018	13,989	4,679	1.78	3.20	39,857

See footnote(s) at end of table.

Table 5-96.—Potted annual bedding and garden plants: Sales and wholesale value for operations with $100,000+ sales, Surveyed States, 2007–2018—Continued

Year	Quantity sold		Wholesale price		Value of sales at wholesale [1]
	Less than 5 inches	5 inches or more	Less than 5 inches	5 inches or more	
	Marigolds				
	1,000 pots	*1,000 pots*	*Dollars*	*Dollars*	*1,000 dollars*
2007	8,372	2,150	0.68	1.59	9,125
2008	7,600	1,704	0.72	1.61	8,185
2009	8,837	1,826	0.78	1.76	10,124
2010	7,901	2,463	0.76	1.88	10,621
2011	7,180	2,272	0.81	1.82	9,947
2012	8,871	1,792	0.79	2.10	10,762
2013	8,637	1,819	0.80	2.09	10,688
2014	9,264	1,273	0.97	2.32	11,922
2015	9,100	1,745	0.97	2.14	12,596
2018	8,020	2,357	1.09	2.39	14,366
	Pansies/violas				
	1,000 pots	*1,000 pots*	*Dollars*	*Dollars*	*1,000 dollars*
2007	28,021	6,145	0.74	2.13	33,788
2008	25,980	5,989	0.75	2.09	31,966
2009	27,054	5,529	0.74	2.06	31,363
2010	23,394	6,159	0.80	2.02	31,035
2011	24,573	6,130	0.80	2.12	32,692
2012	23,416	6,918	0.81	2.19	34,078
2013	21,953	6,155	0.86	2.19	32,308
2014	22,813	6,273	0.86	2.17	33,116
2015	23,029	6,418	0.89	2.17	34,518
2018	14,732	7,522	1.03	2.33	32,646
	Petunias				
	1,000 pots	*1,000 pots*	*Dollars*	*Dollars*	*1,000 dollars*
2007	18,551	6,935	0.98	2.37	34,558
2008	16,310	6,796	1.01	2.27	31,852
2009	18,088	7,527	0.98	2.20	34,301
2010	19,152	9,142	1.07	2.11	39,732
2011	18,212	8,843	1.12	2.07	38,629
2012	20,830	8,651	1.14	2.30	43,546
2013	18,713	8,251	1.23	2.64	44,844
2014	17,627	7,763	1.27	2.70	43,273
2015	17,664	7,815	1.28	2.68	43,536
2018	16,681	10,173	1.30	2.75	49,646
	Other flowering and foliar plants				
	1,000 pots	*1,000 pots*	*Dollars*	*Dollars*	*1,000 dollars*
2007	117,723	50,605	1.13	3.08	288,890
2008	108,251	55,789	1.20	2.65	278,250
2009	93,289	48,271	1.18	3.06	257,709
2010	101,633	57,907	1.26	3.04	301,479
2011	108,661	54,133	1.25	2.96	296,030
2012	127,328	64,961	1.20	3.02	348,961
2013	111,363	50,025	1.32	3.30	309,160
2014	98,436	45,668	1.35	3.33	284,313
2015	106,082	47,534	1.38	3.39	307,799
2018	115,900	64,616	1.45	3.56	398,531
	Vegetable type plants [3]				
	1,000 pots	*1,000 pots*	*Dollars*	*Dollars*	*1,000 dollars*
2007	27,676	3,874	1.01	2.22	36,668
2008	35,998	7,497	1.06	2.49	56,697
2009	38,534	12,794	1.07	2.51	73,307
2010	38,453	14,155	1.12	2.64	80,411
2011	40,176	7,478	1.29	3.19	75,761
2012	31,100	12,211	1.22	2.98	74,478
2013	31,816	10,057	1.24	3.16	71,249
2014	44,491	10,531	1.47	3.21	99,356
2015	36,402	8,174	1.33	2.73	70,721
2018	37,663	7,998	1.43	4.15	87,023

(NA) Not available. [1] Equivalent wholesale value of all sales. [2] Estimates discontinued in 2018. [3] Does not include vegetable transplants grown for use in commercial vegetable production.

NASS, Crops Branch, (202) 720–2127.

Table 5-97.—Potted herbaceous perennial plants: Sales and wholesale value for operations with $100,000+ sales, Surveyed States, 2007–2018

Year	Quantity sold		Wholesale price		Value of sales at wholesale [1]
	Less than 5 inches	5 inches or more	Less than 5 inches	5 inches or more	
	Hardy/Garden Chrysanthemums				
	1,000 pots	*1,000 pots*	*Dollars*	*Dollars*	*1,000 dollars*
2007	9,763	35,148	1.06	2.66	103,831
2008	9,217	34,689	1.10	2.61	100,868
2009	8,049	35,833	1.25	2.81	110,747
2010	11,352	34,531	1.10	2.93	113,620
2011	11,962	36,634	1.03	2.77	113,747
2012	13,327	35,792	1.03	3.08	124,097
2013	15,558	33,176	1.08	2.89	112,552
2014	14,727	33,907	1.04	3.08	119,888
2015	9,326	37,885	1.12	2.99	123,677
2018	15,810	37,243	1.46	3.34	147,494

Year	Quantity sold			Wholesale price			Value of sales at wholesale [1]
	Less than 1 gallon	1-2 gallons	2 gallons or more	Less than 1 gallon	1-2 gallons	2 gallons or more	
	Hosta						
	1,000 pots	*1,000 pots*	*1,000 pots*	*Dollars*	*Dollars*	*Dollars*	*1,000 dollars*
2007	4,374	6,589	271	1.74	3.50	7.69	32,723
2008	4,451	6,793	173	1.91	3.43	9.10	33,391
2009	4,279	6,340	582	2.15	3.36	6.47	34,283
2010	1,448	6,783	337	2.11	3.26	7.54	27,704
2011	2,112	6,270	281	2.27	3.19	8.53	27,195
2012	2,365	5,535	363	2.34	3.40	8.04	27,240
2013	2,511	5,898	382	2.64	3.39	7.98	29,671
2014	5,362	3,870	398	2.73	3.75	7.78	32,242
2015	5,195	4,419	419	2.70	3.92	8.35	34,869
2018	5,128	3,521	162	2.85	4.35	9.11	31,391
	Other Herbaceous Perennials						
	1,000 pots	*1,000 pots*	*1,000 pots*	*Dollars*	*Dollars*	*Dollars*	*1,000 dollars*
2007	68,640	69,843	6,442	1.71	3.33	6.84	394,407
2008	65,928	74,574	7,533	1.59	3.43	6.65	410,867
2009	50,229	80,234	4,975	1.68	3.42	6.92	392,847
2010	53,613	86,180	6,257	1.63	3.38	7.11	423,266
2011	56,970	83,944	5,459	1.75	3.35	7.43	421,276
2012	56,936	65,596	10,001	1.77	3.78	7.33	422,282
2013	62,721	72,430	6,983	1.90	3.90	8.41	460,375
2014	62,508	60,111	5,823	2.19	3.90	8.47	420,547
2015	57,666	62,449	4,271	2.17	4.01	8.75	412,866
2018	69,491	63,028	14,100	2.05	4.06	6.53	489,931

[1] Equivalent wholesale value of all sales.
NASS, Crops Branch, (202) 720–2127.

Table 5-98.—Floriculture: Number of Producers and Area Used for Production by Type of Cover, operations with $10,000+ sales, 15 Program States: 2015 and 2018

State	Total number of producers		Glass greenhouses		Fiberglass and other rigid greenhouses		Film plastic (single/multi) greenhouses	
	2015	2018	2015	2018	2015	2018	2015	2018
	Number		*1,000 square feet*					
Alaska [1]	(NA)	51	(NA)	(D)	(NA)	(D)	(D)	253
California	685	850	10,748	10,387	30,042	30,091	30,091	64,726
Colorado [1]	(NA)	121	(NA)	(D)	(NA)	(D)	(D)	3,854
Connecticut [1]	(NA)	216	(NA)	2,533	(NA)	1,560	1,560	10,067
Florida	710	680	3,054	3,800	8,159	5,468	5,468	34,499
Hawaii [2]	301	(NA)	(D)	(NA)	(D)	(NA)	(NA)	(NA)
Illinois	273	241	2,966	2,695	2,249	1,701	1,701	9,058
Maryland [2]	153	(NA)	1,644	(NA)	1,375	(NA)	(NA)	(NA)
Michigan	556	569	3,458	3,126	3,773	2,926	2,926	41,861
New Jersey	273	303	4,675	4,350	1,031	548	548	13,213
New York	615	585	3,816	3,114	1,223	1,467	1,467	15,156
North Carolina	294	257	6,652	7,662	529	265	265	13,486
Ohio	472	481	8,860	9,455	1,767	2,272	2,272	15,337
Oregon	283	259	2,835	2,367	2,691	2,485	2,485	12,054
Pennsylvania	727	683	2,585	2,616	3,808	3,613	3,613	16,135
South Carolina [2]	72	(NA)	(D)	(NA)	(D)	(NA)	(NA)	(NA)
Texas	251	254	1,361	1,221	3,696	4,977	4,977	25,844
Virginia [1]	(NA)	190	(NA)	574	(NA)	68	68	12,233
Washington	248	277	2,317	1,860	1,099	894	894	5,771
Wisconsin [1]	(NA)	369	(NA)	793	(NA)	1,457	1,457	8,148
Other States [3]	....	....	27	1,326	1,704	3,647	3,647	....
Total	5,913	6,386	54,998	57,879	63,146	63,439	63,439	301,695

State	Total greenhouse cover		Shade and temporary cover		Total covered area		Open ground [4]	
	2015	2018	2015	2018	2015	2018	2015	2018
	1,000 square feet						*Acres*	
Alaska [1]	(NA)	1,063	(NA)	-	(NA)	1,063	(NA)	54
California	104,779	105,204	37,148	30,386	141,927	135,590	9,399	13,327
Colorado [1]	(NA)	8,017	(NA)	188	(NA)	8,205	(NA)	160
Connecticut [1]	(NA)	14,160	(NA)	211	(NA)	14,371	(NA)	503
Florida	51,673	43,767	289,184	392,386	340,857	436,153	6,853	6,527
Hawaii [2]	(D)	(NA)	(D)	(NA)	17,940	(NA)	914	(NA)
Illinois	14,604	13,454	664	619	15,268	14,073	4,272	1,179
Maryland [2]	9,274	(NA)	360	(NA)	9,634	(NA)	618	(NA)
Michigan	46,278	47,913	711	1,742	46,989	49,655	2,063	2,359
New Jersey	23,236	18,111	493	227	23,729	18,338	4,826	2,890
New York	20,760	19,737	433	377	21,193	20,114	722	943
North Carolina	21,640	21,413	1,244	251	22,884	21,664	912	644
Ohio	26,632	27,064	956	538	27,588	27,602	385	431
Oregon	18,861	16,906	2,275	2,408	21,136	19,314	3,903	3,047
Pennsylvania	20,959	22,364	262	187	21,221	22,551	778	802
South Carolina [2]	(D)	(NA)	(D)	(NA)	5,921	(NA)	396	(NA)
Texas	33,109	32,042	6,485	5,694	39,594	37,736	1,215	1,789
Virginia [1]	(NA)	12,875	(NA)	430	(NA)	13,305	(NA)	582
Washington	10,118	8,525	917	286	11,035	8,811	2,786	2,132
Wisconsin [1]	(NA)	10,398	(NA)	431	(NA)	10,829	(NA)	980
Other States [3]	7,425	....	16,436	....	....	....	....	....
Total	409,348	423,013	357,568	436,361	766,916	859,374	40,042	38,358

(D) Withheld to avoid disclosure of individual operations. (NA) Not available. [1] Estimates began in 2018. [2] Estimates discontinued in 2018. [3] Includes data withheld above. [4] Totals may not add due to rounding.

NASS, Crops Branch, (202) 720-2127.

Table 5-99.—Floriculture Crops: Wholesale value of all sales by category, operations with $100,000+ sales: 2015 and 2018

State	Annual bedding/ garden plants		Herbaceous perennial plants		Total bedding/ garden plants [1]	
	2015	2018	2015	2018	2015	2018
	1,000 dollars					
Alaska [2]	(NA)	4,136	(NA)	336	(NA)	4,472
California	193,209	205,623	72,361	126,603	265,570	332,226
Colorado [2]	(NA)	61,486	(NA)	23,647	(NA)	85,133
Connecticut [2]	(NA)	74,025	(NA)	40,683	(NA)	114,708
Florida	96,402	140,090	37,023	63,539	133,425	203,629
Hawaii [3]	2,199	(NA)	1,587	(NA)	3,786	(NA)
Illinois	38,595	40,612	25,619	35,375	64,214	75,987
Maryland [3]	64,704	(NA)	37,527	(NA)	102,231	(NA)
Michigan	208,727	224,469	61,939	69,390	270,666	293,859
New Jersey	77,016	71,187	56,641	49,562	133,657	120,749
New York	86,189	72,076	24,608	21,276	110,797	93,352
North Carolina	140,596	84,195	42,873	58,199	183,469	142,394
Ohio	81,126	69,016	51,844	40,933	132,970	109,949
Oregon	52,586	71,514	30,667	37,857	83,253	109,371
Pennsylvania	67,574	77,783	22,593	31,025	90,167	108,808
South Carolina [3]	8,036	(NA)	46,786	(NA)	54,822	(NA)
Texas	136,112	98,708	32,118	29,868	168,230	128,576
Virginia [2]	(NA)	76,269	(NA)	24,254	(NA)	100,523
Washington	33,511	39,586	27,226	38,449	60,737	78,035
Wisconsin [2]	(NA)	46,440	(NA)	16,595	(NA)	63,035
Other States [4]	....	....	....	....	....	....
Total	1,286,582	1,457,215	571,412	707,591	1,857,994	2,164,806

State	Potted flowering plants		Foliage plants for indoor or patio use		Cut flowers	
	2015	2018	2015	2018	2015	2018
	1,000 dollars					
Alaska [2]	(NA)	(D)	(NA)	(D)	(NA)	163
California	273,537	299,573	114,599	155,649	293,737	288,356
Colorado [2]	(NA)	9,149	(NA)	1,446	(NA)	2,724
Connecticut [2]	(NA)	8,460	(NA)	(D)	(NA)	66
Florida	201,212	151,957	543,447	413,873	2,289	(D)
Hawaii [3]	15,079	(NA)	9,612	(NA)	7,014	(NA)
Illinois	23,875	25,070	1,121	1,746	1,103	(D)
Maryland [3]	7,060	(NA)	(D)	(NA)	470	(NA)
Michigan	31,147	70,435	6,305	8,849	5,312	(D)
New Jersey	29,368	50,723	(D)	12,996	14,675	(D)
New York	29,537	33,433	(D)	2,266	885	(D)
North Carolina	27,545	18,494	(D)	18,078	4,981	(D)
Ohio	68,163	75,458	4,207	7,559	(D)	800
Oregon	14,809	17,186	1,170	4,695	13,350	13,231
Pennsylvania	44,954	47,996	(D)	(D)	(D)	8,513
South Carolina [3]	8,221	(NA)	(D)	(NA)	(D)	(NA)
Texas	27,165	26,040	(D)	14,010	(D)	3,533
Virginia [2]	(NA)	30,130	(NA)	835	(NA)	2,026
Washington	7,988	7,028	(D)	6,486	20,457	21,571
Wisconsin [2]	(NA)	(D)	(NA)	(D)	(NA)	2,799
Other States [4]	....	5,622	33,228	4,591	10,045	31,162
Total	809,660	876,754	713,689	653,079	374,318	374,944

See footnote(s) at end of table.

Table 5-99.—Floriculture Crops: Wholesale value of all sales by category, operations with $100,000+ sales: 2015 and 2018–Continued

State	Cut cultivated greens		Propagative floriculture material		Total wholesale value of all plant categories	
	2015	2018	2015	2018	2015	2018
	1,000 dollars					
Alaska [2]	(NA)	....	(NA)	....	(NA)	5,602
California	15,762	21,105	107,076	102,488	1,070,281	1,199,397
Colorado [2]	(NA)	....	(NA)	27,516	(NA)	125,968
Connecticut [2]	(NA)	....	(NA)	(D)	(NA)	123,667
Florida	61,080	(D)	86,828	90,893	1,028,281	938,886
Hawaii [3]	323	(NA)	1,352	(NA)	37,166	(NA)
Illinois	....	10	1,359	1,633	91,672	105,372
Maryland [3]	....	(NA)	(D)	(NA)	111,163	(NA)
Michigan	(D)	(D)	(D)	96,208	398,113	474,977
New Jersey	(D)	(D)	18,271	21,122	197,001	221,597
New York	(D)	(D)	16,522	17,712	160,167	148,014
North Carolina	....	(D)	(D)	3,432	234,168	188,269
Ohio	....	(D)	(D)	3,142	210,102	196,923
Oregon	2,465	3,318	14,292	10,925	129,339	158,726
Pennsylvania	(D)	(D)	(D)	27,864	169,962	195,620
South Carolina [3]	....	(NA)	(D)	(NA)	63,199	(NA)
Texas	(D)	....	(D)	4,925	216,429	177,084
Virginia [2]	(NA)	(D)	(NA)	(D)	(NA)	140,093
Washington	(D)	44	21,920	13,655	112,761	126,819
Wisconsin [2]	(NA)	(D)	(NA)	2,995	(NA)	75,691
Other States [4]	796	77,520	126,097	6,615	....	....
Total	80,426	101,997	393,717	431,125	4,229,804	4,602,705

- Represents zero. (D) Withheld to avoid disclosure of individual operations.(NA) Not available. [1] Includes Annual Bedding Plants and Herbaceous Perennials. [2] Estimates began in 2018. [3] Estimates discontinued in 2018. [4] Includes data withheld above.

NASS, Crops Branch, (202) 720-2127.

Table 5-100.—Nuts, Pecans: Cold storage holdings, end of month, United States, 2017 and 2018

Month	Pecans			
	Shelled		In-shell	
	2017	2018	2017	2018
	1,000 pounds			
January	39,821	45,662	195,588	162,210
February	44,708	46,991	203,931	196,988
March	48,213	51,950	182,828	184,869
April	52,640	57,156	158,509	161,330
May	51,084	60,151	133,144	136,556
June	50,941	63,314	106,529	111,349
July	55,313	65,379	85,068	89,383
August	56,911	70,019	63,032	57,796
September	53,112	64,493	34,405	33,667
October	46,475	55,475	23,686	25,476
November	41,564	53,219	43,018	47,970
December	44,036	54,259	95,912	94,823

NASS, Livestock Branch, (202) 720-3570.

Table 5-101.—Fruit and orange juice: Cold storage holdings, end of month, United States, 2017 and 2018

Month	Apples		Apricots		Blackberries, IQF		Blackberries, pails & tubs	
	2017	2018	2017	2018	2017	2018	2017	2018
	1,000 pounds							
January	37,963	34,420	6,506	4,295	18,532	14,018	2,114	1,747
February	36,919	35,915	4,103	3,616	16,980	11,789	1,409	1,502
March	38,679	36,968	3,163	2,974	15,269	10,188	1,513	1,518
April	44,495	35,087	2,848	2,275	14,755	9,329	1,382	1,184
May	40,049	32,441	2,279	1,664	12,268	7,962	1,535	1,133
June	37,418	33,715	11,696	8,301	12,541	8,924	1,488	1,106
July	34,995	30,609	11,048	9,538	21,214	25,723	1,424	1,681
August	34,475	24,822	8,512	8,843	22,190	22,340	1,439	1,320
September	29,471	22,366	7,335	8,148	20,717	22,247	1,483	1,344
October	26,836	21,602	6,098	7,549	18,618	21,081	1,607	1,678
November	29,408	23,141	5,506	6,640	17,320	18,770	1,661	1,635
December	32,007	28,276	4,873	6,458	16,208	17,059	1,724	1,420

Month	Blackberries, barrels		Blackberries, concentrate		Blackberries, total		Blueberries	
	2017	2018	2017	2018	2017	2018	2017	2018
	1,000 pounds							
January	8,043	4,356	851	1,281	29,540	21,402	241,947	192,354
February	7,904	3,735	690	1,179	26,983	18,205	223,211	162,564
March	6,715	3,210	654	1,266	24,151	16,182	195,417	134,469
April	6,355	2,976	655	1,262	23,147	14,751	184,367	116,387
May	6,590	2,416	563	1,023	20,956	12,534	157,140	96,891
June	7,363	3,519	693	932	22,085	14,481	147,915	99,912
July	13,494	10,207	781	1,103	36,913	38,714	197,723	175,163
August	10,241	8,707	837	1,080	34,707	33,447	276,632	244,902
September	8,669	7,665	734	1,038	31,603	32,294	266,423	247,396
October	6,792	6,417	1,007	922	28,024	30,098	256,727	228,308
November	6,618	5,900	1,083	764	26,682	27,069	230,843	199,883
December	5,326	5,389	1,191	771	24,449	24,639	222,060	182,857

Month	Boysenberries		Cherries, Tart (RTP)		Cherries, Sweet		Grapes	
	2017	2018	2017	2018	2017	2018	2017	2018
	1,000 pounds							
January	1,499	412	131,911	125,530	20,042	16,935	1,290	2,859
February	1,444	589	121,549	115,381	20,301	14,840	1,166	2,853
March	1,208	437	111,923	108,226	18,044	14,400	1,371	3,015
April	978	430	102,192	98,931	16,530	13,710	1,368	2,525
May	843	347	93,736	88,879	13,998	12,447	2,281	3,055
June	869	835	83,809	74,151	10,511	10,877	2,392	4,464
July	1,224	1,044	155,363	167,724	16,605	16,941	2,790	3,719
August	852	897	166,554	184,463	20,305	22,197	2,764	5,798
September	721	868	158,660	169,664	20,977	20,896	3,031	4,831
October	665	933	154,858	156,443	20,736	16,924	3,155	3,785
November	768	794	142,281	145,503	19,546	14,646	2,897	4,417
December	585	722	134,946	141,203	17,801	15,147	2,977	4,772

Month	Peaches		Raspberries, Black		Red Raspberries, IQF		Red Raspberries, pails & tubs	
	2017	2018	2017	2018	2017	2018	2017	2018
	1,000 pounds							
January	74,285	68,986	1,047	1,756	29,657	33,313	6,498	6,428
February	69,924	60,036	960	1,677	27,875	32,545	5,669	6,678
March	64,477	54,899	1,012	1,703	24,868	29,636	5,273	6,369
April	58,878	46,756	1,021	1,423	22,982	27,388	4,799	5,934
May	53,696	40,717	870	1,306	19,910	24,831	4,795	5,671
June	53,066	35,517	911	2,081	16,999	26,870	4,017	5,419
July	62,003	37,622	2,015	2,718	39,775	55,768	8,718	9,483
August	83,564	47,951	1,995	1,992	43,714	53,168	8,662	9,225
September	87,901	69,188	1,905	1,796	41,073	47,645	7,167	8,784
October	85,238	69,577	1,584	1,625	35,904	43,591	7,281	8,483
November	84,813	64,956	1,590	1,513	36,458	39,721	7,251	7,913
December	76,686	62,532	1,498	1,467	34,781	37,341	7,216	7,627

See footnotes(s) at end of table.

Table 5-101.—Fruit and orange juice: Cold storage holdings, end of month, United States, 2017 and 2018—Continued

Month	Red Raspberries, barrels		Red Raspberries, concentrate		Red Raspberries, total		Strawberries, IQF & Poly	
	2017	2018	2017	2018	2017	2018	2017	2018
	1,000 pounds							
January	21,857	26,466	3,263	1,027	61,275	67,234	116,982	110,933
February	18,119	23,695	3,109	2,037	54,772	64,955	103,960	95,498
March	15,770	19,891	2,984	2,107	48,895	58,003	112,436	95,820
April	13,456	20,758	2,911	2,126	44,148	56,206	119,276	90,021
May	12,400	18,483	2,559	1,912	39,664	50,897	139,991	111,245
June	10,964	14,062	1,838	2,211	33,818	48,562	154,949	141,526
July	32,655	46,228	2,723	1,978	83,871	113,457	180,463	138,909
August	38,161	46,080	2,647	1,896	93,184	110,369	175,380	129,037
September	38,007	44,888	1,058	1,882	87,305	103,199	168,268	126,616
October	36,109	41,770	1,361	1,540	80,655	95,384	149,453	108,659
November	34,380	38,648	1,293	1,519	79,382	87,801	136,248	90,907
December	32,424	38,240	1,193	1,566	75,614	84,774	122,244	86,344

Month	Strawberries, pails & tubs		Strawberries, barrels & drums		Strawberries, juice stock		Strawberries, total	
	2017	2018	2017	2018	2017	2018	2017	2018
	1,000 pounds							
January	84,344	83,607	61,185	46,853	27,111	11,626	289,622	253,019
February	83,362	70,208	57,265	36,151	29,560	14,226	274,147	216,083
March	67,296	57,643	50,287	28,576	25,959	13,841	255,978	195,880
April	65,884	56,735	56,192	27,743	24,854	12,480	266,206	186,979
May	78,498	82,692	69,293	43,875	24,462	11,716	312,244	249,528
June	94,329	126,678	82,286	95,690	26,064	13,339	357,628	377,233
July	109,452	122,929	97,989	100,883	23,337	10,475	411,241	373,196
August	121,832	111,697	84,789	98,137	20,914	11,748	402,915	350,619
September	108,110	94,959	70,672	95,479	16,492	11,123	363,542	328,177
October	101,259	84,202	66,590	81,553	15,748	11,796	333,050	286,210
November	98,398	81,755	60,415	69,646	14,290	10,870	309,351	253,178
December	90,885	73,196	54,950	57,780	12,997	10,113	281,076	227,433

Month	Other fruit		Total frozen fruit		Orange juice	
	2017	2018	2017	2018	2017	2018
	1,000 pounds					
January	764,821	595,561	1,673,422	1,390,288	503,356	517,105
February	738,926	554,544	1,585,755	1,256,166	506,275	500,973
March	665,196	487,759	1,439,934	1,119,005	517,057	563,125
April	604,047	402,212	1,360,500	1,041,047	542,175	632,626
May	543,809	399,596	1,290,956	992,928	575,365	730,886
June	491,595	404,649	1,262,782	1,117,468	544,443	733,849
July	502,270	395,232	1,530,292	1,379,068	505,491	691,110
August	493,106	361,493	1,633,134	1,417,408	471,509	633,390
September	515,569	398,684	1,585,809	1,425,149	495,648	608,983
October	700,422	741,609	1,707,834	1,677,206	493,531	566,387
November	709,259	710,070	1,650,332	1,556,323	468,090	528,895
December	666,624	654,518	1,547,787	1,449,406	505,077	547,910

NASS, Livestock Branch, (202) 720–3570.

CHAPTER VI

STATISTICS OF HAY, SEEDS, AND MINOR FIELD CROPS

Chapter VI deals with hay, pasture, seeds, and various minor field crops.

Table 6-1.—Hay, all: Area, yield, and production, by State and United States, 2017–2019

State	Area harvested			Yield per harvested acre			Production		
	2017	2018	2019	2017	2018	2019	2017	2018	2019
	1,000 acres	*1,000 acres*	*1,000 acres*	*Tons*	*Tons*	*Tons*	*1,000 tons*	*1,000 tons*	*1,000 tons*
Alabama	860	850	700	2.50	2.80	2.50	2,150	2,380	1,750
Alaska [1]	(X)	22	22	(X)	1.30	1.30	(X)	29	29
Arizona	325	300	325	7.96	7.82	7.72	2,586	2,346	2,509
Arkansas	1,293	1,203	1,253	2.00	1.80	2.20	2,591	2,168	2,760
California	1,140	980	1,010	5.60	5.80	5.74	6,388	5,682	5,795
Colorado	1,440	1,420	1,460	2.75	2.55	2.78	3,960	3,621	4,052
Connecticut	48	47	47	2.29	2.34	1.72	110	110	81
Delaware	15	13	14	3.20	2.62	2.21	48	34	31
Florida	300	280	270	2.50	3.10	2.90	750	868	783
Georgia	620	600	560	2.90	2.90	2.75	1,798	1,740	1,540
Idaho	1,430	1,340	1,300	3.59	3.75	3.93	5,128	5,019	5,111
Illinois	490	470	420	3.25	2.79	2.71	1,593	1,309	1,140
Indiana	540	510	520	2.76	2.71	2.48	1,492	1,382	1,290
Iowa	1,060	940	1,020	3.08	3.19	3.05	3,268	2,998	3,116
Kansas	2,470	2,360	2,280	2.22	2.02	2.77	5,472	4,760	6,315
Kentucky	2,125	1,895	1,945	2.43	2.68	2.27	5,170	5,088	4,424
Louisiana	400	380	390	2.60	2.20	2.50	1,040	836	975
Maine	125	110	110	1.93	1.89	2.15	241	208	236
Maryland	190	195	189	2.68	2.83	2.68	509	552	507
Massachusetts	78	79	51	1.78	1.48	2.25	139	117	115
Michigan	870	810	780	2.29	2.24	2.38	1,989	1,812	1,858
Minnesota	1,360	1,220	1,100	2.79	2.52	2.70	3,797	3,077	2,966
Mississippi	610	590	610	2.40	2.10	2.30	1,464	1,239	1,403
Missouri	3,000	3,070	3,360	2.00	1.76	2.19	5,985	5,408	7,367
Montana	2,500	2,900	3,000	1.90	1.93	2.08	4,740	5,595	6,225
Nebraska	2,510	2,700	2,450	2.37	2.59	2.48	5,955	6,985	6,085
Nevada	385	365	435	3.35	3.17	3.60	1,288	1,158	1,565
New Hampshire	45	39	49	1.80	1.77	1.69	81	69	83
New Jersey	108	114	91	2.22	1.93	2.05	240	220	187
New Mexico	285	250	245	4.00	3.73	3.89	1,140	932	954
New York	1,320	1,220	1,180	2.01	2.25	1.90	2,650	2,744	2,240
North Carolina	657	816	816	2.30	2.71	2.30	1,514	2,210	1,877
North Dakota	2,580	2,670	2,420	1.33	1.66	1.70	3,433	4,419	4,116
Ohio	960	970	920	2.47	2.43	2.32	2,371	2,356	2,137
Oklahoma	2,930	3,230	3,005	1.92	1.59	1.98	5,638	5,121	5,935
Oregon	1,085	1,000	970	3.05	3.06	3.47	3,304	3,056	3,362
Pennsylvania	1,420	1,190	1,210	2.61	2.30	2.47	3,709	2,739	2,986
Rhode Island	6	6	5	2.00	2.00	1.40	12	12	7
South Carolina	300	270	270	2.60	2.50	2.10	780	675	567
South Dakota	2,950	3,250	3,350	1.56	1.78	2.09	4,603	5,788	7,003
Tennessee	1,665	1,720	1,763	2.26	2.46	2.31	3,767	4,231	4,073
Texas	4,520	4,740	4,920	2.11	1.77	1.87	9,548	8,374	9,216
Utah	705	650	680	3.74	3.38	3.85	2,636	2,195	2,618
Vermont	185	170	160	1.97	2.15	1.86	364	366	298
Virginia	1,195	1,140	1,145	2.31	2.23	2.23	2,764	2,540	2,555
Washington	740	760	640	4.02	3.64	3.83	2,973	2,764	2,448
West Virginia	567	535	515	1.78	1.72	1.74	1,009	922	894
Wisconsin	1,270	1,360	1,300	2.77	2.17	2.14	3,522	2,953	2,784
Wyoming	1,100	1,090	1,150	2.28	2.20	2.17	2,508	2,393	2,496
United States [2]	52,777	52,839	52,425	2.43	2.34	2.46	128,207	123,600	128,864

(X) Not applicable. [1] Previously was included in the Alaska table. For 2017 data please refer to the Alaska table. [2] Beginning in 2018, United States total includes data for Alaska.
NASS, Crops Branch, (202) 720–2127.

Table 6-2.—Hay, all: Area, yield, production, and value, United States, 2010–2019

Year	Area harvested	Yield per acre	Production	Marketing year average price per ton received by farmers	Value of production
	1,000 acres	*Tons*	*1,000 tons*	*Dollars*	*1,000 dollars*
2010	59,574	2.43	145,000	114.00	14,606,696
2011	55,204	2.35	129,880	178.00	18,085,074
2012	54,653	2.14	117,072	191.00	18,613,183
2013	57,973	2.33	135,198	176.00	19,845,080
2014	57,153	2.45	140,119	172.00	19,147,954
2015	54,529	2.47	134,668	145.00	16,568,121
2016	53,185	2.52	134,082	129.00	15,477,263
2017	52,777	2.43	128,207	142.00	16,109,040
2018	52,839	2.34	123,600	166.00	17,288,215
2019	52,425	2.46	128,864	165.00	18,160,596

NASS, Crops Branch, (202) 720–2127.

Table 6-3.—Alfalfa and alfalfa mixtures for hay: Area, yield, and production, by State and United States, 2017–2019

State	Area harvested			Yield per harvested acre			Production		
	2017	2018	2019	2017	2018	2019	2017	2018	2019
	1,000 acres	*1,000 acres*	*1,000 acres*	*Tons*	*Tons*	*Tons*	*1,000 tons*	*1,000 tons*	*1,000 tons*
Arizona	285	260	280	8.40	8.30	8.30	2,394	2,158	2,324
Arkansas	3	3	3	3.60	2.50	3.20	11	8	10
California	700	620	580	6.80	6.90	7.10	4,760	4,278	4,118
Colorado	720	730	730	3.70	3.40	3.70	2,664	2,482	2,701
Connecticut	8	7	7	2.30	2.50	1.90	18	18	13
Delaware	5	4	3	3.50	2.90	3.00	18	12	9
Idaho	1,060	1,050	1,010	4.00	4.20	4.40	4,240	4,410	4,444
Illinois	230	250	200	4.10	3.30	3.50	943	825	700
Indiana	250	240	220	3.30	3.00	3.00	825	720	660
Iowa	720	620	700	3.50	3.70	3.40	2,520	2,294	2,380
Kansas	570	610	630	3.60	3.50	4.00	2,052	2,135	2,520
Kentucky	185	145	145	3.30	3.10	3.20	611	450	464
Maine	10	10	10	2.20	2.30	2.10	22	23	21
Maryland	35	40	34	3.90	4.50	3.50	137	180	119
Massachusetts	8	9	6	2.50	2.10	2.70	20	19	16
Michigan	610	590	550	2.60	2.40	2.50	1,586	1,416	1,375
Minnesota	870	720	730	3.35	2.85	3.10	2,915	2,052	2,263
Missouri	300	270	260	2.40	2.40	2.70	720	648	702
Montana	1,650	1,900	2,100	2.10	2.05	2.15	3,465	3,895	4,515
Nebraska	860	850	950	3.95	4.30	3.80	3,397	3,655	3,610
Nevada	225	185	225	4.30	4.70	4.90	968	870	1,103
New Hampshire	5	4	4	1.80	2.20	1.50	9	9	6
New Jersey	13	9	11	3.10	3.45	3.20	40	31	35
New Mexico	190	160	160	5.00	4.70	4.90	950	752	784
New York	400	300	290	2.60	2.40	2.20	1,040	720	638
North Carolina	7	6	6	2.70	3.90	2.30	19	23	14
North Dakota	1,380	1,470	1,220	1.35	1.70	1.80	1,863	2,499	2,196
Ohio	350	350	330	3.20	3.10	2.90	1,120	1,085	957
Oklahoma	280	230	205	3.10	2.70	3.00	868	621	615
Oregon	420	420	400	4.70	4.10	4.70	1,974	1,722	1,880
Pennsylvania	430	300	290	3.10	2.90	3.00	1,333	870	870
Rhode Island	1	1	1	2.00	2.00	2.20	2	2	2
South Dakota	1,550	1,750	1,900	1.75	2.15	2.35	2,713	3,763	4,465
Tennessee	15	20	13	3.60	3.30	3.70	54	66	48
Texas	120	140	120	4.40	5.60	4.80	528	784	576
Utah	550	500	510	4.20	3.70	4.30	2,310	1,850	2,193
Vermont	30	20	20	1.80	1.80	2.30	54	36	46
Virginia	65	40	45	3.40	3.00	3.00	221	120	135
Washington	390	350	330	5.20	4.50	4.60	2,028	1,575	1,518
West Virginia	17	15	15	2.70	2.50	2.90	46	38	44
Wisconsin	910	820	880	3.00	2.35	2.40	2,730	1,927	2,112
Wyoming	580	590	620	2.80	2.70	2.70	1,624	1,593	1,674
United States	17,007	16,608	16,743	3.28	3.17	3.28	55,812	52,634	54,875

NASS, Crops Branch, (202) 720–2127.

Table 6-4.—Hay, all other: Area, yield, and production, by State and United States, 2017–2019

State	Area harvested			Yield per harvested acre			Production		
	2017	2018	2019	2017	2018	2019	2017	2018	2019
	1,000 acres	*1,000 acres*	*1,000 acres*	*Tons*	*Tons*	*Tons*	*1,000 tons*	*1,000 tons*	*1,000 tons*
Alabama [1]	860	850	700	2.50	2.80	2.50	2,150	2,380	1,750
Alaska [1 2]	(X)	22	22	(X)	1.30	1.30	(X)	29	29
Arizona	40	40	45	4.80	4.70	4.10	192	188	185
Arkansas	1,290	1,200	1,250	2.00	1.80	2.20	2,580	2,160	2,750
California	440	360	430	3.70	3.90	3.90	1,628	1,404	1,677
Colorado	720	690	730	1.80	1.65	1.85	1,296	1,139	1,351
Connecticut	40	40	40	2.30	2.30	1.70	92	92	68
Delaware	10	9	11	3.00	2.40	2.00	30	22	22
Florida [1]	300	280	270	2.50	3.10	2.90	750	868	783
Georgia [1]	620	600	560	2.90	2.90	2.75	1,798	1,740	1,540
Idaho	370	290	290	2.40	2.10	2.30	888	609	667
Illinois	260	220	220	2.50	2.20	2.00	650	484	440
Indiana	290	270	300	2.30	2.45	2.10	667	662	630
Iowa	340	320	320	2.20	2.20	2.30	748	704	736
Kansas	1,900	1,750	1,650	1.80	1.50	2.30	3,420	2,625	3,795
Kentucky	1,940	1,750	1,800	2.35	2.65	2.20	4,559	4,638	3,960
Louisiana [1]	400	380	390	2.60	2.20	2.50	1,040	836	975
Maine	115	100	100	1.90	1.85	2.15	219	185	215
Maryland	155	155	155	2.40	2.40	2.50	372	372	388
Massachusetts	70	70	45	1.70	1.40	2.20	119	98	99
Michigan	260	220	230	1.55	1.80	2.10	403	396	483
Minnesota	490	500	370	1.80	2.05	1.90	882	1,025	703
Mississippi [1]	610	590	610	2.40	2.10	2.30	1,464	1,239	1,403
Missouri	2,700	2,800	3,100	1.95	1.70	2.15	5,265	4,760	6,665
Montana	850	1,000	900	1.50	1.70	1.90	1,275	1,700	1,710
Nebraska	1,650	1,850	1,500	1.55	1.80	1.65	2,558	3,330	2,475
Nevada	160	180	210	2.00	1.60	2.20	320	288	462
New Hampshire	40	35	45	1.80	1.70	1.70	72	60	77
New Jersey	95	105	80	2.10	1.80	1.90	200	189	152
New Mexico	95	90	85	2.00	2.00	2.00	190	180	170
New York	920	920	890	1.75	2.20	1.80	1,610	2,024	1,602
North Carolina	650	810	810	2.30	2.70	2.30	1,495	2,187	1,863
North Dakota	1,200	1,200	1,200	1.30	1.60	1.60	1,560	1,920	1,920
Ohio	610	620	590	2.05	2.05	2.00	1,251	1,271	1,180
Oklahoma	2,650	3,000	2,800	1.80	1.50	1.90	4,770	4,500	5,320
Oregon	665	580	570	2.00	2.30	2.60	1,330	1,334	1,482
Pennsylvania	990	890	920	2.40	2.10	2.30	2,376	1,869	2,116
Rhode Island	5	5	4	1.90	1.90	1.30	10	10	5
South Carolina [1]	300	270	270	2.60	2.50	2.10	780	675	567
South Dakota	1,400	1,500	1,450	1.35	1.35	1.75	1,890	2,025	2,538
Tennessee	1,650	1,700	1,750	2.25	2.45	2.30	3,713	4,165	4,025
Texas	4,400	4,600	4,800	2.05	1.65	1.80	9,020	7,590	8,640
Utah	155	150	170	2.10	2.30	2.50	326	345	425
Vermont	155	150	140	2.00	2.20	1.80	310	330	252
Virginia	1,130	1,100	1,100	2.25	2.20	2.20	2,543	2,420	2,420
Washington	350	410	310	2.70	2.90	3.00	945	1,189	930
West Virginia	550	520	500	1.75	1.70	1.70	963	884	850
Wisconsin	360	540	420	2.20	1.90	1.60	792	1,026	672
Wyoming	520	500	530	1.70	1.60	1.55	884	800	822
United States [2]	35,770	36,231	35,682	2.02	1.96	2.07	72,395	70,966	73,989

(X) Not applicable. [1] Alfalfa and alfalfa mixtures included in all other hay. [2] Beginning in 2018, United States total includes data for Alaska.
NASS, Crops Branch, (202) 720–2127.

Table 6-5.—Hay, all: Stocks on farms, United States, 2010–2019

Crop year	Dec. 1	May 1 [1]
2010	101,667	20,931
2011	89,723	22,217
2012	75,175	21,381
2013	89,394	14,156
2014	92,172	19,186
2015	94,928	24,537
2016	95,924	25,155
2017	89,422	24,400
2018	79,055	15,348
2019	84,488	14,906

[1] Following year.
NASS, Crops Branch, (202) 720–2127.

Table 6-6.—Hay, all: Marketing year average price and value of production, by State and United States, 2017–2019

State	Marketing year average price per ton, baled [1]			Value of production		
	2017	2018	2019 [2]	2017	2018	2019 [2]
	Dollars	*Dollars*	*Dollars*	*1,000 dollars*	*1,000 dollars*	*1,000 dollars*
Alabama	98.00	95.00	86.00	210,700	226,100	150,500
Alaska [3]	(NA)	355.00	350.00	(NA)	10,295	10,150
Arizona	172.00	209.00	205.00	445,368	488,622	513,420
Arkansas	100.00	108.00	108.00	257,488	234,816	298,920
California	168.00	191.00	193.00	1,067,060	1,083,312	1,097,417
Colorado	172.00	220.00	232.00	688,824	794,138	934,660
Connecticut	171.00	172.00	167.00	17,568	18,960	13,509
Delaware	153.00	168.00	171.00	7,656	5,650	5,315
Florida	157.00	153.00	149.00	117,750	132,804	116,667
Georgia	98.00	82.00	84.00	176,204	142,680	129,360
Idaho	138.00	154.00	157.00	717,832	773,241	799,534
Illinois	129.00	153.00	159.00	200,243	194,260	178,300
Indiana	157.00	154.00	178.00	237,369	211,026	230,100
Iowa	111.00	131.00	128.00	367,396	394,170	406,456
Kansas	111.00	153.00	128.00	536,256	635,950	732,893
Kentucky	131.00	159.00	150.00	624,019	770,610	616,200
Louisiana	95.00	102.00	103.00	98,800	85,272	100,425
Maine	151.00	133.00	164.00	33,395	28,121	38,752
Maryland	150.00	163.00	169.00	76,387	91,092	85,911
Massachusetts	159.00	182.00	166.00	18,696	21,662	19,091
Michigan	145.00	147.00	169.00	296,985	271,980	314,750
Minnesota	103.00	133.00	139.00	398,191	410,294	440,970
Mississippi	90.00	97.00	97.00	131,760	120,183	136,091
Missouri	99.50	121.00	122.00	566,775	631,392	872,477
Montana	141.00	145.00	146.00	665,430	800,860	907,755
Nebraska	91.00	107.00	103.00	526,475	706,705	614,900
Nevada	174.00	174.00	173.00	219,328	202,644	269,359
New Hampshire	153.00	114.00	164.00	10,080	8,103	13,579
New Jersey	127.00	186.00	187.00	31,240	41,032	35,048
New Mexico	178.00	231.00	223.00	201,780	211,832	211,874
New York	148.00	150.00	172.00	446,820	423,976	388,102
North Carolina	117.00	123.00	101.00	177,410	271,897	211,624
North Dakota	99.50	87.00	84.00	315,735	357,969	319,968
Ohio	138.00	145.00	171.00	339,865	354,888	354,816
Oklahoma	86.00	103.00	109.00	495,308	539,127	644,945
Oregon	170.00	195.00	200.00	560,952	590,414	674,280
Pennsylvania	164.00	182.00	191.00	616,101	502,203	579,498
Rhode Island	143.00	140.00	171.00	1,650	1,684	1,199
South Carolina	141.00	139.00	146.00	109,980	93,825	82,782
South Dakota	108.00	104.00	103.00	487,765	588,941	711,345
Tennessee	116.00	120.00	112.00	438,497	510,353	457,095
Texas	116.00	143.00	128.00	1,042,668	1,078,326	1,074,816
Utah	134.00	171.00	182.00	347,356	364,085	461,176
Vermont	137.00	138.00	167.00	48,244	50,412	49,634
Virginia	127.00	139.00	126.00	354,113	347,540	323,185
Washington	172.00	186.00	196.00	515,901	519,277	477,852
West Virginia	120.00	127.00	114.00	120,402	116,446	101,948
Wisconsin	111.00	153.00	189.00	396,066	441,450	524,832
Wyoming	140.00	167.00	175.00	347,152	387,596	427,116
United States [3]	142.00	166.00	165.00	16,109,040	17,288,215	18,160,596

(NA) Not available. [1] Baled hay. [2] Preliminary. [3] Beginning in 2018, United States total includes data for Alaska.
NASS, Crops Branch, (202) 720–2127.

Table 6-7.—Hay: Area and production, by type, United States, 2010–2019

Year	Area harvested			Production		
	Alfalfa	All other hay	All hay	Alfalfa	All other hay	All hay
	1,000 acres	*1,000 acres*	*1,000 acres*	*1,000 tons*	*1,000 tons*	*1,000 tons*
2010	19,968	39,606	59,574	67,977	77,023	145,000
2011	19,044	36,160	55,204	64,815	65,065	129,880
2012	16,795	37,858	54,653	50,600	66,472	117,072
2013	17,699	40,274	57,973	57,307	77,891	135,198
2014	18,406	38,747	57,153	61,487	78,632	140,119
2015	17,810	36,719	54,529	59,060	75,608	134,668
2016	17,029	36,156	53,185	58,601	75,481	134,082
2017	17,007	35,770	52,777	55,812	72,395	128,207
2018	16,608	36,231	52,839	52,634	70,966	123,600
2019	16,743	35,682	52,425	54,875	73,989	128,864

NASS, Crops Branch, (202) 720–2127.

Table 6-8.—Hay: Supply and disappearance, prices, and number of animal units fed annually, United States, 2009–2018[1]

Year beginning May	Farm carryover May 1	Production	Total supply	Disappearance	Roughage-consuming animal units	Supply per animal unit	Disappearance per animal unit	Price received per ton
	Million tons	*Million tons*	*Million tons*	*Million tons*	*Million tons*	*Tons*	*Tons*	*Dollars*
2009[2]	22.1	146.6	170.0	148.8	70	2.41	2.11	108
2010	20.9	143.5	166.0	143.7	69	2.39	2.07	114
2011	22.2	140.3	152.2	130.7	68	2.24	1.92	178
2012	21.4	126.1	138.7	124.3	68	2.05	1.84	191
2013	14.2	132.7	149.5	130.0	67	2.24	1.95	176
2014	19.2	137.0	159.4	134.6	67	2.36	2.00	172
2015	24.5	134.5	159.3	133.9	69	2.29	1.93	145
2016	25.1	133.8	160.1	135.5	71	2.26	1.91	129
2017	....	....	....	....	....	....	....	142
2018	....	....	....	....	....	....	....	164

[1] Excludes trade. [2] Beginning in 2009, supply includes imports.
ERS, Market and Trade Economics Division, (202) 694-5313.

Forage production is the sum of all dry hay production and haylage/greenchop production after converting the haylage/greenchop production to a dry equivalent basis (13 percent moisture) by multiplying the green weight (weight at harvest) by 0.4943. The conversion factor (0.4943) is based on the assumption that one ton of dry hay is 0.87 ton of dry matter, one ton of haylage is 0.45 ton dry matter and one ton of greenchop is 0.25 ton dry matter. The total haylage/greenchop production is assumed to be comprised of 90 percent haylage and 10 percent greenchop. Therefore, the conversion factor used to adjust haylage/greenchop production to a dry equivalent basis = ((0.45*0.9)+(0.25*0.1))/0.87 = 0.4943. The factors assumed here may vary by State and can be adjusted. Adjustments would result in a slightly different conversion factor.

Table 6-9.—All forage: Area harvested, yield, and production, by State and 17 State total, 2017–2019[1]

State	Area harvested			Yield		
	2017	2018	2019	2017	2018	2019
	1,000 acres	*1,000 acres*	*1,000 acres*	*Tons*	*Tons*	*Tons*
California	1,360	1,180	1,190	5.92	5.98	5.93
Idaho	1,495	1,380	1,380	3.74	4.00	4.35
Illinois	515	485	450	3.46	2.92	2.86
Iowa	1,120	995	1,115	3.23	3.31	3.15
Kansas	2,565	2,460	2,345	2.32	2.09	2.85
Michigan	1,050	1,010	990	2.86	2.70	2.99
Minnesota	1,550	1,380	1,330	2.97	2.73	2.82
Missouri	3,060	3,170	3,490	2.02	1.81	2.20
Nebraska	2,535	2,730	2,505	2.42	2.59	2.50
New York	1,800	1,740	1,640	2.73	3.01	2.52
Ohio	1,060	1,035	970	2.72	2.66	2.62
Pennsylvania	1,795	1,465	1,430	2.92	2.77	2.98
South Dakota	3,020	3,330	3,505	1.60	1.83	2.10
Texas	4,655	4,845	5,045	2.20	1.84	1.98
Vermont	290	295	265	3.47	3.76	3.54
Washington	815	830	670	4.35	4.07	4.02
Wisconsin	2,170	2,210	2,330	3.52	2.93	2.63
17 State Total	30,855	30,540	30,650	2.76	2.61	2.71

State	Production		
	2017	2018	2019
	1,000 tons	*1,000 tons*	*1,000 tons*
California	8,052	7,053	7,060
Idaho	5,587	5,516	6,000
Illinois	1,783	1,417	1,285
Iowa	3,619	3,289	3,517
Kansas	5,949	5,140	6,690
Michigan	3,006	2,729	2,959
Minnesota	4,597	3,763	3,745
Missouri	6,193	5,737	7,661
Nebraska	6,125	7,084	6,258
New York	4,913	5,233	4,130
Ohio	2,878	2,757	2,546
Pennsylvania	5,242	4,065	4,265
South Dakota	4,827	6,110	7,365
Texas	10,236	8,910	9,965
Vermont	1,006	1,110	939
Washington	3,542	3,382	2,694
Wisconsin	7,643	6,479	6,135
17 State Total	85,198	79,774	83,214

[1] All forage production is the sum of the following dry equivalents: alfalfa hay harvested as dry hay, all other hay harvested as dry hay, alfalfa haylage and greenchop, all other hay haylage and greenchop; after converting alfalfa and all other haylage and greenchop to a dry equivalent basis.
NASS, Crops Branch, (202) 720–2127.

Table 6-10.—All alfalfa forage: Area harvested, yield, and production, by State and 17 State total, 2017–2019 [1]

State	Area harvested 2017	Area harvested 2018	Area harvested 2019	Yield 2017	Yield 2018	Yield 2019
	1,000 acres	*1,000 acres*	*1,000 acres*	*Tons*	*Tons*	*Tons*
California	740	670	610	6.71	6.75	7.06
Idaho	1,090	1,080	1,060	4.18	4.43	4.86
Illinois	245	260	220	4.45	3.47	3.68
Iowa	770	655	765	3.67	3.84	3.52
Kansas	585	620	645	3.72	3.54	4.05
Michigan	780	780	750	3.23	2.94	3.20
Minnesota	1,040	850	930	3.52	3.13	3.20
Missouri	310	290	290	2.51	2.68	2.69
Nebraska	870	870	990	3.98	4.26	3.75
New York	700	650	530	3.73	3.95	3.47
Ohio	410	390	370	3.60	3.66	3.44
Pennsylvania	645	465	380	3.59	3.65	4.37
South Dakota	1,580	1,800	2,000	1.78	2.21	2.34
Texas	125	145	125	4.47	5.52	4.90
Vermont	50	45	35	4.24	4.27	4.94
Washington	425	355	350	5.32	4.72	4.63
Wisconsin	1,700	1,590	1,680	3.83	3.29	3.00
17 State Total	12,065	11,515	11,730	3.71	3.64	3.61

State	Production 2017	Production 2018	Production 2019
	1,000 tons	*1,000 tons*	*1,000 tons*
California	4,968	4,523	4,308
Idaho	4,561	4,788	5,155
Illinois	1,090	902	810
Iowa	2,828	2,514	2,690
Kansas	2,176	2,194	2,613
Michigan	2,523	2,290	2,403
Minnesota	3,665	2,657	2,975
Missouri	779	778	781
Nebraska	3,463	3,704	3,711
New York	2,611	2,566	1,840
Ohio	1,476	1,428	1,273
Pennsylvania	2,316	1,698	1,661
South Dakota	2,807	3,985	4,682
Texas	559	801	613
Vermont	212	192	173
Washington	2,263	1,676	1,619
Wisconsin	6,519	5,239	5,036
17 State Total	44,816	41,935	42,343

[1] All alfalfa forage production is the sum of alfalfa harvested as dry hay; and alfalfa haylage and greenchop production after converting it to a dry equivalent basis.
NASS, Crops Branch, (202) 720–2127.

Table 6-11.—All haylage and greenchop: Area harvested, yield, and production, by State and 17 State total, 2017–2019[1]

State	Area harvested 2017	Area harvested 2018	Area harvested 2019	Yield 2017	Yield 2018	Yield 2019
	1,000 acres	*1,000 acres*	*1,000 acres*	*Tons*	*Tons*	*Tons*
California	265	250	210	12.70	11.10	12.19
Idaho	100	105	155	9.30	9.57	11.60
Illinois	53	38	49	7.23	5.74	5.96
Iowa	100	80	140	7.12	7.36	5.80
Kansas	135	120	85	7.15	6.42	8.92
Michigan	275	285	290	7.48	6.51	7.68
Minnesota	250	220	265	6.48	6.31	5.95
Missouri	90	155	190	4.68	4.29	3.13
Nebraska	50	40	75	6.88	5.05	4.67
New York	660	710	610	6.94	7.09	6.27
Ohio	205	135	125	5.00	6.00	6.62
Pennsylvania	475	410	390	6.53	6.54	6.64
South Dakota	105	120	190	4.32	5.44	3.85
Texas	199	145	190	7.00	7.48	7.97
Vermont	180	185	165	7.22	8.14	7.85
Washington	125	119	85	9.20	10.50	5.85
Wisconsin	1,190	1,120	1,290	7.01	6.37	5.26
17 State Total	4,457	4,237	4,504	7.21	6.99	6.44

State	Production 2017	Production 2018	Production 2019
	T31,000 tons		
California	3,365	2,774	2,559
Idaho	930	1,005	1,798
Illinois	383	218	292
Iowa	712	589	812
Kansas	965	770	758
Michigan	2,057	1,856	2,227
Minnesota	1,620	1,388	1,576
Missouri	421	665	595
Nebraska	344	202	350
New York	4,578	5,035	3,824
Ohio	1,026	810	828
Pennsylvania	3,101	2,683	2,588
South Dakota	454	653	731
Texas	1,393	1,085	1,515
Vermont	1,300	1,505	1,296
Washington	1,150	1,249	497
Wisconsin	8,337	7,132	6,780
17 State Total	32,136	29,619	29,026

[1] Includes all types of forage harvested as haylage or greenchop (green weight). Forage harvested as dry hay and corn and sorghum silage/greenchop are not included.
NASS, Crops Branch, (202) 720–2127.

Table 6-12.—Alfalfa haylage and greenchop: Area harvested, yield, and production, by State and 17 State total, 2017–2019

State	Area harvested			Yield		
	2017	2018	2019	2017	2018	2019
	1,000 acres	*1,000 acres*	*1,000 acres*	*Tons*	*Tons*	*Tons*
California	70	80	60	6.00	6.20	6.40
Idaho	65	85	115	10.00	9.00	12.50
Illinois	33	24	30	9.00	6.50	7.40
Iowa	80	55	95	7.80	8.10	6.60
Kansas	25	20	25	10.00	6.00	7.50
Michigan	240	260	260	7.90	6.80	8.00
Minnesota	220	180	225	6.90	6.80	6.40
Missouri	20	35	40	6.00	7.50	4.00
Nebraska	20	25	50	6.70	4.00	4.10
New York	410	450	320	7.75	8.30	7.60
Ohio	120	90	90	6.00	7.70	7.10
Pennsylvania	265	250	200	7.50	6.70	8.00
South Dakota	50	75	125	3.80	6.00	3.50
Texas	9	5	10	7.00	7.00	7.50
Vermont	40	45	35	8.00	7.00	7.30
Washington	50	24	40	9.50	8.50	5.10
Wisconsin	1,050	1,000	1,020	7.30	6.70	5.80
17 State Total	2,767	2,703	2,740	7.41	7.08	6.68

State	Production		
	2017	2018	2019
	1,000 tons	*1,000 tons*	*1,000 tons*
California	420	496	384
Idaho	650	765	1,438
Illinois	297	156	222
Iowa	624	446	627
Kansas	250	120	188
Michigan	1,896	1,768	2,080
Minnesota	1,518	1,224	1,440
Missouri	120	263	160
Nebraska	134	100	205
New York	3,178	3,735	2,432
Ohio	720	693	639
Pennsylvania	1,988	1,675	1,600
South Dakota	190	450	438
Texas	63	35	75
Vermont	320	315	256
Washington	475	204	204
Wisconsin	7,665	6,700	5,916
17 State Total	20,508	19,145	18,304

NASS, Crops Branch, (202) 720–2127.

Table 6-13.—Beans, dry edible (clean basis): Production, by classes, United States, 2017–2019[1]

Class	2017	2018	2019
	1,000 cwt	*1,000 cwt*	*1,000 cwt*
Navy (pea beans)	4,161	4,191	3,029
Great northern	1,403	1,188	1,040
Small white	171	155	105
Pinto	13,617	8,778	6,769
Red kidney, light	899	897	915
Red kidney, dark	1,099	1,625	1,489
Pink	332	398	291
Small red	438	701	567
Cranberry	185	244	161
Black	5,120	5,212	5,069
Large lima	255	234	197
Baby lima	204	275	278
Blackeye	437	528	259
Small chickpeas (Garbanzo)	1,969	3,346	1,423
Large chickpeas (Garbanzo)	5,088	9,441	4,814
Chickpeas, all (Garbanzo)	7,057	12,787	6,237
Other[2]	583	532	642
Total	35,961	37,745	20,811

[1] Excludes beans grown for garden seed. [2] Data are included in "Other" class to avoid disclosing data for individual operations.
NASS, Crops Branch, (202) 720–2127.

Table 6-14.—Beans, dry edible: Area, yield, and production, by State and United States, 2017–2019[1]

State	Area planted			Area harvested		
	2017	2018	2019	2017	2018	2019
	1,000 acres	*1,000 acres*	*1,000 acres*	*1,000 acres*	*1,000 acres*	*1,000 acres*
California	50.0	48.0	27.4	49.7	47.7	27.4
Colorado	58.0	42.0	37.0	54.5	30.5	33.8
Idaho	180.0	185.0	47.0	178.0	183.0	45.0
Michigan	220.0	195.0	185.0	218.5	193.0	180.0
Minnesota	170.0	185.0	210.0	163.0	178.0	201.0
Montana[2]	275.0	395.0	(NA)	265.0	386.0	(NA)
Nebraska	180.0	140.2	120.0	155.0	131.2	97.0
North Dakota	705.0	635.0	615.0	685.0	615.0	550.0
Texas[2]	22.0	20.3	(NA)	20.0	18.3	(NA)
Washington	196.0	218.0	25.0	195.0	217.0	25.0
Wyoming	41.0	31.0	21.0	39.0	28.5	17.3
United States	2,097.0	2,094.5	1,287.4	2,022.7	2,028.2	1,176.5

State	Yield per acre (clean basis)			Production (clean basis)		
	2017	2018	2019	2017	2018	2019
	Pounds	Pounds	Pounds	*1,000 cwt*	*1,000 cwt*	*1,000 cwt*
California	2,100	2,490	2,660	1,045	1,190	729
Colorado	2,000	2,120	1,840	1,092	647	623
Idaho	1,610	1,710	2,370	2,873	3,127	1,067
Michigan	2,010	2,400	2,030	4,394	4,635	3,662
Minnesota	2,190	2,360	2,040	3,567	4,200	4,101
Montana[2]	1,000	1,350	(NA)	2,643	5,214	(NA)
Nebraska	2,520	2,480	1,940	3,901	3,254	1,883
North Dakota	1,810	1,760	1,400	12,392	10,806	7,691
Texas[2]	1,100	1,150	(NA)	220	210	(NA)
Washington	1,490	1,780	2,660	2,901	3,857	665
Wyoming	2,390	2,120	2,250	933	605	390
United States	1,778	1,861	1,769	35,961	37,745	20,811

(NA) Not available. [1] Excludes beans grown for garden seed. Beginning 2019, chickpeas are excluded. [2] Estimates discontinued in 2019.
NASS, Crops Branch, (202) 720–2127.

Table 6-15.—Beans, dry edible: Area, yield, production, price, and value, United States, 2010–2019 [1]

Year	Area planted	Area harvested	Yield per acre [2]	Production [2]	Marketing year average price per 100 pounds received by farmers	Value of production
	1,000 acres	*1,000 acres*	*Pounds*	*1,000 cwt.*	*Dollars*	*1,000 dollars*
2010	1,911.4	1,842.7	1,726	31,801	28.00	899,258
2011	1,217.9	1,167.9	1,703	19,890	42.10	851,131
2012	1,742.5	1,690.4	1,889	31,925	38.00	1,235,255
2013	1,361.8	1,315.0	1,868	24,567	39.10	982,385
2014	1,703.1	1,648.6	1,754	28,910	32.30	980,622
2015	1,766.7	1,708.4	1,759	30,057	27.30	866,222
2016	1,664.0	1,558.1	1,842	28,703	29.20	863,431
2017	2,097.0	2,022.7	1,778	35,961	26.70	1,006,353
2018	2,094.5	2,028.2	1,861	37,745	25.40	951,047
2019	1,287.4	1,176.5	1,769	20,811	29.10	608,870

[1] Excludes beans grown for garden seed. [2] Clean basis.
NASS, Crops Branch, (202) 720–2127.

Table 6-16.—Beans, dry edible ((clean basis): Marketing year average price and value of production, by State and United States, 2017–2019

States	Marketing year average price per cwt.			Value of production		
	2017	2018	2019 [1]	2017	2018	2019 [1]
	Dollars	*Dollars*	*Dollars*	*1,000 dollars*	*1,000 dollars*	*1,000 dollars*
California	61.20	69.20	53.30	63,954	82,348	38,856
Colorado	28.90	31.20	33.20	31,559	20,186	20,684
Idaho	27.80	23.50	22.40	79,869	73,485	23,901
Michigan	29.30	27.60	29.80	128,744	127,926	109,128
Minnesota	27.40	26.70	31.90	97,736	112,140	130,822
Montana [2]	33.80	19.30	(NA)	89,333	100,630	(NA)
Nebraska	25.50	(D)	28.50	99,476	(D)	53,666
North Dakota	24.10	22.90	25.70	298,647	247,457	197,659
Texas [2]	34.60	(D)	(NA)	7,612	(D)	(NA)
Washington	29.10	22.70	35.70	84,419	87,554	23,741
Wyoming	26.80	25.90	26.70	25,004	15,670	10,413
United States	26.70	25.40	29.10	1,006,353	951,047	608,870

(D) Withheld to avoid disclosing data for individual operations. (NA) Not available. [1] Preliminary. [2] Estimates discontinued in 2019.
NASS, Crops Branch, (202) 720–2127.

Table 6-17.—Beans, dry edible: Season average price [1] per 100 pounds, 2009–2018

Year beginning September	Lima	Garbanzo	Blackeye	Pinto	Great northern	Small red	Pea bean (Navy)	Black	Red kidney
	Dollars								
2009	43.98	39.18	45.12	39.45	41.57	43.32	40.37	41.57	43.56
2010	40.13	49.69	42.47	36.08	41.81	47.74	41.94	41.81	48.25
2011	57.88	58.42	69.57	62.72	54.75	61.25	58.61	54.75	69.30
2012	48.14	52.32	54.75	45.54	53.96	53.36	45.57	53.96	63.32
2013	53.45	40.63	55.19	45.76	(NA)	52.17	55.25	(NA)	68.88
2014	56.50	38.54	70.00	32.41	48.46	55.10	38.85	48.46	64.84
2015	58.75	45.20	70.00	33.14	32.47	39.80	32.19	32.47	38.37
2016	50.49	47.98	56.86	38.34	40.53	38.00	38.72	40.53	45.04
2017	58.08	63.67	65.62	31.05	33.79	37.25	34.40	33.79	44.67
2018	58.61	28.50	64.16	28.86	36.47	38.38	33.43	36.47	49.00

(NA) Not available. [1] Free-on-board (f.o.b.) dealer prices as reported by USDA, Bean Market News.
ERS, Specialty Crops Branch, (202) 694–5253. Compiled from the Bean Market Summary, Agricultural Marketing Service, U.S. Department of Agriculture, Greeley, Colorado.

Table 6-18.—Beans, dry edible: United States exports to specified countries, 2017–2019 [1]

Country	2017	2018	2019
	Metric tons		
Mexico	102,791	98,855	82,014
Canada	72,101	45,486	49,512
Italy(*)	47,082	38,754	46,174
Dominican Republic	19,636	22,968	26,592
United Kingdom	38,048	28,241	25,371
Saudi Arabia	0	0	19,117
Haiti	10,712	7,888	14,138
Yemen(*)	0	0	10,797
Japan	6,994	7,637	8,003
Colombia	6,348	9,759	7,895
Belgium-Luxembourg(*)	5,262	3,690	6,041
Turkey	1,162	1,006	6,022
Australia(*)	6,382	4,846	5,620
Panama	5,762	5,926	4,944
Spain	4,132	5,034	4,698
Costa Rica	7,630	2,476	4,218
El Salvador	3,043	3,850	4,077
Germany(*)	2,701	4,009	3,900
Jamaica	2,694	3,184	3,242
France(*)	5,834	4,394	3,165
Guatemala	4,114	5,615	2,994
Korea, South	5,877	3,901	2,524
New Zealand(*)	838	431	2,032
United Arab Emirates	1,308	1,965	2,024
Peru	2,650	3,500	1,669
Brazil	2,978	12	1,571
Netherlands	4,650	3,195	1,448
Tanzania	0	1,157	1,060
Niger	0	0	1,052
French West Indies(*)	949	1,152	1,047
Rest of World	29,233	20,722	16,144
World Total	400,908	339,655	369,103

(*) Denotes a country that is a summarization of its component countries. [1] Excluding seed bean exports.
FAS, Office of Global Analysis, (202) 720-6301. Data Source: U.S. Census Bureau Trade Data.

Table 6-19.—Chickpeas & lentils, dried: United States exports by class and quantity, 2017–2019[1]

Country	2017	2018	2019
	Metric tons		
Dried chickpeas:			
Pakistan	18,780	14,744	41,075
Canada	29,348	15,163	34,498
Spain	20,631	19,709	21,915
Portugal	2,835	3,206	13,760
India	17,130	4,323	6,923
Italy(*)	5,863	1,663	5,938
United Arab Emirates	7,600	1,041	2,891
Colombia	1,816	263	2,684
Peru	3,317	1,841	1,562
Jordan	1,446	1,180	1,549
New Zealand(*)	667	760	1,538
Sri Lanka	2,757	1,122	1,473
Lebanon	3,197	1,515	1,402
Israel(*)	620	545	1,197
Turkey	12,348	1,271	1,094
Algeria	6,302	1,688	724
Dominican Republic	150	432	685
Korea, South	766	526	649
Taiwan	419	554	486
Japan	530	652	397
Costa Rica	86	185	305
Netherlands	392	162	247
Philippines	341	500	232
Malaysia	363	111	207
China	527	474	173
Indonesia	23	45	162
Trinidad and Tobago	429	163	139
Panama	259	17	133
Hong Kong	153	159	111
Cyprus	60	48	92
Rest of World	9,793	3,628	873
World Total	148,947	77,689	145,111
Dried lentils:			
Canada	55,795	16,301	77,166
India	22,885	8,272	56,679
Spain	33,869	22,216	31,571
Mexico	23,171	11,698	20,222
Sudan(*)	5,988	21,747	16,700
Peru	18,431	9,650	11,486
China	1,580	6,280	9,661
Colombia	31,974	8,967	9,381
Italy(*)	5,913	2,862	4,261
Greece	3,106	2,427	2,198
Belgium-Luxembourg(*)	3,108	1,244	1,975
United Arab Emirates	4,884	414	1,044
Pakistan	4,152	1,215	966
Dominican Republic	992	918	924
Sierra Leone	220	0	709
Thailand	1,001	1,035	668
Netherlands	1,591	515	667
Ecuador	1,623	328	566
Leeward-Windward Islands(*)	634	495	543
Portugal	230	0	539
French Ind. Ocean Territory(*)	160	83	508
Germany(*)	2,255	837	495
French Pacific Islands(*)	545	524	493
France(*)	769	243	482
Algeria	1,635	240	476
Burkina Faso	400	0	450
Chile	359	0	403
Turkey	5,166	838	375
Korea, South	147	490	314
Laos	170	240	240
Rest of World	13,219	5,942	2,485
World Total	246,048	126,021	254,642

(*) Denotes a country that is a summarization of its component countries. [1] Excluding seed pea exports.
FAS, Office of Global Analysis, (202) 720-6301. Data Source: U.S. Census Bureau Trade Data.

Table 6-20.—Peas, dry: United States exports to specified countries, 2017–2019[1]

Country	2017	2018	2019
	Metric tons		
Canada	16,909	15,422	63,368
Ethiopia(*)	36,511	26,012	22,873
Philippines	16,535	16,791	19,686
Peru	16,587	17,675	16,467
China	58,550	13,550	13,912
India	45,857	15,421	13,717
Djibouti	22,230	12,523	13,625
Kenya	14,591	11,718	10,964
Cameroon	5,594	4,360	10,299
South Africa	12,950	7,295	9,383
Mexico	9,155	10,710	7,950
Somalia	5,075	6,364	7,762
Tanzania	10,233	26,150	6,498
United Arab Emirates	901	258	4,839
Saudi Arabia	47	2,657	4,750
Colombia	2,630	897	3,906
Congo (Kinshasa)	0	160	3,365
Belgium-Luxembourg(*)	473	485	3,308
Pakistan	1,894	1,340	2,964
Togo	1,492	1,994	2,584
Taiwan	2,908	2,861	2,338
Turkey	3,066	411	1,829
Korea, South	220	284	1,237
Chile	547	577	1,228
Madagascar	1,472	0	1,132
Thailand	904	701	1,105
Vietnam	625	935	1,067
Nepal	0	0	1,009
Haiti	780	311	772
Sudan(*)	6,493	2,156	646
Rest of World	48,244	36,628	6,984
World Total	343,472	236,647	261,567

(*) Denotes a country that is a summarization of its component countries. [1] Excluding seed pea exports.
FAS, Office of Global Analysis, (202) 720-6301. Data Source: U.S. Census Bureau Trade Data.

Table 6-21.—Hops: Area, yield, production, price, value, and Sept. 1 stocks, United States, 2010–2019

Year	Area harvested	Yield per acre	Production	Marketing year average price per pound received by farmers	Value of production	Stocks Sept. 1	Stocks Mar. 1
	1,000 acres	*Pounds*	*1,000 pounds*	*Dollars per pound*	*1,000 dollars*	*1,000 pounds*	*1,000 pounds*
2010	31.3	2,093	65,493	3.28	214,589	83,000	102,000
2011	29.8	2,175	64,782	3.14	203,378	87,000	121,000
2012	29.7	1,985	58,911	3.17	186,876	96,000	120,000
2013	35.3	1,962	69,246	3.35	232,308	(NA)	115,000
2014	38.0	1,868	70,996	3.67	260,627	90,000	121,000
2015	43.6	1,807	78,846	4.38	345,388	83,000	119,000
2016	50.9	1,713	87,140	5.72	498,420	85,000	128,000
2017	54.0	1,956	105,622	5.60	591,375	98,000	140,000
2018	55.0	1,943	106,907	5.46	583,444	113,000	169,000
2019	56.5	1,981	112,041	5.68	636,580		

(NA) Not available.
NASS, Crops Branch, (202) 720–2127.

Table 6-22.—Hops: Area, yield, and production, by State and United States, 2017–2019

State	Area harvested			Yield per acre			Production		
	2017	2018	2019	2017	2018	2019	2017	2018	2019
	1,000 acres	*1,000 acres*	*1,000 acres*	*Pounds*	*Pounds*	*Pounds*	*1,000 pounds*	*1,000 pounds*	*1,000 pounds*
Idaho	7,125	8,140	8,358	1,974	1,995	2,034	14,067.3	16,242.8	17,003.1
Oregon	8,216	7,725	7,306	1,518	1,675	1,783	12,470.4	12,936.2	13,023.2
Washington	38,648	39,170	40,880	2,046	1,984	2,006	79,083.8	77,727.7	82,014.9
United States	53,989	55,035	56,544	1,956	1,943	1,981	105,621.5	106,906.7	112,041.2

NASS, Crops Branch, (202) 720–2127.

Table 6-23.—Hops: Marketing year average price and value of production, by State and United States, 2017–2019

State	Marketing year average price per pound			Value of production		
	2017	2018	2019 [1]	2017	2018	2019 [1]
	Dollars	*Dollars*	*Dollars*	*1,000 dollars*	*1,000 dollars*	*1,000 dollars*
Idaho	5.00	5.30	5.25	70,337	86,087	89,266
Oregon	5.00	5.40	5.50	62,352	69,855	71,628
Washington	5.80	5.50	5.80	458,686	427,502	475,686
United States	5.60	5.46	5.68	591,375	583,444	636,580

[1] Preliminary.
NASS, Crops Branch, (202) 720–2127.

Table 6-24.—Hops, including extract: United States exports by country of destination, 2017–2019

Country	2017	2018	2019
	Metric tons		
Belgium-Luxembourg(*)	1,698	2,563	2,528
Canada	1,386	1,752	2,430
United Kingdom	3,392	2,092	2,224
Germany(*)	1,284	1,754	1,806
Brazil	1,001	1,409	1,765
Australia(*)	595	869	836
Mexico	822	923	726
China	764	1,472	600
Argentina	542	593	526
Colombia	678	593	450
Japan	609	469	432
Vietnam	135	270	322
Korea, South	385	254	227
Peru	293	251	225
New Zealand(*)	88	99	194
Chile	44	155	171
Philippines	97	190	156
Ecuador	64	97	111
India	64	124	106
Hong Kong	125	125	106
South Africa	107	113	104
Russia	188	98	99
Dominican Republic	115	96	98
Netherlands	39	14	94
Ireland	64	23	84
Panama	55	69	61
Guatemala	45	48	51
Cambodia	28	23	49
Sweden	5	5	38
Thailand	22	11	36
Rest of World	480	493	437
World Total	15,215	17,125	17,182

(*) Denotes a country that is a summarization of its component countries.
FAS, Office of Global Analysis, (202) 720-6301. Data Source: U.S. Census Bureau Trade Data

CHAPTER VII

STATISTICS OF CATTLE, HOGS, AND SHEEP

This chapter contains information about most kinds of farm livestock and livestock products, with the exception of dairy and poultry. The information relates to inventories, production, disposition, prices, and income for farm animals, and to livestock slaughter, meat production, and market statistics for meat animals.

Table 7-1.—All cattle and calves: Inventory, and value, United States, Jan. 1, 2010-2019

Year	Inventory	Value	
		Per head	Total
	Thousands	*Dollars*	*1,000 dollars*
2010	94,081	833	78,335,410
2011	92,887	947	87,988,337
2012	91,160	1,111	101,252,540
2013	90,095	1,139	101,731,742
2014	88,243	1,223	107,921,189
2015	89,173	1,584	141,250,032
2016	91,888	1,410	129,562,080
2017	93,625	1,109	103,829,681
2018	94,298	1,146	108,065,508
2019	94,805	1,031	97,746,846

NASS, Livestock Branch, (202) 720–3570.

Table 7-2.—All cattle and calves: Number by class, United States, Jan. 1, 2010–2019

Year	All cattle and calves [1]	Cows and heifers that have calved		500 pounds and over					Calves under 500 pounds
				Heifers			Steers	Bulls	
		Beef cows	Milk cows	Beef cow replacements	Milk cow replacements	Other			
	Thousands	*Thousands*	*Thousands*	*Thousands*	*Thousands*	*Thousands*	*Thousands*	*Thousands*	*Thousands*
2010	94,081	31,440	9,087	5,443	4,551	9,784	16,568	2,190	15,019
2011	92,887	30,913	9,156	5,135	4,577	9,938	16,394	2,165	14,610
2012	91,160	30,282	9,236	5,281	4,618	9,546	15,957	2,100	14,141
2013	90,095	29,631	9,221	5,420	4,546	9,281	15,931	2,074	13,983
2014	88,243	28,956	9,208	5,556	4,539	8,824	15,623	2,038	13,498
2015	89,173	29,332	9,312	6,086	4,710	8,469	15,630	2,109	13,523
2016	91,888	30,164	9,312	6,335	4,814	8,753	16,305	2,137	14,067
2017	93,625	31,171	9,369	6,363	4,754	8,995	16,374	2,244	14,356
2018	94,298	31,466	9,432	6,108	4,768	9,341	16,528	2,252	14,401
2019	94,805	31,691	9,353	5,885	4,702	9,624	16,758	2,253	14,540

[1] Totals may not add due to rounding.
NASS, Livestock Branch, (202) 720–3570.

Table 7-3.—All cattle and calves: Inventory and value, by State and United States, Jan. 1, 2018–2019

State	Inventory		Value			
			Value per head		Total value	
	2018	2019	2018	2019	2018	2019
	Thousands	*Thousands*	*Dollars*	*Dollars*	*1,000 dollars*	*1,000 dollars*
Alabama	1,340.0	1,300.0	930	840	1,246,200	1,092,000
Alaska	15.0	16.0	1,280	1,280	19,200	20,480
Arizona	1,020.0	1,020.0	1,100	940	1,122,000	958,800
Arkansas	1,760.0	1,780.0	1,010	890	1,777,600	1,584,200
California	5,200.0	5,150.0	1,230	980	6,396,000	5,047,000
Colorado	2,850.0	2,850.0	1,230	1,100	3,505,500	3,163,500
Connecticut	50.0	47.0	1,210	1,070	60,500	50,290
Delaware	17.0	15.0	1,080	980	18,360	14,700
Florida	1,630.0	1,680.0	1,100	1,000	1,793,000	1,680,000
Georgia	1,060.0	1,070.0	950	950	1,007,000	1,016,500
Hawaii	144.0	142.0	750	700	108,000	99,400
Idaho	2,420.0	2,500.0	1,250	1,050	3,025,000	2,625,000
Illinois	1,150.0	1,190.0	1,220	1,020	1,403,000	1,213,800
Indiana	860.0	880.0	1,070	920	920,200	809,600
Iowa	4,000.0	3,950.0	1,200	1,130	4,800,000	4,463,500
Kansas	6,300.0	6,400.0	1,110	1,070	6,993,000	6,848,000
Kentucky	2,160.0	2,130.0	960	850	2,073,600	1,810,500
Louisiana	820.0	800.0	1,090	950	893,800	760,000
Maine	81.0	78.0	1,190	980	96,390	76,440
Maryland	193.0	197.0	1,070	930	206,510	183,210
Massachusetts	38.0	37.0	1,130	920	42,940	34,040
Michigan	1,160.0	1,160.0	1,140	950	1,322,400	1,102,000
Minnesota	2,350.0	2,320.0	1,080	940	2,538,000	2,180,800
Mississippi	930.0	900.0	950	860	883,500	774,000
Missouri	4,350.0	4,250.0	1,060	970	4,611,000	4,122,500
Montana	2,550.0	2,500.0	1,350	1,310	3,442,500	3,275,000
Nebraska	6,800.0	6,800.0	1,260	1,210	8,568,000	8,228,000
Nevada	465.0	470.0	1,270	1,180	590,550	554,600
New Hampshire	36.0	33.0	1,160	980	41,760	32,340
New Jersey	29.0	30.0	1,160	1,100	33,640	33,000
New Mexico	1,510.0	1,480.0	1,310	1,010	1,978,100	1,494,800
New York	1,480.0	1,450.0	1,130	990	1,672,400	1,435,500
North Carolina	800.0	800.0	900	730	720,000	584,000
North Dakota	1,860.0	1,830.0	1,450	1,340	2,697,600	2,452,200
Ohio	1,300.0	1,310.0	1,090	860	1,417,000	1,126,600
Oklahoma	5,100.0	5,300.0	1,100	1,010	5,610,000	5,353,000
Oregon	1,270.0	1,310.0	1,210	1,090	1,536,700	1,427,900
Pennsylvania	1,620.0	1,600.0	1,060	910	1,717,200	1,456,000
Rhode Island	5.0	4.7	1,280	1,180	6,400	5,546
South Carolina	340.0	350.0	960	820	326,400	287,000
South Dakota	4,000.0	4,050.0	1,350	1,240	5,400,000	5,022,000
Tennessee	1,830.0	1,800.0	940	890	1,720,200	1,602,000
Texas	12,500.0	13,000.0	1,080	990	13,500,000	12,870,000
Utah	790.0	810.0	1,270	1,150	1,003,300	931,500
Vermont	260.0	255.0	1,270	1,000	330,200	255,000
Virginia	1,480.0	1,440.0	940	860	1,391,200	1,238,400
Washington	1,160.0	1,180.0	1,200	930	1,392,000	1,097,400
West Virginia	395.0	390.0	1,000	870	395,000	339,300
Wisconsin	3,500.0	3,450.0	1,140	950	3,990,000	3,277,500
Wyoming	1,320.0	1,300.0	1,330	1,260	1,755,600	1,638,000
United States	94,298.0	94,804.7	1,146	1,031	108,065,508	97,746,846

NASS, Livestock Branch, (202) 720–3570.

Table 7-4.—Cattle and calves, January 1: Number by class, State and United States, 2018–2019

State	Cows and heifers that have calved				Heifers, 500 pounds and over					
	Beef cows		Milk cows		Beef cow replacements		Milk cow replacements		Other	
	2018	2019	2018	2019	2018	2019	2018	2019	2018	2019
	1,000 head									
Alabama	714.0	705.0	6.0	5.0	125.0	116.0	3.0	2.0	37.0	37.0
Alaska	6.1	6.8	0.3	0.2	1.4	1.4	0.1	0.1	0.5	0.7
Arizona	200.0	215.0	210.0	205.0	36.0	35.0	105.0	115.0	29.0	20.0
Arkansas	924.0	935.0	6.0	5.0	160.0	156.0	4.0	4.0	71.0	75.0
California	670.0	630.0	1,740.0	1,730.0	125.0	115.0	780.0	760.0	175.0	215.0
Colorado	812.0	792.0	168.0	178.0	175.0	170.0	100.0	110.0	550.0	570.0
Connecticut	5.0	4.5	20.0	19.5	2.0	1.5	9.5	9.0	1.5	1.5
Delaware	2.5	2.0	5.0	4.5	0.7	0.6	2.0	1.6	0.4	0.3
Florida	886.0	914.0	124.0	116.0	115.0	130.0	40.0	35.0	30.0	25.0
Georgia	485.0	499.0	85.0	81.0	95.0	90.0	25.0	30.0	25.0	30.0
Hawaii	75.0	75.5	2.0	1.5	12.0	11.5	1.0	1.0	5.0	5.0
Idaho	510.0	506.0	600.0	614.0	120.0	110.0	310.0	340.0	210.0	220.0
Illinois	397.0	405.0	93.0	85.0	70.0	70.0	47.0	45.0	98.0	95.0
Indiana	208.0	204.0	187.0	181.0	50.0	45.0	75.0	80.0	45.0	50.0
Iowa	950.0	930.0	220.0	220.0	165.0	155.0	135.0	125.0	550.0	560.0
Kansas	1,504.0	1,529.0	156.0	161.0	280.0	280.0	140.0	170.0	1,490.0	1,420.0
Kentucky	1,033.0	1,017.0	57.0	53.0	145.0	120.0	45.0	45.0	115.0	130.0
Louisiana	473.0	459.0	12.0	11.0	90.0	83.0	4.0	4.0	20.0	23.0
Maine	10.0	11.0	30.0	29.0	4.0	3.0	15.0	14.0	3.0	3.0
Maryland	46.0	50.0	47.0	44.0	12.0	13.0	28.0	30.0	10.0	8.0
Massachusetts	6.5	7.0	11.5	10.5	2.0	2.0	7.0	6.5	1.0	1.0
Michigan	102.0	108.0	428.0	422.0	24.0	25.0	176.0	160.0	30.0	40.0
Minnesota	365.0	370.0	455.0	450.0	100.0	95.0	290.0	255.0	175.0	170.0
Mississippi	501.0	477.0	9.0	8.0	92.0	90.0	7.0	5.0	40.0	40.0
Missouri	2,086.0	2,059.0	84.0	81.0	355.0	335.0	40.0	40.0	205.0	205.0
Montana	1,497.0	1,448.0	13.0	12.0	390.0	380.0	7.0	8.0	223.0	232.0
Nebraska	1,910.0	1,941.0	60.0	59.0	375.0	365.0	15.0	15.0	1,520.0	1,530.0
Nevada	238.0	242.0	32.0	33.0	42.0	42.0	12.0	11.0	30.0	29.0
New Hampshire	4.5	4.0	12.5	12.0	1.5	1.3	7.0	6.5	0.5	0.7
New Jersey	9.0	9.5	6.0	5.5	2.1	2.5	3.2	3.3	1.2	0.7
New Mexico	483.0	480.0	332.0	325.0	105.0	95.0	130.0	125.0	95.0	85.0
New York	105.0	105.0	625.0	625.0	45.0	40.0	350.0	335.0	50.0	45.0
North Carolina	370.0	367.0	45.0	43.0	63.0	60.0	17.0	20.0	22.0	20.0
North Dakota	964.0	975.0	16.0	15.0	191.0	197.0	9.0	8.0	240.0	210.0
Ohio	296.0	307.0	264.0	253.0	70.0	70.0	121.0	125.0	59.0	55.0
Oklahoma	2,088.0	2,150.0	42.0	40.0	410.0	400.0	25.0	20.0	510.0	520.0
Oregon	536.0	535.0	124.0	125.0	95.0	110.0	70.0	65.0	100.0	115.0
Pennsylvania	215.0	225.0	525.0	505.0	60.0	65.0	310.0	290.0	60.0	55.0
Rhode Island	1.6	1.4	0.8	0.7	0.5	0.6	0.5	0.5	0.2	0.2
South Carolina	174.0	186.0	15.0	14.0	28.0	37.0	6.0	5.0	0.0	8.0
South Dakota	1,751.0	1,818.0	119.0	122.0	435.0	385.0	45.0	40.0	500.0	550.0
Tennessee	910.0	914.0	40.0	36.0	135.0	145.0	25.0	25.0	80.0	75.0
Texas	4,520.0	4,655.0	530.0	545.0	800.0	740.0	250.0	260.0	1,470.0	1,690.0
Utah	338.0	340.0	97.0	100.0	70.0	70.0	50.0	50.0	60.0	65.0
Vermont	15.0	14.0	128.0	126.0	5.0	4.5	57.0	55.0	6.0	6.5
Virginia	633.0	631.0	87.0	79.0	100.0	93.0	40.0	37.0	70.0	61.0
Washington	235.0	230.0	275.0	280.0	52.0	57.0	123.0	123.0	115.0	126.0
West Virginia	203.0	198.0	7.0	7.0	37.0	32.0	3.0	3.0	18.0	20.0
Wisconsin	285.0	290.0	1,275.0	1,270.0	80.0	80.0	700.0	680.0	50.0	60.0
Wyoming	714.0	714.0	6.0	6.0	160.0	160.0	4.0	4.0	136.0	126.0
United States	31,466.2	31,690.7	9,432.1	9,353.4	6,108.2	5,884.9	4,768.3	4,701.5	9,341.3	9,623.6

See footnote(s) at end of table.

Table 7-4.—Cattle and calves, January 1: Number by class, State and United States, 2018–2019—Continued

State	Steers, 500 pounds and over		Bulls, 500 pounds and over		Calves under 500 pounds	
	2018	2019	2018	2019	2018	2019
	Thousands	*Thousands*	*Thousands*	*Thousands*	*Thousands*	*Thousands*
Alabama	40.0	45.0	50.0	45.0	365.0	345.0
Alaska	0.5	0.7	2.4	3.0	3.7	3.1
Arizona	275.0	295.0	20.0	20.0	145.0	115.0
Arkansas	110.0	115.0	60.0	60.0	425.0	430.0
California	620.0	610.0	70.0	60.0	1,020.0	1,030.0
Colorado	810.0	830.0	55.0	55.0	180.0	145.0
Connecticut	2.0	1.5	0.5	0.5	9.5	9.0
Delaware	2.1	2.6	0.3	0.4	4.0	3.0
Florida	20.0	20.0	55.0	60.0	360.0	380.0
Georgia	35.0	37.0	35.0	33.0	275.0	270.0
Hawaii	11.0	10.5	4.0	4.0	34.0	33.0
Idaho	310.0	320.0	40.0	40.0	320.0	350.0
Illinois	195.0	245.0	25.0	25.0	225.0	220.0
Indiana	104.0	115.0	16.0	17.0	175.0	188.0
Iowa	1,390.0	1,390.0	70.0	70.0	520.0	500.0
Kansas	2,020.0	2,060.0	95.0	95.0	615.0	685.0
Kentucky	195.0	225.0	70.0	70.0	500.0	470.0
Louisiana	23.0	27.0	31.0	30.0	167.0	163.0
Maine	4.0	4.0	1.5	1.5	13.5	12.5
Maryland	17.0	14.0	4.0	5.0	29.0	33.0
Massachusetts	2.0	2.0	1.0	1.0	7.0	7.0
Michigan	180.0	180.0	15.0	15.0	205.0	210.0
Minnesota	475.0	485.0	35.0	35.0	455.0	460.0
Mississippi	48.0	52.0	38.0	38.0	195.0	190.0
Missouri	410.0	395.0	120.0	125.0	1,050.0	1,010.0
Montana	210.0	240.0	105.0	100.0	105.0	80.0
Nebraska	2,480.0	2,380.0	110.0	110.0	330.0	400.0
Nevada	40.0	39.0	15.0	15.0	56.0	59.0
New Hampshire	2.0	1.5	0.5	0.5	7.5	6.5
New Jersey	2.1	2.5	1.0	1.0	4.4	5.0
New Mexico	130.0	130.0	40.0	35.0	195.0	205.0
New York	47.0	47.0	18.0	18.0	240.0	235.0
North Carolina	33.0	35.0	30.0	30.0	220.0	225.0
North Dakota	260.0	255.0	70.0	65.0	110.0	105.0
Ohio	210.0	215.0	30.0	30.0	250.0	255.0
Oklahoma	990.0	1,050.0	155.0	180.0	880.0	940.0
Oregon	145.0	160.0	40.0	40.0	160.0	160.0
Pennsylvania	130.0	135.0	25.0	25.0	295.0	300.0
Rhode Island	0.5	0.4	0.1	0.1	0.8	0.8
South Carolina	10.0	10.0	16.0	14.0	82.0	76.0
South Dakota	730.0	730.0	110.0	105.0	310.0	300.0
Tennessee	150.0	130.0	60.0	65.0	430.0	410.0
Texas	2,620.0	2,720.0	340.0	340.0	1,970.0	2,050.0
Utah	80.0	85.0	25.0	25.0	70.0	75.0
Vermont	4.0	4.0	3.0	3.0	42.0	42.0
Virginia	160.0	155.0	40.0	39.0	350.0	345.0
Washington	200.0	200.0	20.0	20.0	140.0	150.0
West Virginia	41.0	42.0	15.0	14.0	71.0	74.0
Wisconsin	380.0	360.0	30.0	30.0	700.0	680.0
Wyoming	175.0	150.0	40.0	40.0	85.0	100.0
United States	16,528.2	16,757.7	2,252.3	2,253.0	14,401.0	14,539.9

NASS, Livestock Branch, (202) 720–3570.

Table 7-5.—Cows and calf crop: Cows and heifers that have calved, Jan. 1, 2018–2019, and calves born, by State and United States, 2017–2018

State	Cows and heifers that have calved		Calves born	
	Jan. 1		2017	2018
	2018	2019		
	Thousands	*Thousands*	*Thousands*	*Thousands*
Alabama	720.0	710.0	630.0	620.0
Alaska	6.4	7.0	4.5	5.0
Arizona	410.0	420.0	310.0	320.0
Arkansas	930.0	940.0	790.0	800.0
California	2,410.0	2,360.0	1,880.0	1,860.0
Colorado	980.0	970.0	830.0	840.0
Connecticut	25.0	24.0	17.5	16.5
Delaware	7.5	6.5	7.0	6.0
Florida	1,010.0	1,030.0	790.0	820.0
Georgia	570.0	580.0	480.0	510.0
Hawaii	77.0	77.0	60.0	60.0
Idaho	1,110.0	1,120.0	960.0	960.0
Illinois	490.0	490.0	420.0	430.0
Indiana	395.0	385.0	340.0	350.0
Iowa	1,170.0	1,150.0	1,090.0	1,100.0
Kansas	1,660.0	1,690.0	1,430.0	1,500.0
Kentucky	1,090.0	1,070.0	990.0	970.0
Louisiana	485.0	470.0	370.0	360.0
Maine	40.0	40.0	30.0	29.0
Maryland	93.0	94.0	70.0	75.0
Massachusetts	18.0	17.5	17.0	16.0
Michigan	530.0	530.0	410.0	420.0
Minnesota	820.0	820.0	790.0	800.0
Mississippi	510.0	485.0	400.0	385.0
Missouri	2,170.0	2,140.0	1,960.0	1,940.0
Montana	1,510.0	1,460.0	1,480.0	1,440.0
Nebraska	1,970.0	2,000.0	1,700.0	1,790.0
Nevada	270.0	275.0	220.0	220.0
New Hampshire	17.0	16.0	13.5	12.0
New Jersey	15.0	15.0	9.5	10.0
New Mexico	815.0	805.0	630.0	620.0
New York	730.0	730.0	550.0	550.0
North Carolina	415.0	410.0	365.0	365.0
North Dakota	980.0	990.0	960.0	940.0
Ohio	560.0	560.0	490.0	490.0
Oklahoma	2,130.0	2,190.0	1,950.0	2,050.0
Oregon	660.0	660.0	630.0	620.0
Pennsylvania	740.0	730.0	600.0	610.0
Rhode Island	2.4	2.1	2.2	2.2
South Carolina	189.0	200.0	147.0	164.0
South Dakota	1,870.0	1,940.0	1,840.0	1,880.0
Tennessee	950.0	950.0	850.0	860.0
Texas	5,050.0	5,200.0	4,400.0	4,650.0
Utah	435.0	440.0	375.0	385.0
Vermont	143.0	140.0	105.0	102.0
Virginia	720.0	710.0	640.0	630.0
Washington	510.0	510.0	440.0	440.0
West Virginia	210.0	205.0	195.0	190.0
Wisconsin	1,560.0	1,560.0	1,430.0	1,420.0
Wyoming	720.0	720.0	660.0	670.0
United States	40,898.3	41,044.1	35,758.2	36,312.7

NASS, Livestock Branch, (202) 720–3570.

Table 7-6.—Cattle and calves: All cattle on feed, United States, Jan. 1, 2010–2019 [1]

Year	Inventory
	Thousands
2010	13,727.6
2011	14,131.5
2012	14,355.3
2013	13,703.3
2014	12,949.3
2015	13,024.8
2016	13,156.7
2017	13,108.4
2018	14,146.0
2019	14,367.9

[1] Cattle and calves on feed are steers and heifers for slaughter market being fed a ration of grain or other concentrates and are expected to produce a carcass that will grade select or better.
NASS, Livestock Branch, (202) 720–3570.

Table 7-7.—Cattle and calves: Total number on feed by State and United States, Jan. 1, 2018–2019

State	2018	2019
	1,000 head	*1,000 head*
Arizona	274.0	297.0
California	490.0	535.0
Colorado	1,000.0	1,050.0
Idaho	265.0	295.0
Illinois	220.0	250.0
Indiana	90.0	100.0
Iowa	1,300.0	1,320.0
Kansas	2,450.0	2,430.0
Kentucky	17.0	16.0
Maryland	9.0	9.0
Michigan	140.0	150.0
Minnesota	430.0	410.0
Missouri	80.0	100.0
Montana	45.0	40.0
Nebraska	2,800.0	2,750.0
Nevada	3.0	4.0
New York	22.0	22.0
North Dakota	58.0	59.0
Ohio	140.0	150.0
Oklahoma	330.0	330.0
Oregon	90.0	90.0
Pennsylvania	85.0	100.0
South Dakota	470.0	425.0
Texas	2,650.0	2,750.0
Utah	20.0	23.0
Virginia	18.0	15.0
Washington	215.0	230.0
West Virginia	4.0	4.0
Wisconsin	280.0	280.0
Wyoming	70.0	65.0
Other States [1]	81.0	68.9
United States	14,146.0	14,367.9

[1] Individual state estimates not available for states not shown, but are included in Other States.
NASS, Livestock Branch, (202) 720–3570.

Table 7-8.—Cattle: Average price per 100 pounds, by grades, at Nebraska Direct, Worthing, SD and Louisville, KY, 2010–2019

Year	Nebraska		Worthing, SD		Louisville, KY	
	Choice		Cows [1]		Cows	
	Steers [2]	Heifers [3]	Commercial	Breaking utility	Breaking utility	85-95% Lean
	Dollars	*Dollars*	*Dollars*	*Dollars*	*Dollars*	*Dollars*
2010	95.81	95.41	(NA)	61.49	53.98	41.70
2011	111.52	111.55	74.25	71.34	67.20	53.92
2012	123.11	124.18	83.95	78.90	76.55	62.71
2013	127.13	127.37	84.83	78.52	79.22	71.00
2014	154.03	154.67	108.79	109.08	105.26	83.56
2015	148.71	148.09	100.39	104.29	99.14	78.27
2016	117.74	119.69	82.14	76.40	(NA)	(NA)
2017	121.43	121.92	83.72	71.65	(NA)	(NA)
2018	116.42	117.62	79.15	68.45	(NA)	(NA)
2019	118.47	118.05	84.32	(NA)	(NA)	(NA)

(NA) Not available. [1] All weights; simple average of price range. [2] 1,100 to 1,500 pound weight range; weighted average of price range. [3] 1,000 to 1,300 pound weight range; simple average of price range.
AMS, Livestock and Grain Market News, (202) 720–7316.

Table 7-9.—Cattle and calves: Production, disposition, cash receipts, and gross income, United States, 2009-2018

Year	Calf crop [1]	Death loss		Marketings [2]		Inshipments [3]	Farm slaughter
		Cattle	Calves	Cattle	Calves		Cattle and calves
	1,000 head	*1,000 head*	*1,000 head*	*1,000 head*	*1,000 head*	*1,000 head*	*1,000 head*
2010	35,740	1,736	2,265	44,658	8,874	20,757	157
2011	35,357	1,787	2,230	44,875	8,401	20,357	148
2012	34,469	1,752	2,171	43,578	8,337	20,443	139
2013	33,630	1,730	2,140	43,453	7,996	19,965	128
2014	33,522	1,720	2,130	41,243	7,819	20,443	124
2015	34,087	1,736	2,144	40,487	7,397	20,508	116
2016	35,063	1,736	2,140	41,756	7,656	20,084	123
2017	35,758	1,784	2,144	43,644	7,777	20,380	116
2018	36,313	1,786	2,205	45,031	7,602	20,937	119
2019	36,060	1,865	2,300	45,040	7,541	20,418	123

Year	Production (live weight) [4]	Value of production	Cash receipts [5]	Value of home consumption	Gross income [6]	Average price per 100 pounds received by farmers	
						Cattle	Calves
	1,000 pounds	*1,000 dollars*	*1,000 dollars*	*1,000 dollars*	*1,000 dollars*	*Dollars*	*Dollars*
2010	41,379,839	36,850,474	51,246,136	405,789	51,651,925	92.20	117.00
2011	41,483,945	45,059,200	62,321,217	478,871	62,800,088	113.00	142.00
2012	40,920,479	48,059,904	66,090,126	525,630	66,615,756	121.00	172.00
2013	40,781,761	48,595,712	67,849,440	509,175	68,358,615	125,00	181.00
2014	40,268,012	60,141,507	81,076,720	610,833	81,687,553	152.00	261.00
2015	41,503,073	60,080,918	78,252,807	588,216	78,841,023	147.00	247.00
2016	42,694,001	48,572,501	63,691,327	472,478	64,163,805	119.00	158.00
2017	44,197,461	50,398,374	66,936,726	455,988	67,392,714	120.00	168.00
2018	45,677,452	49,147,588	67,038,059	431,071	67,469,130	116.00	170.00
2019	44,820,270	48,223,046	66,239,043	436,788	66,675,831	116.00	159.00

[1] Calves born during the year. [2] Includes custom slaughter for use on farms where produced and State outshipments, but excludes interfarm sales within the State. [3] Includes cattle shipped in from other States, but excludes cattle for immediate slaughter. [4] Adjustments made for changes in inventory and for inshipments. [5] Receipts from marketings and sale of farm slaughter. [6] Cash receipts from sales of cattle, calves, beef, and veal plus value of cattle and calves slaughtered for home consumption.

NASS, Livestock Branch, (202) 720–3570.

Table 7-10.—Cattle: Weighted average weight and price per 100 pounds, Texas-Oklahoma, Kansas, Colorado, Nebraska, Iowa-So. Minnesota Feedlots, 2010–2019 [1]

Year	Steers SE/CH 65-80%			Steers SE/CH 35-65%		
	Price	Average Weight	Number of Head	Price	Average Weight	Number of Head
	Dollars	*Pounds*		*Dollars*	*Pounds*	
2010	95.00	1,359	561,173	95.95	1,301	1,329,021
2011	114.45	1,364	518,689	114.92	1,304	1,101,808
2012	122.84	1,402	458,382	123.06	1,312	743,859
2013	126.27	1,408	384,642	126.35	1,338	517,782
2014	154.25	1,410	548,667	152.15	1,339	386,051
2015	147.64	1,432	341,078	149.00	1,366	228,126
2016	120.04	1,429	735,708	121.29	1,369	276,086
2017	122.85	1,454	845,341	123.13	1,313	235,130
2018	117.06	1,401	704,101	119.06	1,312	195,726
2019	117.87	1,390	456,517	115.45	1,322	108,332

Year	Heifers SE/CH 65-80%			Heifers SE/CH 35-65%		
	Price	Average Weight	Number of Head	Price	Average Weight	Number of Head
	Dollars	*Pounds*		*Dollars*	*Pounds*	
2010	95.41	1,227	562,788	96.22	1,166	1,159,191
2011	114.05	1,222	508,487	114.64	1,167	928,633
2012	123.38	1,255	412,483	120.01	1,173	577,535
2013	126.09	1,266	320,285	126.36	1,198	335,205
2014	154.37	1,279	322,272	152.18	1,204	218,658
2015	148.20	1,289	220,073	147.73	1,235	97,078
2016	120.99	1,288	400,528	121.67	1,231	103,739
2017	122.87	1,251	404,560	123.25	1,194	86,001
2018	117.74	1,247	353,713	118.80	1,206	73,320
2019	116.62	1,248	246,807	114.29	1,207	38,108

[1] Sales FOB the feedyard. Estimated net weights after 3-4% shrink.

AMS, Livestock and Grain Market News, (202) 720–7316.

Table 7-11.—Cattle: Receipts at selected markets, 2010–2019

Year	Oklahoma City	Fort Collins	Tulia [1]	South St. Joseph	Sioux Falls
	Thousands	*Thousands*	*Thousands*	*Thousands*	*Thousands*
2010	492	63	74	105	153
2011	468	30	60	94	104
2012	399	72	43	121	153
2013	409	46	35	90	156
2014	382	42	37	86	140
2015	368	43	21	88	139
2016	368	51	34	91	179
2017	369	15	39	98	174
2018	388	31	26	91	139
2019	415	32	91	77	203

[1] Changed from Amarillo, Texas to Tulia, Texas
AMS, Livestock & Grain Market News, (202) 720–7316.

Table 7-12.—Cattle and calves: Number slaughtered, United States, 2010–2019

Year	Cattle slaughter					Calf slaughter				
	Commercial			Farm	Total	Commercial			Farm	Total
	Federally inspected	Other	Total [1]			Federally inspected	Other	Total [1]		
	1,000 head									
2010 ...	33,702	547	34,249	124	34,373	864	14	879	33	912
2011 ...	33,555	532	34,087	119	34,205	839	14	853	30	882
2012 ...	32,426	525	32,951	112	33,062	760	12	772	27	800
2013 ...	31,947	515	32,462	103	32,565	751	11	762	26	788
2014 ...	29,682	486	30,168	98	30,266	558	8	566	26	591
2015 ...	28,296	455	28,752	92	28,844	446	7	453	24	476
2016 ...	30,114	464	30,578	98	30,676	480	8	488	25	513
2017 ...	31,704	485	32,189	91	32,281	503	9	512	25	537
2018 ...	32,518	487	33,005	95	33,100	571	9	580	23	604
2019 ...	33,069	486	33,555	101	33,656	579	8	587	22	609

[1] Totals are based on unrounded numbers.
NASS, Livestock Branch, (202) 720-3570.

Table 7-13.—Cattle and calves: Number slaughtered under Federal inspection, and average live weight, 2010–2019

Year	Cattle		Calves	
	Number slaughtered	Average live weight [1]	Number slaughtered	Average live weight [1]
	Thousands	*Pounds*	*Thousands*	*Pounds*
2010	33,702	1,282	864	260
2011	33,555	1,280	839	260
2012	32,426	1,305	760	257
2013	31,947	1,317	751	248
2014	29,682	1,333	558	281
2015	28,296	1,364	446	309
2016	30,114	1,365	480	264
2017	31,704	1,351	503	248
2018	32,518	1,352	571	224
2019	33,069	1,347	579	219

[1] Excludes postmortem condemnations.
NASS, Livestock Branch, (202) 720-3570.

Table 7-14.—Cattle and calves: Number slaughtered commercially, total and average live weight, by State and United States, 2019 [1]

State	Cattle			Calves		
	Number slaughtered	Total live weight [2]	Average live weight [2]	Number slaughtered	Total live weight [2]	Average live weight [2]
	Thousands	*1,000 pounds*	*Pounds*	*Thousands*	*1,000 pounds*	*Pounds*
Alabama	5.9	6,168	1,037	(Y)	(Y)	(Y)
Alaska	0.6	698	1,130	(D)	(D)	(D)
Arizona	551.3	752,983	1,368	(D)	(D)	(D)
Arkansas	5.3	5,068	957	(Y)	(Y)	(Y)
California	1,531.1	2,002,936	1,317	82.0	8,365	104
Colorado	2,469.3	3,384,389	1,372	(D)	(D)	(D)
Delaware-Maryland	37.7	51,736	1,373	(D)	(D)	(D)
Florida	(D)	(D)	(D)	0.8	310	392
Georgia	(D)	(D)	(D)	1.3	575	442
Hawaii	13.4	14,509	1,087	(D)	(D)	(D)
Idaho	503.5	642,342	1,288	40.3	3,545	89
Illinois	(D)	(D)	(D)	1.0	379	383
Indiana	34.2	40,024	1,170	4.5	1,353	300
Iowa	(D)	(D)	(D)	(D)	(D)	(D)
Kansas	6,436.7	8,642,515	1,343	0.5	202	445
Kentucky	39.1	40,870	1,053	(D)	(D)	(D)
Louisiana	5.5	4,356	788	0.2	69	423
Michigan	(D)	(D)	(D)	1.2	369	302
Minnesota	(D)	(D)	(D)	(Y)	(Y)	(Y)
Mississippi	4.4	3,777	863	(D)	(D)	(D)
Missouri	47.6	55,305	1,161	0.3	119	447
Montana	21.7	29,198	1,349	(Y)	(Y)	(Y)
Nebraska	7,666.0	10,727,535	1,401	(D)	(D)	(D)
Nevada	1.4	1,558	1,085	(D)	(D)	(D)
New England [3]	28.4	32,839	1,156	3.2	714	222
New Jersey	41.9	46,537	1,114	22.6	8,568	379
New Mexico	4.9	4,976	1,014	(Y)	(Y)	(Y)
New York	39.6	46,819	1,200	101.1	8,960	89
North Carolina	79.9	98,205	1,234	0.7	213	301
North Dakota	8.8	11,341	1,290	(D)	(D)	(D)
Ohio	64.5	83,771	1,301	154.7	22,345	145
Oklahoma	31.0	33,006	1,065	0.3	142	429
Oregon	17.3	19,443	1,124	(D)	(D)	(D)
Pennsylvania	1,124.4	1,357,158	1,211	108.9	40,209	424
South Carolina	228.7	280,833	1,234	(D)	(D)	(D)
South Dakota	496.1	699,472	1,416	(D)	(D)	(D)
Tennessee	16.8	16,532	997	0.2	86	410
Texas	5,858.5	7,604,107	1,302	2.2	946	423
Utah	699.0	938,615	1,345	(D)	(D)	(D)
Virginia	16.0	16,995	1,060	(D)	(D)	(D)
Washington	1,145.6	1,579,384	1,383	5.8	456	78
West Virginia	10.8	10,695	990	(D)	(D)	(D)
Wisconsin	1,379.4	1,894,770	1,382	50.9	23,598	465
Wyoming	5.4	5,947	1,111	(D)	(D)	(D)
United States	33,555.3	45,011,509	1,344	587.0	128,804	221

(D) Withheld to avoid disclosing data for individual operations. (Y) Less than level of precision shown. [1] Includes slaughter in federally inspected and other slaughter plants; excludes animals slaughtered on farms. Average live weight is based on unrounded numbers. Totals may not add due to rounding. [2] Excludes postmortem condemnations. [3] New England includes Connecticut, Maine, Massachusetts, New Hampshire, Rhode Island, and Vermont.

NASS, Livestock Branch, (202) 720-3570.

Table 7-15.—Cattle and calves: Production, disposition, cash receipts, and gross income, by State and United States, 2019

State	Marketings [1]		Inshipments [2]	Farm slaughter [3]	Production (live weight) [4]	Value of production	Cash receipts [5]	Value of home consumption	Gross income [6]
	Cattle	Calves							
	1,000 head	*1,000 head*	*1,000 head*	*1,000 head*	*1,000 pounds*	*1,000 dollars*	*1,000 dollars*	*1,000 dollars*	*1,000 dollars*
Alabama	526.0	52.0	18.0	2.0	592,458	402,396	406,929	2,106	409,035
Alaska	2.7	0.1	0.4	0.4	4,443	4,884	3,424	441	3,865
Arizona	533.5	95.1	337.0	1.4	484,789	543,422	783,923	2,269	786,192
Arkansas	633.0	234.0	115.0	1.0	510,641	360,750	452,034	3,579	455,613
California	2,027.0	311.0	740.0	7.0	2,312,271	2,426,684	3,064,300	10,074	3,074,374
Colorado	2,364.5	102.5	1,709.0	2.0	1,861,346	1,796,196	3,625,741	13,157	3,638,898
Connecticut	7.4	7.5	1.6	0.2	12,223	13,250	17,255	827	12,413
Delaware	4.0	1.8	0.5	0.1	4,808	5,115	7,497	637	5,638
Florida	220.0	565.5	40.0	1.5	430,506	439,933	507,755	2,862	477,872
Georgia	301.0	162.5	17.0	1.5	398,613	311,266	335,319	2,057	303,448
Hawaii	15.6	42.2	....	0.2	35,038	41,387	45,781	448	43,200
Idaho	1,165.0	160.0	450.0	3.0	1,259,900	1,405,115	1,725,717	10,120	1,745,760
Illinois	492.0	79.0	135.0	7.0	556,181	660,003	595,677	16,656	834,533
Indiana	323.0	122.0	109.0	5.0	283,810	282,568	353,897	14,816	408,778
Iowa	2,403.0	100.5	1,570.0	2.5	2,075,108	2,536,003	4,074,878	14,583	3,946,525
Kansas	5,344.0	4.0	4,200.0	2.0	4,425,147	4,651,116	8,285,905	15,790	8,406,456
Kentucky	551.0	383.0	73.0	3.0	594,091	648,279	738,867	11,167	703,175
Louisana	131.5	217.5	8.0	1.0	202,545	202,975	234,660	1,612	205,903
Maine	12.7	14.1	3.0	0.2	15,242	16,504	20,514	1,684	18,746
Maryland	60.5	21.0	4.1	0.6	73,049	76,424	68,955	2,838	94,487
Massachusetts	9.0	8.0	0.8	0.3	8,092	8,596	9,482	632	11,379
Michigan	377.0	41.0	70.0	3.0	487,465	486,956	553,716	14,249	562,046
Minnesota	1,366.5	105.5	800.0	4.0	1,395,147	1,422,743	2,063,652	18,475	2,014,746
Mississippi	228.0	110.0	15.0	2.0	245,638	191,007	215,709	3,286	175,272
Missouri	903.0	895.0	115.0	7.0	1,445,831	1,880,552	2,170,559	24,470	1,893,181
Montana	1,290.0	150.5	124.0	3.5	1,115,068	1,254,311	1,365,683	13,010	1,368,143
Nebraska	6,408.0	85.0	4,965.0	2.0	5,586,250	5,424,191	10,583,711	15,871	10,562,966
Nevada	215.0	95.0	110.0	1.0	210,394	232,289	326,304	2,386	322,126
New Hampshire	5.9	6.3	0.6	0.4	7,439	8,272	9,696	948	9,826
New Jersey	7.0	5.1	1.4	0.4	7,334	8,080	5,804	1,654	10,984
New Mexico	892.7	101.2	390.0	1.1	632,851	715,030	919,041	4,337	997,630
New York	202.6	300.4	18.5	3.5	261,505	276,247	344,279	12,798	289,042
North Carolina	208.5	119.5	6.0	1.0	291,217	222,816	247,857	2,822	222,057
North Dakota	870.3	103.7	140.0	1.0	794,993	943,461	1,028,871	9,720	993,144
Ohio	475.0	21.0	50.0	6.0	585,650	594,916	575,463	27,365	650,715
Oklahoma	2,332.0	355.0	900.0	3.0	2,117,748	2,578,360	3,308,434	19,133	3,293,410
Oregon	515.0	194.0	140.0	5.0	547,700	625,158	701,269	12,650	749,610
Pennsylvania	410.0	210.7	36.0	7.3	513,029	553,687	586,422	20,313	636,223
Rhode Island	1.1	1.1	0.2	0.2	1,086	1,174	902	493	1,721
South Carolina	141.0	16.0	4.0	2.0	167,087	115,360	125,693	2,159	124,321
South Dakota	1,889.0	500.0	584.0	1.0	1,720,157	2,123,392	2,726,006	10,760	2,739,338
Tennessee	482.0	323.0	30.0	3.0	585,786	476,175	548,804	7,647	495,312
Texas	5,428.0	257.5	1,650.0	4.5	6,181,230	7,256,724	8,624,064	16,041	8,440,074
Utah	376.0	35.5	58.0	1.5	403,998	446,167	449,991	6,405	498,907
Vermont	39.3	61.2	3.4	0.9	55,927	62,520	65,525	2,957	70,574
Virginia	341.5	221.5	12.0	3.0	439,952	347,309	412,529	5,168	349,751
Washington	564.0	6.0	210.0	6.0	658,905	698,751	748,635	13,183	867,111
West Virginia	112.5	76.5	20.0	2.0	145,668	157,535	173,634	5,154	165,886
Wisconsin	1,027.0	375.2	163.0	4.8	1,499,119	1,590,916	1,752,726	31,022	1,693,324
Wyoming	786.0	85.5	270.0	0.5	575,768	695,811	942,966	3,963	892,101
United States	45,040.3	7,541.2	20,417.5	122.5	44,820,270	48,233,046	67,105,197	431,231	66,675,831

[1] Includes custom slaughter for use on farms where produced and State outshipments, but excludes interfarm sales within the State. [2] Includes cattle shipped in from other states, but excludes cattle for immediate slaughter. [3] Excludes custom slaughter for farmers at commercial establishments. [4] Adjustments made for changes in inventory and for inshipments. [5] Includes receipts from marketings and sales of farm-slaughter. [6] Includes cash receipts from sales of cattle, calves, beef, and veal plus value of cattle and calves slaughtered for home consumption.
NASS, Livestock Branch, (202) 720–3570.

Table 7-16.—Cattle and calves: Inventory Jan 1, 2018–2019, and number of operations, 2017, by State and United States[1]

State	January 1 Cattle inventory		Operations with cattle[2]
	2018	2019	2017
	1,000 head	*1,000 head*	*Number*
Alabama	1,340.0	1,000.0	22,046
Alaska	15.0	16.0	118
Arizona	1,020.0	1,020.0	7,057
Arkansas	1,760.0	1,780.0	25,372
California	5,200.0	5,150.0	13,694
Colorado	2,850.0	2,850.0	14,914
Connecticut	50.0	47.0	1,158
Delaware	17.0	15.0	301
Florida	1,630.0	1,680.0	21,469
Georgia	1,060.0	1,070.0	17,387
Hawaii	144.0	142.0	1,218
Idaho	2,420.0	2,500.0	10,076
Illinois	1,150.0	1,190.0	16,269
Indiana	860.0	880.0	17,014
Iowa	4,000.0	3,950.0	25,367
Kansas	6,300.0	6,400.0	26,740
Kentucky	2,160.0	2,130.0	38,657
Louisana	820.0	800.0	13,449
Maine	81.0	78.0	1,756
Maryland	193.0	197.0	3,322
Massachusetts	38.0	37.0	1,267
Michigan	1,160.0	1,160.0	12,221
Minnesota	2,350.0	2,320.0	20,969
Mississippi	930.0	900.0	15,980
Missouri	4,350.0	4,250.0	53,497
Montana	2,550.0	2,500.0	11,400
Nebraska	6,800.0	6,800.0	20,430
Nevada	465.0	470.0	1,621
New Hampshire	36.0	33.0	903
New Jersey	29.0	30.0	1,246
New Mexico	1,510.0	1,480.0	10,880
New York	1,480.0	1,450.0	12,796
North Carolina	800.0	800.0	18,413
North Dakota	1,860.0	1,830.0	8,777
Ohio	1,300.0	1,310.0	25,224
Oklahoma	5,100.0	5,300.0	52,048
Oregon	1,270.0	1,310.0	13,880
Pennsylvania	1,620.0	1,600.0	22,729
Rhode Island	5.0	4.7	214
South Carolina	340.0	350.0	7,868
South Dakota	4,000.0	4,050.0	13,928
Tennessee	1,830.0	1,800.0	37,288
Texas	12,500.0	13,000.0	152,882
Utah	700.0	810.0	8,026
Vermont	260.0	255.0	2,317
Virginia	1,480.0	1,440.0	21,880
Washington	1,160.0	1,180.0	11,311
West Virginia	395.0	390.0	11,774
Wisconsin	3,550.0	3,450.0	27,777
Wyoming	1,320.0	1,300.0	5,702
United States	94,298.0	94,804.7	882,692

[1] An operation is any place having one or more head of cattle on hand on December 31. [2] State level estimates only available in conjunction with the Census of Agriculture every 5 years.
NASS, Livestock Branch, (202) 720–3570.

Table 7-17.—Cattle: Number slaughtered under Federal inspection and percentage distribution, by classes, 2010–2019[1]

Year	Number						Percentage of total					
	Steers	Heif-ers	Cows			Bulls	Steers	Heif-ers	Cows			Bulls
			Dairy cows	Other cows	Total cows				Dairy cows	Other cows	Total cows	
	Thousands						*Percent*					
2010 ...	16,596	10,047	2,807	3,630	6,437	622	49.2	29.8	8.3	10.8	19.1	1.8
2011 ...	16,539	9,726	2,914	3,798	6,712	579	49.3	29.0	8.7	11.3	20.0	1.7
2012 ...	16,160	9,269	3,102	3,344	6,446	551	49.8	28.6	9.6	10.3	19.9	1.7
2013 ...	16,003	9,132	3,125	3,130	6,255	557	50.1	28.6	9.8	9.8	19.6	1.7
2014 ...	15,378	8,377	2,816	2,565	5,380	548	51.8	28.2	9.5	8.6	18.1	1.8
2015 ...	15,331	7,351	2,915	2,236	5,151	462	54.2	26.0	10.3	7.9	18.2	1.6
2016 ...	16,495	7,698	2,886	2,543	5,428	494	54.8	25.6	9.6	8.4	18.0	1.6
2017 ...	16,771	8,611	2,988	2,784	5,773	550	52.9	27.2	9.4	8.8	18.2	1.7
2018 ...	16,637	9,167	3,153	3,024	6,177	538	51.2	28.2	9.7	9.3	19.0	1.7
2019 ...	16,298	9,819	3,224	2,784	6,414	539	49.3	29.7	9.7	8.4	19.4	1.6

[1] Totals and percentages based on unrounded data and may not equal sum of classes due to rounding.
NASS, Livestock Branch, (202) 720-3570.

Table 7-18.—Cattle and calves: Average dressed weight under Federal inspection, 2010–2019[1]

Year	Cattle					Calves
	All cattle	Steers	Heifers	Cows	Bulls	
	Pounds					
2010	773	835	768	607	875	154
2011	773	841	773	596	868	154
2012	790	859	792	608	877	152
2013	796	863	794	620	880	146
2014	808	872	800	627	898	166
2015	829	892	818	644	915	183
2016	829	891	822	643	901	155
2017	817	877	812	642	896	145
2018	818	880	817	645	889	130
2019	813	878	813	639	878	127

[1] Excludes postmortem condemnations.
NASS, Livestock Branch, (202) 720-3570.

Table 7-19.—Beef cows: Inventory Jan 1, 2018 and 2019, and number of operations, 2017, by State and United States [1]

State	January 1 beef cow inventory		Operations with beef cows [2]
	2018	2019	2017
	1,000 head	*1,000 head*	*Number*
Alabama	714.0	705.0	20,004.0
Alaska	6.1	6.8	92.0
Arizona	200.0	215.0	5,560.0
Arkansas	924.0	935.0	23,036.0
California	670.0	630.0	10,254.0
Colorado	812.0	792.0	12,407.0
Connecticut	5.0	4.5	860.0
Delaware	2.5	2.0	235.0
Florida	886.0	914.0	18,493.0
Georgia	485.0	499.0	14,869.0
Hawaii	75.0	75.5	1,047.0
Idaho	510.0	506.0	8,149.0
Illinois	397.0	405.0	13,139.0
Indiana	208.0	204.0	11,753.0
Iowa	950.0	930.0	19,171.0
Kansas	1,504.0	1,529.0	23,682.0
Kentucky	1,033.0	1,017.0	33,864.0
Louisana	473.0	459.0	12,051.0
Maine	10.0	11.0	1,141.0
Maryland	46.0	50.0	2,486.0
Massachusetts	6.5	7.0	879.0
Michigan	102.0	108.0	7,445.0
Minnesota	365.0	370.0	13,339.0
Mississippi	501.0	477.0	14,752.0
Missouri	2,086.0	2,059.0	48,122.0
Montana	1,497.0	1,448.0	10,290.0
Nebraska	1,910.0	1,941.0	17,707.0
Nevada	238.0	242.0	1,356.0
New Hampshire	4.5	4.0	602.0
New Jersey	9.0	9.5	941.0
New Mexico	483.0	480.0	8,991.0
New York	105.0	105.0	7,310.0
North Carolina	370.0	367.0	16,407.0
North Dakota	964.0	975.0	8,245.0
Ohio	296.0	307.0	17,733.0
Oklahoma	2,088.0	2,150.0	46,080.0
Oregon	536.0	535.0	11,548.0
Pennsylvania	215.0	225.0	13,176.0
Rhode Island	1.6	1.4	163.0
South Carolina	174.0	186.0	6,917.0
South Dakota	1,751.0	1,818.0	12,613.0
Tennessee	910.0	914.0	32,960.0
Texas	4,520.0	4,655.0	134,250.0
Utah	000.0	340.0	6,508.0
Vermont	15.0	14.0	1,399.0
Virginia	633.0	631.0	18,453.0
Washington	235.0	230.0	9,295.0
West Virginia	203.0	198.0	10,336.0
Wisconsin	285.0	290.0	13,954.0
Wyoming	714.0	714.0	4,902.0
United States	31,466.2	31,690.7	729,046.0

[1] An operation is any place having one or more beef cows on hand on December 31. [2] State level estimates only available in conjunction with the Census of Agriculture every 5 years.

NASS, Livestock Branch, (202) 720–3570.

Table 7-20.—Hogs and pigs: Inventory and value, Dec. 1, 2018–2019, and number of operations, 2017, by State and United States

State	Inventory		Value				Operations [1]
			Value per head		Total value		
	2018	2019	2018	2019	2018	2019	2017
	Thousands	*Thousands*	*Dollars*	*Dollars*	*1,000 dollars*	*1,000 dollars*	*Number*
Alabama	33.0	36.0	112	110	3,696	3,960	1,074
Alaska	1.9	1.9	221	220	420	418	64
Arizona	170.0	161.0	115	110	19,550	17,710	521
Arkansas	130.0	117.0	110	105	14,300	12,285	1,021
California	101.0	106.0	145	145	14,645	15,370	1,389
Colorado	750.0	760.0	110	105	82,500	78,750	1,227
Connecticut	3.7	4.0	145	145	537	580	214
Delaware	6.5	7.0	110	110	715	770	55
Florida	13.0	10.0	110	112	1,430	1,120	1,810
Georgia	72.0	62.0	100	100	7,200	6,200	1,091
Hawaii	9.0	11.0	170	170	1,530	1,870	226
Idaho	32.0	35.0	110	110	3,520	3,850	606
Illinois	5,400.0	5,500.0	97	102	523,800	545,700	2,153
Indiana	4,250.0	4,450.0	97	102	412,250	438,600	2,570
Iowa	23,600.0	25,100.0	96	102	2,265,600	2,529,600	5,660
Kansas	2,050.0	2,160.0	100	102	205,000	214,000	943
Kentucky	285.0	435.0	95	93	27,075	40,455	1,805
Louisiana	6.0	6.0	112	110	672	660	874
Maine	4.4	4.6	120	120	528	552	429
Maryland	19.0	20.0	120	120	2,280	2,400	562
Massachusetts	8.0	8.0	105	105	840	840	337
Michigan	1,180.0	1,240.0	95	99	112,100	120,780	2,017
Minnesota	9,100.0	9,500.0	97	102	882,700	938,400	3,225
Mississippi	190.0	190.0	108	106	20,520	20,140	784
Missouri	3,650.0	3,400.0	99	103	361,350	334,750	2,687
Montana	192.0	210.0	113	113	21,696	23,730	452
Nebraska	3,550.0	3,850.0	100	103	355,000	386,250	1,230
Nevada	6.0	5.0	121	120	726	600	70
New Hampshire	3.5	3.4	115	115	403	391	281
New Jersey	8.5	7.5	120	120	1,020	900	347
New Mexico	1.3	2.0	115	115	150	230	353
New York	46.0	53.0	105	105	4,830	5,565	1,739
North Carolina	9,200.0	9,500.0	91	96	837,200	883,200	2,426
North Dakota	145.0	142.0	103	100	14,935	14,200	156
Ohio	2,550.0	2,950.0	103	104	272,850	291,200	3,484
Oklahoma	2,200.0	2,280.0	120	116	264,000	263,320	2,264
Oregon	9.0	11.0	115	115	1,035	1,265	1,177
Pennsylvania	1,310.0	1,330.0	95	100	124,450	131,300	2,777
Rhode Island	1.7	1.6	120	120	204	192	60
South Carolina	210.0	195.0	96	95	20,160	18,525	1,005
South Dakota	1,750.0	2,010.0	100	102	175,000	202,980	571
Tennessee	225.0	250.0	91	93	20,475	23,250	1,898
Texas	1,110.0	1,140.0	115	114	127,650	128,820	5,894
Utah	710.0	960.0	105	105	74,550	100,800	561
Vermont	3.7	3.6	135	135	500	486	353
Virginia	345.0	340.0	94	96	32,430	32,640	1,461
Washington	17.0	17.0	115	115	1,955	1,955	1,126
West Virginia	4.0	3.0	112	105	448	315	892
Wisconsin	320.0	340.0	97	101	31,040	36,865	2,198
Wyoming	88.0	94.0	105	110	9,240	10,340	320
United States	75,070.2	79,047.6	98	102	7,356,703	7,888,779	66,439

(D) Withheld to avoid disclosing data for individual operations. [1] State level estimates only available in conjunction with the Census of Agriculture every 5 years. An operation is any place having one or more hogs and pigs on hand December 31. Totals may not add due to rounding.

NASS, Livestock Branch, (202) 720–3570.

Table 7-21.—Hogs and pigs: Operations, inventory and value, United States, Dec. 1, 2010–2019

Year	Inventory	Value	
		Per head	Total
	Thousands	*Dollars*	*1,000 dollars*
2010	64,725	106.00	6,880,179
2011	66,259	123.00	8,145,169
2012	66,224	116.00	7,683,152
2013	64,775	138.00	8,920,314
2014	67,626	144.00	9,731,521
2015	69,019	96.00	6,635,688
2016	71,345	92.00	6,578,419
2017	73,145	99.00	7,206,965
2018	75,070	98.00	7,356,703
2019	79,048	102.00	7,888,779

NASS, Livestock Branch, (202) 720–3570.

Table 7-22.—Sows farrowing and pig crop: Number, United States 2010-2019

Year	Sows farrowing		Pig crop		
	Dec.-May	June-Nov.	Dec.-May	June-Nov.	Total
	Thousands	*Thousands*	*Thousands*	*Thousands*	*Thousands*
2010	5,749	5,824	55,770	57,358	113,128
2011	5,694	5,846	56,469	58,616	115,085
2012	5,759	5,810	57,749	58,906	116,655
2013	5,595	5,670	57,020	58,115	115,135
2014	5,573	5,975	53,821	60,933	114,754
2015	5,749	5,949	59,219	62,221	121,441
2016	5,898	6,098	61,256	64,651	125,907
2017	6,008	6,209	63,026	66,403	129,429
2018	6,041	6,377	64,053	68,515	132,568
2019	6,233	6,540	67,617	72,575	140,192

NASS, Livestock Branch, (202) 720–3570.

Table 7-23.—Hogs and pigs: Number for breeding and market, United States, 2010–2019

Year	All hogs and pigs	Kept for breeding	Market hogs by weight groups				
			Under 50 pounds	50 to 119 pounds	120 to 179 pounds	180 pounds and over	Total
	June 1						
	Thousands	*Thousands*	*Thousands*	*Thousands*	*Thousands*	*Thousands*	*Thousands*
2010	64,650	5,788	19,224	16,832	12,154	10,653	58,862
2011	65,320	5,803	19,423	17,241	12,254	10,599	60,517
2012	66,469	5,862	19,746	17,924	12,243	10,694	60,607
2013	65,188	5,884	19,145	17,068	12,414	10,678	59,304
2014	61,468	5,855	18,254	15,801	11,471	10,086	55,613
2015	67,065	5,926	19,365	17,461	12,935	11,379	61,140
2016	69,281	5,979	20,356	18,198	13,291	11,456	63,302
2017	71,210	6,109	20,647	18,841	13,696	11,917	65,101
2018	72,231	6,320	21,081	18,846	13,898	12,085	65,911
2019	75,725	6,109	22,210	19,693	14,396	13,017	69,316
	Dec. 1						
	Thousands	*Thousands*	*Thousands*	*Thousands*	*Thousands*	*Thousands*	*Thousands*
2010	64,725	5,778	18,864	16,519	12,183	11,381	58,947
2011	66,259	5,803	19,447	16,618	12,473	11,918	60,456
2012	66,224	5,819	19,299	16,752	12,614	11,741	60,405
2013	64,775	5,757	18,389	16,080	12,576	11,972	59,018
2014	67,626	5,939	19,746	17,296	13,000	11,646	61,688
2015	69,019	6,002	20,038	17,262	13,440	12,276	63,017
2016	71,345	6,110	20,862	18,077	13,711	12,585	65,235
2017	73,145	6,179	21,407	18,544	13,925	13,089	66,966
2018	75,020	6,326	21,858	19,369	14,323	13,195	68,745
2019	79,048	6,471	22,648	20,691	15,321	13,916	72,577

NASS, Livestock Branch, (202) 720–3570.

Table 7-24.—Cattle and swine: Production, 2018–2020

Country	2018	2019	2020
	1,000 head		
Cattle:			
India	68,600	69,000	69,400
Brazil	49,500	50,490	51,500
China	47,500	48,500	49,500
United States	36,403	36,300	36,200
European Union	28,800	28,350	28,300
Argentina	14,650	14,780	14,900
Australia	9,100	8,700	8,300
Mexico	7,700	7,900	8,105
Russia	6,566	6,590	6,650
New Zealand	4,895	4,915	4,875
Canada	4,292	4,325	4,400
Uruguay	2,750	2,700	2,810
Ukraine	2,104	2,020	1,950
Egypt	1,930	1,940	1,940
Belarus	1,400	1,400	1,400
Japan	1,224	1,225	1,230
Korea, South	968	991	1,028
Turkey	3,930	0	0
Swine:			
China	685,000	490,000	412,000
European Union	267,000	266,500	270,000
United States	132,568	138,032	142,790
Russia	49,500	50,915	52,600
Brazil	40,954	42,500	44,000
Canada	28,027	28,450	28,900
Mexico	18,750	19,600	20,200
Korea, South	19,118	19,530	19,415
Japan	16,690	17,000	17,030
Ukraine	8,816	8,740	8,750
Belarus	5,050	4,825	4,725

FAS, Office of Global Analysis, (202) 720-6301. Prepared or estimated on the basis of official USDA production, supply, and distribution statistics from foreign governments.

Table 7-25.—Hogs: Number slaughtered, United States, 2010–2019

Year	Commercial			Farm	Total
	Federally inspected	Other	Total [1]		
	Thousands				
2010	109,315	945	110,260	107	110,367
2011	109,956	904	110,860	96	110,956
2012	112,265	898	113,163	83	113,247
2013	111,248	829	112,077	84	112,161
2014	106,123	753	106,876	82	106,958
2015	114,616	810	115,425	87	115,512
2016	117,388	832	118,220	84	118,304
2017	120,516	801	121,317	73	121,390
2018	123,693	739	124,432	76	124,508
2019	129,211	702	129,913	73	129,989

[1] Totals are based on unrounded number.
NASS, Livestock Branch, (202) 720-3570.

Table 7-26.—Sows farrowing and pig crop: Number by State and United States, 2018–2019

State	Sows farrowing							
	December [1]–February		March–May		June–August		September–November	
	2018	2019	2018	2019	2018	2019	2018	2019
	Thousands							
Colorado	72	78	75	78	79	79	75	76
Illinois	254	270	275	275	265	290	280	285
Indiana	130	125	110	120	125	120	130	125
Iowa	530	530	550	530	575	550	570	540
Kansas	79	86	76	86	87	90	85	92
Michigan	53	56	52	54	57	55	54	56
Minnesota	290	300	305	295	300	300	310	310
Missouri	220	245	240	242	255	260	255	265
Nebraska	180	185	190	200	185	194	195	195
North Carolina	445	455	455	460	485	500	475	480
Ohio	91	93	88	98	89	102	99	104
Oklahoma	200	205	205	215	210	230	205	220
Pennsylvania	48	55	50	54	51	51	52	57
South Dakota	113	119	110	123	117	129	127	138
Texas	55	66	64	66	68	71	67	68
Utah	36	40	34	43	39	44	37	41
Other States [2]	181	191	185	194	185	210	189	213
United States [3]	2,977	3,099	3,064	3,133	3,172	3,275	3,205	3,265

State	Pig crop							
	December [1]–February		March–May		June–August		September–November	
	2018	2019	2018	2019	2018	2019	2018	2019
	Thousands							
Colorado	698	718	720	835	751	845	720	806
Illinois	2,692	2,876	2,943	2,956	2,822	3,176	2,982	3,121
Indiana	1,359	1,275	1,133	1,284	1,313	1,320	1,378	1,313
Iowa	5,830	5,936	6,105	6,069	6,440	6,243	6,384	6,129
Kansas	806	912	768	920	948	981	927	989
Michigan	567	610	567	594	616	611	567	608
Minnesota	3,248	3,480	3,416	3,496	3,345	3,585	3,534	3,674
Missouri	2,233	2,585	2,448	2,577	2,665	2,886	2,703	2,942
Nebraska	2,106	2,137	2,147	2,300	2,091	2,260	2,233	2,282
North Carolina	4,406	4,505	4,596	4,830	4,996	5,250	4,821	5,064
Ohio	983	995	968	1,098	970	1,153	1,049	1,186
Oklahoma	2,120	2,183	2,194	2,268	2,237	2,507	2,173	2,387
Pennsylvania	509	594	525	599	546	576	579	630
South Dakota	1,294	1,410	1,207	1,470	1,299	1,529	1,480	1,656
Texas	545	673	627	693	687	774	697	707
Utah	277	368	258	460	429	484	370	472
Other States [2]	1,824	1,906	1,854	2,005	1,864	2,189	1,906	2,231
United States [3]	31,497	33,163	32,556	34,454	34,019	36,369	34,496	36,205

[1] December preceding year. [2] Individual State estimates not available for the 34 other States. [3] Totals may not add due to rounding.

NASS, Livestock Branch, (202) 720–3570.

Table 7-27.—Hogs: Production, disposition, cash receipts, and gross income, United States, 2010–2019

Year	Marketings [1]	Inshipments [2]	Farm slaughter [3]	Production (live weight) [4]	Value of production [5]	Cash receipts [6]	Value of home consumption	Gross income	Average price per 100 pounds received by farmers
	1,000 head	*1,000 head*	*1,000 head*	*1,000 pounds*	*1,000 dollars*	*1,000 dollars*	*1,000 dollars*	*1,000 dollars*	*Dollars*
2010	144,362	40,004	107	30,284,630	16,012,200	17,898,063	38,306	17,936,369	55.10
2011	145,420	40,522	96	30,836,171	20,014,277	21,631,894	44,004	21,675,898	66.50
2012	151,835	44,027	83	32,060,619	20,285,027	22,092,108	40,007	22,132,115	64.20
2013	154,923	47,864	73	32,524,986	21,611,356	23,706,457	37,428	23,743,885	67.20
2014	149,097	47,185	82	32,126,235	24,183,766	26,489,394	43,550	26,532,944	77.10
2015	159,724	50,146	87	34,739,292	18,814,459	20,552,958	31,982	20,584,940	53.50
2016	165,538	52,954	84	35,898,712	17,363,044	19,037,752	28,797	19,066,549	49.60
2017	171,320	55,266	73	36,962,875	19,159,248	21,038,034	29,273	21,067,307	53.60
2018	180,251	61,619	76	38,498,011	18,769,964	20,881,335	27,267	20,908,602	49.90
2019	187,648	63,297	76	40,509,010	19,826,838	22,015,189	28,146	22,043,335	51.90

[1] Includes custom slaughter for use on farms where produced and State outshipments, but excludes interfarm sales within the State. [2] Includes hogs and pigs shipped in from other states but excludes animals for immediate slaughter. [3] Excludes custom slaughter for farmers at commercial establishments. [4] Adjustments made for changes in inventory and for inshipments. [5] Includes allowance for higher average price of State inshipments and outshipments of feeder pigs. [6] Receipts from marketings and sale of farm slaughter.
NASS Livestock Branch, (202) 720–3570.

Table 7-28.—Hogs: Direct receipts at interior markets, 2010–2019

Year	All receipts (live and carcass basis)			
	National	Iowa/ Southern Minnesota [1]	Western Region	Eastern Region
	Thousands	*Thousands*	*Thousands*	*Thousands*
2010	75,104	40,143	48,413	22,896
2011	75,514	41,479	49,649	22,643
2012	75,459	42,343	50,607	22,192
2013	71,599	40,744	48,202	20,929
2014	73,182	41,687	49,180	21,341
2015	78,212	44,997	53,076	22,298
2016	80,716	26,315	32,247	15,922
	Number	*Number*	*Number*	*Number*
2017	2,912,345	1,607,503	1,763,741	1,145,350
2018	3,163,846	1,675,816	1,521,595	1,068,483
2019 [2]	2,845,278	(NA)	(NA)	(NA)

(NA) Not available. [1] Iowa / Southern Minnesota is a subset of the Western Region. [2] Due to confidentiality rules, these numbers are now only tracked on a national basis.
AMS, Livestock & Grain Market News, (202) 720–7316.

Table 7-29.—Hogs and corn: Hog-corn price ratio and average price received by farmers for corn, United States, 2010–2019 [1] [2]

Year	Hog-corn price ratio [1]	Price of corn per bushel [2]
		Dollars
2010	14.4	3.83
2011	11.0	6.02
2012	9.6	6.67
2013	11.3	6.15
2014	18.9	4.11
2015	14.5	3.70
2016	14.2	3.48
2017	15.9	3.36
2018	14.4	3.47
2019	13.8	3.75

[1] Number of bushels of corn equal in value to buy 100 pounds of live hogs at local markets, based on average prices received by farmers for hogs and corn. Annual average is a simple average of monthly ratios for the calendar year. [2] Annual average is a simple average of monthly prices for the calendar year.
NASS, Environmental, Economics, and Demographics Branch, (202) 720–6146.

Table 7-30.—Hogs: Production, disposition, cash receipts, and gross income, by State and United States, 2019

State	Marketings [1]	Inshipments [2]	Farm slaughter [3]	Production (live weight) [4]	Value of production [5]	Cash receipts [5] [6]	Value of home consumption	Gross income
	1,000 head	*1,000 head*	*1,000 head*	*1,000 pounds*	*1,000 dollars*	*1,000 dollars*	*1,000 dollars*	*1,000 dollars*
Alabama	211.0	43.0	0.5	27,958	16,595	20,170	283	18,369
Alaska	3.2	1.3	0.8	982	539	324	109	615
Arizona	276.5	3.0	1.0	67,654	39,957	36,790	294	40,853
Arkansas	1,040.0	21.0	1.0	65,205	51,980	60,345	392	57,411
California	181.0	144.0	3.0	39,830	18,393	27,453	612	27,191
Colorado	3,208.0	140.0	2.0	293,229	176,024	140,519	302	183,910
Connecticut	5.2	1.2	0.1	1,384	672	397	25	693
Delaware	40.0	1.0	0.1	9,869	5,084	3,808	47	5,058
Florida	31.5	9.0	0.5	3,729	1,994	1,836	150	2,415
Georgia	552.0	202.0	2.0	57,982	30,776	39,986	538	36,827
Hawaii	1.7	0.1	1.6	1,044	613	485	180	478
Idaho	108.1	29.2	1.0	28,333	15,854	16,056	294	17,268
Illinois	12,880.0	1,394.0	3.0	2,196,434	1,184,193	1,209,683	825	1,228,867
Indiana	10,063.0	5,493.0	2.0	2,235,725	1,029,649	1,199,559	839	1,239,617
Iowa	54,732.0	35,800.0	5.0	14,455,917	6,651,649	7,616,470	2,099	7,772,961
Kansas	5,245.0	2,023.0	1.0	1,048,275	485,277	518,816	429	549,481
Kentucky	1,003.0	243.0	4.0	194,995	110,057	114,816	1,208	115,567
Louisiana	6.0	4.0	0.5	919	509	865	71	689
Maine	5.8	1.5	0.1	1,436	686	1,088	58	792
Maryland	48.1	13.5	0.1	9,917	4,839	6,809	38	5,939
Massachusetts	15.0	2.5	0.1	3,236	1,608	1,825	25	1,673
Michigan	2,476.0	198.0	2.0	635,011	325,244	502,505	590	330,083
Minnesota	22,302.0	9,600.0	3.0	4,777,656	2,328,552	2,514,681	1,202	2,724,246
Mississippi	995.0	4.0	4.0	61,289	41,421	59,299	695	41,783
Missouri	12,240.9	1,548.9	2.0	1,656,302	866,479	788,932	1,060	927,228
Montana	668.0	5.0	2.0	120,614	69,822	56,717	476	70,255
Nebraska	8,805.0	604.0	3.0	1,509,174	853,620	813,183	1,352	873,673
Nevada	3.4	2.3	0.1	648	289	181	28	530
New Hampshire	6.2	1.5	0.1	1,656	796	866	73	883
New Jersey	13.4	7.5	0.1	1,027	229	616	76	743
New Mexico	5.9	3.8	0.2	957	464	680	52	614
New York	88.3	54.0	0.5	1,432	2,285	6,851	224	6,374
North Carolina	17,968.0	660.0	1.0	4,361,099	2,076,752	2,129,121	020	2,174,162
North Dakota	937.6	143.1	0.3	44,904	41,872	56,962	84	60,660
Ohio	4,916.0	1,100.0	6.0	1,331,230	623,182	667,969	2,973	677,872
Oklahoma	9,433.0	725.0	2.0	2,035,654	921,129	938,522	408	976,075
Oregon	7.3	1.0	1.0	2,170	1,849	1,624	283	1,180
Pennsylvania	2,402.7	225.0	3.3	642,821	272,183	275,440	787	330,148
Rhode Island	2.6	0.1	0.1	638	277	275	22	322
South Carolina	215.0	77.0	1.0	40,077	17,800	17,153	873	24,115
South Dakota	6,860.0	1,250.0	2.0	1,153,511	530,360	585,716	1,385	731,000
Tennessee	640.0	170.0	2.0	100,004	72,280	79,520	574	89,496
Texas	3,232.0	685.0	6.0	487,749	225,405	230,092	2,151	244,389
Utah	1,413.8	73.3	0.5	292,364	128,244	123,783	136	166,359
Vermont	6.1	1.0	0.2	1,624	1,057	1,095	91	867
Virginia	451.0	430.0	2.0	109,527	29,561	43,580	647	61,929
Washington	25.9	1.5	1.0	6,706	4,270	3,972	416	4,016
West Virginia	6.0	0.4	0.2	1,549	750	795	102	885
Wisconsin	1,158.5	155.0	1.0	218,375	112,135	122,706	683	150,741
Wyoming	704.0	1.0	1.0	108,809	57,287	57,122	307	65,674
United States	187,647.7	63,296.7	76.0	40,509,010	19,060,203	21,098,058	21,794	22,043,335

- Represents zero. (D)Withheld to avoid disclosing data for individual operations. [1] Includes custom slaughter for use on farms where produced and State outshipments,but excludes interfarm sales within the State. [2] Includes hogs and pigs shipped in from other states but excludes animals for immediate slaughter. [3] Excludes custom slaughter for farmers at commercial establishments. [4] Adjustments made for changes in inventory and for inshipments. [5] Includes allowance for higher average price of State inshipments and outshipments of feeder pigs. [6] Receipts from marketings and sale of farm-slaughter.

NASS, Livestock Branch, (202) 720–3570.

Table 7-31.—Hogs: Number slaughtered commercially, total and average live weight, by State and United States, 2018[1]

State	Number slaughtered	Total live weight[2]	Average live weight[2]
	Thousands	*1,000 pounds*	*Pounds*
Alabama	37.9	15,514	410
Alaska	1.4	377	269
Arizona	(D)	(D)	(D)
Arkansas	7.2	1,916	266
California	2,133.4	539,959	253
Colorado	20.1	4,933	245
Delaware & Maryland	19.3	5,022	261
Florida	59.0	7,369	125
Georgia	63.6	15,468	243
Hawaii	4.6	1,135	246
Idaho	167.6	44,741	267
Illinois	12,242.9	3,494,184	285
Indiana	8,573.9	2,373,289	277
Iowa	35,033.5	9,908,595	283
Kansas	(D)	(D)	(D)
Kentucky	(D)	(D)	(D)
Louisiana	9.3	1,994	215
Michigan	2,439.2	711,942	292
Minnesota	11,846.5	3,246,540	274
Mississippi	37.6	6,109	163
Missouri	9,049.3	2,612,590	289
Montana	16.8	4,662	277
Nebraska	7,873.1	2,216,027	282
Nevada	1.1	295	267
New England[3]	35.3	9,287	264
New Jersey	102.7	10,222	100
New Mexico	2.6	698	270
New York	28.2	6,771	240
North Carolina	(D)	(D)	(D)
North Dakota	4.0	1,175	292
Ohio	896.1	253,597	284
Oklahoma	5,622.0	1,561,561	278
Oregon	166.3	44,317	267
Pennsylvania	3,351.2	923,584	276
South Carolina	33.9	8,157	241
South Dakota	(D)	(D)	(D)
Tennessee	803.8	363,307	453
Texas	291.4	71,968	247
Utah	58.4	10,286	177
Virginia	(D)	(D)	(D)
Washington	12.1	3,137	259
West Virginia	8.8	2,513	285
Wisconsin	732.3	319,256	437
Wyoming	3.6	964	267
United States[4]	124,435.3	35,232,964	283

(D) Withheld to avoid disclosing data for individual operations. [1] Includes slaughter in federally inspected and other slaughter plants; excludes animals slaughtered on farms. Average live weight is based on unrounded numbers. Totals may not add due to rounding. [2] Excludes postmortem condemnations. [3] Connecticut, Maine, Massachusetts, New Hampshire, Rhode Island, and Vermont. [4] States with no data printed are still included in US total. Data are not printed to avoid disclosing individual operations.

NASS, Livestock Branch, (202) 720-3570.

Table 7-32.—Hogs: Number slaughtered, average dressed and live weights, Federally inspected, 2010–2019[1]

Year	Federally inspected					
	Barrows and gilts			Sows		
	Head	Percent of total	Avg. dressed weight[2]	Head	Percent of total	Avg. dressed weight[2]
	1,000		*Pounds*	*1,000*		*Pounds*
2010	105,983	97.0	201	2,966	2.7	305
2011	106,600	96.9	203	3,027	2.8	305
2012	108,912	97.0	203	3,009	2.7	306
2013	107,965	97.0	205	2,932	2.6	304
2014	102,998	97.1	212	2,788	2.6	305
2015	111,488	97.3	210	2,852	2.5	309
2016	114,184	97.3	209	2,885	2.5	310
2017	117,195	97.2	209	2,952	2.4	308
2018	120,303	97.3	209	3,015	2.4	305
2019	125,844	97.3	211	3,015	2.4	305

Year	Boars			Total		
	Head	Percent of total	Avg. dressed weight[2]	Head	Avg. dressed weight[2]	Avg. live weight[2]
	1,000		*Pounds*	*1,000*	*Pounds*	*Pounds*
2009	419	0.4	199	112,613	203	271
2010	366	0.3	200	109,315	204	273
2011	329	0.3	210	109,956	206	275
2012	344	0.3	208	112,265	206	275
2013	351	0.3	204	111,248	207	277
2014	337	0.3	204	106,123	214	285
2015	276	0.2	207	114,616	213	283
2016	319	0.3	206	117,388	211	282
2017	370	0.3	201	120,516	211	283
2018	376	0.3	192	123,696	212	283

[1] All weights calculated using unrounded totals. Totals and percentages based on unrounded data and may not equal sum of classes due to rounding. [2] Excludes postmortem condemnations.
NASS, Livestock Branch, (202) 720-3570.

Table 7-33.—Lard: Supply and disappearance, United States, 2009–2018

Calendar year	Supply				Disappearance		
	Stocks Jan 1	Production	Imports	Total	Domestic	Exports	Total
	Million lbs	*Million lbs*	*Million lbs*	*Million lbs*	*Million lbs*	*Million lbs*	*Million lbs*
2009	12	860	17	889	788	83	871
2010	18	840	15	873	776	72	847
2011	26	852	13	891	794	77	871
2012	20	871	14	905	830	55	885
2013	20	867	14	901	820	61	881
2014	20	857	16	894	822	52	874
2015	20	902	14	936	881	47	928
2016	9	932	10	951	901	42	943
2017	8	959	13	980	935	38	973
2018	7	987	15	1,008	965	37	1,002

ERS, Market and Trade Economics Division, Field Crops Branch, (202) 694–5300.

Table 7-34.—Lard: United States exports by country of destination, 2017–2019

Country	2017	2018	2019
	Metric tons		
Mexico	15,876	16,173	22,115
Canada	605	264	259
Ireland	97	98	63
Marshall Islands	153	118	55
Singapore	0	12	10
Micronesia	5	4	3
Argentina	4	0	0
Brazil	18	1	0
Chile	0	14	0
Dominican Republic	1	0	0
Guatemala	29	0	0
Guyana	0	24	0
Japan	43	0	0
Korea, South	346	0	0
Norway(*)	0	72	0
Netherlands Antilles(*)	4	2	0
Philippines	0	37	0
Spain	0	5	0
Leeward-Windward Islands(*)	0	3	0
World Total	17,181	16,825	22,506

(*) Denotes a country that is a summarization of its component countries.
FAS, Office of Global Analysis, (202) 720-6301. Data Source: U.S. Census Bureau Trade Data,as of March 17, 2020.

Table 7-35.—Sheep and lambs: Inventory and value, United States, Jan. 1, 2009–2018

Year	Inventory	Value	
		Per head	Total
	1,000 head	Dollars	1,000 dollars
2009	5,747	133.00	765,194
2010	5,620	135.00	761,115
2011	5,470	170.00	929,453
2012	5,375	221.00	1,187,730
2013	5,360	177.00	951,020
2014	5,235	188.00	982,316
2015	5,270	214.00	1,127,157
2016	5,295	202.00	1,071,467
2017	5,270	203.00	1,067,857
2018	5,265	204.00	1,071,378

NASS, Livestock Branch, (202) 720–3570.

Table 7-36.—Sheep and lambs: Number by class, United States, Jan. 1, 2009–2018

Year	All sheep and lambs	Breeding sheep			
		Total [1]	Replacement lambs	1 year and over	
				Ewes	Rams
	1,000 head	1,000 head	1,000 head	1,000 head	1,000 head
2009	5,747	4,247	647	3,405	196
2010	5,620	4,185	655	3,335	195
2011	5,470	4,070	665	3,215	190
2012	5,375	3,995	660	3,165	170
2013	5,360	3,985	670	3,135	180
2014	5,235	3,890	635	3,080	175
2015	5,270	3,925	650	3,100	175
2016	5,295	3,940	665	3,100	175
2017	5,270	3,894	666	3,058	170
2018	5,265	3,865	662	3,033	170

[1] Categories may not add to total due to rounding.
NASS, Livestock Branch, (202) 720–3570.

Table 7-37.—Lamb mutton, goat, etc. meat: U.S. imports, 2017–2019

Country	2017	2018	2019
	Metric tons		
Australia(*)	92,426	97,356	100,917
New Zealand(*)	28,034	26,010	24,465
Canada	1,103	1,200	1,031
Mexico	169	370	917
Chile	1,038	539	504
Uruguay	14	197	188
Iceland	227	203	1
China	0	26	0
Denmark(*)	0	-	0
Mozambique	0	19	0
World Total	123,010	125,919	128,022

(*) Denotes a country that is a summarization of its component countries. Users should use cautious interpretation on quantity reports using mixed units of measure. Quantity line items will only include statistics on the units of measure that are equal to, or are able to be converted to, the assigned unit of measure of the grouped commodities.
FAS, Office of Global Analysis, (202) 720-6301. Data Source: U.S. Census Bureau Trade Data.

Table 7-38.—Breeding sheep: Number by class, State and United States, Jan. 1, 2017–2018

State	Under one year old		One year and over			
	Replacement lambs		Ewes		Rams	
	2017	2018	2017	2018	2017	2018
	1,000 head					
Arizona	23.0	18.0	68.0	67.0	6.0	5.0
California	45.0	45.0	275.0	260.0	10.0	10.0
Colorado	34.0	33.0	160.0	156.0	6.0	6.0
Idaho	41.0	39.0	138.0	141.0	5.0	5.0
Illinois	8.0	8.0	36.0	36.0	2.0	2.0
Indiana	7.0	8.0	38.0	38.0	4.0	4.0
Iowa	20.0	19.0	95.0	91.0	5.0	5.0
Kansas	7.0	0.0	36.0	34.0	2.0	2.0
Kentucky	7.0	8.0	33.0	36.0	2.0	2.0
Michigan	14.0	13.0	44.0	41.0	3.0	3.0
Minnesota	14.0	12.0	72.0	74.0	5.0	4.0
Missouri	13.0	14.0	59.0	63.0	3.0	3.0
Montana	35.0	39.0	159.0	150.0	6.0	6.0
Nebraska	10.0	9.0	58.0	55.0	3.0	3.0
Nevada	9.0	9.0	43.0	43.0	2.0	2.0
New England [1]	8.0	8.0	27.0	30.0	2.0	2.0
New Mexico	18.0	16.0	59.0	58.0	5.0	6.0
New York	13.0	13.0	51.0	55.0	3.0	3.0
North Carolina	4.0	3.0	19.0	16.0	2.0	2.0
North Dakota	8.0	8.0	42.0	39.0	2.0	2.0
Ohio	16.0	16.0	70.0	73.0	6.0	6.0
Oklahoma	7.0	8.0	29.0	31.0	2.0	3.0
Oregon	18.0	20.0	101.0	94.0	5.0	6.0
Pennsylvania	11.0	13.0	59.0	60.0	5.0	5.0
South Dakota	31.0	31.0	146.0	153.0	6.0	6.0
Tennessee	6.0	7.0	29.0	29.0	3.0	2.0
Texas	95.0	100.0	440.0	465.0	35.0	35.0
Utah	42.0	42.0	205.0	200.0	8.0	8.0
Virginia	9.0	9.0	49.0	45.0	3.0	3.0
Washington	9.0	6.0	28.0	27.0	2.0	2.0
West Virginia	4.0	4.0	23.0	23.0	1.0	1.0
Wisconsin	12.0	12.0	48.0	48.0	3.0	3.0
Wyoming	43.0	43.0	225.0	210.0	7.0	7.0
Other States [2]	25.0	23.0	94.0	92.0	6.0	6.0
United States	666.0	662.0	3,058.0	3,033.0	170.0	170.0

[1] New England includes Connecticut, Maine, Massachusetts, New Hampshire, Rhode Island, and Vermont. [2] Individual state estimates not available for states not shown, but are included in Other States.
NASS, Livestock Branch, (202) 720–3570.

Table 7-39.—Sheep and lambs: Average price per 100 pounds at San Angelo, 2010–2019 [1]

Year	Sheep			Slaughter lambs choice & prime			
				Wooled		Shorn	
	Good	Utility	Cull	90-110 lbs	110-130 1bs	90-110 lbs	110-130 1bs
2010	59.51	59.50	41.12	114.66	115.12	115.18	115.68
2011	66.22	66.62	41.43	161.09	161.08	161.53	161.24
2012	64.30	65.80	42.84	113.64	114.01	114.56	114.68
2013	47.68	49.68	28.21	107.34	107.50	107.44	107.69
2014	65.66	67.88	43.76	157.08	157.14	157.19	157.30
2015	79.11	80.63	54.70	143.97	143.97	144.02	144.12
2016	72.12	75.37	45.63	135.18	135.28	135.24	135.58
2017	76.86	77.14	47.63	140.98	140.74	141.07	141.01
2018	65.13	67.16	40.52	126.58	125.48	134.63	133.50
2019	72.96	74.84	42.64	133.03	133.71	133.03	133.67

[1] Simple average of monthly bulk-of-sales prices from data of the livestock reporting service.
AMS, Livestock & Grain Market News, (202) 720–7316.

Table 7-40.—Sheep and lambs: Number of breeding and market sheep, by State and United States, Jan. 1, 2017–2018

State	Breeding sheep and lambs		Market sheep and lambs	
	2017	2018	2017	2018
	1,000 head	*1,000 head*	*1,000 head*	*1,000 head*
Arizona	97.0	90.0	33.0	35.0
California	330.0	315.0	270.0	255.0
Colorado	200.0	195.0	220.0	250.0
Idaho	184.0	185.0	66.0	50.0
Illinois	46.0	46.0	9.0	9.0
Indiana	49.0	50.0	7.0	7.0
Iowa	120.0	115.0	55.0	50.0
Kansas	45.0	42.0	23.0	25.0
Kentucky	42.0	46.0	11.0	12.0
Michigan	61.0	57.0	24.0	23.0
Minnesota	91.0	90.0	39.0	40.0
Missouri	75.0	80.0	20.0	20.0
Montana	200.0	195.0	30.0	30.0
Nebraska	71.0	67.0	12.0	13.0
Nevada	54.0	54.0	9.0	7.0
New England [1]	37.0	40.0	10.0	9.0
New Mexico	82.0	80.0	15.0	16.0
New York	67.0	71.0	13.0	14.0
North Carolina	25.0	21.0	5.0	6.0
North Dakota	52.0	49.0	14.0	21.0
Ohio	92.0	95.0	25.0	24.0
Oklahoma	38.0	42.0	10.0	12.0
Oregon	124.0	120.0	46.0	45.0
Pennsylvania	75.0	78.0	18.0	18.0
South Dakota	183.0	190.0	57.0	60.0
Tennessee	38.0	38.0	8.0	8.0
Texas	570.0	600.0	140.0	150.0
Utah	255.0	250.0	20.0	25.0
Virginia	61.0	57.0	19.0	18.0
Washington	39.0	35.0	9.0	10.0
West Virginia	28.0	28.0	6.0	7.0
Wisconsin	63.0	63.0	13.0	12.0
Wyoming	275.0	260.0	85.0	85.0
Other States [2]	125.0	121.0	35.0	34.0
United States	3,984.0	3,865.0	1,376.0	1,400.0

[1] New England includes Connecticut, Maine, Massachusetts, New Hampshire, Rhode Island, and Vermont. [2] Includes data for States not published in this table.
NASS, Livestock Branch, (202) 720–3570.

Table 7-41.—Lamb crop: Per 100 ewes 1+, number and percent of previous year, by State and United States, 2016–2017

State	Breeding ewes 1 year & older, Jan. 1		Lambs per 100 ewes, Jan. 1		Lamb crop [1]		
	2017	2018	2017	2018	2017	2018	2018 as % of 2017
	1,000 head	*1,000 head*	*Number*	*Number*	*1,000 head*	*1,000 head*	*Percent*
Arizona	68	67	60	66	41	44	107
California	275	260	85	90	235	235	100
Colorado	160	156	116	119	185	185	100
Idaho	138	141	116	113	160	160	100
Illinois	36	36	119	114	43	41	95
Indiana	38	38	121	121	46	46	100
Iowa	95	91	121	121	115	110	96
Kansas	36	34	119	129	43	44	102
Kentucky	33	36	106	103	35	37	106
Michigan	44	41	111	122	49	50	102
Minnesota	72	74	125	122	90	90	100
Missouri	59	63	132	124	78	78	100
Montana	159	150	119	120	190	180	95
Nebraska	58	55	121	118	70	65	93
Nevada	43	43	79	88	34	38	112
New England [2]	27	30	122	117	33	35	106
New Mexico	59	58	76	83	45	48	107
New York	51	55	114	104	58	57	98
North Carolina	19	16	95	106	18	17	94
North Dakota	42	39	117	115	49	45	92
Ohio	70	73	126	121	88	88	100
Oklahoma	29	31	114	103	33	32	97
Oregon	101	94	114	120	115	113	98
Pennsylvania	59	60	114	110	67	66	99
South Dakota	146	153	134	131	195	200	103
Tennessee	29	29	121	114	35	33	94
Texas	440	465	82	78	360	365	101
Utah	205	200	112	118	230	235	102
Virginia	49	45	120	131	59	59	100
Washington	28	27	107	119	30	32	107
West Virginia	23	23	117	113	27	26	96
Wisconsin	48	48	119	119	57	57	100
Wyoming	225	210	104	114	235	240	102
Other States [3]	94	92	87	91	82	84	102
United States	3,058	3,033	106	107	3,230	3,235	100

[1] Lamb crop is defined as lambs born in the Eastern States and lambs docked or branded in the Western States. [2] New England includes Connecticut, Maine, Massachusetts, New Hampshire, Rhode Island, and Vermont. [3] Includes data for States not published in this table.
NASS, Livestock Branch, (202) 720–3570.

Table 7-42.—Sheep and lambs: Receipts at selected markets, 2010–2019

Year	Sioux Falls, SD	Billings, MT	San Angelo, TX	New Holland,PA
	Thousands	*Thousands*	*Thousands*	*Thousands*
2010	41	48	143	92
2011	38	42	156	94
2012	35	53	89	101
2013	48	52	110	109
2014	52	49	107	107
2015	82	63	110	117
2016	57	54	129	133
2017	62	61	141	123
2018	69	52	143	142
2019	55	56	160	38

AMS, Livestock & Grain Market News, (202) 720–7316.

Table 7-43.—Sheep and lambs: Number slaughtered, United States, 2009–2018

Year	Commercial			Farm	Total
	Federally inspected	Other	Total [1]		
	Thousands	*Thousands*	*Thousands*	*Thousands*	*Thousands*
2009	2,323	193	2,516	95	2,611
2010	2,261	196	2,458	95	2,553
2011	2,000	164	2,164	93	2,258
2012	2,012	171	2,183	93	2,275
2013	2,120	199	2,319	94	2,412
2014	2,105	205	2,310	95	2,404
2015	1,998	225	2,224	95	2,319
2016	2,010	228	2,238	95	2,333
2017	1,937	241	2,178	96	2,274
2018	2,000	265	2,265	92	2,357

[1] Totals are based on unrounded numbers.
NASS, Livestock Branch, (202) 720–3570.

Table 7-44.—Sheep and lambs: Number slaughtered, average dressed and live weights, percentage distribution, by class, Federally inspected, 2009–2018 [1]

Year	Federally inspected								
	Lambs and yearlings			Mature sheep			Total		
	Head	Percent of total	Avg. dressed weight [2]	Head	Percent of total	Avg. dressed weight [2]	Head	Avg. dressed weight [2]	Avg. live weight [2]
	1,000		*Pounds*	*1,000*		*Pounds*	*1,000*	*Pounds*	
2009	2,165	93.2	70	158	6.8	64	2,323	70	139
2010	2,105	93.1	69	156	6.9	65	2,261	68	137
2011	1,860	93.0	71	141	7.0	66	2,000	70	141
2012	1,869	92.9	74	143	7.1	64	2,012	74	147
2013	1,988	93.7	69	133	6.3	64	2,120	69	137
2014	1,968	93.5	69	136	6.5	66	2,105	69	137
2015	1,885	94.3	70	113	5.7	67	1,998	70	139
2016	1,902	94.6	69	108	5.4	67	2,010	69	137
2017	1,836	94.8	68	102	5.2	67	1,937	68	136
2018	1,893	94.7	70	107	5.3	67	2,000	70	139

[1] All percents and weights calculated using unrounded totals. [2] Excludes postmortem condemnations.
NASS, Livestock Branch, (202) 720–3570.

Table 7-45.—Sheep and lambs: Number slaughtered commercially, total and average live weight, by State and United States, 2018[1]

State	Number slaughtered	Total live weight	Average live weight[2]
	Thousands	*1,000 pounds*	*Pounds*
Alabama	0.8	67	84
Alaska	(Y)	(Y)	(Y)
Arizona	(D)	(D)	(D)
Arkansas	0.4	41	101
California	321.4	48,535	151
Colorado	738.0	124,656	169
Delaware-Maryland	46.0	4,292	93
Florida	15.0	853	57
Georgia	23.2	1,511	65
Hawaii	1.4	177	131
Idaho	2.5	349	141
Illinois	56.6	5,259	93
Indiana	46.4	5,485	118
Iowa	2.7	446	166
Kansas	5.1	513	100
Kentucky	16.9	2,115	125
Louisiana	3.8	224	59
Michigan	215.5	30,695	142
Minnesota	4.8	491	102
Mississippi	10.2	626	61
Missouri	10.9	931	86
Montana	4.8	672	141
Nebraska	0.6	86	135
Nevada	1.2	173	146
New England[3]	32.4	3,110	96
New Jersey	153.9	12,036	78
New Mexico	8.7	1,274	148
New York	61.8	6,232	101
North Carolina	14.3	1,047	73
North Dakota	0.5	71	138
Ohio	53.6	8,282	155
Oklahoma	8.2	937	115
Oregon	47.2	6,782	144
Pennsylvania	88.0	9,140	104
South Carolina	(D)	(D)	(D)
South Dakota	3.8	562	147
Tennessee	10.5	713	68
Texas	145.4	12,860	88
Utah	21.0	2,902	138
Virginia	9.7	709	73
Washington	16.3	2,243	138
West Virginia	(D)	(D)	(D)
Wisconsin	38.1	6,209	163
Wyoming	1.1	160	140
United States	2,205.0	000,319	135

(D) Withheld to avoid disclosing data for individual operations. (Y) Less than level of precision shown. [1] Includes slaughter in federally inspected and in other slaughter plants; exludes animals slaughtered on farms. Excludes postmortem condemnations. [2] Averages are based on unrounded data. [3] New England includes Connecticut, Maine, Massachusetts, New Hampshire, Rhode Island, and Vermont.

NASS, Livestock Branch, (202) 720–3570.

Table 7-46.—Sheep and lambs: Inventory Jan 1, 2017–2018, and number of operations, 2017, by State and United States[1]

State	January 1 Sheep inventory		Operations with sheep[2]
	2017	2018	2017
	1,000 head	*1,000 head*	*Number*
Alabama	....	....	1,062
Alaska	....	....	49
Arizona	130	125	7,509
Arkansas	....	....	1,053
California	600	570	3,807
Colorado	420	445	1,731
Connecticut	....	....	428
Delaware	....	....	89
Florida	....	....	1,666
Georgia	....	....	1,208
Hawaii	....	....	548
Idaho	250	235	1,447
Illinois	55	55	1,870
Indiana	56	57	2,316
Iowa	175	165	2,801
Kansas	68	67	1,234
Kentucky	53	58	2,818
Louisiana	....	....	785
Maine	....	....	738
Maryland	....	....	925
Michigan	85	80	728
Minnesota	130	130	2,483
Mississippi	....	....	2,248
Missouri	95	100	748
Montana	230	225	3,103
Nebraska	83	80	1,383
Nevada	63	61	1,153
New England[3]	47	49	328
New Hampshire	....	....	502
New Jersey	....	....	1,047
New Mexico	97	96	4,047
New York	80	85	2,113
North Carolina	30	27	1,679
North Dakota	66	70	573
Ohio	117	119	4,123
Oklahoma	48	54	2,216
Oregon	170	165	3,263
Pennsylvania	93	96	3,749
Rhode Island	....	....	108
South Carolina	....	....	738
South Dakota	240	250	1,337
Tennessee	46	46	2,503
Texas	710	750	14,672
Utah	275	275	1,898
Vermont	....	....	704
Virginia	80	75	2,646
Washington	48	45	2,281
West Virginia	34	35	1,226
Wisconsin	76	75	2,845
Wyoming	360	345	859
Other States[4]	160	155	....
United States	5,270	5,265	101,387

[1] An operation is any place having one or more head of sheep on hand December 31. [2] State level estimates only available in conjunction with the Census of Agriculture every 5 years. [3] New England includes Connecticut, Maine, Massachusetts, New Hampshire, Rhode Island, and Vermont. [4] Includes data for States not published in this table.
NASS, Livestock Branch, (202) 720–3570.

Table 7-47.—Wool: Number of sheep shorn, weight per fleece, production, average price per pound received by farmers, value of production, exports, imports, total new supply of apparel wool, and imports of carpet wool, United States, 2009–2018

Year	Sheep and lambs shorn [1]	Weight per fleece	Shorn wool production	Price per pound [2]	Value of production [3]
	Thousands	*Pounds*	*1,000 pounds*	*Cents*	*1,000 dollars*
2009	4,195	7.4	30,860	0.79	24,337
2010	4,180	7.3	30,360	1.15	35,013
2011	4,030	7.3	29,280	1.67	48,920
2012	3,790	7.3	27,630	1.52	41,972
2013	3,700	7.3	26,990	1.45	39,209
2014	3,680	7.3	26,680	1.46	38,909
2015	3,675	7.4	27,015	1.45	39,205
2016	3,585	7.3	26,050	1.45	37,721
2017	3,435	7.2	24,810	1.48	36,774
2018	3,372	7.2	24,400	1.75	42,772

Year	Shorn wool production	Raw wool supply (clean)				
		Domestic production [4]	Exports [5]	Imports for consumption		Total new supply [8]
				48's and Finer [6]	Not Finer than 46's [7]	
	1,000 pounds	*1,000 pounds*	*1,000 pounds*	*1,000 pounds*	*1,000 pounds*	
2009	30,860	16,294	10,207	3,306	6,046	15,439
2010	30,360	16,035	9,973	3,108	4,928	14,098
2011	29,280	15,465	9,586	3,791	4,694	14,364
2012	27,630	14,467	7,741	4,564	4,551	15,841
2013	26,990	14,251	9,998	3,858	3,746	11,857
2014	26,680	14,087	7,916	3,917	3,363	13,247
2015	27,015	14,264	7,847	3,980	3,321	13,718
2016	26,050	13,754	7,826	3,909	2,178	12,015
2017	24,810	13,100	11,002	3,396	2,285	7,779
2018	24,400	12,883	12,250	3,050	2,350	6,033

[1] Includes sheep shorn at commercial feeding yards. [2] Price computed by weighting State average prices for all wool sold during the year by sales of shorn wool. [3] Production by States multiplied by annual average price. [4] Conversion factor from grease basis to clean basis are as follows: Shorn wool production—52.8 percent (Stat. Bull. 616) from 1987-1997. [5] Includes carpet wool exports. [6] Prior to 1989, known as dutiable imports. [7] Prior to 1980, known as duty-free imports. In 1994 includes 24,645,306 pounds of imported raw wool not finer than 46's and 2,182,576 pounds of miscellaneous imported raw wool. [8] Production minus exports plus imports; stocks not taken into consideration.
NASS, Livestock Branch, (202) 720–3570 and ERS, Field Crops Branch, (202) 694–5300. Imports and exports from reports of the U.S. Department of Commerce.

Table 7-48.—Wool: Price-support operations, United States, 2010–2019 [1]

Year	Program price levels per pound		Put under loan		Acquired by CCC under loan program [2]	Owned by CCC at end of marketing year
	Graded wool loan	Nongraded loan	Quantity	Percentage of production		
	Dollars	*Dollars*	*1,000 pounds*	*Percent*	*1,000 pounds*	*1,000 pounds*
2010	1.15	0.40	27.8	0.09	0.0	0.0
2011	1.15	0.40	0.0	0.00	0.0	0.0
2012	1.15	0.40	0.0	0.00	0.0	0.0
2013	1.15	0.40	14.0	0.05	0.0	0.0
2014	1.15	0.40	11.0	0.04	0.0	0.0
2015	1.15	0.40	0.0	0.00	0.0	0.0
2016	1.15	0.40	0.0	0.00	0.0	0.0
2017	1.15	0.40	10.0	0.04	0.0	0.0
2018	1.15	0.40	0.0	0.00	0.0	0.0
2019	1.15	0.40	0.0	0.00	0.0	0.0

[1] Nonrecourse Marketing Loan Program authorized by the Food, Conservation, and Energy Act of 2008, as amended, for marketing years 2008-2013, and the Agricultural Act of 2014, as amended, for marketing years 2014-2018. [2] Acquisitions as of September 30, 2020.
FPAC-BC, Commodity Analysis Branch, (202) 720-4284.

Table 7-49.—Wool: United States imports of raw wool for mill use, clean yield[1], 2014–2018

Year	Finer-than-58s[2]	48s-and-finer[2]	Not-finer-than-46s[3]	Grand total[4]	Share finer-than-58s of grand total raw wool imports
	1,000 pounds				Percent
2015	2,895	3,980	3,321	7,301	39.7
2016	2,692	3,909	2,178	6,087	44.2
2017	2,114	3,396	2,285	5,681	37.2
2018	1,996	3,116	2,348	5,463	36.5

[1] Wool not advanced in any way or by any process of manufacture beyond washed, scoured, or carbonized condition. Imports for consumption include entries for immediate consumption and warehouse withdrawals for consumption. [2] Formerly "Dutiable". [3] Formerly "Duty-free". [4] Grand total includes "48s-and-finer" and "Not-finer-than-46s".
ERS, Field Crops Branch, (202) 694–5300. Source: U.S. Department of Commerce, U.S. Census Bureau.

Table 7-50.—U.S. raw wool imports by country of origin, clean yield, 2016–2018

Country of origin	Not-finer-than 46s			48s-and-finer		
	2016	2017	2018	2016	2017	2018
	1,000 pounds					
Australia	319.5	144.9	32.6	1,446.4	1,362.9	1,681.9
Belgium	233.0	30.3	--	--	0.9	--
Canada	--	35.8	43.6	1,029.1	674.7	176.8
China	43.2	--	167.2	184.1	178.2	125.9
Italy	0.0	0.0	0.2	330.1	366.9	98.5
Germany	70.5	53.0	--	--	23.2	--
Mexico	67.2	--	--	26.5	24.4	59.7
New Zealand	1,124.7	1,340.8	1,456.7	443.4	339.9	435.8
Pakistan	43.8	88.7	90.6	--	--	--
South Africa	38.7	138.7	82.8	77.8	--	74.6
Spain	0.0	65.1	42.3	82.2	246.7	107.3
United Kingdom	183.7	318.8	270.7	21.6	0.0	0.2
Uruguay	--	--	--	266.9	178.0	355.0
Other	53.5	69.3	160.9	1.0	0.2	0.2
Total	2,177.8	2,285.4	2,347.6	3,909.1	3,396.0	3,115.7

(--) No imports. 0.0 = Less than 100 pounds.
ERS, Field Crops Branch, (202) 694–5300. Source: U.S. Department of Commerce, U.S. Census Bureau.

Table 7-51.—Wool: Graded territory shorn wool, and Australian offering prices, 2009–2018[1]

Year	Graded territory shorn wool, clean[1]		Australian offering prices, clean[2]
	64s staple 2-3/4" & up	58s staple 3-1/4" & up	Grade 64s type 63
	U.S. dollars per pound		
2009	2.27	1.73	3.02
2010	3.27	2.15	4.10
2011	4.25	4.07	6.30
2012	2.81	3.46	5.90
2013	4.23	3.01	5.34
2014	4.17	3.00	4.89
2015	3.58	3.04	4.50
2016	3.94	3.21	4.89
2017	4.36	3.24	5.50
2018	6.04	4.43	7.23

[2] Refers to wool principally produced in Texas and the Rocky Mountain States. [2] Free on board (f.o.b.) Australian Wool Corporation's South Carolina warehouse in bond. A duty of 10 cents per pound, clean, should be added to these prices.
ERS, Field Crops Branch, (202) 694–5300. Sources: USDA and International Wool Textile Organization.

Table 7-52.—Wool: Number of sheep shorn, weight per fleece, and production, by State and United States, 2017–2018

State	Sheep		Weight per fleece		Shorn wool production	
	2017	2018	2017	2018	2017	2018
	1,000 head	*1,000 head*	*Pounds*	*Pounds*	*1,000 pounds*	*1,000 pounds*
Arizona	90.0	83.0	6.8	6.9	610	570
California	400.0	380.0	6.3	6.3	2,500	2,400
Colorado	310.0	315.0	6.8	7.0	2,100	2,200
Idaho	185.0	170.0	8.6	8.8	1,600	1,500
Illinois	33.0	32.0	6.1	6.3	200	200
Indiana	38.0	42.0	5.9	6.0	225	250
Iowa	140.0	140.0	5.6	5.4	780	760
Kansas	43.0	43.0	6.6	6.4	205	275
Kentucky	11.0	11.0	6.8	6.8	75	75
Michigan	59.0	55.0	5.8	5.9	345	325
Minnesota	112.0	102.0	6.3	6.3	700	640
Missouri	36.0	40.0	6.1	5.8	220	230
Montana	195.0	180.0	9.0	8.9	1,750	1,610
Nebraska	62.0	58.0	7.1	7.1	440	410
Nevada	46.0	47.0	9.3	9.6	430	450
New England[1]	31.0	27.0	6.8	6.7	210	180
New Mexico	81.0	82.0	7.6	7.6	615	625
New York	48.0	46.0	6.3	5.9	300	270
North Carolina	6.0	6.0	5.8	5.5	35	33
North Dakota	61.0	59.0	6.9	6.9	420	410
Ohio	80.0	79.0	5.8	5.8	460	460
Oklahoma	18.0	19.0	5.6	5.5	100	105
Oregon	130.0	130.0	6.4	6.4	830	830
Pennsylvania	47.0	46.0	6.7	6.7	315	310
South Dakota	230.0	230.0	7.6	7.6	1,750	1,750
Tennessee	10.0	10.0	5.5	5.0	55	50
Texas	240.0	240.0	7.5	7.3	1,800	1,760
Utah	245.0	245.0	9.0	9.1	2,200	2,220
Virginia	23.0	24.0	5.9	6.0	135	145
Washington	31.0	33.0	8.4	8.0	260	265
West Virginia	18.0	17.0	5.8	5.4	105	92
Wisconsin	50.0	50.0	6.6	6.6	330	330
Wyoming	280.0	285.0	8.4	8.4	2,350	2,400
Other States[2]	46.0	46.0	6.1	5.9	280	270
United States	3,435.0	3,372.0	7.2	7.2	24,810	24,400

[1] New England includes Connecticut, Maine, Massachusetts, New Hampshire, Rhode Island, and Vermont. [2] Includes data for States not published in this table.
NASS, Livestock Branch, (202) 720–3570.

Table 7-53.—Wool: Price and value, by State and United States, 2017–2018

State	Price per pound		Value [1]	
	2017	2018	2017	2018
	Dollars	*Dollars*	*1,000 Dollars*	*1,000 dollars*
Arizona	0.90	1.20	549	684
California	1.55	2.00	3,875	4,800
Colorado	1.80	2.10	3,780	4,620
Idaho	1.70	2.02	2,720	3,030
Illinois	0.70	0.65	140	130
Indiana	0.60	0.55	135	138
Iowa	0.52	0.59	406	448
Kansas	0.85	0.95	242	261
Kentucky	0.90	0.80	68	60
Michigan	0.60	0.65	207	211
Minnesota	0.60	0.67	420	429
Missouri	0.86	0.60	189	138
Montana	1.90	2.50	3,325	4,025
Nebraska	0.79	0.88	348	361
Nevada	2.00	2.20	860	990
New England [2]	0.90	0.85	189	153
New Mexico	1.60	2.10	984	1,313
New York	0.90	0.90	270	243
North Carolina	1.10	1.20	39	40
North Dakota	1.09	1.32	458	541
Ohio	0.50	0.40	230	184
Oklahoma	0.80	0.70	80	74
Oregon	1.65	1.65	1,370	1,370
Pennsylvania	0.60	0.60	189	186
South Dakota	1.49	1.83	2,608	3,203
Tennessee	0.90	0.80	50	40
Texas	1.63	1.80	2,934	3,168
Utah	1.80	2.00	3,960	4,440
Virginia	1.45	1.40	196	203
Washington	1.90	2.10	494	557
West Virginia	1.45	1.40	152	129
Wisconsin	0.65	0.60	215	198
Wyoming	2.00	2.50	4,700	6,000
Other States [3]	1.40	1.50	392	405
United States	1.48	1.75	36,774	42,772

[1] Production multiplied by marketing year average price. United States value is the summation of State values. [2] New England includes Connecticut, Maine, Massachusetts, New Hampshire, Rhode Island, and Vermont. [3] Includes data for States not published in this table.

NASS, Livestock Branch, (202) 720–3570.

Table 7-54.—Mohair: Price-support operations, United States, 2010–2019[1]

Year	Program price levels per pound: Loan	Put under loan: Quantity	Put under loan: Percentage of production	Acquired by CCC under loan program[2]	Owned by CCC at end of marketing year
	Dollars	*1,000 pounds*	*Percent*	*1,000 pounds*	*1,000 pounds*
2010	4.20	4.2	0.38	0.0	0.0
2011	4.20	0.0	0.0	0.0	0.0
2012	4.20	0.0	0.0	0.0	0.0
2013	4.20	0.0	0.0	0.0	0.0
2014	4.20	0.0	0.0	0.0	0.0
2015	4.20	0.0	0.0	0.0	0.0
2016	4.20	0.0	0.0	0.0	0.0
2017	4.20	0.0	0.0	0.0	0.0
2018	4.20	0.0	0.0	0.0	0.0
2019	4.20	0.0	0.0	0.0	0.0

[1] Nonrecourse Marketing Loan Program authorized by the Food , Conservation, and Energy Act of 2008, as amended, for marketing years 2008-2013, and the Agricultural Act of 2014, as amended, for marketing years 2014-2018. [2] Acquisitions as of September 30, 2020.
FPAC-BC, Commodity Analysis Branch, (202) 720-4284.

Table 7-55.—Mohair: Goats clipped, production, price, and value, by State and United States, 2017–2018

State	Goats clipped		Average clip per goat		Production		Price per pound		Value[1]	
	2017	2018	2017	2018	2017	2018	2017	2018	2017	2018
	Head	*Head*	*Pounds*	*Pounds*	*1,000 pounds*	*1,000 pounds*	*Dollars*	*Dollars*	*1,000 dollars*	*1,000 dollars*
Arizona	27,000	28,000	3.9	4.5	105	125	1.20	1.30	126	163
California	2,000	2,000	5.0	5.0	10	10	6.00	6.00	60	60
New Mexico	7,000	7,000	4.3	4.3	30	30	1.40	1.60	42	48
Texas	77,000	75,000	6.1	6.2	470	465	6.60	7.20	3,102	3,348
Other States[2]	21,000	21,000	6.0	6.0	125	125	2.65	2.75	331	344
United States	134,000	133,000	5.5	5.7	740	755	4.95	5.25	3,661	3,963

[1] Production multiplied by marketing year average price. U.S. value is summation of State values. [2] Includes data for States not published in this table.
NASS, Livestock Branch, (202) 720–3570.

Table 7-56—Angora goats: Inventory Jan 1, 2017–2018, and number of operations, 2017, by State and United States [1]

State	January 1 angora goats inventory		Operations with angora goats [2]
	2017	2018	2017
	Head	*Head*	*Number*
Alabama			202
Alaska			6
Arizona	35,000	30,000	2,185
Arkansas			25
California	3,400	3,500	363
Colorado			217
Connecticut			70
Delaware			5
Florida			284
Georgia			236
Hawaii			57
Idaho			107
Illinois			82
Indiana			126
Iowa			113
Kansas			75
Kentucky			266
Louisiana			95
Maine			49
Maryland			114
Massachusetts			85
Michigan			238
Minnesota	(NA)	(NA)	157
Mississippi			44
Missouri	(NA)	(NA)	192
Montana			86
Nebraska			61
Nevada			17
New Hampshire			50
New Jersey			129
New Mexico	10,500	9,500	1,196
New York			211
North Carolina			273
North Dakota			20
Ohio			241
Oklahoma			181
Oregon	(NA)	(NA)	295
Pennsylvania			290
Rhode Island			16
South Carolina			147
South Dakota			39
Tennessee			35
Texas	80,000	75,000	1,514
Utah			272
Vermont			65
Virginia			201
Washington			267
West Virginia			93
Wisconsin	(NA)	(NA)	168
Wyoming			33
United States	152,000	144,000	11,293

(NA) Not available. [1] An operation is any place having one or more head of angora goats on hand December 31. [2] State level estimates only available in conjunction with the Census of Agriculture every 5 years. [3] New England includes Connecticut, Maine, Massachusetts, New Hampshire, Rhode Island, and Vermont. [4] Includes data for States not published in this table.

NASS, Livestock Branch, (202) 720–3570.

Table 7-57.—Milk goats: Inventory Jan 1, 2017–2018, and number of operations, 2017, by State and United States [1]

State	January 1 milk goats inventory		Operations with milk goats [2]
	2017	2018	2017
	Head	*Head*	*Number*
Alabama	3,900	3,500	547
Alaska	(NA)		39
Arizona	(NA)		499
Arkansas	4,500	4,000	709
California	41,000	40,000	1,372
Colorado	9,000	9,000	1,124
Connecticut	(NA)	(NA)	280
Delaware	(NA)	(NA)	34
Florida	10,000	10,000	1,410
Georgia	5,000	7,100	809
Hawaii	(NA)		93
Idaho	5,000	8,000	598
Illinois	9,000	10,000	585
Indiana	11,000	11,000	1,120
Iowa	30,500	31,000	753
Kansas	4,700	4,400	525
Kentucky	5,500	6,000	1,078
Louisiana	(NA)	(NA)	368
Maine	(NA)	(NA)	395
Maryland	(NA)	(NA)	343
Massachusetts	(NA)	(NA)	335
Michigan	12,500	11,000	1,246
Minnesota	12,000	14,000	698
Mississippi	(NA)	(NA)	431
Missouri	11,000	12,000	1,382
Montana	(NA)	(NA)	400
Nebraska	3,700	3,500	419
Nevada	(NA)	(NA)	104
New England [3]	14,200	17,000	
New Hampshire	(NA)	(NA)	231
New Jersey	(NA)	(NA)	286
New Mexico	(NA)	(NA)	564
New York	13,700	13,000	1,033
North Carolina	6,400	7,000	849
North Dakota	(NA)	(NA)	164
Ohio	10,000	12,000	1,504
Oklahoma	6,000	7,000	1,142
Oregon	12,600	14,000	1,216
Pennsylvania	15,000	15,000	1,240
Rhode Island	(NA)	(NA)	59
South Carolina	3,000	3,500	479
South Dakota	(NA)	(NA)	235
Tennessee	7,000	7,500	981
Texas	20,000	29,000	3,630
Utah	(NA)	(NA)	397
Vermont	(NA)	(NA)	270
Virginia	6,000	5,500	867
Washington	7,500	7,000	982
West Virginia	(NA)	(NA)	523
Wisconsin	56,000	67,000	1,029
Wyoming	(NA)	(NA)	305
Other States [4]	33,300	31,000	
United States	395,000	420,000	35,682

(NA) Not available. [1] An operation is any place having one or more head of angora goats on hand December 31. [2] State level estimates only available in conjunction with the Census of Agriculture every 5 years. [3] New England includes Connecticut, Maine, Massachusetts, New Hampshire, Rhode Island, and Vermont. [4] Includes data for States not published in this table.

NASS, Livestock Branch, (202) 720–3570.

Table 7-58.—Meat and other goats: Inventory Jan 1, 2017–2018, and number of operations, 2017, by State and United States[1]

State	January 1 meat and other goats inventory		Operations with Meat goats[2]
	2017	2018	2017
	Head	*Head*	*Number*
Alabama	45,000	47,000	1,549
Alaska	(NA)	(NA)	18
Arizona	30,000	30,000	390
Arkansas	34,000	31,000	1,111
California	87,000	85,000	1,343
Colorado	25,000	23,000	1,008
Connecticut	(NA)	(NA)	123
Delaware	(NA)	(NA)	44
Florida	44,000	45,000	1,526
Georgia	57,000	60,000	1,893
Hawaii	(NA)	(NA)	194
Idaho	(NA)	(NA)	585
Illinois	24,000	25,000	867
Indiana	33,000	36,000	1,154
Iowa	35,000	40,000	1,183
Kansas	46,000	41,000	1,093
Kentucky	56,000	57,000	1,768
Louisiana	18,000	15,000	504
Maine	(NA)	(NA)	82
Maryland	(NA)	(NA)	362
Massachusetts	(NA)	(NA)	141
Michigan	(NA)	(NA)	691
Minnesota	22,000	24,000	758
Mississippi	20,000	20,000	837
Missouri	75,000	70,000	1,724
Montana	(NA)	(NA)	256
Nebraska	(NA)	(NA)	657
Nevada	(NA)	(NA)	126
New Hampshire	(NA)	(NA)	83
New Jersey	(NA)	(NA)	361
New Mexico	(NA)	(NA)	535
New York	17,000	16,000	592
North Carolina	50,000	47,000	1,658
North Dakota	(NA)	(NA)	117
Ohio	42,000	44,000	1,942
Oklahoma	92,000	82,000	2,477
Oregon	27,000	29,000	1,048
Pennsylvania	37,000	38,000	1,351
Rhode Island	(NA)	(NA)	18
South Carolina	32,000	34,000	1,216
South Dakota	(NA)	(NA)	282
Tennessee	100,000	96,000	2,875
Texas	760,000	765,000	12,511
Utah	(NA)	(NA)	385
Vermont	(NA)	(NA)	63
Virginia	45,000	41,000	1,356
Washington	18,000	19,000	723
West Virginia	21,000	21,000	809
Wisconsin	(NA)	(NA)	582
Wyoming	(NA)	(NA)	256
Other States[4]	188,000	194,000	....
United States	2,080,000	2,075,000	53,227

(NA) Not available. [1] An operation is any place having one or more head of angora goats on hand December 31. [2] State level estimates only available in conjunction with the Census of Agriculture every 5 years. [3] New England includes Connecticut, Maine, Massachusetts, New Hampshire, Rhode Island, and Vermont. [4] Includes data for States not published in this table.

NASS, Livestock Branch, (202) 720–3570.

Table 7-59.—All goats: Number of operations, 2017, by State and United States[1]

State	2017[2]
	Number
Alabama	3,279
Alaska	73
Arizona	4,721
Arkansas	2,488
California	3,938
Colorado	2,803
Connecticut	592
Delware	121
Florida	4,366
Georgia	4,063
Hawaii	609
Idaho	1,556
Illinios	2,028
Indiana	2,833
Iowa	2,400
Kansas	2,010
Kentucky	4,330
Louisiana	1,501
Maine	583
Maryland	1,085
Massachusetts	719
Michigan	2,614
Minnesota	1,996
Mississippi	2,048
Missouri	4,132
Montana	908
Nebraska	1,341
Nevada	339
New Hampshire	427
New Jersey	969
New Mexico	2,770
New York	2,192
North Carolina	4,084
North Dakota	335
Ohio	4,841
Oklahoma	5,398
Oregon	3,289
Pennsylvania	3,749
Rhode Island	102
South Carolina	2,905
South Dakota	721
Tennessee	5,802
Texas	26,143
Utah	1,392
Vermont	480
Virginia	3,440
Washington	2,609
West Virginia	2,040
Wisconsin	2,586
Wyoming	683
United States	136,442

[1] An operation is any place having one or more head of goats on hand December 31. [2] State level estimates only available in conjunction with the Census of Agriculture every 5 years. [3] New England includes Connecticut, Maine, Massachusetts, New Hampshire, Rhode Island, and Vermont.

NASS, Livestock Branch, (202) 720–3570.

Table 7-60.—Red meat: Production, by class of slaughter, United States, 2009–2018

Year	Commercial		Farm	Total
	Federally inspected	Total		
	Beef			
	Million pounds			
2009	25,598	25,966	90	26,056
2010	25,954	26,305	84	26,389
2011	25,854	26,195	75	26,270
2012	25,573	25,913	76	25,989
2013	25,385	25,720	70	25,790
2014	23,932	24,249	66	24,315
2015	23,395	23,698	63	23,760
2016	24,908	25,221	67	25,288
2017	25,856	26,188	63	26,251
2018	26,536	26,873	66	26,939
	Pork, excluding lard			
	Million pounds			
2009	22,827	22,999	21	23,020
2010	22,275	22,437	19	22,456
2011	22,599	22,758	17	22,775
2012	23,090	23,253	15	23,268
2013	23,040	23,187	16	23,203
2014	22,710	22,843	15	22,858
2015	24.355	24,501	16	24,517
2016	24,789	24,941	16	24,957
2017	25,437	25,584	14	25,598
2018	26,178	26,315	14	26,330
	Veal			
	Million pounds			
2009	135	138	8	147
2010	131	134	8	143
2011	126	130	7	136
2012	115	118	7	125
2013	109	111	6	117
2014	92	94	6	100
2015	81	83	5	88
2016	74	76	6	81
2017	73	74	6	80
2018	74	76	5	80
	Lamb and Mutton			
	Million pounds			
2009	162	171	5	175
2010	154	164	5	168
2011	141	149	5	153
2012	148	156	5	161
2013	146	156	5	161
2014	145	156	5	161
2015	139	151	5	156
2016	138	150	5	155
2017	132	145	5	150
2018	140	153	5	158
	All meat, excluding lard			
	Million pounds			
2009	48,721	49,274	124	49,398
2010	48,514	49,039	116	49,155
2011	48,721	49,232	103	49,335
2012	48,925	49,440	103	49,543
2013	48,679	49,174	97	49,271
2014	46,879	47,342	91	47,433
2015	47,970	48,432	89	48,520
2016	49,909	50,388	93	50,481
2017	51,497	51,992	88	52,079
2018	52,927	53,417	90	53,507

NASS, Livestock Branch, (202) 720–3570.

Table 7-61.—Meat: United States exports and imports into the United States, carcass weight equivalent, 2010–2019 [1]

Year	Exports				Imports			
	Beef and veal	Lamb and mutton	Pork [2]	All meat	Beef & veal	Lamb and mutton	Pork [2]	All meat
	Million pounds							
2010	2,300	16	4,223	6,539	2,298	166	859	3,323
2011	2,785	19	5,196	8,000	2,057	162	803	3,022
2012	2,452	11	5,379	7,842	2,220	154	802	3,175
2013	2,588	7	4,986	7,582	2,250	173	880	3,302
2014	2,574	7	5,092	7,672	2,947	195	1,011	4,153
2015	2,267	4	5,010	7,282	3,368	214	1,116	4,698
2016	2,557	5	5,239	7,801	3,012	216	1,091	4,319
2017	2,859	6	5,632	8,497	2,993	252	1,116	4,361
2018	3,160	6	5,877	9,042	2,998	273	1,042	4,313
2019	3,026	6	6,321	9,353	3,058	272	945	4,275

[1] Carcass weight equivalent of all meat, including the meat content of minor meats and of mixed products. Shipments to U.S. Territories are included in domestic consumption. [2] The pork series has been revised to a dressed weight equivalent rather than "Pork, excluding lard."
ERS, Market and Trade Economics Division, Animal Products and Cost of Production Branch, (202) 694–5409. Data on imports and commercial exports are computed from records of the U.S. Department of Commerce, those on exports by the U.S. Department of Agriculture are separately estimated from deliveries and stocks.

Table 7-62.—International Meat: Production, 2017–2019

Country	2017	2018	2019
	1,000 metric tons		
Beef and veal:			
United States	11,943	12,257	12,383
Brazil	9,550	9,900	10,200
European Union	7,869	8,003	7,928
China	6,346	6,440	6,670
India	4,230	4,240	4,305
Argentina	2,840	3,050	3,125
Australia	2,149	2,306	2,432
Mexico	1,925	1,980	2,030
Pakistan	1,780	1,800	1,820
Russia	1,325	1,357	1,369
Canada	1,201	1,265	1,340
South Africa	1,046	1,027	1,019
Colombia	758	773	770
New Zealand	654	672	713
Uruguay	594	596	562
Swine:			
China	54,518	54,040	42,550
European Union	23,660	24,082	23,960
United States	11,611	11,943	12,543
Brazil	3,725	3,763	3,975
Russia	2,959	3,155	3,321
Vietnam	2,741	2,811	2,380
Canada	1,958	1,955	2,020
Philippines	1,563	1,601	1,585
Mexico	1,267	1,321	1,408
Korea, South	1,280	1,329	1,364
Japan	1,272	1,284	1,279
Taiwan	811	829	820
Ukraine	769	732	745
Argentina	565	621	630
Chile	489	534	530

FAS, Office of Global Analysis, (202) 720-6301. Data Source: USDA FAS PSD Online.

Table 7-63.—Meat: U.S. exports, 2017–2019

Country	2017	2018	2019
	Metric tons		
Beef & veal, prep/pres:			
Canada	25,390	25,666	23,987
Hong Kong	5,629	1,958	5,408
Mexico	1,002	905	1,726
Korea, South	266	686	442
Guatemala	101	143	210
Dominican Republic	189	86	186
Philippines	37	176	146
Trinidad and Tobago	30	67	116
Malaysia	9	99	96
Chile	109	168	89
Japan	16	42	87
Panama	148	218	68
Bahamas, The	51	43	61
Micronesia	57	39	60
Australia(*)	580	105	53
Netherlands Antilles(*)	25	20	52
Leeward-Windward Islands(*)	40	31	43
Bermuda	19	23	40
Jamaica	25	68	38
Albania	0	0	36
Germany(*)	22	29	32
El Salvador	10	21	31
United Arab Emirates	46	24	28
Costa Rica	37	60	27
Netherlands	8	37	24
Colombia	24	4	22
Ireland	0	0	18
Cayman Islands	9	18	17
Belize	8	2	15
China	3	12	15
Rest of World	430	372	178
World Total	34,318	31,118	33,347
Beef & veal, fr/ch/fz:			
Japan	258,194	278,801	248,111
Korea, South	170,248	224,729	241,830
Mexico	131,964	141,591	134,336
Hong Kong	110,657	101,518	73,024
Canada	81,488	78,225	67,804
Taiwan	44,421	59,740	63,509
Philippines	9,306	12,043	13,813
Vietnam	9,874	12,142	12,225
Indonesia	6,403	7,411	10,904
China	2,957	7,189	10,492
Netherlands	12,692	10,771	9,927
Chile	10,548	9,227	9,408
Dominican Republic	5,868	5,979	6,203
United Arab Emirates	5,703	5,638	5,617
Guatemala	4,857	4,965	5,099
Italy(*)	5,216	4,811	3,899
Colombia	2,301	3,262	3,865
Singapore	3,035	2,943	3,431
Bahamas, The	2,935	3,187	3,291
Netherlands Antilles(*)	2,765	2,512	2,767
Kuwait	2,711	2,715	2,541
Costa Rica	1,774	2,320	2,443
Germany(*)	2,821	2,963	2,173
Panama	1,170	1,346	1,947
Jamaica	1,662	2,235	1,817
Peru	1,450	1,360	1,613
Israel(*)	401	908	1,589
Saudi Arabia	144	1,222	1,539
Thailand	637	961	1,499
Cayman Islands	1,449	1,563	1,456
Rest of World	17,398	17,849	15,268
World Total	913,046	1,012,122	963,438

See footnote(s) at end of table.

Table 7-63.—Meat: U.S. exports, 2017–2019—Continued

Country	2017	2018	2019
	Metric tons		
Pork, fr/ch/fz:			
Mexico	621,597	621,631	552,583
China	127,452	104,991	378,025
Japan	365,131	366,626	343,828
Korea, South	157,945	220,401	188,954
Canada	105,128	105,434	119,208
Australia(*)	61,956	72,014	97,716
Colombia	63,097	91,718	94,942
Chile	23,291	26,610	32,421
Honduras	27,041	28,940	31,556
Dominican Republic	27,934	38,087	30,189
Philippines	19,121	20,631	21,741
Hong Kong	43,570	18,197	15,390
Guatemala	13,026	14,191	15,286
Taiwan	9,537	13,091	12,200
Panama	7,060	9,510	12,038
New Zealand(*)	5,105	6,143	8,299
Nicaragua	5,140	6,419	7,475
El Salvador	4,842	6,784	7,034
Costa Rica	3,811	4,691	6,191
Peru	3,843	5,499	4,962
Bahamas, The	4,855	4,023	4,059
Singapore	3,841	2,601	3,720
Vietnam	2,821	5,496	3,566
Trinidad and Tobago	2,130	1,964	2,494
Leeward-Windward Islands(*)	1,585	1,826	2,192
Netherlands Antilles(*)	1,259	1,227	1,535
Albania	900	852	1,214
United Kingdom	944	1,087	923
French Pacific Islands(*)	145	318	634
Ecuador	623	835	561
Rest of World	6,828	6,050	6,394
World Total	1,721,555	1,807,884	2,007,327
Pork, hams/shldrs,cured:			
Canada	18,459	17,705	16,563
Panama	2,231	2,437	2,788
Mexico	3,339	1,387	1,435
Albania	197	587	965
Belize	550	734	782
Netherlands Antilles(*)	486	529	509
Trinidad and Tobago	593	620	457
Bahamas, The	278	397	422
Colombia	440	538	402
Korea, South	203	123	303
Australia(*)	2,339	863	262
Hong Kong	28	299	262
Barbados	181	160	217
Guatemala	47	63	176
Leeward-Windward Islands(*)	161	138	167
Dominican Republic	19	60	134
Thailand	0	0	100
Italy(*)	0	52	88
Philippines	228	95	66
El Salvador	0	51	65
Japan	540	118	63
Honduras	22	63	59
Costa Rica	47	14	47
Haiti	26	32	46
United Kingdom	0	0	40
New Zealand(*)	1	10	24
Turks and Caicos Islands	6	11	17
Netherlands	17	16	14
Guyana	5	4	13
Singapore	30	0	9
Rest of World	572	676	38
World Total	31,044	27,780	26,530

See footnote(s) at end of table.

Table 7-63.—Meat: U.S. exports, 2017–2019—Continued

Country	2017	2018	2019
	Metric tons		
Pork, bacon, cured:			
Mexico	14,912	12,283	13,289
Canada	8,794	7,399	5,870
Korea, South	2,617	3,195	3,848
Japan	3,148	3,316	3,554
Australia(*)	1,186	1,853	1,447
New Zealand(*)	1,246	777	1,304
French Pacific Islands(*)	369	1,152	1,247
Dominican Republic	711	823	643
Hong Kong	602	387	474
Chile	486	345	413
Bahamas, The	183	368	402
Guatemala	503	344	401
Samoa	102	444	393
Colombia	364	421	343
Costa Rica	490	298	292
Panama	340	160	289
Netherlands Antilles(*)	89	134	232
Singapore	274	281	232
El Salvador	120	125	174
Cayman Islands	136	101	162
Leeward-Windward Islands(*)	128	101	155
Honduras	156	107	154
Bermuda	126	102	137
United Arab Emirates	91	35	101
Malaysia	7	0	76
Philippines	26	42	72
Turks and Caicos Islands	50	49	61
Taiwan	24	0	47
Guyana	34	30	37
Trinidad and Tobago	55	83	34
Rest of World	344	156	73
World Total	37,710	34,908	35,954
Pork, prep/pres, nt/cn:			
Canada	56,686	56,827	55,307
Mexico	17,305	11,787	10,622
Japan	4,131	5,899	6,648
Peru	52	101	1,681
Korea, South	875	1,092	1,429
Colombia	883	685	736
Chile	213	620	635
Australia(*)	99	67	631
Panama	223	306	509
Philippines	918	423	495
Dominican Republic	91	136	267
Micronesia	273	227	252
Costa Rica	95	164	226
Hong Kong	327	289	172
El Salvador	126	79	115
Guatemala	82	78	86
Marshall Islands	43	47	84
Netherlands Antilles(*)	99	57	68
Honduras	109	62	49
Bahamas, The	53	60	47
Trinidad and Tobago	73	19	39
Taiwan	33	45	38
Leeward-Windward Islands(*)	45	44	31
Singapore	166	10	31
United Arab Emirates	1	0	28
New Zealand(*)	0	12	27
Nicaragua	25	11	16
Netherlands	1	7	14
Iceland	0	4	12
Barbados	16	25	12
Rest of World	75	63	64
World Total	83,116	79,247	80,371

See footnote(s) at end of table.

Table 7-63.—Meat: U.S. exports, 2017–2019—Continued

Country	2017	2018	2019
	Metric tons		
Pork, prep/pres, canned:			
Philippines	6,566	8,854	6,220
Japan	9,572	6,234	5,364
Australia(*)	4,225	3,896	3,764
Panama	1,699	1,573	1,889
Korea, South	1,966	1,998	1,711
Hong Kong	2,058	1,476	1,580
Dominican Republic	1,373	2,639	1,578
Colombia	385	521	572
Costa Rica	116	325	524
Singapore	361	408	442
New Zealand(*)	578	644	360
Mexico	365	501	302
Chile	59	111	227
Netherlands Antilles(*)	170	179	214
Vietnam	109	127	175
Taiwan	85	81	171
El Salvador	99	98	171
Guatemala	700	147	161
United Arab Emirates	124	89	124
Trinidad and Tobago	145	94	103
Honduras	112	80	88
Indonesia	14	41	82
French Pacific Islands(*)	51	45	75
Canada	311	15	62
Nicaragua	46	52	57
Jamaica	46	48	46
Malaysia	27	40	43
Haiti	13	33	37
Bahamas, The	33	18	37
Belize	32	19	32
Rest of World	272	103	90
World Total	31,709	30,489	26,302
Lamb & mutton; fr/ch/fz:			
Mexico	877	684	765
Bahamas, The	142	219	178
United Arab Emirates	96	361	142
Trinidad and Tobago	60	72	123
Dominican Republic	25	74	104
Canada	224	132	101
Netherlands Antilles(*)	155	83	90
El Salvador	0	1	84
Italy(*)	18	14	65
Bermuda	99	67	65
Leeward-Windward Islands(*)	81	108	60
Panama	49	13	58
Barbados	25	41	39
Jamaica	52	95	39
Guatemala	48	23	34
Turks and Caicos Islands	26	58	32
Spain	10	19	31
Netherlands	30	23	28
Philippines	13	19	25
Egypt	0	0	25
Costa Rica	29	43	23
Japan	41	69	20
Taiwan	37	30	20
Bahrain	0	0	18
Micronesia	0	16	12
Singapore	31	31	12
Saudi Arabia	0	0	12
Guyana	12	7	12
Denmark(*)	4	2	11
Equatorial Guinea	0	0	10
Rest of World	251	97	57
World Total	2,434	2,403	2,294

See footnote(s) at end of table.

Table 7-63.—Meat: U.S. exports, 2017–2019—Continued

Country	2017	2018	2019
	Metric tons		
Sausages & bologna:			
Canada	42,906	42,895	43,346
Japan	21,927	23,444	24,090
Mexico	10,767	10,437	9,991
Korea, South	6,311	5,910	6,267
Philippines	1,912	3,980	3,481
Hong Kong	1,875	1,506	1,759
Belize	1,093	1,134	1,646
Guatemala	869	1,021	1,483
United Kingdom	678	589	746
Chile	297	528	716
Taiwan	329	275	658
Dominican Republic	300	609	621
Panama	734	721	556
Colombia	243	393	547
Netherlands Antilles(*)	304	427	472
Bahamas, The	461	413	463
Singapore	599	337	452
Australia(*)	251	114	448
El Salvador	142	405	389
Honduras	101	209	369
Costa Rica	325	385	291
Peru	121	210	239
Marshall Islands	248	246	215
Leeward-Windward Islands(*)	125	76	166
Samoa	250	290	128
Bermuda	114	113	128
Micronesia	113	140	117
Nicaragua	31	102	114
United Arab Emirates	70	108	91
Trinidad and Tobago	107	76	91
Rest of World	1,044	1,016	898
World Total	94,645	98,109	100,978
Other meat products, prp/ps:			
Canada	3,532	2,876	2,401
Mexico	1,737	1,962	2,138
Philippines	523	432	587
Guatemala	152	152	461
Panama	135	372	286
Korea, South	26	79	265
Colombia	61	137	179
Cayman Islands	6	3	173
Japan	171	144	144
Australia(*)	76	103	117
Taiwan	15	76	92
Leeward-Windward Islands(*)	30	37	72
Ecuador	36	103	68
Jamaica	52	21	63
Suriname	1	0	54
Trinidad and Tobago	8	59	44
Thailand	50	44	43
Indonesia	23	0	33
New Zealand(*)	31	20	31
Kuwait	11	37	29
Belize	17	32	26
Honduras	59	19	25
Hong Kong	32	85	23
Nicaragua	28	18	22
Chile	4	3	22
Netherlands Antilles(*)	10	39	19
United Arab Emirates	0	0	19
Bahamas, The	88	30	19
Haiti	27	6	18
Bahrain	0	2	12
Rest of World	402	234	48
World Total	7,342	7,124	7,532

See footnote(s) at end of table.

Table 7-63.—Meat: U.S. exports, 2017–2019—Continued

Country	2017	2018	2019
		Metric tons	
Variety meats, beef:			
Mexico	104,881	96,596	100,645
Egypt	70,562	61,623	63,449
Japan	49,234	51,602	62,949
Hong Kong	14,449	19,271	14,149
Korea, South	13,631	14,141	13,487
Indonesia	7,322	6,700	12,689
South Africa	11,391	12,448	11,219
Canada	8,674	10,144	8,040
Peru	6,212	6,481	5,886
Philippines	3,598	5,721	4,485
Jamaica	3,325	4,326	4,153
Angola	2,996	3,303	3,550
Colombia	2,771	2,911	2,837
Gabon	2,746	1,986	2,276
Chile	1,804	1,776	1,881
Dominican Republic	285	782	1,649
Trinidad and Tobago	927	759	894
Honduras	1,121	991	753
Mozambique	713	355	723
Ecuador	620	990	713
Cote d'Ivoire	2,232	1,661	690
Guatemala	349	686	575
Nicaragua	18	273	534
Libya	76	134	511
Costa Rica	424	776	482
Vietnam	225	420	480
El Salvador	439	680	456
Guinea	196	141	357
Panama	183	148	263
Turkey	0	0	237
Rest of World	3,808	2,048	1,530
World Total	315,212	309,871	322,538
Variety meats, pork:			
China	147,615	80,974	155,421
Mexico	128,423	112,758	112,792
Hong Kong	139,741	111,637	72,751
Canada	18,587	17,522	16,466
Philippines	11,374	17,298	10,927
Japan	11,039	13,968	10,353
Vietnam	0	9,343	10,045
Korea, South	7,266	12,297	8,556
Chile	3,386	2,752	8,531
Guatemala	2,090	3,056	4,393
Taiwan	3,352	4,822	3,610
Colombia	3,740	2,033	2,757
Panama	1,358	2,343	2,065
Dominican Republic	532	902	1,541
Honduras	423	1,341	1,447
Trinidad and Tobago	656	1,221	1,095
Leeward-Windward Islands(*)	657	402	512
Australia(*)	23	297	423
Costa Rica	194	361	404
El Salvador	250	283	325
Haiti	664	538	324
Peru	559	242	322
Singapore	458	289	218
Italy(*)	0	0	176
Bermuda	0	0	160
Nicaragua	21	102	137
Albania	0	27	119
South Africa	689	487	113
Turks and Caicos Islands	141	43	84
Bahamas, The	62	135	75
Rest of World	1,027	574	389
World Total	484,324	398,074	426,531

See footnote(s) at end of table.

Table 7-63.—Meat: U.S. exports, 2017–2019—Continued

Country	2017	2018	2019
	Metric tons		
Other meat products, fr/ch/fz:			
Leeward-Windward Islands(*)	74	72	153
Vietnam	0	21	99
Mexico	15	75	59
Italy(*)	0	1	30
Jamaica	0	0	28
Venezuela	0	0	28
Korea, South	0	5	17
Trinidad and Tobago	0	0	12
Panama	0	0	12
Cayman Islands	21	2	11
Dominican Republic	0	0	10
Bermuda	1	3	8
United Arab Emirates	17	0	8
Bahamas, The	0	3	2
Saudi Arabia	0	0	2
Singapore	12	1	1
Netherlands Antilles(*)	1	1	1
Turks and Caicos Islands	4	5	1
Netherlands	0	11	1
Estonia	0	0	1
Denmark(*)	0	0	1
Spain	0	0	0
Australia(*)	0	28	0
Barbados	34	26	0
Canada	32	0	0
China	18	0	0
Costa Rica	3	0	0
Ireland	36	0	0
El Salvador	0	19	0
France(*)	0	3	0
Rest of World	144	7	0
World Total	410	281	484

(*)Denotes a country that is a summarization of its component countries. Users should use cautious interpretation on quantity reports using mixed units of measure. Quantity line items will only include statistics on the units of measure that are equal to, or are able to be converted to, the assigned unit of measure of the grouped commodities.

FAS, Office of Global Analysis, (202) 720-6301. Data Source: U.S. Census Bureau Trade Data, as of March 17, 2020.

Table 7-64.—Meat, beef, veal, and swine: International trade, imports and exports, 2018–2020

Country	2018	2019	2020
		1,000 metric tons	
Principle exporters, beef and veal:			
Brazil	2,082	2,356	2,580
India	1,556	1,600	1,700
United States	1,434	1,372	1,499
Australia	1,662	1,825	1,470
Argentina	507	765	840
New Zealand	633	649	642
Canada	502	560	610
Uruguay	466	470	468
Mexico	310	355	390
European Union	352	370	360
Paraguay	365	320	350
Belarus	220	195	195
Nicaragua	158	160	160
Pakistan	66	70	75
Ukraine	60	57	52
Principle importers, beef and veal:			
China	1,467	2,300	2,900
United States	1,360	1,388	1,306
Japan	862	870	890
Korea, South	582	610	625
Russia	495	440	430
Chile	317	380	395
European Union	373	357	355
Hong Kong	541	350	350
Egypt	300	310	320
Canada	245	215	215
Mexico	202	200	205
Taiwan	176	190	200
Malaysia	215	210	195
Israel	132	145	155
Saudi Arabia	134	140	145
Principle exporters, swine:			
European Union	2,933	3,650	3,900
United States	2,665	2,856	3,221
Canada	1,331	1,330	1,400
Brazil	730	860	1,000
Chile	200	240	270
Mexico	178	215	250
China	203	130	100
Russia	45	60	80
Australia	47	40	42
Serbia	14	18	20
South Africa	17	17	17
Argentina	8	11	12
Belarus	14	12	10
Vietnam	35	15	10
Norway	5	6	5
Principle importers, swine:			
China	1,561	2,600	3,700
Japan	1,481	1,510	1,490
Mexico	1,188	1,200	1,235
Korea, South	753	685	695
United States	473	434	401
Hong Kong	423	335	300
Philippines	287	240	300
Canada	233	250	260
Australia	216	260	240
Colombia	129	155	175
Chile	98	130	150
Singapore	125	123	124
Taiwan	109	107	105
Russia	87	130	80
Vietnam	20	50	75

FAS, Office of Global Analysis, (202) 720-6301. Prepared or estimated on the basis of official USDA production, supply, and distribution statistics from foreign governments.

Table 7-65.—Meats: Production and consumption, United States, 2010–2019[1]

Year	Beef			Veal			Lamb and mutton		
	Production	Consumption		Production	Consumption		Production	Consumption	
		Total	Per capita		Total	Per capita		Total	Per capita
	Million pounds	*Million pounds*	*Pounds*	*Million pounds*	*Million pounds*	*Pounds*	*Million pounds*	*Million pounds*	*Pounds*
2010	26,412	26,390	85.2	145	150	0.5	168	318	1.0
2011	26,281	25,538	81.8	136	137	0.4	153	295	0.8
2012	25,989	25,748	81.9	125	123	0.4	161	299	1.0
2013	25,790	25,476	80.5	117	119	0.4	161	324	1.0
2014	24,316	24,682	77.4	100	98	0.3	161	340	1.1
2015	23,760	24,769	77.2	88	88	0.3	155	357	1.1
2016	25,288	25,669	79.4	81	73	0.2	155	381	1.2
2017	26,250	26,492	81.5	80	78	0.2	150	396	1.2
2018	26,942	26,767	81.9	80	89	0.3	158	415	1.3
2019	27,221	27,272	83.0	79	81	0.2	153	422	1.3

Year	Pork			All meats		
	Production	Consumption		Production	Consumption	
		Total	Per capita		Total	Per capita
	Million pounds	*Million pounds*	*Pounds*	*Million pounds*	*Million pounds*	*Pounds*
2010	22,456	19,076	61.6	49,181	45,934	148
2011	22,775	18,382	58.9	49,232	44,351	142
2012	23,268	18,607	59.2	49,543	44,778	142
2013	23,203	19,104	60.4	49,271	45,022	142
2014	22,858	18,836	59.1	47,435	43,955	138
2015	24,517	20,592	64.6	48,520	45,806	143
2016	24,957	20,892	64.6	50,388	47,015	145
2017	25,598	21,034	64.7	51,991	48,000	148
2018	26,330	21,490	65.7	53,417	48,758	149
2019	27,652	22,188	67.5	55,015	49,966	152

[1] Carcass weight equivalent or dressed weight. Beginning 1977, pork production was no longer reported as "pork, excluding lard." This series has been revised to reflect pork production in prior years on a dressed weight basis that is comparable with the method used to report beef, veal, and lamb and mutton. Edible offals are excluded. Shipments to the U.S. territories are included in domestic consumption.
ERS, Animal Products and Cost of Production Branch, (202) 694–5409.

Table 7-66.—Hides, packer: Average price per piece, Central U.S., 2010–2019

Year	Steers				Heifers	
	Heavy native	Heavy Texas	Butt branded	Colorado branded	Heavy native	Branded
	Dollars	*Dollars*	*Dollars*	*Dollars*	*Dollars*	*Dollars*
2010	71.93	72.30	70.77	67.31	63.44	67.57
2011	82.17	81.70	80.77	76.42	74.39	71.17
2012	84.53	84.23	84.28	79.83	71.77	70.19
2013	98.73	95.74	98.56	94.38	84.68	82.90
2014	110.98	106.37	108.95	103.05	93.45	89.68
2015	84.29	77.13	82.57	75.98	65.00	59.76
2016	73.88	68.02	72.37	60.11	58.39	53.00
2017	67.05	59.13	65.21	(NA)	51.77	42.76
2018	68.19	39.29	50.98	39.36	38.17	33.72
2019	24.57	36.96	28.61	21.94	16.00	16.46

(NA) Not available.
AMS, Livestock & Grain Market News, (202) 720–7316.

Table 7-67.—Hides and skins: United States imports by country of origin, 2017–2019

Country of origin	2017	2018	2019
	Number		
Furskins:			
Canada	1,994,609	915,358	1,169,297
Ukraine	184,949	207,500	358,000
Czech Republic	62,050	0	230,000
Uruguay	42,840	46,379	52,745
Finland	48,652	64,193	47,243
Spain	16,269	0	25,121
Poland	24,357	16,251	14,077
Belgium-Luxembourg(*)	121,399	200,362	8,889
Denmark(*)	9,477	6,493	7,415
Latvia	708	1,524	2,139
Netherlands	19,429	2,741	955
Lithuania	842	532	891
Greece	113,477	891	718
China	12,250	752	364
Romania	1,241	3,913	210
Ireland	0	0	111
Italy(*)	810	477	111
Hong Kong	6,887	8	54
France(*)	56	1,742	47
Thailand	0	0	40
Mexico	13,088	12,163	30
United Arab Emirates	788	715	23
Turkey	0	0	11
Moldova	0	0	2
South Africa	4	4	1
Albania	190	0	0
Armenia	107	25	0
Argentina	40	0	0
Bosnia and Herzegovina	1,572	0	0
Bulgaria	10	12	0
Rest of World	114,288	26,017	0
World Total	2,790,389	1,508,052	1,918,494
	Pieces		
Hides and skins:			
Canada	625,09	653,668	347,052
United Kingdom	445,751	426,434	342,439
Belgium-Luxembourg(*)	203,691	196,535	118,831
Mexico	16,644	9,235	31,822
Brazil	18,484	19,641	14,560
Australia(*)	5,200	3,429	8,080
Thailand	5,746	4,747	7,923
Italy(*)	10,209	10,563	6,920
Papua New Guinea	0	0	6,024
Turkey	4	32	5,778
Cote d'Ivoire	2,658	2,139	4,411
New Zealand(*)	4,076	16,504	3,855
Argentina	15,731	15,211	2,719
France(*)	115	6,549	2,669
Colombia	27,050	13,694	2,016
Dominican Republic	1,311	0	1,326
Senegal	200	401	770
Japan	0	27	695
Guinea	177	350	650
Zimbabwe	343	4	628
Netherlands	0	120	626
Denmark(*)	0	32	614
India	311	411	557
Spain	515	13,096	375
Singapore	6	21	300
Austria	0	0	262
China	209	4,939	211
South Africa	124	41	108
Indonesia	211	364	101
Poland	0	1	26
Rest of World	65,857	6,273	83
World Total	1,449,725	1,404,461	912,431

(*) Denotes a country that is a summarization of its component countries.
FAS, Office of Global Analysis, (202) 720–6301. Data as of March 17, 2020.

Table 7-68.—Hides: U.S. trade exports, 2017–2019

Country	2017	2018	2019
	Pieces		
Bovine hides, whole:			
China	10,539,888	8,882,126	8,802,149
Korea, South	2,540,183	2,473,837	2,679,460
Mexico	1,540,934	1,669,958	2,022,979
Thailand	880,929	1,496,653	921,491
Taiwan	556,770	374,302	387,391
Japan	151,841	175,111	181,501
Brazil	34,355	159,598	163,587
Indonesia	228,318	192,279	96,343
Netherlands	33,036	64,156	71,727
Vietnam	50,745	30,249	62,831
Italy(*)	191,691	183,274	60,211
India	19,200	45,512	43,868
Turkey	100,643	114,151	42,311
Cambodia	0	0	23,730
Ethiopia(*)	0	633	21,189
Hong Kong	29,274	11,744	14,005
Bosnia and Herzegovina	83,510	55,347	11,208
Slovenia	4,959	77,747	10,186
Egypt	0	0	9,325
Germany(*)	10,277	3,110	4,178
Belgium-Luxembourg(*)	66,007	2,675	3,560
Austria	960	1,539	3,456
Israel(*)	0	1,211	3,213
Colombia	2,557	0	3,166
Spain	8,796	16,837	2,399
Philippines	0	1,680	1,760
Portugal	0	0	920
Bahamas, The	0	0	708
Ecuador	0	0	365
Haiti	0	900	349
Rest of World	20,184	12,600	531
World Total	17,095,057	16,047,229	15,650,097
Other cattle hides:			
Mexico	1,582,984	1,573,810	363,402
Spain	1,920	38,133	36,036
Japan	42,221	33,131	35,151
Thailand	54,389	65,130	29,731
Hong Kong	12,893	12,465	20,748
China	43,804	36,094	19,656
Korea, South	31,119	9,210	10,721
Vietnam	25,697	7,459	3,541
Italy(*)	0	630	3,199
Austria	0	247	1,669
Cambodia	0	0	1,070
Sweden	188	734	1,039
United Kingdom	0	7,396	963
Portugal	0	0	944
India	981	1,077	935
Taiwan	0	7,210	567
Philippines	0	0	116
Bangladesh	420	199	0
Brazil	7,173	26	0
Dominican Republic	2,750	167	0
Germany(*)	16,404	4,327	0
Greece	523	0	0
Indonesia	171	64	0
Netherlands	28,554	1,120	0
World Total	1,852,191	1,798,629	529,488

See footnote(s) at end of table.

Table 7-68.—Hides: U.S. trade exports, 2017–2019—Continued

Country	2017	2018	2019
	Pieces		
Horse hides, whole:			
China	201,061	98,244	25,616
Korea, South	50,596	69,395	23,746
Netherlands	0	0	2,675
Canada	10,936	8,965	1,762
Togo	0	24	349
Mexico	154,247	21,326	88
Nigeria	60	351	82
Indonesia	2,720	9,852	31
Australia(*)	25	0	0
Bermuda	97	0	0
Costa Rica	135	0	0
Ireland	0	333	0
Germany(*)	0	1	0
Hong Kong	44,146	0	0
Honduras	0	1,757	0
Israel(*)	0	3,507	0
Italy(*)	3,600	0	0
Liberia	0	112	0
New Zealand(*)	0	2,000	0
Sweden	0	223	0
Thailand	19,523	0	0
Taiwan	12,667	14,608	0
United Kingdom	1,520	0	0
Vietnam	7,830	5,418	0
World Total	509,163	263,116	54,349
Calf skins, whole:			
China	1,371,637	1,685,359	1,496,510
Mexico	273,229	393,267	329,255
Korea, South	319,216	690,135	316,701
Italy(*)	171,269	114,591	217,430
Thailand	201,429	125,508	186,439
Netherlands	0	0	42,678
Indonesia	3,897	0	31,248
Costa Rica	73,001	75,133	28,894
Israel(*)	61,728	46,744	27,109
India	58,427	32,319	25,739
Cambodia	0	0	19,810
Vietnam	5,733	5,092	15,844
Spain	0	0	12,724
Hong Kong	9,052	8,481	12,000
Colombia	0	0	3,849
Japan	22,043	7,902	2,726
Germany(*)	7,797	20,765	1,926
Turkey	27,175	13,892	1,800
Brazil	0	4,628	1,600
Dominican Republic	0	0	1,530
Belgium-Luxembourg(*)	0	0	1,360
Ghana	0	424	1,129
Guatemala	0	0	558
Sri Lanka	0	0	174
Nigeria	0	0	119
Kuwait	0	85	56
France(*)	1,078	150	11
Australia(*)	145	0	0
Austria	53	0	0
Bahamas, The	0	96	0
Rest of World	21,444	21,080	0
World Total	2,628,353	3,245,651	2,779,219
Sheep & lamb skins:			
China	818,429	635,279	483,942
Turkey	56,760	116,840	55,153
Russia	19,200	55,860	22,650
Brazil	15,392	13,109	19,515
Mexico	32,089	18,615	18,331
Germany(*)	9,125	11,683	8,000
Spain	0	2,685	3,990
Canada	3,015	2,987	3,920
Poland	3,667	28,310	2,473
Pakistan	0	748	243
Bolivia	0	0	120
Colombia	90	0	0
Italy(*)	500	0	0
Korea, South	2,155	0	0
Netherlands Antilles(*)	667	0	0
United Kingdom	137	2,800	0
World Total	961,226	888,916	618,346

See footnote(s) at end of table.

Table 7-68.—Hides: U.S. trade exports, 2017–2019—Continued

Country	2017	2018	2019
	Pieces		
Other hides & skins:			
Mexico	1,867,504	1,643,008	1,140,446
China	2,042,535	1,437,489	675,774
Thailand	1,651,170	1,285,795	508,765
Vietnam	161,765	52,284	302,451
Korea, South	901,190	500,102	287,340
France(*)	111,452	195,816	183,271
United Kingdom	91,000	106,135	103,746
Singapore	113,034	105,229	103,713
Germany(*)	44,920	66,123	91,136
Italy(*)	174,131	156,409	75,557
Taiwan	1,381,408	396,557	70,056
Indonesia	0	35,479	22,919
Portugal	0	2,985	10,606
Canada	47,778	17,397	8,212
Spain	7,578	0	5,419
India	3,435	0	4,124
Malaysia	7,594	5,973	1,885
Japan	32,371	12,864	1,739
Philippines	0	0	826
Brazil	51,668	17,374	647
Djibouti	0	127	550
Pakistan	1,200	2,449	453
Cambodia	83,899	189,891	242
Guatemala	0	0	200
Bosnia and Herzegovina	0	160	126
Australia(*)	0	0	0
Barbados	0	395	0
Belgium-Luxembourg(*)	1,000	515	0
Bangladesh	972	0	0
Sri Lanka	340	0	0
Rest of World	33,018	41,435	0
World Total	8,810,962	6,271,991	3,600,203
	Number		
Other furskins:			
Canada	491,395	853,684	872,982
China	566,762	427,458	374,809
Hong Kong	95,216	154,208	132,831
Cambodia	10,552	19,878	125,363
Pakistan	15,860	15,900	53,063
Portugal	10,028	45,015	42,789
Belgium-Luxembourg(*)	0	41,077	9,687
Germany(*)	7,247	24,168	3,730
Thailand	0	0	3,156
Italy(*)	1,905	23,707	2,891
Greece	3,663	1,625	2,005
Vietnam	0	3,449	1,362
Turkey	0	416	1,200
Lithuania	0	0	1,005
Mexico	511	0	768
France(*)	13,604	3,697	767
Finland	0	500	600
Chile	0	0	4
Argentina	270	0	0
Costa Rica	128	0	0
Dominican Republic	850	0	0
Haiti	0	0	0
Indonesia	0	685	0
India	6,084	0	0
Japan	396	0	0
Korea, South	6,768	0	0
Latvia	0	0	0
Spain	0	259	0
Switzerland(*)	0	200	0
United Kingdom	0	157	0
Rest of World	1,095	0	0
World Total	1,232,334	1,616,083	1,629,012

(*) Denotes a country that is a summarization of its component countries.
FAS, Office of Global Analysis, (202) 720-6301. Data Source: U.S. Census Bureau Trade Data, as of March 17, 2020.

Table 7-69.—Mink: Farms, pelts produced, average price, and value, United States, 2009–2018

Year	Mink farms	Pelts produced	Average marketing price	Value of mink pelts
	Number	*Number*	*Dollars*	*Dollars*
2009	278	2,866,700	65.10	186,622,170
2010	265	2,840,200	81.90	232,612,380
2011	268	3,091,470	94.30	291,525,621
2012 [1]	(NA)	(NA)	(NA)	(NA)
2013	(NA)	3,544,610	56.30	199,561,543
2014	(NA)	3,741,150	57.70	215,864,355
2015	(NA)	3,682,960	32.00	117,854,720
2016	(NA)	3,454,410	34.70	119,868,027
2017	(NA)	3,305,440	36.30	119,987,472
2018	....	....	....	....

(NA) Not available. [1] Due to sequestration the Mink report was suspended.
NASS, Livestock Branch, (202) 720–3570.

Table 7-70.—Mink pelts: Pelts produced by color class, selected States, and United States, 2017

State	Black	Demi/Wild	Pastel	Sapphire	Blue Iris	Mahogany
	Number	*Number*	*Number*	*Number*	*Number*	*Number*
Idaho	94,000	(D)	14,000	11,500	(D)	165,000
Illinois	51,000	-	-	(D)	-	(D)
Iowa	44,000	-	(D)	2,900	(D)	36,000
Michigan	59,000	-	500	200	(D)	1,200
Minnesota	(D)	(D)	(D)	(D)	(D)	37,000
Montana	(D)	(D)	-	-	-	-
Ohio	(D)	(D)	-	(D)	-	(D)
Oregon	210,000	-	-	(D)	44,000	(D)
Pennsylvania	33,000	(D)	5,500	11,500	(D0	(D)
Utah	280,000	24,000	33,000	45,000	1,900	285,000
Washington	27,000	-	-	-	(D)	(D)
Wisconsin	690,000	(D)	33,000	39,000	116,000	49,000
Other States [1]	151,150	86,010	11,810	88,800	40,730	56,200
United States	1,639,150	110,010	97,810	198,900	184,120	629,400

State	Pearl	Lavender	Violet	White	Other	Total [2]
	Number	*Number*	*Number*	*Number*	*Number*	*Number*
Idaho	-	(D)	(D)	(D)	(D)	313,500
Illinois	(D)	-	-	(D)	-	81,100
Iowa	-	-	-	(D)	-	88,210
Michigan	-	3,500	(D)	7,500	-	77,700
Minnesota	-	-	(D)	31,000	(D)	180,580
Montana	-	-	-	-	-	(D)
Ohio	(D)	(D)	(D)	(D)	-	(D)
Oregon	-	(D)	(D)	-	-	283,670
Pennsylvania	(D)	(D)	(D)	(D)	(D)	68,130
Utah	(D)	(D)	(D)	(D)	(D)	734,260
Washington	-	-	-	-	-	44,000
Wisconsin	-	20,000	(D)	151,000	(D)	1,091,180
Other States [1]	115,510	10,630	42,730	52,730	11,450	343,110
United States	115,510	34,130	42,730	242,230	11,450	3,305,440

- Represents zero. (D) Withheld to avoid disclosing data for individual operations. [1] Other States include New Hampshire, New Jersey, New York, North Carolina, South Dakota, and some pelts from the above listed States that were not published to avoid disclosing individual operations. [2] Published color classes may not add to the State total to avoid disclosing individual operations.
NASS, Livestock Branch, (202) 720–3570.

Table 7-71.—Livestock: Inventory and value, United States, Jan. 1, 2016–2018

Class of livestock and poultry	Inventory			Value					
				Per head [1]			Total		
	2016	2017	2018	2016	2017	2018	2016	2017	2018
	1,000	*1,000*	*1,000*	*Dollars*	*Dollars*	*Dollars*	*1,000 Dollars*	*1,000 Dollars*	*1,000 Dollars*
Angora goats [2]	150	152	144	117	130	124	14,757	16,827	14,584
Cattle	91,888	93,624	94,298	1,410	1,109	1,146	129,562,080	103,829,681	108,065,508
Chickens [3]	500,608	514,838	527,573	4.23	4.20	4.33	2,115,245	2,162,545	2,284,164
Hogs [3]	71,345	73,145	74,915	92	99	98	6,578,419	7,206,965	7,298,943
Sheep and lambs	5,295	5,270	5,265	202	203	204	1,071,467	1,067,857	1,071,378

[1] Based on reporters' estimates of average price per head in their localities. [2] Four-State total for angora goats (Arizona, California, New Mexico, Texas). [3] Dec. 1 of preceding year.
NASS, Livestock Branch, (202) 720–3570.

Table 7-72.—Livestock: Market year for specified commodities

Cattle market year average price received: United States marketing years 2009–2018 [1]

Year	Cows [2]	Steers and heifers	Calves	Beef cattle [3]	Milks cows [4]
	Dollars	*Dollars*	*Dollars*	*Dollars*	*Dollars*
2009	44.80	85.40	105.00	80.30	1,390.00
2010	54.80	97.70	117.00	92.20	1,330.00
2011	71.20	117.00	142.00	113.00	1,420.00
2012	81.70	123.00	172.00	121.00	1,430.00
2013	82.30	126.00	181.00	125.00	1,380.00
2014	107.00	153.00	261.00	152.00	1,830.00
2015	103.00	148.00	247.00	147.00	1,990.00
2016	74.30	121.00	158.00	119.00	1,760.00
2017	69.10	122.00	168.00	120.00	1,620.00
2018	62.60	117.00	170.00	115.00	1,360.00

Hog market year average price received: United States marketing years 2008–2017 [5]

Year	Barrows and gilts	Sows	All Hogs
	Dollars	*Dollars*	*Dollars*
2008	47.90	29.20	47.00
2009	42.00	36.10	41.60
2010	54.40	48.70	54.10
2011	65.70	57.50	65.30
2012	64.60	51.30	64.20
2013	67.30	62.90	67.20
2014	76.50	77.70	76.50
2015	55.70	44.90	55.30
2016	53.50	44.50	53.10
2017	50.50	41.30	50.20

[1] Market year for cattle January 1-December 31 for United States and all States. [2] Cows includes beef cows and cull dairy cows sold for slaughter. [3] All beef includes steer and heifers combined and cows. [4] Milk cow prices are calendar year average. [5] Market year for hogs December 1-November 30 for United States and all States.
NASS, Livestock Branch, (202) 720–3570.

Table 7-74.—Frozen meat: Cold storage holdings, end of month, United States, 2017–2018

Month	Boneless beef		Beef bone-in		Total beef	
	2017	2018	2017	2018	2017	2018
	1,000 pounds					
January	499,000	458,749	39,215	42,995	538,215	501,744
February	463,934	416,438	38,514	42,901	502,448	459,339
March	422,572	426,232	41,429	37,725	464,001	463,957
April	415,592	435,196	42,826	35,964	458,418	471,160
May	376,699	426,089	34,799	38,565	411,498	464,654
June	383,658	407,131	31,668	41,454	415,326	448,585
July	398,071	444,089	33,765	40,159	431,836	484,248
August	438,094	457,392	38,473	43,923	476,567	501,315
September	454,439	458,904	41,576	48,262	496,015	507,166
October	462,093	468,424	44,948	47,150	507,041	515,574
November	443,927	473,863	41,260	40,835	485,187	514,698
December	445,881	462,072	42,176	33,552	488,057	495,624

Month	Picnics		Bellies		Butts	
	2017	2018	2017	2018	2017	2018
	1,000 pounds					
January	8,993	7,074	13,995	43,810	23,243	25,477
February	8,437	8,644	16,153	49,012	22,052	22,503
March	8,783	11,314	20,570	59,202	21,925	20,629
April	7,210	10,094	33,536	64,563	21,264	20,904
May	7,741	10,110	31,589	61,234	19,862	15,313
June	7,698	7,268	22,291	53,279	15,057	15,734
July	6,648	8,157	17,602	38,556	14,502	13,218
August	8,176	8,874	19,213	34,805	16,308	11,498
September	8,745	8,375	20,897	30,354	17,247	13,282
October	8,055	7,879	32,268	26,690	21,249	17,014
November	6,866	6,644	35,164	36,859	25,799	17,623
December	5,982	6,832	39,620	42,251	23,883	16,749

Month	Hams					
	Bone-in		Boneless		Total	
	2017	2018	2017	2018	2017	2018
	1,000 pounds					
January	34,094	35,572	61,271	82,835	95,365	118,407
February	50,874	36,932	74,293	85,811	125,167	122,743
March	28,850	24,234	61,343	72,105	90,193	96,339
April	36,689	23,694	76,126	88,451	112,815	112,145
May	51,222	41,898	92,419	97,397	143,641	139,295
June	74,248	54,794	104,063	93,863	178,311	148,657
July	87,178	71,184	107,790	96,379	194,968	167,563
August	91,736	91,764	112,151	112,999	203,887	204,763
September	99,301	93,281	132,733	121,347	232,034	214,628
October	79,733	76,417	115,594	99,692	195,327	176,109
November	27,715	37,122	70,509	59,253	98,224	96,375
December	15,458	15,714	65,624	57,404	81,082	73,118

Month	Loins					
	Bone-in		Boneless		Total	
	2017	2018	2017	2018	2017	2018
	1,000 pounds					
January	14,212	14,276	25,493	26,497	39,705	40,773
February	13,911	14,638	24,244	24,102	38,155	38,740
March	13,753	13,081	22,608	26,472	36,361	39,553
April	16,365	12,958	26,507	26,872	42,872	39,830
May	15,502	12,205	24,855	24,314	40,357	36,519
June	13,168	9,889	26,729	22,060	39,897	31,949
July	9,826	7,261	24,052	19,353	33,878	26,614
August	10,180	9,810	22,461	20,765	32,641	30,575
September	12,129	11,130	22,162	22,633	34,291	33,763
October	10,971	9,790	25,956	24,426	36,927	34,216
November	9,007	10,279	27,433	23,644	36,440	33,923
December	9,684	11,221	25,445	22,871	35,129	34,092

See footnote(s) at end of table.

Table 7-74.—Frozen meat: Cold storage holdings, end of month, United States, 2017–2018—Continued

Month	Ribs		Trimmings		Other frozen pork	
	2017	2018	2017	2018	2017	2018
	1,000 pounds					
January	128,029	114,366	34,281	48,602	85,023	104,544
February	139,525	131,600	37,339	51,186	86,028	97,215
March	140,639	143,957	40,087	56,318	83,593	93,548
April	136,875	143,717	40,613	57,490	88,858	90,657
May	114,460	119,286	37,308	56,969	91,386	92,610
June	85,993	88,871	32,781	45,132	90,064	85,049
July	77,182	84,171	29,858	40,372	91,725	86,046
August	74,341	77,803	34,811	42,253	99,330	86,905
September	88,032	83,403	34,643	38,499	99,095	81,592
October	94,859	101,369	33,185	42,156	94,458	79,323
November	100,218	108,324	37,484	43,033	93,602	81,265
December	104,264	124,310	43,080	48,441	86,880	78,855

Month	Variety meats		Unclassified pork		Total pork	
	2017	2018	2017	2018	2017	2018
	1,000 pounds					
January	52,415	30,735	43,166	46,926	524,215	580,714
February	50,908	33,161	44,091	55,009	567,855	609,813
March	54,430	35,875	48,882	54,278	545,463	611,013
April	54,471	36,544	51,810	58,778	590,324	634,722
May	49,848	34,681	52,024	57,708	588,216	623,725
June	39,419	34,438	47,499	51,502	559,010	561,879
July	40,879	34,439	47,612	52,893	554,854	552,029
August	37,736	34,307	49,255	49,730	575,698	581,513
September	37,231	37,030	46,348	48,477	618,563	589,403
October	35,495	36,193	46,551	49,968	598,374	570,917
November	28,709	36,001	39,818	47,621	502,324	507,668
December	27,965	34,009	42,162	46,630	490,047	505,287

Month	Veal		Lamb & mutton		Total red meat	
	2017	2018	2017	2018	2017	2018
	1,000 pounds					
January	18,535	19,912	20,361	26,790	1,101,326	1,129,160
February	16,950	21,158	25,694	28,280	1,112,947	1,118,590
March	16,104	20,780	25,792	28,615	1,051,360	1,124,365
April	15,383	20,033	28,603	33,992	1,092,728	1,159,907
May	12,870	18,206	29,859	35,591	1,042,443	1,142,176
June	12,297	14,954	26,177	38,678	1,012,810	1,064,096
July	16,329	18,096	26,770	42,129	1,029,789	1,096,502
August	15,311	14,179	32,383	39,386	1,099,959	1,136,393
September	13,669	13,736	31,415	40,466	1,159,662	1,150,771
October	12,344	9,842	31,594	39,321	1,149,353	1,135,654
November	15,799	9,106	28,977	37,859	1,032,287	1,069,331
December	16,373	8,238	26,714	36,454	1,021,191	1,045,603

NASS, Livestock Branch, (202) 720–3570.

CHAPTER VIII

DAIRY AND POULTRY STATISTICS

Dairy statistics in this chapter include series relating to many phases of production, movement, prices, stocks, and consumption of milk and its products. Two series of number of milk cows on farms are included in this publication. One series is an inventory number of a specific classification estimated as one of the major groups making up the total cattle population on January 1. The other series identified as ''milk cows'' is an annual average number of milk cows during the year (excluding any not yet fresh) and is used in estimating milk production.

In comparing the several series of milk prices, it is important to note that prices received by farmers for all whole milk sold are for milk or milkfat content as actually sold, while certain prices paid by dealers for milk for fluid purposes or for specified manufacturing purposes may be quoted on a 3.5 percent butterfat basis, or for some types of manufacturing milk on the test of the milk used for that particular purpose.

Poultry and poultry products statistics include inventory numbers of chickens by classes; the production, disposition, cash receipts, and gross income from chickens and eggs; poultry and egg receipts at principal markets; commercial broiler production; turkey production, disposition, and gross income; poultry and eggs under Federal inspection; and the National Poultry Improvement Plan. Estimates relating to inventories, production, and income exclude poultry and eggs produced on places not classified as farms.

Table 8-1.—Milk cows and heifers: Number that have calved and heifers 500 pounds and over kept for milk cow replacements, United States, Jan. 1, 2010–2019

Year	Milk cows and heifers that have calved	Heifers 500 pounds and over kept for milk cow replacements
	Thousands	*Thousands*
2010	9,087	4,551
2011	9,156	4,577
2012	9,236	4,618
2013	9,221	4,546
2014	9,209	4,539
2015	9,312	4,710
2016	9,312	4,814
2017	9,369	4,754
2018	9,432	4,768
2019	9,353	4,702

NASS, Livestock Branch, (202) 720–3570.

Table 8-2.—Milk cows and heifers: Number that have calved and heifers 500 pounds and over kept for milk cow replacements, by State and United States, Jan. 1, 2018 and 2019

State	Milk cows and heifers that have calved		Heifers 500 pounds and over kept for milk cow replacements	
	2018	2019	2018	2019
	Thousands	*Thousands*	*Thousands*	*Thousands*
Alabama	6.0	5.0	3.0	2.0
Alaska	0.3	0.2	0.1	0.1
Arizona	210.0	205.0	105.0	115.0
Arkansas	6.0	5.0	4.0	4.0
California	1,740.0	1,730.0	780.0	760.0
Colorado	168.0	178.0	100.0	110.0
Connecticut	20.0	19.5	9.5	9.0
Delaware	5.0	4.5	2.0	1.6
Florida	124.0	116.0	40.0	35.0
Georgia	85.0	81.0	25.0	30.0
Hawaii	2.0	1.5	1.0	1.0
Idaho	600.0	614.0	310.0	340.0
Illinois	93.0	85.0	47.0	45.0
Indiana	187.0	181.0	75.0	80.0
Iowa	220.0	220.0	135.0	125.0
Kansas	156.0	161.0	140.0	170.0
Kentucky	57.0	53.0	45.0	45.0
Louisiana	12.0	11.0	4.0	4.0
Maine	30.0	29.0	15.0	14.0
Maryland	47.0	44.0	28.0	30.0
Massachusetts	11.5	10.5	7.0	6.5
Michigan	428.0	422.0	176.0	160.0
Minnesota	455.0	450.0	290.0	255.0
Mississippi	9.0	8.0	7.0	5.0
Missouri	84.0	81.0	40.0	40.0
Montana	13.0	12.0	7.0	8.0
Nebraska	60.0	59.0	15.0	15.0
Nevada	32.0	33.0	12.0	11.0
New Hampshire	12.5	12.0	7.0	6.5
New Jersey	6.0	5.5	3.2	3.3
New Mexico	332.0	325.0	130.0	125.0
New York	625.0	625.0	350.0	335.0
North Carolina	45.0	43.0	17.0	20.0
North Dakota	16.0	15.0	9.0	8.0
Ohio	264.0	253.0	121.0	125.0
Oklahoma	42.0	40.0	25.0	20.0
Oregon	124.0	125.0	70.0	65.0
Pennsylvania	525.0	505.0	310.0	290.0
Rhode Island	0.8	0.7	0.5	0.5
South Carolina	15.0	14.0	6.0	5.0
South Dakota	119.0	122.0	45.0	40.0
Tennessee	40.0	36.0	25.0	25.0
Texas	530.0	545.0	250.0	260.0
Utah	97.0	100.0	50.0	50.0
Vermont	128.0	126.0	57.0	55.0
Virginia	87.0	79.0	40.0	37.0
Washington	275.0	280.0	123.0	123.0
West Virginia	7.0	7.0	3.0	3.0
Wisconsin	1,275.0	1,270.0	700.0	680.0
Wyoming	6.0	6.0	4.0	4.0
United States	9,432.1	9,353.4	4,768.3	4,701.5

NASS, Livestock Branch, (202) 720–3570.

Table 8-3.—Milk and milkfat production: Number of milk cows, production per cow, and total quantity produced, by State and United States, 2017 [1]

State	Number of milk cows [2]	Production of milk and milkfat [3]				
		Per milk cow		All milk percent of fat	Total	
		Milk	Milkfat		Milk	Milkfat
	Thousands	*Pounds*	*Pounds*	*Percent*	*Million pounds*	*Million pounds*
Alabama	6.0	15,000	579	3.86	90.0	3.5
Alaska	0.3	9,667	379	3.92	2.9	0.1
Arizona	208.0	24,197	876	3.62	5,033.0	182.2
Arkansas	6.0	13,333	496	3.72	80.0	3.0
California	1,749.0	22,755	876	3.85	39,798.0	1,532.2
Colorado	162.0	25,858	954	3.69	4,189.0	154.6
Connecticut	19.0	22,105	871	3.94	420.0	16.5
Delaware	5.0	18,560	716	3.86	92.8	3.6
Florida	124.0	20,129	743	3.69	2,496.0	92.1
Georgia	84.0	21,905	795	3.63	1,840.0	66.8
Hawaii	2.3	16,913	560	3.31	38.9	1.3
Idaho	600.0	24,388	954	3.91	14,633.0	572.2
Illinois	93.0	20,742	796	3.84	1,929.0	74.1
Indiana	187.0	22,754	851	3.74	4,255.0	159.1
Iowa	218.0	23,757	919	3.87	5,179.0	200.4
Kansas	152.0	23,020	866	3.76	3,499.0	131.6
Kentucky	56.0	18,607	700	3.76	1,042.0	39.2
Louisiana	12.0	13,417	521	3.88	161.0	6.2
Maine	30.0	21,000	809	3.85	630.0	24.3
Maryland	48.0	19,917	761	3.82	956.0	36.5
Massachusetts	12.0	17,583	695	3.95	211.0	8.3
Michigan	427.0	26,302	978	3.72	11,231.0	417.8
Minnesota	458.0	21,544	838	3.89	9,867.0	383.8
Mississippi	9.0	15,222	585	3.84	137.0	5.3
Missouri	85.0	14,600	574	3.93	1,241.0	48.8
Montana	13.0	22,154	831	3.75	288.0	10.8
Nebraska	60.0	24,067	924	3.84	1,444.0	55.4
Nevada	32.0	22,156	866	3.91	709.0	27.7
New Hampshire	13.0	21,000	817	3.89	273.0	10.6
New Jersey	6.0	19,833	758	3.82	119.0	4.5
New Mexico	329.0	24,960	909	3.64	8,212.0	298.9
New York	624.0	23,925	921	3.85	14,029.0	574.8
North Carolina	45.0	21,156	793	3.75	952.0	35.7
North Dakota	16.0	21,563	826	3.83	345.0	13.2
Ohio	264.0	21,284	822	3.86	5,619.0	216.9
Oklahoma	40.0	18,200	684	3.76	728.0	27.4
Oregon	124.0	20,395	816	4.00	2,529.0	101.2
Pennsylvania	525.0	20,749	795	3.83	10,893.0	417.2
Rhode Island	0.8	16,250	644	3.96	13.0	0.5
South Carolina	15.0	16,533	637	3.85	248.0	9.5
South Dakota	117.0	22,376	913	4.08	2,618.0	106.8
Tennessee	40.0	17,325	651	3.76	693.0	26.1
Texas	515.0	23,406	946	4.04	12,054.0	487.0
Utah	96.0	23,073	877	3.80	2,215.0	84.2
Vermont	129.0	21,155	819	3.87	2,729.0	105.6
Virginia	87.0	19,954	748	3.75	1,736.0	65.1
Washington	274.0	23,836	953	4.00	6,531.0	261.2
West Virginia	8.0	15,075	602	3.79	127.0	4.8
Wisconsin	1,278.0	23,735	907	3.82	30,333.0	1,158.7
Wyoming	6.0	23,033	838	3.64	138.2	5.0
United States	9,406.0	22,914	880	3.84	215,527.0	8,272.3

[1] May not add due to rounding. [2] Average number during year, excluding heifers not yet fresh. [3] Excludes milk sucked by calves.
NASS, Livestock Branch, (202) 720–3570.

Table 8-4.—Milk and milkfat production: Number of milk cows, production per cow, and total quantity produced, by State and United States, 2018 [1]

State	Number of milk cows [2]	Production of milk and milkfat [3]				
		Per milk cow		All milk percent of fat	Total	
		Milk	Milkfat		Milk	Milkfat
	Thousands	*Pounds*	*Pounds*	*Percent*	*Million pounds*	*Million pounds*
Alabama	5.0	14,600	566	3.88	73.0	2.8
Alaska	0.3	9,333	367	3.93	2.8	0.1
Arizona	208.0	23,933	876	3.66	4,978.0	182.2
Arkansas	6.0	12,333	467	3.79	74.0	2.8
California	1,734.0	23,306	909	3.90	40,413.0	1,576.1
Colorado	176.0	25,892	968	3.74	4,557.0	170.4
Connecticut	19.0	22,474	890	3.96	427.0	16.9
Delaware	4.8	19,063	732	3.84	91.5	3.5
Florida	120.0	19,842	730	3.68	2,381.0	87.6
Georgia	82.0	21,537	784	3.64	1,766.0	64.3
Hawaii	2.0	17,000	588	3.46	34.0	1.2
Idaho	609.0	24,875	985	3.96	15,149.0	599.9
Illinois	90.0	20,867	812	3.89	1,878.0	73.1
Indiana	184.0	22,614	855	3.78	4,161.0	157.3
Iowa	220.0	23,945	943	3.94	5,268.0	207.6
Kansas	159.0	23,321	900	3.86	3,708.0	143.1
Kentucky	55.0	18,345	695	3.79	1,009.0	38.2
Louisiana	11.0	13,818	558	4.04	152.0	6.1
Maine	30.0	20,600	797	3.87	618.0	23.9
Maryland	45.0	20,556	785	3.82	925.0	35.3
Massachusetts	11.0	18,364	731	3.98	202.0	8.0
Michigan	424.0	26,340	1,006	3.82	11,168.0	426.6
Minnesota	453.0	21,784	867	3.98	9,868.0	392.7
Mississippi	9.0	14,333	579	4.04	129.0	5.2
Missouri	83.0	14,386	573	3.98	1,194.0	47.5
Montana	12.0	22,833	868	3.80	274.0	10.4
Nebraska	60.0	24,000	926	3.86	1,440.0	55.6
Nevada	32.0	22,938	906	3.95	734.0	29.0
New Hampshire	12.0	20,750	811	3.91	249.0	9.7
New Jersey	6.0	18,333	697	3.80	110.0	4.2
New Mexico	330.0	25,106	929	3.70	8,285.0	306.5
New York	623.0	23,888	922	3.86	14,882.0	574.4
North Carolina	44.0	21,295	803	3.77	937.0	35.3
North Dakota	15.0	22,267	875	3.93	334.0	13.1
Ohio	259.0	21,359	831	3.89	5,532.0	215.2
Oklahoma	40.0	18,125	692	3.82	725.0	27.7
Oregon	123.0	20,577	835	4.06	2,531.0	102.8
Pennsylvania	519.0	20,549	783	3.81	10,665.0	406.3
Rhode Island	0.7	16,714	674	4.03	11.7	0.5
South Carolina	14.0	17,286	666	3.85	242.0	9.3
South Dakota	121.0	22,355	932	4.17	2,705.0	112.8
Tennessee	37.0	17,135	649	3.79	634.0	24.0
Texas	537.0	23,933	984	4.11	12,852.0	528.2
Utah	100.0	23,220	899	3.87	2,322.0	89.9
Vermont	127.0	21,102	823	3.90	2,680.0	104.5
Virginia	83.0	19,699	745	3.78	1,635.0	61.8
Washington	277.0	24,318	987	4.06	6,736.0	273.5
West Virginia	7.0	15,857	606	3.82	111.0	4.2
Wisconsin	1,274.0	24,002	934	3.89	30,579.0	1,189.5
Wyoming	6.0	23,700	863	3.64	142.2	5.2
United States	9,399.0	23,149	900	3.89	217,575.0	8,466.0

[1] May not add due to rounding. [2] Average number during year, excluding heifers not yet fresh. [3] Excludes milk sucked by calves.
NASS, Livestock Branch, (202) 720–3570.

Table 8-5.—Milk: Quantities used and marketed by producers, by State and United States, 2017[1]

State	Milk used where produced			Milk marketed by producers	
	Fed to calves[2]	Used for milk cream & butter	Total	Total quantity[3]	Fluid grade[4]
	Million pounds	*Million pounds*	*Million pounds*	*Million pounds*	*Percent*
Alabama	0.7	0.3	1.0	89.0	100
Alaska	0.2	0.2	0.4	2.5	100
Arizona	13.0	1.0	14.0	5,019.0	100
Arkansas	1.7	0.3	2.0	78.0	100
California	26.0	4.0	30.0	39,768.0	97
Colorado	21.0	1.0	22.0	4,167.0	100
Connecticut	2.5	0.5	3.0	417.0	100
Delaware	0.9	0.1	1.0	91.8	100
Florida	5.0	1.0	6.0	2,490.0	100
Georgia	7.0	1.0	8.0	1,832.0	100
Hawaii	0.1	0.1	0.2	38.7	100
Idaho	31.0	1.0	32.0	14,601.0	100
Illinois	10.0	2.0	12.0	1,917.0	98
Indiana	23.0	4.0	27.0	4,228.0	100
Iowa	15.0	1.0	16.0	5,163.0	100
Kansas	13.0	1.0	14.0	3,485.0	100
Kentucky	6.0	1.0	7.0	1,035.0	100
Louisiana	2.0	1.0	3.0	158.0	100
Maine	3.0	1.0	4.0	626.0	100
Maryland	7.0	1.0	8.0	948.0	100
Massachusetts	1.5	0.5	2.0	209.0	100
Michigan	33.0	2.0	35.0	11,196.0	100
Minnesota	95.0	4.0	99.0	9,768.0	99
Mississippi	1.0	1.0	2.0	135.0	100
Missouri	17.0	4.0	21.0	1,220.0	97
Montana	3.0	2.0	5.0	283.0	100
Nebraska	5.5	0.5	6.0	1,438.0	100
Nevada	5.0	1.0	6.0	703.0	100
New Hampshire	1.5	0.5	2.0	271.0	100
New Jersey	1.5	0.5	2.0	117.0	100
New Mexico	42.0	3.0	45.0	8,167.0	100
New York	55.0	2.0	57.0	14,872.0	100
North Carolina	5.0	1.0	6.0	948.0	100
North Dakota	4.5	0.5	5.0	340.0	98
Ohio	24.0	5.0	29.0	5,590.0	97
Oklahoma	6.0	1.0	7.0	721.0	100
Oregon	20.0	1.0	21.0	2,508.0	100
Pennsylvania	61.0	14.0	75.0	10,818.0	100
Rhode Island	0.1	-	0.1	12.9	100
South Carolina	2.0	1.0	3.0	245.0	100
South Dakota	7.0	1.0	8.0	2,610.0	100
Tennessee	4.0	1.0	5.0	688.0	100
Texas	25.0	1.0	26.0	12,028.0	100
Utah	12.0	1.0	13.0	2,202.0	100
Vermont	14.0	2.0	16.0	2,713.0	100
Virginia	8.0	2.0	10.0	1,726.0	100
Washington	17.0	1.0	18.0	6,513.0	100
West Virginia	2.0	1.0	3.0	124.0	100
Wisconsin	239.0	14.0	253.0	30,080.0	99
Wyoming	1.3	0.2	1.5	136.7	100
United States	901.0	91.0	992.0	214,535.0	99

- Represents zero. [1] May not add due to rounding. [2] Excludes milk sucked by calves. [3] Milk sold to plants and dealers as whole milk and equivalent amounts of milk for cream. Includes milk produced by dealers' own herds and milk sold directly to consumers. Also includes milk produced by institutional herds. [4] Percentage of milk sold that is eligible for fluid use (Grade A in most States). Includes fluid grade milk used in manufacturing dairy products.

NASS, Livestock Branch, (202) 720–3570.

Table 8-6.—Milk: Quantities used and marketed by producers, by State and United States, 2018[1]

State	Milk used where produced			Milk marketed by producers	
	Fed to calves[2]	Used for milk cream & butter	Total	Total quantity[3]	Fluid grade[4]
	Million pounds	*Million pounds*	*Million pounds*	*Million pounds*	*Percent*
Alabama	0.7	0.3	1.0	72.0	100
Alaska	0.2	0.3	0.5	2.3	100
Arizona	14.0	1.0	15.0	4,963.0	100
Arkansas	1.7	0.3	2.0	72.0	100
California	26.0	4.0	30.0	40,383.0	97
Colorado	21.0	1.0	22.0	4,535.0	100
Connecticut	2.5	0.5	3.0	424.0	100
Delaware	0.9	0.1	1.0	90.5	100
Florida	5.0	1.0	6.0	2,375.0	100
Georgia	7.0	1.0	8.0	1,758.0	100
Hawaii	0.1	0.1	0.2	33.8	100
Idaho	33.0	1.0	34.0	15,115.0	100
Illinois	10.0	2.0	12.0	1,866.0	98
Indiana	23.0	4.0	27.0	4,134.0	100
Iowa	16.0	1.0	17.0	5,251.0	100
Kansas	14.0	1.0	15.0	3,693.0	100
Kentucky	6.0	1.0	7.0	1,002.0	100
Louisiana	2.0	1.0	3.0	149.0	100
Maine	3.0	1.0	4.0	614.0	100
Maryland	7.0	1.0	8.0	917.0	100
Massachusetts	1.5	0.5	2.0	200.0	100
Michigan	34.0	2.0	36.0	11,132.0	100
Minnesota	95.0	4.0	99.0	9,769.0	99
Mississippi	1.0	1.0	2.0	127.0	100
Missouri	17.0	4.0	21.0	1,173.0	97
Montana	2.0	2.0	4.0	270.0	100
Nebraska	6.5	0.5	7.0	1,433.0	100
Nevada	5.0	1.0	6.0	728.0	100
New Hampshire	1.5	0.5	2.0	247.0	100
New Jersey	1.5	0.5	2.0	108.0	100
New Mexico	60.0	3.0	63.0	8,222.0	100
New York	55.0	2.0	57.0	14,825.0	100
North Carolina	5.0	1.0	6.0	931.0	100
North Dakota	3.5	0.5	4.0	330.0	98
Ohio	24.0	5.0	29.0	5,503.0	97
Oklahoma	6.0	1.0	7.0	718.0	100
Oregon	20.0	1.0	21.0	2,510.0	100
Pennsylvania	58.0	12.0	70.0	10,595.0	100
Rhode Island	0.1	-	0.1	11.6	100
South Carolina	2.0	1.0	3.0	239.0	100
South Dakota	7.0	1.0	8.0	2,697.0	100
Tennessee	4.0	1.0	5.0	629.0	100
Texas	27.0	1.0	28.0	12,824.0	100
Utah	13.0	1.0	14.0	2,308.0	100
Vermont	14.0	2.0	16.0	2,664.0	100
Virginia	8.0	2.0	10.0	1,625.0	100
Washington	17.0	1.0	18.0	6,718.0	100
West Virginia	1.0	1.0	2.0	109.0	100
Wisconsin	245.0	14.0	259.0	30,320.0	99
Wyoming	1.3	0.2	1.5	140.7	100
United States	929.0	89.0	1,018.0	216,556.0	99

- Represents zero. [1] May not add due to rounding. [2] Excludes milk sucked by calves. [3] Milk sold to plants and dealers as whole milk and equivalent amounts of milk for cream. Includes milk produced by dealers' own herds and milk sold directly to consumers. Also includes milk produced by institutional herds. [4] Percentage of milk sold that is eligible for fluid use (Grade A in most States). Includes fluid grade milk used in manufacturing dairy products.

NASS, Livestock Branch, (202) 720–3570.

Table 8-7.—Milk and cream: Marketings and income, by State and United States, 2017 [1]

State	Milk utilized	All milk Average returns per cwt [2]	Returns per lb milkfat	Cash receipts from marketings
	Million pounds	*Dollars*	*Dollars*	*1,000 dollars*
Alabama	89.0	18.60	4.82	16,554
Alaska	2.5	22.00	5.61	550
Arizona	5,019.0	16.70	4.61	838,173
Arkansas	78.0	18.70	5.03	14,586
California	39,768.0	16.50	4.29	6,561,720
Colorado	4,167.0	18.10	4.91	754,227
Connecticut	417.0	18.60	4.72	77,562
Delaware	91.8	17.60	4.56	16,157
Florida	2,490.0	21.50	5.83	535,350
Georgia	1,832.0	19.00	5.23	348,080
Hawaii	38.7	28.60	8.64	11,068
Idaho	14,601.0	17.20	4.40	2,511,372
Illinois	1,917.0	18.30	4.77	350,811
Indiana	4,228.0	17.70	4.73	748,356
Iowa	5,163.0	18.10	4.68	934,503
Kansas	3,485.0	16.90	4.49	588,965
Kentucky	1,035.0	18.90	5.03	195,615
Louisiana	158.0	18.70	4.82	29,546
Maine	626.0	19.50	5.06	122,070
Maryland	948.0	17.80	4.66	168,744
Massachusetts	209.0	18.80	4.76	39,292
Michigan	11,196.0	16.40	4.41	1,836,144
Minnesota	9,768.0	17.80	4.58	1,738,704
Mississippi	135.0	18.90	4.92	25,515
Missouri	1,220.0	18.70	4.76	228,140
Montana	283.0	17.50	4.67	49,525
Nebraska	1,438.0	18.20	4.74	261,716
Nevada	703.0	17.90	4.58	125,837
New Hampshire	271.0	18.50	4.76	50,135
New Jersey	117.0	18.30	4.79	21,411
New Mexico	8,167.0	16.30	4.48	1,331,221
New York	14,872.0	18.20	4.73	2,706,704
North Carolina	946.0	18.80	5.01	177,848
North Dakota	340.0	17.60	4.60	59,840
Ohio	5,590.0	18.40	4.77	1,028,560
Oklahoma	721.0	19.20	5.11	138,432
Oregon	2,508.0	19.00	4.95	496,584
Pennsylvania	10,818.0	18.60	4.86	2,012,148
Rhode Island	12.9	18.50	4.67	2,387
South Carolina	245.0	19.10	4.96	46,795
South Dakota	2,610.0	18.80	4.61	490,680
Tennessee	688.0	18.90	5.03	130,032
Texas	12,028.0	18.40	4.55	2,213,152
Utah	2,202.0	17.70	4.66	389,754
Vermont	2,713.0	18.60	4.81	504,018
Virginia	1,726.0	19.40	5.17	334,844
Washington	6,513.0	18.20	4.55	1,185,366
West Virginia	124.0	18.00	4.75	22,320
Wisconsin	30,080.0	18.10	4.74	5,444,480
Wyoming	136.7	17.90	4.92	24,469
United States	214,535.0	17.69	4.61	37,940,662

[1] May not add due to rounding. [2] Cash receipts divided by milk or milkfat in combined marketings.
NASS, Livestock Branch, (202) 720–3570.

Table 8-8.—Milk and cream: Marketings and income, by State and United States, 2018[1]

State	Milk utilized	All milk Average returns per cwt[2]	Returns per lb milkfat	Cash receipts from marketings
	Million pounds	*Dollars*	*Dollars*	*1,000 dollars*
Alabama	72.0	16.60	4.28	11,952
Alaska	2.3	22.00	5.60	506
Arizona	4,963.0	15.50	4.23	769,265
Arkansas	72.0	17.00	4.49	12,240
California	40,383.0	15.78	4.05	6,372,437
Colorado	4,535.0	16.70	4.47	757,345
Connecticut	424.0	17.10	4.32	72,504
Delaware	90.5	16.10	4.19	14,571
Florida	2,375.0	19.90	5.41	472,625
Georgia	1,758.0	17.10	4.70	300,618
Hawaii	33.8	28.00	8.09	9,464
Idaho	15,115.0	15.70	3.96	2,373,055
Illinois	1,866.0	16.50	4.24	307,890
Indiana	4,134.0	15.70	4.15	649,038
Iowa	5,251.0	16.50	4.19	866,415
Kansas	3,693.0	15.30	3.96	565,029
Kentucky	1,002.0	17.50	4.62	175,350
Louisiana	149.0	17.20	4.26	25,628
Maine	614.0	18.10	4.68	111,134
Maryland	917.0	16.20	4.24	148,554
Massachusetts	200.0	17.40	4.37	34,800
Michigan	11,132.0	14.90	3.90	1,658,668
Minnesota	9,769.0	16.50	4.15	1,611,885
Mississippi	127.0	17.10	4.23	21,717
Missouri	1,173.0	16.90	4.25	198,237
Montana	270.0	16.00	4.21	43,200
Nebraska	1,433.0	16.20	4.20	232,146
Nevada	728.0	16.40	4.15	119,392
New Hampshire	247.0	17.00	4.35	41,990
New Jersey	108.0	16.20	4.26	17,496
New Mexico	8,222.0	14.70	3.97	1,208,634
New York	14,825.0	16.70	4.33	2,475,775
North Carolina	931.0	17.30	4.59	161,063
North Dakota	330.0	16.20	4.12	53,460
Ohio	5,503.0	16.40	4.22	902,492
Oklahoma	718.0	17.80	4.66	127,804
Oregon	2,510.0	18.70	4.61	469,370
Pennsylvania	10,595.0	16.80	4.41	1,779,960
Rhode Island	11.6	17.20	4.27	1,995
South Carolina	239.0	17.40	4.52	41,586
South Dakota	2,697.0	17.30	4.15	466,581
Tennessee	629.0	17.40	4.59	109,446
Texas	12,824.0	16.90	4.11	2,167,256
Utah	2,308.0	16.10	4.16	371,588
Vermont	2,664.0	17.10	4.38	455,544
Virginia	1,625.0	17.50	4.63	284,375
Washington	6,718.0	16.80	4.14	1,128,624
West Virginia	109.0	16.40	4.29	17,876
Wisconsin	30,320.0	16.50	4.24	5,002,800
Wyoming	140.7	16.30	4.48	22,934
United States	216,556.0	16.28	4.19	35,244,314

[1] May not add due to rounding. [2] Cash receipts divided by milk or milkfat in combined marketings.
NASS, Livestock Branch, (202) 720–3570.

Table 8-9.—Milk production: Value, by State and United States, 2017[1]

State	Used for milk, cream, & butter by producers		Gross producer income[3]	Value of milk produced[2 4]
	Milk utilized	Value[2]		
	Million pounds	*1,000 dollars*	*1,000 dollars*	*1,000 dollars*
Alabama	0.3	56	16,610	16,740
Alaska	0.2	44	594	638
Arizona	1.0	167	838,340	840,511
Arkansas	0.3	56	14,642	14,960
California	4.0	660	6,562,380	6,566,670
Colorado	1.0	181	754,408	758,209
Connecticut	0.5	93	77,655	78,120
Delaware	0.1	18	16,175	16,333
Florida	1.0	215	535,565	536,640
Georgia	1.0	190	348,270	349,600
Hawaii	0.1	29	11,097	11,125
Idaho	1.0	172	2,511,544	2,516,876
Illinois	2.0	366	351,177	353,007
Indiana	4.0	708	749,064	753,135
Iowa	1.0	181	934,684	937,399
Kansas	1.0	169	589,134	591,331
Kentucky	1.0	189	195,804	196,938
Louisiana	1.0	187	29,733	30,107
Maine	1.0	195	122,265	122,850
Maryland	1.0	178	168,922	170,168
Massachusetts	0.5	94	39,386	39,668
Michigan	2.0	328	1,836,472	1,841,884
Minnesota	4.0	712	1,739,416	1,756,326
Mississippi	1.0	189	25,704	25,893
Missouri	4.0	748	228,888	232,067
Montana	2.0	350	49,875	50,400
Nebraska	0.5	91	261,807	262,808
Nevada	1.0	179	126,016	126,911
New Hampshire	0.5	93	50,228	50,505
New Jersey	0.5	92	21,503	21,777
New Mexico	3.0	489	1,331,710	1,338,556
New York	2.0	364	2,707,068	2,717,078
North Carolina	1.0	188	178,036	178,976
North Dakota	0.5	88	59,928	60,720
Ohio	5.0	920	1,029,480	1,033,896
Oklahoma	1.0	192	138,624	139,776
Oregon	1.0	198	496,782	500,742
Pennsylvania	14.0	2,604	2,014,752	2,026,098
Rhode Island	-	-	2,387	2,405
South Carolina	1.0	191	46,986	47,368
South Dakota	1.0	188	490,868	492,104
Tennessee	1.0	189	130,221	130,977
Texas	1.0	184	2,213,336	2,217,936
Utah	1.0	177	389,931	392,055
Vermont	2.0	372	504,990	507,594
Virginia	2.0	388	335,232	336,784
Washington	1.0	182	1,185,548	1,188,642
West Virginia	1.0	180	22,500	22,860
Wisconsin	14.0	2,534	5,447,014	5,490,273
Wyoming	0.2	36	24,505	24,738
United States	91.0	16,594	37,957,256	38,119,254

- Represents zero. [1] May not add due to rounding. [2] Value at average returns per 100 pounds of milk in combined marketings of milk and cream. [3] Cash receipts from marketings of milk and cream plus value of milk used for home consumption. [4] Includes value of milk fed to calves.

NASS, Livestock Branch, (202) 720–3570.

Table 8-10.—Milk production: Value, by State and United States, 2018[1]

State	Used for milk, cream, & butter by producers		Gross producer income[3]	Value of milk produced[2 4]
	Milk utilized	Value[2]		
	Million pounds	*1,000 Dollars*	*1,000 Dollars*	*1,000 Dollars*
Alabama	0.3	50	12,002	12,118
Alaska	0.3	66	572	616
Arizona	1.0	155	769,420	771,590
Arkansas	0.3	51	12,291	12,580
California	4.0	631	6,373,068	6,377,171
Colorado	1.0	167	757,512	761,019
Connecticut	0.5	86	72,590	73,017
Delaware	0.1	16	14,587	14,732
Florida	1.0	199	472,824	473,819
Georgia	1.0	171	300,789	301,986
Hawaii	0.1	28	9,492	9,520
Idaho	1.0	157	2,373,212	2,378,393
Illinois	2.0	330	308,220	309,870
Indiana	4.0	628	649,666	653,277
Iowa	1.0	165	866,580	869,220
Kansas	1.0	153	565,182	567,324
Kentucky	1.0	175	175,525	176,575
Louisiana	1.0	172	25,800	26,144
Maine	1.0	181	111,315	111,858
Maryland	1.0	162	148,716	149,850
Massachusetts	0.5	87	34,887	35,148
Michigan	2.0	298	1,658,966	1,664,032
Minnesota	4.0	660	1,612,545	1,628,220
Mississippi	1.0	171	21,888	22,059
Missouri	4.0	676	198,913	201,786
Montana	2.0	320	43,520	43,840
Nebraska	0.5	81	232,227	233,280
Nevada	1.0	164	119,556	120,376
New Hampshire	0.5	85	42,075	42,330
New Jersey	0.5	81	17,577	17,820
New Mexico	3.0	441	1,209,075	1,217,895
New York	2.0	334	2,476,109	2,485,294
North Carolina	1.0	173	161,236	162,101
North Dakota	0.5	81	53,541	54,108
Ohio	5.0	820	903,312	907,248
Oklahoma	1.0	178	127,982	129,050
Oregon	1.0	187	469,557	473,297
Pennsylvania	12.0	2,016	1,781,976	1,791,720
Rhode Island	-	-	1,995	2,012
South Carolina	1.0	174	41,760	42,108
South Dakota	1.0	173	466,754	467,965
Tennessee	1.0	174	109,620	110,316
Texas	1.0	169	2,167,425	2,171,988
Utah	1.0	161	371,749	373,842
Vermont	2.0	342	455,886	458,280
Virginia	2.0	350	284,725	286,125
Washington	1.0	168	1,128,792	1,131,648
West Virginia	1.0	164	18,040	18,204
Wisconsin	14.0	2,310	5,005,110	5,045,535
Wyoming	0.2	33	22,967	23,179
United States	89.0	14,814	35,259,128	35,411,485

- Represents zero. [1] May not add due to rounding. [2] Value at average returns per 100 pounds of milk in combined marketings of milk and cream. [3] Cash receipts from marketings of milk and cream plus value of milk used for home consumption. [4] Includes value of milk fed to calves.
NASS, Livestock Branch, (202) 720–3570.

Table 8-11.—Milk cows, milk, and fat in cream: Average prices received by farmers, United States, 2009–2018

Year	Milk cows, per head [1]	Milk per 100 pounds [2]					
		Eligible for fluid market [3]		Of manufacturing grade		All milk wholesale	
		Price per 100 lb.	Fat test	Price per 100 lb.	Fat test	Price per 100 lb.	Fat test
	Dollars	*Dollars*	*Percent*	*Dollars*	*Percent*	*Dollars*	*Percent*
2009	1,390.00	12.94	3.67	12.03	4.00	12.93	3.67
2010	1,330.00	16.37	3.65	14.56	4.00	16.35	3.66
2011	1,420.00	(NA)	(NA)	(NA)	(NA)	20.24	3.71
2012	1,430.00	(NA)	(NA)	(NA)	(NA)	18.56	3.72
2013	1,380.00	(NA)	(NA)	(NA)	(NA)	20.11	3.76
2014	1,830.00	(NA)	(NA)	(NA)	(NA)	24.07	3.74
2015	1,990.00	(NA)	(NA)	(NA)	(NA)	17.21	3.75
2016	1,760.00	(NA)	(NA)	(NA)	(NA)	16.34	3.79
2017	1,620.00	(NA)	(NA)	(NA)	(NA)	17.69	3.84
2018	1,360.00	(NA)	(NA)	(NA)	(NA)	16.28	3.89

(NA) Not available. [1] Simple average of quarterly prices, by States, weighted by the number of milk cows on farms Jan. 1 of the current year. [2] Average price at average fat test for all milk sold at wholesale to plants and dealers, based on reports from milk-market administrators, cooperative milk-market associations, whole-milk distributors, and milk-products manufacturing plants, f.o.b. plant or receiving station (whichever is the customary place for determining prices) before hauling costs are deducted and including all premiums. [3] Includes fluid milk surplus diverted to manufacturing.
NASS, Livestock Branch, (202) 720–3570.

Table 8-12—Milk-feed price ratios: All milk price; Dairy feed price, 16% protein; Milk-feed price ratios, United States, annual 2009–2018

Year	All milk price	Dairy feed price 16% protein [1]	Milk-feed price ratio [2]
	Dollars/cwt	*Dollars/ton*	*Pounds*
2009	12.93	293	1.78
2010	16.35	274	2.26
2011	20.24	369	1.90
2012	18.56	442	1.52
2013	20.11	481	1.75
2014	24.07	502	2.54
2015	17.21	(NA)	2.14
2016	16.34	(NA)	2.26
2017	17.69	(NA)	2.42
2018	16.28	(NA)	2.05

[1] Commercially prepared 16%protein dairy ration price collected from March annual Prices Paid Survery. Discontinued beginning 2015. [2] Annual ratios based on average of monthly ratios. Pounds of 16% protein mixed dairy feed equal in value to one pound of whole milk. Feed price component (16% protein) calculated using U.S. price received for corn (51 lbs), soybeans (8 lb), and alfalfa hay (41 lbs).
NASS, Environmental, Economics, and Demographics Branch, (202) 720–6146.

Table 8-13.—Fluid beverage milk: Total sales and per capita consumption, United States, 2009–2018

Year	Consumption	
	Total	Per capita
	Million pounds	*Pounds*
2009	54,850	179
2010	55,003	178
2011	54,296	174
2012	53,443	170
2013	52,286	165
2014	50,773	159
2015	50,041	156
2016	49,713	154
2017	48,650	149
2018	47,672	146

ERS, Animal Products and Cost of Production Branch, (202) 694–5171.

Table 8-14.—Federal milk order markets[1]: Measures of growth, 2013–2019[2]

Year	Population of Federal milk marketing areas	Number of handlers[3]	Number of producers[4]	Receipts of producer milk	Producer milk used in Class I	Percentage of producer milk used in Class I
	Thousands	*Number*	*Number*	*Million pounds*	*Million pounds*	*Percent*
2013	251,201	225	40,043	132,100	42,742	32.4
2014	255,184	223	39,146	129,420	41,420	32.0
2015	256,526	214	36,112	126,126	41,206	32.7
2016	258,172	216	34,689	133,846	41,140	30.7
2017	262,240	217	32,981	135,502	40,642	30.0
2018	302,089	233	32,061	141,684	40,945	28.9
2019	303,067	230	29,474	156,510	43,882	28.0

Year	Prices at 3.5 percent butterfat content per hundredweight[5]		Receipts as percentage of milk sold to plants and dealers		Daily deliveries of milk per producer	Gross value of receipts of producer milk[6]	
	Class I	Blend	Fluid grade	All milk		Per producer	All producer
	Dollars	*Dollars*	*Percent*	*Percent*	*Pounds*	*Dollars*	*1,000 dollars*
2013	21.80	19.44	67	66	9,039	641,295	25,682,588
2014	26.14	23.54	63	63	9,074	793,728	30,472,016
2015	19.21	16.70	61	61	9,559	583,173	21,063,042
2016	17.70	15.38	64	64	10,557	593,364	20,585,571
2017	19.31	16.96	64	63	11,244	696,651	22,981,139
2018	17.70	15.51	66	65	12,449	685,389	21,974,258
2019	19.74	17.35	33	72	14,507	921,305	27,154,539

[1] The California Federal Milk Marketing Order became effective on November 1, 2018. [2] Over this period, handler selected periodically not to pool substantial volumes of milk that normally would have been pooled under Federal orders. This decision resulted from disadvantageous blend/class price relationships and qualification circumstances. This fact should be kept in mind if year-to-year comparisons are made using the various "producer deliveries" measures of growth. [3] End of year. [4] Average for year. [5] Prices are weighted averages. [6] Based on blend (uniform) price adjusted for butterfat content, and in later years, other milk components of producer milk.
AMS, Dairy Programs, (202) 720–7461.

Table 8-15.—Milk production: Marketings, income and value, United States, 2009–2018

Year	Combined marketings of milk and cream: Milk utilized	Average returns[1]: Per 100 pounds milk	Average returns[1]: Per pound milkfat	Cash receipts from marketings	Used for milk, cream, and butter on farms where produced: Milk utilized	Used on farms: Value[2]	Gross farm income from dairy products[3]	Farm value of all milk produced[2] [4]
	Million pounds	*Dollars*	*Dollars*	*1,000 dollars*	*Million pounds*	*1,000 dollars*	*1,000 dollars*	*1,000 dollars*
2009	188,189	12.93	3.52	24,321,032	112	15,224	24,336,256	24,455,900
2010	191,897	16.35	4.47	31,372,346	107	18,269	31,390,615	31,535,575
2011	195,290	20.24	5.46	39,531,306	98	20,561	39,551,867	39,730,346
2012	199,687	18.56	4.99	37,064,731	98	18,779	37,083,510	37,247,542
2013	200,283	20.11	5.35	40,282,881	100	20,629	40,303,510	40,482,699
2014	205,083	24.07	6.44	49,351,199	92	22,699	49,373,898	49,588,283
2015	207,536	17.21	4.59	35,716,849	91	16,291	35,733,140	35,888,595
2016	211,457	16.34	4.31	34,546,316	94	15,784	34,562,100	34,712,099
2017	214,535	17.69	4.61	37,940,662	91	16,594	37,957,256	38,119,254
2018	216,556	16.28	4.19	35,244,314	89	14,814	35,259,128	35,411,485

[1] Cash receipts divided by milk or milkfat represented in combined marketings. [2] Valued at average returns per 100 pounds of milk in combined marketings of milk and cream. [3] Cash receipts from marketings of milk and cream plus value of milk used for home consumption. [4] Includes value of milk fed to calves.
NASS, Livestock Branch, (202) 720–3570.

Table 8-16.—Official Dairy Herd Information test plans: Numbers of herds and cows and milk, fat, and protein production, United States, 2010–2019

Year	Herds	Cows	Cows per herd	Average production			Cows with protein information	Average protein production	Average protein production
				Milk	Fat	Fat			
	Number	*Number*	*Number*	*Pounds*	*Percent*	*Pounds*	*Percent*	*Percent*	*Pounds*
2010 ...	15,067	3,746,177	248.6	22,765	3.66	836	98	3.09	706
2011 ...	14,490	3,800,410	262.3	22,961	3.71	855	98	3.11	714
2012 ...	13,894	3,762,925	270.8	23,328	3.72	871	98	3.12	728
2013 ...	13,329	3,712,080	278.5	23,695	3.77	894	98	3.13	742
2014 ...	13,043	3,829,273	293.6	24,101	3.76	907	98	3.14	757
2015 ...	12,440	3,822,370	307.3	24,403	3.75	917	98	3.13	764
2016 ...	11,745	3,836,074	326.6	24,651	3.79	934	98	3.13	773
2017 ...	10,932	3,809,695	348.5	24,776	3.84	951	99	3.16	783
2018 ...	9,787	3,715,872	379.7	24,660	3.87	956	99	3.16	781
2019 ...	8,710	3,636,877	417.6	24,787	3.91	970	100	3.18	789

Council on Dairy Cattle Breeding, (240) 334–4164, https://www.uscdcb.com.

Table 8-17.—Milk and milkfat production: Number of producing cows, production per cow, and total quantity produced, United States, 2009–2018

Year	Number of milk cows [1]	Production of milk and milkfat [2]				
		Per milk cow		Percentage of fat in all milk produced	Total	
		Milk	Milkfat		Milk	Milkfat
	Thousands	*Pounds*	*Pounds*	*Percent*	*Million pounds*	*Million pounds*
2009	9,202	20,561	755	3.67	189,202	6,944
2010	9,123	21,142	774	3.66	192,877	7,054
2011	9,199	21,334	791	3.71	196,255	7,284
2012	9,237	21,722	808	3.72	200,642	7,463
2013	9,224	21,819	820	3.76	201,260	7,558
2014	9,261	22,249	832	3.74	206,048	7,698
2015	9,320	22,372	839	3.75	208,508	7,810
2016	9,334	22,761	003	3.79	212,451	8,054
2017	9,406	22,914	880	3.84	215,527	8,272
2018	9,399	23,149	900	3.89	217,575	8,466

[1] Average number during year, excluding heifers not yet fresh. [2] Excludes milk sucked by calves.
NASS, Livestock Branch, (202) 720–3570.

Table 8-18.—Milk: Quantities used and marketed by farmers, United States, 2009–2018

Year	Milk used on farms where produced			Milk marketed by producers	
	Fed to calves [1]	Consumed as fluid milk or cream	Total	Total [2]	Fluid grade [3]
	Million pounds	*Million pounds*	*Million pounds*	*Million pounds*	*Percent*
2009	901	112	1,013	188,189	98
2010	873	107	980	191,897	98
2011	867	98	965	195,290	99
2012	858	98	956	199,687	99
2013	877	100	977	200,283	99
2014	874	92	966	205,083	99
2015	880	91	971	207,536	99
2016	900	94	994	211,457	99
2017	901	91	992	214,535	99
2018	929	89	1,018	216,556	99

[1] Excludes milk sucked by calves. [2] Milk sold to plants and dealers as whole milk and equivalent amounts of milk for cream. Includes milk produced by dealers' own herds and small amounts sold directly to consumers. Also includes milk produced by institutional herds. [3] Percentage of milk sold that is eligible for fluid use (Grade A in most States). Includes fluid-grade milk used in manufacturing dairy products.
NASS, Livestock Branch, (202) 720–3570.

Table 8-19.—Milk markets under Federal order program: Whole milk and fat-reduced milk products sold for fluid consumption within defined marketing areas, 2017–2019 [1]

Federal milk order marketing area	Whole milk products [2]		Fat-reduced milk products [3]		Total fluid milk products	
	Quantity	Butterfat content	Quantity	Butterfat content	Quantity	Butterfat content
	Million pounds	*Percent*	*Million pounds*	*Percent*	*Million pounds*	*Percent*
			2017			
Northeast	3,249	3.27	4,782	1.18	8,031	2.03
Appalachian	1,157	3.29	2,005	1.34	3,162	2.05
Florida	1,152	3.23	1,579	1.31	2,731	2.12
Southeast	1,692	3.30	2,651	1.33	4,343	2.10
Upper Midwest	698	3.29	2,864	1.23	3,562	1.64
Central	1,164	3.30	2,918	1.30	4,082	1.87
Mideast	1,468	3.30	3,787	1.35	5,255	1.89
Pacific Northwest	596	3.33	1,307	1.36	1,903	1.98
Southwest	1,735	3.32	2,650	1.33	4,385	2.12
Arizona	346	3.29	671	1.31	1,017	1.99
Combined areas	13,256	3.29	25,214	1.29	38,471	1.98
			2018			
Northeast	3,306	3.28	4,539	1.21	7,846	2.08
Appalachian	1,206	3.29	1,960	1.36	3,166	2.10
Florida	1,161	3.19	1,515	1.36	2,676	2.15
Southeast	1,704	3.31	2,517	1.36	4,221	2.15
Upper Midwest	712	3.29	2,715	1.25	3,427	1.67
Central	1,197	3.30	2,773	1.34	3,970	1.93
Mideast	1,514	3.30	3,685	1.37	5,209	1.94
California [4]	334	3.38	556	1.44	890	2.17
Pacific Northwest	613	3.32	1,229	1.37	1,842	2.02
Southwest	1,775	3.28	2,528	1.35	4,303	2.15
Arizona	363	3.29	657	1.33	1,020	2.03
Combined areas	13,886	3.29	24,673	1.32	38,568	2.03
			2019			
Northeast	3,313	3.28	4,070	1.22	7,382	2.15
Appalachian	1,220	3.30	1,785	1.37	3,005	2.16
Florida	1,170	3.24	1,392	1.37	2,562	2.22
Southeast	1,707	3.32	2,255	1.38	3,962	2.22
Upper Midwest	733	3.30	2,460	1.27	3,194	1.73
Central	1,215	3.26	2,499	1.36	3,714	1.98
Mideast	1,579	3.31	3,467	1.41	5,046	2.01
California [4]	2,001	3.44	3,067	1.42	5,069	2.22
Pacific Northwest	613	3.32	1,077	1.38	1,690	2.08
Southwest	1,787	3.30	2,392	1.36	4,179	2.19
Arizona	360	3.31	596	1.37	956	2.10
Combined areas	15,699	3.31	25,060	1.35	40,759	2.10

[1] In-area sales include total sales in each of the areas by handlers regulated under the respective order, by handlers regulated under other orders, by partially regulated handlers, by exempt handlers, and by producer-handlers. Sales routes of handlers may extend outside defined marketing areas; therefore, some handlers' in-area sales are partially estimated. [2] Plain, organic, flavored, and miscellaneous whole milk products, and eggnog. [3] Plain, fortified, organic, and flavored reduced fat milk (2%), low fat milk (1%), and fat-free milk (skim), and miscellaneous fat-reduced milk products, and buttermilk. [4] The California Federal Milk Order became effective November 1, 2018.

AMS, Dairy Programs, (202) 720–7461.

Table 8-20.—Milk markets under Federal order program: Uniform and Class I milk prices at 3.5 percent fat test, number of producers, producer milk receipts, producer milk used in Class I, Class I percentage, daily milk deliveries per producer, average fat test of producer milk receipts, by markets, 2017–2019

Federal milk order marketing area	Class I $ / cwt [1]	Uniform $ / cwt [1] [2]	Average number of producers	Receipts of producer milk	Producer milk used in Class I	Class I utilization	Daily milk deliveries per producer	Average fat test of producer milk
	Dollars	*Dollars*	*Number*	*Million pounds*	*Million pounds*	*Percent*	*Pounds*	*Percent*
				2017				
Northeast [3]	19.71	17.43	11,170	27,397	8,799	32.1	6,722	3.85
Appalachian [4]	19.87	18.79	1,990	5,801	4,002	69.0	8,002	3.76
Florida [5]	21.87	20.92	143	2,602	2,169	83.3	49,877	3.69
Southeast [6]	20.27	19.13	1,672	5,451	3,767	69.1	8,936	3.74
Upper Midwest [7] [8]	18.26	16.28	9,431	32,312	3,244	10.0	9,345	3.84
Central [8] [9]	18.46	16.35	2,565	15,879	4,839	30.5	16,967	3.82
Mideast [8] [10]	18.46	16.56	4,968	20,241	6,430	31.8	11,160	3.78
Pacific Northwest [8] [11]	18.36	16.18	467	7,661	1,891	24.7	44,854	3.99
Southwest [8] [12]	19.46	17.16	486	13,092	4,217	32.2	73,541	3.86
Arizona [13]	18.81	16.39	89	5,065	1,284	25.4	155,410	3.62
All markets combined	19.31	16.96	32,981	135,502	40,642	30.0	11,244	3.82
				2018				
Northeast [3]	18.10	16.09	10,574	27,109	8,701	32.1	7,026	3.86
Appalachian [4]	18.25	17.29	1,704	5,735	3,984	69.5	9,243	3.79
Florida [5]	20.24	19.37	143	2,565	2,144	83.6	49,152	3.68
Southeast [6]	18.64	17.71	1,672	5,204	3,705	71.2	8,541	3.80
Upper Midwest [7] [8]	16.63	14.75	8,883	33,323	2,990	9.0	10,263	3.92
Central [8] [9]	16.85	14.87	2,433	16,613	4,792	28.8	18,722	3.89
Mideast [8] [10]	16.86	15.21	4,513	19,603	6,374	32.5	11,905	3.84
California [11]	17.39	15.18	1,081	4,117	927	22.5	62,481	4.01
Pacific Northwest [12]	16.76	14.86	495	8,558	1,851	21.6	47,288	4.07
Southwest [8] [13]	17.86	15.77	482	13,727	4,221	30.8	77,613	3.94
Arizona [14]	17.19	15.09	81	5,133	1,265	24.6	173,295	3.66
All markets combined	17.70	15.51	32,081	141,687	40,954	28.9	12,449	3.88
				2019				
Northeast [3]	20.23	18.11	9,760	26,752	8,283	31.0	7,510	3.89
Appalachian [4]	20.38	19.38	1,552	5,327	3,746	70.3	9,414	3.80
Florida [5]	22.35	21.39	125	2,510	2,091	83.3	55,174	3.66
Southeast [6]	20.76	19.75	1,540	4,903	3,438	70.1	8,733	3.80
Upper Midwest [7] [8]	18.79	16.70	7,981	32,310	2,720	8.4	10,961	3.93
Central [8] [9]	18.96	16.70	2,370	15,260	4,605	30.2	17,595	3.92
Mideast [8] [10]	18.99	17.20	4,164	18,942	6,560	34.6	12,456	3.86
California [11]	19.08	16.79	993	24,272	5,321	21.9	66,953	3.86
Pacific Northwest [12]	18.88	16.74	458	8,496	1,728	20.3	50,847	4.08
Southwest [8] [13]	19.97	17.40	457	12,900	4,147	32.2	77,184	3.99
Arizona [14]	19.35	17.23	74	4,840	1,241	25.6	177,338	3.74
All markets combined	19.74	17.35	29,474	156,510	43,882	28.0	14,507	3.90

[1] Prices are for milk of 3.5 percent butterfat content and for the principal pricing point of the market. See footnotes 3-13. [2] For those orders that use the component pricing system for paying producers (orders 1, 30, 32, 33, 124,and 126), the figures are the statistical uniform price (the sum of the producer price differential and the Class III price). For those orders that use the skim milk/butterfat pricing system for paying producers (orders 5, 6, 7, and 131), the figures are the uniform price (the sum of the uniform butterfat price times 3.5 and the uniform skim milk price times 0.965). [3] Suffolk Co. (Boston), MA. [4] Mecklenburg Co. (Charlotte), NC. [5] Hillsborough Co. (Tampa), FL. [5] Fulton Co. (Atlanta), GA. [7] Cook Co. (Chicago), IL. [8] Due to the disadvantageous intraorder class and uniform price relationships in some months in these markets, handlers elected not to pool milk that normally would have been pooled under these orders. [9] Jackson Co. (Kansas City), MO. [10] Cuyahoga Co. (Cleveland), OH. [11] The California Federal Milk Marketing Order became effective on November 1, 2018. [12] King Co. (Seattle), WA. [13] Dallas Co. (Dallas), TX. [14] Maricopa Co. (Phoenix), AZ.

AMS, Dairy Programs, (202) 720–7461.

Table 8-21.—Dairy products: Quantities manufactured, United States, 2014–2018

Product	2014	2015	2016	2017	2018
	1,000 pounds				
Butter	1,855,315	1,849,519	1,839,399	1,847,473	1,891,007
Cheese:					
American types	4,588,023	4,694,471	4,768,888	5,072,129	5,253,833
Cheddar	3,317,038	3,393,111	3,434,498	3,721,468	3,802,508
Other American	1,270,985	1,301,360	1,334,390	1,350,661	1,451,325
Blue and Gorgonzola	92,845	94,489	90,872	91,316	94,648
Brick	2,942	3,449	2,845	2,424	2,276
Cream and Neufchatel	851,713	876,286	908,972	918,071	914,824
Feta	105,622	112,424	126,849	122,470	129,823
Gouda	55,911	58,364	58,601	65,400	65,252
Hispanic	249,579	254,291	264,941	286,521	311,916
Italian types	4,950,235	5,081,826	5,304,355	5,395,248	5,556,850
Mozzarella	3,924,925	3,988,936	4,117,746	4,167,492	4,351,361
Parmesan	301,848	339,003	407,319	450,640	424,491
Provolone	361,088	379,316	401,589	393,792	397,786
Ricotta	245,284	243,464	252,231	245,912	249,461
Romano	45,021	55,034	52,448	58,302	58,058
Other Italian types	72,069	76,073	73,022	79,110	75,693
Muenster cheese	163,650	177,540	181,354	189,167	191,269
Swiss cheese	297,802	312,015	311,977	316,654	332,303
All other types	153,783	166,240	161,889	180,562	171,593
Total cheese [1]	11,512,105	11,831,395	12,181,543	12,639,962	13,024,587
Cottage cheese:					
Curd [2]	381,146	400,634	406,428	390,409	402,362
Creamed [3]	303,113	317,531	329,444	330,484	352,785
Lowfat [4]	364,614	363,004	367,815	344,421	342,084
Sour cream	1,302,900	1,325,629	1,374,059	1,387,149	1,403,411
Yogurt plain & flavored	4,756,562	4,645,594	4,458,399	4,478,204	4,388,088
Bulk condensed milk:					
Skim, sweetened	43,593	52,935	77,158	90,157	120,873
Skim, unsweetened	1,661,446	1,672,557	1,651,169	1,570,819	1,468,374
Whole, sweetened	88,607	99,867	116,563	142,602	144,659
Whole, unsweetened	65,596	173,701	97,204	62,259	66,023
Condensed or evaporated buttermilk	109,044	105,676	105,968	113,035	109,612
Canned milk:					
Evaporated and condensed whole [5]	315,290	452,780	456,695	379,193	412,599
Evaporated skim	27,856	43,940	16,897	9,156	15,144
Dry milk products:					
Dry buttermilk, total	111,097	98,364	109,641	112,904	118,075
Dry skim milk animal	11,303	9,953	9,287	11,862	14,071
Dry whole milk	103,122	108,522	98,174	122,397	143,654
Milk protein concentrate, total	126,017	157,309	125,685	139,047	145,632
Nonfat dry milk, human	1,764,632	1,822,348	1,752,634	1,835,277	1,773,540
Skim milk powder, total [6]	543,504	446,324	559,175	529,633	566,504
Dry whey, total	869,701	977,568	955,141	1,035,414	999,356
	1,000 gallons				
Ice cream, regular, total	865,753	896,688	906,680	871,157	840,028
Ice cream, lowfat, total [7]	411,701	438,991	435,868	461,414	451,103
Ice cream, nonfat, total	18,303	13,575	12,438	11,427	11,266
Sherbet, total	48,353	44,743	44,262	42,975	40,206
Frozen yogurt, total	66,456	74,229	66,814	62,911	50,277

[1] Excluding cottage cheese. [2] Mostly used for processing into creamed or lowfat cottage cheese. [3] Fat content 4 percent or more. [4] Fat content less than 4 percent. [5] Combined to avoid disclosing individual plant operations. [6] Includes protein standardized and blends. [7] Includes freezer-made milkshake.

NASS, Livestock Branch, (202) 720–3570.

Table 8-22.—Dairy Products: Factory production of specified items, by State and United States, 2017–2018

State	Butter		Total American cheese [1]		Total cheese [2]	
	2017	2018	2017	2018	2017	2018
	1,000 pounds	*1,000 pounds*	*1,000 pounds*	*1,000 pounds*	*1,000 pounds*	*1,000 pounds*
California	534,378	578,624	632,677	630,164	2,513,336	2,543,368
Idaho			605,555	625,427	958,687	991,239
Illinois					82,389	82,288
Iowa			155,111	182,094	256,737	296,396
Minnesota			589,516	622,884	712,988	740,601
New Jersey					57,727	59,087
New Mexico					766,804	895,779
New York	27,581	24,688	132,273	139,560	829,410	802,331
Ohio					222,044	239,267
Oregon			205,733	208,767	206,679	209,829
Pennsylvania	92,329	86,062			411,552	433,750
South Dakota					282,304	293,455
Vermont					142,941	146,953
Wisconsin			1,016,702	1,025,766	3,376,769	3,422,895
Other States [3]	1,193,185	1,201,633	1,734,562	1,819,161	1,819,595	1,867,349
United States	1,847,473	1,891,007	5,072,129	5,253,833	12,639,962	13,024,587

State	Ice cream, regular (hard)		Nonfat dry milk for human food	
	2017	2018	2017	2018
	1,000 Gallons	*1,000 Gallons*	*1,000 Pounds*	*1,000 Pounds*
California	73,643	66,328	562,017	587,059
Connecticut	12,206	12,614		
Missouri	32,404	37,350		
New Jersey	1,390	1,183		
New York	38,422	29,547		
Ohio	26,122	27,984		
Oregon	12,104	14,380		
Pennsylvania	41,064	37,595	183,766	181,158
Tennessee	25,711	22,704		
Utah	26,283	29,667		
Wisconsin	19,211	9,708		
Other States [3]	422,602	429,382	1,089,494	1,005,323
United States	731,162	718,532	1,835,277	1,773,540

[1] Includes Cheddar, Colby, washed curd, stirred curd, Monterey, and Jack. [2] Excluding cottage cheese. [3] States not shown when fewer than 3 plants reported or individual plant operations could be disclosed.
NASS, Livestock Branch, (202) 720–3570.

Table 8-23.—Dairy products: Average price per pound for specified products, 2014–2018

Item and market	2014	2015	2016	2017	2018
	Dollars	*Dollars*	*Dollars*	*Dollars*	*Dollars*
Butter, Chicago Mercantile Exchange, Grade AA:					
High [1]	3.0600	3.1350	2.3675	2.7375	2.4175
Low [1]	1.5325	1.5400	1.7550	2.0625	2.0675
Butter, Agricultural Marketing Service, Grade AA: [2]	2.1361	2.0670	2.0777	2.3303	2.2572
Cheese, Cheddar, Chicago Mercantile Exchange, Barrels:					
High [1]	2.4900	1.7550	1.8800	1.7600	1.6675
Low [1]	1.4200	1.4100	1.2700	1.3375	1.2345
Cheese, Cheddar, Chicago Mercantile Exchange, 40-lb blocks:					
High [1]	2.4500	1.8000	1.9425	1.8500	1.6905
Low [1]	1.5200	1.4000	1.2700	1.3600	1.3540
Cheese, Cheddar, Agricultural Marketing Service, Barrels: [3]	2.1376	1.6241	1.5961	1.5860	1.4659
Cheese, Cheddar, Agricultural Marketing Service, 40-lb blocks: [3]	2.1439	1.6389	1.5897	1.6513	1.5825
Nonfat dry milk, Agricultural Marketing Service:					
Low/medium heat [2]	1.7682	0.9016	0.8292	0.8666	0.7945
Dry whey, Agricultural Marketing Service:					
Edible nonhygroscopic [2]	0.6538	0.3804	0.2875	0.4437	0.3422

[1] Figures are the high and low prices for any trading day during the year. [2] Simple average of the product prices from the Class and Component Prices Announcement. [3] Simple average of the block and barrel prices used in the calculation of the cheese price on the Class and Component Prices Announement. Historical data are available at: https://www.ams.usda.gov/rules-regulations/mmr/dmr.
AMS, Dairy Programs, (202) 720–4392.

Table 8-24.—Dairy products: Manufacturers' stocks, end of month, United States, 2017–2018 [1]

Month	Evaporated and condensed whole milk [2]		Dry whole milk		Nonfat dry milk, human	
	2017	2018	2017	2018	2017	2018
	1,000 pounds	*1,000 pounds*	*1,000 pounds*	*1,000 pounds*	*1,000 pounds*	*1,000 pounds*
January	43,940	51,472	18,034	33,232	227,052	300,828
February	55,613	48,558	21,660	37,328	263,021	296,991
March	50,777	49,050	22,284	46,035	246,484	297,296
April	63,792	53,147	23,060	47,243	267,375	273,346
May	69,730	73,770	22,961	59,625	280,078	270,489
June	76,890	73,123	21,224	56,604	297,773	303,301
July	79,138	79,064	21,864	51,876	295,906	317,447
August	82,905	88,565	15,948	42,387	312,929	280,494
September	75,947	79,977	20,608	32,589	320,765	261,646
October	61,202	64,953	22,070	18,733	316,826	252,648
November	41,983	43,053	27,878	17,559	316,969	289,199
December	37,191	42,112	31,007	15,573	320,046	276,527

[1] Stocks held by manufacturers at all points and in transit. [2] Combined to avoid disclosing individual plant operations.
NASS, Livestock Branch, (202) 720–3570.

Table 8-25.—Dairy products: Total disappearance, and total and per capita consumption, United States, 2009–2018 [1]

Year	Butter			Cheese [2]			Condensed and evaporated milk [3]		
	Total disappearance	Consumption		Total disappearance	Consumption		Total disappearance	Consumption	
		Total	Per capita		Total	Per capita		Total	Per capita
	Million pounds	*Million pounds*	*Pounds*	*Million pounds*	*Million pounds*	*Pounds*	*Million pounds*	*Million pounds*	*Pounds*
2009	1,574	1,522	5.0	10,248	9,917	32.3	771	704	2.3
2010	1,623	1,521	4.9	10,605	10,136	32.7	718	610	2.0
2011	1,795	1,676	5.4	10,893	10,300	33.0	711	600	1.9
2012	1,829	1,730	5.5	11,123	10,461	33.3	715	629	2.0
2013	1,915	1,732	5.5	11,364	10,580	33.4	722	597	1.9
2014	1,887	1,753	5.5	11,784	10,887	34.2	537	451	1.4
2015	1,841	1,800	5.6	12,049	11,268	35.1	782	701	2.2
2016	1,881	1,843	5.7	12,492	11,776	36.4	741	662	2.0
2017	1,903	1,853	5.7	12,861	12,018	36.9	662	570	1.8
2018	1,959	1,898	5.8	13,265	12,407	37.9	700	618	1.9

Year	Reg hard ice cream (product weight)			Dry whole milk			Nonfat dry milk (human food)		
	Total disappearance	Consumption		Total disappearance	Consumption		Total disappearance	Consumption	
		Total	Per capita		Total	Per capita		Total	Per capita
	Million pounds	*Million pounds*	*Pounds*	*Million pounds*	*Million pounds*	*Pounds*	*Million pounds*	*Million pounds*	*Pounds*
2009	4,030	3,994	13.1	97	78	0.3	1,789	1,227	4.0
2010	3,851	3,808	12.4	86	64	0.2	1,864	998	3.2
2011	3,762	3,712	12.0	85	67	0.2	1,926	942	3.0
2012	3,765	3,705	12.0	80	53	0.2	2,132	1,137	3.6
2013	3,722	3,640	11.8	87	51	0.2	2,159	918	2.9
2014	3,607	3,523	11.3	103	63	0.2	2,209	997	3.1
2015	3,647	3,571	11.3	140	107	0.3	2,306	1,051	3.3
2016	3,676	3,602	11.3	129	87	0.3	2,292	961	3.0
2017	3,441	3,365	10.5	151	109	0.3	2,272	902	2.8
2018	3,384	3,298	10.4	175	115	0.4	2,386	794	2.4

[1] Total disappearance is based on production, imports, and change in stocks during the year. Production statistics for these commodities appear in other tables in this chapter. The total apparent consumption was obtained by subtracting ending stocks, shipments, and exports, from the total supply. The per capita consumption for each year was obtained by dividing the total apparent consumption by the number of persons. [2] Includes all kinds of cheese except cottage cheese. [3] The evaporated milk is unskimmed, unsweetened, case goods. The condensed milk is unsweetened, unskimmed, bulk goods; and sweetened condensed milk, unskimmed, case and bulk goods.
ERS, Animal Products and Cost of Production Branch, (202) 694–5171.

Table 8-26.—Dairy products: December 31 stocks, United States, 2009–2018

Year	Butter [1] [2]	Cheese [1] [3]	Condensed and evaporated milk	Dry whole milk	Nonfat dry milk for human consumption [1]
	Million pounds	*Million pounds*	*Million pounds*	*Million pounds*	*Million pounds*
2009	133	967	45	7	132
2010	82	1,048	52	8	145
2011	107	992	37	7	165
2012	153	1,023	38	7	183
2013	112	1,009	37	8	135
2014	105	1,018	32	23	240
2015	155	1,146	43	11	204
2016	166	1,198	42	13	226
2017	169	1,280	37	31	320
2018	179	1,345	42	16	277

[1] Includes Government holdings. [2] Includes anhydrous milkfat and butter oil. [3] Excludes cottage cheese.
ERS, Animal Products and Cost of Production Branch, (202) 694–5171.

Table 8-27.—International dairy: Butter production, 2018–2020

Country	2018	2019	2020
	1,000 metric tons		
India	5,600	5,850	6,100
European Union	2,345	2,425	2,410
United States	858	861	885
New Zealand	530	530	525
Russia	256	254	255
Mexico	228	231	233
Canada	116	112	115
Belarus	115	110	105
China	99	102	104
Ukraine	106	103	90
Brazil	85	86	87
Japan	60	61	62
Australia	93	65	60
Argentina	33	30	32

FAS, Office of Global Analysis, (202) 720-6301. Prepared or estimated on the basis of official USDA production, supply, and distribution statistics from foreign governments.

Table 8-28.—International dairy: Cheese production, 2018–2020

Country	2018	2019	2020
	1,000 metric tons		
European Union	10,160	10,275	10,350
United States	5,900	5,950	6,100
Russia	970	970	970
Brazil	760	780	795
Canada	510	519	525
Argentina	444	439	455
Mexico	419	436	454
Australia	367	370	375
New Zealand	355	360	365
Belarus	275	300	325
China	272	281	287
Ukraine	192	195	197
Japan	45	45	46
Korea, South	37	40	43
Philippines	2	2	2

FAS, Office of Global Analysis, (202) 720-6301. Prepared or estimated on the basis of official USDA production, supply, and distribution statistics from foreign governments.

Table 8-29.—Dairy products: United States imports by country of origin, 2017–2019

Commodity and country of origin	2017	2018	2019
	Metric tons		
Licensed cheese items 1:			
Netherlands	6,459	6,500	6,905
United Kingdom	3,981	5,409	5,269
Ireland	1,920	2,366	3,193
Australia(*)	1,326	1,711	1,815
Denmark(*)	1,702	1,940	1,783
New Zealand(*)	4,701	1,459	1,707
Germany(*)	1,141	1,387	1,366
Canada	946	1,243	787
Jamaica	474	498	450
Italy(*)	279	408	397
France(*)	306	307	288
Dominican Republic	197	193	183
Bahrain	148	138	157
Finland	115	185	137
India	140	115	75
Spain	26	62	45
Poland	43	39	43
Estonia	17	85	25
Lithuania	27	33	22
Philippines	11	7	20
Belgium-Luxembourg(*)	6	1	13
Greece	3	9	12
Chile	0	1	9
Mexico	0	0	3
Croatia	2	1	3
Portugal	3	3	2
Japan	1	1	1
Switzerland(*)	0	0	1
Austria	1	0	0
Egypt	0	1	0
Rest of World	0	42	0
World Total	23,971	24,143	24,712
Licensed cheese items 2:			
France(*)	18,330	20,168	21,441
Italy(*)	18,599	19,749	18,589
Switzerland(*)	8,152	9,130	8,740
Netherlands	8,034	7,380	7,827
Germany(*)	7,718	7,787	6,793
Norway(*)	4,736	5,969	6,328
Spain	6,458	6,506	6,074
Denmark(*)	5,126	6,327	5,194
Nicaragua	2,118	1,964	5,008
Ireland	4,331	4,146	4,922
Canada	5,945	5,583	4,171
Finland	4,078	4,395	3,861
Mexico	3,387	3,386	3,308
New Zealand(*)	3,498	2,804	2,368
Lithuania	454	461	2,145
Poland	1,534	1,913	2,041
Australia(*)	1,792	1,647	1,716
United Kingdom	1,033	1,273	1,233
Austria	973	1,365	887
Uruguay	782	749	802
Belgium-Luxembourg(*)	616	741	643
Greece	466	621	588
Egypt	440	465	571
Israel(*)	428	522	540
Rest of World	671	526	490
Uruguay	312	371	472
Belgium-Luxembourg(*)	442	298	409
Greece	76	171	377
Egypt	261	351	370
Israel(*)	2,701	40	329
Rest of World	3,323	2,014	2,183
World Total	116,813	118,822	120,419

See footnote(s) at end of table.

Table 8-29.—Dairy products: United States imports by country of origin, 2017–2019—Continued

Commodity and country of origin	2017	2018	2019
	Metric tons		
Non-licensed cheese:			
Italy(*)	17,428	11,948	15,392
Spain	5,318	5,776	6,013
Greece	3,405	3,611	4,004
France(*)	3,151	3,942	3,199
Bulgaria	2,583	2,814	2,558
Israel(*)	553	584	617
Cyprus	461	516	467
United Kingdom	693	385	433
Romania	486	301	366
Norway(*)	428	383	364
Turkey	190	397	345
Netherlands	197	160	211
Mexico	2	0	180
El Salvador	207	357	90
Switzerland(*)	14	214	82
Albania	0	0	81
Jordan	13	114	66
Portugal	28	26	25
Armenia	0	15	23
Croatia	4	20	23
Georgia	16	34	23
Hungary	11	10	19
Republic of North Macedonia	140	11	18
Egypt	27	77	14
Bosnia and Herzegovina	5	6	9
Germany(*)	2,379	4	8
Austria	2	6	6
Brazil	0	1	2
Kuwait	0	0	1
Poland	2	1	1
Rest of World	3,876	1,536	4
World Total	41,617	33,246	34,641
Casein:			
New Zealand(*)	30,658	23,161	22,933
Ireland	7,468	7,456	10,703
Netherlands	10,664	8,149	6,965
France(*)	2,890	4,306	5,339
Poland	3,888	2,442	4,053
Denmark(*)	3,886	3,701	3,293
Argentina	2,298	3,568	2,180
India	1,500	2,249	2,136
Germany(*)	2,295	1,482	1,700
Australia(*)	0	0	1,466
Uganda	1,020	476	353
Ukraine	0	0	20
Belgium-Luxembourg(*)	0	54	15
Switzerland(*)	0	24	15
Italy(*)	4	4	0
Sweden	0	0	0
Japan	0	0	-
Canada	6	0	0
Mexico	1	2	0
United Kingdom	0	19	0
World Total	66,584	57,092	61,172

See footnote(s) at end of table.

Table 8-29.—Dairy products: United States imports by country of origin, 2017–2019—Continued

Commodity and country of origin	2017	2018	2019
	Metric tons		
Non-licensed dairy, misc.:			
Canada	10,194	10,246	16,334
Chile	12,832	14,280	14,189
Peru	11,560	11,973	7,441
Mexico	5,625	8,541	6,066
New Zealand(*)	9,628	5,677	4,981
France(*)	2,502	3,245	4,524
Denmark(*)	2,559	2,104	2,046
Norway(*)	1,907	1,238	1,929
Ireland	153	1,300	1,593
Netherlands	1,127	965	1,510
Italy(*)	565	1,845	1,312
United Kingdom	430	244	1,138
Germany(*)	890	973	1,069
Brazil	3,722	496	655
Ukraine	568	431	448
Colombia	220	202	336
Israel(*)	611	215	318
Iceland	0	145	316
Malaysia	65	83	256
Belgium-Luxembourg(*)	178	196	227
Australia(*)	956	87	214
Argentina	252	98	156
Russia	69	95	137
China	0	-	94
Poland	152	112	75
Lithuania	40	48	73
India	119	72	67
Turkey	74	64	61
Greece	23	80	50
Yemen(*)	0	18	18
Rest of World	196	154	57
World Total	67,215	65,222	67,688
Misc. Dairy Quota:			
Canada	181,210	186,239	197,536
New Zealand(*)	49,953	38,842	43,433
Mexico	21,020	20,344	21,316
Italy(*)	14,654	13,429	14,096
Nicaragua	7,250	11,464	12,391
Korea, South	10,454	10,030	11,434
Germany(*)	3,297	5,305	9,108
Guatemala	5,094	6,417	5,720
France(*)	4,493	6,238	5,521
Ireland	2,192	5,184	5,356
Belgium-Luxembourg(*)	6,416	4,920	5,149
Netherlands	304	2,691	3,221
Thailand	1,450	3,082	2,772
India	1,878	2,385	2,560
Austria	1,889	1,844	1,766
Australia(*)	3,453	2,740	1,368
South Africa	1,411	1,263	1,192
Taiwan	675	945	1,182
Malaysia	1,278	1,129	1,126
Singapore	626	742	849
Denmark(*)	148	780	844
Israel(*)	1,480	831	775
Russia	114	202	768
Uruguay	565	399	706
Japan	397	515	636
Hungary	306	2,094	552
Lithuania	465	590	504
Switzerland(*)	332	755	477
Brazil	201	365	466
Philippines	270	181	432
Rest of World	11,053	4,419	4,928
World Total	334,328	336,363	358,181

See footnote(s) at end of table.

Table 8-29.—Dairy products: United States imports by country of origin, 2017–2019—Continued

Commodity and country of origin	2017	2018	2019
	Metric tons		
Licensed dairy, misc :			
Mexico	28,056	21,884	45,746
Canada	28,364	29,326	28,027
Germany(*)	3,930	2,127	3,630
Chile	9,211	6,753	2,423
Netherlands	16,802	2,242	1,716
Belgium-Luxembourg(*)	655	742	1,063
Denmark(*)	1,018	864	1,003
Ireland	2,242	2,690	940
New Zealand(*)	2,051	1,129	928
Australia(*)	365	270	754
Honduras	344	351	477
Peru	313	306	468
Italy(*)	204	570	467
Korea, South	245	662	356
France(*)	205	426	345
Colombia	164	174	193
Brazil	129	185	188
Argentina	69	142	135
Portugal	29	192	130
Malaysia	0	0	102
Singapore	104	33	76
Switzerland(*)	11	16	72
India	40	452	64
Costa Rica	30	71	32
Poland	36	11	30
Greece	62	29	23
United Kingdom	76	46	19
Africa, not elsewhere specified(*)	0	2	16
Venezuela	0	3	14
United Arab Emirates	224	122	8
Rest of World	130	811	27
World Total	95,110	76,632	89,472
Lactose:			
Germany(*)	2,165	1,853	1,394
Canada	503	203	1,035
Netherlands	1,045	421	735
New Zealand(*)	86	127	177
India	2	0	80
China	34	24	11
Australia(*)	16	0	7
Belarus	5	0	5
Ukraine	4	0	5
Japan	1	1	1
Belgium-Luxembourg(*)	0	3	0
Switzerland(*)	8	1	0
Argentina	0	5	0
Bosnia and Herzegovina	0	3	0
Ireland	-	0	0
France(*)	0	45	0
Italy(*)	1	11	0
Lithuania	0	2	0
Poland	5	0	0
Russia	12	0	0
South Africa	0	1	0
Singapore	0	3	0
Taiwan	1	0	0
United Kingdom	0	0	0
World Total	3,887	2,704	3,450

(*) Denotes a country that is a summarization of its component countries. Note: All zeroes for a data item may show that statistics exist in the other import type. Consumption or General. Users should use cautious interpretation on quantity reports using mixed units of measure. Quantity line items will only include statistics on the units of measure that are equal to, or are able to be converted to the assigned unit of measure of the grouped commodities.
FAS, Office of Global Analysis, (202) 720-6301. Data Source: U.S. Census Bureau Trade Data.

Table 8-30.—Dairy products: United States exports by area/partners of destination, 2017–2019

Commodity and destination	2017	2018	2019
		Metric tons	
Condensed & evap milk:			
Oceania	111	174	104
Micronesia	9	16	28
Australia(*)	22	101	26
Marshall Islands	35	34	23
Palau	19	21	21
French Pacific Islands(*)	3	2	3
Other Pacific Islands, NEC(*)	10	0	3
New Zealand(*)	14	1	0
Non-fat dry milk:			
Oceania	2,878	8,287	6,722
New Zealand(*)	600	7,998	6,119
Australia(*)	2,277	287	604
Samoa	1	0	0
Other Pacific Islands, NEC(*)	0	1	0
Dry whole milk & cream:			
Oceania	453	1,286	677
New Zealand(*)	0	577	489
Australia(*)	435	708	175
Micronesia	3	2	7
Palau	11	0	6
Marshall Islands	3	0	1
Other Pacific Islands, NEC(*)	1	0	0
Whey:			
Oceania	29,213	24,761	36,797
New Zealand(*)	23,057	20,579	30,364
Australia(*)	6,155	4,182	6,419
French Pacific Islands(*)	1	0	14
Casein:			
Oceania	298	432	416
Australia(*)	298	432	416
New Zealand(*)	0	0	0
Ice cream:			
Oceania	5,732	7,680	6,334
Australia(*)	5,150	7,024	5,622
Micronesia	322	257	308
New Zealand(*)	0	113	176
Marshall Islands	161	130	120
Palau	76	38	52
Other Pacific Islands, NEC(*)	6	116	48
British Pacific Islands(*)	0	0	7
French Pacific Islands(*)	18	3	1
Samoa	0	0	1
Cheese and curd:			
Oceania	32,546	27,263	24,268
Australia(*)	30,145	24,648	21,157
New Zealand(*)	2,325	2,434	2,988
French Pacific Islands(*)	52	141	90
Micronesia	10	22	16
Samoa	12	11	9
Marshall Islands	2	5	6
Palau	1	1	2
Other Pacific Islands, NEC(*)	0	0	1
		Liters	
Fluid milk and cream:			
Oceania	287,237	254,182	261,916
Micronesia	108,232	124,384	136,819
French Pacific Islands(*)	11,111	22,905	59,531
Marshall Islands	21,777	23,616	38,227
Australia(*)	64,165	14,473	16,608
Palau	45,435	49,793	6,507
New Zealand(*)	8,268	8,655	4,224
Other Pacific Islands, NEC(*)	28,249	10,356	0

(*) Denotes a country that is a summarization of its component countries. Note: Users should use cautious interpretation on quantity reports using mixed units of measure. Quantity line items will only include statistics on the units of measure that are equal to, or are able to be converted to, the assigned unit of measure of the grouped commodities.

FAS, Office of Global Analysis, (202) 720-6301. Data Source: U.S. Census Bureau Trade Data, as of March 17, 2020.

Table 8-31.—Chickens: Layers, pullets, and other chickens, by State and United States, December 1, 2017 and 2018

State	Total layers		Total pullets		Other Chickens	
	2017	2018	2017	2018	2017	2018
	Thousands	*Thousands*	*Thousands*	*Thousands*	*Thousands*	*Thousands*
Alabama	9,348	9,962	5,792	6,342	973	1,071
Arkansas	14,175	14,690	8,372	8,596	1,009	1,060
California	14,582	15,021	3,237	4,025	54	54
Colorado	4,635	5,141	1,254	1,124	36	55
Florida	7,383	7,352	2,087	1,618	20	25
Georgia	20,134	20,222	8,822	9,644	1,101	894
Illinois	5,635	6,476	433	365	22	19
Indiana	34,082	34,631	9,202	9,693	72	49
Iowa	56,337	58,188	13,243	14,313	107	78
Kentucky	5,644	5,942	2,541	2,418	214	216
Louisiana	2,014	2,078	735	637	75	99
Maryland	2,858	2,831	1,400	1,260	9	8
Massachusetts	140	154	9	30	-	-
Michigan	14,737	16,149	3,655	3,476	4	4
Minnesota	10,458	11,174	3,427	2,974	33	37
Mississippi	5,684	5,536	3,531	3,651	501	508
Missouri	10,509	12,537	4,527	5,600	191	199
Montana	942	1,000	244	236	-	-
Nebraska	7,670	8,453	1,814	1,711	52	28
New York	5,626	5,628	1,095	996	6	11
North Carolina	15,294	13,434	7,319	7,399	894	851
Ohio	35,542	32,967	8,395	10,632	51	1
Oklahoma	2,951	3,105	1,103	1,192	232	179
Oregon	2,404	2,279	553	725	-	-
Pennsylvania	29,391	28,758	4,737	5,161	165	182
South Carolina	4,055	4,263	1,399	1,334	156	125
South Dakota	2,682	2,665	882	777	-	-
Tennessee	1,872	1,658	915	1,019	170	147
Texas	22,549	22,747	6,559	6,533	404	349
Utah	5,036	4,713	1,178	1,139	-	-
Vermont	202	190	20	6	-	2
Virginia	2,675	2,735	1,011	1,283	151	165
Washington	6,770	6,772	1,721	1,339	-	-
West Virginia	1,251	1,207	770	632	99	93
Wisconsin	7,383	7,284	1,679	1,509	22	26
Other States [1]	18,156	18,928	3,512	4,746	36	34
United States	390,806	396,870	117,173	124,135	6,859	6,568

- Represents zero. [1] Alaska, Arizona, Connecticut, Delaware, Hawaii, Idaho, Kansas, Maine, New Hampshire, New Jersey, New Mexico, Nevada, North Dakota, Rhode Island, and Wyoming combined to avoid disclosing individual operations.
NASS, Livestock Branch, (202) 720–3570.

Table 8-32.—Chickens: Inventory number and value, United States, Dec. 1, 2009–2018 [1]

Year	Total layers	Total pullets	Other chickens	All chickens	Value per head	Total value
	Thousands	*Thousands*	*Thousands*	*Thousands*	*Dollars*	*1,000 dollars*
2009	342,058	104,069	8,487	454,614	3.32	1,510,038
2010	342,782	107,025	7,390	457,197	3.58	1,637,016
2011	343,283	104,159	6,922	454,364	3.79	1,721,671
2012	354,977	105,140	6,827	466,944	4.04	1,885,904
2013	367,356	108,919	6,853	483,128	4.15	2,007,374
2014	374,880	108,044	6,403	489,327	4.13	2,020,748
2015	356,312	120,007	7,211	483,530	4.38	2,115,982
2016	380,610	113,239	6,759	500,608	4.23	2,115,245
2017	390,806	117,173	6,859	514,838	4.20	2,162,545
2018	396,870	124,135	6,568	527,573	4.33	2,284,164

[1] Excludes commercial broilers.
NASS Livestock Branch, (202) 720-3570.

Table 8-33.—Chicken inventory: Number, value per head, and total value, by State and United States, December 1, 2017 and 2018 [1]

State	Number		Value per bird		Total value	
	2017	2018	2017	2018	2017	2018
	1,000 Head	*1,000 Head*	*Dollars*	*Dollars*	*1,000 Dollars*	*1,000 Dollars*
Alabama	16,113	17,375	7.40	9.20	119,236	159,850
Arkansas	23,556	24,346	7.90	8.50	186,092	206,941
California	17,873	19,100	3.70	3.80	66,130	72,580
Colorado	5,925	6,320	2.50	2.40	14,813	15,168
Florida	9,490	8,995	2.30	2.70	21,827	24,287
Georgia	30,057	30,760	6.20	6.60	186,353	203,016
Illinois	6,090	6,860	2.70	2.60	16,443	17,836
Indiana	43,356	44,373	1.90	2.30	82,376	102,058
Iowa	69,687	72,579	2.30	2.40	160,280	174,190
Kentucky	8,399	8,576	4.80	5.00	40,315	42,880
Louisiana	2,824	2,814	5.20	5.50	14,685	15,477
Maryland	4,267	4,099	4.00	3.90	17,068	15,986
Massachusetts	149	184	7.50	9.50	1,118	1,748
Michigan	18,396	19,629	2.20	2.60	40,471	51,035
Minnesota	13,918	14,185	2.30	2.30	32,011	32,626
Mississippi	9,716	9,695	8.80	8.60	85,501	83,377
Missouri	15,227	18,336	4.10	4.20	62,431	77,011
Montana	1,186	1,236	5.70	8.60	6,760	10,630
Nebraska	9,536	10,192	3.70	4.10	35,283	41,787
New York	6,727	6,635	2.40	2.90	16,145	19,242
North Carolina	23,507	21,684	7.70	8.70	181,004	188,651
Ohio	43,988	43,600	4.40	3.80	193,547	165,680
Oklahoma	4,286	4,476	7.00	7.50	30,002	33,570
Oregon	2,957	3,004	5.00	4.90	14,785	14,720
Pennsylvania	34,293	34,101	4.20	3.60	144,031	122,764
South Carolina	5,610	5,722	4.70	5.00	26,367	28,610
South Dakota	3,564	3,442	3.50	3.50	12,474	12,047
Tennessee	2,957	2,824	9.40	9.10	27,796	25,698
Texas	29,512	29,629	4.40	4.80	129,853	142,219
Utah	6,214	5,852	2.20	2.30	13,671	13,460
Vermont	222	198	8.60	7.20	1,909	1,426
Virginia	3,837	4,183	7.30	6.50	28,010	27,190
Washington	8,491	8,111	3.90	4.20	33,115	34,066
West Virginia	2,120	1,932	7.50	7.90	15,900	15,263
Wisconsin	9,084	8,818	2.40	2.50	21,802	22,045
Other States [2]	21,704	23,708	3.82	2.91	82,941	69,030
United States	514,838	527,573	4.20	4.33	2,162,545	2,284,164

Totals may not add due to rounding. [1] Excludes commercial broilers. [2] Alaska, Arizona, Connecticut, Delaware, Hawaii, Idaho, Kansas, Maine, New Hampshire, New Jersey, New Mexico, Nevada, North Dakota, Rhode Island and Wyoming combined to avoid disclosing data for individual operations.
NASS, Livestock Branch, (202) 720-3570.

Table 8-34.—Mature chickens: Lost, sold for slaughter, price, and value, United States, 2009–2018 [1]

Year	Number		Pounds (live weight) sold [3]	Price per pound live weight [3]
	Lost [2]	Sold [3]		
	1,000 head	*1,000 head*	*1,000 pounds*	*1,000 dollars*
2009	99,596	176,266	910,333	65,381
2010	108,356	173,404	903,750	73,099
2011	106,361	182,153	943,142	81,110
2012	103,758	179,162	901,411	79,208
2013	102,105	186,486	940,635	89,497
2014	106,166	192,334	970,852	96,840
2015	132,625	198,648	1,010,070	104,828
2016	106,166	207,923	1,060,677	87,949
2017	125,941	189,841	1,001,685	46,999
2018	136,698	189,603	1,019,695	49,365

[1] Annual estimates cover the period December 1 previous year through November 30. Excludes broilers. [2] Includes rendered, died, destroyed, composted, or disappeared for any reason (excluding sold for slaughter) during the 12-month period.
NASS, Livestock Branch, (202) 720–3570.

Table 8-35.—Chickens: Lost, sold for slaughter, and value of sales, by State and United States, 2017 and 2018 [1]

State	Number lost [2]		Number sold		Pounds sold		Value of sales	
	2017	2018	2017	2018	2017	2018	2017	2018
	1,000 head				1,000 pounds		1,000 dollars	
Alabama	3,195.9	3,476.2	11,002.1	11,650.7	87,466.7	92,856.1	6,472.5	7,057.1
Arkansas	3,474.2	3,513.9	16,212.7	15,524.2	121,595.3	115,034.3	8,633.3	8,282.5
California	5,978.1	7,143.7	3,013.3	2,671.1	11,058.8	9,909.8	132.7	109.0
Colorado	2,313.7	2,240.8	1,553.0	1,286.7	7,873.7	6,973.9	338.6	341.7
Florida	5,378.0	5,022.6	380.5	401.7	2,891.8	3,000.7	214.0	216.1
Georgia	6,131.3	6,425.8	15,484.6	17,214.4	108,701.9	118,262.9	7,283.0	7,805.4
Illinois	1,221.4	1,487.4	1,911.5	2,505.2	7,301.9	9,519.8	109.5	123.8
Indiana	14,310.9	13,820.0	11,245.3	12,441.1	39,246.1	44,041.5	196.2	220.2
Iowa	28,024.3	31,854.6	6,376.6	9,608.6	22,063.0	33,534.0	110.3	100.6
Kentucky	992.6	1,085.1	4,506.6	5,181.5	26,138.3	30,260.0	1,437.6	1,664.3
Louisiana	315.0	403.5	1,879.4	1,930.1	11,953.0	12,410.5	729.1	769.5
Maryland	280.0	809.6	1,525.3	508.1	5,613.1	2,118.8	67.4	50.9
Massachusetts	9.2	89.2	75.4	0.2	254.1	0.7	(Z)	(Z)
Michigan	1,069.5	3,959.0	9,756.2	5,674.0	32,976.0	19,518.6	33.0	19.5
Minnesota	3,902.3	4,729.9	4,058.2	3,571.8	15,705.2	15,394.5	267.0	431.0
Mississippi	1,399.8	1,406.8	5,525.2	5,812.7	40,555.0	43,072.1	2,798.3	3,058.1
Missouri	3,209.7	2,418.0	8,703.9	6,790.5	41,865.8	34,971.1	1,632.8	1,573.7
Montana	322.6	629.9	52.3	5.1	176.3	17.5	(Z)	(Z)
Nebraska	791.9	1,272.1	5,814.8	4,035.2	19,886.6	14,042.5	59.7	28.1
New York	509.2	586.4	3,903.2	4,532.3	13,192.8	15,681.8	13.2	15.7
North Carolina	4,056.5	4,059.9	14,993.5	17,210.5	103,305.2	112,900.9	6,818.1	7,112.8
Ohio	10,930.4	11,193.0	12,950.4	12,662.9	46,491.9	46,219.6	371.9	416.0
Oklahoma	736.2	775.1	2,562.1	2,251.2	20,112.5	18,144.7	1,488.3	1,397.1
Oregon	1,625.6	1,710.8	14.1	14.9	47.5	51.3	(Z)	(Z)
Pennsylvania	2,781.9	2,855.3	11,201.6	11,911.9	41,670.0	45,146.1	541.7	632.0
South Carolina	1,961.7	1,993.0	1,916.2	2,269.1	12,608.6	15,611.4	807.0	1,046.0
South Dakota	904.6	1,091.5	1,072.3	140.3	3,613.7	481.2	3.6	0.5
Tennessee	521.1	467.9	1,802.3	1,917.2	14,076.0	14,800.8	1,041.6	1,095.3
Texas	4,156.5	3,686.8	14,270.9	14,350.6	69,784.7	72,470.5	2,861.2	3,116.2
Utah	1,598.2	1,127.0	2,648.0	2,271.9	8,923.8	7,815.3	8.9	7.8
Vermont	19.2	25.2	103.2	142.2	390.1	594.4	5.9	14.3
Virginia	1,536.5	1,326.4	2,116.9	2,092.1	17,041.0	16,841.4	1,278.1	1,279.9
Washington	4,852.1	5,113.0	33.3	36.3	112.2	129.6	(Z)	(Z)
West Virginia	286.7	276.3	1,690.7	1,740.5	13,153.6	13,680.3	973.4	1,026.0
Wisconsin	1,093.4	2,951.1	2,540.6	2,157.1	9,781.3	9,340.2	166.3	261.5
Other States [3]	6,050.5	5,670.9	6,944.5	7,088.7	24,057.8	24,845.7	104.2	90.9
United States	125,940.7	136,697.7	189,840.7	189,602.6	1,001,685.3	1,019,694.5	46,999.0	49,364.4

(Z) Less than half of the unit shown. [1] Annual estimates cover the period December 1 previous year through November 30. Exclude broilers. Totals may not add due to rounding. [2] Includes rendered, died, destroyed, composted, or disappeared for any reason except sold during the 12-month period. [3] Alaska, Arizona, Connecticut, Delaware, Hawaii, Idaho, Kansas, Maine, Nevada, New Hampshire, New Jersey, New Mexico, North Dakota, Rhode Island, and Wyoming combined to avoid disclosing data for individual operations.

NASS, Livestock Branch, (202) 720–3570.

Table 8-36.—Chickens: Production, commercial storage, exports, and consumption, United States, 2010–2019

Year	Production			Commercial storage at beginning of year	Exports	Commercial storage at end of year	Consumption	
	Commercial broilers	Other chickens	Total [1]				Total [1 2]	Per capita
	Million pounds							Pounds
2010	36,515	504	37,018	618	6,840	777	30,130	97
2011	36,804	521	37,325	777	7,069	592	30,549	98
2012	36,643	516	37,159	592	7,363	652	29,850	95
2013	37,425	523	37,948	652	7,453	675	30,597	97
2014	38,153	521	38,673	675	7,406	683	31,378	98
2015	39,620	522	40,142	683	6,465	840	33,652	105
2016	40,261	548	40,809	840	6,803	786	34,194	106
2017	41,217	535	41,751	786	6,916	861	34,890	107
2018	42,145	539	42,684	861	7,153	850	35,683	109
2019	43,435	528	43,963	850	7,190	942	36,814	112

[1] Totals may not add due to rounding. [2] Shipments to territories now included in total consumption.

ERS Markets and Trade Economics Division, Animal Products and Cost of Production Branch, (202) 694–5308. Data as of March 13, 2020.

Table 8-37.—Broilers: Production and value, United States, 2009–2018[1] [2] [3]

Year	Number produced	Pounds produced	Value of production
	1,000 head	*1,000 pounds*	*1,000 dollars*
2009	8,550,200	47,752,300	21,822,804
2010	8,623,600	49,152,600	23,691,553
2011	8,607,600	50,082,400	22,987,822
2012	8,463,000	49,655,600	24,827,800
2013	8,533,800	50,678,200	30,761,669
2014	8,545,000	51,378,700	32,728,234
2015	8,688,700	53,376,200	28,716,398
2016	8,776,700	54,259,100	25,935,852
2017	8,913,800	55,573,900	30,232,203
2018	9,037,100	56,791,100	31,746,230

[1] December 1, previous year through November 30, current year. [2] Broiler production including other domestic meat-type strains. [3] Excludes States producing less than 500,000 broilers.
NASS, Livestock Branch, (202) 720–3570.

Table 8-38.—Broilers: Production and value, States and United States, 2017 and 2018[1]

State	2017			2018		
	Number produced	Pounds produced	Value of production	Number produced	Pounds produced	Value of production
	1,000 head	*1,000 pounds*	*1,000 dollars*	*1,000 head*	*1,000 pounds*	*1,000 dollars*
Alabama	1,095,400	6,134,200	3,337,005	1,123,700	6,180,400	3,454,844
Arkansas	1,059,000	6,989,400	3,802,234	1,092,000	7,316,400	4,089,868
Delaware	259,800	1,870,600	1,017,606	263,600	1,924,300	1,075,684
Florida	65,200	371,600	202,150	65,400	385,900	215,718
Georgia	1,363,400	8,044,100	4,375,990	1,361,400	8,168,400	4,566,136
Kentucky	295,800	1,893,100	1,029,846	303,300	1,971,500	1,102,069
Maryland	306,700	1,840,200	1,001,069	289,400	1,736,400	970,648
Minnesota	59,700	358,200	194,861	59,100	360,500	201,520
Mississippi	741,100	4,743,000	2,580,192	747,800	4,711,100	2,633,505
Missouri	291,100	1,426,400	775,962	293,100	1,465,500	819,215
North Carolina	830,800	6,563,300	3,570,435	873,600	6,901,400	3,857,883
Ohio	99,300	526,300	286,307	107,900	561,100	313,655
Oklahoma	204,500	1,370,200	745,389	196,800	1,318,600	737,097
Pennsylvania	185,200	1,037,100	564,182	200,100	1,140,600	637,595
South Carolina	243,100	1,798,900	978,602	237,800	1,807,300	1,010,281
Tennessee	171,500	909,000	494,496	177,300	939,700	525,292
Texas	651,200	4,102,600	2,231,814	653,500	4,247,800	2,374,520
Virginia	277,400	1,608,900	875,242	278,900	1,673,400	935,431
West Virginia	86,100	335,800	182,675	83,300	316,500	176,924
Wisconsin	53,800	226,000	122,944	55,800	228,800	127,899
Other States[2]	573,700	3,425,000	1,863,202	573,300	3,435,500	1,920,446
United States	8,913,800	55,573,900	30,232,203	9,037,100	56,791,100	31,746,230

[1] Annual estimates cover the period December 1 previous year through November 30. Broiler production including other domestic meat-type strains. Excludes States producing less than 500,000 broilers. [2] Includes State estimates not shown and States whithheld to avoid disclosing data for individual operations.
NASS, Livestock Branch, (202) 720–3570.

Table 8-39.—Poultry: Slaughtered under Federal inspection, by class, United States, 2016–2018

Class	Number slaughtered			Total live weight		
	2016	2017	2018	2016	2017	2018
	Thousands	*Thousands*	*Thousands*	*Thousands*	*Thousands*	*Thousands*
Young chickens	8,768,399	8,916,083	9,034,504	54,036,929	55,314,913	56,541,518
Mature chickens	140,587	134,619	126,406	848,287	822,578	816,199
Total chickens	8,908,986	9,050,702	9,160,910	54,885,216	56,137,491	57,357,717
Young turkeys	241,418	240,014	235,198	7,412,058	7,420,122	7,310,114
Old turkeys	1,837	1,666	1,662	51,966	48,973	48,981
Total turkeys	243,255	241,680	236,860	7,464,024	7,469,095	7,359,095
Ducks	27,268	26,628	27,647	186,715	184,338	192,980
Other poultry [1]	(NA)	(NA)	(NA)	4,054	4,211	3,872
Total poultry	(NA)	(NA)	(NA)	62,540,009	63,795,135	64,913,664

Class	Pounds condemned					
	Ante-mortem (live weight)			Post-mortem (Carcass and parts)		
	2016	2017	2018	2016	2017	2018
	Thousands	*Thousands*	*Thousands*	*Thousands*	*Thousands*	*Thousands*
Young chickens	124,994	124,241	130,452	356,808	342,149	322,994
Mature chickens	10,156	9,563	8,167	30,365	25,923	20,727
Total chickens	135,150	133,804	138,619	387,173	368,072	343,721
Young turkeys	18,680	18,798	19,090	86,939	84,726	82,278
Old turkeys	662	543	494	1,900	2,025	1,944
Total turkeys	19,342	19,341	19,584	88,839	86,751	84,222
Ducks	528	592	797	3,633	3,531	3,667
Other poultry [2]	4	5	5	28	40	35
Total poultry	155,024	153,742	159,005	479,673	458,394	431,645

Class	Pounds certified (ready-to-cook)		
	2016	2017	2018
	Thousands	*Thousands*	*Thousands*
Young chickens	40,696,114	41,662,394	42,600,735
Mature chickens	548,567	535,291	539,362
Total chickens	41,244,681	42,197,685	43,140,097
Young turkeys	5,942,076	5,943,827	5,841,082
Old turkeys	39,025	36,750	37,009
Total turkeys	5,981,101	5,980,577	5,878,091
Ducks	135,821	134,313	140,936
Other poultry [2]	2,655	2,727	2,563
Total poultry	47,364,258	48,315,302	49,161,687

(NA) Not available. [1] Includes geese, guineas, ostriches, emus, rheas, and squab. [2] Includes geese, guineas, and squab.
NASS, Livestock Branch, (202) 720–3570.

Table 8-40.—Poultry: Feed-price ratios, United States, 2009–2018

Year	Ratios [1]		
	Egg-feed	Broiler-feed	Turkey-feed
	Pounds	*Pounds*	*Pounds*
2009	7.2	4.1	5.0
2010	7.5	4.5	6.2
2011	6.0	3.1	4.9
2012	5.4	3.1	4.7
2013	6.5	3.7	4.6
2014	10.2	5.0	6.3
2015	17.1	5.0	8.5
2016	5.9	4.7	9.2
2017	7.7	5.4	7.2
2018	11.3	5.6	5.5

[1] Number of pounds of poultry feed equivalent in value at local market prices to 1 dozen market eggs, or 1 pound of broiler or 1 pound of turkey live weight. Simple average of monthly feed-price ratios. Egg feed= corn (75 lbs) and soybeans (25 lbs); broiler feed= corn (58 lbs); soybeans (42 lbs); turkey feed= corn (51 lbs), soybeans (28 lbs), and wheat (21 lbs). Monthly equivalent prices of commercial prepared feeds are based on current U.S. prices received for corn, soybeans, and wheat.
NASS, Environmental, Economics, and Demographics Branch, (202) 720–6146.

Table 8-41.—Turkeys: Production, commercial storage, exports, and consumption, United States, 2010–2019

Year	Production	Commercial storage at beginning of year	Exports	Commercial storage at end of year	Consumption	
					Total [1 2]	Per capita
	Million pounds					*Pounds*
2010	5,570	262	581	192	5,084	16
2011	5,715	192	703	211	5,013	16
2012	5,889	211	797	296	5,028	16
2013	5,729	296	741	237	5,068	16
2014	5,756	237	775	193	5,052	16
2015	5,627	193	529	201	5,135	16
2016	5,981	201	569	279	5,384	17
2017	5,981	279	622	310	5,352	16
2018	5,878	310	611	303	5,293	16
2019	5,818	303	639	233	5,261	16

[1] Totals may not add due to rounding. [2] Shipments to territories now included in consumption.
ERS Markets and Trade Economics Division, Animal Products and Cost of Production Branch, (202) 694–5409. Data as of March 13, 2020.

Table 8-42.—Turkeys: Production and value, United States, 2009–2018

Year	Number raised	Pounds (live weight) produced	Value of production [1]
	1,000 head	*1,000 pounds*	*1,000 dollars*
2009	247,359	7,149,314	3,573,324
2010	244,188	7,108,222	4,372,438
2011	248,500	7,313,205	4,987,608
2012	253,500	7,561,905	5,452,135
2013	240,000	7,277,536	4,839,562
2014	237,500	7,217,006	5,304,501
2015	233,100	7,038,136	5,707,928
2016	244,000	7,486,978	6,184,247
2017	245,200	7,554,397	4,873,677
2018	244,750	7,598,289	3,875,131

NASS, Livestock Branch, (202) 720–3570.

Table 8-43.—Turkeys: Production and value, by State and United States, 2017–2018 [1]

State	2017			2018		
	Number raised	Pounds produced	Value of production	Number raised	Pounds produced	Value of production
	1,000 head	*1,000 pounds*	*1,000 dollars*	*1,000 head*	*1,000 pounds*	*1,000 dollars*
Arkansas	29,500	587,050	379,234	31,500	595,350	303,629
California	11,500	319,700	206,526	11,000	317,900	162,129
Indiana	20,000	792,000	511,632	20,000	768,000	391,680
Iowa	12,000	484,800	313,181	11,900	477,190	243,367
Michigan	5,100	206,040	133,102	5,300	222,070	113,256
Minnesota	42,000	1,058,400	683,726	42,000	1,113,000	567,630
Missouri	18,500	614,200	396,773	19,000	640,300	326,553
North Carolina	32,500	1,144,000	739,024	32,500	1,196,000	609,960
Ohio	6,700	280,730	181,352	6,700	282,070	143,856
Pennsylvania	7,500	204,750	132,269	7,000	195,300	99,603
South Dakota	4,100	176,300	113,890	4,250	179,350	91,469
Utah	5,200	134,160	86,667	(D)	(D)	(D)
Virginia	16,800	458,640	296,281	16,800	462,000	235,620
West Virginia	3,700	111,000	71,706	3,100	96,410	49,169
Other States [2]	30,100	972,621	628,314	33,700	1,053,349	537,210
United States	245,200	7,544,391	4,873,677	244,750	7,598,289	3,875,131

(D) Withheld to avoid disclosing data for individual operations. [1] Based on turkeys placed September 1 through August 31. Excludes young turkeys lost. [2] Includes State estimates not shown and States withheld to avoid disclosing data for individual operations.
NASS, Livestock Branch, (202) 720–3570.

Table 8-44.—Turkeys: Net poults placements, United States, Monthly, 2017–2018 [1]

Month	Total all breeds		Percent of Previous Year
	2017	2018	
	Thousands	*Thousands*	*Percent*
January	23,046	22,642	98
February	22,078	21,340	97
March	23,636	22,793	96
April	22,237	22,335	100
May	22,639	22,168	98
June	23,950	22,597	94
July	23,987	25,652	107
August	24,321	23,362	96
September	20,670	20,512	99
October	22,030	22,377	102
November	21,399	21,108	99
December	20,766	19,915	96
Total	270,759	266,801	99

[1] Includes imports and excludes exports.
NASS, Livestock Branch, (202) 720–3570.

Table 8-45.—Turkeys: Poults hatched by commercial hatcheries, United States by Month, 2017–2018

Month	2017	2018	Percent of Previous Year
	Thousands	*Thousands*	*Percent*
January	25,412	24,406	96
February	23,679	22,654	96
March	25,812	24,180	94
April	23,278	23,482	101
May	24,169	23,503	97
June	25,125	23,337	93
July	24,691	25,730	104
August	24,868	23,888	96
September	23,530	22,443	95
October	24,393	24,295	100
November	24,532	29,089	119
December	22,272	23,176	104
Total	291,761	290,183	99

NASS, Livestock Branch, (202) 720–3570.

Table 8-46.—Eggs: Supply, distribution, and per capita consumption, United States, 2010–2019 [1]

Year	Total egg production	Storage at beginning of the year [1]	Imports [2]	Exports [2]	Storage at end of the year [2]	Eggs used for hatching	Consumption	
							Total [3]	Per capita
	Million dozen							*Number*
2010	7,656	93	22	295	98	982	6,396	248
2011	7,715	98	21	305	120	950	6,459	248
2012	7,884	120	19	336	85	941	6,660	254
2013	8,233	85	17	425	63	964	6,884	261
2014	8,509	63	35	414	76	981	7,136	269
2015	8,144	76	132	342	74	996	6,941	259
2016	8,668	74	130	304	142	1,010	7,415	275
2017	8,947	142	34	355	88	1,035	7,646	282
2018	9,205	88	18	333	79	1,058	7,841	287
2019	9,447	79	15	334	109	1,079	8,019	292

[1] Calendar years. [2] Shell eggs and the approximate shell-egg equivalent of egg product. [3] Shipments to territories now included in total consumption.
ERS Markets and Trade Economics Division, Animal Products and Cost of Production Branch, (202) 694–5409. Data as of March 13, 2020.

Table 8-47.—Eggs, shell: Average price per dozen on consumer Grade A cartoned white eggs to volume buyers, store-door delivery, New York, 2010–2019

Year	Large
	Cents
2010	106.29
2011	115.31
2012	117.46
2013	124.69
2014	142.33
2015	181.74
2016	85.70
2017	100.96
2018	137.58
2019	94.00

AMS, Livestock, Poultry and Seed Programs, Livestock, Poultry and Grain Market News Division, (515) 284-4460.

Table 8-48.—Total layers and egg production: Annual average number of layers, eggs per layer, and total production, by State and United States, 2017–2018 [1]

State	Average number of layers		Eggs per layer [2]		Total egg production	
	2017	2018	2017	2018	2017	2018
	Thousands	*Thousands*	*Number*	*Number*	*Millions*	*Millions*
Alabama	9,112	9,556	227	223	2,072.3	2,133.3
Arkansas	14,147	14,668	243	241	3,431.0	3,534.7
California	13,202	14,542	285	295	3,759.6	4,294.6
Colorado	4,642	4,866	305	305	1,414.5	1,482.9
Florida	7,587	7,340	276	273	2,095.7	2,005.4
Georgia	19,565	19,607	256	248	5,010.6	4,871.1
Illinois	5,088	6,004	295	294	1,500.4	1,764.1
Indiana	33,553	33,794	294	286	9,869.7	9,658.6
Iowa	55,867	57,614	289	282	16,155.2	16,273.8
Kentucky	5,190	5,690	262	252	1,360.5	1,434.4
Louisiana	1,984	2,004	242	258	480.8	517.5
Maryland	2,852	2,689	295	290	840.1	780.6
Massachusetts	124	142	324	304	40.2	43.1
Michigan	14,272	15,387	296	296	4,225.5	4,548.1
Minnesota	10,462	10,812	294	290	3,070.7	3,131.8
Mississippi	5,587	5,673	249	250	1,392.8	1,418.6
Missouri	10,764	11,937	292	291	3,146.3	3,473.9
Montana	523	900	294	325	153.8	292.5
Nebraska	8,167	7,829	305	305	2,489.1	2,388.8
New York	5,660	5,553	303	298	1,717.8	1,656.5
North Carolina	15,295	14,573	259	254	3,956.2	3,705.4
Ohio	33,773	32,848	289	285	9,754.6	9,364.9
Oklahoma	2,931	3,051	236	228	691.8	697.1
Oregon	2,369	2,382	314	307	744.6	732.4
Pennsylvania	28,232	28,477	295	296	8,337.3	8,423.1
South Carolina	3,922	4,331	272	267	1,068.3	1,156.2
South Dakota	2,701	2,603	290	307	784.3	797.9
Tennessee	1,642	1,798	229	216	376.6	388.8
Texas	21,781	22,563	267	271	5,820.3	6,108.5
Utah	5,153	4,793	294	293	1,512.9	1,403.4
Vermont	158	201	292	307	46.1	61.7
Virginia	2,698	2,676	265	268	716.0	716.7
Washington	6,994	6,959	301	302	2,103.7	2,102.1
West Virginia	1,244	1,284	221	230	274.7	295.9
Wisconsin	6,428	7,271	289	286	1,860.1	2,077.8
Other States [3]	17,506	18,894	284	289	4,967.5	5,455.9
United States	381,175	391,311	281	279	107,241.6	109,192.1

[1] Annual estimates cover the period December 1 previous year through November 30. Totals may not add due to rounding. [2] Total egg production divided by average number of layers on hand. [3] Alaska, Arizona, Connecticut, Delaware, Hawaii, Idaho, Kansas, Maine, New Hampshire, New Jersey, New Mexico, Nevada, North Dakota, Rhode Island, and Wyoming combined to avoid disclosing data for individual operations.

NASS, Livestock Branch, (202) 720–3570.

Table 8-49.—Eggs: Broken under Federal inspection, United States, 2017–2018

Item	Quantity	
	2017	2018
	1,000 dozen	*1,000 dozen*
Shell eggs broken	2,307,023	2,399,762
	1,000 pounds	1,000 pounds
Edible product from shell eggs broken		
Whole	1,837,087	1,911,501
White	771,207	788,037
Yolk	383,655	390,716
Total	2,991,949	3,090,254
Inedible product from shell eggs broken	239,584	260,875

NASS, Livestock Branch, (202) 720–3570.

Table 8-50.—Eggs: Number, rate of lay, production, and value, United States, 2009–2018 [1]

Year	Layers average number	Eggs per layer [2]	Total egg production	Value of production
	Thousands	*Number*	*Millions*	*1,000 dollars*
2009	338,846	268	90,737	6,191,040
2010	341,505	269	91,811	6,553,087
2011	340,598	271	92,450	7,355,873
2012	394,844	274	94,364	7,929,104
2013	358,313	275	98,481	8,745,404
2014	368,193	277	101,816	10,342,687
2015	356,370	276	98,291	13,762,519
2016	369,949	279	103,202	6,591,359
2017	381,175	281	107,242	7,635,001
2018	391,311	279	109,192	10,586,262

[1] Annual estimates cover the period December 1 previous year through November 30. [2] Total egg production divided by average number of layers on hand.
NASS, Livestock Branch, (202) 720–3570.

Table 8-51.—Total Eggs: Production and value by State and United States, 2017–2018 [1]

State	Eggs produced		Value of production	
	2017	2018	2017	2018
	Millions	*Millions*	*1,000 dollars*	*1,000 dollars*
Alabama	2,072.3	2,133.3	349,437	382,196
Arkansas	3,431.0	3,534.7	482,651	527,651
California	3,759.6	4,294.6	267,690	503,663
Colorado	1,414.5	1,482.9	77,227	113,657
Florida	2,095.7	2,005.4	112,225	154,784
Georgia	5,010.6	4,871.1	587,500	656,656
Illinois	1,500.4	1,764.1	87,784	147,870
Indiana	9,869.7	9,658.6	543,793	796,467
Iowa	16,155.2	16,273.8	868,838	1,327,106
Kentucky	1,360.5	1,434.4	122,051	158,458
Louisiana	480.8	517.5	53,102	63,196
Maryland	840.1	780.6	45,389	60,686
Massachusetts	40.2	43.1	2,023	3,194
Michigan	4,225.5	4,548.1	220,431	364,078
Minnesota	3,070.7	3,131.8	171,173	262,646
Mississippi	1,392.8	1,418.6	211,051	230,685
Missouri	3,146.3	3,473.9	207,485	297,684
Montana	153.8	292.5	11,192	33,674
Nebraska	2,489.1	2,388.8	130,912	198,202
New York	1,717.8	1,656.5	90,433	127,359
North Carolina	3,956.2	3,705.4	461,195	509,017
Ohio	9,754.6	9,364.9	524,196	762,538
Oklahoma	691.8	697.1	80,090	92,177
Oregon	744.6	732.4	50,436	85,136
Pennsylvania	8,337.3	8,423.1	482,082	673,940
South Carolina	1,068.3	1,156.2	92,746	118,383
South Dakota	784.3	797.9	40,556	63,795
Tennessee	376.6	388.8	68,552	70,558
Texas	5,820.3	6,108.5	395,521	546,249
Utah	1,512.9	1,403.4	102,395	163,332
Vermont	46.1	61.7	2,787	5,218
Virginia	716.0	716.7	91,300	100,668
Washington	2,103.7	2,102.1	141,321	240,515
West Virginia	274.7	295.9	50,249	54,681
Wisconsin	1,860.1	2,077.8	108,619	176,103
Other States [2]	4,967.5	5,455.9	300,569	514,040
United States	107,241.6	109,192.1	7,635,001	10,586,262

Totals may not add due to rounding. [1] Annual estimates cover the period December 1 previous year through November 30. Includes hatching and market (table) eggs. [2] Alaska, Arizona, Connecticut, Delaware, Hawaii, Idaho, Kansas, Maine, Nevada, New Hampshire, New Jersey, New Mexico, North Dakota, Rhode Island, and Wyoming combined to avoid disclosing individual operations.
NASS, Livestock Branch, (202) 720–3570.

Table 8-52.—Poultry and poultry products: Cold storage holdings, end of month, United States, 2017– 2018

Month	Frozen eggs							
	Whites		Yolks		Whole & mixed		Unclassified	
	2017	2018	2017	2018	2017	2018	2017	2018
	1,000 pounds							
January	4,364	4,028	1,025	689	13,170	13,136	18,354	13,188
February	5,200	4,917	1,039	677	13,177	12,782	21,655	13,932
March	5,707	3,155	828	629	13,416	11,341	21,960	13,050
April	4,628	2,479	920	715	12,296	12,596	23,332	11,973
May	3,530	3,296	914	688	13,109	13,000	21,480	13,252
June	4,773	3,207	1,340	1,031	14,034	12,837	21,565	13,630
July	5,244	3,220	1,228	1,095	14,592	13,169	19,129	12,307
August	4,651	2,734	675	799	13,290	14,498	16,550	13,959
September ...	4,685	2,521	1,200	1,157	13,174	11,231	14,875	14,026
October	4,138	2,308	672	704	12,884	13,721	15,234	13,534
November	4,597	2,503	733	485	11,217	13,974	11,364	12,641
December	4,760	2,688	642	814	11,734	13,869	13,026	12,005

Month	Frozen eggs, total		Frozen chicken					
			Broilers (Whole)		Hens		Breast and breast meat	
	2017	2018	2017	2018	2017	2018	2017	2018
	1,000 pounds							
January	36,913	31,041	17,357	12,841	7,918	4,735	191,811	200,238
February	41,071	32,308	16,274	14,010	6,490	4,305	191,083	201,580
March	41,911	28,175	16,783	15,641	4,926	3,869	178,702	184,218
April	41,176	27,763	21,761	14,436	4,629	3,923	186,900	182,862
May	39,033	30,236	20,662	14,402	6,090	3,808	184,393	186,418
June	41,712	30,705	22,744	15,370	7,846	3,907	182,935	181,547
July	40,193	29,791	22,807	16,379	8,799	6,310	172,907	170,472
August	35,166	31,990	22,154	20,407	8,538	5,270	169,854	173,958
September ...	33,934	28,935	22,269	21,073	6,567	6,150	170,582	177,388
October	32,928	30,267	20,281	17,073	6,065	4,545	175,209	184,127
November	27,911	29,603	16,350	17,119	4,562	4,223	184,012	186,937
December	30,162	29,376	11,990	17,712	4,613	5,615	188,070	188,311

Month	Frozen chicken							
	Drumsticks		Leg quarters		Legs		Thigh and thigh quarters	
	2017	2018	2017	2018	2017	2018	2017	2018
	1,000 pounds							
January	16,621	25,870	100,617	88,635	12,620	15,918	8,473	7,030
February	18,146	26,997	112,677	81,742	17,379	15,490	12,162	8,492
March	16,672	27,613	113,069	86,768	21,830	14,423	9,916	8,853
April	19,942	29,793	116,017	89,943	24,220	13,176	8,502	8,575
May	21,240	31,983	119,333	87,863	23,665	15,390	8,106	9,627
June	20,500	36,304	131,323	85,540	21,861	17,291	8,362	10,214
July	25,124	36,503	125,073	81,554	18,937	15,527	7,186	9,182
August	24,359	37,194	114,455	97,914	17,842	19,163	9,177	12,812
September ...	22,835	40,085	128,744	104,410	18,386	18,012	9,101	11,892
October	21,869	38,655	120,762	90,698	20,317	16,693	8,225	11,576
November	24,930	38,884	113,777	70,030	18,843	17,217	9,046	13,449
December	31,185	37,552	104,563	61,435	13,220	11,749	10,274	12,572

Month	Frozen chicken							
	Thigh meat		Wings		Paws and feet		Other	
	2017	2018	2017	2018	2017	2018	2017	2018
	1,000 pounds							
January	26,635	26,054	71,783	64,627	18,650	28,853	293,562	402,530
February	24,497	26,396	71,523	70,655	15,328	32,100	300,314	418,109
March	21,697	24,368	64,942	68,347	17,706	26,899	298,341	410,474
April	18,937	24,544	61,818	71,639	22,781	25,402	310,387	403,241
May	15,936	23,611	56,609	79,955	21,337	30,233	307,465	391,898
June	15,170	21,872	60,502	81,488	19,136	36,553	315,086	397,898
July	16,597	23,595	60,238	88,979	21,353	33,573	319,099	395,575
August	15,861	21,861	63,417	97,436	20,841	33,837	315,555	406,395
September ...	17,285	22,721	66,850	104,951	22,784	28,189	332,687	423,132
October	21,082	22,435	70,364	97,318	24,602	27,422	385,432	429,754
November	23,241	25,906	76,187	98,708	26,569	26,216	399,085	430,447
December	26,122	24,145	74,113	86,813	26,665	31,460	396,407	404,262

See end of table.

Table 8-52.—Poultry and poultry products: Cold storage holdings, end of month, United States, 2017–2018—Continued

Month	Total chicken		Frozen turkey					
			Toms		Hens		Total whole	
	2017	2018	2017	2018	2017	2018	2017	2018
	1,000 pounds							
January	775,077	877,334	57,392	84,346	67,075	74,187	124,467	158,533
February	785,873	899,876	71,510	97,875	83,670	90,466	155,180	188,341
March	764,673	871,473	79,721	106,625	101,494	112,223	181,215	218,848
April	795,894	867,534	101,509	125,408	115,587	123,467	217,096	248,875
May	784,836	875,188	130,431	149,736	141,572	134,593	272,003	284,329
June	805,465	887,984	146,273	160,846	161,610	145,418	307,883	306,264
July	798,120	877,649	171,608	181,480	174,669	147,906	346,277	329,386
August	782,053	926,247	175,578	192,601	173,123	155,216	348,701	347,817
September ...	818,090	958,003	181,048	192,267	151,266	138,460	332,314	330,727
October	874,208	940,296	154,342	150,034	103,223	101,861	257,565	251,895
November	896,602	929,136	61,513	51,307	47,543	41,267	109,056	92,574
December	887,222	881,626	61,288	49,213	48,356	53,181	109,644	102,394

Month	Frozen turkey							
	Breasts		Legs		Mechanically deboned meat		Other	
	2017	2018	2017	2018	2017	2018	2017	2018
	1,000 pounds							
January	73,909	85,313	17,522	11,588	6,252	6,546	32,038	31,208
February	87,836	101,384	16,497	11,069	5,825	6,607	30,166	31,787
March	97,176	100,335	15,289	11,744	6,479	5,983	33,736	32,596
April	105,780	102,215	12,257	11,231	7,290	7,497	32,206	29,018
May	106,663	104,830	12,492	12,325	8,512	7,831	29,679	30,241
June	105,260	99,023	10,463	14,972	8,438	9,466	29,246	33,116
July	103,097	99,010	10,518	14,039	6,428	10,182	27,784	34,366
August	101,706	90,558	10,393	14,710	6,559	9,155	31,039	30,738
September ...	92,471	79,241	7,311	13,077	6,501	7,857	32,976	29,151
October	71,492	66,522	9,344	11,641	6,189	8,003	33,077	24,755
November	64,000	72,068	11,958	12,465	5,943	7,673	28,675	25,294
December	73,195	77,143	13,076	14,117	6,302	8,118	31,140	30,586

Month	Frozen turkey				Ducks		Total frozen poultry	
	Unclassified		Total turkey					
	2017	2018	2017	2018	2017	2018	2017	2018
	1,000 pounds							
January	85,305	82,000	339,493	375,188	4,492	2,802	1,119,062	1,255,324
February	82,866	88,430	378,370	427,618	5,329	2,697	1,169,572	1,330,191
March	94,857	93,479	428,752	462,985	5,325	3,623	1,198,750	1,338,081
April	96,855	95,008	471,484	493,844	3,872	3,645	1,271,250	1,365,023
May	100,555	96,470	529,904	536,026	3,365	3,850	1,318,105	1,415,064
June	103,833	99,017	565,123	561,858	3,307	3,625	1,373,895	1,453,467
July	101,519	107,944	595,623	594,927	3,903	4,285	1.397,646	1,476,861
August	101,615	113,381	600,013	606,359	3,868	3,974	1,385,934	1,536,580
September ...	98,390	104,693	569,963	564,746	3,682	3,563	1,391,735	1,526,312
October	83,189	82,243	460,856	445,059	3,651	3,402	1,338,715	1,388,757
November	68,904	64,092	288,536	274,166	2,877	2,949	1,188,015	1,206,251
December	76,268	70,405	309,625	302,763	2,373	2,942	1,199,220	1,187,331

NASS, Livestock Branch, (202) 720–3570.

Table 8-53.—Dairy products: Cold storage holdings, end of month, United States, 2017–2018

Month	Butter		American cheese	
	2017	2018	2017	2018
	1,000 pounds			
January	221,556	226,694	722,449	741,772
February	269,857	265,756	744,640	762,770
March	272,500	273,955	772,702	766,628
April	292,284	307,325	804,645	780,256
May	313,593	338,492	816,266	804,075
June	310,158	336,625	810,234	800,379
July	307,359	318,325	831,538	823,342
August	280,194	290,851	800,994	787,435
September	255,839	282,379	780,466	803,750
October	217,918	231,223	740,404	811,593
November	159,258	154,366	733,378	798,970
December	168,787	179,333	746,846	800,336
Month	Swiss cheese		Other	
	2017	2018	2017	2018
	1,000 pounds			
January	23,930	28,733	445,787	508,132
February	26,999	27,884	454,818	527,077
March	26,053	29,080	463,489	529,020
April	26,962	29,193	471,721	535,831
May	26,242	31,424	466,421	549,441
June	25,495	31,312	480,969	556,947
July	27,009	32,189	510,959	557,449
August	26,831	31,211	505,726	541,843
September	25,408	30,848	502,198	545,105
October	24,277	30,775	503,269	532,781
November	24,933	29,866	500,319	523,903
December	26,367	29,775	507,271	514,683
Month	Total natural cheese			
	2017		2018	
	1,000 pounds			
January	1,192,166		1,278,637	
February	1,226,457		1,317,731	
March	1,262,244		1,324,728	
April	1,303,328		1,345,280	
May	1,308,929		1,384,940	
June	1,316,698		1,388,638	
July	1,369,506		1,412,980	
August	1,333,551		1,360,489	
September	1,308,072		1,379,703	
October	1,267,950		1,375,149	
November	1,258,630		1,352,739	
December	1,280,484		1,344,794	

NASS, Livestock Branch, (202) 720–3570.

CHAPTER IX

FARM RESOURCES, INCOME, AND EXPENSES

The statistics in this chapter deal with farms, farm resources, farm income, and expenses. Many of the series are estimates developed in connection with economic research activities of the Department.

Table 9-1.—Economic trends: Data relating to agriculture, United States, 2009–2018

Year	Prices paid by farmers [1]		Prices received by farmers [1]	Farm income [2]		
	Total including interest, taxes, and wage rates (PPITW)	Production items		Gross farm income [3]	Production expenses	Net farm income
	Index numbers 2011=100	*Index numbers 2011=100*	*Index numbers 2011=100*	*Billion dollars*	*Billion dollars*	*Billion dollars*
2009	86.4	84.8	80.6	336.6	274.4	62.2
2010	89.0	87.7	86.8	356.5	279.4	77.1
2011	100.0	100.0	100.0	420.4	306.9	113.6
2012	104.8	105.4	105.0	449.8	353.4	96.4
2013	106.7	107.4	107.0	484.1	360.4	123.7
2014	113.1	114.1	107.9	483.3	391.0	92.2
2015	111.6	112.0	99.2	440.8	359.2	81.6
2016	105.7	104.7	90.6	412.3	350.0	62.3
2017	106.3	104.5	93.3	425.4	350.4	75.1
2018	108.7	106.4	90.9	427.6	343.8	83.8

Year	National income [4]	Personal income [4]	Industrial production [5]	Consumer prices all items [6]	Producer prices consumer foods [6]
	Billion dollars	*Billion dollars*	*Index numbers 2012=100*	*Index numbers 1982–84=100*	*Index numbers 1982=100*
2009	12,027.2	12,059.1	89.2	214.6	175.5
2010	12,735.8	12,551.6	94.1	218.1	182.4
2011	13,357.7	13,326.8	97.1	224.9	193.9
2012	14,094.7	14,010.1	100.0	229.6	199.1
2013	14,494.7	14,181.1	102.0	233.0	203.5
2014	15,245.5	14,991.8	105.2	236.7	212.5
2015	15,783.0	15,719.5	104.1	237.0	209.7
2016	16,058.9	16,125.1	102.1	240.0	204.6
2017	16,756.1	16,830.9	104.4	245.1	207.2
2018	17,529.4	17,569.5	108.6	251.1	207.4

[1] U.S. Department of Agriculture - NASS. [2] U.S. Department of Agriculture - ERS. [3] Includes cash receipts from farm marketings, government payments, nonmoney income (gross rental value of dwelling and value of home consumption), other income (machine hire custom work and recreational income), and value of change in farm inventories. [4] Department of Commerce, Bureau of Economic Analysis. [5] Major Industry groups Federal Reserve Board. [6] U.S. Department of Labor, Bureau of Labor Statistics retrieved from FRED, Federal Reserve Bank of St. Louis.
ERS, Farm Economy Branch, (202) 694–5476. E-mail contact is Dipak Subedi at dipak.subedi@usda.gov.

Table 9-2.—Farms: Number, land in farms, and average size of farm, United States, 2010–2019

Year	Farms [1]	Land in farms	Average size farm
	Number	*1,000 acres*	*Acres*
2010	2,149,520	915,660	426
2011	2,131,240	914,420	429
2012	2,109,810	914,600	433
2013	2,100,350	911,720	434
2014	2,082,440	908,920	436
2015	2,063,890	905,790	439
2016	2,055,340	902,680	439
2017	2,042,000	900,370	441
2018	2,029,200	899,500	443
2019	2,023,400	897,400	444

[1] A farm is any establishment from which $1,000 or more of agricultural products were produced and sold or normally would have been sold during the year.
NASS, Environmental, Economics, and Demographics Branch, (202) 720–6146.

Table 9-3.—Farms: Percent of farms and land in farms, and average size, by economic sales class, United States, 2018–2019

Economic sales class	Percent of total				Average size farm	
	Farms		Land in farms		2018	2019
	2018	2019	2018	2019		
	Percent	*Percent*	*Percent*	*Percent*	*Acres*	*Acres*
$ 1,000 - $ 9,999	51.0	51.1	9.4	9.4	81	81
$ 10,000 - $ 99,999	30.5	30.4	20.8	20.8	302	304
$100,000 - $249,999	6.7	6.7	14.8	14.7	987	976
$250,000 - $499,999	4.4	4.4	14.3	14.3	1,450	1,448
$500,000 - $999,999	3.6	3.5	15.4	15.4	1,925	1,940
$1,000,000 or more	3.9	3.9	25.3	25.4	2,897	2,910
Total [1]	100.0	100.0	100.0	100.0	443	444

[1] May not add due to rounding.
NASS, Environmental, Economics, and Demographics Branch, (202) 720–6146.

Table 9-4.—Land in farms: Classification by tenure of operator, United States, 1935–2012

Year	Land in farms	Tenure of operator			
		Full owners	Part owners	Managers	All tenants
	Acres	*Percent*	*Percent*	*Percent*	*Percent*
1935 [1]	1,054,515,111	37.1	25.2	5.8	31.9
1940	1,065,113,774	35.9	28.2	6.5	29.4
1945 [1]	1,141,615,364	36.1	32.5	9.3	22.0
1950	1,161,419,720	36.1	36.4	9.2	18.3
1954 [1]	1,158,191,511	34.2	40.7	8.6	16.5
1959	1,123,507,574	31.0	44.0	9.8	14.8
1964	1,110,187,000	28.7	48.0	10.2	13.1
1969	1,062,892,501	35.3	51.8		13.0
1974	1,017,030,357	35.3	52.6		12.0
1978	1,014,777,234	32.7	55.3		12.0
1982	986,796,579	34.7	53.8		11.5
1987	964,470,625	32.9	53.9		13.2
1992	945,531,506	31.3	55.7		13.0
1997	931,795,255	33.9	54.5		11.6
2002 [2]	938,279,056	38.0	52.8		9.2
2007 [2]	922,095,843	37.3	53.8		8.9
2012 [2]	914,527,657	36.8	53.7		9.5

[1] Excludes Alaska and Hawaii. [2] The 2002 Census of Agriculture introduced new methodology to account for all farms in the United States. All 2002 published census items were reweighted for undercoverage. Strictly speaking, data for 2002 and subsequent years are not fully comparable with data from earlier years.
ERS, Resource and Rural Economics Division, (202) 694–5572. Data from the Census of Agriculture, National Agricultural Statistics Service.

Table 9-5.—Number of farms and land in farms by economic sales class by State and United States, 2018–2019

State	Economic Sales Class: $1,000-$9,999			
	Number of Farms		Land in Farms	
	2018	2019	2018	2019
	Number	*Number*	*1,000 Acres*	*1,000 Acres*
Alabama	22,600	21,800	2,100	1,900
Alaska	540	590	80	80
Arizona	14,300	14,200	4,800	4,800
Arkansas	20,700	20,500	1,800	1,750
California	26,400	27,200	1,400	1,300
Colorado	21,900	22,000	2,100	2,200
Connecticut	3,650	3,650	130	130
Delaware	820	820	20	20
Florida	29,000	28,900	1,300	1,300
Georgia	23,300	23,200	2,300	2,300
Hawaii	4,250	4,250	70	70
Idaho	13,500	13,300	700	650
Illinois	27,900	27,700	1,200	1,200
Indiana	25,800	26,100	900	1,000
Iowa	25,400	25,000	900	900
Kansas	21,800	21,300	2,000	1,900
Kentucky	44,300	44,000	3,100	3,000
Louisiana	15,300	15,400	1,100	1,100
Maine	4,800	4,800	390	390
Maryland	6,700	6,700	260	260
Massachusetts	4,500	4,500	190	190
Michigan	24,000	24,500	1,200	1,250
Minnesota	25,400	24,900	1,600	1,600
Mississippi	19,700	19,600	2,300	2,200
Missouri	44,400	44,500	3,300	3,200
Montana	11,600	11,400	1,900	2,000
Nebraska	11,500	11,300	800	800
Nevada	1,700	1,700	500	520
New Hampshire	2,750	2,750	170	170
New Jersey	6,400	6,400	160	160
New Mexico	16,800	17,000	5,100	5,000
New York	15,400	15,500	1,100	1,100
North Carolina	26,100	25,900	1,500	1,400
North Dakota	7,200	7,400	1,100	1,200
Ohio	40,400	41,400	1,600	1,900
Oklahoma	39,800	40,300	4,100	4,200
Oregon	23,400	23,500	1,000	1,100
Pennsylvania	25,000	24,900	1,300	1,300
Rhode Island	630	630	20	20
South Carolina	16,500	16,400	1,600	1,500
South Dakota	7,200	7,000	900	1,000
Tennessee	43,800	43,600	2,700	2,700
Texas	156,500	156,500	15,600	15,200
Utah	11,000	10,800	600	600
Vermont	3,750	3,750	280	280
Virginia	24,100	24,100	1,700	1,700
Washington	21,800	21,700	800	800
West Virginia	17,000	16,600	1,600	1,600
Wisconsin	28,800	29,000	1,800	1,900
Wyoming	5,600	5,600	1,200	1,200
United States	1,035,690	1,034,540	84,370	83,940

See footnote(s) at end of table.

Table 9-5.—Number of farms and land in farms by economic sales class by State and United States, 2018–2019—Continued

State	Economic Sales Class: $10,000-$99,999			
	Number of Farms		Land in Farms	
	2018	2019	2018	2019
	Number	*Number*	*1,000 Acres*	*1,000 Acres*
Alabama	12,500	12,500	3,200	3,200
Alaska	360	360	450	450
Arizona	3,550	3,450	5,300	5,200
Arkansas	14,700	14,500	3,700	3,700
California	22,500	22,600	4,000	4,300
Colorado	11,200	10,800	7,100	7,000
Connecticut	1,400	1,400	100	100
Delaware	510	510	50	50
Florida	13,500	13,500	2,100	2,100
Georgia	11,500	11,500	2,700	2,700
Hawaii	2,500	2,500	200	200
Idaho	6,500	6,500	1,800	1,800
Illinois	20,200	20,000	2,600	2,500
Indiana	16,600	16,100	1,800	1,700
Iowa	26,200	25,800	3,700	3,600
Kansas	21,300	21,500	7,100	7,200
Kentucky	24,200	24,200	4,400	4,500
Louisiana	8,800	8,700	1,900	1,900
Maine	2,050	2,050	350	350
Maryland	3,300	3,300	390	390
Massachusetts	1,950	1,950	160	160
Michigan	14,400	14,000	1,700	1,600
Minnesota	20,400	20,500	3,600	3,600
Mississippi	10,700	10,600	3,000	3,000
Missouri	37,200	37,300	8,600	8,600
Montana	8,000	8,100	10,400	10,300
Nebraska	14,500	14,300	5,000	4,900
Nevada	970	980	500	530
New Hampshire	1,100	1,100	170	170
New Jersey	2,350	2,350	170	170
New Mexico	6,100	6,000	10,400	10,200
New York	11,400	11,500	1,800	1,800
North Carolina	12,700	12,700	1,800	1,800
North Dakota	7,400	7,300	4,000	4,100
Ohio	23,000	22,000	2,700	2,900
Oklahoma	29,000	28,500	11,400	11,400
Oregon	9,000	8,900	3,000	2,900
Pennsylvania	16,700	16,700	2,200	2,200
Rhode Island	340	340	20	20
South Carolina	5,900	6,000	1,300	1,400
South Dakota	9,300	9,400	4,600	4,500
Tennessee	21,700	21,600	3,900	3,800
Texas	72,800	72,800	38,300	39,000
Utah	5,100	5,000	1,900	1,900
Vermont	1,950	1,950	310	310
Virginia	14,000	13,900	2,800	2,800
Washington	8,300	8,300	1,800	1,700
West Virginia	5,600	5,500	1,400	1,400
Wisconsin	20,100	20,200	2,900	2,900
Wyoming	3,700	3,800	4,000	4,100
United States	619,030	615,340	186,770	187,100

See footnote(s) at end of table.

Table 9-5.—Number of farms and land in farms by economic sales class by State and United States, 2018–2019—Continued

State	Economic Sales Class: $100,000-$249,999			
	Number of Farms		Land in Farms	
	2018	2019	2018	2019
	Number	*Number*	*1,000 Acres*	*1,000 Acres*
Alabama	1,050	1,150	750	810
Alaska	40	40	210	210
Arizona	530	510	10,300	10,400
Arkansas	1,350	1,400	950	950
California	6,450	6,500	3,200	3,200
Colorado	2,550	2,600	5,900	5,800
Connecticut	190	190	30	30
Delaware	130	130	40	40
Florida	1,900	1,900	1,200	1,100
Georgia	1,450	1,400	690	710
Hawaii	270	270	130	130
Idaho	1,700	1,700	1,700	1,700
Illinois	8,000	8,000	2,700	2,700
Indiana	5,000	5,200	1,700	1,600
Iowa	11,100	11,000	3,600	3,600
Kansas	6,300	6,100	6,600	6,500
Kentucky	2,900	3,000	1,200	1,200
Louisiana	950	950	790	790
Maine	320	320	100	100
Maryland	720	720	210	210
Massachusetts	340	340	40	40
Michigan	3,150	3,200	1,200	1,300
Minnesota	7,700	7,700	2,900	2,900
Mississippi	920	940	610	620
Missouri	5,800	5,800	3,500	3,500
Montana	3,100	3,150	10,200	10,300
Nebraska	6,400	6,500	5,700	5,900
Nevada	220	220	900	960
New Hampshire	(D)	(D)	(D)	(D)
New Jersey	450	450	110	110
New Mexico	820	810	6,300	6,200
New York	3,000	2,850	880	880
North Carolina	1,650	1,700	600	700
North Dakota	3,100	3,200	4,700	4,600
Ohio	6,400	6,500	2,200	2,000
Oklahoma	4,250	4,250	6,300	6,400
Oregon	1,850	1,800	2,600	2,500
Pennsylvania	5,100	5,000	1,100	1,100
Rhode Island	(D)	(D)	(D)	(D)
South Carolina	630	630	320	300
South Dakota	4,450	4,500	6,800	6,900
Tennessee	1,800	1,800	850	850
Texas	7,500	7,400	20,200	19,200
Utah	900	890	1,300	1,300
Vermont	470	470	140	140
Virginia	1,750	1,700	950	950
Washington	1,800	1,800	3,100	3,000
West Virginia	370	370	270	270
Wisconsin	6,900	7,000	2,100	2,100
Wyoming	1,200	1,200	5,400	5,300
Other States [1]	190	190	40	40
United States	135,110	135,440	133,310	132,140

See footnote(s) at end of table.

Table 9-5.—Number of farms and land in farms by economic sales class by State and United States, 2018–2019—Continued

State	Economic Sales Class: $250,000-$499,999			
	Number of Farms		Land in Farms	
	2018	2019	2018	2019
	Number	*Number*	*1,000 Acres*	*1,000 Acres*
Alabama	650	650	560	580
Alaska	(D)	(D)	(D)	(D)
Arizona	210	200	1,700	1,600
Arkansas	1,050	1,100	750	800
California	3,900	4,000	2,300	2,200
Colorado	1,450	1,500	5,700	5,800
Connecticut	110	110	20	20
Delaware	110	110	50	50
Florida	1,000	1,000	850	850
Georgia	1,050	1,100	610	690
Hawaii	120	120	170	170
Idaho	1,200	1,200	1,500	1,500
Illinois	6,200	6,100	4,000	4,000
Indiana	3,350	3,250	2,000	2,000
Iowa	8,900	9,200	5,500	5,500
Kansas	4,050	4,150	7,600	7,500
Kentucky	1,450	1,400	900	900
Louisiana	540	570	610	610
Maine	180	180	100	100
Maryland	490	490	230	230
Massachusetts	(D)	(D)	(D)	(D)
Michigan	2,200	2,150	1,200	1,300
Minnesota	5,800	5,800	3,900	4,000
Mississippi	600	580	590	580
Missouri	2,950	2,950	2,900	2,900
Montana	2,300	2,250	13,400	13,300
Nebraska	5,000	5,100	7,800	7,900
Nevada	240	200	1,000	900
New Hampshire	70	70	30	30
New Jersey	280	280	80	80
New Mexico	390	390	6,400	6,300
New York	1,750	1,700	780	780
North Carolina	1,250	1,250	700	700
North Dakota	3,000	3,000	6,500	6,600
Ohio	3,300	3,000	1,900	1,600
Oklahoma	2,050	2,100	4,600	4,600
Oregon	1,150	1,150	2,900	2,800
Pennsylvania	3,150	3,100	980	980
Rhode Island	(D)	(D)	(D)	(D)
South Carolina	280	280	270	230
South Dakota	3,700	3,800	8,700	8,800
Tennessee	1,000	1,000	660	660
Texas	3,650	3,600	14,700	14,800
Utah	520	510	2,000	2,000
Vermont	320	320	130	130
Virginia	910	960	680	680
Washington	1,250	1,250	2,100	2,200
West Virginia	130	130	120	110
Wisconsin	4,300	4,250	2,000	2,100
Wyoming	810	810	6,200	6,100
Other States [1]	250	250	130	130
United States	88,610	88,660	128,500	128,390

See footnote(s) at end of table.

Table 9-5.—Number of farms and land in farms by economic sales class by State and United States, 2018–2019—Continued

State	Economic Sales Class: $500,000-$999,999			
	Number of Farms		Land in Farms	
	2018	2019	2018	2019
	Number	*Number*	*1,000 Acres*	*1,000 Acres*
Alabama	1,200	1,100	690	660
Alaska	30	30	20	20
Arizona	200	220	1,000	1,000
Arkansas	1,350	1,400	1,200	1,200
California	3,550	3,200	2,200	2,300
Colorado	900	920	4,500	4,700
Connecticut	70	70	20	20
Delaware	260	260	110	110
Florida	900	900	650	650
Georgia	1,800	1,850	1,400	1,400
Hawaii	70	70	210	210
Idaho	800	800	1,800	1,750
Illinois	5,300	5,200	6,100	6,000
Indiana	2,450	2,500	2,800	2,700
Iowa	8,000	7,900	7,800	7,800
Kansas	3,000	2,900	9,200	9,200
Kentucky	1,000	1,000	900	900
Louisiana	710	730	1,050	1,050
Maine	110	110	70	70
Maryland	520	520	330	330
Massachusetts	140	140	30	30
Michigan	1,550	1,500	1,500	1,400
Minnesota	4,800	4,800	5,100	5,100
Mississippi	880	880	900	900
Missouri	2,400	2,400	3,700	3,700
Montana	1,300	1,250	12,200	12,100
Nebraska	4,400	4,300	9,400	9,200
Nevada	140	110	700	640
New Hampshire	30	30	10	10
New Jersey	200	200	90	90
New Mexico	260	260	6,300	6,200
New York	930	930	640	640
North Carolina	1,450	1,450	900	900
North Dakota	2,800	2,700	9,100	8,800
Ohio	2,550	2,650	2,300	2,200
Oklahoma	1,150	1,100	3,600	3,600
Oregon	850	870	2,800	2,800
Pennsylvania	1,700	1,650	750	750
Rhode Island	20	20	10	10
South Carolina	410	380	400	400
South Dakota	2,700	2,600	8,900	8,800
Tennessee	830	830	890	890
Texas	3,000	3,100	14,500	14,800
Utah	310	320	1,000	1,000
Vermont	140	140	80	80
Virginia	830	850	670	670
Washington	1,100	1,100	2,300	2,300
West Virginia	150	160	100	110
Wisconsin	2,550	2,400	1,900	1,800
Wyoming	390	380	6,100	6,100
United States	72,180	71,170	138,920	138,090

See footnote(s) at end of table.

Table 9-5.—Number of farms and land in farms by economic sales class by State and United States, 2018–2019—Continued

State	Economic Sales Class: $1,000,000 or more			
	Number of Farms		Land in Farms	
	2018	2019	2018	2019
	Number	*Number*	*1,000 Acres*	*1,000 Acres*
Alabama	1,700	1,600	1,200	1,150
Alaska	(D)	(D)	(D)	(D)
Arizona	410	420	3,100	3,200
Arkansas	3,350	3,400	5,500	5,600
California	6,600	6,400	11,200	11,000
Colorado	900	880	6,500	6,300
Connecticut	80	80	80	80
Delaware	470	470	260	260
Florida	1,200	1,200	3,600	3,700
Georgia	2,500	2,450	2,400	2,400
Hawaii	90	90	320	320
Idaho	1,100	1,100	4,100	4,100
Illinois	4,400	4,400	10,400	10,600
Indiana	2,900	2,850	5,800	5,900
Iowa	6,400	6,400	9,100	9,200
Kansas	2,450	2,550	13,300	13,400
Kentucky	1,250	1,200	2,400	2,400
Louisiana	1,100	1,050	2,550	2,550
Maine	140	140	290	290
Maryland	670	670	580	580
Massachusetts	(D)	(D)	(D)	(D)
Michigan	1,700	1,650	3,000	2,950
Minnesota	4,400	4,300	8,400	8,300
Mississippi	1,900	1,900	3,000	3,100
Missouri	2,250	2,250	5,700	5,700
Montana	600	650	9,900	10,000
Nebraska	4,100	4,200	16,300	16,200
Nevada	130	140	2,500	2,550
New Hampshire	(D)	(D)	(D)	(D)
New Jersey	220	220	140	140
New Mexico	330	340	6,000	6,100
New York	920	920	1,700	1,700
North Carolina	3,250	3,200	2,900	2,900
North Dakota	2,600	2,500	13,900	14,000
Ohio	2,150	2,250	3,200	3,000
Oklahoma	1,050	1,050	4,200	4,200
Oregon	950	980	3,700	3,700
Pennsylvania	1,350	1,350	970	970
Rhode Island	(D)	(D)	(D)	(D)
South Carolina	880	910	910	970
South Dakota	2,250	2,300	13,300	13,200
Tennessee	870	870	1,900	1,900
Texas	3,550	3,600	23,700	23,500
Utah	270	280	3,900	3,900
Vermont	170	170	260	260
Virginia	910	890	1,000	1,000
Washington	1,450	1,450	4,600	4,600
West Virginia	150	150	110	110
Wisconsin	2,150	2,050	3,600	3,500
Wyoming	200	210	6,100	6,200
Other States [1]	120	120	60	60
United States	78,580	78,250	227,630	227,740

(D) Withheld to avoid disclosing data for individual operations. [1] Includes data withheld above.
NASS, Environmental, Economics, and Demographics Branch, (202) 720–6146.

Table 9-6.—Number of farms and land in farms by State and United States, 2018–2019

State	Number of Farms [1]		Land in farms		Average farm size	
	2018	2019	2018	2019	2018	2019
	Number	*Number*	*1,000 acres*	*1,000 acres*	*Acres*	*Acres*
Alabama	39,700	38,800	8,500	8,300	214	214
Alaska	1,000	1,050	850	850	850	810
Arizona	19,200	19,000	26,200	26,200	1,365	1,379
Arkansas	42,500	42,300	13,900	14,000	327	331
California	69,400	69,900	24,300	24,300	350	348
Colorado	38,900	38,700	31,800	31,800	817	822
Connecticut	5,500	5,500	380	380	69	69
Delaware	2,300	2,300	530	530	230	230
Florida	47,500	47,400	9,700	9,700	204	205
Georgia	41,600	41,500	10,100	10,200	243	246
Hawaii	7,300	7,300	1,100	1,100	151	151
Idaho	24,800	24,600	11,600	11,500	468	467
Illinois	72,000	71,400	27,000	27,000	375	378
Indiana	56,100	56,000	15,000	14,900	267	266
Iowa	86,000	85,300	30,600	30,600	356	359
Kansas	58,900	58,500	45,800	45,700	778	781
Kentucky	75,100	74,800	12,900	12,900	172	172
Louisiana	27,400	27,400	8,000	8,000	292	292
Maine	7,600	7,600	1,300	1,300	171	171
Maryland	12,400	12,400	2,000	2,000	161	161
Massachusetts	7,200	7,200	500	500	69	69
Michigan	47,000	47,000	9,800	9,800	209	209
Minnesota	68,500	68,000	25,500	25,500	372	375
Mississippi	34,700	34,500	10,400	10,400	300	301
Missouri	95,000	95,200	27,700	27,600	292	290
Montana	26,900	26,800	58,000	58,000	2,156	2,164
Nebraska	45,900	45,700	45,000	44,900	980	982
Nevada	3,400	3,350	6,100	6,100	1,794	1,821
New Hampshire	4,100	4,100	430	430	105	105
New Jersey	9,900	9,900	750	750	76	76
New Mexico	24,700	24,800	40,500	40,000	1,640	1,613
New York	33,400	33,400	6,900	6,900	207	207
North Carolina	46,400	46,200	8,400	8,400	181	182
North Dakota	26,100	26,100	39,300	39,300	1,506	1,506
Ohio	77,800	77,800	10,900	10,600	170	176
Oklahoma	77,300	77,300	34,200	34,400	442	445
Oregon	37,200	37,200	16,000	15,800	430	425
Pennsylvania	53,000	52,700	7,300	7,300	138	139
Rhode Island	1,100	1,100	60	60	55	55
South Carolina	24,600	24,600	4,800	4,800	195	195
South Dakota	29,600	29,600	43,200	43,200	1,459	1,459
Tennessee	70,000	69,700	10,900	10,800	156	155
Texas	247,000	247,000	127,000	126,500	514	512
Utah	18,100	17,800	10,700	10,700	591	601
Vermont	6,800	6,800	1,200	1,200	176	176
Virginia	42,500	42,400	7,800	7,800	184	184
Washington	35,700	35,600	14,700	14,600	412	410
West Virginia	23,400	22,900	3,600	3,500	154	153
Wisconsin	64,800	64,900	14,300	14,300	221	220
Wyoming	11,900	12,000	29,000	29,000	2,437	2,417
United States	2,029,200	2,023,400	899,500	897,400	443	444

[1] A farm is any establishment from which $1,000 or more of agricultural products were produced and sold or would normally have been sold during the year.

NASS, Environmental, Economics, and Demographics Branch, (202) 720–6146.

Table 9-7.—Farms: Classification by tenure of operator, United States, 1940–2017

Year	Farms	Tenure of operator			
		Full owners	Part owners	Managers	All tenants
	Number	*Percent*	*Percent*	*Percent*	*Percent*
1940	6,102,417	50.6	10.1	0.6	38.8
1945 [1]	5,859,169	56.4	11.3	0.7	31.7
1950	5,388,437	57.4	15.3	0.4	26.9
1954 [1]	4,783,021	57.4	18.2	0.4	24.0
1959	3,710,503	57.1	21.9	0.6	20.5
1964	3,157,857	57.6	24.8	0.6	17.1
1969	2,730,250	62.5	24.6	....	12.9
1974	2,314,013	61.5	27.2	....	11.3
1978	2,257,775	57.5	30.2	....	12.3
1982	2,240,976	59.2	29.3	....	11.6
1987	2,087,759	59.3	29.2	....	11.5
1992	1,925,300	57.7	31.0	....	11.3
1997	1,911,859	60.0	30.0	....	10.0
2002 [2]	2,128,982	67.1	25.9	....	7.0
2007 [2]	2,204,792	69.0	24.6	....	6.4
2012 [2]	2,109,303	67.7	25.3	....	7.0
2017	2,042,220	69.0	24.1	....	6.9

[1] Excludes Alaska and Hawaii. [2] The 2002 Census of Agriculture introduced new methodology to account for all farms in the United States. All 2002 published census items were reweighted for undercoverage. Strictly speaking, data for 2002 and subsequent years are not fully comparable with data from earlier years.

NASS, Environmental, Economics, and Demographics Branch, (202) 720-6146.

Table 9-8.—Farmland Rented: Classification by tenants and part owners, United States, 1920–2017

Year	Land in farms	Land rented by tenure of operator [1]			Percentage of land rented
		Tenants	Part owners	Total	
	Million acres	*Million acres*	*Million acres*	*Million acres*	*Percent*
1920	958.7	[3]265.0	[4]54.7	319.7	33.3
1925	924.3	264.9	96.3	361.2	39.1
1930	990.1	307.3	125.2	432.5	43.7
1935	1,054.5	336.8	134.3	471.1	44.7
1940	1,065.1	313.2	155.9	469.1	44.0
1945	1,141.6	251.6	178.9	430.5	37.7
1950	1,161.4	212.2	196.2	408.4	35.2
1954	1,158.2	192.6	212.3	404.9	35.0
1959	1,123.0	166.8	234.1	400.9	35.7
1964	1,110.2	144.9	248.1	[5]393.0	35.4
1969	1,063.3	137.6	241.8	379.4	35.7
1974	1,017.0	122.3	258.4	380.7	37.4
1978	1,029.7	124.1	282.2	406.2	39.4
1982	986.2	113.6	269.9	383.5	38.9
1987	964.5	126.9	275.4	402.3	41.7
1992	945.5	122.7	282.2	404.9	42.8
1997	931.8	108.1	270.0	378.1	40.6
2002 [6]	938.3	86.5	266.8	353.3	37.7
2007 [6]	922.1	81.8	269.0	350.8	38.0
2012 [6]	914.5	87.0	268.1	355.1	38.8
2017	900.2	86.9	274.2	361.1	39.4

[1] Columns 3, 4, and 5 refer only to land rented from others and operated, so subleased land is not included. Acres of land rented are comparable in the same year, but definitions change over time. Basic sources are 1969 Census of Agriculture, table 5, p.14; 1974 Census of Agriculture, table 3, pp.1-6; 1978 Census of Agriculture, vol. 1, part 51, table 5, pp. 124-127; 1982 Census of Agriculture, vol. 1, part 51, table 48, p. 49; 1987 Census of Agriculture vol. 1 part 51, table 48, p. 49; 1992 Census of Agriculture vol. 1, part 51, table 46, p. 53; 1997 Census of Agriculture, vol. 1, part 51, chapter 1, table 46, p. 57; 2002 Census of Agriculture, vol. 1, part 51, chapter 1, table 61, p. 214; 2007 Census of Agriculture, vol. 1, part 51, chapter 1, table 65, p. 262; 2012 Census of Agriculture, vol. 1, part 51, table 70, p. 231; and earlier census volumes as noted. [2] Assumes land leased by part-owners is the difference between the average size of full-owner and part-owner farms. Acreage leased by part-owners is this difference times the number of part-owners. 1910 Census of Agriculture, chapter 11, table 1 and 3, pp.97-99. [3] 1920 Census of Agriculture, vol. VI, part 1, table 5, p. 19. [4] Assumes same proportion of owner and part-owner as in 1910. [5] 1964 Census of Agriculture, vol. II, chapter 8, p.757. [6] The 2002 Census of Agriculture introduced new methodology to account for all farms in the United States. All 2002 published census items were reweighted for undercoverage. Strictly speaking, data for 2002 and subsequent years are not fully comparable with data from earlier years.

NASS, Environmental, Economics, and Demographics Branch, (202) 720-6146.

Table 9-9.—Land: Utilization, by State and United States, 2012

State	Cropland			Grassland pasture	Forest land
	Used for crops	Idle	Used only for pasture		
	1,000 acres	*1,000 acres*	*1,000 acres*	*1,000 acres*	*1,000 acres*
Alabama	2,231	415	161	2,892	22,800
Alaska	31	45	4	696	91,817
Arizona	908	142	84	43,580	13,000
Arkansas	7,466	585	184	4,127	18,544
California	8,316	780	481	26,667	16,991
Colorado	8,013	2,218	437	31,734	15,138
Connecticut	104	9	9	22	1,346
Delaware	420	11	7	18	331
Florida	2,122	452	260	5,100	15,827
Georgia	3,799	457	129	1,680	24,352
Hawaii	161	189	22	770	1,299
Idaho	4,790	789	221	18,391	16,771
Illinois	22,672	1,175	88	1,728	4,772
Indiana	12,216	414	80	1,656	4,748
Iowa	24,750	1,738	225	2,879	2,968
Kansas	25,545	2,598	449	17,781	2,402
Kentucky	5,400	641	328	4,742	11,886
Louisiana	3,497	869	218	2,275	14,645
Maine	328	55	8	159	17,191
Maryland	1,254	108	15	447	2,329
Massachusetts	130	14	5	79	2,088
Michigan	7,192	483	91	1,982	19,262
Minnesota	20,394	1,887	171	3,568	15,929
Mississippi	4,372	638	163	2,715	19,495
Missouri	13,455	1,591	580	9,792	15,085
Montana	12,522	3,181	902	47,629	18,429
Nebraska	20,442	1,090	326	23,677	1,470
Nevada	478	42	57	52,329	5,417
New Hampshire	73	18	2	116	4,341
New Jersey	403	29	16	78	1,116
New Mexico	1,183	534	231	54,344	13,278
New York	3,816	318	113	2,397	15,920
North Carolina	4,085	294	95	1,579	18,078
North Dakota	24,081	2,718	322	13,336	517
Ohio	10,190	530	109	2,144	7,864
Oklahoma	9,155	1,123	1,011	19,756	7,656
Oregon	3,522	834	308	23,863	24,116
Pennsylvania	3,952	446	119	1,287	16,242
Rhode Island	19	4	2	7	290
South Carolina	1,540	308	55	976	13,025
South Dakota	17,624	1,203	528	24,972	1,789
Tennessee	4,479	374	408	3,424	13,500
Texas	21,598	4,773	2,844	104,603	14,357
Utah	1,090	246	140	32,774	9,810
Vermont	379	19	15	305	4,476
Virginia	2,636	205	148	2,794	15,385
Washington	5,558	1,856	125	7,314	18,081
West Virginia	685	42	54	1,351	11,780
Wisconsin	9,301	607	164	2,864	16,727
Wyoming	1,523	207	256	46,086	7,002
United States [1]	339,900	39,306	12,769	655,486	631,682

[1] Distributions may not sum to totals due to rounding.
NASS, Environmental, Economics, and Demographics Branch, (202) 720–6146. See notes to Table 9-11 for definitions and data sources. Estimates developed for years coinciding with a Census of Agriculture.

Table 9-10.—Land in farms: Irrigated land, by State and United States, 1982–2012[1]

State	1982	1987	1992	1997	2002	2007	2012
	1,000 acres	*1,000 acres*	*1,000 acres*	*1,000 acres*	*1,000 acres*	*1,000 acres*	*1,000 acres*
Alabama	66	84	82	80	109	113	113
Alaska	1	2	2	3	3	4	2
Arizona	1,098	914	956	1,075	932	876	881
Arkansas	2,022	2,406	2,702	3,785	4,150	4,461	4,804
California	8,461	7,596	7,571	8,887	8,709	8,016	7,862
Colorado	3,201	3,014	3,170	3,374	2,591	2,868	2,517
Connecticut	7	7	6	8	10	10	9
Delaware	44	61	62	75	97	105	127
Florida	1,585	1,623	1,783	1,874	1,815	1,552	1,493
Georgia	575	640	725	773	871	1,018	1,125
Hawaii	146	149	134	77	69	59	82
Idaho	3,450	3,219	3,260	3,544	3,289	3,300	3,365
Illinois	166	208	328	352	391	474	522
Indiana	132	170	241	256	313	397	437
Iowa	91	92	116	133	142	190	172
Kansas	2,675	2,463	2,680	2,696	2,678	2,763	2,881
Kentucky	23	38	28	60	37	59	74
Louisiana	694	647	898	961	939	954	1,093
Maine	6	6	10	22	20	21	31
Maryland	39	51	57	69	81	93	105
Massachusetts	17	20	20	27	24	23	23
Michigan	286	315	366	407	456	500	592
Minnesota	315	354	370	403	455	506	524
Mississippi	431	637	883	1,110	1,176	1,369	1,652
Missouri	403	535	709	921	1,033	1,200	1,181
Montana	2,023	1,997	1,978	2,102	1,976	2,013	1,903
Nebraska	6,039	5,682	6,312	7,066	7,625	8,559	8,297
Nevada	830	779	556	764	747	691	688
New Hampshire	1	3	2	3	2	2	3
New Jersey	83	91	80	94	97	95	88
New Mexico	807	718	738	852	845	830	680
New York	52	51	47	74	75	68	60
North Carolina	81	138	113	156	264	232	175
North Dakota	163	168	187	183	203	236	218
Ohio	28	32	29	35	41	38	47
Oklahoma	492	478	512	509	518	535	480
Oregon	1,808	1,648	1,622	1,963	1,908	1,845	1,630
Pennsylvania	18	30	23	40	43	38	39
Rhode Island	2	4	3	3	4	4	4
South Carolina	81	81	76	89	96	132	159
South Dakota	376	362	371	367	401	374	379
Tennessee	18	38	37	47	61	81	146
Texas	5,576	4,271	4,912	5,764	5,075	5,010	4,489
Utah	1,082	1,161	1,143	1,218	1,091	1,134	1,104
Vermont	1	2	2	3	2	2	4
Virginia	43	79	62	86	99	82	69
Washington	1,638	1,519	1,641	1,787	1,823	1,736	1,634
West Virginia	1	3	3	4	2	2	2
Wisconsin	259	285	331	358	386	377	422
Wyoming	1,565	1,518	1,465	1,750	1,542	1,551	1,436
United States	49,003	46,386	49,404	56,289	55,316	56,599	55,822
Puerto Rico	42	36	46	35	43	40	52
Virgin Islands	(3)	(3)	(3)	(3)	(2)	(2)	(3)
Total	49,002	46,386	49,404	55,058	55,360	56,639	55,874

[1] Distributions may not sum to totals due to rounding. [2] Less than 500 acres. [3] Not available.

NASS, Environmental, Economics, and Demographics Branch, (202) 720–6146. 1982-1992 data from the Census of Agriculture, U.S. Department of Commerce. Beginning in 1997 from the Census of Agriculture, U.S. Department of Agriculture. Estimates developed for years coinciding with a Census of Agriculture.

Table 9-11.—Land utilization, United States, selected years, 1987–2012

Major land uses	1987	1992	1997	2002	2007	2012
	Million acres	*Million acres*	*Million acres*	*Million acres*	*Million acres*	*Million acres*
Cropland used for crops [1]	331	338	349	340	335	340
Idle cropland	68	56	39	40	37	39
Cropland used for pasture [2]	65	67	68	62	36	13
Grassland pasture [3]	591	591	580	587	614	655
Forest land [4]	648	648	641	651	671	632
Special uses [5]	279	281	286	297	313	316
Urban areas [6]	57	59	66	60	61	70
Other land [7]	227	224	236	228	197	196
Total land area [8]	2,265	2,263	2,263	2,264	2,264	2,260

[1] Cropland harvested, crop failure, and cultivated summer fallow. [2] The 2007 and 2012 estimates declined due to a change in the methodology for determining cropland used for pasture. [3] Grassland and other nonforest pasture and range. [4] Excludes reserved and other forest land duplicated in parks and special uses of land. Includes forested grazing land. [5] Includes rural transportation areas, Federal and State areas used primarily for recreation and wildlife purposes, military areas, farmsteads, and farm roads and lanes. [6] The 2002 urban acreage estimate is not directly comparable to estimates in prior years due to a change in the definition of urban areas in the 2000 Census of Population and Housing. The apparent change in "urban" acreage between 1997 and 2002 reflects a definitional change, rather than a decline in acreage. [7] Miscellaneous areas such as marshes, open swamps, bare rock areas, deserts, and other uses not inventoried. [8] Remeasurement and increases in reservoirs account for changes in total land areas.

NASS, Environmental, Economics, and Demographics Branch, (202) 720–6146. Estimates developed for years coinciding with a Census of Agriculture.

Table 9-12.—Farm real estate: Value of farmland and buildings, Region, State, and United States, 2016–2019[1]

Region and State	Total value of land and buildings			
	2016	2017	2018	2019
	Million dollars	*Million dollars*	*Million dollars*	*Million dollars*
Northeast:				
Connecticut	4,641	4,598	4,674	4,636
Delaware	4,311	4,373	4,457	4,744
Maine	2,873	3,081	3,081	3,133
Maryland	14,940	15,240	15,720	16,120
Massachusetts	5,350	5,292	5,450	5,550
New Hampshire	1,982	2,090	2,107	2,141
New Jersey	9,709	9,782	10,125	10,125
New York	21,770	21,804	22,287	22,425
Pennsylvania	42,486	44,019	45,625	47,231
Rhode Island	876	894	912	936
Vermont	4,080	4,164	4,248	4,356
Lake States:				
Michigan	48,020	48,412	48,608	48,608
Minnesota	122,624	124,185	123,675	123,420
Wisconsin	65,088	69,641	70,070	70,785
Corn Belt:				
Illinois	197,100	193,320	196,560	196,560
Indiana	101,767	98,700	98,700	98,042
Iowa	225,522	224,910	222,462	220,014
Missouri	89,838	86,736	93,626	93,840
Ohio	83,580	84,140	86,180	85,544
Northern Plains:				
Kansas	87,478	86,562	84,730	89,572
Nebraska	130,050	126,900	123,750	127,965
North Dakota	68,775	68,382	67,203	68,382
South Dakota	94,827	90,720	89,424	89,424
Appalachian:				
Kentucky	46,020	47,840	48,633	49,278
North Carolina	38,675	38,472	38,976	39,312
Tennessee	41,093	41,856	42,728	43,092
Virginia	35,313	35,802	36,036	36,270
West Virginia	9,432	9,768	9,540	9,380
Southeast:				
Alabama	24,252	25,026	25,330	25,730
Florida	52,896	56,842	57,230	57,715
Georgia	34,100	35,600	35,451	35,394
South Carolina	15,264	15,228	15,888	16,320
Delta States:				
Arkansas	41,700	43,229	43,924	46,480
Louisiana	22,960	23,680	24,320	24,960
Mississippi	27,195	27,664	28,496	29,120
Southern Plains:				
Oklahoma	57,967	59,850	61,560	64,328
Texas	234,600	243,840	260,350	268,180
Mountain:				
Arizona[2]	24,929	26,058	26,493	26,608
Colorado	47,550	48,972	49,608	49,926
Idaho	30,044	31,941	33,292	34,500
Montana	52,443	53,278	53,128	53,070
Nevada[2]	5,829	5,722	5,722	5,722
New Mexico[2]	20,586	20,977	21,100	20,982
Utah[2]	15,512	15,983	16,290	17,019
Wyoming	20,481	20,648	21,054	21,460
Pacific:				
California	200,384	219,765	227,205	243,000
Oregon	35,840	37,760	38,880	39,500
Washington	39,396	40,572	41,748	41,172
United States[3]	2,602,148	2,644,318	2,686,656	2,732,071

[1] Total value of land and buildings is derived by multiplying average value per acre of farm real estate by the land in farms. [2] Value of all land and buildings adjusted to include American Indian reservation land value. [3] Excludes Alaska and Hawaii.

NASS, Environmental, Economics, and Demographics Branch, (202) 720–6146.

Table 9-13.—Farm real estate: Average value per acre - Region, State, and United States, 2016–2019

Region and State	2016	2017	2018	2019
	Dollars	*Dollars*	*Dollars*	*Dollars*
Northeast:	5,270	5,380	5,550	5,690
Connecticut	11,900	12,100	12,300	12,200
Delaware	8,290	8,250	8,410	8,950
Maine	2,210	2,370	2,370	2,410
Maryland	7,470	7,620	7,860	8,060
Massachusetts	10,700	10,800	10,900	11,100
New Hampshire	4,610	4,860	4,900	4,980
New Jersey	13,300	13,400	13,500	13,500
New York	3,110	3,160	3,230	3,250
Pennsylvania	5,820	6,030	6,250	6,470
Rhode Island	14,600	14,900	15,200	15,600
Vermont	3,400	3,470	3,540	3,630
Lake:	4,730	4,880	4,890	4,900
Michigan	4,900	4,940	4,960	4,960
Minnesota	4,790	4,870	4,850	4,840
Wisconsin	4,520	4,870	4,900	4,950
Corn Belt:	6,100	5,990	6,110	6,100
Illinois	7,300	7,160	7,280	7,280
Indiana	6,830	6,580	6,580	6,580
Iowa	7,370	7,350	7,270	7,190
Missouri	3,220	3,120	3,380	3,400
Ohio	5,970	6,010	6,200	6,290
Northern Plains:	2,200	2,150	2,110	2,170
Kansas	1,910	1,890	1,850	1,960
Nebraska	2,890	2,820	2,750	2,850
North Dakota	1,750	1,740	1,710	1,740
South Dakota	2,190	2,100	2,070	2,070
Appalachian:	3,880	3,970	4,030	4,080
Kentucky	3,540	3,680	3,770	3,820
North Carolina	4,550	4,580	4,640	4,680
Tennessee	3,770	3,840	3,920	3,990
Virginia	4,470	4,590	4,620	4,650
West Virginia	2,620	2,640	2,650	2,680
Southeast:	3,830	3,990	4,050	4,090
Alabama	2,820	2,910	2,980	3,100
Florida	5,510	5,860	5,900	5,950
Georgia	3,410	3,560	3,510	3,470
South Carolina	3,180	3,240	3,310	3,400
Delta:	2,830	2,920	3,000	3,100
Arkansas	3,000	3,110	3,160	3,320
Louisiana	2,870	2,960	3,040	3,120
Mississippi	2,590	2,660	2,740	2,800
Southern Plains:	1,810	1,880	2,000	2,070
Oklahoma	1,690	1,750	1,800	1,870
Texas	1,840	1,920	2,050	2,120
Mountain:	1,140	1,170	1,200	1,220
Arizona [1]	3,570	3,770	3,780	3,800
Colorado	1,500	1,540	1,560	1,570
Idaho	2,590	2,730	2,870	3,000
Montana	898	917	916	915
Nevada [1]	1,040	1,020	1,020	1,020
New Mexico [1]	540	558	565	570
Utah [1]	2,160	2,230	2,310	2,420
Wyoming	699	712	726	740
Pacific:	4,960	5,440	5,610	5,900
California	8,080	8,970	9,350	10,000
Oregon	2,240	2,360	2,430	2,500
Washington	2,680	2,760	2,840	2,820
United States [2]	2,990	3,030	3,100	3,160

[1] Excludes American Indian Reservation Land. [2] Excludes Alaska and Hawaii.
NASS, Environmental, Economics, and Demographics Branch, (202) 720–6146.

Table 9-14.—Land values, cropland and pasture average value per acre: Region, State, and United States, 2016–2019

Region and State	Cropland			
	2016	2017	2018	2019
	Dollars	*Dollars*	*Dollars*	*Dollars*
Northeast:	5,650	5,700	5,940	6,040
Delaware	8,090	7,960	8,120	8,600
Maryland	6,910	7,050	7,280	7,370
New Jersey	13,500	13,600	13,700	13,700
New York	2,690	2,740	2,800	2,810
Pennsylvania	6,450	6,470	6,890	7,030
Other States [1]	7,290	7,630	7,650	7,900
Lake:	4,750	4,840	4,810	4,760
Michigan	4,590	4,580	4,510	4,500
Minnesota	4,840	4,920	4,950	4,810
Wisconsin	4,660	4,870	4,740	4,850
Corn Belt:	6,500	6,380	6,370	6,360
Illinois	7,350	7,210	7,280	7,300
Indiana	6,690	6,300	6,210	6,210
Iowa	7,510	7,440	7,290	7,260
Missouri	3,570	3,560	3,490	3,490
Ohio	6,070	6,150	6,320	6,400
Northern Plains:	2,900	2,760	2,740	2,790
Kansas	2,080	2,010	2,060	2,160
Nebraska	4,750	4,430	4,380	4,390
North Dakota	1,910	1,890	1,870	1,920
South Dakota	3,430	3,200	3,120	3,130
Appalachian:	3,980	4,070	4,140	4,190
Kentucky	3,980	4,140	4,250	4,300
North Carolina	4,060	4,090	4,130	4,180
Tennessee	3,670	3,730	3,830	3,910
Virginia	4,610	4,730	4,760	4,720
West Virginia	3,220	3,250	3,250	3,280
Southeast:	4,030	4,060	4,160	4,120
Alabama	3,080	3,170	3,300	3,430
Florida	6,860	6,940	7,040	7,190
Georgia	3,420	3,430	3,430	3,210
South Carolina	2,610	2,700	2,790	2,830
Delta:	2,690	2,770	2,840	2,920
Arkansas	2,660	2,730	2,780	2,850
Louisiana	2,590	2,700	2,790	2,880
Mississippi	2,810	2,900	3,000	3,080
Southern Plains:	1,700	1,780	1,820	1,860
Oklahoma	1,530	1,590	1,630	1,670
Texas	1,770	1,850	1,890	1,930
Mountain:	1,820	1,860	1,910	1,980
Arizona [2]	7,800	7,720	7,610	7,600
Colorado	2,020	2,070	2,100	2,160
Idaho	3,420	3,570	3,740	3,930
Montana	1,010	1,010	1,020	1,040
Nevada [2]	(D)	(D)	(D)	(D)
New Mexico [2]	1,500	1,560	1,580	1,550
Utah [2]	3,530	3,690	3,830	3,970
Wyoming	1,450	1,460	1,490	1,520
Pacific:	6,350	6,650	6,830	7,190
California	11,160	11,630	12,170	12,830
Oregon	2,780	2,920	3,000	3,080
Washington	2,590	2,660	2,630	2,630
United States [3]	4,040	4,030	4,050	4,100

See footnote(s) at end of table.

Table 9-14.—Land values, cropland and pasture average value per acre: Region, State, and United States, 2016–2019—Continued

Region, State, and land type	Irrigated and Non-Irrigated Cropland			
	2016	2017	2018	2019
	Dollars	*Dollars*	*Dollars*	*Dollars*
Corn Belt:				
Missouri all cropland	3,570	3,560	3,490	3,490
Irrigated	4,830	4,940	4,770	4,770
Non-irrigated	3,470	3,450	3,380	3,350
Northern Plains:				
Kansas all cropland	2,080	2,010	2,060	2,160
Irrigated	3,050	2,910	2,980	3,320
Non-irrigated	1,970	1,910	1,960	2,050
Nebraska all cropland	4,750	4,430	4,380	4,390
Irrigated	6,430	6,010	5,930	5,850
Non-irrigated	3,720	3,450	3,430	3,490
South Dakota all cropland	3,430	3,200	3,120	3,130
Irrigated	(D)	(D)	(D)	(D)
Non-irrigated	3,410	3,180	3,100	3,100
Southeast:				
Florida all cropland	6,860	6,940	7,040	7,190
Irrigated	7,750	7,860	7,980	8,160
Non-irrigated	6,020	6,070	6,160	6,280
Georgia all cropland	3,420	3,430	3,430	3,210
Irrigated	4,010	4,080	4,560	4,030
Non-irrigated	3,210	3,190	3,020	2,870
Delta:				
Arkansas all cropland	2,660	2,730	2,780	2,850
Irrigated	3,150	3,230	3,290	3,340
Non-irrigated	1,920	1,960	1,990	2,060
Louisiana all cropland	2,590	2,700	2,790	2,880
Irrigated	2,520	2,660	2,750	2,820
Non-irrigated	2,620	2,710	2,810	2,900
Mississippi all cropland	2,810	2,900	3,000	3,080
Irrigated	3,300	3,440	3,580	3,620
Non-irrigated	2,580	2,640	2,720	2,770
Southern Plains:				
Oklahoma all cropland	1,530	1,590	1,630	1,670
Irrigated	(D)	(D)	(D)	(D)
Non-irrigated	1,520	1,580	1,610	1,650
Texas all cropland	1,770	1,850	1,890	1,930
Irrigated	1,920	2,020	2,160	2,230
Non-irrigated	1,750	1,820	1,840	1,880
Mountain:				
Arizona all cropland [2]	7,800	7,720	7,610	7,600
Irrigated	7,800	7,720	7,610	7,600
Colorado all cropland	2,020	2,070	2,100	2,160
Irrigated	4,860	4,950	5,050	5,100
Non-irrigated	1,320	1,360	1,370	1,370
Idaho all cropland	3,420	3,570	3,740	3,930
Irrigated	5,180	5,410	5,690	6,020
Non-irrigated	1,470	1,530	1,590	1,650
Montana all cropland	1,010	1,010	1,020	1,040
Irrigated	2,970	2,970	2,990	3,010
Non-irrigated	818	827	836	835
Nevada all cropland [2]	(D)	(D)	(D)	(D)
Irrigated	(D)	(D)	(D)	(D)
New Mexico all cropland [2]	1,500	1,560	1,580	1,550
Irrigated	4,080	4,140	4,190	4,200
Non-irrigated	405	463	469	475
Utah all cropland [2]	3,530	3,690	3,830	3,970
Irrigated	5,660	5,930	6,160	6,360
Non-irrigated	1,240	1,270	1,320	1,400
Wyoming all cropland	1,450	1,460	1,490	1,520
Irrigated	2,330	2,340	2,390	2,430
Non-irrigated	816	820	836	840
Pacific:				
California all cropland	11,160	11,630	12,170	12,830
Irrigated	13,200	13,700	14,300	15,100
Non-irrigated	4,400	4,740	5,090	5,400
Oregon all cropland	2,780	2,920	3,000	3,080
Irrigated	4,730	4,950	5,180	5,290
Non-irrigated	2,060	2,170	2,200	2,220
Washington all cropland	2,590	2,660	2,630	2,630
Irrigated	7,760	8,000	7,930	7,690
Non-irrigated	1,250	1,270	1,260	1,260

See footnote(s) at end of table.

Table 9-14.—Land values, cropland and pasture average value per acre: Region, State, and United States, 2016–2019-Continued

Region and State	Pasture			
	2016	2017	2018	2019
	Dollars	*Dollars*	*Dollars*	*Dollars*
Northeast:	3,550	3,640	3,770	3,870
Maryland	6,450	6,580	(D)	(D)
New Jersey	13,000	13,100	13,300	13,400
New York	1,460	1,480	1,560	1,530
Pennsylvania	2,860	3,020	3,140	3,290
Other States [1]	6,040	6,160	6,410	6,530
Lake:	2,020	2,050	2,080	2,080
Michigan	2,650	2,620	2,600	2,590
Minnesota	1,680	1,740	1,750	1,700
Wisconsin	2,190	2,200	2,260	2,310
Corn Belt:	2,330	2,260	2,320	2,330
Illinois	3,350	3,240	3,200	3,170
Indiana	2,480	2,430	2,430	2,450
Iowa	3,190	2,850	2,790	2,720
Missouri	1,830	1,830	1,920	1,980
Ohio	3,250	3,240	3,370	3,350
Northern Plains:	1,000	1,020	1,040	1,090
Kansas	1,310	1,310	1,320	1,390
Nebraska	891	904	975	1,050
North Dakota	794	804	776	820
South Dakota	993	1,020	1,040	1,050
Appalachian:	3,440	3,500	3,530	3,540
Kentucky	2,880	2,970	3,000	3,030
North Carolina	4,810	4,840	4,830	4,810
Tennessee	3,610	3,670	3,870	3,860
Virginia	4,090	4,150	4,050	4,020
West Virginia	2,060	2,100	2,090	2,120
Southeast:	4,000	4,030	4,180	4,180
Alabama	2,280	2,360	2,470	2,590
Florida	5,200	5,240	5,380	5,360
Georgia	3,540	3,570	3,660	3,730
South Carolina	3,120	3,180	3,260	3,240
Delta:	2,420	2,480	2,550	2,620
Arkansas	2,410	2,460	2,530	2,610
Louisiana	2,570	2,660	2,750	2,830
Mississippi	2,300	2,350	2,410	2,430
Southern Plains:	1,480	1,490	1,540	1,620
Oklahoma	1,380	1,350	1,380	1,460
Texas	1,500	1,520	1,570	1,660
Mountain:	636	647	667	683
Arizona [2]	(D)	(D)	(D)	(D)
Colorado	803	818	835	845
Idaho	1,350	1,420	1,490	1,560
Montana	649	658	667	680
Nevada [2]	(D)	(D)	(D)	(D)
New Mexico [2]	363	379	394	417
Utah [2]	1,100	1,130	1,160	1,240
Wyoming	540	550	561	575
Pacific:	1,660	1,680	1,680	1,750
California	2,760	2,780	2,810	3,010
Oregon	692	715	728	750
Washington	790	782	766	766
United States [3]	1,320	1,330	1,370	1,400

(D) Withheld to avoid disclosing data for individual operations. [1] Includes: Connecticut, Delaware, Maine, Maryland (beginning in 2018), Massachusetts, New Hampshire, Rhode Island, and Vermont. [2] Excludes American Indian Reservation land. [3] Excludes Alaska and Hawaii.

NASS, Environmental, Economics, and Demographics Branch, (202) 720–6146.

Table 9-15.—Cash rents, cropland and pasture: By State, 2018–2019

State	2018				2019			
	Cropland	Irrigated cropland	Non-irrigated cropland	Pasture	Cropland	Irrigated cropland	Non-irrigated cropland	Pasture
	Dollars							
Alabama	61.50	111.00	59.00	22.00	63.50	125.00	60.00	22.00
Arizona	253.00	253.00	....	....	249.00	249.00	....	2.00
Arkansas	111.00	136.00	49.00	18.00	105.00	131.00	49.00	19.00
California	340.00	528.00	....	13.00	423.00	543.00	35.00	13.00
Colorado	74.50	144.00	....	....	79.50	151.00	29.00	6.10
Connecticut	....	....	....	....	....	....	60.00	....
Delaware	112.00	....	....	....	119.00	161.00	97.00	....
Florida	115.00	232.00	53.00	17.00	110.00	216.00	58.00	15.50
Georgia	116.00	190.00	65.00	27.00	126.00	208.00	67.00	30.00
Hawaii	....	....	....	....	271.00	375.00	180.00	16.00
Idaho	160.00	216.00	56.00	11.00	159.00	216.00	56.00	11.00
Illinois	223.00	240.00	223.00	39.00	224.00	241.00	224.00	41.00
Indiana	198.00	244.00	196.00	....	194.00	238.00	193.00	43.00
Iowa	231.00	....	231.00	54.00	230.00	235.00	230.00	59.00
Kansas	66.50	131.00	58.00	19.50	64.50	128.00	57.00	19.00
Kentucky	149.00	....	148.00	....	151.00	220.00	150.00	27.00
Louisiana	89.00	104.00	73.00	18.00	94.50	111.00	75.00	20.00
Maine	....	....	....	....	....	....	62.00	....
Maryland	113.00	....	106.00	....	109.00	196.00	100.00	44.00
Massachusetts	....	....	....	....	88.50	240.00	71.00	....
Michigan	123.00	232.00	115.00	....	127.00	220.00	120.00	30.00
Minnesota	167.00	192.00	166.00	31.00	164.00	205.00	163.00	28.00
Mississippi	120.00	143.00	84.00	19.00	123.00	148.00	87.00	20.00
Missouri	132.00	180.00	125.00	33.00	130.00	186.00	122.00	32.00
Montana	32.00	....	26.50	6.30	32.50	82.00	27.00	6.60
Nebraska	195.00	238.00	150.00	22.50	191.00	237.00	144.00	24.50
Nevada	....	....	....	....	164.00	164.00	....	10.00
New Hampshire	....	....	....	....	44.00	....	40.00	....
New Jersey	77.50	....	....	....	82.00	139.00	65.00	45.00
New Mexico	....	....	....	....	80.50	136.00	17.50	2.80
New York	63.00	....	62.00	....	66.00	145.00	65.00	26.00
North Carolina	87.00	110.00	86.00	28.00	90.50	105.00	90.00	26.00
North Dakota	65.00	163.00	64.00	17.00	70.00	164.00	69.00	17.50
Ohio	152.00	....	152.00	....	155.00	199.00	155.00	28.00
Oklahoma	34.00	72.00	32.00	13.50	34.50	78.00	32.00	13.50
Oregon	159.00	215.00	93.00	12.00	152.00	215.00	95.00	11.00
Pennsylvania	80.50	....	80.00	....	94.00	173.00	93.00	27.00
South Carolina	48.50	90.00	44.00	....	47.00	94.00	42.00	18.00
South Dakota	119.00	189.00	117.00	23.00	119.00	194.00	117.00	26.00
Tennessee	98.00	165.00	95.00	20.00	103.00	180.00	99.00	21.00
Texas	42.50	91.00	30.00	6.70	42.50	92.00	30.00	6.80
Utah	64.00	92.00	....	....	75.50	108.00	24.00	4.30
Vermont	....	....	....	....	51.00	....	50.00	29.00
Virginia	63.00	100.00	61.00	21.00	59.00	100.00	57.00	21.00
Washington	203.00	358.00	75.00	....	201.00	360.00	75.00	8.00
West Virginia	45.00	....	45.00	....	43.00	....	43.00	14.00
Wisconsin	140.00	238.00	134.00	40.00	142.00	237.00	137.00	40.00
Wyoming	....	....	....	....	57.50	81.00	16.00	4.40

NASS, Environmental, Economics, and Demographics Branch, (202) 720–6146.

Table 9-16.—Farm assets and claims: Comparative balance sheet of the farming sector, excluding operator households, United States, Dec. 31, 2014–2018

Item	2014	2015	2016	2017	2018
Assets	*Billion dollars*	*Billion dollars*	*Billion dollars*	*Billion dollars*	*Billion dollars*
Physical assets:					
Real estate	2,364.5	2,364.3	2,400.3	2,471.9	2,519.0
Non-real estate:					
Livestock and poultry [1]	127.8	118.2	109.0	107.1	97.1
Machinery and motor vehicles [2]	245.7	239.5	255.4	272.3	271.0
Crops [3]	61.7	52.5	55.7	56.8	59.7
Purchased inputs	20.1	16.4	14.9	15.8	16.1
Financial	102.8	80.2	70.8	72.9	65.4
Total	2,930.6	2,878.6	2,913.4	3,005.0	3,026.7
Debt					
Liabilities:					
Real estate	196.8	208.8	226.0	236.2	245.7
Non-real estate	148.4	148.0	148.2	154.2	156.3
Total Debt [4]	345.2	356.7	374.2	390.4	402.0
Equity	2,585.4	2,521.9	2,539.2	2,614.6	2,624.7
	Percent	*Percent*	*Percent*	*Percent*	*Percent*
Ratio:					
Debt/equity	13.4	14.1	14.7	14.9	15.3
Debt/assets	11.8	12.4	12.8	13.0	13.3

Note: Data as of February 5, 2020. [1] The U.S. total exceeds the sum of the states because NASS does not release state data for some minor producing states due to disclosure issues. Horses and mules are excluded. [2] Includes only farm share value for trucks and autos. [3] All non-CCC crops held on farms plus the value above loan rate for crops held under CCC. [4] Excludes debt for nonfarm purposes.

ERS, Farm Income Team@ers.usda.gov. http://www.ers.usda.gov/data-products/farm-income-and-wealth-statistics.aspx.

Table 9-17.—Farm labor: Number of workers on farms and average wage rates, United States, 2009–2018

Year	Hired workers [1]	Wage rate [2]
	Thousands	*Dollars Per Hour*
2009		
Jan	603	10.93
Apr	694	10.86
July	892	10.66
Oct	829	10.93
Annual average	754.5	10.83
2010		
Jan	612	11.08
Apr	746	10.82
July	885	10.79
Oct	827	11.13
Annual average	767.5	10.95
2011		
Jan	603	11.30
Apr	(3)	(3)
July	834	10.93
Oct	828	11.15
Annual average	748.8	11.07
2012		
Jan	575	11.52
Apr	748	11.41
July	906	11.36
Oct	876	11.75
Annual average	776.3	11.51
2013		
Jan	596	12.02
Apr	736	11.89
July	906	11.68
Oct	871	11.96
Annual average	777.3	11.87
2014		
Jan	540	12.23
Apr	690	12.01
July	838	11.96
Oct	782	12.12
Annual average	712.5	12.07
2015		
Jan	549	12.53
Apr	687	12.28
July	872	12.47
Oct	841	12.82
Annual average	737.3	12.54
2016		
Jan	582	12.83
Apr	703	12.75
July	840	13.02
Oct	798	13.25
Annual average	730.8	12.98
2017		
Jan	533	13.43
Apr	673	13.23
July	879	13.23
Oct	840	13.42
Annual average	731.3	13.32
2018		
Jan	534	14.08
Apr	648	13.72
July	843	14.28
Oct	784	14.47
Annual average	702.3	14.17

[1] Includes all workers, other than agricultural service workers, who were paid for at least one hour of agricultural work on a farm or ranch during the survey week. [2] Applies to hired workers only (excludes pay for agricultural service workers). [3] The Agricultural (Farm) Labor Survey was not conducted for this quarter.
NASS, Economic, Environmental and Demographics Branch, (202) 720–6146.

Table 9-18.—Farm labor: Number of hired workers on farms and average wage rates, by regions and United States, 2018[1]

Region[2]	Workers on farms	Farm wage rates			
		Type of worker			
	Hired	Field	Livestock	Field and livestock	All hired workers[3]
	Thousands	*Dollars per hour*	*Dollars per hour*	*Dollars per hour*	*Dollars per hour*
January 7–13, 2018					
Northeast I	28	14.00	13.12	13.45	14.70
Northeast II	27	13.57	12.88	13.25	14.19
Appalachian I	19	12.49	11.57	12.15	13.30
Appalachian II	17	11.68	11.53	11.60	12.89
Southeast	20	10.74	11.33	10.95	11.86
Florida	37	10.80	10.80	10.80	11.64
Lake	35	12.18	12.35	12.30	13.06
Cornbelt I	31	13.09	13.20	13.15	14.29
Cornbelt II	16	13.37	13.08	13.20	13.85
Delta	19	12.35	10.83	11.50	12.23
Northern Plains	25	14.76	13.47	14.05	14.82
Southern Plains	40	11.68	12.48	12.05	12.65
Mountain I	17	13.18	13.14	13.15	14.54
Mountain II	13	12.16	13.93	13.40	14.57
Mountain III	17	12.04	12.33	12.15	13.31
Pacific	37	14.06	14.23	14.10	15.31
California	129	13.55	14.40	13.73	15.61
Hawaii	7	14.35	15.40	14.52	16.20
United States	534	12.84	12.89	12.86	14.08
April 8–14, 2018					
Northeast I	35	13.44	13.03	13.25	14.46
Northeast II	33	13.37	12.68	13.10	13.89
Appalachian I	24	11.87	11.80	11.85	12.69
Appalachian II	18	11.56	11.64	11.60	12.69
Southeast	30	10.35	11.03	10.55	11.23
Florida	38	11.20	12.20	11.25	11.89
Lake	43	12.28	12.41	12.35	13.02
Cornbelt I	42	12.49	13.20	12.75	13.71
Cornbelt II	21	12.74	13.43	13.05	13.64
Delta	32	11.30	10.91	11.15	11.62
Northern Plains	32	14.52	13.47	14.00	14.70
Southern Plains	44	11.40	12.13	11.75	12.26
Mountain I	26	13.16	13.02	13.10	13.84
Mountain II	15	12.08	13.59	13.05	14.13
Mountain III	16	11.77	12.09	11.90	13.13
Pacific	53	14.16	14.10	14.15	14.97
California	140	13.45	14.15	13.58	15.10
Hawaii	6	14.55	15.70	14.77	16.71
United States	648	12.72	12.78	12.74	13.72

See footnote(s) at end of table.

Table 9-18.—Farm labor: Number of hired workers on farms and average wage rates, by regions and United States, 2018 [1]—Continued

Region [2]	Workers on farms	Type of worker			
	Hired	Field	Livestock	Field and livestock	All hired workers [3]
	Thousands	*Dollars per hour*	*Dollars per hour*	*Dollars per hour*	*Dollars per hour*
July 8–14, 2018					
Northeast I	34	13.14	12.92	13.05	13.74
Northeast II	42	12.57	12.83	12.65	13.45
Appalachian I	40	12.17	12.54	12.25	12.73
Appalachian II	31	11.52	11.77	11.60	12.33
Southeast	27	11.75	10.85	11.50	12.32
Florida	30	11.40	11.40	11.40	12.49
Lake	70	13.76	14.05	13.90	14.49
Cornbelt I	45	13.20	13.36	13.25	14.29
Cornbelt II	24	13.48	12.62	13.15	13.84
Delta	31	11.33	11.67	11.40	11.85
Northern Plains	42	15.12	13.80	14.40	15.14
Southern Plains	57	12.33	12.28	12.30	13.12
Mountain I	27	13.53	14.23	13.85	14.34
Mountain II	21	13.15	13.01	13.10	13.79
Mountain III	18	11.30	12.67	11.95	12.49
Pacific	120	15.39	14.40	15.30	15.69
California	178	14.10	14.15	14.11	15.43
Hawaii	6	14.35	17.00	14.82	16.58
United States	843	13.58	13.22	13.48	14.28
October 7–13, 2018					
Northeast I	36	13.58	12.81	13.30	13.95
Northeast II	35	13.77	13.70	13.75	14.45
Appalachian I	37	12.52	12.68	12.55	13.07
Appalachian II	30	11.63	11.84	11.70	12.39
Southeast	27	11.92	10.82	11.60	12.48
Florida	31	11.60	11.60	11.60	12.63
Lake	66	14.81	14.39	14.60	15.14
Cornbelt I	45	13.93	13.47	13.80	14.76
Cornbelt II	23	13.94	13.65	13.85	14.53
Delta	28	11.32	11.46	11.35	11.83
Northern Plains	40	15.93	13.55	14.80	15.49
Southern Plains	53	12.67	12.73	12.70	13.53
Mountain I	31	13.05	14.11	13.55	13.95
Mountain II	20	12.91	13.26	13.05	13.87
Mountain III	19	11.45	12.67	12.00	12.53
Pacific	90	15.62	14.58	15.50	16.02
California	167	14.10	14.25	14.12	15.50
Hawaii	6	14.55	16.20	14.02	16.26
United States	784	13.74	13.38	13.64	14.47

[1] Includes all workers, other than agricultural service workers, who were paid for at least one hour of agricultural work on a farm or ranch during the survey week. [2] Multi-state regions consist of the following: Northeast I: Connecticut, Maine, Massachusetts, New Hampshire, New York, Rhode Island, Vermont; Northeast II: Delaware, Maryland, New Jersey, Pennsylvania; Appalachian I: North Carolina, Virginia; Appalachian II: Kentucky, Tennessee, West Virginia; Southeast: Alabama, Georgia, South Carolina; Lake: Michigan, Minnesota, Wisconsin; Cornbelt I: Illinois, Indiana, Ohio; Cornbelt II: Iowa, Missouri; Delta: Arkansas, Louisiana, Mississippi; Northern Plains: Kansas, Nebraska, North Dakota, South Dakota; Southern Plains: Oklahoma, Texas; Mountain I: Idaho, Montana, Wyoming; Mountain II: Colorado, Nevada, Utah; Mountain III: Arizona, New Mexico; Pacific: Oregon, Washington. [3] Includes field workers, livestock workers, supervisors, and others, excluding agricultural service workers.

NASS, Economic, Environmental and Demographics Branch, (202) 720–6146.

Table 9-19.—Hired farmworkers: Number of Workers and Median Weekly Earnings, 2017–2019

Characteristics	Workers [1]			Median Weekly Earnings [2]		
	2017	2018	2019	2017	2018	2019
	Thousands	*Thousands*	*Thousands*	*Dollars*	*Dollars*	*Dollars*
All workers	964	950	965	500	540	560
15–19 years old	69	78	66	300	300	175
20–24 years old	104	108	91	442	459	500
25–34 years old	216	191	215	560	576	560
35–44 years old	199	204	229	520	576	560
45–54 years old	192	169	157	550	570	576
55 years old and older	185	201	207	600	550	560
Male	776	744	744	554	577	576
Female	189	206	220	430	440	480
White [3]	456	426	426	600	597	600
Black and other races [3]	50	55	47	*	*	*
Hispanic	459	469	492	480	528	540
Schooling completed						
Less than 5th grade	51	68	70	464	460	520
5th-8th grade	175	165	157	461	492	500
9th-12th grade (no diploma)	165	183	151	450	480	480
High school diploma	318	300	346	560	600	580
Beyond high school	255	235	241	650	600	673
Full-time (35 or more hours per week) [4]	836	798	819	574	580	585
Part-time (less than 35 hours per week) [4]	126	148	142	240	220	200

* Insufficient number of reports to publish data. [1] Represents annual average number of persons 15 years old and over in the civilian noninstitutional population who were employed as hired farm managers, supervisors, or laborers. Employment estimates based on 12 monthly Current Population Survey microdata files. Earnings estimates based on 12 monthly Current Population Survey Outgoing Rotation Group microdata files. [2] "Median weekly earnings" is the earnings value that divides farmworkers into two equal-sized groups, one group having earnings above the median and the other group having earnings below the median. "Earnings" refers to the weekly earnings the farmworker usually earns at a farmwork job, before deductions, and includes any overtime pay or commissions. [3] Excludes persons of Hispanic origin. [4] The sum of full-time and part-time workers will not equal the total because usual hours worked varies for some individuals.

ERS, Rural Economy Branch, (202) 694–5416.

Table 9-20.—Crops: Area, United States, 2009–2018

Year	Principal crops				Commercial vegetables, harvested area	Fruits and nuts, bearing area [4]
	Area harvested			Area planted total [3]		
	Feed grains [1]	Food grains [2]	Total [3]			
	1,000 acres	*1,000 acres*	*1,000 acres*	*1,000 acres*	*1,000 acres*	*1,000 acres*
2009	89,446	53,195	301.172	319,022	2,946.6	4,050.5
2010	89,984	50,768	303,619	315,414	2,827.2	4,091.5
2011	90,940	48,543	292,652	314,343	2,682.0	4,132.6
2012	96,639	51,687	306,855	324,304	2,762.0	4,113.1
2013	98,095	48,073	303,764	324,937	2,681.2	4,306.1
2014	93,079	49,576	308,368	326,673	2,669.6	4,375.9
2015	93,037	50,267	304,814	319,047	2,637.1	4,398.3
2016	96,455	47,356	305,826	318,977	2,636.2	4,770.4
2017	90,543	40,229	301,779	318,340	2,572.5	4,818.5
2018	89,648	42,800	300,566	319,579	2,498.1	4,056.1

[1] Corn for grain, oats, barley, and sorghum for grain. [2] Wheat, rye, and rice. [3] Crops included in area planted and area harvested are corn, sorghum, oats, barley, winter wheat, rye, durum wheat, other spring wheat, rice, soybeans, peanuts, sunflower, cotton, dry edible beans, potatoes, canola, proso millet, and sugarbeets. Harvested acreage for all hay, tobacco, and sugarcane are used in computing total area planted. [4] Includes the following fruits and nuts: Citrus fruits—oranges, tangerines, Temples, grapefruit, lemons and tangelos; area is for the year of harvest; deciduous fruits—commercial apples, peaches, pears, grapes, cherries, plums, prunes, apricots, bananas, nectarines, figs, kiwifruit, olives, avocados, papayas, dates, berries, guavas, cranberries, pineapples (discontinued as of 2007 crop) and strawberries; nuts—almonds, hazelnuts, macadamias, pistachios, and walnuts.

NASS, Crops Branch, (202) 720–2127.

Table 9-21.—Crops: Area harvested and yield, United States, 2018–2019

Crop	Area harvested		Yield per acre		
	2018	2019	Unit	2018	2019
	1,000 acres	*1,000 acres*			
Grains and hay:					
Barley	1,982	2,221	Bushels	77.5	73.0
Corn for grain	81,740	81,337	Bushels	176.4	167.5
Corn for silage	6,113	6,615	Tons	19.9	20.2
Hay, all	52,839	52,425	Tons	2.34	2.46
Alfalfa	16,608	16,743	Tons	3.17	3.28
All other	36,231	35,682	Tons	1.96	2.07
Oats	865	828	Bushels	64.9	64.3
Proso millet	403	465	Bushels	29.7	35.7
Rice	2,915	2,477	Pounds	7,692	7,473
Rye	273	310	Bushels	30.9	34.3
Sorghum for grain	5,061	4,675	Bushels	72.1	73.0
Sorghum for silage	264	339	Tons	12.6	11.9
Wheat, all	39,612	37,394	Bushels	47.6	51.7
Winter	24,742	24,592	Bushels	47.9	53.6
Durum	1,974	1,177	Bushels	39.5	45.8
Other spring	12,896	11,625	Bushels	48.3	48.3
Oilseeds:					
Canola	1,942.5	1,909.0	Pounds	1,861	1,781
Cottonseed	....	....	Tons	....	....
Flaxseed	198.0	284.0	Bushels	22.6	19.8
Mustard Seed	97.8	90.0	Pounds	749	706
Peanuts	1,373.5	1,389.7	Pounds	4,001	3,934
Rapeseed	5.4	10.4	Pounds	1,524	2,160
Safflower	156.4	151.5	Pounds	1,512	1,273
Soybeans for beans	87,594	74,939	Bushels	50.6	47.4
Sunflower	1,217.4	1,253.5	Pounds	1,731	1,560
Cotton, tobacco and sugar crops:					
Cotton, all	9,990.8	11,612.5	Pounds	882	823
Pima	248.8	223.5	Pounds	1,545	1,472
Upland	9,742.0	11,389.0	Pounds	865	810
Sugarbeets	1,096.4	980.1	Tons	30.4	29.2
Sugarcane	899.7	913.2	Tons	38.1	35.0
Tobacco	291.4	227.1	Pounds	1,830	2,060
Dry beans, peas and lentils [1]:					
Austrian winter peas	10.9	(NA)	Cwt	1,138	(NA)
Dry edible beans [2]	2,016.0	1,174.3	Cwt	1,860	1,768
Chickpeas, all	846.5	404.5	Cwt	1,511	1,547
Large	623.9	313.2	Cwt	1,513	1,553
Small	222.6	91.3	Cwt	1,503	1,524
Lentils	718.0	425.0	Cwt	1,171	1,250
Peas, Dry edible [2]	807.9	1,046.0	Cwt	1,972	2,123
Peas, Wrinkled seed	....	....	Cwt	....	....
Potatoes and miscellaneous:					
Hops	55.0	56.5	Pounds	1,943	1,981
Maple Syrup	....	....	Pounds	....	....
Mushrooms	....	....	Pounds	....	....
Peppermint oil	58.5	52.4	Pounds	92	104
Potatoes, all	1,014.8	937.3	Cwt	443	453
Spring	51.8	....	Cwt	343	....
Summer	56.4	....	Cwt	315	....
Fall	906.6	....	Cwt	457	....
Spearmint oil	20.8	18.3	Pounds	124	131
Sweet potatoes	144.4	....	Cwt	190	....
Taro (Hawaii)	0.3	....	Pounds	9,630	....

(NA) Not available. [1] Beginning in 2019, Austrian winter peas and wrinkled seed peas are included in dry edible peas. [2] Yield in pounds.
NASS, Crops Branch, (202) 720–2127.

Table 9-22.—Crops: Production and value, United States, 2018–2019

Crop	Production			Value of production	
	Unit	2018	2019	2018	2019
		Thousands	*Thousands*	*1,000 dollars*	*1,000 dollars*
Grains and hay:					
Barley	Bushels	153,527	172,499	697,598	761,152
Corn for grain	Bushels	14,340	13,620	52,102	52,911
Corn for silage	Bushels	121,564	133,522	....	....
Hay, all	Tons	123,600	128,864	17,288	18,161
Alfalfa	Tons	52,634	54,875	8,583,806	9,184,257
All other	Tons	70,966	73,989	8,704,409	8,976,339
Oats	Bushels	56,130	53,258	167,640	162,711
Proso millet	Bushels	11,595	16,608	60,566	82,907
Rice	Cwt	223,833	185,104	2,903,041	2,459,035
Rye	Bushels	8,432	10,622	52,870	64,863
Sorghum for grain	Bushels	364,986	341,460	1,180,847	1,151,709
Sorghum for silage	Bushels	3,326	4,019	....	....
Wheat, all	Bushels	1,885,156	1,932,017	9,661,916	8,882,766
Winter	Bushels	1,183,939	1,316,963	5,985,308	5,999,460
Durum	Bushels	77,985	53,959	412,749	257,103
Other Spring	Bushels	623,232	561,095	3,263,859	2,626,203
Oilseeds:					
Canola	Pounds	3,615,440	3,400,865	568,622	494,295
Cottonseed	Tons	5,631	5,945	878,254	1,021,832
Flaxseed	Bushels	4,466	5,625	43,533	56,062
Mustard Seed	Pounds	73,297	63,580	20,974	16,748
Peanuts	Pounds	5,495,935	5,466,487	1,169,953	1,129,584
Rapeseed	Pounds	8,230	22,464	1,526	4,509
Safflower	Pounds	236,270	192,900	47,976	38,361
Soybeans for beans	Bushels	4,428,150	3,551,908	36,819,008	31,202,680
Sunflower	Pounds	2,107,045	1,956,035	370,446	358,408
Cotton, tobacco and sugar crops:					
Cotton, all	Bales	18,367	19,912	6,375,167	6,012,662
Upland	Bales	17,566	19,227	5,931,451	5,631,849
American Pima	Bales	801	685	443,716	380,813
Sugarbeets	Tons	33,282	28,650	1,177,992	1,099,574
Sugarcane	Tons	32,934	30,287	1,100,218	1,144,859
Tobacco	Pounds	533,241	467,956	1,093,418	946,252
Dry Beans, peas and lentils [1]:					
Austrian winter peas	Cwt	124	(NA)	1,830	(NA)
Dry edible beans [2]	Cwt	37,745	20,756	951,047	608,870
Chickpeas, all	Cwt	12,787	6,256	281,451	117,056
Large	Cwt	9,441	4,865	209,744	93,037
Small	Cwt	3,346	1,391	71,677	24,019
Lentils	Cwt	8,408	5,311	131,739	78,799
Peas, dry edible [2]	Cwt	15,929	22,210	163,963	212,328
Peas, wrinkled seed	Cwt	389	(NA)	13,564	(NA)
Potatoes and miscellaneous:					
Hops	Pounds	106,906.7	112,041.2	583,444	636,580
Maple Syrup	Gallons	4,199	4,180	141,825	129,479
Mushrooms	Pounds	917,235	....	1,131,564	....
Peppermint oil	Pounds	5,377	5,452	106,489	105,439
Potatoes, all	Cwt	450,020	424,419	4,006,340	....
Spring	Cwt	17,757	....	282,093	....
Summer	Cwt	17,764	....	207,518	....
Fall	Cwt	414,499	....	3,516,729	....
Spearmint oil	Pounds	2,571	2,400	43,178	40,765
Sweet potatoes	Cwt	27,378	31,972	634,228	588,125
Taro (Hawaii) [3]	Pounds	2,985	(NA)	1,970	....

(NA) Not available. [1] Beginning in 2019, Austrian winter peas and wrinkled seed peas are included in dry edible peas. [2] Yield in pounds. [3] Estimates discontinued in 2019.
NASS, Crops Branch, (202) 720–2127.

Table 9-23.—Fruits and nuts: Bearing acreage and yield, United States, 2017–2018

Crop	Bearing acreage		Yield per acre		
	2017	2018	Unit	2017	2018
	Acres	*Acres*			
Noncitrus fruits:					
Apples, Commerical	328,200	291,200	Tons	17.60	17.61
Apricots	11,300	10,600	Tons	4.04	3.73
Avocados	58,140	53,640	Tons	3.23	3.46
Bananas (Hawaii) [1 2]	950	....	Tons	3.50	....
Blackberries Cultivated (Oregon) [1 2]	6,300	....	Tons	3.19	....
Blueberries Cultivated [1]	83,900	89,200	Tons	3.06	3.15
Blueberries Wild (Maine) [1]	17,000	18,800	Tons	1.99	1.34
Boysenberries (Oregon) [1 2]	330	....	Tons	3.03	....
Cherries, Sweet	92,500	85,000	Tons	4.73	4.05
Cherries, Tart	35,300	35,200	Tons	3.68	4.24
Coffee (Hawaii)	7,200	7,100	Tons	1.77	1.92
Cranberries	39,900	39,300	Tons	10.46	11.36
Dates	13,400	13,100	Tons	3.23	3.13
Figs (California) [2]	6,700	....	Tons	4.66	....
Grapes	997,800	937,000	Tons	7.40	8.11
Kiwifruit (California)	3,600	3,900	Tons	9.33	9.70
Nectarines	17,000	14,000	Tons	8.34	8.60
Olives (California)	40,000	37,500	Tons	4.81	1.43
Papayas (Hawaii) [1]	1,100	800	Tons	11.64	6.50
Peaches	91,950	74,500	Tons	7.62	8.74
Pears	46,200	46,300	Tons	16.00	17.40
Plums (California)	15,000	14,000	Tons	7.86	7.16
Prunes (California)	45,000	44,000	Tons	7.22	6.36
Raspberries [1]	19,960	16,900	Tons	5.65	6.47
Strawberries [1]	53,200	49,220	Tons	25.57	29.03
Tree nuts:					
Almonds (California) [3]	1,030,000	1,090,000	Tons	1.79	1.69
Hazelnuts (Oregon) [3]	40,000	44,000	Tons	0.80	1.16
Macadamia (Hawaii) [3]	17,000	16,900	Tons	1.44	1.04
Pecans [3]	404,800	409,900	Tons	0.38	0.30
Pistachios (California) [3]	250,000	264,000	Tons	1.20	1.87
Walnuts (California) [3]	335,000	350,000	Tons	1.88	1.93
Citrus fruits:					
Grapefruit [4]	59,600	54,800	Boxes	285	228
Lemons [4]	54,300	54,300	Boxes	406	409
Oranges [4]	527,500	517,500	Boxes	225	176
Tangerines and Mandarins [4]	68,400	71,300	Boxes	372	280

[1] Harvested acreage. For 2017, yield based on utilized production. For 2018, yield based on total production. [2] Estimates discontinued in 2018. [3] Yield based on utilized production on an in-shell basis. [4] Crop year begins with bloom in one year and ends with completion of harvest the following year. Citrus production is for the the year of harvest.

NASS, Crops Branch, (202) 720–2127.

Table 9-24.—Fruits and nuts: Production and value, United States, 2017–2018

Crop	Total production		Value of utilized production	
	2017	2018	2017	2018
	1,000 tons [1]	*1,000 tons* [1]	*1,000 dollars*	*1,000 dollars*
Noncitrus fruits:				
Apples, Commerical	5,776.9	5,128.5	3,601,447	3,013,713
Apricots	45.7	39.6	44,556	48,465
Avocados	187.7	185.8	392,012	400,354
Bananas (Hawaii) [2]	3.3	....	6,028	....
Blackberries Cultivated (Oregon)) [2]	20.1	....	31,115	....
Blueberries Cultivated	259.3	281.2	815,908	797,295
Blueberries Wild (Maine)	33.9	25.2	17,561	23,155
Boysenberries (Oregon)) [2]	1.0	....	1,693	....
Cherries, Sweet	437.6	344.4	891,652	637,700
Cherries, Tart	129.8	149.2	56,868	56,635
Coffee	12.7	13.7	43,774	50,160
Cranberries	419.7	446.3	252,088	222,440
Dates	43.3	41.1	150,959	152,175
Figs (California)) [2]	31.2	....	28,568	....
Grapes	7,383.9	7,596.0	6,507,849	6,615,121
Kiwifruit (California)	33.6	37.8	34,860	32,886
Nectarines	141.9	120.5	128,255	104,626
Olives (California)	192.3	53.6	186,649	40,523
Papayas (Hawaii)	12.8	5.2	9,400	5,702
Peaches	700.8	651.5	599,862	511,226
Pears	737.5	805.5	519,290	428,940
Plums (California)	117.9	100.0	114,897	92,570
Prunes (California)	325.5	279.6	207,900	194,832
Raspberries	113.4	109.4	493,945	367,001
Strawberries [3]	1,360.4	1,428.9	2,895,813	2,670,523
Tree Nuts:				
Almonds, shelled (California) [4]	1,892.5	1,872.5	5,603,950	5,468,040
Hazelnuts, in-shell (Oregon) [5]	(NA)	(NA)	73,600	91,800
Macadamia, in-shell (Hawaii) [5]	(NA)	(NA)	53,900	42,007
Pecans, in-shell [5]	(NA)	(NA)	709,218	425,331
Pistachios, in-shell (California) [5]	(NA)	(NA)	1,014,507	2,615,550
Walnuts, in-shell (California) [5]	(NA)	(NA)	1,568,700	878,800
Citrus fruits [3]:				
Grapefruit	698	509	256,917	207,970
Lemons	882	888	763,446	715,761
Oranges	5,088	3,875	1,943,678	1,830,445
Tangerines and mandarins	1,029	804	568,084	575,976

(NA) Not available. [1] Tons refers to the 2,000 lb. short Tons. [2] Estimates discontinued in 2018. [3] Value of production is packinghouse-door equivalent. [4] Value is based on the edible portion of the crop only. [5] Only utilized production estimated.

NASS, Crops Branch, (202) 720–2127.

Table 9-25.—Vegetables, commercial: Area harvested and yield, United States, 2017–2018

Crop	Total area harvested		Total yield per harvested acre		
	2017	2018	Unit	2017	2018
	Acres	*Acres*			
Artichokes	7,200	6,900	Cwt	130.0	145.0
Asparagus	26,300	21,700	Cwt	32.0	36.0
Beans, lima	24,100	23,750	Cwt	27.8	28.7
Beans, snap	212,100	221,500	Cwt	85.2	79.4
Broccoli	128,600	113,900	Cwt	158.5	151.7
Cabbage	60,600	54,200	Cwt	393.2	359.9
Cantaloupes	63,250	60,700	Cwt	243.4	240.6
Carrots	75,900	79,800	Cwt	408.4	413.8
Cauliflower	45,800	43,900	Cwt	198.1	211.5
Celery	31,800	30,200	Cwt	505.9	589.4
Corn, sweet	464,600	473,100	Cwt	162.9	154.9
Cucumbers	117,200	110,900	Cwt	161.4	139.3
Garlic	33,000	32,800	Cwt	155.0	175.0
Honeydews	11,600	14,900	Cwt	290.0	310.0
Lettuce					
Head	140,700	120,300	Cwt	351.1	337.2
Leaf	67,200	69,300	Cwt	203.5	162.7
Romaine	117,400	99,600	Cwt	309.3	293.5
Onions	151,500	130,200	Cwt	543.8	556.1
Pea, green	134,200	131,100	Cwt	44.8	38.7
Peppers, bell	42,200	39,700	Cwt	341.0	324.8
Peppers, chile	16,000	14,200	Cwt	208.5	187.7
Pumpkins	72,300	65,900	Cwt	220.2	228.5
Spinach	64,730	61,450	Cwt	125.0	138.0
Squash	45,900	44,800	Cwt	174.5	165.0
Tomatoes	310,500	321,900	Cwt	791.2	863.8
Watermelons	107,800	111,400	Cwt	378.3	350.5

NASS, Crops Branch, (202) 720–2127.

Table 9-26.—Vegetables, commercial: Production and value, United States, 2017–2018

Crop	Total production			Total value of utilized production	
	Unit	2017	2018	2017	2018
		Thousands	*Thousands*	*1,000 dollars*	*1,000 dollars*
Artichokes	Cwt	936.0	1,000.5	65,520	63,032
Asparagus	Cwt	841.1	781.8	100,672	87,584
Beans, lima	Cwt	671.0	681.7	19,493	21,622
Beans, snap	Cwt	18,076.3	17,595.2	349,445	363,506
Broccoli	Cwt	20,384.0	17,273.0	925,716	738,527
Cabbage	Cwt	23,826.0	19,507.5	431,307	409,446
Cantaloupes	Cwt	15,394.8	14,607.0	295,975	331,542
Carrots	Cwt	31,001.0	33,018.0	696,129	731,504
Cauliflower	Cwt	9,074.5	9,286.0	415,737	425,350
Celery	Cwt	16,089.0	17,799.0	322,047	444,013
Corn, sweet	Cwt	75,674.4	73,279.7	892,179	858,862
Cucumbers	Cwt	18,912.8	15,450.4	392,013	332,867
Garlic	Cwt	5,115.0	5,740.0	390,021	452,599
Honeydews	Cwt	3,364.0	4,619.0	94,192	90,532
Lettuce					
Head	Cwt	49,395.5	40,561.0	1,774,522	1,219,857
Leaf	Cwt	13,675.0	11,277.0	833,077	585,299
Romaine	Cwt	36,308.0	29,233.0	1,628,136	901,186
Onions	Cwt	82,389.0	72,409.0	1,042,090	817,496
Pea, green	Cwt	6,012.4	5,071.0	85,475	64,901
Peppers, bell	Cwt	14,390.0	12,895.0	625,577	533,307
Peppers, chile	Cwt	3,336.0	2,665.0	113,562	94,767
Pumpkins	Cwt	15,919.6	15,058.4	196,541	190,162
Spinach	Cwt	8,090.6	8,480.5	470,860	422,879
Squash	Cwt	8,009.1	7,392.5	235,613	192,922
Tomatoes	Cwt	245,654.5	278,071.0	1,677,960	1,856,280
Watermelons	Cwt	40,781.5	39,045.0	594,033	656,655

NASS, Crops Branch, (202) 720–2127.

Table 9-27.—Livestock and livestock products: Production and value, United States, 2016–2018

Product	Production [1]			Value of production		
	2016	2017	2018	2016	2017	2018
	Millions	*Millions*	*Millions*	*1,000 dollars*	*1,000 dollars*	*1,000 dollars*
Eggs	103,202	107,242	109,192	6,591,359	7,635,359	10,586,262
	1,000 pounds	*1,000 pounds*	*1,000 pounds*	*1,000 dollars*	*1,000 dollars*	*1,000 dollars*
Cattle and calves	42,694,001	44,197,461	46,318,583	48,572,501	50,398,374	49,844,530
Hogs	35,898,712	36,962,875	38,829,022	17,363,044	19,159,248	19,060,203
Broilers [2]	54,259,100	55,573,900	56,791,100	25,935,852	30,232,203	31,746,230
Mature chickens	1,060,677	1,001,386	1,019,695	87,949	46,999	49,364
Turkeys [3]	7,486,978	7,544,391	7,598,289	6,184,247	4,873,677	3,875,131
Milk	212,451,000	215,527,000	217,575,000	34,712,099	38,119,254	35,411,485
Catfish [3 4]	320,174	342,241	358,604	385,985	379,713	360,401
Trout [3 4]	60,933	55,709	49,772	113,904	120,302	110,554
Honey	162,246	148,980	152,348	343,962	334,166	333,482
Wool (shorn)	25,795	24,810	24,00	37,423	36,774	42,772
Mohair	800	740	755	3,650	3,661	3,963

[1] For cattle, sheep, and hogs, the quantity of net production is the live weight actually produced during the year, adjustments having been made for animals shipped in and changes in inventory. Estimates for broilers and eggs cover the 12-month period Dec. 1, previous year through Nov. 30. [2] Young chickens of meat–type strains raised for meat production. [3] Live weight. [4] Value of fish sold, excludes eggs.
NASS, Livestock Branch, (202) 720–3570.

Table 9-28.—Farm product prices: Marketing year average prices received by farmers; Parity prices, United States, 2017–2018

Commodity	Unit	Marketing year average price [1]		Parity price [2]	
		2017	2018	2017	2018
		Dollars	*Dollars*	*Dollars*	*Dollars*
Basic commodities:					
Cotton:					
Upland	pound	0.686	0.703	1.93	2
Extra long staple(American Pima)	pound	1.39	1.15	3.83	3.99
Wheat	bushel	4.72	5.16	17.7	17.6
Rice	cwt	12.9	12.3	39.5	39.9
Corn	bushel	3.36	3.61	13	13.2
Peanuts	pound	0.229	0.215	0.663	0.675
Tobacco:					
Flue-cured, types (class 1)	pound	2.004	1.933	5.21	5.46
Types 21	pound	(NA)	(NA)	(NA)	(NA)
Burley, type 31	pound	1.935	1.96	5.13	5.34
Maryland, type 32 [3]	pound	1.8	1.8	4.9	5.05
Dark air-cured, types 35–36	pound	(NA)	(NA)	(NA)	(NA)
Sun-cured, type 37	pound	(NA)	(NA)	(NA)	(NA)
Pa., seedleaf, type 41	pound	2.36	2.14	5.5	5.78
Cigar binder type 51	pound	(NA)	(NA)	(NA)	(NA)
Puerto Rican filler, type 46	pound	(NA)	(NA)	(NA)	(NA)
Cigar wrapper, type 61	pound	(NA)	(NA)	(NA)	(NA)
Designated nonbasic commodities:					
All milk, sold to plants	cwt	17.69	16.28	51.9	52.2
Honey, all	pound	2.200	2.166	4.72	5.14
Wool and mohair:					
Wool [4]	pound	1.48	1.75	3.63	3.87
Mohair [5]	pound	4.95	5.25	11.4	11.9
Other nonbasic commodities:					
Field crops and miscellaneous:					
Austrian winter peas	cwt	12.7	16.4	(NA)	(NA)
Barley	bushel	4.47	4.62	14.3	14.9
Beans, dry edible	cwt	26.7	25.4	93.3	96
Cottonseed	ton	142	155	591	593
Crude pine gum	barrel	(NA)	(NA)	400	408
Flaxseed	bushel	9.53	(NA)	33.1	33.8
Hay, all, baled	ton	142	166	424	431
Hops	pound	5.6	5.46	10.6	11.6
Lentils	cwt	25.9	17.7	73.5	77.8
Oats	bushel	2.59	2.66	8.41	8.57
Peas, dry edible	cwt	11.8	10.5	54.5	55.5
Peppermint oil	pounds	18.3	19.8	58.8	60.8
Popcorn, shelled basis	cwt	(NA)	(NA)	52.1	53.1
Potatoes	cwt	9.17	8.9	24.6	(NA)
Rye	bushel	4.7	6.27	18.2	18.5
Sorghum grain	cwt	5.75	5.82	22.2	22.3
Soybeans	bushel	9.33	8.48	31.4	32.6
Spearmint oil	pound	16.2	16.8	49	50.8
Sweet potatoes	cwt	18.4	23.2	59.3	60.5
Fruits:					
Citrus (equiv. on-tree): [6]					
Grapefruit	box	12.48	14.24	19.2	21.7
Lemons	box	28.5	26.03	50.4	54.9
Oranges	box	13.32	16.86	25.4	26.7
Tangerines	box	18.76	25.39	51.6	53.7
Deciduous and other:					
Apples:					
For fresh consumption [7]	pound	0.407	0.394	0.98	1.03
For processing [8]	ton	248	206	545	575
Apricots:					
For fresh consumption [9]	ton	1,400	1,540	3400	3,400
Dried, California (dried basis) [8]	ton	(D)	(D)	7630	8,750
For processing (excl dried) [8]	ton	(NA)	(NA)	1160	1,230
Avocados [9]	ton	2,110	2,190	5100	5,370

See footnote(s) at end of table.

Table 9-28.—Farm product prices: Marketing year average prices received by farmers; Parity prices, United States, 2017–2018—Continued

Commodity	Unit	Marketing year average price [1]		Parity price [2]	
		2017	2018	2017	2018
		Dollars	*Dollars*	*Dollars*	*Dollars*
Deciduous and other—Continued					
Berries for processing:					
Blackberries (Oregon)	pound	0.692	....	17.90	18.20
Boysenberries (Oregon)	pound	0.835	....	2.54	2.58
Gooseberries	pound	....	....	1.07	1.09
Loganberries (Oregon)	pound	....	....	1.73	1.76
Raspberries, black (California, Oregon & Washington)	pound	....	....	3.05	3.11
Raspberries, red (California, Oregon & Washington)	pound	....	....	2.42	2.47
Cherries:					
Sweet	ton	2,060	1,860	5,930	6,250
Tart	pound	0.224	0.196	0.922	0.939
Cranberries [10]	barrel	30.20	25.10	121	119
Dates [9]	ton	3,510	3,800	4,260	4,230
Grapes:					
For all sales	ton	881	871	....	....
Raisin varieties dried, California (dried basis) [8]	ton	1,840	....	4,090	4,110
Wine dried grapes	ton	928	....	1,860	2,010
Kiwi	ton	1,050	870	2,780	3,050
Nectarines					
For fresh consumption [17]	ton	943	(D)	1,830	1,970
For processing [18]	ton	144	(D)	121	124
Olives (California): [11]					
For all sales	ton	974	766	....	....
Crushed for oil	ton	810	566	1,690	1,800
For all sales (excl crushed)	ton	....	....	2,520	2,610
For canning	ton	1,320	1,270	2,790	2,910
Papayas	pound	0.422	0.554	1.15	1.20
Peaches:					
For all sales	ton	864	801	....	....
For fresh consumption [7]	ton	1,350	1,250	2,490	2,660
Dried, California (dried basis) [8]	ton	(NA)	....	1,320	1,280
For processing California (excl dried):					
Clingstone [11]	ton	474	480	980	1,060
Freestone [8]	ton	393	410	798	869
Pears:					
For all sales	ton	710	536	....	....
For fresh consumption [7]	ton	875	610	1,670	1,770
For processing (excl dried) [8]	ton	384	367	....	....
Plums (California):					
For all sales [9]	ton	1,000	935	....	....
For fresh consumption [17]	ton	(D)	(D)	1,840	1,910
For processing [18]	ton	(D)	(D)	....	....
Prunes, dried (California) [8]	ton	1,980	....	4,520	4,700
Prunes and plums (excl California):					
For fresh consumption [12]	ton	....	....	1,760	1,800
For processing (excl dried) [8]	ton	....	....	686	699
Strawberries:					
For fresh consumption [13]	cwt	125	106	253	282
For processing [8]	cwt	37.20	43.60	101	106
Sugar crops:					
Sugarbeets	ton	41.2	35.5	150	150
Sugarcane for sugar	ton	31	33.4	99.70	102
Tree nuts: [14]					
Almonds	pound	2.53	2.44	6.60	6.93
Hazelnuts	ton	2,300	1,800	6,250	6,840
Macadamia	pound	1.10	1.19	....	....
Pecans, all	pound	2.33	1.75	4.98	(NA)
Pistachios	pound	1.69	2.65	6.63	6.93
Walnuts	ton	2,490	1,300	6,680	6,870

See footnote(s) at end of table.

Table 9-28.—Farm product prices: Marketing year average prices received by farmers; Parity prices, United States, 2017–2018—Continued

Commodity	Unit	Marketing year average price[1]		Parity price[2]	
		2017	2018	2017	2018
		Dollars	*Dollars*	*Dollars*	*Dollars*
Vegetables for fresh market:[13]					
Artichokes, California	cwt	70	63	131	134
Asparagus	cwt	132	122	323	335
Beans, snap	cwt	57.1	59.8	130	132
Broccoli	cwt	46	43.1	111	115
Cabbage	cwt	19.8	22.9	39.8	40.5
Cantaloupes	cwt	19.2	22.7	61.4	62.5
Carrots[15]	cwt	30.2	27.3	78.7	81.9
Cauliflower[15]	cwt	46.8	46.1	130	135
Celery[15]	cwt	20.5	25.9	58.8	58.1
Cucumbers	cwt	29.4	28.6	65.7	66.9
Eggplant	cwt	(NA)	(NA)	69.4	70.7
Escarole/Endive	cwt	(NA)	(NA)	89.3	91
Garlic	cwt	184	190	84.4	86
Green peppers[15]	cwt	48.7	44.3	104	106
Honeydew melons	cwt	28	19.6	55.6	59.3
Lettuce	cwt	35.9	30.1	66.3	71.3
Onions[15]	cwt	14.4	13.5	39.8	41.4
Spinach	cwt	68.8	59	114	116
Sweet corn	cwt	29.2	29.3	76.3	79.8
Tomatoes	cwt	36.8	41.5	116	119
Watermelons	cwt	14.8	16.9	24.4	24.8
Vegetables for processing:[8]					
Asparagus	ton	1570	1,580	42100	4,340
Beets	ton	(NA)	(NA)	224	229
Cabbage	ton	202	123	173	176
Cucumbers	ton	352	352	(NA)	(NA)
Green peas	ton	250	251	977	989
Lima beans	ton	561	625	19300	1,970
Snap beans	ton	188	182	645	660
Spinach	ton	196	197	418	426
Sweet corn	ton	78.5	79.7	305	311
Tomatoes	ton	82.7	81.5	235	243
Livestock and livestock products:					
All beef cattle	cwt	120	115	320	335
Cows	cwt	69.1	62.6	(NA)	(NA)
Steers and heifers	cwt	122	117	(NA)	(NA)
Calves	cwt	168	170	464	484
Chickens:					
Broilers, live[18]	pound	0.545	0.567	1.44	1.5
All Eggs	dozen	0.863	1.15	2.94	2.96
Hogs	cwt	53.1	50.2	161	166
Milk cows[16]	head	1,620	1,360	(NA)	(NA)
Turkeys, live	pound	0.645	0.51	187	194

(NA) Not available. [1] Unless otherwise noted, these prices are for marketing year average or calendar year average computed by weighing State prices by quantities sold, or by production for those commodities for which the production is sold. [2] Parity prices are for January of the year shown as published in the January issue of Agricultural Prices. [3] Previous year. [4] Average local market price for wool sold excluding incentive payment. [5] Average local market price for mohair sold excluding incentive payment. [6] Crop year begins with bloom in one year and ends with completion of harvest the following year. Prices refer to the year harvest begins. [7] Equivalent packinghouse-door returns for California, Oregon (pears only), Washington, and New York (apples only), and prices as sold for other States. [8] Equivalent returns at processing plant-door. [9] Equivalent returns at packinghouse-door. [10] Weighted average of co-op and independent sales. Co-op prices represent pool proceeds excluding returns from non-cranberry products and before deductions for capital stock and other retains. [11] Equivalent per unit returns for bulk fruit at first delivery point. [12] Average price as sold. [13] FOB shipping point when available. Weighted average of prices at points of first sale. [14] Prices are in-shell basis except almonds which are shelled basis. [15] Includes some processing. [16] Simple average of States weighted by estimated Jan. 1 head for U.S. average. [17] Prices for fresh and processing breakdown no longer published to avoid disclosure of individual operations. [18] Live weight equivalent price.

NASS, Environmental, Economics, and Demographics Branch (202) 720–6146.

Table 9-29.—Producer prices: Index numbers, by groups of commodities, United States, 2010–2019

[1982=100]

Year	Total finished goods	Consumer foods	Personal consumption goods [1]	Total intermediate materials	Unprocessed Goods for intermediate demand [2]
2010	179.8	182.4	189.1	183.4	212.2
2011	190.7	193.9	203.3	199.8	249.4
2012	194.3	199.1	207.5	200.7	241.4
2013	196.7	203.5	210.3	200.8	246.7
2014	200.4	212.5	214.7	201.9	249.3
2015	193.9	209.7	204.4	188.0	189.1
2016	191.9	204.6	201.3	182.2	173.4
2017	198.0	207.2	209.2	190.7	190.8
2018	204.1	207.4	216.8	200.9	200.1
2019	205.7	211.6	217.5	198.1	185.9

ERS, Food Marketing Branch, (202) 694–5349. Compiled from reports of the U.S. Department of Labor.

Table 9-30.—Prices received by farmers: Index numbers by groups of commodities and parity ratio, United States, 2008–2018 [1]

[1910–14=100]

Year	Food grain	Feed grain	Cotton	Tobacco	Oilseed	Fruit & tree nut [2]	Vegetable & melon	Other crop
2008	820	1,010	515	1,409	1,107	1,038	1,076	604
2009	590	579	416	1,569	971	977	1,153	609
2010	560	587	601	1,557	944	1,031	1,161	622
2011	758	902	745	1,497	1,225	1,162	1,224	645
2012	779	1,010	673	1,576	1,356	1,339	1,040	649
2013 [3]	759	943	651	1,760	1,343	1,311	1,330	645

Year	Potato & dry edible bean	Crop Production	Meat animal	Dairy	Poultry & egg	Livestock Production	Agricultural Production	Parity ratio [4]
2009	761	747	1,075	790	390	857	832	35
2010	708	690	1,256	1,000	427	1,002	850	35
2011	867	872	1,540	1,239	422	1,161	1,032	38
2012	846	933	1,633	1,140	459	1,190	1,083	38
2013	901	922	1,669	1,230	515	1,260	1,104	38
2014	(3)	805	(3)	(3)	(3)	1,495	1,113	37
2015	(3)	759	(3)	(3)	(3)	1,317	1,024	34
2016	(3)	752	(3)	(3)	(3)	1,096	935	32
2017	(3)	752	(3)	(3)	(3)	1,160	963	33
2018	(3)	609	(3)	(3)	(3)	1,095	938	32

[1] These indexes are computed using the price estimates of averages for all classes and grades for individual commodities being sold in local farm markets. In computing the group indexes, prices of individual commodities have been compared with 2011 weighted average prices. The resulting ratios are seasonally weighted by average quantities sold for the most recent 5–year period. For example, 2013 indexes use quantities sold for the period 2007–11. Then, the 2011 indexes are used to adjust the 1910–14 base period. [2] Fresh market for noncitrus, and fresh market and processing for citrus. [3] Data series discontinued after 2013. [4] Ratio of Index of Prices Received to the Index of Prices Paid by Farmers for Commodities and Services, Interest, Taxes, and Farm Wage Rates.

NASS, Environmental, Economics, and Demographics Branch, (202) 720–6146.

Table 9-31.—Prices received by farmers: Index numbers by groups of commodities and ratio, United States, 2009–2018[1]

(2011=100)

Year	Food grain	Feed grain	Cotton[2]	Tobacco[2]	Oilseed	Fruit & tree nut[3]	Vegetable & melon	Other crop
2009	78.5	65.1	55.9	99.7	83.5	83.9	102.8	94.1
2010	74.4	66.0	80.6	98.9	81.2	88.5	103.5	95.9
2011	100.0	100.0	....	....	100.0	100.0	100.0	100.0
2012	103.8	110.8	....	....	111.9	112.4	91.9	102.7
2013	101.5	102.4	....	....	111.6	119.1	103.8	100.5
2014	90.4	69.1	....	....	98.8	136.3	103.3	94.7
2015	75.5	62.7	....	....	76.0	138.6	108.8	84.3
2016	62.1	58.6	....	....	75.0	138.8	103.9	79.1
2017	65.5	56.5	....	....	75.1	133.8	113.6	81.5
2018	74.8	58.3	....	....	73.5	132.4	107.3	88.5

Year	Potato[4] & dry edible bean[5]	Crop Production	Meat animal	Dairy product	Poultry & egg	Livestock Production	Agricultural Production	Parity ratio[6]
2009	88.3	85.7	73.8	63.7	93	69.9	80.6	92
2010	82.1	87.0	85.7	80.7	101.6	81.6	86.8	96
2011	....	100.0	100	100.0	100	100	100	100
2012	....	107.0	102.5	92.1	109	103.9	105	100
2013	....	105.7	108.5	99.8	123.3	106.8	107	100
2014	....	92.3	128.7	119.2	133.1	131.1	107.9	96
2015	....	87.0	113.4	85.2	127.8	119.8	99.2	90
2016	....	86.2	94.4	81.1	100.4	97.9	90.6	85
2017	....	86.8	99.9	87.8	107.5	100.5	93.3	87
2018	....	86.8	94.3	80.9	116.3	95.8	90.9	83

[1] These indexes are computed using the price estimates of averages for all classes and grades for individual commodities being sold in local farm markets. In computing the group indexes, prices of individual commodities have been compared with 2011 weighted average prices. The resulting ratios are seasonally weighted by average quantities sold for the most recent previous 5-year period. For example, 2013 indexes use quantities sold for the period 2007–11. [2] Included in Other crop index group beginning in 2010. [3] Fresh market for noncitrus, and fresh market and processing for citrus. [4] Included in Vegetable and melon index group beginning 2010. [5] Included in Food grain index group beginning 2010. [6] Ratio of Index of Prices Received (2011=100) to Index of Prices Paid by Farmers for Commodities & Services, Interest, Taxes, and Wage Rates (2007–11=100).

NASS, Environmental, Economics, and Demographics Branch, (202) 720–6146.

Table 9-32.—Prices paid by farmers: Index numbers, by groups of commodities, United States, 2009–2018

(2011=100)

Year	Production indexes[1]								
	Production all commodities	Feed	Livestock & Poultry	Seeds	Fertilizer	Agricultural chemicals	Fuels	Supplies & Repairs	Autos & trucks
2010	87.7	79.7	86.0	93.4	76.8	99.5	78.3	96.1	97.3
2011	100.0	100.0	100.0	100.0	100.0	100.0	100.0	100.0	100.0
2012	105.4	115.3	106.6	105.5	101.4	105.4	99.3	102.9	101.9
2013	107.4	117.5	108.3	110.2	96.7	108.5	98.4	103.8	103.4
2014	114.1	114.9	153.6	113.5	94.5	109.5	97.9	105.7	104.4
2015	112.0	106.1	147.1	124.6	87.2	106.5	63.5	105.8	105.5
2016	104.7	101.4	105.2	121.4	71.8	107.7	55.6	106.0	106.0
2017	104.5	94.8	107.0	119.9	66.2	104.0	63.2	107.9	106.0
2018	106.4	99.9	105.8	118.5	66.7	100.7	71.1	111.6	105.5
2019	84.8	82.5	74.6	90.1	83.8	102.5	63.1	94.3	94.9

Year	Production indexes[1] - continued				Interest	Taxes	Wage rates	Production, interest, taxes, & wage rates	Family living	Commodities, interest, taxes, & wage rates[2]
	Farm machinery	Building materials	Farm services	Rent						
2009	91.2	95.4	95.3	89.6	94.2	91.9	97.9	86.4	95.4	87.3
2010	94.3	96.6	98.1	92.6	91.6	95.9	98.9	89.0	96.9	90.0
2011	100.0	100.0	100.0	100.0	100.0	100.0	100.0	100.0	100.0	100.0
2012	105.3	102.6	101.8	101.7	99.3	101.0	102.9	104.8	102.1	104.4
2013	108.1	104.6	105.5	105.6	93.3	103.4	106.3	106.7	103.6	106.3
2014	112.0	106.9	109.1	114.2	93.1	116.3	108.0	113.1	105.3	112.0
2015	114.6	107.4	113.7	130.3	98.4	109.9	111.9	111.6	105.4	110.7
2016	115.4	107.6	115.6	123.8	103.9	114.7	115.9	105.8	106.7	105.9
2017	117.7	110.4	112.4	123.8	111.9	116.3	119.1	106.3	109.0	106.6
2018	120.0	116.1	114.5	119.5	117.6	117.1	126.3	108.7	111.7	109.1

[1] Annual price index computed using annual weights. Base period (2011=100) are now being published to one decimal digit. [2] Family Living component included.

NASS, Environmental, Economics, and Demographics Branch, (202) 720–6146.

Table 9-33.—Prices paid by farmers: Index numbers, by groups of commodities, United States, 2009–2018[1]

[1910–14=100]

Year	Family living	Production indexes							
		Production all commodities	Feed	Livestock & poultry	Seed	Fertilizer	Agricultural chemicals	Fuels	Supplies & repairs
2009	2,038	1,766	909	1,472	2,960	1,009	921	1,765	1,113
2010	2,071	1,825	879	1,698	3,070	925	893	2,191	1,134
2011	2,136	2,082	1,102	1,974	3,286	1,204	898	2,797	1,180
2012	2,181	2,193	1,270	2,104	3,468	1,221	946	2,779	1,214
2013	2,213	2,237	1,295	2,137	3,622	1,164	974	2,752	1,225
2014	2,249	2,376	1,266	3,032	3,729	1,138	983	2,739	1,247
2015	2,252	2,331	1,168	2,904	4,096	1,050	957	1,775	1,248
2016	2,280	2,179	1,118	2,076	3,990	864	967	1,556	1,251
2017	2,328	2,175	1,045	2,113	3,940	797	934	1,768	1,272
2018	2,385	2,214	1,100	2,089	3,893	803	904	1,988	1,316

Year	Production indexes—Continued				Interest	Taxes	Wage rates	Production, interest, taxes, & wage rates	Commodities, interest, taxes, & wage rates[2]
	Autos & trucks	Farm machinery	Building materials	Farm services & rent					
2009	2,917	5,575	2,218	1,976	3,436	5,453	7,007	2,435	2,364
2010	2,992	5,762	2,248	2,036	3,339	5,694	7,079	2,509	2,434
2011	3,074	6,111	2,326	2,123	3,646	5,935	7,161	2,820	2,706
2012	3,131	6,432	2,387	2,162	3,620	5,993	7,366	2,954	2,824
2013	3,179	6,609	2,434	2,241	3,402	6,137	7,607	3,010	2,877
2014	3,209	6,845	2,486	2,360	3,394	6,904	7,731	3,190	3,031
2015	3,243	7,003	2,497	2,554	3,587	6,520	8,015	3,146	2.996
2016	3,259	7,051	2,504	2,524	3,789	6,808	8,295	2,983	2,866
2017	3,259	7,190	2,569	2,486	4,082	6,904	8,529	2,996	2,885
2018	3,242	7,329	2,700	2,474	4,288	6,952	9,047	3,066	2,954

[1] Based on Consumer Price Index-Urban of Bureau of Labor Statistics. [2] The index known as the Parity Index is the Index of Prices Paid by Farmers for Commodities and Services, Interest, Taxes, and Wage Rates expressed on the 1910–14=100 base.

NASS, Environmental, Economics, and Demographics Branch, (202) 720–6146.

Table 9-34.—Grazing fees: Rates for cattle by selected States and regions, 2017–2018

State	Monthly lease rates for private non-irrigated grazing land[1]					
	Animal unit[2]		Cow-calf		Per head	
	2017	2018	2017	2018	2017	2018
	Dollars per month	*Dollars per month*	*Dollars per month*	*Dollars per month*	*Dollars per month*	*Dollars per month*
Arizona	9.50	10.00	(S)	(S)	(S)	(S)
California	20.60	22.40	28.00	29.00	19.50	21.00
Colorado	19.00	19.50	23.00	23.00	18.00	18.50
Idaho	18.00	18.00	22.00	22.50	18.50	19.00
Kansas	21.00	21.00	27.00	27.00	24.50	22.00
Montana	24.50	24.50	27.00	26.00	24.00	24.50
Nebraska	39.80	46.00	45.00	52.00	39.00	35.00
Nevada	9.90	9.50	18.10	(S)	15.50	15.20
New Mexico	15.50	16.00	(S)	(S)	16.00	16.50
North Dakota	19.00	24.50	23.00	32.00	19.00	19.00
Oklahoma	12.50	12.50	(S)	(S)	11.50	13.00
Oregon	16.50	17.50	19.50	21.00	19.50	21.50
South Dakota	31.50	31.50	39.00	40.50	35.00	34.00
Texas	12.50	12.50	(S)	(S)	11.50	14.50
Utah	16.50	17.00	20.00	19.00	18.50	18.50
Washington	14.00	14.50	16.50	16.50	16.00	16.00
Wyoming	21.50	22.00	23.50	24.00	22.00	23.00
17-State[3]	20.20	21.30	23.70	25.20	20.60	21.00
16-State[4]	22.60	24.00	26.40	28.40	23.40	23.00
11-State[5]	19.30	19.70	22.80	22.80	19.80	20.50
9-State[6]	20.50	21.70	23.80	25.70	20.70	21.00

(S) Insufficient number of reports to establish an estimate. [1] The average rates are estimates (rates over $10.00 are rounded to the nearest dime) based on survey indications of monthly lease rates for private, non-irrigated grazing land from the January Cattle Survey. [2] Includes animal unit plus cow-calf rates. Cow-calf rate converted to animal unit (AUM) using (1 aum=cow-calf *0.833). [3] Seventeen Western States: All States listed. [4] Sixteen Western States: All States, except Texas. [5] Eleven Western States: Arizona, California, Colorado, Idaho, Montana, Nevada , New Mexico, Oregon, Utah, Washington and Wyoming. [6] Nine Great Plains States: Colorado, Kansas, Nebraska, New Mexico, North Dakota, Oklahoma, South Dakota, Texas and Wyoming.

NASS, Environmental, Economics, and Demographics Branch, (202) 720–6146.

Table 9-35.—Agricultural commodities: Support prices per unit, United States, 2015–2019[1]

Commodity	Unit	2015	2016	2017	2018	2019
		Dollars	*Dollars*	*Dollars*	*Dollars*	*Dollars*
Basic commodities:						
Corn:						
Target/reference price	Bushel	3.70	3.70	3.70	3.70	3.70
Loan rate	do	1.95	1.95	1.95	1.95	2.20
Cotton:						
American upland:						
Loan rate	do	52.00	52.00	49.49	52.00	52.00
Extra-long staple:						
Loan rate	do	79.77	79.77	79.77	79.77	95.00
Peanuts:						
Target/reference price	Short tons	535.00	535.00	535.00	535.00	535.00
Loan rate	do	355.00	355.00	355.00	355.00	355.00
Rice:						
Target/reference price[2]	Cwt	14.00	14.00	14.00	14.00	14.00
Loan rate	do	6.50	6.50	6.50	6.50	7.00
Wheat:						
Target/reference price	Bushel	5.50	5.50	5.50	5.50	5.50
Loan rate	do	2.94	2.94	2.94	2.94	3.38
Barley:						
Target/reference price	Bushel	4.95	4.95	4.95	4.95	4.95
Loan rate	do	1.95	1.95	1.95	1.95	2.50
Sorghum grain:						
Target/reference price	Cwt	7.05	7.05	7.05	7.05	7.05
Loan rate	do	3.48	3.48	3.48	3.48	2.20
Oats:						
Target/reference price	Bushel	2.40	2.40	2.40	2.40	2.40
Loan rate	do	1.39	1.39	1.39	1.39	2.00
Other oilseeds:[3]						
Target/reference price	Cwt	20.15	20.15	20.15	20.15	20.15
Loan rate	do	10.09	10.09	10.09	10.09	10.09
Soybeans:						
Target/reference price	Bushel	8.40	8.40	8.40	8.40	8.40
Loan rate	do	5.00	5.00	5.00	5.00	6.20
Dry Peas:						
Target/reference price	Cwt	11.00	11.00	11.00	11.00	11.00
Loan rate	do	5.40	5.40	5.40	5.40	6.15
Small chick peas:						
Target/reference price	Cwt	19.04	19.04	19.04	19.04	19.04
Loan rate	do	7.43	7.43	7.43	7.43	10.00
Large chick peas:						
Target/reference price	Cwt	21.54	21.54	21.54	21.54	21.54
Loan rate	do	11.28	11.28	11.28	11.28	14.00
Lentils:						
Target/reference price	do	19.97	19.97	19.97	19.97	19.97
Loan rate	do	11.28	11.28	11.28	11.28	13.00
Sugar, raw cane:						
Loan rate	Pound	0.188	0.188	0.188	0.188	0.1975
Sugar, refined beet:						
Loan rate	do	0.241	0.241	0.241	0.241	0.2538
Honey, extracted:						
Loan rate	Pound	0.69	0.69	0.69	0.69	0.69
Mohair:						
Loan rate	do	4.20	4.20	4.20	4.20	4.20
Wool, graded:						
Loan rate	Pound	1.15	1.15	1.15	1.15	1.15
Wool, nongraded:						
Loan rate	Pound	0.40	0.40	0.40	0.40	0.40

[1] National averages during the marketing years for the individual crops. [2] Target and reference price shown is for long grain and medium (including short) grain rice. The reference price for temporate japonica rice is $16.10 per Cwt beginning with crop year 2014 and $17.30 per Cwt beginning with crop year 2019. The loan rate for temperate japonica is the same as for other types of rice, at 7.00 per Cwt. [3] Other oilseeds are flaxseed, sunflower seed (oil and other types), safflower, rapeseed, canola, mustard seed, crambe, and sesame seed.
FPAC-BC, Commodity Analysis Branch.

Table 9-36.—Farm income: Cash receipts by commodity groups and selected commodities, United States, 2014–2018[1]

Commodity	2014	2015	2016	2017	2018
	Thousand dollars				
All commodities	423,970,804	377,431,136	358,481,892	370,427,404	372,741,074
Animals and products	212,290,239	189,515,589	162,730,663	175,559,718	176,529,725
Cattle and calves	81,076,720	78,252,807	63,691,327	66,936,726	67,105,197
Hogs	26,489,394	20,552,958	19,037,752	21,038,034	21,098,058
Sheep and lambs	(NA)	(NA)	(NA)	(NA)	(NA)
Dairy products	49,351,199	35,716,849	34,546,316	37,940,662	35,244,314
Broilers	32,728,234	28,716,398	25,935,852	30,232,203	31,746,230
Farm chickens	96,840	104,828	87,949	46,999	49,364
Chicken eggs	10,342,687	13,762,519	6,591,359	7,635,001	10,586,262
Turkeys	5,304,501	5,707,928	6,184,247	4,873,677	3,875,131
Miscellaneous animals and products	6,900,663	6,701,302	6,655,861	6,856,416	6,825,169
Crops	211,680,565	187,915,547	195,751,229	194,867,686	196,211,349
Food grains	16,058,149	12,296,220	11,288,344	11,201,209	12,149,091
Feed crops	65,888,944	56,930,107	55,443,315	53,920,441	57,687,345
Cotton	7,111,320	4,756,100	5,496,889	7,573,587	7,821,649
Tobacco	1,728,991	1,606,619	1,337,542	1,378,695	1,246,889
Oil crops	42,624,290	35,518,959	44,042,747	41,094,011	39,609,416
Vegetables	18,951,858	20,358,992	19,542,550	20,494,457	18,539,199
Fruits/nuts	32,248,510	28,447,492	29,698,085	30,588,949	29,030,320
All other crops	27,068,502	28,001,057	28,901,756	28,616,339	30,127,440

Data as of February 5, 2020. (NA) Not available [1] USDA estimates and publishes individual cash receipt values only for major commodities and major producing States. The U.S. receipts for individual commodities, computed as the sum of the reported States, may understate the value of sales for some commodities, with the balance included in the appropriate category labeled "other" or "miscellaneous". The degree of underestimation in some of the minor commodities can be substantial.

ERS, Farm Income Team, (202) 694–5344. FarmIncomeTeam@ers.usda.gov. http://www.ers.usda.gov/data-products/farm-income-and-wealth-statistics.aspx.

Table 9-37.—Farm income: United States, 2014–2018

Item	2014	2015	2016	2017	2018
	Thousand dollars				
Total gross farm income	483,287,883	440,793,623	412,252,228	425,410,799	427,588,978
Value of production	473,521,038	429,989,137	399,272,552	413,879,188	413,919,968
Crops	206,311,808	184,329,250	189,302,127	187,926,642	188,574,697
Livestock and product	214,340,139	194,143,948	165,429,595	176,896,045	177,519,121
Services and forestry	52,869,092	51,515,939	44,540,830	49,056,501	47,826,150
Direct government payments	9,766,845	10,804,486	12,979,677	11,531,611	13,669,010
Total production expenses[1]	391,049,856	359,207,751	349,989,196	350,350,914	343,812,385
Net farm income	92,238,027	81,585,872	62,263,032	75,059,885	83,776,593
Gross cash income	470,303,009	422,611,802	399,352,723	413,164,535	415,534,849
Cash expenses	338,997,507	315,828,783	303,783,582	311,891,580	311,309,474
Net cash income	131,305,503	106,783,019	95,569,141	101,272,955	104,225,375

Data as of February 5, 2020. [1] Includes expenses associated with operator dwellings.

ERS, Farm Income Team, (202) 694–5344. FarmIncomeTeam@ers.usda.gov. http://www.ers.usda.gov/data-products/farm-income-and-wealth-statistics.aspx.

Table 9-38.—Expenses: Farm production expenses, United States, 2015–2018

Item	2015	2016	2017	2018
	Thousand dollars			
Total production expenses [1]	359,207,751	349,989,196	350,350,914	343,812,385
Feed purchased	58,538,814	55,636,890	54,538,086	53,837,596
Livestock and poultry purchased	30,277,335	22,060,469	27,413,658	29,069,564
Seed purchased	21,323,225	21,823,770	22,515,616	21,915,200
Fertilizer and lime	25,544,606	23,541,108	22,032,717	23,234,502
Pesticides	14,629,651	15,230,869	15,716,091	15,415,784
Fuel and oil	13,166,472	12,155,180	12,761,072	13,187,914
Electricity	5,722,547	5,585,083	5,805,753	6,052,989
Other [2]	66,511,167	65,592,758	67,236,565	67,274,025
Interest [1]	16,382,490	17,337,685	18,567,706	20,637,498
Contract and hired labor expenses	32,102,649	34,425,216	36,266,282	34,148,554
Net rent to landlords [3]	20,078,115	19,470,908	17,640,729	15,466,212
Capital consumption [1]	41,413,697	44,498,283	36,382,881	30,015,271
Property taxes [1]	13,516,985	12,630,978	13,473,759	13,557,276

[1] Includes expenses associated with operator dwellings. [2] Includes repair and maintenance, machine hire and custom work, marketing, storage and transportation, insurance premiums, and miscellaneous other expenses. [3] Data includes landlord capital consumption.

ERS, Farm Income Team, (202) 694-5344. FarmIncomeTeam@ers.usda.gov. http://www.ers.usda.gov/data-products/farm-income-and-wealth-statistics.aspx. Data as of February 5, 2020.

Table 9-39.—Principal farm operator household finances, United States, 2016–2019

Item	2016	2017	2018	2019 [1]
Number of family farms	2,027,269	1,989,574	1,979,368	1,979,368
	Income, median dollars per household			
Farm income	(940)	(1,035)	(1,735)	(1,383)
Off-farm income	66,468	67,500	65,841	67,314
Earned income	40,000	43,225	37,500	38,537
Unearned income	24,902	19,000	20,404	20,778
Household income	76,250	74,707	72,481	76,810
U.S. household income [2]	59,039	61,372	63,179	(NA)
	Income, average dollars per household			
Farm income	24,731	21,842	18,425	24,700
Off-farm income	93,187	89,747	93,786	96,012
Earned income	65,680	61,360	65,596	67,110
Unearned income	27,506	28,387	28,190	28,892
Household income	117,918	111,589	112,210	120,712
U.S. household income [2]	83,143	86,220	90,021	(NA)

(NA) Not available. [1] Forecast. [2] Estimates of U.S. Household Income are produced by the U.S. Census Bureau, Current Population Reports, p60-263, *Income and Poverty in the United States: 2018 (and earlier editions)*.

ERS, Farm Economy Branch, farmincometeam@usda.gov. Source: USDA, Economic Research Service and National Agricultural Statistics Service, 2016-2018 Agricultural Resource Management Survey. Data as of February 5, 2020.

CHAPTER X

INSURANCE, CREDIT, AND COOPERATIVES

The statistics in this chapter deal with insurance, agricultural credit and farm cooperatives. Some of the series were developed in connection with research activities of the Department, while others, such as data from agricultural credit agencies, are primarily records of operations.

Table 10-1.—Crop losses: Average percentage of indemnities attributed to specific hazards, by crops, 1948–2019

Crop	Year	Drought heat (excess)	Hail	Precip. (excess poor drainage)	Frost freeze, (other cold damage)	Flood	Cyclone, tornado, wind, hot wind	Insects	Disease	Decline in price	Other
		Percent									
Adj. gross revenue	2004-2014	9	10	9	22	0	2	0	0	48	0
Adj. gross revenue-lite	2004-2014	8	10	10	31	1	1	0	1	39	0
Alfalfa seed	2002-2019	35	8	18	17	0	15	6	0	0	0
All other citrus trees	2001-2018	0	0	4	9	0	25	0	0	0	63
All other grapefruit	2003-2009	0	0	0	11	0	89	0	0	0	0
Almonds	1981-2019	8	3	49	35	0	4	0	0	0	0
Annual Forage	2014-2019	0	0	0	0	0	0	0	0	0	0
Apiculture	2009-2019	0	0	0	0	0	0	0	0	0	0
Apples	1963-2019	7	28	6	55	0	2	0	0	0	1
Avocado trees	1996-2018	0	0	6	1	0	94	0	0	0	0
Avocados	1998-2019	52	0	1	24	0	16	0	0	1	6
Banana	2012-2013	100	0	0	0	0	0	0	0	0	0
Barley	1956-2019	41	16	31	5	0	2	2	2	0	0
Blueberries	1995-2019	5	4	11	70	0	4	1	1	0	4
Buckwheat	2010-2019	38	30	21	9	0	2	0	0	0	0
Burley tobacco	1997-2019	37	3	46	2	6	2	0	3	0	1
Cabbage	1999-2019	21	1	40	24	1	5	3	3	0	2
Camelina	2012-2015	100	0	0	0	0	0	0	0	0	0
Canning beans	1988-1997	44	5	26	13	0	3	1	6	0	1
Canning peaches	1986-1987	4	0	92	0	0	0	0	0	0	4
Canola	1995-2019	22	9	53	11	0	3	1	1	1	0
Carambola trees	2001-2018	0	0	17	0	0	83	0	0	0	0
Cherries	1963-2019	14	3	38	33	0	2	0	0	8	0
Chile peppers	2001-2016	1	26	11	19	6	22	9	5	0	1
Cigar:											
binder tobacco	1997-2019	11	18	26	3	0	2	0	39	0	1
filler tobacco	1998-2019	88	0	9	0	0	0	0	3	0	0
wrapper tobacco	1997-2018	0	0	44	1	0	0	0	56	0	0
Citrus	1952-1997	2	1	1	94	0	2	0	0	0	0
Citrus I	1998-2012	0	0	0	6	0	94	0	0	0	0
Citrus II	2000-2013	0	0	0	25	0	74	0	0	0	0
Citrus III	2005-2013	0	0	0	12	0	88	0	0	0	0
Citrus IV	1998-2011	0	6	0	6	0	88	0	0	0	0
Citrus V	1999-2013	0	4	0	35	0	61	0	0	0	0
Citrus VI	2005-2006	0	0	0	0	0	100	0	0	0	0
Citrus VII	1998-2013	0	3	0	14	0	83	0	0	0	0
Citrus VIII	2009-2012	0	13	0	87	0	0	0	0	0	0
Citrus tree	1990-1997	0	0	0	100	0	0	0	0	0	0
Citrus trees	1984-1986	0	0	0	100	0	0	0	0	0	0
Citrus trees I	2008-2010	0	0	66	0	0	34	0	0	0	0
Citrus trees II	2008-2010	0	0	100	0	0	0	0	0	0	0
Citrus trees III	2010	0	0	100	0	0	0	0	0	0	0
Citrus trees IV	2004-2010	0	0	100	0	0	0	0	0	0	0
Citrus trees V	2010	0	0	100	0	0	0	0	0	0	0
Clams	2001-2019	0	0	0	26	0	8	0	2	0	64
Clary sage	2016-2019	5	1	75	3	0	16	0	0	0	0
Coffee	2009-2019	45	0	13	0	0	17	4	0	0	21
Corn	1948-2019	47	5	30	3	2	2	0	1	9	0
Cotton	1948-2019	53	12	14	4	1	13	1	0	2	0
Cotton ex long staple	1984-2019	81	3	5	7	1	2	1	0	0	0
Crambe	1999-2003	31	8	35	10	0	11	0	5	0	0
Cranberries	1984-2019	14	16	19	39	2	2	3	1	0	5
Cucumbers	2014-2019	11	2	79	4	0	4	0	1	0	0
Cultivated wild rice	1999-2019	42	10	8	8	1	15	1	1	0	14
Dark air tobacco	1997-2019	14	2	71	0	2	3	0	6	0	2
Dry beans	1948-2019	16	20	45	13	0	2	0	2	1	0
Dry peas	1963-2019	45	23	23	4	0	1	0	1	3	0

See note(s) at end of table.

Table 10-1.—Crop losses: Average percentage of indemnities attributed to specific hazards, by crops, 1948–2019—Continued

Crop	Year	Drought heat (excess)	Hail	Precip. (excess poor drainage)	Frost freeze, (other cold damage)	Flood	Cyclone, tornado, wind, hot wind	Insects	Disease	Decline in price	Other
		Percent									
Early & midseason oranges	1998-2017	0	7	23	37	0	32	0	0	0	0
Figs	1988-2019	22	0	41	35	0	2	0	0	0	0
Fire cured tobacco	1997-2019	14	6	58	2	5	5	0	4	0	6
Flax	1948-2019	38	8	43	8	0	2	1	1	0	0
Flue cured tobacco	1997-2019	30	4	30	2	0	20	0	13	0	0
Forage production	1979-2019	67	2	7	22	0	0	1	0	0	0
Forage seeding	1978-2019	26	0	20	51	1	2	0	0	0	0
Fresh:											
Apricots	1997-2019	8	11	26	52	0	3	0	0	0	0
Freestone peaches	1997-2019	13	18	20	46	0	2	0	0	0	0
Market beans	2001-2019	3	0	68	13	0	9	0	7	0	0
Market sweet corn	1985-2019	12	2	34	27	0	17	3	1	0	2
Market tomatoes	1984-2019	7	4	47	27	0	8	1	5	0	0
Nectarines	1997-2019	7	27	23	42	0	1	0	0	0	0
Plum	1990-1997	1	32	41	25	0	0	0	0	0	0
Grain sorghum	1959-2019	74	3	11	4	1	4	1	0	2	0
Grapefruit	1997-2019	6	1	4	10	0	79	0	0	0	0
Grapefruit trees	2001-2018	0	0	7	5	0	14	0	0	0	74
Grapes	1967-2019	21	5	15	53	0	2	0	0	0	4
Grass Seed	2012-2019	54	2	42	2	0	0	0	0	0	0
Green peas	1962-2019	44	4	39	9	0	2	0	1	0	0
Hybrid corn seed	1983-2019	57	5	21	2	2	11	0	1	0	0
Hybrid seed rice	2016-2019	76	0	24	0	0	0	0	0	0	0
Hybrid sorghum seed	1988-2019	25	20	8	18	0	28	0	0	0	0
Hybrid sweet corn seed	2018-2019	64	0	0	33	0	3	0	0	0	0
Income protection corn	1996-1996	3	0	93	3	0	0	0	0	0	0
Income protection cotton	1996-1996	96	0	4	0	0	0	0	0	0	0
Income protection wheat	1996-1996	9	0	90	0	1	0	0	0	0	0
Late oranges	1998-2017	0	11	24	24	0	41	0	0	0	0
Lemon trees	2005-2018	0	0	0	0	0	100	0	0	0	0
Lemons	1997-2019	17	2	2	75	0	4	0	0	0	0
Lime trees	1998-2005	0	0	0	0	0	0	0	0	0	100
Macadamia nuts	1996-2019	63	0	7	7	0	10	5	0	0	7
Macadamia trees	2005-2012	0	0	0	0	0	82	0	0	0	18
Mandarins	1997-2014	17	2	1	77	0	4	0	0	0	0
Mandarins/ tangerines	2015-2019	54	2	5	30	0	9	0	0	0	0
Mango trees	1997-2018	0	0	8	2	0	90	0	0	0	0
Maryland tobacco	1997-2019	68	9	6	4	0	6	0	7	0	0
Millet	1996-2019	64	20	12	2	0	1	0	0	0	0
Minneola tangelos	1998-2014	11	0	5	80	0	3	0	0	0	0
Mint	2001-2019	35	4	24	31	1	2	1	2	0	0
Mustard	1999-2019	50	20	21	6	0	3	1	0	0	0
Navel oranges	1998-2014	19	2	2	76	0	1	0	0	1	0
Nursery (container)	1987-1999	9	1	18	19	11	21	8	14	0	0
Nursery (fg&c)	2001-2019	1	6	4	12	4	70	3	1	0	0
Oats	1956-2019	56	10	25	5	0	2	1	1	0	0
Olives	2012-2019	23	2	11	58	0	5	0	0	0	0
Onions	1988-2019	21	7	45	10	1	2	0	13	0	0
Orange trees	1996-2018	0	0	6	5	0	31	0	0	0	58
Oranges	1958-2019	16	1	3	18	0	63	0	0	0	0
Orlando tangelos	1998-2012	0	0	0	100	0	0	0	0	0	0
Papaya	2007-2018	0	0	16	0	0	10	4	45	0	25
Papaya tree	2014-2018	0	0	20	3	0	24	0	22	0	31
Pastures/Range-land forage	2007-2019	0	0	0	0	0	0	0	0	0	0
Peaches	1957-2019	2	12	2	79	0	0	0	0	0	4
Peanuts	1962-2019	66	1	20	3	0	4	0	5	0	1
Pears	1989-2019	18	22	12	44	0	2	0	1	0	0
Pecans	1998-2019	19	5	14	21	0	37	0	1	2	0
Peppers	1984-2019	1	4	62	20	0	11	0	2	0	0
Pistachios	2012-2019	78	1	15	5	0	2	0	0	0	0
Plums	1998-2019	14	23	19	41	0	3	0	0	0	0
Popcorn	1984-2019	38	20	26	6	2	3	0	1	3	0
Potatoes	1962-2019	24	5	42	16	1	2	0	10	0	0

See note(s) at end of table.

Table 10-1.—Crop losses: Average percentage of indemnities attributed to specific hazards, by crops, 1948–2019—Continued

Crop	Year	Drought heat (excess)	Hail	Precip. (excess poor drainage)	Frost freeze, (other cold damage)	Flood	Cyclone, tornado, wind, hot wind	Insects	Disease	Decline in price	Other
		Percent									
Prevented planting endorse	1990-1994	31	0	11	5	53	0	0	0	0	0
Prevented planting	1982-1985	0	0	97	0	3	0	0	0	0	0
Prevented planting endorse	1986	0	0	24	0	76	0	0	0	0	0
Processing:											
Apricots	1997-2019	11	5	35	45	0	4	0	0	0	0
Beans	1998-2019	43	7	41	5	0	2	0	2	0	0
Cling peaches	1997-2019	19	13	32	34	0	2	0	0	0	0
Cucumbers	2001-2005	34	3	49	3	0	1	2	6	0	0
Freestone	1998-2019	19	6	30	45	0	1	0	0	0	0
Prunes	1986-2019	38	2	32	19	0	8	0	0	0	0
Pumpkins	2009-2019	10	0	57	32	0	0	0	1	1	0
Raisins	1961-2018	0	0	100	0	0	0	0	0	0	0
Rangeland	1999-2008	0	0	0	0	0	0	0	0	0	100
Raspberry and blackberry	2002-2006	10	0	0	62	0	28	0	0	0	0
Revenue coverage corn	1996-1996	5	35	47	4	7	1	0	0	0	0
Revenue coverage soybeans	1996-1996	7	22	51	5	12	0	0	2	0	0
Rice	1960-2019	22	0	60	3	4	6	0	2	3	0
Rio red & star ruby	1998-2017	0	5	31	33	0	30	0	0	0	0
Ruby red grapefruit	1998-2017	0	12	36	17	0	35	0	0	0	0
Rye	1980-2019	34	13	33	17	0	1	0	0	0	0
Safflower	1964-2019	54	5	18	13	0	7	2	2	0	0
Sesame	2011-2019	53	2	36	3	1	5	0	0	0	1
Silage sorghum	2005-2019	75	7	2	3	0	12	0	0	0	0
Soybeans	1955-2019	40	6	37	4	3	1	0	0	8	0
Special citrus	1992-1994	7	13	0	80	0	0	0	0	0	0
Stonefruit	1988-1996	3	12	59	19	0	2	0	0	0	4
Strawberries	2001-2015	22	1	33	24	0	0	3	17	0	0
Sugar beets	1965-2019	10	4	49	25	1	5	1	6	0	0
Sugarcane	1967-2019	26	0	17	37	1	8	3	8	0	1
Sunflowers	1976-2019	25	8	49	8	0	3	1	3	1	2
Sweet corn	1978-2019	47	2	29	16	0	4	0	1	0	1
Sweet oranges	1998-2014	20	0	5	72	0	4	0	0	0	0
Sweet potatoes	2011-2019	1	0	99	0	0	0	0	0	0	0
Sweet potatoes	1998-2009	36	0	45	0	0	15	3	0	0	0
Table grapes	1984-2019	41	7	28	22	0	1	0	1	0	0
Tangelos	1997-2019	31	2	0	34	0	20	0	0	0	0
Tangors	2014-2019	0	0	0	1	0	99	0	0	0	0
Tobacco	1948-1996	32	10	32	2	1	11	0	11	0	1
Tomatoes	1963-2019	34	6	38	9	1	1	3	8	0	0
Triticale	2018-2019	24	15	5	53	0	3	0	0	0	0
Tung Nuts	1965-1970	0	0	0	100	0	0	0	0	0	0
Valencia oranges	1998-2014	18	2	2	74	0	3	0	0	0	0
Walnuts	1984-2019	27	6	33	20	1	4	0	0	0	0
Watermelons	1999-1999	22	2	11	5	0	7	0	48	0	6
Wheat	1948-2019	43	12	23	13	0	3	0	2	3	0
Whole Farm Revenue Protection	2015-2019	19	7	18	13	1	5	0	1	33	0
Winter squash	1999-2005	35	4	54	1	5	0	0	0	0	2

GRP crops do not have any specific cause of loss.
RMA, Requirements, Analysis and Validation Branch, (816) 926–7910.

Table 10-2.—Crop insurance programs: Coverage, amount of premiums and indemnities, by crops, United States, 2017–2019

Commodity and year	Coverage				Amount of premium	Indemnities		
	County programs	Insured units	Area insured	Maximum insured production		Number	Area in-demnified	Amount
	Number	*Number*	*1,000 acres*	*1,000 dollars*	*1,000 dollars*		*1,000 acres*	*1,000 dollars*
Alfalfa seed:								
2017	32	711	52	76,116	5,126	312	18	17,394
2018	35	659	43	54,257	3,969	273	12	8,672
2019	35	399	25	33,697	2,124	17	2	469
All other citrus trees:								
2017	28	292	0	36,871	523	1	0	2
2018	28	231	0	36,047	488	45	0	1,871
2019	28	228	0	36,777	498	0	0	0
All other grapefruit:								
2017	3	0	0	0	0	0	0	0
Almonds:								
2017	32	6,424	757	2,577,514	95,471	623	44	36,404
2018	32	6,729	787	2,132,999	64,965	1,049	76	51,712
2019	32	7,252	837	2,148,677	61,947	658	36	20,406
Annual Forage:								
2017	744	2,968	481	134,131	33,843	1,455	0	41,000
2018	744	3,963	646	151,485	37,106	2,899	0	65,037
2019	744	4,545	679	171,425	42,594	2,207	0	28,907
Apiculture:								
2017	2,059	9,901	0	115,519	25,870	5,673	0	29,928
2018	3,069	7,706	0	166,403	35,815	4,187	0	30,628
2019	3,069	9,986	0	223,377	49,371	3,650	0	20,761
Apples:								
2017	600	7,093	225	1,277,810	119,894	1,754	32	92,521
2018	600	7,434	229	1,402,830	123,343	1,446	23	75,356
2019	612	7,566	230	1,432,848	113,771	708	8	26,919
Avocado trees:								
2017	1	153	0	30,708	1,111	0	0	0
2018	1	129	0	24,734	806	113	0	7,877
2019	1	116	0	29,526	1,042	0	0	0
Avocados:								
2017	7	1,012	34	82,984	5,550	338	1	13,104
2018	16	1,026	33	80,362	5,092	179	4	5,064
2019	16	974	34	87,208	5,692	373	11	20,560
Banana tree:								
2017	4	0	0	0	0	0	0	0
2018	4	2	0	508	14	0	0	0
2019	4	2	0	537	15	0	0	0
Bananas:								
2017	4	2	0	764	4	0	0	0
2018	4	4	0	1,867	41	0	0	0
2019	4	4	0	1,870	41	0	0	0
Barley:								
2017	5,379	13,262	1,679	314,923	39,464	3,876	416	29,921
2018	5,379	12,029	1,586	295,185	36,160	2,175	237	20,102
2019	5,391	12,790	1,780	319,382	39,136	2,080	221	17,339
Blueberries:								
2017	169	1,287	67	222,476	13,781	619	18	40,308
2018	171	1,372	69	247,212	16,455	536	17	35,283
2019	171	1,557	70	289,466	22,169	370	10	21,187
Buckwheat:								
2017	32	86	9	1,399	262	10	1	77
2018	33	120	10	1,748	298	37	3	297
2019	33	121	11	1,813	317	13	1	73
Burley tobacco:								
2017	497	5,810	69	179,551	35,347	3,555	49	78,449
2018	497	4,370	51	132,360	23,121	2,651	35	54,792
2019	497	3,724	42	113,355	25,071	545	6	10,955
Cabbage:								
2017	31	341	15	32,068	2,210	62	2	1,797
2018	31	314	13	31,065	2,165	80	2	2,468
2019	31	342	13	33,590	2,498	44	1	1,481
Camelina:								
2017	52	2	0	16	3	0	0	0
2018	52	0	0	0	0	0	0	0
2019	52	0	0	0	0	0	0	0
Canola:								
2017	1,005	13,780	1,990	400,010	80,867	5,034	684	58,027
2018	1,005	12,304	1,891	421,000	84,009	2,486	320	28,481
2019	1,011	12,996	1,976	426,045	76,034	2,732	389	42,719

See footnote(s) at end of table.

Table 10-2.—Crop insurance programs: Coverage, amount of premiums and indemnities, by crops, United States, 2017–2019—Continued

Commodity and year	Coverage				Amount of premium	Indemnities		
	County programs	Insured units	Area insured	Maximum insured production		Number	Area indemnified	Amount
	Number	*Number*	*1,000 acres*	*1,000 dollars*	*1,000 dollars*		*1,000 acres*	*1,000 dollars*
Carambola trees:								
2017	2	10	0	1,834	65	0	0	0
2018	2	9	0	2,772	101	5	0	87
2019	2	10	0	3,232	113	0	0	0
Cattle:								
2017	20	38	0	17,432	683	3	0	11
2018	20	9	0	964	42	5	0	32
2019	20	17	0	1,314	42	4	0	24
Cherries:								
2017	64	3,428	84	487,051	56,097	970	22	43,691
2018	64	3,521	85	495,677	61,345	1,178	31	59,074
2019	64	3,531	86	505,657	66,393	1,253	29	82,508
Chile Peppers:								
2017	3	17	2	739	29	0	0	0
2018	3	11	1	457	14	0	0	0
2019	3	9	1	354	11	0	0	0
Cigar binder tobacco:								
2017	21	355	3	19,093	5,213	82	1	2,634
2018	21	389	3	25,294	7,162	70	0	1,923
2019	21	413	4	29,753	8,815	13	0	450
Cigar filler tobacco:								
2017	3	11	0	291	5	0	0	0
2018	3	11	0	331	5	1	0	4
2019	3	46	0	484	13	12	0	38
Cigar wrapper tobacco:								
2017	5	10	0	1,393	179	4	0	306
2018	5	13	0	1,387	175	3	0	24
2019	5	13	0	1,350	181	6	0	0
Clams:								
2017	9	66	0	14,062	367	0	0	0
2018	9	61	0	17,652	485	23	0	1,589
2019	9	116	0	17,936	476	6	0	231
Clary sage:								
2017	4	199	22	15,356	1,671	77	7	1,670
2018	4	154	13	8,172	883	26	1	216
2019	4	59	6	4,178	421	28	3	377
Coffee:								
2017	4	105	4	16,815	413	24	0	129
2018	4	125	4	19,699	430	40	1	1,048
2019	4	118	4	19,783	398	3	0	25
Coffee tree:								
2017	4	67	0	20,944	85	0	0	0
2018	4	79	0	23,621	98	0	0	0
2019	4	72	0	34,942	159	0	0	0
Corn:								
2017	17,232	677,695	78,907	39,436,068	3,454,064	137,707	12,531	1,267,248
2018	18,722	655,986	78,153	40,324,052	3,161,033	109,356	11,744	1,370,558
2019	18,728	718,627	86,914	43,646,616	3,746,041	193,371	18,658	3,601,555
Cotton:								
2017	5,922	153,430	11,740	4,954,984	935,615	42,954	6,487	651,346
2018	5,938	169,337	13,182	5,719,055	1,137,383	88,632	15,735	1,629,098
2019	5,938	142,332	13,096	5,473,628	956,110	33,018	6,363	777,437
Cotton exlong staple:								
2017	58	1,228	253	298,072	21,070	261	50	16,093
2018	58	1,048	247	208,039	15,424	209	51	22,056
2019	58	1,050	221	185,511	13,607	263	45	14,710
Cranberries:								
2017	30	642	32	111,701	3,236	86	3	3,432
2018	30	606	31	102,716	2,682	49	1	1,929
2019	30	597	31	133,213	3,282	65	3	3,991
Cucumbers:								
2017	72	405	27	18,755	1,588	81	4	1,226
2018	72	334	25	17,155	1,379	91	5	1,920
2019	72	395	26	18,757	1,609	40	3	633
Cultivated wild rice:								
2017	22	102	25	24,906	1,301	8	1	359
2018	22	81	22	14,196	811	9	1	175
2019	22	68	20	13,431	687	7	2	527

See footnote(s) at end of table.

Table 10-2.—Crop insurance programs: Coverage, amount of premiums and indemnities, by crops, United States, 2017–2019—Continued

Commodity and year	Coverage				Amount of premium	Indemnities		
	County programs	Insured units	Area insured	Maximum insured production		Number	Area indemnified	Amount
	Number	*Number*	*1,000 acres*	*1,000 dollars*	*1,000 dollars*		*1,000 acres*	*1,000 dollars*
Dairy cattle:								
2017	48	1,080	0	303,454	6,533	461	0	4,951
2018	48	1,370	0	319,088	6,131	609	0	5,409
2019	48	734	0	128,607	2,149	125	0	2,339
Dark air tobacco:								
2017	59	973	6	27,357	1,315	155	1	2,652
2018	59	1,094	9	38,553	1,861	265	4	9,802
2019	59	1,104	9	41,972	2,533	134	2	5,759
Dry beans:								
2017	938	14,302	1,345	526,639	74,036	3,138	248	42,090
2018	940	11,274	1,083	419,456	56,548	1,965	178	32,438
2019	982	11,598	1,192	435,467	64,260	3,512	332	65,990
Dry Peas:								
2016	725	16,381	2,400	444,950	75,608	2,829	399	37,907
2017	725	16,752	2,593	480,369	85,658	8,961	1,447	128,614
2018	725	14,172	2,258	443,844	78,944	4,045	721	75,559
Early and Midseason oranges:								
2016	3	181	4	3,590	143	28	0	96
2017	3	175	4	3,750	148	31	0	143
Fed cattle:								
2016	37	236	0	32,643	1,315	126	0	1,106
2017	37	221	0	23,053	993	20	0	74
2018	37	128	0	13,328	473	23	0	57
Feeder cattle:								
2016	38	1,852	0	159,594	6,154	1,345	0	8,685
2017	38	2,559	0	173,357	7,853	449	0	1,791
2018	38	1,385	0	110,163	4,036	596	0	2,260
Figs:								
2016	4	56	4	7,081	265	2	0	110
2017	4	70	5	8,220	254	2	0	130
2018	4	60	4	8,241	225	2	0	133
Fired cured tobacco:								
2016	63	1,315	12	67,518	3,345	627	6	18,237
2017	63	1,474	15	87,470	5,065	253	3	7,890
2018	63	1,519	16	88,939	5,262	205	3	6,833
Flax:								
2016	265	3,432	339	38,247	5,462	438	41	2,207
2017	265	2,658	261	31,799	4,720	1,460	145	7,852
2018	265	1,713	177	23,938	3,974	378	36	2,265
Flue cured tobacco:								
2016	291	11,750	210	666,273	56,540	4,465	86	131,728
2017	291	11,475	206	638,033	61,882	3,492	66	95,645
2018	291	11,686	205	657,775	69,268	5,319	119	215,500
Forage production:								
2016	1,404	17,893	2,447	446,137	38,824	4,923	846	36,320
2017	1,404	15,935	2,222	277,277	25,828	6,969	1,112	44,962
2018	1,404	14,905	2,108	261,146	25,916	1,838	174	9,668
Forage seeding:								
2016	589	3,743	167	28,623	3,871	1,515	62	6,876
2017	590	3,068	151	25,507	3,238	1,065	52	5,181
2018	590	3,556	176	31,942	3,779	100	8	842
Fresh apricots:								
2016	29	136	3	10,645	1,395	13	0	369
2017	29	130	3	12,292	1,654	43	1	1,899
2018	29	125	3	11,484	1,378	38	1	1,620
Fresh freestone peaches:								
2016	25	709	17	58,519	1,484	47	0	445
2017	25	695	19	68,755	1,625	96	1	1,521
2018	25	713	19	79,585	2,152	76	1	1,200
Fresh market beans:								
2016	15	27	4	2,192	193	16	2	538
2017	15	26	5	3,441	378	4	1	151
2018	15	26	6	4,117	494	10	3	440
Fresh market sweet corn:								
2016	230	688	48	48,107	3,513	108	4	2,513
2017	230	622	49	45,647	3,374	86	4	2,988
2018	230	609	47	45,411	3,236	119	4	2,582
Fresh market tomatoes:								
2016	57	521	33	122,698	13,060	173	5	12,273
2017	57	455	31	120,434	12,636	151	4	12,711
2018	59	408	29	103,266	10,490	184	4	15,134

See footnote(s) at end of table.

Table 10-2.—Crop insurance programs: Coverage, amount of premiums and indemnities, by crops, United States, 2017–2019—Continued

Commodity and year	Coverage				Amount of premium	Indemnities		
	County programs	Insured units	Area insured	Maximum insured production		Number	Area indemnified	Amount
	Number	*Number*	*1,000 acres*	*1,000 dollars*	*1,000 dollars*		*1,000 acres*	*1,000 dollars*
Fresh nectarines:								
2017	24	705	15	58,196	3,322	132	2	2,015
2018	24	686	14	59,278	3,498	116	2	3,026
2019	24	702	14	66,307	3,783	84	1	1,429
Grain sorghum:								
2017	7,074	54,432	4,141	679,196	150,570	9,965	812	49,723
2018	7,077	54,688	4,191	713,915	151,795	14,442	1,332	87,503
2019	7,077	52,552	4,076	713,655	155,099	9,659	790	53,996
Grapefruit:								
2017	53	668	37	54,735	2,383	147	0	5,219
2018	56	897	45	68,091	4,798	363	28	26,315
2019	56	895	44	74,058	6,628	97	3	1,713
Grapefruit trees:								
2017	31	1,019	0	163,430	3,972	0	0	0
2018	31	960	0	166,336	4,207	47	0	3,573
2019	31	913	0	190,360	4,830	0	0	0
Grapes:								
2017	200	16,695	573	1,507,208	49,831	2,179	49	43,833
2018	226	16,890	558	1,571,585	51,202	1,201	23	25,148
2019	226	17,354	560	1,722,760	55,872	1,035	20	33,937
Grass seed:								
2017	20	106	29	7,134	620	12	1	208
2018	20	96	32	8,862	628	14	4	460
2019	20	113	44	12,403	845	4	0	130
Green peas:								
2017	321	1,624	117	56,858	6,490	402	31	7,723
2018	321	1,570	118	55,071	6,642	729	51	10,406
2019	303	1,699	122	55,922	7,395	625	42	8,841
Hybrid corn seed:								
2017	462	5,769	382	300,169	17,751	243	15	2,601
2018	462	4,615	310	245,526	13,245	226	18	2,810
2019	462	5,029	331	258,157	13,745	141	9	2,840
Hybrid seed rice:								
2017	50	160	17	18,125	1,486	11	3	59
2018	50	246	19	26,058	2,335	83	10	5,591
2019	50	338	26	33,126	2,690	19	2	459
Hybrid sorghum seed:								
2017	52	346	25	9,057	804	46	3	684
2018	52	437	32	13,870	1,258	52	3	687
2019	52	444	35	15,211	1,377	37	4	500
Hybrid sweet corn seed:								
2017	15	0	0	0	0	0	0	0
2018	16	122	2	2,510	233	19	0	137
2019	16	127	3	4,572	389	1	0	68
Lamb:								
2017	28	88	0	18,223	842	79	0	3,347
2018	28	282	0	50,139	1,430	267	0	5,582
2019	28	85	0	9,740	235	7	0	31
Late oranges:								
2017	3	62	1	1,102	125	4	0	27
Lemon trees:								
2017	2	0	0	0	0	0	0	0
2018	3	8	0	1,297	29	3	0	410
2019	3	15	0	3,854	95	0	0	0
Lemons:								
2017	34	859	44	153,560	9,540	22	1	1,881
2018	34	861	43	161,178	11,541	45	3	2,176
2019	34	874	44	196,247	11,724	23	0	666
Lime trees:								
2017	5	5	0	927	17	0	0	0
2018	5	4	0	985	16	0	0	0
2019	5	5	0	1,026	14	0	0	0
Macadamia nuts:								
2017	3	39	12	17,289	220	8	0	818
2018	3	54	12	18,035	244	0	0	0
2019	3	51	11	20,718	385	29	4	1,715
Macadamia trees:								
2017	3	50	12	51,874	298	0	0	0
2018	3	53	12	52,808	308	0	0	0
2019	4	162	982	67,031	347	0	0	0
Mandarins/ Tangerines:								
2017	53	989	48	265,366	23,135	55	0	4,109
2018	53	1,044	50	302,843	24,517	184	7	11,093
2019	53	1,137	52	319,870	24,250	52	2	6,022

See footnote(s) at end of table.

Table 10-2.—Crop insurance programs: Coverage, amount of premiums and indemnities, by crops, United States, 2017–2019—Continued

Commodity and year	Coverage				Amount of premium	Indemnities		
	County programs	Insured units	Area insured	Maximum insured production		Number	Area indemnified	Amount
	Number	*Number*	*1,000 acres*	*1,000 dollars*	*1,000 dollars*		*1,000 acres*	*1,000 dollars*
Mango trees:								
2017	1	20	0	837	33	0	0	0
2018	1	20	0	876	32	14	0	217
2019	1	17	0	858	32	0	0	0
Maryland tobacco:								
2017	6	0	0	0	0	0	0	0
2018	6	0	0	0	0	0	0	0
2019	6	1	0	20	1	1	0	19
Milk:								
2019	50	9,373	0	5,872,319	95,073	278	0	5,513
Millet:								
2017	138	4,266	348	20,277	4,876	1,171	96	3,114
2018	138	4,019	329	21,884	5,499	1,217	103	3,766
2019	138	4,477	394	27,488	6,026	954	89	3,264
Mint:								
2017	48	270	19	16,947	856	67	3	1,211
2018	48	246	17	15,953	747	65	3	662
2019	48	222	17	14,607	765	52	2	550
Mustard:								
2017	75	318	63	6,083	1,683	154	26	1,418
2018	75	309	48	5,704	1,529	90	10	793
2019	75	308	54	6,870	1,539	88	20	1,518
Nursery (FG&C):								
2017	2,799	2,420	0	1,259,008	23,755	27	0	2,537
2018	2,799	2,468	0	1,402,807	26,316	547	0	97,245
2019	2,799	2,539	0	1,553,851	31,388	26	0	3,193
Oats:								
2017	2,805	8,500	436	42,135	7,554	3,390	194	12,899
2018	2,805	7,764	400	39,856	6,730	1,507	70	4,304
2019	2,805	7,955	430	45,016	7,700	2,064	93	6,230
Olives:								
2017	13	429	24	36,379	3,627	16	1	516
2018	17	379	23	36,689	3,535	271	14	17,084
2019	17	369	23	45,858	4,510	26	1	828
Onions:								
2017	176	1,708	101	218,824	39,813	688	24	32,301
2018	178	1,935	104	237,697	44,901	849	27	41,677
2019	178	1,428	86	209,519	25,834	270	9	15,347
Orange trees:								
2017	31	2,332	0	1,078,270	12,255	0	0	0
2018	62	1,994	0	1,122,148	11,910	214	0	26,655
2019	31	2,085	0	1,271,216	13,337	0	0	0
Oranges:								
2017	63	6,082	438	639,287	29,346	237	0	3,446
2018	66	6,385	415	581,035	26,795	1,818	182	76,788
2019	66	6,995	442	689,178	31,666	279	8	6,197
Oysters:								
2017	9	0	0	0	0	0	0	0
2018	9	0	0	0	0	0	0	0
2019	9	0	0	0	0	0	0	0
Papaya:								
2017	4	36	0	1,340	32	1	0	41
2018	4	19	0	859	22	8	0	187
2019	4	2	0	229	10	0	0	0
Papaya tree:								
2017	4	15	0	403	5	3	0	40
2018	4	8	0	347	4	2	0	63
2019	4	4	0	238	2	0	0	0
Pasture/Rangeland/Forage:								
2017	3,069	140,701	74,936	1,744,753	380,381	64,227	0	341,241
2018	3,069	159,751	98,289	2,378,024	520,182	64,869	0	500,039
2019	3,069	181,901	140,389	2,625,886	581,814	55,378	0	292,255
Peaches:								
2017	383	1,406	31	81,985	22,494	748	20	44,018
2018	383	1,411	32	82,433	24,273	426	12	18,629
2019	390	1,461	31	94,552	29,183	416	9	15,842
Peanuts:								
2017	2,139	27,993	1,645	859,863	71,577	4,989	256	60,384
2018	2,139	22,605	1,302	643,672	55,079	4,786	241	56,550
2019	2,139	23,055	1,327	706,008	60,100	5,070	253	65,761
Pears:								
2017	29	1,944	33	177,840	4,216	235	4	5,813
2018	29	1,960	33	194,705	4,299	128	4	6,406
2019	29	1,982	33	199,901	4,344	228	2	5,960
Pecan trees:								
2018	233	18	0	5,204	25	0	0	0
2019	233	21	0	7,430	27	0	0	0
Pecans:								
2017	138	1,823	163	286,170	16,313	191	15	6,104
2018	139	1,897	166	315,144	17,246	1,086	89	79,137
2019	139	1,929	169	320,243	17,573	259	15	13,479

See footnote(s) at end of table.

Table 10-2.—Crop insurance programs: Coverage, amount of premiums and indemnities, by crops, United States, 2017–2019—Continued

Commodity and year	Coverage				Amount of premium	Indemnities		
	County programs	Insured units	Area insured	Maximum insured production		Number	Area indemnified	Amount
	Number	*Number*	*1,000 acres*	*1,000 dollars*	*1,000 dollars*		*1,000 acres*	*1,000 dollars*
Peppers:								
2017	13	127	6	26,651	3,643	52	2	8,024
2018	13	123	5	19,960	2,834	50	2	6,810
2019	13	106	4	17,431	2,928	31	1	4,698
Pistachios:								
2017	24	806	146	377,099	20,628	138	26	13,404
2018	24	930	168	559,132	43,018	20	2	1,587
2019	24	970	177	549,767	45,798	144	23	28,816
Plums:								
2017	23	663	13	39,746	3,898	128	2	2,144
2018	23	615	12	40,769	3,960	97	1	1,662
2019	23	577	12	41,287	3,876	75	1	1,790
Popcorn:								
2017	3,297	1,963	200	124,903	8,763	366	34	3,894
2018	3,297	1,853	189	116,536	7,412	149	16	2,596
2019	3,300	1,837	197	121,011	8,431	360	32	10,001
Potatoes:								
2017	531	5,101	725	1,089,700	80,957	503	34	30,120
2018	531	5,070	739	1,123,089	85,521	1,032	73	71,894
2019	531	5,351	754	1,206,255	83,877	671	49	47,873
Processing apricots:								
2017	13	61	3	6,946	1,055	15	0	1,003
2018	13	53	3	5,895	840	25	1	1,513
2019	13	41	2	4,373	569	3	0	29
Processing beans:								
2017	258	1,394	88	47,272	4,533	240	11	3,655
2018	258	1,371	89	43,703	4,583	401	22	5,196
2019	258	1,447	89	45,345	4,824	290	16	3,326
Processing cling peaches:								
2017	10	835	14	59,892	2,344	75	1	1,370
2018	10	784	13	51,741	1,905	115	2	1,790
2019	10	735	11	45,875	1,756	46	1	728
Processing freestone:								
2017	8	97	2	11,516	277	7	0	293
2018	8	91	2	10,280	289	10	0	356
2019	8	89	2	8,000	282	1	0	16
Prunes:								
2017	28	722	40	109,723	23,759	123	7	7,561
2018	28	686	39	94,170	21,272	262	14	17,073
2019	28	640	37	85,507	20,381	115	6	8,010
Pumpkins:								
2017	22	201	10	6,675	462	68	4	1,291
2018	22	138	6	3,874	201	8	0	83
2019	22	165	8	5,269	449	63	2	1,003
Raisins:								
2017	7	1,828	0	96,395	3,061	662	0	3,158
2018	7	1,805	0	175,544	5,334	122	0	513
2019	7	236	0	17,356	294	0	0	0
Rice:								
2017	999	18,623	2,385	1,261,043	75,293	4,909	646	182,093
2018	1,089	21,318	2,550	1,664,522	87,492	3,689	472	82,653
2019	1,089	20,709	2,814	1,564,345	97,722	6,688	994	268,039
Rio Red & Star Ruby:								
2017	3	313	12	16,686	2,319	43	0	609
Ruby red grapefruit:								
2017	3	39	1	433	49	9	0	34
Rye:								
2017	89	406	36	2,948	511	150	12	730
2018	89	483	35	3,446	616	209	13	686
2019	97	672	54	6,837	1,217	238	13	1,176
Safflower:								
2017	164	594	108	10,710	1,731	173	25	1,622
2018	164	556	102	11,314	1,715	105	16	711
2019	164	584	86	7,820	1,359	167	23	1,519

See footnote(s) at end of table.

Table 10-2.—Crop insurance programs: Coverage, amount of premiums and indemnities, by crops, United States, 2017–2019—Continued

Commodity and year	Coverage				Amount of premium	Indemnities		
	County programs	Insured units	Area insured	Maximum insured production		Number	Area indemnified	Amount
	Number	*Number*	*1,000 acres*	*1,000 dollars*	*1,000 dollars*		*1,000 acres*	*1,000 dollars*
Sesame:								
2017	102	322	21	1,865	614	154	8	471
2018	102	710	58	6,215	1,830	345	25	2,121
2019	138	866	70	8,247	2,458	269	19	1,494
Silage Sorghum:								
2017	194	542	47	11,055	1,321	51	3	395
2018	194	626	58	14,577	1,741	102	11	1,403
2019	194	796	73	17,557	2,196	124	14	1,423
Soybeans:								
2017	14,265	700,986	79,882	28,412,875	2,556,484	125,741	11,206	766,516
2018	15,790	671,493	78,853	28,884,196	2,244,330	161,487	16,650	1,286,277
2019	15,818	647,449	71,399	24,603,865	1,880,887	180,844	15,893	1,737,081
Strawberries:								
2017	7	5	0	4,883	89	0	0	0
2018	7	3	0	4,345	206	0	0	0
2019	7	3	0	1,718	63	0	0	0
Sugar beets:								
2017	239	13,145	992	848,993	46,781	773	47	9,196
2018	239	13,001	982	944,362	49,201	2,124	158	47,690
2019	243	13,154	1,011	983,182	53,701	3,294	249	151,656
Sugarcane:								
2017	62	4,739	767	320,763	5,861	117	5	921
2018	62	4,831	789	357,470	6,717	165	8	1,671
2019	62	4,835	801	348,538	6,152	29	3	495
Sunflowers:								
2017	1,794	6,843	1,221	245,512	47,067	1,771	249	27,654
2018	1,806	5,786	1,146	216,862	42,885	1,425	249	22,148
2019	1,806	6,286	1,275	241,243	44,208	1,595	239	29,090
Sweet corn:								
2017	332	2,388	199	90,157	4,397	231	16	4,340
2018	332	2,345	198	86,002	4,225	412	28	5,383
2019	326	2,477	200	90,760	4,439	358	25	5,181
Sweet potatoes:								
2017	9	22	7	8,268	983	2	1	385
2018	9	20	7	6,334	638	3	0	978
2019	9	19	9	10,699	1,380	1	1	405
Swine:								
2017	85	190	0	22,732	1,144	41	0	296
2018	85	126	0	18,649	767	63	0	1,430
2019	85	85	0	16,273	920	46	0	1,205
Table grapes:								
2017	10	1,177	77	326,189	9,269	234	6	16,190
2018	10	1,212	77	360,317	11,310	197	6	17,811
2019	10	1,206	77	362,398	11,178	104	3	9,458
Tangelos:								
2017	49	382	8	20,811	1,586	36	0	626
2018	49	344	7	20,638	1,404	78	1	820
2019	49	336	7	21,721	1,368	12	0	502
Tangerine trees:								
2017	3	12	0	411	16	0	0	0
2018	3	13	0	381	14	0	0	0
2019	3	12	0	658	20	0	0	0
Tangors:								
2017	29	185	4	9,690	491	8	0	248
2018	29	138	3	7,139	357	105	3	4,919
2019	29	133	3	5,168	268	1	0	11
Tomatoes:								
2017	148	2,656	232	490,700	11,418	216	16	9,439
2018	148	2,694	240	512,868	10,854	102	8	4,165
2019	148	2,500	228	525,788	10,999	121	13	12,457
Triticale:								
2018	116	196	23	2,702	309	49	3	157
2019	135	285	30	3,529	361	54	5	348
Walnuts:								
2017	52	1,835	158	249,534	5,985	182	8	3,973
2018	52	1,884	169	303,864	6,036	113	4	3,045
2019	52	1,963	180	222,496	4,045	112	6	2,390
Wheat:								
2017	15,522	344,489	37,247	5,892,115	893,223	85,034	10,664	752,014
2018	15,672	337,418	38,712	6,906,618	997,826	86,841	9,159	573,754
2019	15,738	327,592	38,692	7,218,143	1,108,877	94,725	10,860	874,655
Whole Farm Revenue Protection:								
2017	3,140	2,729	0	2,829,150	142,167	831	0	159,610
2018	3,140	2,492	0	2,671,630	137,063	613	0	125,007
2019	3,140	2,118	0	2,319,039	132,695	80	0	2,659

RMA, Requirements, Analysis and Validation Branch, (816) 926–7910.

Table 10-3.—Farm real estate debt: Amount outstanding by lender, United States, Dec. 31, 2009–2018 [1]

Year	Farm Credit System	Farm Service Agency	Farmer Mac	Commercial banks [1]
	Billion dollars	*Billion dollars*	*Billion dollars*	*Billion dollars*
2009	69.1	2.6	2.1	44.2
2010	72.5	3.5	3.6	51.2
2011	75.3	3.3	3.8	52.9
2012	80.3	3.7	3.8	64.6
2013	85.3	3.7	4.5	68.9
2014	88.8	4.3	4.7	73.3
2015	96.7	4.9	4.8	79.2
2016	103.7	5.9	5.5	84.4
2017	107.2	6.0	6.2	88.4
2018	113.0	6.6	6.5	92.8

Year	Individuals and others [1]	Life insurance companies	Storage facility loans	Total farm mortgage debt
	Billion dollars	*Billion dollars*	*Billion dollars*	*Billion dollars*
2009	14.2	13.3	0.5	146.0
2010	10.2	12.4	0.6	154.1
2011	18.1	13.0	0.7	167.2
2012	8.7	11.5	0.7	173.4
2013	10.1	12.0	0.7	185.2
2014	12.5	12.4	0.8	196.8
2015	10.0	12.5	0.8	208.8
2016	12.5	13.2	0.7	226.0
2017	12.6	15.0	0.8	236.2
2018	9.9	15.9	0.8	245.7

Data as of February 5, 2020.
[1] Beginning with 2012 estimates, farm sector debt held by savings associations is reported with the commercial bank lender group instead of the individuals and others grouping.
ERS, Farm Farm Income Team, (202) 694–5586. FarmIncomeTeam@ers.usda.gov. http://www.ers.usda.gov/data-products/farm-income-and-wealth-statistics.aspx.

Table 10-4.—Nonreal estate farm debt: Amount outstanding, by lender, United States, Dec. 31, 2009–2018

Year	Commericial banks [1]	Farm Credit System	Farm Service Agency	Individuals and others [1]	Total nonreal estate debt
	Billion dollars	*Billion dollars*	*Billion dollars*	*Billion dollars*	*Billion dollars*
2009	57.2	39.0	3.3	22.9	122.4
2010	56.2	39.2	3.6	25.8	124.9
2011	59.2	41.1	3.5	23.5	127.3
2012	59.9	42.7	3.4	18.2	124.2
2013	63.7	44.0	2.8	19.6	130.2
2014	70.7	47.9	3.6	26.2	148.4
2015	73.2	48.3	3.7	22.8	148.0
2016	73.2	40.4	3.8	21.8	148.2
2017	73.3	51.1	4.0	25.8	154.2
2018	74.9	53.4	3.9	24.2	156.3

Data as of February 5, 2020.
[1] Beginning with 2012 estimates, farm sector debt held by savings associations is reported with the commercial bank lender group instead of the individuals and others grouping.
ERS, Farm Farm Income Team, (202) 694–5586. FarmIncomeTeam@ers.usda.gov. http://www.ers.usda.gov/data-products/farm-income-and-wealth-statistics.aspx.

Table 10-5.—Farm Service Agency: Credit assistance made to individuals, entities, and associations for farming purposes, and amount outstanding, United States and Territories, 2010–2019[1]

Year	Direct loans and loan guarantees				
	Farm ownership			Soil and water	Recreation
	Obligations (initial and subsequent)	Loans made	Outstanding Jan. 1	Outstanding Jan. 1	Outstanding Jan. 1
	Number	*1,000 dollars*	*1,000 dollars*	*1,000 dollars*	*1,000 dollars*
2010	8,837	2,313,902	10,875,039	10,364	4,632
2011	8,516	2,498,626	11,872,786	8,053	208
2012	7,088	2,029,778	12,498,221	6,585	191
2013	6,086	1,946,988	12,842,052	5,483	133
2014	10,106	3,012,450	13,768,000	4,617	102
2015	9,970	3,050,383	14,985,868	4,082	79
2016	10,712	3,489,028	16,560,650	3,579	64
2017	10,405	3,322,717	18,195,830	2,864	46
2018	10,667	3,264,634	19,753,319	2,333	45
2019	10,607	3,528,293	21,505,224	1,912	19

Year	Direct loans and loan guarantees					
	Operating			Emergency		
	Obligations (initial and subsequent)	Loans made	Outstanding Jan. 1	New borrowers	Loans made	Outstanding Jan. 1
	Number	*1,000 dollars*	*1,000 dollars*	*Number*	*1,000 dollars*	*1,000 dollars*
2010	27,337	2,934,097	7,047,105	340	35,598	661,950
2011	23,411	2,285,131	6,953,778	176	32,610	578,846
2012	24,667	2,103,112	6,594,239	309	31,436	537,640
2013	23,667	1,960,150	6,254,820	382	33,387	479,869
2014	26,862	2,201,420	6,214,490	177	18,106	428,304
2015	27,523	2,617,000	6,352,898	124	13,383	385,951
2016	28,562	2,832,984	6,778,399	376	42,725	379,094
2017	27,888	2,650,932	7,135,916	124	15,131	343,455
2018	23,935	2,198,126	7,119,181	96	12,713	313,088
2019	21,635	2,199,657	7,380,820	103	13,170	284,989

Year	Loans to associations			Economic opportunity individual loans	Economic emergency loans
	Indian tribe land acquisition	Grazing association	Irrigation, drainage, and soil conservation		
	Outstanding Jan. 1	Outstanding Jan. 1	Outstanding Jan. 1	Outstanding Jan. 1	Outstanding Jan. 1
	1,000 dollars				
2010	34,306	2,232	707	6	100,515
2011	29,539	1,848	605	6	85,915
2012	25,112	1,618	511	6	76,843
2013	24,246	1,014	468	6	65,040
2014	19,825	798	284	6	57,053
2015	15,590	673	227	6	49,517
2016	11,619	408	181	5	42,545
2017	10,461	365	152	4	39,216
2018	9,227	326	121	4	33,651
2019	7,450	256	91	0	29,180

[1] Includes loans made directly by FSA and those guaranteed by the Agency. Amounts of loans made represent new obligations (initial and subsequent) for the fiscal year displayed. Amounts outstanding are less principal repayments for loans made directly by the Agency.

FSA, Loan Making Division, (202) 720–3889.

Table 10-6.—Loans to farmers' cooperative organizations: Outstanding amounts held by the agricultural credit bank classified by type of loan, United States, Jan. 1, 2010-2019

Year	Operating capital loans	Facility loans
	1,000 dollars	*1,000 dollars*
2010	10,743,647	33,430,718
2011	10,871,732	35,413,410
2012	32,789,008	39,191,450
2013	32,449,687	41,153,688
2014	32,171,519	48,210,977
2015	35,316,639	53,723,941
2016	39,243,137	56,015,144
2017	35,681,814	63,583,691
2018	39,317,966	65,175,889
2019	33,662,950	75,191,303

FCA, Office of Information Technology, (703) 883–4260.

Table 10-7.—Farmers' marketing, farm supply, and related service cooperatives: Number, memberships, and business volume, United States, 2010–2019

Year [1]	Cooperatives [2]				Estimated memberships [4]			
	Marketing	Farm supply	Related service [3]	Total	Marketing	Farm supply	Related service [3]	Total
	Number				*1,000 members*			
2010	1,215	974	125	2,314	737	1,463	35	2,234
2011	1,222	935	128	2,285	846	1,398	36	2,279
2012	1,200	916	120	2,236	652	1,426	37	2,115
2013	1,195	871	120	2,186	655	1,284	37	1,977
2014	1,114	876	116	2,106	627	1,333	35	1,996
2015	1,079	874	94	2,047	591	1,296	34	1,921
2016	1,040	827	86	1,953	584	1,280	37	1,901
2017	1,010	777	84	1,871	604	1,251	35	1,890
2018	961	760	85	1,806	594	1,262	33	1,880
2019	931	759	89	1,779	677	1,184	38	1,900

Year [1]	Marketing volume		Farm supply volume		Service Receipts [7]	Total marketing and farm supply volume and service receipts	
	Gross [5]	Net [6]	Gross [5]	Net [6]		Gross [5]	Net [6]
	Billion dollars						
2010	103.031	95.756	63.842	47.118	4.930	171.803	147.805
2011	128.041	121.784	80.898	57.322	4.453	213.391	187.100
2012	140.900	133.200	92.200	64.700	4.700	237.800	202.600
2013	144.615	135.810	95.933	67.175	5.572	246.120	208.557
2014	147.731	138.340	92.624	65.638	6.315	246.670	210.293
2015	124.892	115.409	81.709	59.023	5.458	212.059	179.890
2016	114.587	108.603	71.048	51.589	5.440	191.075	165.632
2017	119.807	112.754	71.754	51.516	5.579	197.141	169.849
2018	126.333	118.962	71.728	53.634	5.753	203.814	178.349
2019	124.916	119.497	71.041	53.220	7.090	203.047	179.807

[1] Reports of cooperatives are included for their fiscal year ending in calendar year. [2] Includes independent local cooperatives, centralized cooperatives, federations of cooperatives, and cooperatives with mixed organizational structures. Cooperatives are classified according to their major activity. If, for example, more than 50 percent of a cooperative's business is derived from marketing activities, it is included as a marketing cooperative. [3] Includes cooperatives whose major activity is providing services related to marketing and farm supply activities. [4] Includes members (those entitled to vote for directors) but does not include nonvoting patrons. (Some duplication exists because some farmers belong to more than one cooperative.) [5] Estimated gross business includes all business reported between cooperatives, such as the wholesale business of farm supply cooperatives with other cooperatives or terminal market sales for local cooperatives. [6] Estimated net business represents the value at the first level at which cooperatives transact business for farmers, adjusted for duplication resulting from intercooperative business. [7] Services related to marketing or purchasing but not included in the volumes reported for those activities, plus other operating and non-operating income and losses and extraordinary items.

Rural Development, Cooperative Services Branch, (202) 720-7395.

Table 10-8.—Farmers' cooperatives: Business volume of marketing, farm supply, and related service cooperatives, United States, 2018–2019

Item	Gross business		Net business [1]	
	2018	2019	2018	2019
	Billion dollars			
Products marketed:				
Beans and peas (dry edible)	0.225	0.232	0.218	0.224
Cotton and cotton products	3.549	2.954	3.420	2.866
Dairy products	40.835	43.559	37.887	42.396
Fish	0.239	0.232	0.239	0.232
Fruits and vegetables	9.391	8.095	7.531	6.721
Grain and oilseeds [2]	51.318	49.704	50.211	48.444
Livestock and livestock products	3.990	3.835	3.990	3.835
Nuts	1.725	1.672	1.725	1.672
Poultry products	1.796	0.943	1.796	0.943
Rice	1.694	1.713	1.694	1.713
Sugar products	5.941	6.055	4.964	4.875
Tobacco	0.340	0.316	0.340	0.316
Wool and mohair	0.012	0.012	0.012	0.012
Other products [3]	5.276	5.594	4.933	5.247
Total farm products	126.333	124.916	118.962	119.497
Supplies purchased:				
Crop protectants	8.941	8.119	6.208	5.599
Feed	11.859	11.759	9.905	9.932
Fertilizer	13.367	13.632	10.438	10.714
Petroleum	26.886	26.885	19.037	18.905
Seed	5.861	5.576	3.689	3.443
Other supplies [4]	4.814	5.070	4.356	4.627
Total farm supplies	71.728	71.041	53.634	53.220
Receipts for services: [5]				
Trucking, cotton ginning, storage, grinding, locker plants, miscellaneous	5.440	7.090	5.440	7.090
Total business	203.501	203.047	178.035	179.807

[1] Represents value at the first level at which cooperatives transact business for farmers; adjusted for inter-cooperative business. [2] Excludes oilseed meal and oil. Oilseed meal is included in feed sales while oil sales are included in other products sales. [3] Includes coffee, forest products, hay, hops, seed marketed for growers, nursery stock, other farm products not separately classified, and sales of farm products not received directly from member-patrons. Also includes manufactured food products and resale items marketed by cooperatives. [4] Includes automotive supplies, building material, chicks, containers, farm machinery and equipment, hardware, meats and groceries, and other supplies not separately classified. [5] Trucking, cotton ginning, storage, grinding, locker plants, and/or miscellaneous services related to marketing or purchasing but not included in the volume reported for those activities, plus other operating and non-operating income and losses and extraordinary items.

Rural Development, Cooperative Services Branch, (202) 720–7395.

Table 10-9.—Farmers' cooperatives: Number of cooperatives, memberships, and business volume of marketing, farm supply, and related service cooperatives, by State, United States and Foreign, 2018–2019

State	Cooperatives headquartered in State		Memberships in State [1]		Net business [2]	
	2018	2019	2018	2019	2018	2019
	Number	*Number*	*Number*	*Number*	*Million dollars*	*Million dollars*
Alabama	43	46	24,873	25,337	1,018.76	1,013.75
Arkansas	27	28	38,173	38,245	2,274.61	2,281.82
California	101	100	34,963	37,068	13,692.10	13,895.45
Colorado	25	25	18,702	19,771	2,526.49	2,724.75
Florida	23	22	21,082	21,229	2,364.74	2,263.83
Georgia	9	9	13,784	13,229	1,155.42	1,047.59
Hawaii	9	8	488	370	17.66	20.97
Idaho	20	17	13,449	12,996	2,303.20	2,365.99
Illinois	89	85	109,333	103,970	11,129.04	11,064.73
Indiana	26	25	49,953	45,939	3,891.75	4,241.68
Iowa	73	73	99,594	102,510	18,315.75	17,211.97
Kansas	75	78	104,930	106,894	6,869.97	7,300.06
Kentucky	20	21	161,973	161,425	1,403.25	1,421.89
Louisiana	25	26	7,731	7,197	1,320.14	1,408.04
Maine	21	20	5,574	5,429	277.22	294.13
Maryland	11	11	35,614	35,691	431.34	430.08
Massachusetts	7	6	4,959	5,108	342.86	348.36
Michigan	33	34	42,817	44,223	4,645.24	5,446.39
Minnesota	160	157	125,853	134,226	16,172.06	16,874.28
Mississippi	38	39	42,886	44,512	1,351.86	1,358.83
Missouri	50	50	93,482	94,789	4,972.42	4,699.04
Montana	42	42	18,768	18,542	1,408.91	1,437.63
Nebraska	38	39	60,174	69,826	8,318.59	7,776.52
New Jersey	11	11	1,715	1,770	313.13	314.29
New York	42	41	10,284	10,450	3,930.56	4,393.65
North Carolina	11	11	21,887	21,955	778.95	778.95
North Dakota	120	119	67,092	69,755	6,732.53	6,674.53
Ohio	33	34	39,060	40,573	4,808.19	4,779.95
Oklahoma	47	45	42,154	42,155	1,993.07	1,625.07
Oregon	24	24	29,422	30,150	3,596.39	3,136.84
Pennsylvania	24	20	12,471	12,376	3,107.33	2,994.28
South Dakota	63	61	55,687	57,193	5,100.20	4,869.19
Tennessee	57	56	66,935	66,252	1,318.92	1,427.37
Texas	157	151	75,180	74,403	5,865.18	6,057.12
Utah	10	10	9,299	8,589	737.35	791.20
Virginia	42	41	116,081	111,179	1,736.94	1,698.42
Washington	50	46	25,569	27,060	7,367.93	7,495.80
West Virginia	9	9	58,231	58,537	102.15	103.33
Wisconsin	100	99	102,182	92,096	8,765.69	9,419.76
Wyoming	7	6	4,765	4,150	437.99	135.15
Other States [3]	34	34	21,172	21,884	4,251.96	4,954.91
United States	1,806	1,779	1,888,340	1,899,056	167,155.87	168,877.88
Foreign [4]	....	....	561	569	11,193.54	10,929.11
Total	1,806	1,779	1,888,901	1,899,625	170,049.40	179,807.00

[1] Actual memberships in State. [2] Represents value at the first level at which cooperatives transact business for farmers; adjusted for inter-cooperative business. Totals may not add due to rounding. [3] Dollar volume or membership is not shown to avoid disclosing operations of individual cooperatives. [4] Sales outside the United States and sales of certain products not received directly from member-patrons.

Rural Development, Cooperative Services Branch, (202) 720–7395.

CHAPTER XI

STABILIZATION AND PRICE-SUPPORT PROGRAMS

The statistics in this chapter relate to activities of the Commodity Credit Corporation (CCC), loan and inventory acquisition and disposition programs, the CCC and Farm Service Agency payment programs, and marketing agreements and order programs for fruits and vegetables. Statistics for Federal Milk Marketing Order programs are contained in chapter VIII.

Table 11-1.—Commodity Credit Corporation: Price-supported commodities owned as of September 2019 [1] (Inventory quantity)

Year	Corn Meal	Sorghum and products	Milk and products	Rice and products	Peanut and products	Cotton
	Million pounds	*Million bushels*	*Million pounds*	*Million cwt*	*Million pounds*	*Million pounds/ bales*
2010	0	(3)	7	(3)	0	0
2011	0	(3)	0	(2)	0	0
2012	0	0	0	0	0	0
2013	0	(3)	0	(3)	0	0
2014	0	0	0	(3)	4	0
2015	0	0	0	0	168	0
2016	0	0	0	0	0	0
2017	8	0	0	(3)	55	0
2018	2	(3)	0	0	133	0
2019	1	0	0	(3)	26	(2)

Year	Beans, dry edible	Dry whole peas	Wheat	Blended Foods	Vegetable Oil Products	Value of all commodities owned
	Million bushels	*Million cwt*	*Million bushels*	*Million pounds*	*Million pounds*	*Million dollars*
2010	(4)	0	(2)	16	5	48
2011	(2)	0	0	16	33	53
2012	0	0	0	2	12	14
2013	0	0	0	25	23	71
2014	0	0	0	18	32	40
2015	0	2	2	13	23	55
2016	0	0	0	27	10	24
2017	0	0	0	0	21	35
2018	0	0	0	12	15	45
2019	(2)	(3)	0	14	4	23

Cotton and Dry whole peas were added to the table. This table represents the total value of all commodities owned by CCC, including price-supported commodities not shown and commodities acquired under programs other than price-support programs, less reserve for losses on inventory. [1] Commodities with data consistently zero for 2010-2019 are not listed. [2] Less than 50,000 units. [3] Less than 500,000 units. [4] Less than 500 units.
FPAC, Business Center, Budget Division, Program Budget Branch, CCC Program Section, (202) 720-4697.

Table 11-2.—Commodity Credit Corporation: Loans pledged, by quantity and face amount, United States and Territories, by crop year 2018–2019 [1]

Commodity [2]	Unit [3]	2018 Quantity pledged	2018 Face amount	2019 Quantity pledged	2019 Face amount
		1,000	*1,000 dollars*	*1,000*	*1,000 dollars*
Barley	1,000 bushels	1,711	3,196	2,001	4,709
Canola Seed	1,000 cwt	464	4,666	208	2,103
Chickpeas	1,000 cwt	109	1,183	747	8,325
Corn	1,000 bushels	78,890	152,614	66,091	130,973
Cotton, ELS & Upland	1,000 bales	260	67,888	393	105,291
Dry Whole Peas	1,000 cwt	277	1,478	578	3,413
Flaxseed	1,000 cwt	19	196	1	13
Grain sorghum	1,000 bushels	469	928	702	1,494
Honey	1,000 pounds	3,711	2,561	4,517	3,117
Lentil Dry	1,000 cwt	242	2,702	460	5,355
Mustard Seed	1,000 cwt	26	269		
Oats	1,000 bushels	273	365	452	876
Peanuts	1,000 pounds	538,966	95,856	470,553	83,563
Rice	1,000 bushels	2,064	13,470	2,381	15,773
Safflower Seed	1,000 cwt			4	34
Seed cotton, ELS & Upland	1,000 pounds	6	1,892		
Soybeans	1,000 bushels	7,272	36,013	16,609	81,810
Sunflower Seed	1,000 cwt	85	843	37	378
Sunflower Seed (non-oil)	1,000 cwt	18	183	2	18
Wheat	1,000 bushels	28,113	85,570	35,251	119,227

[1] Includes loans pledged directly by Commodity Credit Corporation. [2] Commodities with no pledges for 2018 and 2019 were removed. [3] Includes Upland & ELS Bales and CELS Pounds.
FPAC, Business Center, Budget Division, Program Budget Branch, CCC Program Section, (202) 720-4697.

Table 11-3.—Commodity Credit Corporation: Loan transactions for fiscal year 2019, by commodities [1]

Commodity	Unit [5]	Loans outstanding Oct. 1, 2018 [2]	New loans made	Loan repayments	Collateral acquired in settlement [3]	Loans written off and transferred to accounts receivable [4]	Loans outstanding Sept. 30, 2019	
							Value	Quantity collateral remaining pledged
		1,000 dollars						
Basic commodities:								
Corn	Bushel	152,614	1,752,104	(1,768,021)		(5,723)	66,091	130,973
Cotton (Upland and ELS)	Bale	69,779	2,286,948	(2,115,069)	(123,454)	(12,912)	394	105,291
Peanuts	Pound	95,856	933,790	(824,355)	(34,560)	(87,168)	470,553	83,563
Rice	Cwt	13,470	230,708	(228,228)		(178)	2,381	15,773
Seed cotton	Pound		31,611	(31,512)		(99)		
Wheat	Bushel	85,570	220,863	(187,170)		(36)	35,251	119,227
Total [6]		417,289	5,456,024	(5,154,355)	(158,014)	(106,116)	574,670	454,827
Designated nonbasic commodities								
Barley	Bushel	3,196	11,599	(10,086)			2,001	4,709
Canola seed	Cwt	4,666	14,626	(17,190)			208	2,103
FlaxSeed	Cwt	196	381	(564)			1	13
Honey	Pound	2,561	5,619	(5,063)			4,517	3,117
Mustard seed	Cwt	269	340	(609)				
Oats	Bushel	365	1,125	(600)		(14)	452	876
Raw sugar, cane	Pound		348,916	(348,916)				
Raw sugar beet	Pound		233,832	(233,832)				
Refined sugar beet	Pound		442,296	(441,347)		(949)		
Safflower seed	Cwt		34				4	34
Sorghum	Bushel	928	4,824	(4,258)			702	1,494
Sunflower seed (oil)	Cwt	843	5,264	(5,729)			37	378
Sunflower seed, non oil	Cwt	183	687	(852)			2	18
Total [5]		13,207	1,069,543	(1,069,046)		(963)	7,924	12,742
Other nonbasic commodities:								
Chickpeas	Pound	1,183	14,894	(7,752)			747	8,325
Lentils	Pound	2,702	11,188	(8,534)			460	5,355
Peas, dry whole	Pound	1,478	6,303	(4,369)			578	3,413
Soybeans	Bushel	36,013	1,082,992	(1,032,718)		(4,477)	16,609	81,810
Total [5]		41,376	1,115,377	(1,053,373)		(4,477)	18,394	98,903
Grand total [5]		471,872	7,640,944	(7,276,774)	(158,014)	(111,556)	600,988	566,472

[1] Loans made directly by Commodity Credit Corporation. [2] Book value of outstanding loans; includes face amounts and any charges paid. [3] Includes Commodity Certificate Exchanges. [4] Includes transfers to accounts receivable. [5] Totals do not include allowance for losses.

Commodities with no loan activity from October 1, 2018 to September 30, 2019 were eliminated.

FPAC, Business Center, Budget Division, Program Budget Branch, CCC Program Section, (202) 720-4697.

Table 11-4.—Commodity Credit Corporation: Selected inventory transactions, programs and commodities, as of September 30, 2019

Program and commodity	Quantity						
	Unit	Inventory Oct. 1, 2018	Purchases	Collateral acquired from loans	Other addition deduction	Sales and other dispositions [1]	Inventory Sept. 30, 2019
		Thousands					
Feed grains:							
Corn products	Pound	2,172	63,114	0	0	(64,759)	527
Grain sorghum	Bushel	396	9,797	0	0	(10,193)	0
Food grains, cotton and tobacco:							
Wheat	Bushel	5	13,319	0	0	(13,324)	0
Wheat flour	Pound	0	(4)	0	0	4	0
Rice, milled	Cwt	0	1,679	0	0	(1,525)	154
Upland cotton	Bale [2]	0	0	42,481	0	(42,462)	20
Oils and oilseeds:							
Peanut butter	Pound	0	0	0	2,649	(2,649)	0
Peanuts	Pound	132,952	0	194,167	(243,370)	(57,603)	26,146
Soybean products	Pound	0	88,183	0	0	(88,183)	0
Dry edible beans	Cwt	0	433	0	....	(400)	34
Blended foods	Pound	12,119	95,497	0	0	(94,109)	13,508
Dry whole peas and lentils	Cwt	248	2,083	0	0	(2,233)	98
Sugar cane and beet	Pound	240	0	0	0	(240)	0
Vegetable oil products	Pound	14,828	335,234	0	0	(346,515)	3,547
Other	....	0	2,337	0	0	(2,337)	0
Total inventory operations	....	162,960	611,672	236,648	(240,721)	(726,528)	44,034

Program and commodity	Value						
	Unit	Inventory Oct. 1, 2018	Purchases	Collateral acquired from loans	Other addition deduction	Sales and other dispositions [1]	Inventory Sept. 30, 2019
		1,000 dollars					
Feed grains:							
Corn products	Pound	542	12,049	0	(121)	(12,364)	106
Grain sorghum	Bushel	2,877	50,405	0	(899)	(52,384)	0
Food grains, cotton and tobacco:							
Wheat	Bushel	14	137,161	0	0	(137,175)	0
Wheat flour	Pound	0	(1)	0	0	1	0
Rice, milled	Cwt	0	37,191	0	0	(33,977)	3,215
Upland cotton	Bale [2]	0	0	122,065	236	(117,784)	4,517
Oils and oilseeds:							
Peanut butter	Pound	0	0	0	3,304	(3,304)	0
Peanuts	Pound	24,039	0	34,560	(43,484)	(10,401)	4,713
Soybean products	Pound	0	15,625	0	0	(15,625)	0
Dry edible beans	Cwt	0	17,072	0	0	(15,631)	1,441
Blended foods	Pound	4,166	42,613	0	679	(42,970)	4,487
Dry whole peas and lentils	Cwt	5,476	41,616	0	(637)	(44,307)	2,148
Sugar, cane and beet	Pound	0	0	0	0	0	0
Vegetable oil products	Pound	8,463	142,054	0	(426)	(147,851)	2,240
Other	....	471	801,235	0	0	(800,773)	933
Total inventory operations	....	46,048	1,297,020	156,625	(41,348)	(1,434,545)	23,800

[1] Includes sales, commodity donations, transfers to other government agencies and inventory adjustment. [2] Includes Upland Bales and CFLS Pounds.
Selected inventory transactions, programs and commodities without activity from October 1, 2018 to September 30, 2019 were eliminated.
FPAC, Business Center, Budget Division, Program Budget Branch, CCC Program Section, (202) 720-4697.

Table 11-5.—Commodity Credit Corporation: Cost value of export and domestic commodity dispositions, by type of disposition, fiscal year 2019

(In Thousands)

Commodity [1]	Domestic				
	Dollar sales (Costs)	Transfers to other Government agencies	Donations [2]	Inventory adjustments and other recoveries (domestic)	Total domestic
Feed grains:					
Corn products	0	0	0	0	0
Grain sorghum	0	0	0	0	0
Food grains, cotton and tobacco:					
Wheat	0	0	0	0	0
Wheat flour	0	0	0	0	0
Rice, milled	0	0	0	0	0
Cotton, extra long staple & upland	0	0	0	117,784	117,784
Oils and oilseeds:					
Peanuts	0	0	0	10,401	10,401
Peanut butter	0	0	3,304	0	3,304
Soya flour	0	0	0	(2)	(2)
Soybeans & Soybean products	0	0	0	0	0
Grains and seeds:					
Lentils dry	0	0	0	0	0
Dry edible beans	0	0	0	0	0
Vegetable oil products	0	0	0	0	0
Other (miscellaneous,tallow & TMP-Food Distribution)	0	0	0	796,157	796,157
Total	0	0	3,304	924,340	927,644

Commodity [1]	Export				Total export and domestic
	Dollar sales (Costs)	Public law 480 (Costs)	Donations [1]	Total export	
Feed grains:					
Corn products	0	0	12,364	12,364	12,364
Grain sorghum	0	0	52,384	52,384	52,384
Food grains, cotton and tobacco:					
Wheat	0	15,044	122,117	137,175	137,175
Wheat flour	0	0	(1)	(1)	(1)
Rice, milled	0	19,743	14,234	33,977	33,977
Cotton, extra long staple & upland	0	0	0	0	117,784
Oils and oilseeds:					
Peanuts	0	0	0	0	10,401
Peanut butter	0	0	0	0	3,304
Soya flour	0	0	42,973	42,970	42,968
Soybeans & Soybean products	0	15,625	0	15,625	15,625
Grains and seeds:					
Lentils dry	0	0	8,069	8,069	8,069
Dry edible beans	0	0	15,631	15,631	15,631
Peas, dried whole	....	0	36,238	36,238	36,238
Vegetable oil products	0	47,691	100,160	147,852	147,852
Other (miscellaneous, tallow & TMP-Food Distribution)	0	1,123	3,494	4,616	800,773
Total	0	99,227	407,662	506,900	1,434,544

[1] Commodities without any activity were removed from the table. [2] Includes donations under section 202,407,416, Section 210, P.L. 85-540, miscellaneous donations under various other authorizations.
FPAC, Business Center, Budget Division, Program Budget Branch, CCC Program Section, (202) 720-4697.

Table 11-6.—Commodity Credit Corporation: Investment in price-support operations, March 31 and June 30, 2008–2019 [1]

Year Month	Inventory investment	Loan investment	Total investment
	Million dollars	*Million dollars*	*Million dollars*
2008:			
March	168	5,926	6,094
June	11	3,335	3,346
2009:			
March	174	4,647	4,821
June	209	2,215	2,424
2010:			
March	119	4,054	4,173
June	70	1,996	2,066
2011:			
March	41	3,259	3,300
June	66	1,588	1,654
2012:			
March	63	2,740	2,803
June	27	1,260	1,287
2013:			
March	28	2,981	3,009
June	43	1,664	1,707
2014:			
March	188	2,094	2,282
June	94	890	984
2015:			
March	32	2,734	2,766
June	41	1,572	1,613
2016:			
March	25	3,934	3,959
June	23	1,956	1,979
2017:			
March	11	4,142	4,153
June	24	2,095	2,119
2018:			
March	7	4,192	4,199
June	13	2,291	2,304
2019:			
March	57	4,028	4,885
June	51	2,826	2,877

[1] Reflects total CCC loans and inventories investment.
FPAC, Business Center, Budget Division, Program Budget Branch, CCC Program Section, (202) 720-4697.

Table 11-7.—Commodity Credit Corporation: Loans made in fiscal year 2019 as of September 30, by State and Territories [1]

State or Territory	Barley	Corn	Cotton-bales	Dry whole peas	Flaxseed
	1,000 dollars				
Alabama		1,573	24,143		
Alaska	6				
Arizona		1,854			
Arkansas		12,109	155,902		
California			496,048		
Colorado	160	17,958			
Connecticut					
Delaware		603			
Florida					
Georgia		7,473	5,670		
Hawaii					
Idaho	2,823	384		620	
Illinois		136,940	76		
Indiana		147,402			
Iowa		359,405			
Kansas City Commodity					
Kansas		22,601			
Kentucky	50	40,004			
Louisiana		4,729	19,620		
Maine	327	60			
Maryland		7,425			
Massachusetts		15			
Michigan		54,438			
Minnesota	1,012	372,489		30	17
Mississippi		12,004	571,146		
Missouri		45,644	6,906		
Montana	3,742			20,387	212
Nebraska		146,310		419	
Nevada					
New Hampshire		21			
New Jersey		559			
New Mexico		1,100			
New York		30,115			
North Carolina	23	3,281	38,827		
North Dakota	3,086	50,991		7,509	152
Ohio		76,141			
Oklahoma		1,137	128		
Oregon					
Pennsylvania		10,708			
Rhode Island					
South Carolina		3,596			
South Dakota	62	90,795		239	
Tennessee		10,407	215,194		
Texas		12,327	753,236		
Utah	45	45			
Vermont					
Virginia	24	5,215	49		
Washington	61	515		3,180	
West Virginia		1,349			
Wisconsin		61,503			
Wyoming	180	880			
Total	11,601	1,752,105	2,286,945	32,384	381

See footnote(s) at end of table.

Table 11-7.—Commodity Credit Corporation: Loans made in fiscal year 2019 as of September 30, by State and Territories [1]—Continued

State or Territory	Honey	Oats	Oilseeds	Peanuts	Rice	Seed Cotton
	1,000 dollars					
Alabama				6,462		
Alaska						
Arizona						568
Arkansas	56				96,765	69
California	457				88,391	
Colorado	4		108			
Connecticut						
Delaware						
Florida	48			24,349		
Georgia				745,593		
Hawaii						
Idaho	364		602			
Illinois		29				
Indiana						
Iowa	103	6				
Kansas City Commodity						
Kansas		56				8,698
Kentucky						
Louisiana	53				5,716	
Maine		98				
Maryland						
Massachusetts						
Michigan		33				
Minnesota	713	68	1,029			
Mississippi				3,376	16,582	2,077
Missouri					10,157	3,928
Montana	758	75	1,174			
Nebraska	65	24				
Nevada						
New Hampshire						
New Jersey						
New Mexico				1,623		
New York	22	3				
North Carolina				35,395		
North Dakota	96	169	14,062			
Ohio						
Oklahoma				1,080		8,111
Oregon	88					
Pennsylvania		60				
Rhode Island						
South Carolina		18		2,217		
South Dakota	1,605	459	3,976			
Tennessee	15				896	
Texas	981	14		46,307	12,201	8,158
Utah	33					
Vermont						
Virginia				67,387		
Washington	108					
West Virginia						
Wisconsin	50	11				
Wyoming						
Total	5,619	1,123	20,951	933,789	230,708	31,609

See footnote(s) at end of table.

Table 11-7.—Commodity Credit Corporation: Loans made in fiscal year 2019 as of September 30, by State and Territories [1]—Continued

State or Territory	Sorghum	Soybeans	Sugar	Wheat
	1,000 dollars			
Alabama		689		49
Alaska				
Arizona				
Arkansas		25,952		
California				
Colorado	171	84	126,168	6,161
Connecticut				
Delaware		304		
Florida			95,002	
Georgia		232		57
Hawaii				
Idaho			310,925	6,117
Illinois		76,279		490
Indiana		116,369		114
Iowa		184,417		
Kansas City Commodity				
Kansas	1,419	14,047		7,840
Kentucky		29,953		2,765
Louisiana		3,551	253,914	
Maine				
Maryland		3,420		903
Massachusetts				
Michigan		40,002	83,279	1,476
Minnesota		190,475	138,909	30,599
Mississippi		25,634		
Missouri	376	50,721		1,115
Montana				50,930
Nebraska	199	48,227		1,630
Nevada				
New Hampshire				
New Jersey		399		32
New Mexico				676
New York		12,019		1,349
North Carolina		3,318		63
North Dakota		48,803		71,769
Ohio		88,693		195
Oklahoma	249	878		4,798
Oregon				3,962
Pennsylvania		5,788		649
Rhode Island				
South Carolina		1,197		42
South Dakota	1,044	68,246		12,113
Tennessee		10,316		62
Texas	1,367			631
Utah				795
Vermont				
Virginia		4,517		166
Washington				12,247
West Virginia		1,450		
Wisconsin		27,012		228
Wyoming			16,848	843
Total	4,825	1,082,992	1,025,045	220,866

[1] Loans made directly by Commodity Credit Corporation. As much as possible, loans have been distributed according to the location of producers receiving the loans. Direct loans to cooperative associations for the benefit of members have been distributed according to the location of the association.

FPAC, Business Center, Budget Division, Program Budget Branch, CCC Program Section, (202) 720-4697.

Table 11-8.—Farm Service Agency programs: Payments to producers, by program and commodity, United States, calendar year 2018–2019 [1]

Program and commodity	2018	2019
	1,000 dollars	*1,000 dollars*
Additional risk coverage	1,116,830	712,051
Auto conservation reserve program (CRP)-cost shares	90,391	54,708
Biomass crop assistance	392	283
Cotton ginning cost share	215,831	100
Cotton transition program	12	1
CRP annual rental	1,816,927	1,796,319
CRP incentives	44,661	21,730
CRP transition incentive	3,964	3,906
Dairy indemnity	91	4,141
Direct and counter cyclical program	164	29
Emergency Assistance program	64,889	39,211
Emergency conservation program	65,008	27,822
Emergency forest restoration	2,354	1,478
Grasslands reserve program	1,993	2,055
Geographic disadvantaged program [2]	9,755	7,829
Livestock forage program	460,377	166,362
Livestock indemnity program	38,299	63,366
Loan deficiency	23	6,729
Margin protection-Dairy	253,615	15,105
Milk income loss II	1	1
Noninsured assistance program	176,955	145,560
Pima cotton trust fund program	14,814	0
Price loss coverage	2,075,956	1,959,025
Tree assistance program	43,514	(12,277)
Trade mitigation programs	5,096,102	15,335,595
Upland cotton assistance	11,258	14,403
Wool manufacturers trust fund	27,942	(2)
Grand Total	11,632,118	20,365,530

[1] Programs with no payment activity in CY2018 and CY2019 were eliminated. [2] Geographic Disadvantaged Program, $1,870, was added to CY2018 since it was not included previously.
FPAC, Business Center, Budget Division, Program Budget Branch, CCC Program Section, (202) 720-4697.

Table 11-9.—Farm Service Agency programs: Payments received, by States, calendar year 2018–2019 [1]

State [2]	Payments	
	2018	2019
	1,000 dollars	*1,000 dollars*
Alabama	80,429	201,733
Alaska	668	806
Arizona	31,898	75,775
Arkansas	487,565	862,715
California	165,820	277,831
Colorado	184,745	229,389
Connecticut	2,157	1,420
Delaware	6,619	28,224
District of Columbia	492	32,998
Florida	61,318	71,877
Georgia	218,521	502,953
Hawaii	7,888	5,369
Idaho	136,985	137,290
Illinois	1,001,352	1,635,341
Indiana	473,037	806,481
Iowa	1,126,699	1,976,908
Kansas	725,996	1,338,962
Kentucky	138,711	300,094
Louisiana	211,632	319,776
Maine	4,946	2,915
Maryland	26,566	94,521
Massachusetts	3,144	7,700
Michigan	209,462	316,651
Minnesota	734,829	1,175,432
Mississippi	262,839	482,918
Missouri	519,580	1,001,744
Montana	288,699	268,341
Nebraska	610,895	1,027,961
Nevada	3,904	6,849
New Hampshire	1,621	974
New Jersey	5,192	15,538
New Mexico	74,241	89,466
New York	64,557	75,096
North Carolina	86,801	321,014
North Dakota	648,477	947,515
Ohio	421,416	635,538
Oklahoma	268,081	361,741
Oregon	74,157	92,057
Pennsylvania	65,184	118,353
Rhode Island	394	296
South Carolina	30,429	97,331
South Dakota	693,308	698,320
Tennessee	107,568	288,942
Texas	737,820	1,637,917
Utah	36,165	30,671
Vermont	11,189	6,045
Virginia	49,121	112,464
Washington	159,642	184,782
West Virginia	2,872	6,322
Wisconsin	252,092	373,876
Wyoming	19,136	22,758
KCCO	83,252	1,053,496
Puerto Rico	11,369	3,866
Virgin Islands	389	46
Guam	154	53
North Mariana Islands Nat	33	48
American Samoa	64	28
Total [3]	11,632,120	20,365,527

[1] Only for programs listed on Table 11-8. [2] Geographic Disadvantaged Program, $1,870, was added to CY2018 since it was not included previously. [3] Immaterial rounding differences of ($.02) and $.03 are due to presenting information by programs on Table 11-8 and by State on Table 11-9. This addition affected the totals for Alaska, Hawaii, North Dakota, KCCO, Puerto Rico, Virgin Island, Guam, North Mariana Islands and American Samoa.
FPAC, Business Center, Budget Division, Program Budget Branch, CCC Program Section, (202) 720-4697.

Table 11-10.—Value of marketing order commodities, 2018-19 season [1]

Commodity	Crop Value	Number of producers
	1,000 dollars	*Number*
Citrus fruits		
Oranges, grapefruit, tangerines, and tangelos (FL)	121,070	500
Oranges and grapefruit (TX)	89,797	170
Deciduous fruits		
Olives (CA)	40,523	800
Desert grapes (CA) [2]	....	38
Kiwifruit (CA)	55,566	140
Avocados (FL)	15,278	400
Apricots (WA)	9,414	315
Cherries, sweet (WA)	407,360	1,450
Pears (OR and WA) [3]	351,596	2,327
Cherries, tart (7 States) [4]	56,635	400
Cranberries (10 States) [5]	245,762	1,100
Dried fruits		
Dates (CA)	86,109	70
Plums (CA)	194,832	800
Raisins (CA)	661,063	2,600
Vegetables [6]		
Tomatoes (FL)	328,468	75
Onions (ID-Eastern OR)	105,613	250
Onions (South TX)	39,695	60
Onions (Vidalia, GA)	90,013	62
Onions (Walla Walla, WA and OR)	1,855	30
Potatoes (CO)	144,913	166
Potatoes (ID-Eastern OR)	260,125	450
Potatoes (WA)	82,731	267
Nuts and Spearmint Oil		
Almonds (CA)	5,602,500	6,800
Pecans (15 States) [7]	421,531	2,500
Pistashios (CA, AZ and NM) [8]	2,615,550	1,236
Walnuts (CA)	916,650	5,000
Hazelnuts (OR and WA) [9]	91,800	800
Spearmint oil (WA, ID, OR, parts of UT and NV) [10]	34,675	133
Subtotal	10,071,124	28,939
Apples (export act) [11]	2,954,219	25,591
Grapes (export act) [12]	1,271,435	25,892
Peanuts(Nationwide standards) [13]	1,169,953	6,182
Grand total [14]	18,466,731	86,604

[1] Programs under the oversight authority of the Marketing Order and Agreement Division, Specialty Crops Program, Agricultural Marketing Service.

[2] California Desert Grape crop value data is not available.

[3] Includes fresh and processed pears.

[4] The marketing order regulates the handling of tart cherries in the states of Michigan, Utah, Wisconsin, Washington, New York, Pennsylvania, and Oregon. The crop value shown is for the sum of the values for 5 states, excluding Pennsylvania and Oregon, for which NASS does not publish data.

[5] The marketing order regulates the handling of cranberries in Wisconsin, Massachusetts, Oregon, New Jersey, Washington, Rhode Island, Connecticut, Michigan, Minnesota, Oregon, and Long Island in New York. The crop value shown is the sum of crop values for the first 4 states listed and excludes the other six states for which NASS does not publish crop value data.

[6] Sources: For tomatoes, Florida Tomato Committee, 2019 Annual Report. For the four onion marketing orders, NASS annual prices for dry onions in Idaho, Texas, Georgia, and Washington, respectively, were multiplied by shipment quantity data from the market order committees. For two of the three potato marketing orders (Colorado and Idaho-Eastern Oregon), NASS annual prices for fresh potato utilization for Colorado and Idaho, respectively, were multiplied by shipment quantity data from the marketing order committees. The Washington potato marketing order crop value is based on the state season average grower price for all potatoes (fresh and processed utilization combined), since NASS does not publish a price for Washington fresh potato utilization.

[7] The crop value shown is the sum of values for eight states for which NASS pecan crop data is published: New Mexico, Georgia, Texas, Arizona, Oklahoma, California, Louisiana, Alabama.

[8] NASS publishes pistachio crop value only for California.

[9] NASS publishes hazelnut crop value only for Oregon.

[10] The spearmint crop value shown is the sum of values for Washington, Idaho, and Oregon, and excludes the minor level of production in Nevada and Utah, which is not published by NASS.

[11] Value of U.S. utilized apple production, fresh and processed combined.

[12] Value of utilized production of California table-type grapes.

[13] Value of U.S. production of peanuts. The Farm Security and Rural Investment Act of 2002 terminated the Peanut Administrative Committee (which locally administered Marketing Agreement No. 146). As a result, the marketing agreement was terminated and new quality standards were established for domestic and imported peanuts, administered by the Peanut Standards Board.

[14] The number of producers is likely overstated to a moderate extent, since some producers may grow more than one of the commodities listed in this table.

AMS, Specialty Crops Programs, Promotion and Economics Division, (202) 720–9915.

CHAPTER XII

AGRICULTURAL CONSERVATION AND FORESTRY STATISTICS

Statistics in this chapter concern conservation of various natural resources, particularly soil, water, timber, wetlands, wildlife, and improvement of water quality. Forestry statistics include area of private and public-owned forest land, timber production, imports and exports, pulpwood consumption and paper and board production, area burned over by forest fires, livestock grazing, and recreational use of national forest lands.

Conservation Practices on Active CRP Contracts, September 2019

Practice code	Practice	Acres
CP1	Introduced grasses and legumes	3,157,028
CP2	Native grasses	5,308,305
CP3	Tree planting	670,717
CP4	Wildlife habitat with woody vegetation	1,472,170
CP5	Field windbreaks	63,164
CP6	Diversions	4
CP7	Erosion control structures	8
CP8	Grass waterways	121,083
CP9	Shallow water areas for wildlife	26,467
CP10	Existing grasses and legumes[1]	2,353,928
CP11	Existing trees	170,280
CP12	Wildlife food plots	33,248
CP15	Contour grass strips	59,188
CP16	Shelterbelts	21,285
CP17	Living snow fences	4,508
CP18	Salinity reducing vegetation	181,252
CP21	Filter strips (grass)	716,815
CP22	Riparian buffers (trees)	617,179
CP23	Wetland restoration	1,244,049
CP24	Cross wind trap strips	58
CP25	Rare and declining habitat	1,185,314
CP26	Sediment retention	40
CP27	Farmable wetland pilot (wetland)	98,113
CP28	Farmable wetland pilot (upland)	217,308
CP29	Wildlife habitat buffer (marginal pasture)	92,650
CP30	Wetland buffer (marginal pasture)	35,741
CP31	Bottomland hardwood	160,049
CP32	Hardwood trees	1
CP33	Upland bird habitat buffers	221,431
CP34	Flood control structure	69
CP36	Longleaf pine	159,255
CP37	Duck nesting habitat	450,312
CP38	State acres for wildlife enhancement	1,981,161
CP39	FWP--Constructed wetlands	489
CP40	FWP--Aquaculture wetlands	16,711
CP41	FWP--Flooded praire wetlands	63,073
CP42	Pollinator Habitat[2]	505,566
CP87	Grasslands-Native grass	80,579
CP88	Grasslands-Introduced grass	836,716
	Total	22,325,377

[1] Includes both introduced grasses and legumes and native grasses. [2] Does not include about 40,000 acres from Signup 39 before CP42 was implemented.
FSA, Conservation and Environmental Programs Division, (202) 690-1612.

CRP enrollment by sign up and initial contract year [1], as of September 2019

Sign up	Before 2011	2011	2012	2013	2014	2015
26	41,999					
28	75,299					
29	261,405					
30	232,408					
31	207,346					
32	1,332,375	232,765				
33	179,678					
35	221,624					
36	269,913					
37	437,450			69		
38	211,545	376,960				
39		3,625,346				
40		169,231	304,394			
41			2,460,237			
42			114,484	481,202		
43				3,408,222		
44				22,808	497,144	
45					1,523,621	
46					3,221	515,169
47						171,859
48						
49						
50						
51						
52						
All	3,71,041	4,404,303	2,879,115	3,912,300	2,023,986	687,028

Sign up	2016	2017	2018	2019	Total
26					41,999
28					75,299
29					261,405
30					232,408
31					207,346
32					1,565,140
33					179,678
35					221,624
36					269,913
37					437,518
38					588,505
39					3,625,346
40					473,626
41					2,460,237
42					595,686
43					3,408,222
44					519,951
45					1,523,621
46					518,390
47	689,463				861,322
48	511,630	812,501	7,403		1,331,534
49		384,461			384,461
50		30,833	1,297,213	1,016	1,329,062
51			11,019	281,080	292,099
52				434	434
200	464	87,908	448,580	40	536,992
201				383,558	383,558
All	1,201,557	1,315,704	1,764,215	666,127	22,325,377

[1] For CRP, contract year is the same as fiscal year, which begins Ocer 1.
General Signup Numbers: 1-13, 15, 16, 18, 20, 26, 29, 33, 39, 41, 43, 459. Continuous Sign-up Numbers: 14, 17, 19, 21-25, 27, 28, 30, 31, 35-38, 40, 42, 44, 46, 47, 48, 50, Grasslands Signup Number: 200.
FSA, Conservation and Environmental Programs Division, (202) 690-1612.

Table 12-1.—Conservation Reserve Program (CRP): Enrollment by practice, under contract, September 2019

(CP1 and CP2)

State	CP1 Establishment of permanent introduced grasses and legumes			CP2 Establishment of permanent native grasses		
	Total acres treated	Total cost share	Avg cost share per acre treated [1]	Total acres treated	Total cost share	Avg cost share per acre treated [1]
Alabama	13,863	727,739	67.69	2,816	146,574	88.14
Alaska	1,100	0	...	...	0	...
Arkansas	3,769	150,055	61.48	3,153	255,877	101.71
California	19,659	748,616	156.26	157	2,100	300.00
Colorado	66,712	3,065,157	64.69	838,186	47,533,518	70.39
Delaware	31	11,105	358.23	23	16,310	700.00
Florida	28	0	...	108	3,718	143.00
Georgia	803	69,876	114.21	47	10,962	812.00
Hawaii	...	0	...	...	0	...
Idaho	202,381	13,379,637	78.41	40,652	2,586,011	81.00
Illinois	182,777	8,545,423	61.92	43,202	6,281,955	198.21
Indiana	17,172	916,726	72.85	11,842	1,491,913	178.75
Iowa	230,226	7,352,062	41.65	126,002	18,013,567	218.92
Kansas	12,164	371,324	42.96	630,031	24,948,861	44.94
Kentucky	31,551	2,839,304	122.66	19,859	1,691,694	128.04
Louisiana	599	75,107	147.01	1,140	142,567	186.41
Maine	2,229	419,335	199.99	...	0	...
Maryland	6,702	584,703	164.51	1,893	223,307	226.76
Massachusetts	...	0	...	...	0	...
Michigan	14,798	1,359,871	123.78	8,278	1,264,473	195.69
Minnesota	63,508	2,100,222	45.09	41,903	1,746,665	78.32
Mississippi	21,756	169,068	89.61	2,178	43,101	109.40
Missouri	429,071	18,322,183	82.37	126,038	11,338,994	158.94
Montana	382,816	5,664,584	27.08	226,141	3,494,928	33.76
Nebraska	29,554	1,557,301	70.09	241,110	15,060,891	76.68
Nevada	130	12,810	98.39	...	0	...
New Jersey	...	0	...	40	0	...
New Mexico	52,423	4,116,452	92.59	264,440	23,440,110	115.22
New York	4,989	1,148,645	270.72	373	76,595	294.23
North Carolina	937	35,607	64.72	94	7,590	126.69
North Dakota	129,466	5,208,293	49.00	13,296	949,362	89.23
Ohio	11,412	542,495	87.71	45,456	2,884,682	113.28
Oklahoma	114,410	5,120,419	60.33	290,602	14,823,509	68.31
Oregon	200,695	13,014,823	72.89	59,392	5,043,263	94.88
Pennsylvania	69,518	6,577,229	146.14	24,633	2,622,255	181.33
South Carolina	574	18,132	145.79	182	0	...
South Dakota	47,425	1,095,566	34.86	63,650	2,886,085	71.09
Tennessee	31,612	1,264,267	96.78	20,500	1,816,199	166.71
Texas	272,022	15,181,070	88.11	1,617,861	261,887,673	201.63
Utah	70,812	2,123,996	42.51	13,760	966,370	73.69
Vermont	7	0	...	...	0	...
Virginia	2,014	283,804	242.16	726	143,654	326.54
Washington	263,084	13,389,590	63.30	502,985	33,300,930	93.15
West Virginia	160	17,778	337.15	...	0	...
Wisconsin	54,309	3,986,378	93.81	22,419	2,381,405	170.56
Wyoming	97,754	1,636,834	28.13	3,136	83,701	48.28
United States	3,157,028	140,200,583	66.13	5,308,305	489,611,379	120.42

[1] Not including acres which receive no cost share.
Total acres treated may not add due to rounding.
FSA, Conservation and Environmental Programs Division, (202) 690-1612.

Table 12-2.—Conservation Reserve Program (CRP): Enrollment by practice, under contract, September 2019

(CP3 and CP4)

State	CP3 Tree planting			CP4 Permanent wildlife habitat		
	Total acres treated	Total cost share	Avg cost share per acre treated [1]	Total acres treated	Total cost share	Avg cost share per acre treated [1]
Alabama	97,158	8,298,216	110.41	4,378	839,066	330.73
Alaska	0	0	....	0	0	....
Arkansas	28,952	2,050,423	107.74	1,663	90,233	70.97
California	14	0	....	9,651	1,028	250.12
Colorado	14	0	....	281,654	16,294,208	88.66
Delaware	2,120	643,674	335.32	554	152,488	371.22
Florida	13,708	611,605	158.68	330	0	....
Georgia	54,564	5,790,762	135.64	1,358	241,242	234.47
Hawaii	13	55,854	4,168.21	0	0	....
Idaho	5,277	435,214	90.29	58,991	2,030,200	49.10
Illinois	32,899	7,656,378	311.02	80,727	22,946,709	462.74
Indiana	12,032	2,550,320	340.19	6,185	546,839	187.92
Iowa	16,813	4,084,624	316.81	106,996	2,619,306	144.43
Kansas	312	29,133	186.93	321,479	15,524,830	57.25
Kentucky	3,016	658,153	278.07	243	23,200	105.15
Louisiana	36,352	2,377,857	101.84	32,354	2,267,511	104.88
Maine	90	84,326	938.00	38	0	....
Maryland	978	181,604	529.46	1,229	78,493	179.54
Massachusetts	0	0	....	0	0	....
Michigan	4,520	612,974	197.86	7,806	273,894	116.39
Minnesota	20,337	1,601,888	120.85	115,783	1,225,071	85.01
Mississippi	224,477	3,604,599	108.33	2,262	155,844	821.62
Missouri	12,964	1,061,813	202.82	2,185	157,100	159.67
Montana	31	0	....	11,175	554,464	293.74
Nebraska	520	30,263	185.44	36,855	1,412,498	63.07
Nevada	0	0	....	0	0	....
New Jersey	0	0	....	0	0	....
New Mexico	0	0	....	140	16,800	120.00
New York	457	380,129	962.42	439	257,229	766.68
North Carolina	20,906	3,768,847	229.08	637	347,358	700.81
North Dakota	418	33,298	179.18	200,305	12,250,080	78.30
Ohio	6,406	1,447,887	429.72	9,061	259,484	94.10
Oklahoma	37	0	....	756	30,492	99.25
Oregon	1,353	165,728	381.56	8,415	885,094	158.36
Pennsylvania	373	236,316	963.77	4,036	894,803	328.88
South Carolina	18,919	605,289	71.30	595	55,411	226.49
South Dakota	21	946	220.00	36,322	1,135,065	58.58
Tennessee	23,151	1,576,439	164.94	2,246	45,211	146.09
Texas	1,199	49,708	95.48	13,310	329,993	97.20
Utah	0	0	....	13	0	....
Vermont	0	0	....	0	0	....
Virginia	5,574	378,483	94.01	223	23,965	118.70
Washington	2,412	164,864	73.63	107,464	7,190,271	111.62
West Virginia	16	4,102	431.79	0	0	....
Wisconsin	22,310	3,627,471	328.43	3,071	206,535	190.76
Wyoming	2	0	....	1,223	41,451	81.81
United States	670,717	54,859,187	165.84	1,472,170	91,403,464	102.13

[1] Not including acres which receive no cost share.
Total acres treated may not add due to rounding.
FSA, Conservation and Environmental Programs Division, (202) 690-1612.

Table 12-3.—Conservation Reserve Program (CRP): Enrollment by practice, under contract, September 2019

(CP5, CP6, and CP7)

State	CP5 Establishment of field windbreaks			CP6 Diversions			CP7 Erosion control structures		
	Total acres treated	Total cost share	Avg cost share per acre treated [1]	Total acres treated	Total cost share	Avg cost share per acre treated [1]	Total acres treated	Total cost share	Avg cost share per acre treated [1]
Alabama	0	0	...	...	0	...	...	0	...
Alaska	0	0	...	...	0	...	...	0	...
Arkansas	0	0	...	...	0	...	...	0	...
California	0	0	...	...	0	...	...	0	...
Colorado	906	439,785	768.99	...	0	...	...	0	...
Delaware	0	0	...	...	0	...	...	0	...
Florida	0	0	...	...	0	...	...	0	...
Georgia	0	0	...	...	0	...	...	0	...
Hawaii	0	0	...	...	0	...	...	0	...
Idaho	55	81,853	2,041.73	...	0	...	...	0	...
Illinois	1,908	339,124	259.64	3	0	...	4	0	...
Indiana	1,202	178,224	235.30	...	0	...	0	0	...
Iowa	5,579	970,988	304.58	...	0	...	1	0	...
Kansas	1,054	285,102	483.06	...	0	...	...	0	...
Kentucky	0	0	...	...	0	...	...	0	...
Louisiana	0	0	...	...	0	...	...	0	...
Maine	0	0	...	...	0	...	...	0	...
Maryland	0	0	...	...	0	...	...	0	...
Massachusetts	0	0	...	...	0	...	...	0	...
Michigan	1,694	344,221	269.40	1	0	...	...	0	...
Minnesota	5,343	843,703	228.34	...	0	...	0	0	...
Mississippi	0	0	...	...	0	...	...	0	...
Missouri	31	2,327	323.19	...	0	...	1	0	...
Montana	53	10,115	511.38	...	0	...	...	0	...
Nebraska	20,592	5,299,859	634.85	...	0	...	...	0	...
Nevada	0	0	...	...	0	...	...	0	...
New Jersey	2	16,537	6,695.14	...	0	...	...	0	...
New Mexico	0	0	...	...	0	...	...	0	...
New York	0	0	...	...	0	...	...	0	...
North Carolina	8	161	84.74	...	0	...	...	0	...
North Dakota	2,706	1,314,948	717.93	...	0	...	...	0	...
Ohio	3,164	600,463	381.06	...	0	...	...	0	...
Oklahoma	31	0	...	...	0	...	...	0	...
Oregon	0	0	...	...	0	...	...	0	...
Pennsylvania	0	0	...	...	0	...	...	0	...
South Carolina	11	115	42.71	...	0	...	...	0	...
South Dakota	18,627	7,436,516	630.09	...	0	...	...	0	...
Tennessee	0	0	...	...	0	...	...	0	...
Texas	0	0	...	...	0	...	...	0	...
Utah	0	0	...	...	0	...	...	0	...
Vermont	0	0	...	...	0	...	...	0	...
Virginia	0	500	1,250.00	...	0	...	...	0	...
Washington	6	0	...	...	0	...	...	0	...
West Virginia	0	0	...	...	0	...	...	0	...
Wisconsin	88	14,400	514.84	...	0	...	1	0	...
Wyoming	104	1,986	139.98	...	0	...	...	0	...
United States	63,164	18,180,928	518.55	4	...	...	8	...	...

[1] Not including acres which receive no cost share.
Total acres treated may not add due to rounding.
FSA, Conservation and Environmental Programs Division, (202) 690-1612.

Table 12-4.—Conservation Reserve Program (CRP): Enrollment by practice, under contract, September 2019

(CP8 and CP9)

State	CP8 Grass waterways			CP9 Shallow water areas for wildlife		
	Total acres treated	Total cost share	Avg cost share per acre treated [1]	Total acres treated	Total cost share	Avg cost share per acre treated [1]
Alabama	0	0	....	107	30,233	700.00
Alaska	0	0	....	....	0	....
Arkansas	5	66	12.74	466	4,520	57.10
California	0	0	....	....	0	....
Colorado	468	6,687	189.65	12	0	....
Delaware	1	0	....	202	233,472	1,725.59
Florida	0	0	....	....	0	....
Georgia	23	4,265	947.78	13	14,424	1,109.54
Hawaii	0	0	....	....	0	....
Idaho	0	0	....	23	224	70.00
Illinois	30,961	24,028,568	1,387.41	4,102	1,539,973	821.10
Indiana	18,084	37,798,209	5,150.67	864	179,191	937.49
Iowa	35,517	12,301,680	595.93	10,146	741,722	167.08
Kansas	7,301	2,373,462	549.04	884	235,285	655.99
Kentucky	5,029	7,287,877	1,999.87	1,751	607,557	1,458.20
Louisiana	2	0	....	476	65,580	342.74
Maine	45	250,347	7,988.11	....	0	....
Maryland	220	553,355	6,450.10	1,017	971,070	2,820.58
Massachusetts	0	0	....	....	0	....
Michigan	423	547,555	3,360.68	1,195	398,098	555.81
Minnesota	3,178	530,426	444.88	159	1,799	56.95
Mississippi	52	0	....	469	62,858	2,104.39
Missouri	1,803	1,031,369	1,480.73	1,692	28,515	285.46
Montana	58	270	40.30	11	0	....
Nebraska	1,128	329,270	530.35	147	36,997	574.58
Nevada	0	0	....	....	0	....
New Jersey	162	1,651,843	11,847.96	....	0	....
New Mexico	0	0	....	....	0	....
New York	37	47,389	2,163.87	3	3,462	1,018.24
North Carolina	200	255,006	1,659.98	167	40,583	366.93
North Dakota	81	12,985	362.00	....	0	....
Ohio	11,472	23,302,687	6,301.21	473	143,879	1,111.98
Oklahoma	133	297	23.17	53	1,685	168.50
Oregon	16	54	100.00	....	0	....
Pennsylvania	200	266,442	2,529.60	31	6,200	984.13
South Carolina	15	510	1,020.00	34	41,000	2,113.40
South Dakota	1,388	261,165	324.50	41	0	....
Tennessee	164	148,667	2,119.88	57	10,660	640.24
Texas	1,160	796,914	1,202.60	83	6,806	680.60
Utah	6	0	....	....	0	....
Vermont	15	12,315	1,021.15	....	0	....
Virginia	83	340,173	4,767.00	52	119,189	3,144.83
Washington	335	1,912	47.28	50	0	....
West Virginia	0	0	....	....	0	....
Wisconsin	1,313	990,678	2,678.96	1,688	525,949	1,165.77
Wyoming	0	0	....	....	0	....
United States	121,083	115,132,444	1,847.79	26,467	6,050,932	615.71

[1] Not including acres which receive no cost share.
Total acres treated may not add due to rounding.
FSA, Conservation and Environmental Programs Division, (202) 690-1612.

Table 12-5.—Conservation Reserve Program (CRP): Enrollment by practice, under contract, September 2019

(CP10, CP11, and CP12)

State	CP10 Vegetative-cover-grass-already established			CP11 Vegetative-cover-trees-already established			CP12 Wildlife food plots		
	Total acres treated	Total cost share	Avg cost share per acre treated [1]	Total acres treated	Total cost share	Avg cost share per acre treated [1]	Total acres treated	Total cost share	Avg cost share per acre treated [1]
Alabama	9,806	566,605	80.87	26,138	2,018,213	129.57	758	0	....
Alaska	1,414	0	....	....	0	....	....	0	....
Arkansas	3,774	78,450	148.75	7,487	89,297	200.38	292	0	....
California	8,851	0	....	....	0	....	1	0	....
Colorado	450,400	4,770,261	32.65	11	0	....	110	0	....
Delaware	....	0	....	....	0	....	3	0	....
Florida	133	0	....	6,051	12,500	690.61	19	0	....
Georgia	694	24,000	568.72	12,149	383,241	146.69	102	0	....
Hawaii	....	0	....	....	0	....	....	0	....
Idaho	52,190	22,063	11.50	291	0	....	71	0	....
Illinois	26,023	15,485	55.73	3,647	3,194	48.32	3,631	0	....
Indiana	4,338	4,282	13.52	1,430	0	....	311	30	50.00
Iowa	52,144	1,364,208	112.97	1,324	99,572	549.45	4,006	0	....
Kansas	76,198	77,585	10.26	54	0	....	2,931	12	....
Kentucky	2,723	4,358	33.25	272	536	43.23	462	0	....
Louisiana	369	0	....	5,134	0	....	479	0	....
Maine	823	0	....	212	0	....	....	0	....
Maryland	336	0	....	114	0	....	28	0	....
Massachusetts	....	0	....	....	0	....	....	0	....
Michigan	4,121	9,757	92.75	1,346	21,343	67.28	578	0	....
Minnesota	38,710	21,078	52.45	4,423	113,014	388.58	3,400	263	43.75
Mississippi	9,254	0	....	67,718	445,158	389.97	1,676	0	....
Missouri	43,823	88,363	65.58	1,043	39,151	588.73	2,784	0	....
Montana	170,900	35,515	19.09	131	0	....	715	0	....
Nebraska	57,588	441,716	32.90	290	32,019	1,351.01	424	50	....
Nevada	....	0	....	....	0	....	....	0	....
New Jersey	14	0	....	....	0	....	....	0	....
New Mexico	12,240	4,382	9.68	....	0	....	196	0	....
New York	3,555	152,349	107.42	147	9,360	248.28	33	0	....
North Carolina	452	0	....	6,788	1,350,364	399.83	10	0	....
North Dakota	121,649	1,384,791	19.71	102	61	45.19	1,787	0	....
Ohio	4,085	9,222	39.66	790	0	....	331	0	....
Oklahoma	169,527	487,199	10.19	84	0	....	666	0	....
Oregon	57,599	7,740,499	327.97	281	151,417	1,202.10	99	0	....
Pennsylvania	4,597	265,094	135.20	21	0	....	736	142	106.77
South Carolina	898	0	....	10,356	96,362	48.96	85	0	....
South Dakota	67,206	16,437	16.68	60	0	....	2,263	500	100.00
Tennessee	10,928	621	17.91	5,212	3,444	50.38	252	0	....
Texas	626,801	11,202,662	112.20	1,142	0	....	2,378	1,880	100.00
Utah	74,361	5,454	3.00	....	0	....	8	0	....
Vermont	....	0	....	....	0	....	....	0	....
Virginia	568	56,629	422.26	1,615	79,937	246.11	20	0	....
Washington	96,132	114,542	23.36	423	3,923	55.01	713	80	....
West Virginia	....	0	....	....	0	....	....	0	....
Wisconsin	17,085	151,666	83.73	3,981	70,358	408.04	009	0	....
Wyoming	71,618	0	....	12	0	....	18	0	....
United States	2,353,928	29,175,270	65.00	170,280	5,031,464	186.97	33,248	2,815	88.70

[1] Not including acres which receive no cost share.
Total acres treated may not add due to rounding.
FSA, Conservation and Environmental Programs Division, (202) 690-1612.

Table 12-6.—Conservation Reserve Program (CRP): Enrollment by practice, under contract, September 2019

(CP15, CP16, and CP17)

State	CP15 Contour grass strips			CP16 Shelter belts			CP17 Living snow fences		
	Total acres treated	Total cost share	Avg cost share per acre treated [1]	Total acres treated	Total cost share	Avg cost share per acre treated [1]	Total acres treated	Total cost share	Avg cost share per acre treated [1]
Alabama	0	0	....	0	0	....	0	0	....
Alaska	0	0	....	0	0	....	0	0	....
Arkansas	0	0	....	0	0	....	0	0	....
California	0	0	....	0	0	....	0	0	....
Colorado	9	0	....	2,166	1,271,744	693.66	23	9,084	925.05
Delaware	0	0	....	0	0	....	0	0	....
Florida	0	0	....	0	0	....	0	0	....
Georgia	0	0	....	0	0	....	0	0	....
Hawaii	0	0	....	0	0	....	0	0	....
Idaho	180	1,007	10.58	18	14,551	1,549.63	0	0	....
Illinois	844	21,088	59.80	96	9,515	292.59	41	3,491	170.130
Indiana	20	170	113.33	19	3,057	285.70	0	48	266.67
Iowa	11,202	526,961	143.99	1,792	943,105	785.74	672	125,998	255.57
Kansas	2,690	88,386	69.82	492	132,585	459.73	35	12,644	630.00
Kentucky	30	0	....	0	0	....	0	0	....
Louisiana	0	0	....	0	0	....	0	0	....
Maine	0	0	....	0	0	....	0	0	....
Maryland	1	0	....	0	0	....	0	0	....
Massachusetts	0	0	....	0	0	....	0	0	....
Michigan	2	0	....	25	1,986	198.80	11	0	....
Minnesota	739	16,682	56.65	2,874	539,787	258.06	2,410	366,745	202.00
Mississippi	40	0	....	0	0	....	0	0	....
Missouri	735	9,054	83.31	48	24,328	859.65	0	0	....
Montana	0	0	....	103	16,097	825.49	188	9,022	405.30
Nebraska	277	4,763	47.44	1,033	269,121	410.49	89	3,617	291.46
Nevada	0	0	....	0	0	....	0	0	....
New Jersey	1	4,391	7,841.07	0	0	....	0	0	....
New Mexico	0	0	....	0	0	....	0	0	....
New York	0	0	....	0	0	....	0	0	....
North Carolina	0	0	....	5	0	....	0	0	....
North Dakota	1	0	....	2,917	1,780,325	765.20	472	243,695	667.20
Ohio	14	0	....	67	11,514	290.75	0	0	....
Oklahoma	0	0	....	21	0	....	0	0	....
Oregon	0	0	....	0	0	....	0	0	....
Pennsylvania	44	1,492	78.65	0	0	....	0	0	....
South Carolina	0	0	....	0	0	....	0	0	....
South Dakota	25	111	30.25	9,597	4,103,060	674.34	556	227,728	643.83
Tennessee	20	0	....	0	0	....	0	0	....
Texas	71	0	....	0	0	....	0	0	....
Utah	18	0	....	0	0	....	0	0	....
Vermont	0	0	....	0	0	....	0	0	....
Virginia	2	286	130.00	0	0	....	0	0	....
Washington	41,679	110,992	46.91	8	1,750	5,833.33	0	0	....
West Virginia	0	0	....	0	0	....	0	0	....
Wisconsin	484	7,568	205.15	3	842	701.67	10	616	150.30
Wyoming	0	0	....	2	0	....	0	0	....
United States	59,188	792,951	95.46	21,285	9,123,367	623.52	4,508	1,002,689	321.69

[1] Not including acres which receive no cost share.
Total acres treated may not add due to rounding.
FSA, Conservation and Environmental Programs Division, (202) 690-1612.

Table 12-7.—Conservation Reserve Program (CRP): Enrollment by practice, under contract, September 2019

(CP18 and CP21)

State	CP18 Salt tolerant grasses			CP21 Alternative perennials		
	Total acres treated	Total cost share	Avg cost share per acre treated [1]	Total acres treated	Total cost share	Avg cost share per acre treated [1]
Alabama	0	0	....	230	10,105	218.25
Alaska	0	0	....	0	0	....
Arkansas	0	0	....	4,540	339,518	227.64
California	0	0	....	0	0	....
Colorado	7	0	....	97	10,325	398.96
Delaware	0	0	....	497	131,930	351.21
Florida	0	0	....	0	0	....
Georgia	0	0	....	308	25	10.87
Hawaii	0	0	....	0	0	....
Idaho	0	0	....	615	49,449	90.97
Illinois	4	261	104.40	100,765	7,274,242	118.57
Indiana	0	0	....	43,721	2,144,531	126.50
Iowa	0	0	....	185,578	14,875,995	149.10
Kansas	562	0	....	19,559	972,195	88.46
Kentucky	0	0	....	16,041	738,722	101.32
Louisiana	0	0	....	307	3,984	99.01
Maine	0	0	....	57	0	....
Maryland	0	0	....	22,444	1,319,777	159.65
Massachusetts	0	0	....	20	14,274	714.77
Michigan	0	0	....	22,681	2,193,851	130.16
Minnesota	4,355	186,013	59.75	110,523	5,797,455	88.43
Mississippi	0	0	....	4,533	110,385	105.80
Missouri	0	0	....	22,647	453,491	114.75
Montana	63,854	133,644	30.16	174	2,331	23.59
Nebraska	449	3,588	42.57	13,665	693,169	72.17
Nevada	0	0	....	0	0	....
New Jersey	0	0	....	317	50,597	217.43
New Mexico	0	0	....	0	0	....
New York	0	0	....	316	110,455	415.67
North Carolina	0	0	....	785	166,919	512.18
North Dakota	93,173	1,392,640	41.48	7,055	220,936	48.45
Ohio	0	0	....	67,932	2,634,815	91.50
Oklahoma	1,514	10,961	78.01	471	38	3.52
Oregon	0	0	....	1,456	103,321	239.00
Pennsylvania	0	0	....	711	26,143	132.98
South Carolina	0	0	....	1,031	19,113	133.54
South Dakota	16,897	564,407	41.23	9,467	273,166	42.10
Tennessee	0	0	....	4,220	319,442	218.69
Texas	436	20	0.13	556	36,000	160.46
Utah	0	0	....	0	0	....
Vermont	0	0	....	123	23,956	217.31
Virginia	0	0	....	2,416	145,492	124.87
Washington	0	0	....	32,404	1,184,609	82.04
West Virginia	0	0	....	577	197,278	885.85
Wisconsin	0	0	....	17,976	1,383,955	159.31
Wyoming	0	0	....	0	0	....
United States	181,252	2,201,504	41.52	716,815	44,031,988	118.35

[1] Not including acres which receive no cost share.
Total acres treated may not add due to rounding.
FSA, Conservation and Environmental Programs Division, (202) 690-1612.

Table 12-8.—Conservation Reserve Program (CRP): Enrollment by practice, under contract, September 2019

(CP22 and CP23)

State	CP22 Riparian buffer			CP23 Wetland restoration		
	Total acres treated	Total cost share	Avg cost share per acre treated [1]	Total acres treated	Total cost share	Avg cost share per acre treated [1]
Alabama	23,095	1,641,914	185.66	5	0	....
Alaska	50	0	....	0	0	....
Arkansas	53,342	2,119,927	111.02	66,364	15,068,268	532.47
California	576	266,400	576.36	572	0	....
Colorado	429	171,836	1,008.90	1,472	68,183	86.98
Delaware	57	8,125	273.57	192	230,544	1,651.22
Florida	64	0	....	0	0	....
Georgia	566	146,111	703.78	403	0	....
Hawaii	1,248	3,820,840	4,800.05	0	0	....
Idaho	2,916	247,240	244.81	401	2,125	83.99
Illinois	95,106	14,660,211	212.01	44,690	7,726,575	210.60
Indiana	4,729	524,778	250.74	11,910	1,478,243	214.50
Iowa	40,874	7,689,384	320.62	133,104	19,979,513	194.41
Kansas	2,311	100,966	178.09	9,822	597,435	99.96
Kentucky	15,326	3,511,550	302.27	220	75,113	1,264.95
Louisiana	3,717	189,122	138.93	137,637	7,341,961	192.92
Maine	30	38,163	8,875.12	0	0	....
Maryland	10,196	2,214,231	812.85	2,153	1,158,729	1,319.36
Massachusetts	0	0	....	0	0	....
Michigan	1,399	427,775	446.16	18,327	3,201,036	223.43
Minnesota	24,337	2,076,123	151.05	345,009	28,002,708	101.87
Mississippi	156,268	2,824,887	81.58	21,350	884,848	184.90
Missouri	20,259	1,057,093	296.99	21,059	2,629,322	268.34
Montana	2,229	89,279	136.02	1,827	744	8.01
Nebraska	1,345	265,377	431.06	13,008	715,447	99.34
Nevada	0	0	....	0	0	....
New Jersey	265	231,946	963.43	0	0	....
New Mexico	1,694	485,455	454.29	0	0	....
New York	7,019	5,489,707	1,499.78	60	4,616	1,394.56
North Carolina	6,367	669,667	179.42	842	122,078	219.95
North Dakota	238	116,408	717.99	196,362	1,821,549	45.60
Ohio	6,590	878,875	400.96	12,726	5,763,135	931.69
Oklahoma	1,027	286,109	495.08	1,825	83,439	60.93
Oregon	31,186	15,552,083	825.95	268	120,166	776.42
Pennsylvania	19,075	14,181,685	1,337.05	649	368,426	981.11
South Carolina	8,821	146,305	51.60	172	0	....
South Dakota	4,277	1,146,044	566.92	187,125	3,909,643	35.095
Tennessee	4,551	528,443	431.35	673	31,976	106.26
Texas	13,390	1,604,445	258.72	8,860	95,837	52.877
Utah	26	0	....	0	0	....
Vermont	2,267	2,651,935	1,565.28	0	0	....
Virginia	17,536	14,464,214	1,658.10	141	14,895	450.00
Washington	18,776	6,562,370	965.54	62	4,636	111.44
West Virginia	4,918	4,988,056	1,179.51	0	0	....
Wisconsin	6,637	842,512	556.19	4,761	414,666	357.89
Wyoming	1,922	458,683	420.19	0	0	....
United States	617,179	115,376,273	421.58	1,244,049	101,915,855	146.64

[1] Not including acres which receive no cost share.
Total acres treated may not add due to rounding.
FSA, Conservation and Environmental Programs Division, (202) 690-1612.

Table 12-9.—Conservation Reserve Program (CRP): Enrollment by practice, under contract, September 2019

(CP25, CP26, and CP27)

State	CP25 Rare and declining habitat			CP26 Sediment retention			CP27 Farmable wetland pilot (wetland)		
	Total acres treated	Total cost share	Avg cost share per acre treated [1]	Total acres treat-ed	Total cost share	Avg cost share per acre treated [1]	Total acres treated	Total cost share	Avg cost share per acre treated [1]
Alabama	393	17,622	142.46	...	0	...	...	0	...
Alaska	...	0	...	...	0	...	...	0	...
Arkansas	...	0	...	...	0	...	...	0	...
California	...	0	...	...	0	...	...	0	...
Colorado	1,604	28,812	65.28	...	0	...	2	0	...
Delaware	...	0	...	...	0	...	...	0	...
Florida	...	0	...	...	0	...	...	0	...
Georgia	...	0	...	...	0	...	...	0	...
Hawaii	...	0	...	...	0	...	...	0	...
Idaho	79	4,120	100.00	...	0	...	4	606	173.14
Illinois	543	180,583	392.06	...	0	...	663	149,991	244.48
Indiana	1,961	347,801	183.99	...	0	...	302	378,092	1,970.67
Iowa	140,601	29,935,876	263.95	...	0	...	26,932	3,404,380	179.20
Kansas	596,427	30,049,124	61.21	...	0	...	800	8,071	78.31
Kentucky	32,089	6,276,111	210.60	...	0	...	...	0	...
Louisiana	...	0	...	...	0	...	335	0	...
Maine	...	0	...	...	0	...	...	0	...
Maryland	596	145,883	252.70	...	0	...	...	0	...
Massachusetts	...	0	...	...	0	...	...	0	...
Michigan	35	462	65.00	40	117,708	3,372.73	22	995	199.00
Minnesota	84,060	6,859,021	98.93	...	0	...	12,955	1,107,871	118.82
Mississippi	...	0	...	...	0	...	40	5,109	129.34
Missouri	22,297	2,556,724	182.29	...	0	...	2	0	...
Montana	57,886	1,868,715	51.92	...	0	...	175	240	27.59
Nebraska	147,376	9,283,939	92.51	...	0	...	1,373	45,536	87.83
Nevada	...	0	...	...	0	...	...	0	...
New Jersey	...	0	...	...	0	...	...	0	...
New Mexico	...	0	...	...	0	...	...	0	...
New York	...	0	...	...	0	...	...	0	...
North Carolina	...	0	...	...	0	...	...	0	...
North Dakota	10,315	722,501	74.13	...	0	...	26,405	1,026,362	60.55
Ohio	4,055	1,020,575	409.76	...	0	...	88	377,774	5,261.48
Oklahoma	16,736	1,071,949	72.69	...	0	...	9	7,316	2,090.29
Oregon	41,733	1,583,892	110.24	...	0	...	...	0	...
Pennsylvania	...	0	...	...	0	...	...	0	...
South Carolina	...	0	...	...	0	...	...	0	...
South Dakota	13,267	898,518	95.16	...	0	...	27,952	613,396	46.11
Tennessee	...	0	...	...	0	...	...	0	...
Texas	...	0	...	...	0	...	...	0	...
Utah	...	0	...	...	0	...	...	0	...
Vermont	...	0	...	...	0	...	...	0	...
Virginia	...	0	...	...	0	...	...	0	...
Washington	1,162	62,911	128.02	...	0	...	2	0	...
West Virginia	...	0	...	...	0	...	...	0	...
Wisconsin	11,417	2,030,802	218.14	...	0	...	55	003	118.24
Wyoming	685	10,517	00.00	...	0	...	...	0	...
United States	1,185,314	94,986,458	103.40	40	117,708	3,372.73	98,113	7,126,343	118.50

[1] Not including acres which receive no cost share.
Total acres treated may not add due to rounding.
FSA, Conservation and Environmental Programs Division, (202) 690-1612.

Table 12-10.—Conservation Reserve Program (CRP): Enrollment by practice, under contract, September 2019

(CP28, CP29, and CP30)

State	CP28 Farmable wetland pilot (buffer)			CP29 Wildlife habitat buffer (marginal pastureland)			CP30 Wetland buffer (marginal pastureland)		
	Total acres treated	Total cost share	Avg cost share per acre treated [1]	Total acres treated	Total cost share	Avg cost share per acre treated [1]	Total acres treated	Total cost share	Avg cost share per acre treated [1]
Alabama	0	0	....	374	1,400	250.00	....	0	....
Alaska	....	0	....	....	0	....	140	12,252	2,005.24
Arkansas	0	0	....	268	126,723	919.61	2,706	26,865	107.59
California	....	0	....	....	0	....	....	0	....
Colorado	4	0	....	58	0	....	32	0	....
Delaware	....	0	....	....	0	....	....	0	....
Florida	....	0	....	....	0	....	....	0	....
Georgia	....	0	....	26	0	....	....	0	....
Hawaii	....	0	....	....	0	....	....	0	....
Idaho	2	62	31.00	194	46,728	768.43	142	15,406	137.31
Illinois	1,128	187,737	179.26	246	36,587	307.74	33	4,143	134.12
Indiana	558	51,555	129.88	56	21,965	480.63	41	7,366	180.54
Iowa	65,063	7,251,713	158.71	6,245	1,259,714	339.09	1,537	179,455	223.91
Kansas	1,555	45,161	47.84	4	224	56.00	....	0	....
Kentucky	....	0	....	49,408	7,625,012	166.91	....	0	....
Louisiana	0	0	....	....	0	....	176	0	....
Maine	....	0	....	5	18,088	36,176.00	11	33,012	2,895.79
Maryland	....	0	....	1,054	208,240	354.66	154	5,630	499.56
Massachusetts	....	0	....	....	0	....	....	0	....
Michigan	47	3,149	185.02	4	0	....	300	280,626	1,113.90
Minnesota	26,974	2,120,552	107.24	230	11,055	98.43	5,000	240,467	116.47
Mississippi	157	20,462	130.17	40	3,266	85.01	37	746	78.53
Missouri	8	0	....	1,114	227,152	500.68	1,614	288,725	461.76
Montana	134	149	27.59	....	0	....	....	0	....
Nebraska	1,845	67,808	72.46	1,051	107,765	199.17	291	18,611	276.29
Nevada	....	0	....	....	0	....	....	0	....
New Jersey	....	0	....	....	0	....	....	0	....
New Mexico	....	0	....	....	0	....	....	0	....
New York	....	0	....	1,998	1,082,908	1,037.43	1,171	950,223	1,006.44
North Carolina	0	0	....	27	41,592	8,318.40	....	0	....
North Dakota	60,423	2,763,118	75.52	35	0	....	....	0	....
Ohio	208	16,258	100.05	2,951	185,541	145.43	127	151,075	3,417.99
Oklahoma	21	465	62.84	....	0	....	....	0	....
Oregon	....	0	....	15,841	2,245,064	562.81	540	799,528	1,481.54
Pennsylvania	....	0	....	1,138	296,111	523.54	417	113,085	542.89
South Carolina	....	0	....	35	19,137	694.63	61	7,189	116.99
South Dakota	59,107	2,508,835	59.21	4,269	199,985	97.94	20,642	240,483	43.32
Tennessee	....	0	....	74	6,761	535.34	....	0	....
Texas	....	0	....	1,674	124,797	99.90	2	2,973	1,351.36
Utah	....	0	....	....	0	....	....	0	....
Vermont	....	0	....	....	0	....	1	1,612	2,302.86
Virginia	....	0	....	733	1,093,764	1,861.09	....	0	....
Washington	8	0	....	695	31,340	519.73	543	669,128	1,309.40
West Virginia	....	0	....	....	0	....	....	0	....
Wisconsin	67	796	118.81	1,149	161,369	234.26	22	13,446	619.63
Wyoming	....	0	....	1,314	173,350	432.08	....	0	....
United States	217,308	15,037,820	101.53	92,650	15,355,639	242.00	35,741	4,062,046	333.84

[1] Not including acres which receive no cost share.
Total acres treated may not add due to rounding.
FSA, Conservation and Environmental Programs Division, (202) 690-1612.

Table 12-11.—Conservation Reserve Program (CRP): Enrollment by practice, under contract, September 2019

(CP31, CP32, and CP33)

State	CP31 Bottomland hardwood			CP32 Hardwood trees			CP33 Upland bird habitat buffers		
	Total acres treated	Total cost share	Avg cost share per acre treated [1]	Total acres treated	Total cost share	Avg cost share per acre treated [1]	Total acres treated	Total cost share	Avg cost share per acre treated [1]
Alabama	1,206	88,081	122.64	....	0	....	681	65,527	130.75
Alaska	....	0	....	....	0	....	....	0	....
Arkansas	19,446	814,459	121.52	....	0	....	3,390	87,443	126.98
California	....	0	....	....	0	....	....	0	....
Colorado	....	0	....	....	0	....	1,434	70,329	95.75
Delaware	....	0	....	....	0	....	....	0	....
Florida	....	0	....	....	0	....	....	0	....
Georgia	....	0	....	....	0	....	393	22,057	126.00
Hawaii	....	0	....	....	0	....	....	0	....
Idaho	....	0	....	....	0	....	....	0	....
Illinois	6,240	1,184,922	233.59	....	0	....	59,801	6,479,795	123.57
Indiana	9,382	1,976,975	246.67	....	0	....	9,660	651,385	107.74
Iowa	3,947	951,187	318.92	....	0	....	24,200	3,922,324	239.87
Kansas	216	31,663	223.97	....	0	....	25,592	1,143,921	76.03
Kentucky	651	173,220	281.12	....	9	....	5,605	653,030	149.75
Louisiana	51,364	2,767,813	99.06	....	0	....	134	8,478	97.56
Maine	....	0	....	....	0	....	....	0	....
Maryland	....	0	....	....	0	....	415	38,587	140.83
Massachusetts	....	0	....	....	0	....	....	0	....
Michigan	....	0	....	....	0	....	571	69,660	146.70
Minnesota	798	35,868	133.79	....	0	....	495	26,644	92.10
Mississippi	61,153	1,210,382	98.08	....	0	....	1,304	26,232	264.09
Missouri	2,030	112,948	184.33	....	0	....	24,385	1,563,423	109.87
Montana	....	0	....	....	0	....	404	30,974	82.00
Nebraska	9	4,794	542.92	....	0	....	9,315	418,737	94.91
Nevada	....	0	....	....	0	....	....	0	....
New Jersey	....	0	....	....	0	....	....	0	....
New Mexico	....	0	....	....	0	....	....	0	....
New York	2	2,000	869.57	....	0	....	....	0	....
North Carolina	57	1,978	139.30	....	0	....	3,311	113,691	125.50
North Dakota	....	0	....	....	0	....	....	0	....
Ohio	109	24,427	336.00	....	0	....	10,291	648,591	131.82
Oklahoma	443	70,970	169.46	....	0	....	368	976	61.00
Oregon	....	0	....	....	0	....	....	0	....
Pennsylvania	....	0	....	....	0	....	292	25,869	158.76
South Carolina	....	0	....	....	0	....	1,124	11,271	56.44
South Dakota	....	0	....	....	0	....	1,447	76,582	69.35
Tennessee	2,616	185,702	126.31	....	0	....	3,421	230,468	91.68
Texas	381	2,925	65.73	....	0	....	30,800	1,153,553	123.81
Utah	....	0	....	....	0	....	....	0	....
Vermont	....	0	....	....	0	....	....	0	....
Virginia	....	0	....	....	0	....	836	52,804	141.12
Washington	....	0	....	....	0	....	1,553	39,395	110.52
West Virginia	....	0	....	....	0	....	....	0	....
Wisconsin	....	0	....	1	0	....	208	5,869	170.66
Wyoming	....	0	....	....	0	....	....	0	....
United States	160,049	9,640,013	142.94	1	....	....	221,431	17,637,615	129.22

[1] Not including acres which receive no cost share.
Total acres treated may not add due to rounding.
FSA, Conservation and Environmental Programs Division, (202) 690-1612.

Table 12-12.—Conservation Reserve Program (CRP): Enrollment by practice, under contract, September 2019

(CP34, CP36, and CP37)

State	CP34 Flood control structure			CP36 Longleaf pine			CP37 Duck nesting habitat		
	Total acres treated	Total cost share	Avg cost share per acre treated [1]	Total acres treated	Total cost share	Avg cost share per acre treated [1]	Total acres treated	Total cost share	Avg cost share per acre treated [1]
Alabama	....	0	....	13,749	2,752,896	228.91	....	0	....
Alaska	....	0	....	....	0	....	....	0	....
Arkansas	....	0	....	....	0	....	....	0	....
California	....	0	....	....	0	....	....	0	....
Colorado	....	0	....	....	0	....	....	0	....
Delaware	....	0	....	....	0	....	....	0	....
Florida	....	0	....	2,354	766,268	349.37	....	0	....
Georgia	....	0	....	121,098	22,609,126	297.92	....	0	....
Hawaii	....	0	....	....	0	....	....	0	....
Idaho	....	0	....	....	0	....	....	0	....
Illinois	....	0	....	....	0	....	....	0	....
Indiana	....	0	....	....	0	....	....	0	....
Iowa	....	0	....	....	0	....	2,441	202,038	123.83
Kansas	....	0	....	....	0	....	....	0	....
Kentucky	....	0	....	....	0	....	....	0	....
Louisiana	....	0	....	34	3,560	105.01	....	0	....
Maine	....	0	....	....	0	....	....	0	....
Maryland	....	0	....	....	0	....	....	0	....
Massachusetts	....	0	....	....	0	....	....	0	....
Michigan	....	0	....	....	0	....	....	0	....
Minnesota	69	5,617	112.90	....	0	....	24,028	1,965,905	92.38
Mississippi	....	0	....	147	5,621	142.30	....	0	....
Missouri	....	0	....	....	0	....	....	0	....
Montana	....	0	....	....	0	....	3,394	20,229	16.39
Nebraska	....	0	....	....	0	....	....	0	....
Nevada	....	0	....	....	0	....	....	0	....
New Jersey	....	0	....	....	0	....	....	0	....
New Mexico	....	0	....	....	0	....	....	0	....
New York	....	0	....	....	0	....	....	0	....
North Carolina	....	0	....	7,325	1,226,074	270.61	....	0	....
North Dakota	....	0	....	....	0	....	188,594	6,304,196	49.68
Ohio	....	0	....	....	0	....	....	0	....
Oklahoma	....	0	....	....	0	....	....	0	....
Oregon	....	0	....	....	0	....	....	0	....
Pennsylvania	....	0	....	....	0	....	....	0	....
South Carolina	....	0	....	14,169	1,485,470	144.00	....	0	....
South Dakota	....	0	....	....	0	....	231,855	7,395,357	41.57
Tennessee	....	0	....	....	0	....	....	0	....
Texas	....	0	....	....	0	....	....	0	....
Utah	....	0	....	....	0	....	....	0	....
Vermont	....	0	....	....	0	....	....	0	....
Virginia	....	0	....	378	42,172	122.84	....	0	....
Washington	....	0	....	....	0	....	....	0	....
West Virginia	....	0	....	....	0	....	....	0	....
Wisconsin	....	0	....	....	0	....	....	0	....
Wyoming	....	0	....	....	0	....	....	0	....
United States	69	5,617	112.90	159,255	28,891,187	274.18	450,312	15,887,724	48.30

[1] Not including acres which receive no cost share.
Total acres treated may not add due to rounding.
FSA, Conservation and Environmental Programs Division, (202) 690-1612.

Table 12-13.—Conservation Reserve Program (CRP): Enrollment by practice, under contract, September 2019

(CP38, CP39, and CP40)

State	CP38 State acres for wildlife enhancement			CP39 Constructed wetlands			CP40 Aquaculture wetlands		
	Total acres treated	Total cost share	Avg cost share per acre treated [1]	Total acres treated	Total cost share	Avg cost share per acre treated [1]	Total acres treated	Total cost share	Avg cost share per acre treated [1]
Alabama	2,114	126,966	116.01	0	0	....	14	504	36.52
Alaska	....	0	....	0	0	....	0	0	....
Arkansas	18,585	1,008,913	155.26	0	0	....	2,012	517,991	293.64
California	....	0	....	0	0	....	0	0	....
Colorado	73,121	3,956,024	81.25	0	0	....	0	0	....
Delaware	....	0	....	0	0	....	0	0	....
Florida	....	0	....	0	0	....	0	0	....
Georgia	15,804	1,010,174	126.63	0	0	....	0	0	....
Hawaii	....	0	....	0	0	....	0	0	....
Idaho	145,740	10,557,754	78.18	0	0	....	0	0	....
Illinois	27,398	4,268,487	207.62	30	0	....	0	0	....
Indiana	57,476	6,337,791	132.39	0	0	....	0	0	....
Iowa	288,933	42,170,420	159.53	263	60,060	280.27	0	0	....
Kansas	204,027	8,153,305	63.59	7	830	350.21	0	0	....
Kentucky	15,355	1,365,495	177.85	0	0	....	0	0	....
Louisiana	477	33,668	92.75	1	138	156.82	3,220	559,700	173.79
Maine	2,099	368,072	417.21	0	0	....	0	0	....
Maryland	....	0	....	0	0	....	0	0	....
Massachusetts	....	0	....	0	0	....	0	0	....
Michigan	19,530	4,226,316	280.82	0	0	....	0	0	....
Minnesota	98,506	7,869,876	97.39	89	32,044	358.11	0	0	....
Mississippi	11,847	1,683,120	305.88	0	0	....	11,182	1,300,930	158.67
Missouri	56,949	5,862,955	196.51	0	0	....	222	0	....
Montana	88,093	4,829,742	97.67	0	0	....	0	0	....
Nebraska	129,155	8,396,087	80.15	0	0	....	0	0	....
Nevada	....	0	....	0	0	0	0	....	
New Jersey	979	148,196	189.13	0	0		0	0	....
New Mexico	2,600	0	....	0	0	....	0	0	....
New York	2,279	328,881	215.85	0	0	....	0	0	....
North Carolina	875	103,413	212.24	0	0	....	58	692	197.71
North Dakota	158,613	4,225,643	46.78	0	0	....	0	0	....
Ohio	37,202	3,129,045	155.46	84	54,829	2,383.89	0	0	....
Oklahoma	8,319	2,647,326	573.36	0	0	....	0	0	....
Oregon	5,450	304,550	63.21	0	0	....	0	0	....
Pennsylvania	....	0	....	0	0	....	0	0	....
South Carolina	1,066	176,990	227.65	0	0	....	0	0	....
South Dakota	164,544	5,090,484	46.93	14	0	....	3	0	....
Tennessee	9,968	1,204,328	144.98	0	0	....	0	0	....
Texas	178,067	14,250,046	102.32	0	0	....	0	0	....
Utah	....	0	....	0	0	....	0	0	....
Vermont	....	0	....	0	0	....	0	0	....
Virginia	510	48,548	114.23	0	0	....	0	0	....
Washington	112,365	14,582,732	165.87	0	0	....	0	0	....
West Virginia	....	0	....	0	0	....	0	0	....
Wisconsin	31,959	4,080,676	179.73	0	0	....	0	0	....
Wyoming	9,831	850,961	87.95	0	0	....	0	0	....
United States	1,979,835	163,396,986	112.31	489	147,901	448.16	16,711	2,379,817	180.28

[1] Not including acres which receive no cost share.
Total acres treated may not add due to rounding.
FSA, Conservation and Environmental Programs Division, (202) 690-1612.

Table 12-14.—Conservation Reserve Program (CRP): Enrollment by practice, under contract, September 2019

(CP41 and CP42)

State	CP41 Flooded prairie wetlands			CP42 Pollinator Habitat [1]		
	Total acres treated	Total cost share	Avg cost share per acre treated [1]	Total acres treated	Total cost share	Avg cost share per acre treated [2]
Alabama	0	0	....	85	10,259	122.73
Alaska	0	0	....	0	0	....
Arkansas	0	0	....	50	6,553	412.14
California	0	0	....	1,819	0	....
Colorado	0	0	....	19,046	2,295,663	152.02
Delaware	0	0	....	4	2,800	700.00
Florida	0	0	....	0	0	....
Georgia	0	0	....	27	3,847	167.48
Hawaii	0	0	....	0	0	....
Idaho	0	0	....	7,830	658,264	101.40
Illinois	0	0	....	105,702	45,233,686	433.40
Indiana	0	0	....	5,244	802,537	162.85
Iowa	125	21,879	196.91	219,435	112,321,932	520.62
Kansas	0	0	....	5,533	226,826	68.78
Kentucky	0	0	....	4,715	1,223,038	266.90
Louisiana	0	0	....	22	1,850	82.42
Maine	0	0	....	0	0	....
Maryland	0	0	....	32	2,889	300.00
Massachusetts	0	0	....	0	0	....
Michigan	0	0	....	5,487	874,254	163.93
Minnesota	1,052	72,521	80.59	14,495	3,935,145	279.41
Mississippi	0	0	....	0	0	....
Missouri	0	0	....	45,055	6,002,455	222.44
Montana	0	0	....	5,492	234,469	56.97
Nebraska	0	0	....	28,172	1,940,360	82.37
Nevada	0	0	....	16	2,795	173.61
New Jersey	0	0	....	14	63,891	4,656.78
New Mexico	0	0	....	857	83,328	120.00
New York	0	0	....	44	21,152	530.38
North Carolina	0	0	....	20	5,145	643.13
North Dakota	48,175	1,394,833	40.09	4,635	797,319	180.46
Ohio	0	0	....	3,305	235,721	117.86
Oklahoma	0	0	....	146	7,967	107.11
Oregon	0	0	....	353	15,304	94.87
Pennsylvania	0	0	....	8	1,371	285.03
South Carolina	0	0	....	0	0	....
South Dakota	13,720	568,939	47.07	4,438	735,424	174.61
Tennessee	0	0	....	4,988	669,949	164.48
Texas	0	0	....	11,993	946,285	130.43
Utah	0	0	....	743	62,006	83.48
Vermont	0	0	....	0	0	....
Virginia	0	0	....	196	28,764	359.64
Washington	0	0	....	3,096	300,202	117.44
West Virginia	0	0	....	0	0	....
Wisconsin	0	0	....	2,236	648,036	398.21
Wyoming	0	0	....	230	43,386	188.40
United States	63,073	2,058,172	42.98	505,566	180,444,870	394.89

[1] Not including acres which receive no cost share.
Total acres treated may not add due to rounding.
FSA, Conservation and Environmental Programs Division, (202) 690-1612.

Table 12-15.—Conservation Reserve Program (CRP): Enrollment by practice, under contract, September 2019

(CP87 and CP88)

State	CP87 Grasslands-Native Grass			CP88 Grasslands-Introduced grass		
	Total acres treated	Total cost share	Avg cost share per acre treated [2]	Total acres treated	Total cost share	Avg cost share per acre treated [1]
Alabama	2,035	0	....	166	482,528	2,904.35
Alaska	....	0	....	....	0	....
Arkansas	....	0	....	60	0	....
California	847	0	....	588	0	....
Colorado	1,401	16,368	100.00	81,153	506,386	46.81
Delaware	....	0	....	....	0	....
Florida	378	0	....	....	0	....
Georgia	1,350	2,624	17.01	....	0	....
Hawaii	....	0	....	....	0	....
Idaho	....	0	....	23,784	861,429	49.28
Illinois	450	0	....	3	0	....
Indiana	54	0	....	47	0	....
Iowa	2,256	0	....	793	0	....
Kansas	607	261	25.02	24,206	13,818	25.00
Kentucky	3,376	0	....	51	0	....
Louisiana	1,217	0	....	165	0	....
Maine	....	0	....	....	0	....
Maryland	894	11,899	46.53	35	0	....
Massachusetts	....	0	....	....	0	....
Michigan	6,360	70,255	255.56	....	0	....
Minnesota	752	0	....	1,781	0	....
Mississippi	420	0	....	156	0	....
Missouri	1,171	0	....	784	0	....
Montana	4,773	0	....	43,114	33,648	14.04
Nebraska	21,164	7,426	43.87	310,770	648,942	61.51
Nevada	....	0	....	....	0	....
New Jersey	154	0	....	....	0	....
New Mexico	1,944	0	....	93,196	804,034	70.35
New York	1,607	230,331	472.65	2	0	....
North Carolina	538	0	....	7	0	....
North Dakota	2,966	0	....	22,894	14,088	30.29
Ohio	4,069	13,627	152.55	61	0	....
Oklahoma	1,577	0	....	33,347	8,629	27.57
Oregon	1,145	0	....	15,930	0	....
Pennsylvania	425	29,178	850.17	110	301	15.00
South Carolina	101	7,708	76.26	....	0	....
South Dakota	6,440	13,555	143.11	128,732	517,821	37.62
Tennessee	2,279	5,609	67.96	1,022	0	....
Texas	1,731	27,059	88.72	27,885	564,081	124.23
Utah	85	0	....	797	0	....
Vermont	....	0	....	....	0	....
Virginia	987	20,272	111.85	80	0	....
Washington	276	0	....	4,850	0	....
West Virginia	2,140	16,682	51.07	....	0	....
Wisconsin	821	0	....	23	0	....
Wyoming	1,709	0	....	20,125	0	....
United States	80,579	473,154	173.07	836,716	4,455,705	61.46

[1] Not including acres which receive no cost share.
Total acres treated may not add due to rounding.
FSA, Conservation and Environmental Programs Division, (202) 690-1612.

Table 12-16.—Emergency Conservation Program: Assistance, fiscal years 2010–2019 [1]

Year	Emergency Conservation Program
	1,000 dollars
2010	76,735
2011	32,262
2012	56,114
2013	41,206
2014	22,548
2015	24,001
2016	26,017
2017	56,353
2018	94,038
2019	71,852

[1] Totals are from unrounded data.
FSA, Conservation and Environmental Protection Division, (202) 690-1612.

Table 12-17.—Conservation Reserve Program (CRP): Enrollment by State, September 2019

State [1]	Number of contracts	Number of farms	Acres	Annual rent ($1,000)	Avg Payments [2] ($/acre)
Alabama	4,851	3,635	199,170	9,148	45.93
Alaska	14	13	2,704	103	38.09
Arkansas	5,259	3,051	220,324	17,170	77.93
California	172	129	42,735	2,253	52.71
Colorado	9,919	5,355	1,820,532	63,068	34.64
Connecticut	*	*	*	*	*
Delaware	323	191	3,684	523	141.89
Florida	561	467	23,173	1,121	48.39
Georgia	6,356	4,403	209,729	13,443	64.10
Hawaii	27	18	1,261	61	48.59
Idaho	3,590	2,041	541,835	28,481	52.56
Illinois	76,531	42,768	853,668	167,270	195.94
Indiana	33,276	18,756	218,638	40,663	185.99
Iowa	107,327	54,040	1,744,748	387,369	222.02
Kansas	34,812	20,498	1,946,905	85,868	44.10
Kentucky	12,326	6,482	207,775	32,870	158.20
Louisiana	4,464	2,921	275,713	25,073	90.94
Maine	243	170	5,641	265	47.03
Maryland	4,834	2,773	50,493	10,895	215.77
Massachusetts	6	3	20	3	153.65
Michigan	9,381	5,508	120,929	15,827	130.88
Minnesota	55,355	29,157	1,058,276	133,995	126.62
Mississippi	14,565	9,617	598,515	44,682	74.66
Missouri	26,714	16,112	841,875	100,395	119.25
Montana	6,265	2,857	1,063,871	32,565	30.61
Nebraska	20,100	11,874	1,068,595	71,645	67.05
Nevada	*	*	*	*	*
New Hampshire	*	*	*	*	*
New Jersey	337	203	1,947	174	89.48
New Mexico	1,688	1,086	429,730	13,595	31.64
New York	1,574	1,135	24,533	2,279	92.90
North Carolina	3,459	2,477	50,417	3,659	72.58
North Dakota	20,826	10,890	1,293,082	67,215	51.98
Ohio	35,223	19,546	242,527	42,545	175.42
Oklahoma	5,475	3,826	642,121	21,265	33.12
Oregon	3,687	2,053	441,752	28,033	63.46
Pennsylvania	7,785	5,204	127,015	16,573	130.48
Puerto Rico	5	5	515	27	51.55
Rhode Island	*	*	*	*	*
South Carolina	2,734	1,592	58,251	2,362	40.55
South Dakota	29,252	13,597	1,141,377	101,455	88.89
Tennessee	5,258	3,569	127,955	12,276	95.94
Texas	18,895	13,665	2,811,809	103,526	36.82
Utah	793	514	160,627	5,483	34.13
Vermont	370	271	2,413	276	114.34
Virginia	3,744	2,898	34,691	2,353	67.84
Washington	10,901	5,052	1,191,082	71,449	59.99
West Virginia	502	414	7,811	503	64.43
Wisconsin	13,765	8,778	204,964	30,530	148.95
Wyoming	768	490	209,765	5,139	24.50
United States	604,317	340,109	22,325,377	1,815,477	81.32

*Data withheld to avoid disclosure of individual operations. [1] State in which land is administered. [2] Payments made October, 2019.
FSA, Conservation and Environmental Programs Division, (202) 690-1612.

Table 12-18.—Forest land: Total forest land and area and ownership of timberland, by regions, Jan. 1, 2017

Region	Total forest land [1]	Timberland [2]							
		All ownerships	Federal			State, county, and municipal	Private		
			Total	National forest	Other		Total	Private corporate	Private non-corporate [3]
	1,000 acres	*1,000 acres*	*1,000 acres*	*1,000 acres*	*1,000 acres*	*1,000 acres*	*1,000 acres*	*1,000 acres*	*1,000 acres*
Northeast	84,727	78,539	2,852	2,355	498	10,103	65,586	22,090	43,496
North Central	91,062	86,355	8,495	7,792	704	15,549	62,310	8,106	54,204
North	175,789	164,894	11,348	10,146	1,202	15,650	127,896	30,196	97,700
Southeast	89,692	85,754	7,016	5,061	1,955	5,618	73,119	27,283	45,836
South Central	155,821	122,338	9,380	7,197	2,183	3,942	109,016	36,220	72,795
South	245,513	208,092	16,397	12,258	4,138	9,561	182,135	63,504	118,632
Great Plains	6,797	6,084	1,217	1,051	166	265	4,602	202	4,400
Intermountain	123,844	63,569	45,894	43,154	2,740	2,927	14,748	4,890	9,858
Rocky Mountains	130,641	69,654	47,111	44,206	2,905	3,193	19,350	5,091	14,259
Alaska	128,735	12,996	4,874	3,848	1,025	4,810	3,313	2,827	486
Pacific Northwest	51,827	41,462	19,200	16,802	2,397	3,637	18,625	10,903	7,722
Pacific Southwest [4]	32,986	17,326	9,249	8,877	372	245	7,833	4,634	3,198
Pacific Coast	213,549	71,784	33,323	29,527	3,795	8,691	29,771	18,364	11,406
All regions	765,493	514,425	108,178	96,138	12,040	47,095	359,152	117,155	241,997

Source: Forest Resources of the United States 2017 (a periodic compilation of the USDA Forest Service's continuous forest inventory, the next edition of which is due in 2022). Data may not add to totals because of rounding. [1] Forest land is land at least 10 percent stocked by forest trees of any size, including land that formerly had such tree cover and that will be naturally or artificially regenerated. Forest land includes transition zones, such as areas between heavily forested and non-forested lands that are at least 10 percent stocked with forest trees, and forest areas. The minimum area for classification of forest land is 1 acre. Roadside, streamside, and shelterbelt strips of timber must have a crown width at least 120 feet wide to qualify as forest land. Unimproved roads and trails, streams, and clearings in forest areas are classified as forest if less than 120 feet in width. [2] Timberland is forest land that is producing or is capable of producing crops of industrial wood and that is not withdrawn from timber utilization by statute or administrative regulation. Areas qualifying as timberland have the capability of producing more than 20 cubic feet per acre per year of industrial wood. Currently inaccessible and inoperable areas are included. [3] Includes Indian lands. [4] Includes Hawaii.

Prepared by Forest Service Research and Development, Washington Office, IMAR Staff.

Table 12-19.—Timber volume: Net volume of growing stock on timberland, by softwoods and hardwoods, and regions, 2017

Region	Growing stock [1]		
	All species	Softwoods	Hardwoods
	Million cubic feet		
Northeast	152,780	37,108	115,672
North Central	117,261	23,494	93,768
North	270,041	60,601	209,440
Southeast	142,603	67,540	75,063
South Central	176,485	73,767	102,717
South	319,088	141,307	177,781
Great Plains	4,487	1,885	2,601
Intermountain	125,518	117,217	8,301
Rocky Mountains	130,005	119,102	10,903
Alaska	37,140	33,761	3,379
Pacific Northwest	159,238	146,480	12,758
Pacific Southwest [2]	69,726	59,273	10,452
Pacific Coast	266,104	239,515	26,589
All regions	985,238	560,526	424,712

Source: Forest Resources of the United States 2017 (a periodic compilation of the USDA Forest Service's continuous forest inventory, the next edition of which is due in 2022). Data may not add to totals because of rounding. [1] Live trees of commercial species meeting specified standards of quality or vigor. Cull trees are excluded. Includes only trees 5.0-inches diameter or larger at 4½ feet above ground. [2] Includes Hawaii.

Prepared by Forest Service Research and Development, Washington Office, IMAR Staff.

Table 12-20.—Total volume of roundwood harvested in the United States, by sources and category, 2016

Category	All sources			Growing stock [1]			Other sources [2]		
	All species	Softwoods	Hardwoods	All species	Softwoods	Hardwoods	All species	Softwoods	Hardwoods
	Million cubic feet								
Roundwood products:									
Sawlogs	5,521	4,075	1,446	5,334	3,959	1,374	187	115	72
Pulpwood	5,368	3,640	1,728	4,772	3,280	1,493	596	360	235
Veneer logs	660	590	69	648	582	65	12	8	4
Other products [3]	728	575	153	563	423	141	165	153	12
Fuelwood	1,695	599	1,096	332	149	183	1,363	450	913
Total	13,972	9,480	4,493	11,650	8,393	3,257	2,323	1,086	1,236
Logging residue [4]	3,758	1,942	1,815	1,126	451	676	2,631	1,492	1,139
Other removals [5]	510	134	376	274	67	207	236	67	169
Total	4,268	2,076	2,191	1,400	518	883	2,867	1,559	1,308

Source: Forest Resources of the United States 2017 (a periodic compilation of the USDA Forest Service's continuous forest inventory, the next edition of which is due in 2022). Data may not add to totals because of rounding. [1] Includes live trees of commercial species meeting specified standards of quality or vigor. Cull trees are excluded. Includes only trees 5.0-inches diameter or larger at 4½ feet above ground. [2] Includes salvable dead trees, rough and rotten trees, trees of noncommercial species, trees less than 5.0-inches diameter at 4½ feet above ground, tops, and roundwood harvested from nonforest land (for example, fence rows). [3] Includes poles, pilings, posts, and miscellaneous products. [4] Net of wet rot or limbs. [5] Unutilized wood volume from cut or otherwise killed growing stock, from nongrowing stock sources on timberland (for example, precommercial thinnings), or from timberland clearing. Does not include volume removed from inventory through reclassification of timberland to reserved timberland.

Prepared by Forest Service Research and Development, Washington Office, IMAR Staff.

Table 12-21.—Net annual growth, removals, and mortality of growing stock on timberland in the United States, 2016

Region	Growth [1]			Removals [2]			Mortality [3]		
	All species	Softwoods	Hardwoods	All species	Softwoods	Hardwoods	All species	Softwoods	Hardwoods
	Million cubic feet								
Northeast	3,264	917	2,347	1,176	377	799	1,242	336	906
North Central	2,668	629	2,039	1,315	277	1,038	1,379	231	1,147
North	5,932	1,546	4,386	2,491	654	1,837	2,621	567	2,053
Southeast	6,393	4,285	2,108	3,527	2,736	790	1,085	528	557
South Central	7,371	4,983	2,388	4,333	2,911	1,422	1,845	630	1,215
South	13,764	9,268	4,496	7,859	5,647	2,212	2,930	1,150	1,772
Great Plains	57	(2)	59	34	29	6	82	43	39
Intermountain	242	192	50	370	367	3	2,487	2,354	133
Rocky Mountain	299	189	109	404	396	9	2,570	2,397	173
Alaska	254	133	121	39	39	-	302	275	27
Pacific Northwest	3,707	3,423	284	1,891	1,811	81	1,201	1,030	171
Pacific Southwest [4]	1,054	909	145	355	355	-	574	472	102
Pacific Coast	5,015	4,465	550	2,286	2,204	82	2,078	1,777	300
All regions	25,009	15,468	9,542	13,041	8,901	4,140	10,198	5,900	4,299

Source: Forest Resources of the United States 2017 (a periodic compilation of the USDA Forest Service's continuous forest inventory, the next edition of which is due in 2022). Data may not add to totals because of rounding. [1] The net increase in the volume of trees during a specified year. Components include the increment in net volume of trees at the beginning of the specific year surviving to its end, plus the net volume of trees reaching the minimum size class during the year, minus the volume of trees that died during the year, and minus the net volume of trees that became cull trees during the year. [2] The net volume of trees removed from the inventory during a specified year by harvesting, cultural operations such as timber stand improvement, or land clearing. [3] The volume of sound wood in trees that died from natural causes during a specified year. [4] Includes Hawaii.

Prepared by Forest Service Research and Development, Washington Office, IMAR Staff.

Table 12-22.—Net volume of growing stock on timberland in the Western United States, region and species, 2017

Species	Total West	Inter-mountain	Alaska	Pacific Northwest	Pacific Southwest [1]	Great Plains
	Million cubit feet					
Softwoods:						
Douglas-fir	128,235	30,003	0	79,650	18,582	0
Ponderosa and Jeffrey pines	42,389	17,118	0	12,389	11,143	1,739
True fir	54,703	23,272	17	16,791	14,624	0
Western hemlock	34,770	1,486	13,009	20,175	101	0
Sugar pine	3,684	0	0	675	3,009	0
Western white pine	1,057	418	0	318	321	0
Redwood	5,904	0	0	21	5,883	0
Sitka spruce	12,149	0	10,536	1,405	208	0
Engelmann and other spruces	24,408	18,601	4,302	1,505	0	0
Western larch	6,242	4,117	3	2,122	0	0
Incense cedar	4,381	0	0	873	3,508	0
Lodgepole pine	19,765	15,661	84	2,960	1,060	0
Other softwoods	20,931	6,544	5,811	2,260	834	146
Total	358,617	117,217	33,761	146,480	59,273	2,021
Hardwoods:						
Cottonwood and aspen	10,990	8,082	1,126	748	46	988
Red alder	6,711	20	140	6,220	331	0
Oak	5,175	0	0	608	4,114	453
Other	14,615	199	2,114	5,181	5,961	1,160
Total	37,492	8,301	3,379	12,758	10,452	2,601
All species	396,109	125,518	37,140	159,238	69,726	4,487

Source: Forest Resources of the United States 2017 (a periodic compilation of the USDA Forest Service's continuous forest inventory, the next edition of which is due in 2022). International ¼-inch rule. Data may not add to totals because of rounding. [1] Includes Hawaii.
Prepared by Forest Service Research and Development, Washington Office, IMAR Staff.

Table 12-23.—Net volume of softwood growing stock on timberland in the Eastern United States, by region and species, 2017

Species	Total East	North		South	
		Northeast	North Central	Southeast	South Central
	Million cubit feet				
Softwoods:					
Longleaf and slash pines	17,820	0	0	13,320	4,500
Loblolly and shortleaf pines	105,748	882	1,093	42,253	61,520
Other yellow pines	8,585	1,784	358	4,690	1,752
White and red pines	25,508	12,945	9,620	2,350	592
Jack pine	912	6	906	0	0
Spruce and balsam fir	13,646	9,202	4,374	70	0
Eastern hemlock	11,252	9,005	1,342	413	493
Cypress	7,309	11	11	3,969	3,318
Other	11,128	3,273	5,789	474	1,592
Total	201,909	37,108	23,494	67,540	73,767
Hardwoods:					
Select white oaks	35,869	5,885	10,132	7,680	12,172
Select red oaks	28,764	12,064	7,007	3,489	6,204
Other white oaks	23,036	5,670	2,187	5,659	9,520
Other red oaks	45,323	6,047	8,109	11,746	19,421
Hickory	23,104	4,146	5,533	3,896	9,529
Yellow birch	4,585	3,778	731	72	3
Hard maple	26,937	13,899	10,049	531	2,097
Soft maple	41,951	22,095	11,229	5,266	3,360
Beech	8,570	4,921	1,059	922	1,668
Sweetgum	20,431	686	251	8,407	11,086
Tupelo and black gum	11,743	829	337	5,846	4,732
Ash	18,948	6,941	6,310	1,823	3,874
Basswood	6,349	2,012	3,527	361	449
Yellow-poplar	33,998	7,554	3,046	14,594	8,804
Cottonwood and aspen	15,539	3,756	11,125	121	537
Black walnut	3,130	479	1,859	253	540
Black cherry	10,655	6,752	2,593	509	800
Other	28,292	8,157	8,325	3,888	7,921
Total	387,221	115,672	93,768	75,063	102,717
All species	589,129	152,780	117,261	142,603	176,485

Source: Forest Resources of the United States 2017 (a periodic compilation of the USDA Forest Service's continuous forest inventory, the next edition of which is due in 2022). International ¼-inch rule. Data may not add to totals because of rounding.
Prepared by Forest Service Research and Development, Washington Office, IMAR Staff.

Table 12-24.— National Forest System: National Forest System lands and other lands in States and Territories, as of September 30, 2019

State or other area	Gross acreage	National Forest System acreage [1]	Other acreage [2]
	1,000 acres		
USA Total	234,023	192,994	41,029
Alabama	1,290	671	620
Alaska	23,932	22,139	1,793
Arizona	11,813	11,179	633
Arkansas	3,549	2,593	955
California	24,288	20,811	3,477
Colorado	15,960	14,487	1,472
Connecticut	0.02	0.02	0
Florida	1,423	1,203	220
Georgia	1,796	868	929
Idaho	21,714	20,449	1,266
Illinois	958	305	653
Indiana	647	204	443
Kansas	109	109	0
Kentucky	2,205	818	1,387
Louisiana	1,032	609	423
Maine	94	54	41
Michigan	4,887	2,876	2,011
Minnesota	5,488	2,845	2,642
Mississippi	2,374	1,191	1,183
Missouri	3,093	1,508	1,585
Montana	19,190	17,195	1,994
Nebraska	562	351	211
Nevada	6,288	5,761	528
New Hampshire	851	754	97
New Mexico	10,249	9,225	1,024
New York	17	16	0
North Carolina	3,027	1,257	1,770
North Dakota	1,103	1,103	0
Ohio	856	244	612
Oklahoma	759	400	359
Oregon	17,654	15,698	1,956
Pennsylvania	741	514	227
South Carolina	1,381	635	746
South Dakota	2,436	2,007	429
Tennessee	1,291	723	568
Texas	2,002	757	1,245
Utah	9,205	8,192	1,013
Vermont	837	411	426
Virginia	3,254	1,669	1,586
Washington	11,990	9,336	2,654
West Virginia	1,893	1,047	846
Wisconsin	2,003	1,525	478
Wyoming	9,726	9,226	500
Puerto Rico	56	29	27
Virgin Islands	0.14	0.14	0

Source: Land Areas of the National Forest System 2019 (https://www.fs.fed.us/land/staff/lar-index.shtml).

[1] *National Forest System acreage.*—A nationally significant system of Federally owned units of forest, range, and related land consisting of national forests, purchase units, national grasslands, land utilization project areas, experimental forest areas, experimental range areas, designated experimental areas, other land areas; water areas, and interests in lands that are administered by USDA Forest Service or designated for administration through the Forest Service.

National forests.—Units formally established and permanently set aside and reserved for national forest purposes.

Purchase units.—Units designated by the Secretary of Agriculture or previously approved by the National Forest Reservation Commission for purposes of Weeks Law Acquisition.

National grasslands.—Units designated by the Secretary of Agriculture and permanently held by the Department of Agriculture under Title III of the Bankhead-Jones Farm Tenant Act.

Land utilization projects.—Units designated by the Secretary of Agriculture for conservation and utilization under Title III of the Bankhead-Jones Farm Tenant Act.

Research and experimental areas.—Units reserved and dedicated by the Secretary of Agriculture for forest or range research and experimentation.

Other areas.—Units administered by the Forest Service that are not included in the above groups.

[2] *Other acreage.*—Lands within the unit boundaries in private, State, county, and municipal ownership and Federal lands over which the Forest Service has no jurisdiction. Areas of such lands which have been offered to the United States and have been approved for acquisition and subsequent Forest Service administration, but to which title had not yet been accepted by the United States.

Prepared by Forest Service Research and Development, Washington Office, IMAR Staff.

Table 12-25.—Forest products cut on National Forest System lands: Volume and value of timber cut and value of all products, United States, fiscal years 2010–2019

Year	Timber cut [1]		Value of non-covertible products [3]	Total value including free-use timber
	Volume	Value [2]		
	Million bd. ft.	*1,000 dollars* [4]	*1,000 dollars* [4, 5]	*1,000 dollars* [4]
2010	2,138	72,174	3,263	104,809
2011	2,440	105,869	2,603	131,904
2012	2,500	112,943	2,748	140,428
2013	2,408	114,878	2,850	143,383
2014	2,437	122,794	2,618	148,979
2015	2,543	129,186	3,346	162,651
2016	2,537	162,444	2,962	165,406
2017	2,596	175,847	2,906	178,753
2018	2,797	185,285	3,480	188,765
2019	2,556	164,208	2,547	166,755

Source: USDA Forest Service, Forest Products Cut and Sold from the National Forests. (https://www.fs.fed.us/forestmanagement/products/cut-sold/index.shtml). [1] Commercial and cost sales and land exchanges. [2] Includes collections for forest restoration or improvement under the Knutson-Vandenberg Act, 1930. [3] Includes materials not measurable in board feet, such as Christmas trees, tanbark, turpentine, seedlings, Spanish moss, etc. [4] Nominal dollars not adjusted for inflation. [5] 2010-2015 revised in 2019.

Prepared by Forest Service Research and Development, Washington Office, IMAR Staff.

Table 12-26.—Lumber: Production, United States, 2010–2019

Year	Total	Softwoods	Hardwoods [1]
	Million bd. ft.		
2010	30,461	24,802	5,659
2011	33,304	26,754	6,550
2012	34,791	28,256	6,535
2013	37,321	29,982	7,339
2014	39,810	31,490	8,320
2015 [2]	42,085	32,028	9,538
2016 [2]	42,085	32,535	9,550
2017	43,538	33,888	9,650
2018	44,508	34,908	9,600
2019	45,423	35,919	9,504

Source: Howard, James L.; Liang, Shaobo, 2019. U.S. timber production, trade, consumption, and price statistics, 1965-2017. USDA Forest Service Research Paper FPL-RP-701. [1] In-house estimate. [2] Revised in 2019.

Prepared by Forest Service Research and Development, Washington Office, IMAR Staff.

Table 12-27.—Timber products: Production, imports, exports, and consumption, United States, 2009–2018

Year	Industrial roundwood used for—										
	Lumber				Plywood and veneer				Pulpwood chip		Other industrial products, production and consumption [1]
	Production	Imports	Exports	Consumption	Production	Imports	Exports	Consumption	Imports	Exports	
	Million cu. ft., roundwood equivalent										
2009	4,576	1,347	288	5,636	616	146	34	728	9	196	294
2010	4,569	1,422	341	5,650	655	137	55	736	9	235	294
2011	5,005	1,403	387	6,022	651	139	52	738	9	235	294
2012	5,219	1,480	374	6,324	679	139	57	761	9	235	294
2013	5,607	1,675	406	6,911	703	147	55	796	9	234	294
2014	5,995	1,869	406	7,458	693	187	46	834	9	234	294
2015	6,065	2,100	371	7,793	683	222	38	867	9	235	294
2016	6,143	2,426	527	8,042	703	263	43	923	6	262	732
2017	6,338	2,328	580	8,086	729	274	47	967	2	280	822
2018	6,467	2,953	694	8,726	716	361	44	1,033	2	290	912

Year	Industrial roundwood used for—									
	Pulpwood-based products				Logs		Total			
	Production	Imports [2]	Exports [2]	Consumption	Imports	Exports	Production	Imports	Exports	Consumption
	Million cu. ft.									
2009	4,733	902	785	4,849	17	322	10,737	2,421	1,625	11,532
2010	4,779	911	832	4,857	20	407	10,938	2,498	1,870	11,566
2011	4,748	887	899	4,736	19	485	11,418	2,457	2,058	11,817
2012	5,805	883	875	5,815	28	432	12,663	2,539	1,972	13,231
2013	5,959	942	1,073	5,827	26	463	13,260	2,799	2,231	13,862
2014	6,562	1,205	1,340	6,427	22	444	14,222	3,292	2,470	15,044
2015	6,569	1,172	1,348	6,392	22	279	14,124	3,524	2,272	15,376
2016	5,099	896	995	5,000	24	390	13,329	3,615	2,216	14,727
2017	5,081	875	1,013	4,943	32	393	13,643	3,511	2,315	14,851
2018	5,228	916	1,051	5,093	26	378	13,991	4,258	2,457	15,792

Year	Fuelwood production and consumption	Production, all products	Consumption, all products
	Million cu. ft.		
2009	1,400	12,137	12,932
2010	1,380	12,318	12,946
2011	1,366	12,784	13,183
2012	1,440	14,103	14,671
2013	1,520	14,780	15,382
2014	1,566	15,788	16,610
2015	1,566	15,690	16,942
2016	2,195	15,524	16,922
2017	2,273	15,917	17,124
2018	2,528	16,519	18,320

Source: Howard, James L.; Liang, Shaobo, 2019. U.S. timber production, trade, consumption, and price statistics, 1965-2017. [1] Includes cooperage logs, poles and piling, fence posts, hewn ties, round mine timbers, excelsior bolts, chemical wood, shingle bolts, and miscellaneous items. [2] Includes both pulpwood and the pulpwood equivalent of wood pulp, paper, and board.

Prepared by Forest Service Research and Development, Washington Office, IMAR Staff.

Table 12-28.—Timber products: Producer price indexes, selected products, United States, 2010–2019

[2009=100]

Year	Lumber	Softwood plywood	Woodpulp	Paper	Paperboard
2010	112.0	114.7	123.8	101.4	108.5
2011	111.5	108.1	129.7	106.5	111.2
2012	115.4	127.2	123.8	106.7	110.0
2013	133.0	137.7	120.3	106.2	117.6
2014	143.8	142.7	122.3	107.3	120.0
2015	133.4	136.4	120.9	105.7	117.3
2016	133.9	122.8	115.6	103.3	108.8
2017	145.4	136.6	107.5	103.8	124.3
2018	155.4	159.7	143.7	110.0	132.0
2019	140.8	129.6	115.8	111.7	129.4

Source: Federal Reserve Bank of St. Louis Economic Data Service (https://fred.stlouisfed.org/).
Prepared by Forest Service Research and Development, Washington Office, IMAR Staff.

Table 12-29.—Timber products: Pulpwood consumption, woodpulp production, and paper and board production and consumption, United States, 2010–2019

Year	Pulpwood consumption [1]	Woodpulp production [2]	Paper and board [3]		
			Production	Consumption or new supply [4]	Per capita consumption
	1,000 cords [5]	*1,000 tons*	*1,000 tons*	*1,000 tons*	*Pounds*
2010	80,307	55,343	82,968	85,331	551
2011	80,040	55,125	81,519	82,858	531
2012	81,422	55,475	80,916	82,321	524
2013	91,251	54,466	80,478	78,603	497
2014	92,186	53,367	79,488	78,046	490
2015	93,141	*52,646	79,024	77,444	481
2016	92,004	*52,701	78,342	76,002	484
2017	90,873	*52,485	78,445	76,625	470
2018	90,281	*51,840	78,114	*75,862	*465
2019	87,632	50,699	78,114	73,096	446

Source: 2009-2016--Howard, James L.; Liang, Shaobo. 2019. U.S. timber production, trade, consumption, and price statistics, 1965-2017. USDA Forest Service Research Paper FPL-RP-701. 2017-2019--In house estimate. All series compiled from U.S. Department of Commerce and American Forest and Paper Association.

*Revised in 2020. [1] Includes changes in stocks. [2] Excludes defibrated and exploded woodpulp used for hard pressed board, dissolving and special Alpha, and wood pulp used for construction paper & board. [3] Excludes hardboard. Includes wet machine board and construction grades. [4] Production plus imports and minus exports (excludes products); changes in inventories not taken into account. [5] One cord equals 128 cubic feet.

Prepared by Forest Service Research and Development, Washington Office, IMAR Staff.

Table 12-30.—Lumber and competing engineered wood products: Production by type of product, 2010–2019

Year	Laminated veneer lumber	Wood glulam	Structural Panels		Lumber	
			Oriented strandboard	Softwood Plywood	Hardwood [1]	Softwood
	Million cubic feet	*Million board feet*	*Million square feet (3/8-in. basis)*	*Million square feet (3/8-in. basis)*	*Billion board feet*	*Billion board feet*
2010	37	176	10,299	9,131	5.7	24.8
2011	38	184	10,039	8,980	6.6	26.8
2012	46	204	11,038	9,181	6.5	28.3
2013	54	230	12,492	9,346	7.3	30.0
2014	60	233	13,008	8,985	8.3	31.5
2015	61	252	13,283	8,751	8.3	32.0
2016	65	257	13,922	8,809	9.6	32.5
2017	73	271	14,609	9,026	9.7	33.8
2018	71	281	15,129	8,869	9.6	34.9
2019 [2]	71	281	15,181	8,679	9.5	35.9

Sources: APA-The Engineered Wood Association; US Department of Commerce, Bureau of the Census; American Forest and Paper Association; Luppold and Dempsey. Hardwood Market Report: 2008-present.

[1] 2016 data revised in 2020. [2] Preliminary estimates.

Prepared by Forest Service Research and Development, Washington Office, IMAR Staff.

CHAPTER XIII

CONSUMPTION AND FAMILY LIVING

The statistics in this chapter deal with the consumption of food by both rural and urban people, retail price levels, and other aspects of family living of farm people. Data presented here on quantities of food available for consumption are based on material presented in the earlier commodity chapters, but they are shown here at the retail level, a form that is more useful for an analysis of the demand situation faced by the producer. Data on quantities of farm-produced food consumed directly by farm households are presented in the commodity chapters. Its value and the rental value of the farm home are given in the section on farm income.

Table 13-1.—Population estimates for the United States, Jan. 1 and July 1, 2011-2019

Year	Jan. 1	July 1
2011	309,335,215	310,362,359
2012	311,584,613	312,634,059
2013	313,844,886	314,815,159
2014	316,078,106	317,160,490
2015	318,474,252	319,546,159
2016	320,808,676	321,868,857
2017	323,032,791	323,956,506
2018	325,032,134	325,980,513
2019	327,044,416	327,971,597

Note: The monthly estimates beginning with August 1, 2018 are short-term projections.
Monthly Population Estimates for the United States: April 1, 2010 to December 1, 2019. Source: U.S. Census Bureau, Population Division. Release Date: December 2018.
ERS, Rural Economy Branch (202) 694–5435.

Table 13-2.—Consumers' prices: Index number of prices paid for goods and services, United States, 2010–2019[1]

[1982–84=100]

Year	Food	Nonfood items					All items
		Apparel and upkeep	Housing		Transportation	Medical care	
			Total	Rent			
2010	219.6	119.5	216.3	258.8	193.4	388.4	218.1
2011	227.8	122.1	219.1	262.2	212.4	400.3	224.9
2012	233.8	126.3	222.7	267.8	217.3	414.9	229.6
2013	237.0	127.4	227.4	274.0	217.4	425.1	233.0
2014	242.7	127.5	233.2	281.8	215.9	435.3	236.7
2015	247.2	125.9	238.1	290.4	199.1	446.8	237.0
2016	247.9	126.0	244.0	300.3	194.9	463.7	240.0
2017	250.1	125.6	251.2	310.3	201.6	475.3	245.1
2018	253.6	125.7	258.5	320.7	210.7	484.7	251.1
2019	258.3	124.0	265.9	331.6	210.1	498.4	255.7

[1] Reflects retail prices of goods and services usually bought by average families in urban areas of the United States. This index is the official index released monthly by the U.S. Department of Labor. Data are for all urban consumers.
ERS, Food Markets Branch, (202) 694–5349. Compiled from data of the U.S. Department of Labor.

Table 13-3.—Consumption: Per capita consumption of major food commodities, United States, 2012–2016 [1]

Commodity	2012	2013	2014	2015	2016
	Pounds	*Pounds*	*Pounds*	*Pounds*	*Pounds*
Red meats [2]	98.0	98.0	95.0	98.6	100.5
Beef	54.5	53.6	51.5	51.4	52.9
Veal	0.3	0.3	0.2	0.2	0.2
Lamb and mutton	0.6	0.7	0.7	0.7	0.8
Pork	42.6	43.5	42.6	46.3	46.6
Fish	14.3	14.5	15.5	14.9	16.1
Canned	3.7	3.3	3.7	3.3	3.7
Fresh and frozen	10.4	10.9	11.5	11.3	12.0
Cured	0.3	0.3	0.3	0.3	0.3
Poultry	69.3	70.3	71.3	75.2	76.3
Chicken	56.7	57.7	58.8	62.6	63.2
Turkey	12.6	12.6	12.5	12.6	13.1
Eggs	32.7	33.2	34.2	33.0	35.0
Dairy products [3]					
Total dairy products	615.1	607.3	616.0	630.1	645.7
Fluid milk and cream	188.6	184.6	178.6	174.7	172.0
Plain and flavored whole milk	46.5	46.2	45.9	47.6	49.8
Plain reduced fat and light milk (2%, 1%, and 0.5%)	84.7	82.6	79.8	76.8	74.2
Plain fat free milk (skim)	24.8	22.6	20.0	17.7	15.6
Flavored lower fat free milk	12.5	12.3	12.0	12.1	12.3
Buttermilk	1.5	1.6	1.5	1.6	1.6
Eggnog	0.4	0.4	0.4	0.4	0.4
Yogurt (excl. frozen)	14.0	15.0	14.9	14.4	13.8
Sour cream and dip	4.1	4.1	4.1	4.1	4.3
Cheese (excluding cottage) [4]	33.3	33.4	34.2	35.1	36.4
American	13.3	13.4	13.7	14.0	14.4
Cheddar	9.6	9.6	9.8	10.2	10.4
Italian	13.8	13.8	14.2	14.5	15.2
Mozzarella	10.7	10.7	11.2	11.3	11.7
Cottage cheese	2.3	2.1	2.1	2.1	2.1
Condensed and evaporated milk	7.3	7.2	6.8	7.7	7.4
Ice cream	13.2	13.0	12.5	12.9	12.9
Butter	5.5	5.5	5.5	5.6	5.7
Fruits and vegetables [5]	636.0	636.6	636.6	631.9	651.7
Fruits	244.6	254.6	250.1	252.7	256.4
Fresh	131.8	136.3	136.3	136.1	142.3
Citrus	23.5	23.9	23.3	22.7	24.0
Noncitrus	108.3	112.4	113.1	113.4	118.3
Processing	112.8	118.2	113.8	116.6	114.1
Citrus	52.6	55.1	52.6	52.7	51.9
Noncitrus	60.2	63.1	61.2	63.8	62.2
Vegetables	391.4	382.1	386.5	379.2	395.3
Fresh	188.7	184.6	186.4	186.4	199.5
Processing	202.7	197.5	200.1	192.9	195.8
Flour and cereal products	174.1	174.7	174.4	172.9	171.9
Wheat flour [6]	134.3	135.0	134.7	133.0	131.7
Corn products	33.9	33.9	34.0	34.0	34.2
Oat products	4.7	4.5	4.5	4.6	4.6
Barley and rye products	1.1	1.2	1.2	1.3	1.4
Caloric sweeteners (dry weight basis)	129.3	128.2	129.1	129.1	128.1
Sugar (refined)	66.6	68.0	68.4	69.1	69.7
Corn sweeteners [7]	61.0	58.4	58.5	57.8	56.5
Honey and edible syrups	1.8	1.9	2.1	2.1	1.9
Others					
Coffee (green bean equivalent)	9.7	9.9	10.0	10.2	NA
Cocoa (chocolate liquor equivalent) [8]	4.2	4.2	4.1	4.3	NA
Tea (dry leaf equivalent)	0.9	0.9	0.9	0.9	NA
Peanuts (shelled)	6.7	6.9	7.0	7.4	7.2
Tree nuts (shelled)	4.2	4.0	4.1	4.1	4.9

[1] Quantity in pounds, retail weight unless otherwise shown. Totals may not add due to rounding. [2] Boneless, trimmed weight equivalent. [3] Total dairy products reported on a milk-equivalent, milkfat basis. All other dairy categories reported on a product weight basis. [4] Natural equivalent of cheese and cheese products. [5] Farm weight. [6] White, whole wheat, semolina, and durum flour. [7] High fructose, glucose, and dextrose. [8] Chocolate liquor is what remains after cocoa beans have been roasted and hulled; it is sometimes called ground or bitter chocolate.

ERS, Food Economics Division, (202) 694-5400. Historical consumption and supply-disappearance data for food may be found at https://www.ers.usda.gov/data-products/food-availability-per-capita-data-system.

Table 13-4.—USDA Food plans: Cost of food at home at four levels, U.S. average, December 2019[1]

Age-gender groups	Weekly cost[2]				Monthly cost[2]			
	Thrifty plan	Low-cost plan	Moderate-cost plan	Liberal plan	Thrifty plan	Low-cost plan	Moderate-cost plan	Liberal plan
	Dollars	*Dollars*	*Dollars*	*Dollars*	*Dollars*	*Dollars*	*Dollars*	*Dollars*
Individuals:[3]								
Child:								
1 year	21.80	29.40	33.40	40.50	94.70	127.30	144.60	175.70
2-3 years	23.90	30.90	37.00	45.00	103.60	133.70	160.40	195.10
4-5 years	25.20	31.70	39.60	47.90	109.30	137.20	171.40	207.40
6-8 years	32.00	44.60	53.90	63.50	138.70	193.10	233.60	275.10
9-11 years	36.30	47.80	62.50	72.80	157.10	207.30	271.00	315.30
Male:								
12-13 years	38.80	55.20	69.00	81.20	168.10	239.00	298.80	351.90
14-18 years	40.00	56.00	70.90	81.90	173.20	242.50	307.10	354.90
19-50 years	42.90	55.50	69.60	85.20	185.90	240.60	301.50	369.10
51-70 years	39.10	52.50	65.50	79.10	169.40	227.70	283.70	342.90
71+ years	39.30	51.50	64.30	79.20	170.20	223.30	278.50	343.00
Female:								
12-13 years	38.60	47.40	57.60	70.30	167.20	205.50	249.60	304.70
14-18 years	38.00	47.40	56.70	70.20	164.90	205.30	245.60	304.20
19-50 years	38.10	48.20	59.10	75.70	165.10	208.80	256.10	328.00
51-70 years	37.80	47.00	58.50	70.70	163.60	203.60	253.40	306.50
71+ years	36.90	46.30	57.80	69.70	160.10	200.60	250.40	301.90
Families:								
Family of 2 (Male and Female)[4]								
19-50 years	89.10	114.10	141.50	177.00	386.10	494.40	613.30	766.80
51-70 years	84.50	109.50	136.30	164.80	366.30	474.30	590.80	714.30
Family of 4:								
Couple (Male and Female), 19-50 years and children—								
2-3 and 4-5 years	130.10	166.30	205.30	253.80	563.90	720.40	889.40	1,000.60
6-8 and 9-11 years	149.30	196.10	245.10	297.10	646.80	849.80	1,062.10	1,287.50

[1] The Food Plans represent a nutritious diet at four different cost levels. The nutritional bases of the Food Plans are the 1997-2005 Dietary Reference Intakes, 2005 Dietary Guidelines for Americans, and 2005 MyPyramid food intake recommendations. In addition to cost, differences among plans are in specific foods and quantities of foods. Another basis of the Food Plans is that all meals and snacks are prepared at home. For specific foods and quantities of foods in the Food Plans, see *Thrifty Food Plan, 2006* (2007) and *The Low-Cost, Moderate-Cost, and Liberal Food Plans, 2007* (2007). All four Food Plans are based on 2001-02 data and updated to current dollars by using the Consumer Price Index for specific food items.

[2] All costs are rounded to nearest 10 cents.

[3] The costs given are for individuals in 4–person families. For individuals in other size families, the following adjustments are suggested: 1 person-add 20 percent; 2 person-add 10 percent; 3 person-add 5 percent; 4 person-no adjustment; 5- or 6-person–subtract 5 percent; 7- (or more) person-subtract 10 percent. To calculate overall household food costs, (1) adjust food costs for each person in household and then (2) sum these adjusted food costs.

[4] Ten percent added for family size adjustment.

Food and Nutrition Service, Center for Nutrition Policy and Promotion, (703) 305 7600. This file and the referenced Food Plans may be accessed at https://www.fns.usda.gov/cnpp/usda-food-plans-cost-food-reports-monthly-reports.

Table 13-5.—Food and Nutrition Service program benefits: Cash payments made under the National School Lunch, School Breakfast, Child and Adult Care, Summer Food and Special Milk Programs and the value of food benefits provided under the SNAP, WIC, Commodity Distribution and The Emergency Feeding Food Assistance Programs, fiscal year 2019[1]

State/Territory	Child Nutrition Program (cash payments only)[2]					Special Supplemental Food (WIC)	SNAP (formerly Food Stamp Program)[4]	Emergency food assistance (TEFAP)	Commodity distribution[3]	Total[4]
	Child and Adult Care Food	Summer Food	Special Milk	National School Lunch	School Breakfast					
	1,000 dollars									
Alabama	56,169	8,534	23	214,638	79,599	65,412	1,084,563	10,381	24,822	1,544,141
Alaska	8,868	1,372	0	38,061	13,090	11,519	187,357	958	3,808	265,034
Amer. Samoa[4]	0	0	0	0	0	4,588	0	0	0	4,588
Arizona	49,479	3,154	43	275,940	94,481	68,824	1,210,430	12,600	38,091	1,753,042
Arkansas	50,411	3,108	0	136,045	55,619	37,571	480,473	6,890	17,449	787,564
California	445,135	18,903	281	1,511,917	523,067	524,633	6,332,718	65,288	199,424	9,621,366
Colorado	25,073	4,427	199	133,410	48,214	37,816	668,611	6,857	17,023	941,630
Connecticut	17,248	4,146	98	105,335	32,726	24,981	614,968	5,210	10,556	815,268
Delaware	17,213	1,994	16	36,215	13,982	7,289	196,899	2,157	7,159	282,923
District of Columbia	10,025	2,017	2	28,446	11,693	6,362	188,433	1,407	3,294	251,679
Florida	275,203	37,357	14	895,124	281,088	235,464	5,763,763	33,621	94,622	7,616,257
Georgia	111,871	13,816	29	529,911	195,953	103,556	2,336,788	16,985	52,118	3,361,028
Guam	458	0	0	8,781	3,258	6,067	106,449	337	35	125,384
Hawaii	6,302	594	0	46,003	10,849	17,507	469,434	1,314	2,481	554,485
Idaho	7,693	3,704	68	53,053	18,476	13,334	199,514	2,630	8,368	306,841
Illinois	137,943	11,834	1,843	465,650	145,542	122,293	2,777,949	23,883	51,998	3,738,935
Indiana	55,385	7,839	118	269,034	82,086	58,130	867,533	11,295	39,071	1,390,491
Iowa	25,079	3,860	61	110,968	27,599	22,738	446,260	4,459	15,679	656,703
Kansas	28,307	4,284	55	106,106	31,698	22,032	293,540	4,048	14,968	505,037
Kentucky	41,876	9,127	18	232,259	95,413	46,085	853,987	8,040	30,615	1,317,420
Louisiana	87,481	7,311	0	249,066	89,640	63,153	1,297,322	10,470	38,492	1,842,935
Maine	8,803	2,266	12	33,863	12,783	9,205	218,218	2,303	6,742	294,196
Maryland	50,419	9,015	263	178,763	69,287	60,309	910,099	6,771	24,080	1,309,004
Massachusetts	61,383	7,258	162	198,670	65,838	49,103	1,159,119	9,073	27,268	1,577,874
Michigan	66,437	10,222	189	311,190	115,102	94,028	1,894,037	17,223	53,189	2,561,618
Minnesota	61,527	9,783	706	168,385	53,671	53,687	544,420	6,455	27,849	926,485
Mississippi	45,888	7,261	4	170,248	63,861	52,239	679,723	6,338	23,749	1,049,310
Missouri	53,835	13,515	428	212,151	79,070	47,697	1,061,334	10,287	34,492	1,512,809
Montana	10,316	2,101	6	28,992	10,432	6,966	158,390	1,525	8,258	226,986
Nebraska	28,553	2,685	56	75,709	19,848	17,487	229,206	2,342	14,230	390,117
Nevada	12,153	1,760	45	103,538	40,361	26,357	614,242	5,771	13,228	817,454
New Hampshire	4,624	910	145	21,594	5,440	4,601	101,470	1,530	5,054	145,369
New Jersey	81,397	11,683	254	262,359	94,775	94,730	1,012,654	15,104	34,614	1,607,570
New Mexico	31,249	5,115	0	101,740	43,961	21,086	638,422	4,731	15,940	862,245
New York	228,288	55,304	532	780,949	253,988	265,486	4,526,971	33,888	73,864	6,219,270
North Carolina	93,476	12,384	103	376,307	134,776	112,992	1,870,952	17,474	48,333	2,666,797
North Dakota	8,725	923	22	21,861	5,986	6,707	75,391	1,029	10,248	130,892
Northern Marianas[4]	0	0	0	0	0	1,164	0	0	0	1,164
Ohio	89,366	11,939	373	365,742	126,136	77,957	2,078,237	19,519	46,181	2,815,450
Oklahoma	59,598	4,363	21	180,185	64,053	39,836	832,653	6,601	45,209	1,232,520
Oregon	32,473	5,001	83	116,417	39,990	37,084	937,799	7,455	15,246	1,191,550
Pennsylvania	118,880	12,422	269	400,460	125,440	116,512	2,592,184	20,372	65,100	3,451,639
Puerto Rico[4]	19,558	6,621	0	110,809	25,885	121,030	0	9,410	15,280	308,594
Rhode Island	8,796	1,356	37	30,642	10,072	9,979	0	1,600	4,417	66,900
South Carolina	35,138	7,833	6	210,630	81,158	49,018	943,922	8,632	20,286	1,356,625
South Dakota	7,600	1,511	17	29,497	7,763	8,666	131,113	988	10,198	197,353
Tennessee	64,484	9,154	18	284,612	113,758	60,847	1,424,891	10,515	30,967	1,999,246
Texas	398,515	27,630	12	1,518,148	597,506	238,069	5,525,177	44,055	179,761	8,528,871
Utah	26,410	545	39	101,112	22,811	22,498	258,536	3,178	16,107	451,237
Vermont	5,789	1,207	26	16,022	6,651	6,202	106,782	1,113	2,940	146,732
Virginia	48,603	9,798	101	254,641	95,123	42,115	1,051,801	10,753	25,426	1,538,363
Virgin Islands	655	280	0	2,296	300	2,473	86,936	335	600	93,875
Washington	46,069	5,377	212	199,785	57,388	69,292	1,268,735	12,112	27,942	1,686,912
West Virginia	15,523	1,617	11	81,167	42,364	16,685	440,299	4,102	10,848	612,616
Wisconsin	35,791	8,389	842	171,279	53,871	41,990	816,882	7,740	31,533	1,168,318
Wyoming	4,327	801	22	14,863	4,155	3,502	40,676	1,073	2,815	72,234
DoD[5]	0	0	0	6,146	16	0	0	0	1,997	8,160
Total[4]	3,321,867	415,410	7,885	12,586,736	4,397,694	3,386,954	60,608,261	540,227	1,644,069	86,909,103

[1] Excludes all administrative and program evaluation costs. [2] Excludes totals for Food Safety Education and Team Nutrition. [3] Includes distribution of bonus and entitlement commodities to the National School Lunch, Child and Adult Care, Summer Food Service, Charitable Institutions, Summer Camps, Food Distribution on Indian Reservations, Nutrition Services Incentive Program (NSIP, formerly Nutrition Program for the Elderly), Commodity Supplemental Food, and Disaster Feeding Programs. Also includes cash-in-lieu of commodities for the National School Lunch and the Child and Adult Care Food programs (NSIP cash grants were transferred to the Agency on Aging, DHHS, in FY 2003). [4] Excludes Nutrition Assistance grants for Puerto Rico, Northern Marianas, and American Samoa. [5] Dept. of Defense represents food service to children of armed forces personnel in overseas schools.

FNS, Budget Division/Program Reports, Analysis and Monitoring Branch (703) 305–2165.

Table 13-6.—Food and Nutrition Service Programs: Persons participating, fiscal years 2010–2019

Fiscal year	National School Lunch Program [1]	School Breakfast Program [1]	Child and Adult Care Program [2]	Summer Food Service [3]	WIC Program [4]
	Thousands	*Thousands*	*Thousands*	*Thousands*	*Thousands*
2010	31,753	11,669	3,411	2,304	9,175
2011	31,842	12,175	3,431	2,278	8,961
2012	31,653	12,868	3,571	2,348	8,908
2013	30,683	13,203	3,681	2,428	8,663
2014	30,460	13,636	3,897	2,663	8,258
2015	30,496	14,049	4,181	2,570	8,024
2016	30,361	14,564	4,407	2,569	7,696
2017	29,992	14,658	4,530	2,646	7,286
2018	29,624	14,681	4,629	2,689	6,870
2019	29,519	14,730	4,706	2,679	6,400

[1] Average monthly participation (excluding summer months). [2] Average daily attendance (data reported quarterly). [3] Average daily attendance for peak month (July). [4] Average monthly participation. WIC is an abbreviation for the Special Supplemental Food Program for Women, Infants and Children.

FNS, Budget Division/Program Reports, Analysis and Monitoring Branch, (703) 305–2165.

Table 13-7.—Food and Nutrition Service Programs: Federal costs of the National School Lunch, School Breakfast, Child Care Food, Summer Food Service, WIC, Special Milk, and Food Distribution Programs, fiscal years 2010–2019 [1]

Fiscal year [2]	Child Nutrition					WIC [6]	Special Milk	Food Distribution Programs [7]
	Cash payments				Cost of food distribution programs [5]			
	School Lunch	School Breakfast	Child & Adult Care [3]	Summer Food [4]				
	1,000 dollars	*1,000 dollars*	*1,000 dollars*	*1,000 dollars*	*1,000 dollars*	*1,000 dollars*	*1,000 dollars*	*1,000 dollars*
2010	9,751,742	2,859,231	2,397,545	314,794	1,223,249	6,689,911	11,926	895,761
2011	10,105,029	3,034,159	2,471,494	327,232	1,298,925	7,180,750	12,296	829,719
2012	10,414,295	3,276,989	2,589,619	350,378	1,278,804	6,801,320	12,295	755,894
2013	11,057,635	3,513,985	2,720,122	375,781	1,288,858	6,501,668	10,721	997,936
2014	11,356,023	3,685,352	2,848,901	409,418	1,437,493	6,356,356	10,495	938,923
2015	11,695,742	3,891,787	3,008,620	427,797	1,457,385	6,239,931	10,515	839,975
2016	12,258,568	4,211,848	3,216,683	417,789	1,466,849	6,020,420	9,061	977,274
2017	12,250,693	4,252,279	3,239,578	423,756	1,545,880	5,695,963	8,284	991,625
2018	12,579,977	4,396,483	3,321,813	416,040	1,401,743	6,445,103	7,888	995,869
2019	12,000,585	4,526,623	3,424,292	416,200	1,484,499	5,184,189	7,376	1,157,153

[1] See table 13-8 for Special Nutrition Assistance Program costs. [2] October 1–September 30. [3] Includes sponsor administrative, audit, and startup costs. [4] Includes sponsor administrative, State administrative and health clinic costs. [5] Includes entitlement commodities, bonus commodities, and cash-in-lieu for the National School Lunch, School Breakfast, Child and Adult Care Food, and Summer Food Service Programs. [6] Includes food costs, administrative costs, program evaluation funds, special grants, and Farmer's Market projects for the Special Supplemental Food Program for Women, Infants and Children. [7] Includes entitlement and bonus commodities, cash-in-lieu of commodities, and administrative costs of the following programs: Food Distribution to Indian Reservations, Nutrition Services Incentive Program (formerly Nutrition Program for the Elderly), Commodity Supplemental Food, Charitable Institutions, Summer Camps, Emergency Food Assistance Program (TEFAP), Disaster Feeding, Bureau of Federal Prisons, Veteran Affairs Administration, and the Food Stamp Program Elderly Pilot Project.

FNS, Budget Division/Program Reports, Analysis and Monitoring Branch, (703) 305–2165.

Table 13-8.—SNAP: Participation and federal costs, fiscal years 2010–2019

Fiscal year [1]	Average monthly participation [2]		Recipient benefits	Total cost [3]	Average monthly benefit	
	Persons	Housholds			Per person	Per household
	1,000	*1,000*	*1,000 dollars*	*1,000 dollars*	*Dollars*	*Dollars*
2010	40,302	18,618	64,702,165	68,283,468	133.79	289.60
2011	44,709	21,072	71,810,924	75,686,540	133.85	283.99
2012	46,609	22,330	74,619,345	78,411,096	133.41	278.48
2013	47,636	23,052	76,066,319	79,859,028	133.07	274.98
2014	46,664	22,744	69,998,836	74,060,327	125.01	256.47
2015	45,767	22,522	69,645,138	73,946,652	126.81	257.09
2016	44,220	21,778	66,539,269	70,913,549	125.40	254.61
2017	42,228	20,901	63,711,051	68,174,548	125.73	254.02
2018	39,431	19,566	58,996,500	63,524,579	124.68	251.27
2019	34,474	17,374	53,761,254	58,277,365	129.96	257.86

SNAP is the Special Nutrition Assistance Program, formerly known as the Food Stamp Program. [1] October 1 to September 30. [2] Participation data are 12-month averages. [3] Total cost includes matching funds for state administrative expenses (e.g., certification of households, quality control, anti-fraud activities; employment and training); and for other Federal costs (e.g., benefit redemption processing; computer support; electronic benefit transfer systems; retailer redemption and monitoring; certification of SSI recipients; nutrition education and program information).

FNS, Budget Division/Program Reports, Analysis and Monitoring Branch, (703) 305–2165.

CHAPTER XIV

STATISTICS OF FERTILIZERS AND PESTICIDES

This chapter contains statistics on percentages of crop acres treated by various types of fertilizers and pesticides. Nitrogen, phosphate, potash, and sulfur are the most common fertilizers; herbicides, insecticides, fungicides, and other chemicals are the main categories of pesticides. Other chemicals include soil fumigants, vine killers, and desiccants. The tables show data for field crops for 2010-2019, fruits for 2019, and vegetables for 2018. NASS collects data for field crops on an annual basis. The surveyed States are generally the major producing States for each crop shown in the tables and represent 65-95 percent of the U.S. planted acres, depending on the selected crop.

Application data for specific pesticide active ingredients and additional fertilizer data are available in the series of NASS ''Agricultural Chemical Usage'' reports and data sets.

Table 14-1.—Field crops: Fertilizer, and percent of area receiving applications, all States surveyed, 2010–2019 [1]

Crop	Nitrogen	Phosphate	Potash	Sulfur
	Percent	*Percent*	*Percent*	*Percent*
2010:				
Corn	97	78	61	15
Cotton, Upland	90	62	52	42
Potatoes, Fall	99	96	90	73
2011:				
Barley	86	68	28	30
Sorghum	81	54	9	16
2012:				
Soybeans	27	37	37	7
Wheat, Durum	98	89	12	12
Wheat, Other Spring	97	87	27	20
Wheat, Winter	85	55	13	19
2013:				
Rice	97	75	54	23
Peanuts	40	42	42	17
2014:				
Corn	97	80	65	29
Potatoes, Fall	99	97	90	79
2015:				
Cotton	78	56	42	30
Oats	76	62	40	24
Soybeans	28	39	38	8
Wheat, Spring (Excl Durum)	97	89	40	30
Wheat, Spring Durum	98	95	32	31
Wheat, Winter	88	60	16	22
2016:				
Corn	97	79	65	33
Potatoes, Fall	98	92	00	76
2017:				
Cotton	78	59	45	38
Soybeans	31	41	42	9
Wheat, Durum	98	91	28	36
Wheat, Other Spring	96	89	34	38
Wheat, Winter	83	58	15	25
2018:				
Corn	98	79	63	32
Peanuts	32	32	33	12
Soybeans	29	42	43	10
2019:				
Barley	86	72	26	48
Sorghum	89	58	10	21
Wheat, Spring (Excl Durum)	97	89	31	32
Wheat, Spring Durum	98	84	11	24
Wheat, Winter	88	63	15	27

[1] Refers to percent of planted acres receiving one or more applications of a specific fertilizer ingredient. See tables 14-2 through 14-21 for surveyed States.

Note: See planted acreage estimates in tables 1-56 for barley, 1-36 for corn, 2-2 for upland and all cotton, 1-48 for oats, 3-16 for peanuts, 1-27 for rice, 1-65 for sorghum, 3-32 for soybeans and 1-8 for wheat.

NASS, Environmental, Economics, and Demographics Branch, (202) 720–6146.

Table 14-2.—Barley: Pesticide usage, 2011 and 2019 [1]

State and Year	Percent treated and amount applied							
	Herbicide		Insecticide		Fungicide		Other Chemicals	
	Area applied	Pounds applied	Area applied	Pounds applied	Area applied	Pounds applied	Area applied	Pounds applied
	Percent	*Thousands*	*Percent*	*Thousands*	*Percent*	*Thousands*	*Percent*	*Thousands*
Arizona:								
2011	37	16	*	*	....	....	....	....
2019	*	*	*	*	....	....	....	....
California:								
2011	39	48	*	*	....	....	....	....
2019	21	7	*	*	....	....	....	....
Colorado:								
2011	96	36	22	1	25	2	....	....
2019	90	23	*	*	*	*	....	....
Idaho:								
2011	91	302	11	1	18	11	14	27
2019	89	326	6	2	11	7	9	6
Minnesota:								
2011	58	19	10	2	32	3	....	....
2019	89	24	34	1	68	11	....	....
Montana:								
2011	92	1,065	*	*	26	16	*	*
2019	84	949	*	*	3	5	*	*
North Dakota:								
2011	95	236	6	4	48	26	....	....
2019	94	304	*	*	63	52	*	*
Oregon:								
2011	74	21	*	*	31	1	*	*
2019	70	33	*	*	*	*	*	*
Pennsylvania:								
2011	39	7	*	*	3	**	....	....
2019	61	7	*	*	6	**	....	....
South Dakota:								
2019	*	*	....	....	....	....	....	....
Virginia:								
2011	59	29	20	**	15	1	*	*
2019	71	17	*	*	18	1	....	....
Washington:								
2011	93	111	....	....	19	2	....	....
2019	96	68	*	*	10	1	....	....
Wisconsin:								
2011	25	4	....	....	....	....	....	....
2019	17	2	*	*	....	....	*	*
Wyoming:								
2011	76	32	*	*	13	1	....	....
2019	68	30	22	**	16	1	....	....

*Insufficient number of reports to publish data. **Amount applied is less than 500 lbs. [1] Data not available for all States for all years.

Note: Planted acres are in table 1-56.

NASS, Environmental, Economics, and Demographics Branch, (202) 720–6146.

Table 14-3.—Barley: Fertilizer usage, 2011 and 2019 [1]

State	Percent treated and amount applied							
	Nitrogen		Phosphate		Potash		Sulfur	
	Area applied	Pounds applied	Area applied	Pounds applied	Area applied	Pounds applied	Area applied	Pounds applied
	Percent	*Millions*	*Percent*	*Millions*	*Percent*	*Millions*	*Percent*	*Millions*
Arizona								
2011	97	8.2	39	1.5	*	*	21	0.3
2019	96	1.6	34	0.5	....	....	*	*
California:								
2011	41	2.6	*	*	....	....	14	0.2
2019	38	1.5	23	0.4	*	*	*	*
Colorado:								
2011	82	7.2	40	1.5	28	0.6	36	0.4
2019	89	5.0	81	3.3	*	*	*	*
Idaho:								
2011	93	44.2	66	10.0	37	4.9	65	9.6
2019	93	42.2	57	12.2	21	4.9	69	6.6
Minnesota:								
2011	60	3.3	56	1.3	44	1.0	11	0.1
2019	89	5.5	77	2.2	78	2.0	43	0.3
Montana:								
2011	90	29.1	83	16.6	37	3.6	16	1.2
2019	84	33.0	79	18.2	32	3.5	55	4.3
North Dakota:								
2011	96	28.3	92	11.1	16	1.0	4	0.1
2019	92	42.0	85	18.8	20	1.5	29	1.7
Oregon:								
2011	77	1.6	26	0.1	*	*	36	0.1
2019	100	2.7	6	0.6	*	*	60	0.2
Pennsylvania:								
2011	64	1.9	32	0.8	32	0.8	10	0.1
2019	72	1.2	16	0.3	16	0.2	28	0.1
South Dakota:								
2019	63	1.8	60	0.8	....	....	*	*
Virginia:								
2011	77	4.9	39	1.7	35	1.7	24	0.3
2019	56	1.0	19	0.2	18	0.4	15	0.1
Washington:								
2011	91	9.0	59	1.1	9	0.2	90	1.6
2019	94	6.4	81	1.2	20	0.3	82	1.2
Wisconsin:								
2011	34	0.2	*	*	34	1.0	14	0.1
2019	23	0.3	15	0.1	23	0.5	8	**
Wyoming:								
2011	73	5.2	55	1.8	30	0.8	18	0.4
2019	93	6.2	79	2.0	58	1.5	20	0.3

*Insufficient number of reports to publish data. **Area applied is less than 0.5 percent. [1] Data not available for all States for all years.

Note: Planted acres are in table 1-56.

NASS, Environmental, Economics, and Demographics Branch, (202) 720–6146.

Table 14-4.—Corn: Pesticide usage, 2014–2018 [1] [2]

State	Percent treated and amount applied							
	Herbicide		Insecticide [2]		Fungicide [2]		Other Chemicals	
	Area applied	Pounds applied	Area applied	Pounds applied	Area applied	Pounds applied	Area applied	Pounds applied
	Percent	*Thousands*	*Percent*	*Thousands*	*Percent*	*Thousands*	*Percent*	*Thousands*
Colorado:								
2016	85	3,819	23	94	(D)	(D)	(D)	(D)
2018	93	2,978	11	69	6	46	(D)	(D)
Georgia:								
2016	98	1,417	22	38	31	30	....	....
2018	....	....	....	....	....	....	....	....
Illinois:								
2014	98	26,870	23	237	21	321	(D)	(D)
2016	99	32,524	18	146	19	256	(D)	(D)
2018	97	31,289	20	149	31	604	(D)	(D)
Indiana:								
2014	100	14,609	9	45	12	80	(D)	(D)
2016	99	14,689	17	78	16	144	(D)	(D)
2018	98	14,345	12	25	28	1,481	(D)	(D)
Iowa:								
2014	95	30,240	13	122	19	296	(D)	(D)
2016	97	35,858	10	280	22	438	(D)	(D)
2018	95	32,371	18	274	32	706	(D)	(D)
Kansas:								
2014	97	11,432	10	244	3	13	....	....
2016	98	18,892	6	500	(D)	(D)	(D)	(D)
2018	98	16,373	5	175	5	39	....	....
Kentucky:								
2014	94	4,102	29	15	11	19	(D)	(D)
2016	95	6,263	30	26	26	49	(D)	(D)
2018	97	4,787	20	22	16	82	(D)	(D)
Michigan:								
2014	98	5,710	4	5	12	36	....	....
2016	93	4,845	6	21	(D)	(D)	(D)	(D)
2018	98	4,999	8	13	5	71	4	7
Minnesota:								
2014	98	13,596	2	26	(D)	(D)	(D)	(D)
2016	97	16,461	7	43	3	32	....	....
2018	99	15,885	8	50	4	63	(D)	(D)
Missouri:								
2014	98	8,517	24	43	14	61	....	....
2016	92	10,121	12	16	(D)	(D)	....	....
2018	92	11,451	19	102	12	70	(D)	(D)
Nebraska:								
2014	95	21,320	16	213	10	118	(D)	(D)
2016	95	27,905	15	186	10	142	(D)	(D)
2018	99	30,070	16	618	20	309	(D)	(D)
New York:								
2016	98	2,370	(D)	(D)	....	....	(D)	(D)
2018	93	2,279	5	4	....	....	(D)	(D)
North Carolina:								
2016	95	3,447	5	3	(D)	(D)	(D)	(D)
2018	96	3,082	16	15	13	53	(D)	(D)
North Dakota:								
2014	97	4,489	(D)	(D)	4	16	....	....
2016	100	6,242	(D)	(D)	(D)	(D)	....	....
2018	99	5,481	(D)	(D)	(D)	(D)	(D)	(D)
Ohio:								
2014	99	9,231	13	64	9	81	(D)	(D)
2016	98	9,025	17	45	13	39	(D)	(D)
2018	100	10,650	19	32	12	124	6	336
Pennsylvania:								
2014	97	4,080	20	46	4	6	4	2
2016	96	4,446	23	12	9	17	(D)	(D)
2018	92	3,840	23	10	9	12	(D)	(D)
South Dakota:								
2014	98	10,803	(D)	(D)	9	47	....	....
2016	99	13,157	(D)	(D)	(D)	(D)	....	....
2018	99	13,471	(D)	(D)	(D)	(D)	(D)	(D)
Texas:								
2014	89	4,338	14	528	23	27	(D)	(D)
2016	84	5,992	13	364	26	40	....	....
2018	92	4,027	16	492	13	61	5	48
Wisconsin:								
2014	90	6,952	8	22	(D)	(D)	(D)	(D)
2016	98	8,572	12	24	5	6	....	....
2018	97	7,344	8	21	6	30	(D)	(D)

(D) Withheld to avoid disclosing data for individual operations. [1] Data not available for all States for all years. [2] Amount applied excludes Bt (bacillus thuringiensis) and other biologicals.

Note: Planted acres are in table 1-36.

NASS, Environmental, Economics, and Demographics Branch, (202) 720–6146.

Table 14-5.—Corn: Fertilizer usage, 2014–2018 [1]

State and Year	Percent treated and amount applied							
	Nitrogen		Phosphate		Potash		Sulfur	
	Area applied	Pounds applied	Area applied	Pounds applied	Area applied	Pounds applied	Area applied	Pounds applied
	Percent	*Millions*	*Percent*	*Millions*	*Percent*	*Millions*	*Percent*	*Millions*
Colorado:								
2016	96	149.8	66	31.3	13	2.9	38	8.4
2018	92	206.5	77	51.7	32	16.3	47	12.8
Georgia:								
2016	97	74.2	84	23.4	88	46.8	43	4.0
2018	....	....	....	....	....	....	....	....
Illinois:								
2014	99	1,918.3	85	938.4	81	1,066.9	8	17.5
2016	98	1,908.8	86	892.7	81	1,036.9	15	43.1
2018	98	1,851.6	87	1,042.6	77	1,139.2	20	40.0
Indiana:								
2014	96	877.7	81	351.1	79	530.5	22	16.0
2016	98	895.1	78	321.4	85	517.6	30	21.1
2018	100	842.0	91	310.9	80	455.0	43	38.2
Iowa:								
2014	96	1,842.2	64	600.5	63	705.3	18	40.2
2016	98	2,036.1	67	701.1	70	938.8	21	45.3
2018	97	1,784.3	71	698.2	70	823.4	22	51.0
Kansas:								
2014	98	549.6	87	148.5	35	60.5	29	10.1
2016	99	721.2	88	165.1	48	61.3	33	10.6
2018	100	798.2	75	246.2	39	117.5	31	21.3
Kentucky:								
2014	98	214.1	88	109.0	87	119.0	14	4.5
2016	96	249.7	82	97.0	87	121.4	23	9.6
2018	98	195.0	90	106.9	88	128.1	19	5.3
Michigan:								
2014	98	338.7	84	89.2	82	192.6	25	7.4
2016	94	276.0	80	83.9	71	141.2	35	11.6
2018	97	322.4	79	86.1	71	156.4	29	7.5
Minnesota:								
2014	94	1,091.8	86	491.4	80	570.2	51	72.5
2016	96	1,126.0	86	442.8	75	495.2	43	63.8
2018	96	1,041.9	79	462.6	72	517.2	37	56.1
Missouri:								
2014	98	603.3	81	191.1	83	228.0	32	16.2
2016	97	590.7	69	173.0	74	213.9	40	20.1
2018	98	577.9	83	208.4	82	226.8	27	16.7
Nebraska:								
2014	99	1,359.9	77	329.9	29	100.8	42	71.6
2016	100	1,400.1	79	314.6	35	65.3	41	68.6
2018	99	1,569.9	73	361.0	26	75.3	38	74.7
New York:								
2016	98	77.6	70	25.2	60	31.7	24	4.0
2018	97	103.0	79	30.9	69	46.6	16	2.2
North Carolina:								
2016	91	127.7	63	32.6	68	62.8	35	7.5
2018	94	125.7	74	39.4	76	63.2	26	10.1
North Dakota:								
2014	99	349.7	88	132.1	44	34.7	43	12.3
2016	97	446.5	92	195.4	59	63.6	56	32.4
2018	97	444.3	88	165.7	62	66.1	40	20.3
Ohio:								
2014	98	558.8	85	228.9	80	282.2	15	5.1
2016	99	585.4	87	225.6	79	302.4	31	22.9
2018	99	604.7	81	225.5	68	258.1	26	12.8
Pennsylvania:								
2014	96	137.7	67	39.7	66	40.5	35	5.6
2016	91	124.4	41	23.8	46	30.4	47	11.2
2018	94	155.6	55	30.7	48	34.6	34	7.3
South Dakota:								
2014	97	684.8	83	216.4	50	113.2	35	24.0
2016	99	715.9	87	249.9	52	136.1	44	36.2
2018	99	657.0	88	258.1	60	147.0	44	52.0
Texas:								
2014	95	310.5	77	77.9	37	19.2	43	10.7
2016	87	313.3	60	59.5	22	12.7	36	11.4
2018	97	301.8	73	68.1	40	23.0	41	10.2
Wisconsin:								
2014	98	407.6	85	127.9	88	222.2	49	31.7
2016	96	427.2	78	103.8	84	217.3	55	36.0
2018	97	426.2	80	116.6	79	232.2	38	29.9

[1] Data not available for all States for all years.
Note: Planted acres are in table 1-36.
NASS, Environmental, Economics, and Demographics Branch, (202) 720–6146.

Table 14-6.—Cotton, Upland: Pesticide usage, 2017–2019[1]

State and Year	Percent treated and amount applied							
	Herbicide		Insecticide[2]		Fungicide		Other Chemicals	
	Area applied	Pounds applied	Area applied	Pounds applied	Area applied	Pounds applied	Area applied	Pounds applied
	Percent	*Thousands*	*Percent*	*Thousands*	*Percent*	*Thousands*	*Percent*	*Thousands*
Alabama:								
2017	99	1,422	66	120	(D)	(D)	100	919
2019	100	1,900	78	166	....	....	97	954
Arizona:								
2019	91	329	63	41	....	....	91	82
Arkansas:								
2017	86	1,681	94	786	6	7	100	1,400
2019	98	2,210	98	1,057	8	15	100	1,895
California:								
2019	99	609	96	226	(D)	(D)	85	620
Georgia:								
2017	99	4,409	71	348	1	9	99	3,185
2019	100	4,445	73	486	8	31	91	2,574
Louisiana:								
2019	99	1,297	97	496	(D)	(D)	100	592
Mississippi:								
2017	99	3,017	93	1,271	(D)	(D)	96	1,675
2019	100	3,116	89	1,321	(D)	(D)	96	1,438
Missouri:								
2017	100	1,037	92	382	18	9	100	730
2019	100	1,126	90	485	(D)	(D)	100	1,205
North Carolina:								
2017	98	1,378	81	140	(D)	(D)	91	699
2019	100	2,002	95	343	(D)	(D)	99	896
Oklahoma:								
2017	59	765	38	112	....	....	15	173
2019	90	2,501	48	247	(D)	(D)	71	767
South Carolina:								
2019	94	1,153	87	86	(D)	(D)	91	716
Tennessee:								
2017	98	1,266	96	429	(D)	(D)	100	739
2019	98	1,711	100	385	(D)	(D)	97	786
Texas:								
2017	90	14,554	23	881	....	....	58	4,366
2019	88	21,076	32	2,412	(D)	(D)	41	3,744

(D) Withheld to avoid disclosing data for individual operations. [1] Data not available for all States for all years. [2] Amount applied excludes Bt (bacillus thuringiensis) and other biologicals.

Note: Planted acres are in table 2-2.

NASS, Environmental, Economics, and Demographics Branch, (202) 720–6146.

Table 14-7.—Cotton, Upland: Fertilizer usage, 2017–2019[1]

State and Year	Percent treated and amount applied							
	Nitrogen		Phosphate		Potash		Sulfur	
	Area applied	Pounds applied	Area applied	Pounds applied	Area applied	Pounds applied	Area applied	Pounds applied
	Percent	*Millions*	*Percent*	*Millions*	*Percent*	*Millions*	*Percent*	*Millions*
Alabama:								
2017	93	42.0	72	19.5	81	29.3	38	2.6
2019	98	57.0	78	23.9	96	46.2	48	5.0
Arizona:								
2019	96	23.3	28	2.3	(D)	(D)	(D)	(D)
Arkansas:								
2017	97	69.2	74	17.5	79	35.3	53	4.8
2019	99	89.9	83	28.1	94	53.3	36	5.4
California:								
2019	95	31.5	26	2.0	(D)	(D)	(D)	(D)
Georgia:								
2017	100	143.5	81	58.0	91	103.7	63	14.3
2019	98	140.0	88	71.2	93	125.1	41	10.9
Louisiana:								
2019	94	23.9	70	11.6	69	18.9	61	2.3
Mississippi:								
2017	99	72.4	47	15.2	60	34.6	37	3.7
2019	97	82.7	43	18.9	73	54.1	36	3.4
Missouri:								
2017	98	33.3	87	12.4	96	20.5	62	3.3
2019	100	41.6	91	15.8	86	26.1	41	1.8
North Carolina:								
2017	96	30.6	67	12.4	87	32.0	56	6.6
2019	97	45.3	52	13.3	89	43.7	41	7.7
Oklahoma:								
2017	54	31.8	44	11.4	19	4.8	7	0.3
2019	63	47.5	58	14.8	29	3.6	11	0.9
South Carolina:								
2019	92	28.3	59	8.5	88	30.9	45	2.6
Tennessee:								
2017	100	35.0	99	19.0	95	29.9	82	3.3
2019	100	40.7	94	21.2	100	38.4	84	4.5
Texas:								
2017	68	363.7	52	133.2	25	35.1	31	26.0
2019	79	316.8	54	113.4	22	17.7	42	27.8

(D) Withheld to avoid disclosing data for individual operations. [1] Data not available for all States for all years.
Note: Planted acres are in table 2-3.
NASS, Environmental, Economics, and Demographics Branch, (202) 720–6146.

Table 14-8.—Peanuts: Pesticide usage, 2013 and 2018[1]

State and Year	Percent treated and amount applied							
	Herbicide		Insecticide		Fungicide		Other Chemicals	
	Area applied	Pounds applied	Area applied	Pounds applied	Area applied	Pounds applied	Area applied	Pounds applied
	Percent	*Thousands*	*Percent*	*Thousands*	*Percent*	*Thousands*	*Percent*	*Thousands*
Alabama:								
2013	99	219	32	33	95	632	*	*
2018	99	312	37	13	95	469	....	1
Florida:								
2013	93	237	59	28	100	670	*	*
2018	96	250	47	34	94	471	(D)	(D)
Georgia:								
2013	100	853	48	177	97	1,692	*	*
2018	98	1,187	40	78	98	2,738	5	2
North Carolina:								
2013	99	190	71	54	87	144	*	*
2018	97	299	58	38	92	173	27	18
South Carolina:								
2013	96	150	60	33	81	261	....	....
2018	95	232	34	13	80	221	(D)	(D)
Texas:								
2013	65	93	11	2	33	42	....	....
2018	73	123	4	1	38	38	(D)	(D)

*Insufficient number of reports to publish data. (D) Withheld to avoid disclosing data for individual operations. [1] Data not available for all States for all years.
Note: Planted acres are in table 3-16.
NASS, Environmental, Economics, and Demographics Branch, (202) 720–6146.

Table 14-9.—Peanuts: Fertilizer usage, 2013 and 2018[1]

State and Year	Percent treated and amount applied							
	Nitrogen		Phosphate		Potash		Sulfur	
	Area applied	Pounds applied	Area applied	Pounds applied	Area applied	Pounds applied	Area applied	Pounds applied
	Percent	*Millions*	*Percent*	*Millions*	*Percent*	*Millions*	*Percent*	*Millions*
Alabama:								
2013	48	1.5	54	3.0	57	5.2	19	0.6
2018	41	1.5	41	3.0	41	3.9	8	0.2
Florida:								
2013	81	2.2	86	4.9	93	11.7	36	1.3
2018	40	1.6	36	2.5	40	7.0	(D)	(D)
Georgia:								
2013	27	2.1	31	6.5	26	6.5	*	*
2018	22	2.6	26	6.8	26	10.4	7	0.8
North Carolina:								
2013	21	0.5	22	0.7	51	4.1	23	0.5
2018	(D)	(D)	(D)	(D)	56	5.4	14	0.2
South Carolina:								
2013	13	0.5	14	0.4	22	1.5	*	*
2018	(D)	(D)	(D)	(D)	10	0.9	(D)	(D)
Texas:								
2013	57	5.3	47	2.4	34	1.4	37	0.7
2018	74	7.1	66	3.3	48	2.5	43	0.8

*Insufficient number of reports to publish data. (D) Withheld to avoid disclosing data for individual operations. [1] Data not available for all States for all years.
Note: Planted acres are in table 3-16.
NASS, Environmental, Economics, and Demographics Branch, (202) 720–6146.

Table 14-10.—Oats: Pesticide usage, 2005 and 2015[1]

State and Year	Percent treated and amount applied					
	Herbicide		Insecticide		Fungicide	
	Area applied	Pounds applied	Area applied	Pounds applied	Area applied	Pounds applied
	Percent	*Thousands*	*Percent*	*Thousands*	*Percent*	*Thousands*
California:						
2005	36	59	....	....	....	....
Idaho:						
2005	26	17	....	....	....	....
Illinois:						
2005	7	1	....	....	....	....
2015	(D)	(D)	....	....	(D)	(D)
Iowa:						
2005	3	2	....	....	....	....
2015	(D)	(D)	....	....	(D)	(D)
Kansas:						
2005	27	13	....	....	....	....
2015	41	28	....	....	(D)	(D)
Michigan:						
2005	61	26	....	....	....	....
2015	66	33	(D)	(D)	(D)	(D)
Minnesota:						
2005	21	26	....	....	....	....
2015	43	66	(D)	(D)	13	4
Montana:						
2005	34	18	....	....	....	....
Nebraska:						
2005	7	4	....	....	....	....
2015	35	21	....	....	(D)	(D)
New York:						
2005	51	23	....	....	....	....
2015	63	26	(D)	(D)	(D)	(D)
North Dakota:						
2005	54	167	....	....	....	....
2015	82	186	(D)	(D)	9	2
Ohio:						
2015	59	22	....	....	....	....
Pennsylvania:						
2005	58	46	....	....	....	....
2015	60	43	(D)	(D)	....	....
South Dakota:						
2005	37	52	....	....	....	....
2015	81	130	(D)	(D)	21	9
Texas:						
2005	26	80	18	35	....	....
2015	45	95	14	20	9	10
Wisconsin:						
2005	18	25	....	....	....	....
2015	30	37	(D)	(D)	6	2

(D) Withheld to avoid disclosing data for individual operations. [1] Data not available for all States for all years.
Note: Planted acres are in table 1-48.
NASS, Environmental, Economics, and Demographics Branch, (202) 720–6146

Table 14-11.—Oats: Fertilizer usage, 2005 and 2015[1]

State and Year	Percent treated and amount applied							
	Nitrogen		Phosphate		Potash		Sulfur	
	Area applied	Pounds applied	Area applied	Pounds applied	Area applied	Pounds applied	Area applied	Pounds applied
	Percent	*Millions*	*Percent*	*Millions*	*Percent*	*Millions*	*Percent*	*Millions*
California:								
2005	26	4.4						
Idaho:								
2005	42	1.6	22	1.4	5	0.1	12	0.2
Illinois:								
2005	15	0.4	12	0.4	26	1.7		
2015	28	0.4	20	0.5	28	0.9	(D)	(D)
Iowa:								
2005	31	1.8	30	2.5	40	6.9		
2015	27	1.4	26	2.1	28	2.7	11	0.3
Kansas:								
2005	84	4.4	39	1.4	17	0.8		
2015	87	4.5	33	0.9	12	0.3	(D)	(D)
Michigan:								
2005	82	2.6	72	2.8	77	3.4		
2015	81	2.0	75	1.7	78	2.0	6	(Z)
Minnesota:								
2005	28	4.2	22	2.4	28	5.9	5	0.2
2015	60	8.3	50	3.6	53	6.7	21	0.7
Montana:								
2005	53	2.0	35	1.0	14	0.4	9	0.1
Nebraska:								
2005	68	4.5	24	1.3	7	0.1	5	
2015	77	5.1	65	2.6	36	0.8	29	0.4
New York:								
2005	75	1.9	72	2.7	72	2.8		
2015	66	1.3	63	1.7	62	1.8	(D)	(D)
North Dakota:								
2005	71	15.8	49	5.7	9	0.7	5	0.1
2015	88	12.1	70	7.2	27	0.9	22	0.6
Ohio:								
2015	70	1.3	69	2.2	66	2.7	(D)	(D)
Pennsylvania:								
2005	90	4.5	81	4.9	82	5.1	2	0.1
2015	81	2.2	76	2.9	75	2.7	(D)	(D)
South Dakota:								
2005	64	11.8	46	5.6	17	1.7		
2015	91	22.1	74	9.2	20	1.1	17	0.7
Texas:								
2005	79	45.4	56	12.7	39	4.9	25	1.7
2015	97	27.8	82	12.1	39	3.2	51	3.0
Wisconsin:								
2005	23	2.1	24	3.9	35	15.1	8	0.4
2015	51	3.9	36	2.9	45	8.4	21	1.0

(D) Withheld to avoid disclosing data for individual operations. (Z) Less than half the rounding unit. [1] Data not available for all States for all years.

Note: Planted acres are in table 1-48.

NASS, Environmental, Economics, and Demographics Branch, (202) 720–6146.

Table 14-12.—Potatoes, Fall: Pesticide usage, 2010–2016 [1]

State and Year	Percent treated and amount applied							
	Herbicide		Insecticide [2]		Fungicide		Other Chemicals	
	Area applied	Pounds applied	Area applied	Pounds applied	Area applied	Pounds applied	Area applied	Pounds applied
	Percent	*Thousands*	*Percent*	*Thousands*	*Percent*	*Thousands*	*Percent*	*Thousands*
Colorado:								
2010	92	173	93	108	98	191	74	5,156
2014	78	83	50	37	96	120	74	5,696
2016	73	73	77	8	74	87	(D)	(D)
Idaho:								
2010	98	829	67	190	93	983	63	36,080
2014	89	717	89	287	95	1,618	57	36,437
2016	92	662	65	81	99	846	49	23,552
Maine:								
2010	93	36	91	8	100	373	73	30
2014	97	30	84	9	90	329	78	37
2016	90	46	93	5	99	402	22	31
Michigan:								
2010	90	70	90	18	96	298	67	46
2014	99	86	96	32	99	442	73	35
2016	99	118	100	24	99	511	....	....
Minnesota:								
2010	90	44	99	9	100	586	48	3,099
2014	91	34	93	13	91	612	52	4,067
2016	90	90	94	7	98	879	(D)	(D)
North Dakota:								
2010	89	71	85	13	96	874	60	6,872
2014	90	71	89	10	99	801	30	1,653
2016	98	103	96	33	100	1,943	(D)	(D)
Washington:								
2010	98	376	97	392	99	1,197	80	16,901
2014	92	566	98	489	99	1,109	87	16,635
2016	100	662	98	205	98	1,472	56	14,517
Wisconsin:								
2010	82	73	91	12	96	866	92	2,742
2014	95	96	99	16	100	987	96	4,913
2016	99	120	84	39	100	825	48	4,502

(D) Withheld to avoid disclosing data for individual operations. [1] Data not available for all States for all years. [2] Amount applied excludes Bt (bacillus thuringiensis) and other biologicals.
NASS, Environmental, Economics, and Demographics Branch, (202) 720–6146.

Table 14-13.—Potatoes, Fall: Fertilizer usage, 2010–2016[1]

State and Year	Percent treated and amount applied							
	Nitrogen		Phosphate		Potash		Sulfur	
	Area applied	Pounds applied	Area applied	Pounds applied	Area applied	Pounds applied	Area applied	Pounds applied
	Percent	*Millions*	*Percent*	*Millions*	*Percent*	*Millions*	*Percent*	*Millions*
Colorado:								
2010	97	10.0	92	10.4	66	3.9	93	5.2
2014	94	9.2	93	7.2	70	1.6	94	2.6
2016	93	7.8	93	9.1	86	6.3	92	2.3
Idaho:								
2010	100	75.0	96	53.2	91	35.9	81	30.0
2014	99	78.1	98	47.5	85	36.3	90	23.6
2016	100	88.3	94	62.5	94	43.3	83	29.3
Maine:								
2010	99	8.8	99	8.2	95	10.2	(D)	(D)
2014	98	8.3	98	7.1	98	8.7	12	0.1
2016	98	8.5	96	7.0	98	10.4	5	(Z)
Michigan:								
2010	100	8.6	98	3.5	100	8.6	(D)	(D)
2014	100	7.9	99	3.8	100	9.6	52	1.7
2016	100	8.8	99	2.8	99	10.0	87	2.2
Minnesota:								
2010	98	9.2	100	4.6	100	14.6	80	1.3
2014	100	6.2	88	2.8	80	5.9	66	0.9
2016	99	6.7	98	3.0	91	5.7	73	1.7
North Dakota:								
2010	100	15.1	89	7.9	84	14.3	44	1.3
2014	100	12.3	97	8.9	100	8.7	79	1.7
2016	100	16.0	99	8.8	81	14.0	52	1.3
Washington:								
2010	100	32.6	99	24.9	94	36.0	90	9.7
2014	100	29.2	100	20.1	97	18.2	82	7.2
2016	95	30.6	75	19.0	81	18.3	80	8.1
Wisconsin:								
2010	100	16.5	100	5.3	93	17.7	91	3.9
2014	100	15.0	96	5.4	99	20.8	89	4.2
2016	100	15.5	100	5.9	98	20.5	90	4.5

(D) Withheld to avoid disclosing data for individual operations. (Z) Less than half of rounding unit for data item shown (see data item definition for rounding unit). [1] Data not available for all States for all years.
NASS, Environmental, Economics, and Demographics Branch, (202) 720–6146.

Table 14-14.—Rice: Pesticide usage, 2006 and 2013[1]

State and Year	Percent treated and amount applied							
	Herbicide		Insecticide		Fungicide		Other Chemicals	
	Area applied	Pounds applied	Area applied	Pounds applied	Area applied	Pounds applied	Area applied	Pounds applied
	Percent	*Thousands*	*Percent*	*Thousands*	*Percent*	*Thousands*	*Percent*	*Thousands*
Arkansas:								
2006	95	3,054	10	14	37	109	5	269
2013	97	2,646	30	10	45	103	5	251
California:								
2006	93	2,500	14	2	50	738	....	....
2013	96	2,986	28	6	45	553	*	*
Louisiana:								
2006	96	475	42	49	46	30	....	....
2013	99	680	17	13	73	82	*	*
Mississippi:								
2006	100	502	55	14	46	16	3	36
2013	100	364	51	2	35	9	6	37
Missouri:								
2006	100	454	....	....	25	12	....	....
2013	100	512	18	1	55	22	20	159
Texas:								
2006	97	496	77	83	55	21	....	....
2013	88	263	35	3	35	11	*	*

* Insufficient number of reports to publish data. [1] Data not available for all States for all years.
Note: Planted acres are in table 1-27.
NASS, Environmental, Economics, and Demographics Branch, (202) 720–6146.

Table 14-15.—Rice: Fertilizer usage, 2006 and 2013[1]

State and Year	Percent treated and amount applied							
	Nitrogen		Phosphate		Potash		Sulfur	
	Area applied	Pounds applied	Area applied	Pounds applied	Area applied	Pounds applied	Area applied	Pounds applied
	Percent	*Millions*	*Percent*	*Millions*	*Percent*	*Millions*	*Percent*	*Millions*
Arkansas:								
2006	97	281.2	68	54.7	60	64.9	9	6.0
2013	96	195.8	76	53.2	56	51.3	14	2.1
California:								
2006	94	61.4	75	18.2	40	7.2	31	4.0
2013	98	83.9	81	21.2	38	7.2	41	4.4
Louisiana:								
2006	99	52.8	78	14.6	75	16.2	4	0.3
2013	100	63.9	87	16.0	79	23.0	14	1.3
Mississippi:								
2006	99	35.8	29	2.5	4	0.5	42	1.6
2013	100	23.3	13	0.8	*	*	50	1.2
Missouri:								
2006	100	45.2	47	5.5	42	5.7	29	0.7
2013	100	32.7	56	4.7	*	*	29	0.6
Texas:								
2006	97	29.2	92	5.8	89	6.0	30	0.6
2013	90	22.3	82	5.5	79	5.4	11	0.1

* Insufficient number of reports to publish data. [1] Data not available for all States for all years.
Note: Planted acres are in table 1-27.
NASS, Environmental, Economics, and Demographics Branch, (202) 720–6146.

Table 14-16.—Sorghum: Pesticide usage, 2011 and 2019[1]

State and Year	Percent treated and amount applied							
	Herbicide		Insecticide		Fungicide		Other chemicals	
	Area applied	Pounds applied	Area applied	Pounds applied	Area applied	Pounds applied	Area applied	Pounds applied
	Percent	*Thousands*	*Percent*	*Thousands*	*Percent*	*Thousands*	*Percent*	*Thousands*
Colorado:								
2011	75	285	....	....	....	....	....	....
2019	96	1,129	....	....	....	....	....	....
Kansas:								
2011	96	9,411	4	3	....	....	....	....
2019	94	9,471	(D)	(D)	....	....	(D)	(D)
Missouri:								
2019	....	....	(D)	(D)	(D)	(D)	....	....
Nebraska:								
2011	84	362	(D)	(D)	....	....	....	....
2019	100	760	(D)	(D)	(D)	(D)	....	....
New Mexico:								
2019	....	....	(D)	(D)	....	....	....	....
Oklahoma:								
2011	74	505	(D)	(D)	....	....	....	....
2019	87	539	(D)	(D)	(D)	(D)	....	....
South Dakota:								
2011	89	289	(D)	(D)	....	....	....	....
2019	100	786	(D)	(D)	....	....	....	....
Texas:								
2011	72	1,901	10	9	(D)	(D)	....	....
2019	78	2,891	27	192	(D)	(D)	(D)	(D)

(D) Withheld to avoid disclosing data for individual operations. [1] Data not available for all States for all years.
Note: Planted acres are in table 1-65.
NASS, Environmental, Economics, and Demographics Branch, (202) 720–6146.

Table 14-17.—Sorghum: Fertilizer usage, 2011 and 2019[1]

State	Percent treated and amount applied							
	Nitrogen		Phosphate		Potash		Sulfur	
	Area applied	Pounds applied	Area applied	Pounds applied	Area applied	Pounds applied	Area applied	Pounds applied
	Percent	*Millions*	*Percent*	*Millions*	*Percent*	*Millions*	*Percent*	*Millions*
Colorado:								
2011	75	7.4	41	1.5	(D)	(D)	(D)	(D)
2019	57	7.9	(D)	(D)	....	....	20	0.7
Kansas:								
2011	83	135.7	51	32.8	8	2.9	9	1.5
2019	97	198.9	65	34.4	(D)	(D)	19	1.9
Missouri:								
2019	....	....	....	....	....	....	(D)	(D)
Nebraska:								
2011	88	11.0	41	1.9	15	0.2	22	0.4
2019	94	16.2	58	5.0	191	0.2	45	0.6
New Mexico:								
2019	(D)	(D)	(D)	(D)	....	....	(D)	(D)
Oklahoma:								
2011	81	11.9	58	3.8	13	0.2	13	0.3
2019	85	14.9	67	7.3	5	0.1	(D)	(D)
South Dakota:								
2011	88	8.9	45	1.9	(D)	(D)	(D)	(D)
2019	(D)	(D)	77	5.0	(D)	(D)	(D)	(D)
Texas:								
2011	77	94.1	63	27.2	11	3.7	29	5.1
2019	83	99.0	50	23.2	22	6.2	25	3.5

(D) Withheld to avoid disclosing data for individual operations. [1] Data not available for all States for all years.
Note: Planted acres are in table 1-65.
NASS, Environmental, Economics, and Demographics Branch, (202) 720–6146.

Table 14-18.—Soybeans: Pesticide usage, 2017 and 2018 [1]

State and Year	Percent treated and amount applied							
	Herbicide		Insecticide [2]		Fungicide		Other Chemicals [2]	
	Area applied	Pounds applied	Area applied	Pounds applied	Area applied	Pounds applied	Area applied	Pounds applied
	Percent	*Thousands*	*Percent*	*Thousands*	*Percent*	*Thousands*	*Percent*	*Thousands*
Arkansas:								
2017	97	7,898	33	350	13	76	(D)	(D)
2018	95	9,729	26	244	17	328	....	....
Illinois:								
2017	95	20,547	19	98	22	399	5	22
2018	98	23,531	16	98	24	643	(D)	(D)
Indiana:								
2017	98	14,058	15	48	16	209	6	7
2018	97	12,624	16	28	18	172	6	1
Iowa:								
2017	95	19,887	19	221	17	280	(D)	(D)
2018	100	21,526	19	283	19	357	(D)	(D)
Kansas:								
2017	93	9,362	15	87	4	22	(D)	(D)
2018	100	12,629	19	165	11	109	(D)	(D)
Kentucky:								
2017	97	3,759	33	87	21	55	5	2
2018	95	4,826	18	11	12	32	7	1
Louisiana:								
2015	97	4,186	63	....	43	107	(D)	(D)
2018	96	4,296	59	512	46	659	3	(Z)
Michigan:								
2017	98	3,986	5	9	7	24	(D)	(D)
2018	99	4,026	6	59	(D)	(D)	3	(Z)
Minnesota:								
2017	94	12,240	38	577	13	203	(D)	(D)
2018	99	12,060	30	637	21	299	....	....
Mississippi:								
2017	100	8,596	50	493	40	135	14	498
2018	100	8,582	26	85	35	291	8	163
Missouri:								
2017	92	10,982	21	222	12	102	3	(Z)
2018	97	12,082	17	93	6	201	(D)	(D)
Nebraska:								
2017	98	11,089	6	189	9	105	(D)	(D)
2018	99	12,978	8	18	13	244	....	....
North Carolina								
2017	97	3,264	38	77	18	52	(D)	(D)
2018	97	4,726	23	27	14	33	(D)	(D)
North Dakota								
2017	94	11,454	13	241	6	82	(D)	(D)
2018	99	10,056	(D)	(D)	(D)	(D)	(D)	(D)
Ohio:								
2017	96	9,448	11	20	18	126	4	6
2018	100	9,726	8	12	11	123	(D)	(D)
South Dakota								
2017	98	11,515	(D)	(D)	3	18	(D)	(D)
2018	99	11,044	....	....	(D)	(D)	(D)	(D)
Tennessee:								
2015	100	4,427	22	14	15	40	(D)	(D)
2018	100	4,790	15	11	14	37	(D)	(D)
Virginia:								
2015	96	1,224	37	25	16	19	(D)	(D)
2018	100	1,124	27	12	24	33	(D)	(D)
Wisconsin:								
2017	96	3,058	(D)	(D)	14	47	(D)	(D)
2018	98	3,705	(D)	(D)	14	49	....	....

(D) Withheld to avoid disclosing data for individual operations. (Z) Less than the rounding unit. [1] Data not available for all States for all years. [2] Amount applied excludes Bt (bacillus thuringiensis) and other biologicals.
Note: Planted acres are in table 3-32.
NASS, Environmental, Economics, and Demographics Branch, (202) 720–6146.

Table 14-19.—Soybeans: Fertilizer usage, 2017 and 2018[1]

State and Year	Percent treated and amount applied							
	Nitrogen		Phosphate		Potash		Sulfur	
	Area applied	Pounds applied	Area applied	Pounds applied	Area applied	Pounds applied	Area applied	Pounds applied
	Percent	*Millions*	*Percent*	*Millions*	*Percent*	*Millions*	*Percent*	*Millions*
Arkansas:								
2017	13	18.9	51	106.7	59	205.0	2	2.6
2018	7	8.1	51	113.3	56	155.0	7	4.0
Illinois:								
2017	25	63.8	36	279.8	53	713.6	5	7.4
2018	25	60.0	43	350.6	61	733.9	5	9.7
Indiana:								
2017	31	57.3	39	144.2	62	417.2	6	8.4
2018	28	32.0	33	111.1	50	309.5	10	2.9
Iowa:								
2017	13	14.4	23	145.0	34	357.1	6	8.1
2018	13	17.2	21	125.9	32	276.3	8	16.3
Kansas:								
2017	49	40.6	54	118.0	26	65.4	14	4.7
2018	29	22.8	38	76.9	18	48.7	10	4.7
Kentucky:								
2017	28	13.7	68	94.4	70	130.2	7	2.5
2018	32	21.3	74	109.9	85	186.7	5	3.0
Louisiana:								
2015	(D)	(D)	29	22.0	29	27.9	7	1.8
2018	10	4.3	41	31.1	51	51.8	10	2.0
Michigan:								
2017	48	15.9	49	49.2	74	141.0	11	1.8
2018	50	16.9	48	45.7	77	155.6	18	8.9
Minnesota:								
2017	26	35.2	28	95.0	34	161.0	6	5.1
2018	29	32.8	35	124.9	36	191.4	11	11.5
Mississippi:								
2017	4	0.7	17	20.6	38	66.6	4	1.6
2018	6	2.6	31	43.8	44	99.9	6	1.8
Missouri:								
2017	20	32.4	46	143.9	55	272.0	11	7.4
2018	11	11.6	33	89.1	44	193.0	6	2.9
Nebraska:								
2017	43	34.4	46	128.1	16	28.1	19	14.2
2018	36	29.5	43	154.2	18	53.1	17	11.0
North Carolina								
2017	54	20.3	46	30.1	72	95.5	15	4.2
2018	46	17.5	45	28.4	70	83.8	9	3.1
North Dakota								
2017	45	48.7	50	167.4	11	19.2	12	13.4
2018	55	39.1	62	145.7	18	20.4	12	6.6
Ohio:								
2017	32	25.2	30	72.0	61	329.5	8	15.9
2018	33	22.8	37	107.5	57	295.1	4	1.4
South Dakota								
2017	40	22.4	56	124.1	26	50.3	4	5.7
2018	42	28.9	55	141.4	28	53.1	13	5.6
Tennessee:								
2015	48	22.1	66	78.1	70	116.5	17	2.9
2018	65	26.7	76	89.3	72	107.4	21	3.1
Virginia:								
2015	58	9.2	64	19.6	79	40.6	25	2.0
2018	53	6.3	56	15.4	65	34.7	27	1.1
Wisconsin:								
2017	59	24.3	56	52.5	80	156.0	31	9.1
2018	37	15.9	50	70.0	74	171.9	29	11.7

(D) Withheld to avoid disclosing data for individual operations. [1] Data not available for all States for all years.
Note: Planted acres are in table 3-32.
NASS, Environmental, Economics, and Demographics Branch, (202) 720–6146.

Table 14-20.—Wheat: Pesticide usage, 2017 and 2019 [1]

State and Year	Percent treated and amount applied							
	Herbicide		Insecticide		Fungicide [2]		Other Chemicals [2]	
	Area applied	Pounds applied	Area applied	Pounds applied	Area applied	Pounds applied	Area applied	Pounds applied
	Percent	*Thousands*	*Percent*	*Thousands*	*Percent*	*Thousands*	*Percent*	*Thousands*
Winter								
Colorado:								
2017	83	3,230	(D)	(D)	24	63	(D)	(D)
2019	79	2,910	(D)	(D)	30	65	(D)	(D)
Idaho:								
2017	95	496	15	20	60	79	(D)	(D)
2019	96	506	(D)	(D)	17	52	(D)	(D)
Illinois:								
2017	59	39	33	5	46	61	(D)	(D)
2019	54	32	46	8	65	87	11	6
Kansas:								
2017	69	4,917	(D)	(D)	21	250	....	....
2019	72	3,486	(D)	(D)	14	121	(D)	(D)
Michigan:								
2017	66	80	40	4	67	67	11	5
2019	79	123	34	4	62	88	19	9
Missouri:								
2017	62	133	33	12	44	54	(D)	(D)
2019	54	64	24	4	39	33	....	....
Montana:								
2017	96	4,105	....	....	21	47	....	....
2019	99	3,703	(D)	(D)	20	39	(D)	(D)
Nebraska:								
2017	69	1,424	(D)	(D)	31	45	....	....
2019	75	917	(D)	(D)	36	77	(D)	(D)
North Dakota:								
2017	81	53	(D)	(D)	25	2	....	....
2019	80	33	....	....	(D)	(D)	....	....
Ohio:								
2017	41	44	17	4	29	28	....	....
2019	26	34	16	2	39	32	(D)	(D)
Oklahoma:								
2017	37	1,534	(D)	(D)	6	52	....	....
2019	36	899	8	60	10	64	(D)	(D)
Oregon:								
2017	98	1,525	(D)	(D)	39	53	(D)	(D)
2019	100	1,106	(D)	(D)	55	64	(D)	(D)
South Dakota:								
2017	60	542	(D)	(D)	25	22	....	....
2019	60	409	(D)	(D)	(D)	(D)	....	....
Texas:								
2017	23	607	6	109	17	91	....	....
2019	40	1,924	13	173	8	27	....	....
Washington:								
2017	99	1,885	(D)	(D)	67	222	(D)	(D)
2019	95	1,326	(D)	(D)	48	183	....	....
Durum								
Arizona:								
2017	72	14	....	....	(D)	(D)	(D)	(D)
2019	84	5	....	....	....	....	....	....
California:								
2019	77	23	(D)	(D)	....	....	(D)	(D)
Idaho:								
2017	96	11	(D)	(D)	(D)	(D)	....	....
Montana:								
2017	87	944	....	....	11	7	(D)	(D)
2019	98	710	(D)	(D)	16	11	....	....
North Dakota:								
2017	100	1,358	(D)	(D)	55	77	(D)	(D)
2019	96	613	(D)	(D)	53	59	(D)	(D)
Other Spring								
Idaho:								
2017	93	211	16	2	45	27	(D)	(D)
2019	100	310	9	1	23	12	(D)	(D)
Minnesota:								
2017	96	538	37	16	86	199	....	....
2019	99	537	29	8	79	226	....	....
Montana:								
2017	94	3,603	....	....	7	27	....	....
2019	98	3,971	(D)	(D)	5	10	(D)	(D)
North Dakota:								
2017	99	4,467	12	48	57	416	....	....
2019	95	4,595	7	20	58	631	(D)	(D)
South Dakota:								
2017	89	613	13	3	28	22	....	....
2019	97	317	10	2	57	92	....	....
Washington:								
2019	100	441	(D)	(D)	42	29	....	....

(D) Withheld to avoid disclosing data for individual operations. [1] Data not available for all States for all years. [2] Amount applied excludes biologicals.

Note: Planted acres are in table 1-8.

NASS, Environmental, Economics, and Demographics Branch, (202) 720–6146.

Table 14-21.—Wheat: Fertilizer usage, 2017 and 2019[1]

State and Year	Nitrogen		Phosphate		Potash		Sulfur[2]	
	Area applied	Pounds applied	Area applied	Pounds applied	Area applied	Pounds applied	Area applied	Pounds applied
	Percent	*Millions*	*Percent*	*Millions*	*Percent*	*Millions*	*Percent*	*Millions*
Winter Wheat								
Colorado:								
2017	63	50.2	39	19.6	(D)	(D)	22	2.4
2019	85	63.7	67	31.6	(D)	(D)	14	1.0
Idaho:								
2017	92	88.2	80	17.6	37	7.2	76	15.3
2019	99	71.4	19	7.4	(D)	(D)	15	5.7
Illinois:								
2017	92	52.5	86	35.0	70	40.1	14	2.3
2019	94	63.9	88	41.5	78	56.3	20	3.5
Kansas:								
2017	85	466.0	62	137.5	(D)	(D)	18	10.9
2019	99	528.9	81	152.9	6	8.7	25	17.0
Michigan:								
2017	92	47.1	62	13.4	80	23.4	46	4.5
2019	96	57.6	81	23.8	78	28.9	53	4.7
Missouri:								
2017	98	65.4	66	27.2	65	30.6	29	3.2
2019	84	49.9	75	26.2	75	33.0	29	2.9
Montana:								
2017	95	133.4	94	57.1	42	11.6	43	6.7
2019	98	128.1	96	56.0	28	7.0	35	5.1
Nebraska:								
2017	79	46.8	50	18.0	14	1.7	25	2.3
2019	88	65.0	68	23.1	12	2.5	42	4.0
North Dakota:								
2017	87	5	70	2.0	(D)	(D)	(D)	(D)
2019	94	6.4	78	2.2	60	1.2	(D)	(D)
Ohio:								
2017	97	45.6	81	21.7	82	28.2	39	3.6
2019	89	39.1	72	24.4	65	21.2	46	4.6
Oklahoma:								
2017	92	294.5	53	63.6	12	11.6	(D)	(D)
2019	93	277.0	63	75.3	13	9.6	8	1.2
Oregon:								
2017	96	39.2	39	3.8	9	0.8	36	3.2
2019	100	55.9	21	6.6	(D)	(D)	29	5.3
South Dakota:								
2017	86	51.0	76	31.3	22	3.9	15	1.6
2019	60	38.4	30	8.4	(D)	(D)	(D)	(D)
Texas:								
2017	65	166.8	42	45.5	5	5.7	22	6.0
2019	57	164.9	34	35.9	6	10.9	26	13.2
Washington:								
2017	97	138.3	59	13.1	10	1.4	66	13.5
2019	100	124.3	46	16.1	(D)	(D)	75	15.2
Durum								
Arizona:								
2017	98	21.4	(D)	(D)	(D)	(D)	(D)	(D)
2019	88	6.1	(D)	(D)	(D)	(D)	(D)	(D)
California:								
2017	....	....	....	....	(D)	(D)	(D)	(D)
2019	94	3.8	....	....	(D)	(D)	(D)	(D)
Idaho:								
2017	96	3.1	(D)	(D)	(D)	(D)	91	0.4
Montana:								
2017	97	64.0	92	23.7	31	4.0	42	3.9
2019	97	35.0	84	11.7	14	0.9	22	0.9
North Dakota:								
2017	100	108.2	95	38.3	29	3.8	33	3.4
2019	100	63.8	(D)	(D)	10	0.8	28	1.6
Other Spring								
Idaho:								
2017	94	51.5	55	11.7	21	3.4	61	8.2
2019	95	70.4	74	16.0	47	7.9	50	4.7
Minnesota:								
2017	98	134.3	96	52.3	59	25.2	31	4.0
2019	100	170.8	91	55.9	66	23.8	40	4.2
Montana:								
2017	92	145.2	90	68.9	31	8.6	43	9.4
2019	96	153.7	90	71.3	22	11.5	34	6.5
North Dakota:								
2017	99	566.5	92	201.2	32	29.2	34	18.1
2019	96	747.5	89	262.9	25	43.2	24	16.5
South Dakota:								
2017	92	87.1	81	33.6	32	7.4	46	5.7
2019	99	59.5	91	24.0	43	7.8	20	1.0

Note: Planted acres are in table 1-8.
(D) Withheld to avoid disclosing data for individual operations. [1] Data not available for all States for all years.
NASS, Environmental, Economics, and Demographics Branch, (202) 720–6146.

Table 14-22.—Fruits, Pesticides: Percent of bearing acres receiving applications, for surveyed States, 2019[1]

Crop	Herbicide	Insecticide	Fungicide	Other
	Percent			
Apples	36	88	85	86
Apricots	35	58	67	37
Avocados	58	44	4	47
Blueberries	63	91	91	47
Cherries, Sweet	43	85	85	80
Cherries, Tart	46	94	97	80
Dates	9	(D)	(D)	(D)
Grapefruit	70	90	86	88
Grapes, All	51	55	84	46
Grapes, Juice	81	(D)	38	31
Grapes, Raisin	51	71	95	52
Grapes, Table	31	65	96	66
Grapes, Wine	54	51	80	41
Kiwifruit	53	24	36	53
Lemons	61	82	56	79
Nectarines	52	80	79	73
Olives	41	28	57	18
Oranges	69	92	81	87
Peaches	54	86	88	67
Pears	35	89	90	93
Plums	46	65	53	66
Prunes	53	56	70	39
Raspberries	51	91	86	48
Strawberries	19	92	93	53
Tangerines	54	77	55	67

(D) Withheld to avoid disclosing data for individual operations. [1] Refers to acres receiving one or more applications of a specific agricultural chemical.
NASS, Environmental, Economics, and Demographics Branch, (202) 720–6146.

Table 14-23.—Fruit, Fertilizers: Percent of acres receiving applications, for surveyed States, 2019[1]

Crop	Nitrogen	Phosphate	Potash	Sulfur
	Percent			
Apples	62	38	56	34
Apricots	87	55	14	(D)
Avocados	77	54	67	28
Blueberries	84	79	83	37
Cherries, Sweet	81	00	68	25
Cherries, Tart	79	33	63	19
Dates	37	(D)	(D)	(D)
Grapefruit	72	46	55	31
Grapes, All	73	27	62	(D)
Grapes, Juice	48	33	46	14
Grapes, Raisin	43	10	25	(D)
Grapes, Table	42	30	50	38
Grapes, Wine	82	29	69	(D)
Kiwifruit	66	44	60	38
Lemons	80	57	66	44
Nectarines	30	49	49	(D)
Olives	71	22	57	(D)
Oranges	39	64	74	38
Peaches	59	42	54	20
Pears	63	54	48	33
Plums	30	41	42	7
Prunes	54	21	37	14
Raspberries	79	67	68	39
Strawberries	95	49	58	(D)
Tangerines	82	81	85	74

(D) Withheld to avoid disclosing data for individual operations. [1] Refers to acres receiving one or more applications of a specific agricultural chemical.
NASS, Environmental, Economics, and Demographics Branch, (202) 720–6146.

Table 14-24.—Vegetables, Pesticides: Percent of acres receiving applications, for surveyed States, 2018[1]

Crop	Herbicide	Insecticide	Fungicide	Other
	Percent			
Asparagus	65	64	39	(D)
Beans, Snap	79	59	56	1
Broccoli	43	77	55	2
Cabbage	(D)	(D)	(D	(D)
Carrots	34	23	51	17
Cauliflower	53	77	11	(D)
Celery	50	79	69	4
Cucumbers, Fresh	39	67	83	2
Garlic	77	47	77	(D)
Lettuce, Excl head	33	63	54	(D)
Lettuce, Head	44	73	68	(D)
Melons, Cantaloupe	(D)	76	(D)	13
Melons, Honeydew	35	98	93	(D)
Melons, Watermelon	52	73	77	9
Onions, Dry	(D)	(D)	(D)	(D)
Peas, Green	88	28	(D)	....
Peppers, Bell	(D)	(D)	(D)	(D)
Pumpkins	(D)	(D)	(D)	(D)
Spinach	(D)	68	83	(D)
Squash	37	79	68	5
Sweet Corn	(D)	(D)	(D)	(D)
Tomatoes, in the open	(D)	81	82	(D)

(D) Withheld to avoid disclosing data for individual operations. [1] Refers to acres receiving one or more applications of a specific agricultural chemical.

NASS, Environmental, Economics, and Demographics Branch, (202) 720–6146.

Table 14-25.—Vegetables, Fertilizers: Percent of acres receiving applications, for surveyed States, 2018[1]

Crop	Nitrogen	Phosphate	Potash	Sulfur
	Percent			
Asparagus	80	30	60	22
Beans, Snap	88	82	84	57
Broccoli	88	80	22	60
Cabbage	(D)	(D)	(D)	(D)
Carrots	83	64	46	30
Cauliflower	97	80	54	18
Celery	100	70	68	74
Cucumbers	99	93	92	63
Garlic	92	46	3	(D)
Lettuce, excluding Head	98	89	(D)	(D)
Lettuce, Head	88	85	(D)	(D)
Melons, Cantatoupe	99	89	(D)	(D)
Melons, Honeydew	95	89	(D)	(D)
Melons, Watermelon	86	82	62	6
Onions, dry	(D)	(D)	(D)	(D)
Peas, Green	71	29	34	47
Peppers, Bell	(D)	(D)	(D)	(D)
Pumpkins	(D)	(D)	(D)	(D)
Spinach	94	94	(D)	(D)
Squash	89	82	85	24
Sweet Corn	(D)	(D)	(D)	(D)
Tomatoes, in the open	99	73	49	(D)

(D) Withheld to avoid disclosing data for individual operations. [1] Refers to acres receiving one or more applications of a specific agricultural chemical.

NASS, Environmental, Economics, and Demographics Branch, (202) 720–6146.

CHAPTER XV

MISCELLANEOUS AGRICULTURAL STATISTICS

This chapter contains miscellaneous data which do not fit into the preceding chapters. Included here are summary tables on foreign trade in agricultural products; statistics on fishery products; tables on refrigerated warehouses; and statistics on crops in Alaska.

Foreign Agricultural Trade Statistics

Agricultural products, sometimes referred to as food and fiber products, cover a broad range of goods from unprocessed bulk commodities like soybeans, feed corn and wheat to highly-processed, high-value foods and beverages like sausages, bakery goods, ice cream, or beer sold in retail stores and restaurants. All of the products found in Chapters 1-24 (except for fishery products in Chapter 3) of the U.S. Harmonized Tariff Schedule are considered agricultural products. These products generally fall into the following categories: grains, animal feeds, and grain products (like bread and pasta); oilseeds and oilseed products (like canola oil); livestock, poultry and dairy products including live animals, meats, eggs, and feathers; horticultural products including all fresh and processed fruits, vegetables, tree nuts, as well as nursery products and beer and wine; unmanufactured tobacco; and tropical products like sugar, cocoa, and coffee. Certain other products are considered ''agricultural,'' the most significant of which are essential oils (Chapter 33), protein isolates and modified starches (Chapter 35), raw rubber (Chapter 40), raw animal hides and skins (Chapter 41), and wool and cotton (Chapters 51-52). Manufactured products derived from plants or animals, but which are not considered ''agricultural'' by USDA's definition are cotton yarn, textiles and clothing; leather and leather articles of apparel; and cigarettes and spirits. The World Trade Organization's definition of agricultural products varies in that it includes some products like spirits and tobacco products.

U.S. foreign agricultural trade statistics are based on documents filed by exporters and importers and compiled by the Bureau of the Census. Puerto Rico is a Customs district within the U.S. Customs territory, and its trade with foreign countries is included in U.S. export and import statistics. U.S. export and import statistics include merchandise trade between the U.S. Virgin Islands and foreign countries even though the Virgin Islands of the United States are not officially a part of the U.S. Customs territory.

The export value, the value at the port of exportation, is based on the selling price and includes inland freight, insurance, and other charges to the port. The country of destination is the country of ultimate destination or where the commodities are consumed or further processed.

Agricultural products, like manufactured goods, are often transhipped from the one country to another. Shippers are asked to identify the ultimate destination of a shipment. However, transhipment points are often recorded as the ultimate destination even though the actual point of consumption may be in a neighboring state. Thus, exports to countries which act as transhipment points are generally overstated, while exports to neighboring countries are often understated. Major world transhipment points include the Netherlands, Hong Kong, and Singapore. In such cases, exports to the Netherlands are over reported, but under reported for Germany, Belgium and the United Kingdom. Exports to Hong Kong are overstated, but under reported to China, and exports to Singapore are overstated, but understated to Malaysia and Indonesia.

Imports for consumption are a combination of entries for immediate consumption and withdrawals from bonded warehouses for consumption. The import value, defined generally as the market value in the foreign country, excludes import duties, ocean freight, and marine insurance. The country of origin is defined as the country where the commodities were grown or processed. Where the country of origin is not known, the imports are credited to the country of shipment.

Table 15-1.—Foreign trade: Value of total agricultural exports and imports, United States, fiscal years 2010–2019

Fiscal year Oct. 1-Sep. 30	U.S. total domestic exports			U.S. total imports for consumption, customs value			Surplus agricultural exports over agricultural imports
	Total merchandise exports	Agricultural exports [1]	Agricultural exports share of total exports	Total merchandise imports	Agricultural imports	Agricultural imports share of total imports	
	Million dollars	*Million dollars*	*Percent*	*Million dollars*	*Million dollars*	*Percent*	*Million dollars*
2010	1,077,045	108,529	10	1,832,595	78,963	4	29,566
2011	1,268,437	137,465	11	2,128,266	94,511	4	42,955
2012	1,343,129	135,907	10	2,248,129	103,371	5	32,536
2013	1,360,350	141,139	10	2,235,764	103,871	5	37,269
2014	1,398,923	152,326	11	2,304,072	109,258	5	43,068
2015	1,327,349	139,757	11	2,267,135	113,633	5	26,124
2016	1,222,350	129,597	11	2,160,641	114,439	5	15,158
2017	1,283,329	140,215	11	2,273,403	120,964	5	19,251
2018	1,402,288	143,414	10	2,506,195	128,678	5	14,736
2019	1,396,075	135,470	10	2,538,445	130,945	5	4,525

[1] Includes food exported for relief or charity by individuals and private agencies.
ERS, Market and Trade Economics Division, (202) 694–5257.

Table 15-2.—Foreign trade: Value and quantity of bulk commodity exports, United States, fiscal years 2010–2019 [1]

Fiscal year	Wheat, unmilled	Rice, milled	Feed grains [2]	Oilseeds [3]	Tobacco unmanufactured	Cotton and linters	Bulk commodities
				Value			
				Million dollars			
2010	5,840	2,296	9,806	17,951	1,223	4,836	41,951
2011	11,504	2,117	13,969	21,571	1,116	8,982	59,260
2012	8,376	1,963	11,719	21,101	1,051	6,551	50,761
2013	10,126	2,212	6,198	22,456	1,193	5,649	47,834
2014	8,260	2,002	12,480	25,758	1,114	4,614	54,228
2015	5,914	2,036	11,057	23,175	1,250	4,146	47,578
2016	5,136	1,834	10,768	21,923	1,042	3,451	44,154
2017	6,198	1,714	10,798	25,313	1,029	5,866	50,917
2018	5,086	1,636	12,238	23,175	1,093	6,624	49,852
2019	6,233	1,826	9,484	18,515	755	6,076	42,889
				Quantity			
				1,000 metric tons			
2010	25,698	4,260	53,849	42,499	185	2,746	129,236
2011	34,583	3,920	49,170	41,365	174	3,113	132,325
2012	26,969	3,578	40,024	39,247	167	2,731	112,716
2013	31,110	3,848	20,460	35,862	165	2,921	94,366
2014	27,091	3,355	56,630	46,050	152	2,202	135,480
2015	21,398	3,971	56,316	51,212	177	2,535	135,610
2016	22,538	3,789	59,075	55,146	156	2,202	142,904
2017	28,078	3,986	61,708	60,755	150	3,298	157,976
2018	21,155	3,052	68,475	57,924	155	3,661	154,422
2019	26,567	3,599	51,651	49,120	105	3,433	134,475

[1] Fiscal years, Oct. 1–Sept. 30. [1] Corn, barley, sorghum, rye, and oats. [3] Soybeans, peanuts, rapeseed, cottonseed, sunflowerseed, safflowerseed, and others.
ERS, Market and Trade Economics Division, (202) 694–5257.

Table 15-3.—Agricultural exports: Value to top 50 countries of destination, United States, fiscal years 2017–2019 [1]

Country	2017	2018	2019
		Million dollars	
Canada	20,444.0	20,701.0	20,997.3
Mexico	18,605.9	18,869.4	18,996.7
EU27+UK	11,552.5	12,707.6	12,615.2
Japan	11,856.7	12,655.0	12,146.7
China	21,838.8	16,262.9	10,115.9
South Korea	6,851.2	7,958.9	7,819.6
Taiwan	3,399.7	3,812.2	3,611.4
Vietnam	2,559.2	3,895.2	3,596.3
Hong Kong	4,043.3	4,198.3	3,512.5
Indonesia	2,968.4	3,091.5	2,888.8
Philippines	2,627.4	2,836.1	2,868.8
Colombia	2,554.2	2,750.1	2,664.5
Thailand	1,781.7	2,143.6	1,884.6
India	1,504.3	1,579.3	1,782.3
Egypt	772.0	1,703.0	1,473.2
Australia	1,368.7	1,425.8	1,443.9
Saudi Arabia	1,588.0	1,330.0	1,318.0
Guatemala	1,081.8	1,202.5	1,307.2
Dominican Republic	1,231.6	1,272.2	1,295.4
Turkey	1,711.5	1,706.5	1,180.7
Malaysia	903.1	959.6	1,147.7
United Arab Emirates	1,071.5	1,033.2	1,115.7
Pakistan	834.0	1,433.4	1,082.1
Peru	1,187.8	1,325.4	1,021.3
Chile	912.3	942.7	1,013.1
Singapore	824.0	792.1	955.4
Bangladesh	892.4	858.6	935.8
Argentina	174.2	350.5	765.4
Costa Rica	691.4	723.3	733.2
Panama	661.7	668.1	716.9
Honduras	597.7	679.0	694.6
Israel	527.7	665.9	622.1
Brazil	725.7	584.1	582.4
El Salvador	487.1	503.5	567.7
Nigeria	500.5	326.5	551.0
New Zealand	379.7	463.3	534.6
Ecuador	271.4	343.7	460.7
Switzerland	454.1	386.2	406.5
Jamaica	376.8	393.6	397.7
Haiti	390.2	394.2	384.4
South Africa	360.6	323.8	361.7
Trinidad and Tobago	331.4	341.7	346.2
Iraq	106.8	335.2	303.4
Morocco	485.2	587.6	276.0
Cuba	266.1	230.0	270.7
The Bahamas	254.0	261.6	262.3
Nicaragua	218.5	214.1	240.2
Kuwait	222.1	237.1	238.9
Netherlands Antilles	219.7	219.9	224.7
Jordan	282.8	208.0	219.7
Other Countries	4,264.0	4,527.2	4,519.3
World Total [2]	140,215.4	143,414.3	135,469.5

[1] Fiscal years Oct. 1–Sept. 30. [2] Totals may not add due to rounding.
ERS, Market and Trade Economics Divison, (202) 694–5257.

Table 15-4.—Foreign trade in agricultural products: Value of exports by principal commodity groups, United States, fiscal years 2016–2019 [1]

Commodity	2016	2017	2018	2019
	1,000 dollars	*1,000 dollars*	*1,000 dollars*	*1,000 dollars*
Total Merchandise Exports	1,427,982,211	1,427,401,788	1,410,626,357	1,419,857,072
Nonagricultural U.S. Exports (Na)	1,298,385,211	1,287,186,788	1,267,212,357	1,284,387,072
Total Agricultural exports	129,597,000	140,215,000	143,414,000	135,470,000
Animals and animal products	24,915,038	28,269,536	29,939,818	29,561,343
Animals, live	457,572	542,795	643,031	642,476
Cattle	67,762	158,462	274,713	236,937
Horses,mules,burros-live	372,184	361,631	342,864	388,276
Swine, live	13,709	18,930	21,672	14,516
Sheep, live	2,280	2,551	2,424	1,518
Other live Animals	1,637	1,221	1,358	1,230
Red meat and products	12,265,093	14,155,005	15,328,372	15,390,245
Beef and Veal	5,196,925	6,173,070	7,342,105	7,283,838
Beef and Veal, fresh/frozen	4,966,796	5,960,005	7,128,147	7,082,067
Beef prep/pres	230,129	213,065	213,958	201,771
Horsemeat, fresh/frozen	204	806	52	25
Lamb and Goat, fr/frozen	11,525	14,851	14,401	14,398
Pork	4,737,457	5,227,433	5,440,608	5,516,852
Pork, fresh/frozen	3,992,969	4,477,735	4,681,686	4,774,617
Pork, prep/pres	744,488	749,698	758,922	742,235
Variety meats	1,660,265	1,884,164	1,731,062	1,674,419
Beef variety meats	897,749	896,036	878,777	956,960
Pork variety meats	689,246	905,847	757,189	604,853
Other variety meats	73,270	82,281	95,096	112,605
Other meats, fresh/frozen	658,718	854,681	800,144	900,714
Poultry and products	4,551,342	4,908,080	5,253,058	5,136,394
Poultry, live	165,604	196,218	216,294	281,246
Baby chicks	148,859	179,075	199,965	264,571
Other live poultry	16,745	17,143	16,329	16,675
Poultry meats	3,595,801	3,845,509	4,097,399	3,988,541
Chickens, fresh/frozen	2,587,149	2,788,146	3,006,205	2,962,248
Turkeys, fresh/frozen	437,249	429,313	411,995	477,315
Other poultry, fresh/frozen	4,944	6,246	4,160	4,597
Poultry meats, prep	566,458	621,804	675,039	544,381
Poultry, misc	235,963	313,388	342,756	283,923
Eggs	553,973	552,965	596,610	582,684
Dairy products	4,622,845	5,403,069	5,653,344	5,743,420
Evaporated/condensed milk	35,198	34,029	36,169	31,741
Nonfat dry milk	1,184,268	1,372,886	1,450,475	1,562,918
Butter and milkfat	48,924	103,698	144,731	97,360
Cheese	1,173,091	1,415,408	1,475,577	1,488,204
Whey,fluid/dried	548,497	695,162	669,284	632,879
Other dairy products	1,632,866	1,781,886	1,877,108	1,930,318
Fats, oils, and greases	489,611	606,058	585,151	633,131
Lard	55,835	97,809	89,440	55,430
Tallow, inedible	206,771	256,221	216,773	206,860
Other animal fats	227,005	252,028	278,938	370,841
Hides and skins	1,887,730	1,931,099	1,580,560	1,108,071
Bovine hides, whole	1,018,548	1,128,521	884,918	635,347
Other cattle hides	12,945	18,177	17,377	13,138
Calf skins, whole	47,385	102,640	127,187	65,453
Horse hides, whole	80,186	23,742	12,703	3,312
Sheep and lamb skins	14,100	15,106	12,977	5,944
Other hides and Skin	421,596	428,034	373,222	267,023
Furskins	292,969	214,880	152,175	117,855
Mink pelts	272,258	199,224	136,433	99,989
Other furskins	20,712	15,656	15,741	17,866
Wool and mohair	18,459	23,191	27,089	18,262
Sausage casings	245,525	277,883	397,712	413,083
Bull semen	160,576	162,648	187,376	204,169
Miscellaneous animal products	216,285	259,708	284,125	272,092
Grains and feeds	29,800,241	30,507,690	31,455,366	30,189,075
Wheat,unmilled	5,136,021	6,197,654	5,086,206	6,233,349
Wheat flour	171,611	161,392	126,867	152,450
Other wheat products	153,565	135,736	147,170	154,064
Rice-paddy, milled	1,834,482	1,714,013	1,636,179	1,826,348
Feed grains and products	11,224,817	11,284,328	12,730,294	9,980,880
Feed grain	10,767,971	10,798,005	12,238,048	9,483,652
Barley	40,168	31,233	28,462	29,944
Corn	9,124,474	9,683,360	11,267,677	8,995,926
Grain sorghum	1,590,054	1,071,130	931,433	447,888
Oats	7,248	8,817	6,703	5,453
Rye	6,027	3,465	3,772	4,441
Feed grain products	456,846	486,322	492,246	497,229

See footnote(s) at end of table.

Table 15-4.—Foreign trade in agricultural products: Value of exports by principal commodity groups, United States, fiscal years 2016–2019[1]—Continued

Commodity	2016	2017	2018	2019
	1,000 dollars	*1,000 dollars*	*1,000 dollars*	*1,000 dollars*
Grains and feeds--Continued				
Popcorn	95,115	120,465	114,481	108,538
Blended food products	50,173	53,526	48,644	58,921
Other grain products	3,670,714	3,636,125	3,694,067	3,848,457
Feeds and fodders	7,463,743	7,204,451	7,871,458	7,826,068
Corn by-products	624,823	625,418	689,629	613,705
Alfalfa meal and cubes	73,599	65,790	51,828	41,649
Beef pulp	97,747	94,493	108,913	95,146
Citrus pulp pellets	1,056	26	171	649
Other feeds and fodders	6,666,518	6,418,724	7,020,916	7,074,919
Fruit and prep	6,138,011	6,307,658	6,394,412	5,945,527
Fruits, fresh	4,491,929	4,676,914	4,721,795	4,333,844
Citrus fruits	983,861	1,016,248	971,950	851,023
Grapefruit	106,136	94,411	61,519	69,161
Lemons and limes	180,093	187,091	179,081	166,040
Oranges and tangerines	679,606	723,164	711,014	593,263
Other citrus	18,026	11,582	20,335	22,559
Noncitrus Fruits	3,508,068	3,660,666	3,749,846	3,482,821
Apples	894,191	958,313	1,079,704	866,106
Berries	677,923	673,549	707,141	699,652
Cherries	476,419	643,770	518,453	493,936
Grapes	765,229	748,231	769,626	784,394
Melons,	153,556	159,605	160,001	136,461
Peaches	140,184	118,491	125,311	129,860
Pears	176,004	144,820	153,922	168,276
Plums	59,080	59,358	60,312	53,853
Other noncitrus	165,481	154,528	175,376	150,283
Fruits, dried	577,168	544,301	529,393	467,384
Raisin	321,685	304,912	296,012	264,451
Prunes	165,000	142,980	145,288	128,715
Other dried fruits	90,483	96,409	88,093	74,218
Fruits, canned	605,718	641,843	683,241	661,165
Fruits, frozen	135,414	122,974	128,448	134,263
Other fruits, prep	327,782	321,626	331,535	348,871
Fruits, juices	1,096,074	984,370	910,098	821,094
Apple juice	46,510	49,840	57,847	51,852
Grape juice	68,295	60,481	77,132	65,653
Grapefruit juice	36,797	36,307	39,811	30,073
Orange juice	382,748	339,569	252,361	221,844
Other fruit juices	561,724	489,173	482,947	451,672
Wine	1,528,841	1,416,818	1,459,096	1,326,576
Nuts and prep	8,235,776	8,760,134	9,431,264	9,635,246
Almonds	4,647,338	4,199,529	4,584,942	4,749,005
Filberts	74,184	94,898	85,562	90,393
Peanuts	595,969	549,844	570,107	640,757
Pistachios	775,538	1,514,356	1,532,628	2,181,500
Walnuts	1,250,986	1,371,122	1,516,684	1,152,906
Pecans	465,097	617,955	688,822	472,933
Other nuts	426,664	412,430	444,459	447,752
Vegetables and prep	7,148,372	7,328,379	7,014,224	7,160,559
Vegetables fresh	2,480,008	2,505,050	2,549,031	2,705,787
Asparagus	48,250	62,297	81,600	78,540
Broccoli	117,248	103,280	102,709	98,018
Carrots	111,240	110,804	111,203	109,581
Cabbage	48,456	59,473	76,006	84,407
Celery	96,764	87,452	79,716	119,225
Cauliflower	135,060	147,424	158,826	161,420
Corn sweet	46,765	49,819	49,762	44,149
Cucumbers	14,493	15,871	13,409	16,688
Garlic	14,949	17,064	14,526	14,018
Lettuce	488,803	499,952	480,983	518,966
Mushrooms	26,848	25,313	34,588	39,156
Onions and shallots	196,622	170,173	185,070	243,554
Peppers	79,938	77,494	76,595	84,519
Potatoes	202,462	232,420	233,197	252,740
Tomatoes	122,977	113,004	110,721	114,172
Other fresh vegetables	729,133	733,211	740,030	726,633

See footnote(s) at end of table.

Table 15-4.—Foreign trade in agricultural products: Value of exports by principal commodity groups, United States, fiscal years 2016–2019 [1]—Continued

Commodity	2016	2017	2018	2019
	1,000 dollars	*1,000 dollars*	*1,000 dollars*	*1,000 dollars*
Vegetables and prep--Continued				
Vegetables, frozen	1,482,153	1,534,695	1,515,472	1,549,597
Corn, sweet	107,487	113,027	107,473	104,392
Potatoes	1,137,484	1,165,600	1,166,940	1,218,771
Other frozen vegetables	237,182	256,068	241,059	226,433
Vegetables, canned	633,919	587,393	546,558	533,012
Pulses	776,779	869,549	620,087	615,291
Dried Beans	298,078	312,475	307,206	288,712
Dried Peas	255,952	189,915	118,899	110,925
Dried Lentils	173,308	256,208	93,798	120,351
Dried chickpeas	49,441	110,952	100,184	95,304
Other vegetables, prep/pres	1,775,513	1,831,692	1,783,076	1,756,872
Oilseeds and products	29,192,243	32,460,021	31,197,490	25,608,461
Oilcake and meal	4,225,951	3,933,033	4,998,037	4,457,068
Bran and residues	12,558	13,443	23,488	26,733
Corn oilcake and meal	3,033	928	666	726
Soybean meal	4,155,007	3,873,278	4,933,693	4,392,407
Other oilcake and meal	55,354	45,385	40,189	37,203
Oilseeds	21,922,530	25,312,750	23,174,724	18,514,702
Rapeseed	106,103	98,775	99,409	120,687
Safflower seeds	981	826	658	1,045
Soybeans	20,426,101	23,808,967	21,688,843	16,996,612
Sunflowerseeds	101,451	78,666	72,975	62,724
Peanuts, oilstock	213,436	128,468	119,082	109,766
Other oilseeds	82,948	141,310	126,429	100,589
Protein substances	991,510	1,055,738	1,067,327	1,123,280
Vegetable oils	3,043,762	3,214,238	3,024,729	2,636,691
Soybean oil	842,844	953,402	896,256	676,486
Cottonseed oil	21,495	32,402	40,470	31,614
Sunflower oil	51,519	42,165	47,232	67,164
Corn oil	430,201	469,927	289,143	212,613
Peanut oil	11,611	11,974	11,547	8,828
Rapeseed oil	94,427	110,214	96,362	83,778
Safflower oil	26,555	17,632	16,569	14,418
Other vegetable oils/waxes	1,565,109	1,576,521	1,627,149	1,541,789
Tobacco, unmfg	1,042,410	1,028,510	1,093,423	754,574
Tobacco, light air	160,616	144,913	126,818	127,995
Tobacco, flue	671,652	651,849	753,509	424,761
Other tobacco, unmfg	210,142	231,748	213,096	201,818
Cotton, excluding linters	3,443,196	5,849,567	6,609,963	6,069,606
Cotton linters	7,475	16,604	13,916	6,577
Essential oils	1,834,209	1,969,901	2,109,209	2,155,531
Seeds, field and garden	1,572,761	1,698,435	1,809,101	1,855,830
Sugar and tropical products	5,034,548	4,927,713	5,050,073	4,883,652
Sugar and related products	1,734,404	1,680,134	1,790,203	1,651,656
Sugar, cane or beet	73,142	65,737	110,215	45,109
Related sugar products	1,661,263	1,614,397	1,679,988	1,606,547
Coffee	937,513	865,479	875,950	875,092
Cocoa	235,822	208,762	188,476	182,628
Chocolate and prep	1,511,799	1,558,390	1,565,361	1,582,761
Tea, including herbal	381,918	363,421	371,115	362,107
Spices	184,499	189,334	198,006	193,393
Rubber, crude	45,130	56,934	54,740	31,379
Fibers, excluding cotton	3,463	5,259	6,222	4,636
Other hort products	6,276,107	6,389,997	6,606,411	7,263,532
Hops, including extract	243,674	275,051	339,993	378,929
Starches, not wheat/corn	135,604	132,609	138,844	144,033
Yeasts	92,762	103,112	104,468	100,937
Misc hort products	5,804,067	5,879,225	6,023,106	6,639,633
Nursery & greenhouse	401,839	417,315	439,295	438,862
Beverages, excluding juice	1,930,038	1,882,792	1,881,144	1,793,461

[1] Fiscal years, Oct. 1–Sept. 30. Totals may not add due to rounding.
ERS, Market and Trade Economics Division, (202) 694–5257.
Compiled from reports of the U.S. Department of Commerce.

Table 15-5.—Foreign trade in agricultural products: Value of imports by principal groups, United States, fiscal years 2016–2019 [1]

Product	2016	2017	2018	2019
	1,000 dollars	*1,000 dollars*	*1,000 dollars*	*1,000 dollars*
Total merchandise imports	2,177,103,456	2,288,033,279	2,499,691,523	2,532,820,540
Non-agricultural U.S. imports	2,062,664,456	2,167,069,279	2,371,013,523	2,401,875,540
Total agricultural imports	114,439,000	120,964,000	128,678,000	130,945,000
Animals & prods.	16,594,053	15,778,997	16,539,892	17,105,618
Animals - live, excluding poultry	2,634,280	2,495,026	2,563,143	2,714,394
Cattle and calves	1,688,912	1,487,359	1,564,249	1,749,673
Horses, mules, burros	548,516	629,370	627,365	594,314
Swine	334,417	323,244	313,365	310,585
Sheep, Live	1,224	498	281	491
Other live animals	61,212	54,555	57,883	59,331
Red meat & products	8,239,788	8,164,540	8,697,188	8,920,077
Beef & veal	5,371,892	5,114,995	5,584,110	5,790,777
Beef & veal - fresh or frozen	4,997,263	4,741,504	5,147,596	5,309,413
Beef & veal - prep. or pres.	374,629	373,490	436,513	481,363
Pork	1,658,024	1,705,340	1,644,300	1,499,146
Pork - fr. or froz.	1,335,915	1,375,854	1,287,052	1,101,118
Pork - prep. or pres.	322,109	329,486	357,248	398,028
Mutton, goat & lamb	775,142	924,135	989,037	1,089,420
Horsemeat - fr. or froz.	1,875	1,872	2,161	2,200
Variety meats - fr. or froz.	300,613	260,150	292,845	354,887
Other meats - fr. or froz.	45,336	54,502	64,743	65,661
Other meats & prods.	86,906	103,547	119,992	117,986
Poultry and prods.	863,321	742,801	777,094	809,823
Poultry - live	50,020	49,383	43,571	42,971
Poultry meat	527,524	470,456	511,912	513,302
Eggs	169,880	83,937	65,077	79,926
Poultry, misc.	115,897	139,026	156,535	173,625
Dairy products	3,395,862	2,939,582	2,958,006	3,117,193
Milk & cream, fresh or dried	105,049	105,885	125,388	124,081
Butter & butterfat mixtures	185,582	185,665	282,931	380,630
Cheese	1,274,575	1,167,399	1,279,347	1,345,586
Casein & mixtures	529,484	513,472	437,491	424,203
Other dairy prods.	1,301,171	967,160	832,848	842,693
Fats, oils, & greases	183,266	221,047	216,482	293,755
Hides & skins	177,594	101,926	58,432	44,154
Sheep & lamb skins	357	443	554	375
Other hides & skins	41,474	31,714	26,750	15,194
Furskins	135,763	69,768	31,128	28,584
Wool - unmfg.	17,726	15,283	14,872	17,223
Apparel grade wool	8,904	6,970	8,604	10,360
Carpet grade wool	8,822	8,312	6,268	6,863
Sausage casings	182,695	193,893	205,042	91,416
Bull semen	43,400	42,404	37,287	35,446
Misc. animal prods	855,872	862,324	1,012,166	1,061,983
Silk, raw	240	171	180	154
Grains & feeds	11,075,221	11,714,644	13,360,868	13,976,050
Wheat, ex. seed	511,095	590,408	830,545	483,128
Corn, unmilled	371,116	298,698	191,980	175,477
Oats, unmilled	318,305	314,107	318,819	312,927
Barley, unmilled	100,797	53,789	39,266	31,713
Rice	666,836	638,352	857,185	970,571
Biscuits & wafers	0,020,489	4,260,520	4,752,985	5,258,279
Pasta & noodles	593,509	565,327	579,635	596,133
Other grains & preps.	3,002,326	3,262,538	3,719,637	4,038,802
Feeds & fodders, excluding oilcake	1,687,748	1,730,905	2,070,816	2,109,020
Fruits & preps.	14,870,410	16,218,914	17,049,053	17,929,435
Fruits - fr. or froz.	12,058,808	13,356,022	13,837,119	14,774,616
Apples, fresh	264,706	237,266	201,279	211,171
Avocados	1,717,897	2,605,107	2,431,484	2,693,030
Berries, excl. strawberries	1,986,251	2,065,450	2,367,284	2,841,018
Bananas & plantains - fresh or frozen	2,271,361	2,296,646	2,415,952	2,425,164
Citrus, fresh	955,802	1,060,013	1,276,777	1,253,876
Grapes, fresh	1,449,269	1,618,416	1,574,652	1,615,883
Kiwifruit, fresh	127,963	121,492	137,271	129,835
Mangoes	545,951	544,045	531,911	562,518
Melons	691,252	664,403	686,521	679,591
Peaches	76,867	69,564	72,513	67,765
Pears	111,125	116,337	131,800	117,204
Pineapples - fr. or froz.	663,304	682,451	678,408	653,966
Plums	53,915	43,707	46,530	43,066
Strawberries - fr. or froz.	725,167	800,018	800,798	1,002,682
Other fruits - fr. or froz.	417,980	431,107	483,942	477,847
Fruits - prep. or pres.	2,811,602	2,862,892	3,211,934	3,154,819
Bananas & plantains - prep. or pres.	143,414	147,902	169,265	168,765
Pineapples - canned or prep.	389,838	355,656	285,608	275,220
Other fruits - prep. or pres.	2,270,050	2,359,334	2,757,061	2,710,834

See footnote(s) at end of table.

Table 15-5.—Foreign trade in agricultural products: Value of imports by principal groups, United States, fiscal years 2016–2019 [1]—Continued

Product	2016	2017	2018	2019
	1,000 dollars	*1,000 dollars*	*1,000 dollars*	*1,000 dollars*
Fruit juices	1,760,525	1,937,797	2,169,101	2,192,542
Apple juice	476,474	438,970	466,608	468,591
Grape juice	73,353	64,472	74,796	82,643
Grapefruit juice	1,293	4,777	14,985	27,627
Lemon juice	114,142	122,661	123,017	113,109
Lime juice	30,173	33,404	31,678	29,038
Orange juice	556,712	774,656	932,206	786,953
Pineapple juice	118,602	110,346	65,011	59,891
Other fruit juice	389,776	388,511	460,800	624,690
Nuts & preps	2,724,812	3,328,514	3,495,030	3,279,495
Brazil nuts	72,546	72,164	52,713	42,559
Cashew nuts	1,234,762	1,688,328	1,682,998	1,344,366
Chestnuts	15,386	13,069	12,855	10,790
Coconut meat	220,925	237,845	260,888	222,111
Filberts	34,799	41,382	46,484	48,756
Macadamia nuts	140,624	146,812	183,488	258,117
Pecans	484,073	634,622	673,506	750,953
Pistachio nuts	10,803	12,490	15,385	15,167
Other nuts	510,894	481,802	566,713	586,676
Vegetables & preps.	13,159,109	13,276,028	14,310,805	14,970,887
Vegetables, fresh	8,009,144	7,697,210	8,362,234	8,909,062
Tomatoes	2,221,247	2,074,235	2,389,574	2,290,915
Asparagus	609,777	696,162	623,357	698,110
Beans	121,866	116,219	142,839	144,701
Cabbage	47,584	40,715	48,171	75,285
Carrots	94,992	85,766	119,131	111,440
Cauliflower & broccoli, fresh	267,797	294,325	286,323	342,627
Celery,	26,576	35,409	30,149	65,944
Cucumbers	704,241	657,350	740,890	815,986
Eggplant	68,154	60,366	64,131	67,282
Endive	3,978	3,843	4,073	4,976
Garlic	205,356	223,076	166,354	155,577
Lettuce	276,595	280,764	275,231	350,093
Okra	25,721	29,511	40,617	43,934
Onions	469,759	412,694	440,544	438,233
Peas	74,879	73,099	87,917	76,331
Peppers	1,451,384	1,305,923	1,460,992	1,673,748
Potatoes	186,601	214,670	229,433	198,462
Radishes	21,181	23,436	34,521	28,060
Squash	383,247	324,765	365,447	373,030
Other fresh vegetables	748,209	744,880	812,540	954,329
Vegetables - prep. or pres.	3,030,523	3,312,934	3,435,521	3,507,678
Bamboo shoots, preserved	26,263	27,520	24,890	24,697
Cucumbers, preserved	57,176	58,068	63,991	61,757
Garlic, dried	73,450	113,801	61,118	30,674
Olives - prep. or pres.	415,202	424,214	451,788	485,664
Mushrooms, canned	109,120	106,592	106,288	107,763
Mushrooms, dried	28,285	28,487	31,930	25,903
Onions, preserved	48,921	52,457	54,781	61,320
Artichokes - prep.	138,255	159,755	144,717	136,927
Asparagus- prep.	20,962	19,137	16,265	13,117
Tomatoes, incl. paste & sauce	204,822	211,682	231,258	245,933
Waterchestnuts	21,440	28,136	31,620	22,871
Peppers & pimentos, prep.	110,100	98,398	112,113	85,103
Veg Starches, excluding wheat & corn	171,854	174,291	216,435	229,452
Soups & sauces	464,535	493,133	529,448	589,076
Other vegetables - prep. or pres.	1,140,140	1,317,264	1,358,878	1,387,420
Vegetables, frozen	1,867,923	1,999,431	2,230,941	2,306,262
Tomatoes	7,109	6,680	7,919	10,363
Asparagus	16,021	14,847	16,967	14,879
Beans	69,359	75,322	75,364	70,817
Carrots	7,796	10,193	9,567	8,338
Cauliflower & broccoli	356,639	356,391	399,808	422,818
Okra	16,494	12,757	15,975	12,852
Peas	40,940	39,411	44,503	54,080
Potatoes	772,005	844,154	937,181	953,136
Other frozen vegetables	581,562	639,677	723,656	758,981
Pulses	251,519	266,453	282,109	247,885
Dried peas	44,483	44,534	63,257	46,822
Dried beans	143,998	145,849	129,266	128,430
Dried lentils	28,149	33,538	36,037	35,019
Dried chickpeas	34,889	42,531	53,550	37,614
Sugar & related prods.	4,469,243	4,612,790	4,743,534	4,529,220
Sugar - cane & beet	1,652,713	1,692,323	1,703,807	1,469,245
Molasses	161,512	118,625	140,918	146,024
Confectionery prods.	1,727,605	1,764,973	1,891,008	1,918,303
Other sugar & related prods.	927,413	1,036,869	1,007,801	995,648

See footnote(s) at end of table.

Table 15-5.—Foreign trade in agricultural products: Value of imports by principal groups, United States, fiscal years 2016–2019 [1]—Continued

Product	2016	2017	2018	2019
	1,000 dollars	*1,000 dollars*	*1,000 dollars*	*1,000 dollars*
Cocoa & products	4,939,220	5,243,686	4,630,500	4,934,897
Coffee & products	5,934,064	6,617,179	6,086,250	6,163,421
Tea	750,078	718,611	703,749	727,971
Spices & herbs	1,859,806	1,979,025	2,044,202	1,981,417
Pepper	991,728	788,970	639,041	607,083
Other spices & herbs	868,078	1,190,055	1,405,161	1,374,334
Drugs, crude & natural	1,792,016	1,826,458	1,993,616	1,968,408
Essential oils	2,627,381	3,056,600	3,176,003	2,997,727
Fibers, excl. cotton	127,817	126,249	122,501	136,156
Rubber & gums	1,306,736	1,700,050	1,583,821	1,513,865
Tobacco - unmfg.	793,605	673,127	661,243	672,243
Tobacco - filler	763,423	650,975	643,234	640,239
Tobacco - scrap	10,770	8,104	7,543	10,701
Other tobacco	19,412	14,048	10,466	21,303
Beverages, ex. fruit juice	13,958,618 5	14,386,991	15,816,195	16,371,913
Wine	5,526,951	5,965,998	6,312,581	6,430,661
Malt beverages	4,831,814	4,988,000	5,368,737	5,548,108
Other beverages	3,599,853	3,432,993	4,134,877	4,393,144
Oilseeds & products	826,295	823,299	860,675	738,299
Oilseeds & oilnuts	826,295	823,298	860,675	738,300
Flaxseed	68,941	64,319	80,859	86,685
Rapeseed	186,040	239,698	262,597	201,357
Soybeans	361,252	331,919	325,567	224,338
Sunflower seeds	45,170	47,145	58,645	71,056
Other oilseeds & oilnuts	164,892	140,217	133,007	154,864
Oils & waxes - vegetable	6,154,477	7,072,533	7,213,267	6,411,556
Castor oil	69,675	80,424	94,989	93,986
Coconut oil	774,366	880,867	753,511	588,115
Cottonseed oil	2,508	30	40	35
Olive oil	1,323,409	1,387,740	1,491,105	1,362,684
Palm oil	828,848	1,024,315	1,103,296	930,837
Palm kernel oil	351,795	477,117	447,027	284,145
Peanut oil	29,633	37,847	33,114	21,397
Rapeseed oil	1,516,558	1,795,063	1,690,628	1,574,250
Soybean oil	99,425	118,820	120,632	136,497
Sesame oil	76,695	83,187	91,067	95,435
Other vegetable oils	1,081,566	1,187,113	1,387,858	1,324,176
Oilcake & meal	1,252,360	1,153,467	1,314,220	1,397,552
Cotton, excl. linters	11,226	3,422	2,803	1,158
Cotton, linters	1,868	4	1,105	269
Seeds - field & garden	1,003,105	1,020,561	1,074,994	979,217
Cut flowers	1,103,005	1,170,801	1,228,519	1,306,724
Nursery stock, bulbs, etc.	719,339	761,010	821,155	897,890
Other hort products	3,202,738	3,878,187	6,507,369	7,660,907
Hops, including extract	58,478	60,811	71,692	72,973
Starches, ex wheat/corn	127,563	133,901	141,229	140,937
Yeasts	300,568	307,041	339,760	346,186
Misc horticultural products	2,716,129	3,376,434	5,954,688	7,100,871

[1] Fiscal years, Oct. 1–Sept. 30.

ERS, Market and Trade Economics Division, (202) 694–5257. Compiled from reports of the U.S. Department of Commerce.

Table 15-6.—Agricultural exports: Value of U.S. exports to the top market, Canada, by commodity, fiscal years 2017–2019[1]

Commodity	Value		
	2017	2018	2019
	1,000 dollars	*1,000 dollars*	*1,000 dollars*
Total agricultural exports	20,444,018	20,701,022	20,997,341
Animals and animal products	3,521,050	3,556,417	3,396,708
Animals Live, ex. Poultry	118,319	219,700	222,476
Cattle, live	75,336	171,803	175,721
Horses, live	40,717	46,012	43,886
Swine, live	1,676	1,262	2,443
Sheep, live	29	34	13
Other live animals	562	589	414
Red meat and products	1,853,003	1,798,750	1,705,840
Beef and veal	772,534	748,139	649,459
Beef and Veal, fresh or frozen	604,536	574,381	497,476
Beef, prep or pres	167,998	173,759	151,983
Lamb, goat, fresh or frozen	2,009	924	823
Pork	774,217	741,233	762,367
Pork-fresh or frozen	385,612	343,782	369,272
Pork-prep or pres	388,604	397,451	393,094
Variety meats, Ed Offals	36,415	37,284	35,908
Beef variety meats	15,788	19,477	14,380
Pork variety meats	18,149	16,034	18,980
Other variety meats	2,478	1,773	2,548
Other meats-fr or froz	267,829	271,169	257,284
Poultry and poultry products	619,161	612,590	538,925
Poultry-Live	58,019	63,556	63,471
Baby chicks	48,178	55,716	55,278
Other live poultry	9,841	7,839	8,193
Poultry meats	469,024	427,453	366,489
Chickens, fresh or frozen	301,494	278,670	238,547
Turkeys, fresh or frozen	13,936	7,942	7,884
Other poultry, fresh or frozen	2,141	1,159	747
Poultry meats, prep or pres.	151,453	139,681	119,310
Poultry misc.	580	1,791	4,862
Eggs	91,538	119,790	104,103
Dairy prods	735,613	690,724	721,965
Evap and condensed milk	973	952	1,242
Nonfat dry milk	13,852	14,583	12,200
Butter and Milkfat	64,164	62,642	46,126
Cheese	67,460	54,993	54,115
Whey, fluid or dried	77,200	50,387	50,726
Other dairy products	511,964	507,166	557,556
Fats, oils and greases	58,478	65,580	53,157
Lard	963	436	342
Tallow, inedible	16,372	19,386	22,877
Other animal fats	41,143	45,758	29,938
Hides and skins include furs	72,425	94,748	69,937
Bovine hides, whole	916	-	-
Calf skins, whole	89	-	-
Horse hides whole	200	126	31
Sheep and lamb skins	118	117	133
Other hides and skins, ex. furs	4,531	2,042	1,372
Furskins	66,572	92,463	68,400
Mink pelts	59,275	85,112	60,916
Other furskins	7,297	7,352	7,484
Wool and Mohair	180	136	142
Sausage casings	7,826	9,028	16,689
Bull semen	8,747	9,642	8,476
Misc animal products-other	47,298	55,519	59,101
Grains and feeds	3,706,872	3,947,684	4,250,047
Wheat, unmilled	18,898	19,755	28,622
Wheat flour	54,658	35,620	33,520
Other wheat products	66,394	80,034	85,346
Rice-paddy,milled parb	147,904	164,642	191,046
Feed grains and products	235,837	362,021	484,961
Feed grains	128,366	275,578	406,106
	16,886	9,917	6,288
Corn	106,920	262,669	397,288
Grain sorghums	1,122	1,118	905
Oats	3,297	1,754	1,518
Rye	140	120	107
Feed grain products	107,471	86,443	78,855
Other grain prods	2,039,040	2,085,880	2,170,594
Feeds and fodders, ex. oilcakes	1,036,670	1,113,289	1,177,103
Corn by-products	39,164	49,952	36,336
Alfalfa meal and cubes	716	721	231
Beet pulp	6,099	5,998	6,906
Other feeds and fodder	990,691	1,056,617	1,133,629

See footnote(s) at end of table.

Table 15-6.—Agricultural exports: Value of U.S. exports to the top market, Canada, by commodity, fiscal years 2017–2019 [1]—Continued

Commodity	Value		
	2017	2018	2019
	1,000 dollars	*1,000 dollars*	*1,000 dollars*
Fruits and prep. excluding juice	2,061,354	2,048,514	1,984,441
Fruits, fresh	1,577,670	1,542,893	1,468,075
Citrus fruits	231,301	228,024	198,053
Grapefruit	19,812	16,379	15,492
Lemons and limes	54,745	52,180	45,270
Oranges and tangerines	156,474	159,062	136,834
Other citrus fruits	270	402	457
Noncitrus fruits	1,346,369	1,314,869	1,270,022
Apple	168,027	163,733	157,992
Berries	506,409	518,982	513,635
Cherries	136,890	118,502	120,774
Grapes	213,514	205,789	190,014
Melons	131,858	124,946	110,903
Peaches	65,315	60,767	61,028
Pears	46,811	45,781	44,446
Plums	21,672	20,570	19,116
Other noncitrus	55,872	55,800	52,113
Fruits, dried	65,457	66,832	67,319
Raisins	33,856	30,478	30,675
Prunes	12,479	12,997	11,513
Other dried fruits	19,122	23,357	25,131
Fruits-canned, excluding juice	226,846	238,548	224,372
Fruits-frozen, excluding juice	53,818	51,224	62,933
Other fruits, prep. or pres	137,563	149,017	161,742
Fruit juices, including frozen	386,070	374,536	339,086
Apple juice	18,105	19,267	17,930
Grape juice	26,045	28,387	25,092
Grapefruit juice	6,837	8,063	9,576
Orange juice	193,390	173,817	155,499
Other fruit juices	141,693	145,002	130,989
Wine	395,769	427,823	405,505
Nuts and prep	860,085	894,622	926,053
Almonds	257,811	266,920	282,858
Filberts	21,590	11,201	44,831
Peanuts, shelled or prep	170,668	168,724	169,863
Pistachios	77,738	92,091	103,109
Walnuts	72,491	98,696	74,352
Pecans	81,695	71,404	63,192
Other nuts	178,092	185,586	187,848
Vegetables and prep	3,158,525	3,064,511	3,198,944
Vegetables, fresh	1,852,596	1,843,346	2,017,741
Asparagus	9,232	10,782	10,268
Broccoli	67,701	74,152	78,284
Carrots	97,198	97,799	97,934
Cabbage	56,802	70,706	81,148
Celery	67,483	61,038	103,699
Cauliflower	123,159	131,332	140,130
Corn, sweet	46,476	44,291	41,881
Cucumbers	15,698	13,337	16,600
Garlic	11,231	9,693	10,219
Lettuce	428,991	412,552	448,759
Mushrooms	19,510	29,374	33,841
Onion and Shallots	103,944	109,519	136,943
Peppers	74,233	73,214	80,404
Potatoes	102,399	96,419	114,053
Tomatoes	103,030	103,317	107,775
Other fresh vegetables	525,417	505,820	515,775
Vegetables, frozen	191,681	192,001	195,550
Corn, sweet	14,534	10,044	7,975
Potatoes	76,050	72,486	75,979
Other frozen vegetables	101,097	109,471	111,596
Vegetables, canned	172,755	164,340	160,671
Pulses	138,886	79,824	104,829
Dried beans	52,725	38,120	38,414
Dried peas	7,659	3,383	21,930
Dried lentils	56,979	14,587	26,222
Dried chick peas	21,524	23,734	18,262
Other vegetables, prep or pres	781,083	761,266	701,891

See footnote(s) at end of table.

Table 15-6.—Agricultural exports: Value of U.S. exports to the top market, Canada, by commodity, fiscal years 2017–2019[1]—Continued

Commodity	Value		
	2017	2018	2019
	1,000 dollars	*1,000 dollars*	*1,000 dollars*
Oilseeds and products	1,286,945	1,327,118	1,437,675
Oilcake and meal	306,201	360,766	339,350
Bran and residues	4,683	4,482	2,863
Soybean meal	294,600	350,413	331,131
Other oilcake and meal	6,918	5,870	5,356
Oilseeds	434,487	443,826	610,404
Rapeseed	86,245	85,257	105,761
Safflower seeds	694	577	876
Soybeans	133,680	162,911	304,724
Sunflowerseeds	16,205	16,031	17,704
Peanuts, including oilstock	7,069	7,558	8,621
Other oilseeds	14,323	11,549	11,555
Protein substances	176,271	159,943	161,163
Vegetable oils	546,257	522,526	487,921
Soybean oil	25,193	23,756	24,551
Cottonseed oil	5,832	6,845	5,863
Sunflower oil	26,747	27,329	27,845
Corn oil	14,596	12,971	11,414
Peanut oil	4,313	5,168	4,103
Rapeseed oil	38,758	19,124	21,122
Safflower oil	2,558	2,209	1,982
Other Vegetable oils and Waxes	428,258	425,125	391,041
Tobacco-unmanufactured	7,256	15,920	6,522
Cotton, excluding linters	635	683	619
Cotton linters	33	29	26
Essential oils	434,192	446,512	437,528
Seeds-field and garden	329,534	335,894	355,579
Sugar and tropical products	2,020,813	1,987,685	1,888,585
Sugar and related products	546,820	541,957	506,078
Sugar, cane or beet	6,706	7,211	9,546
Related sugar product	540,114	534,746	496,531
Coffee	529,885	540,086	498,730
Cocoa	131,133	121,892	116,108
Chocolate and prep	619,875	598,634	580,902
Tea, including herbal	124,209	124,874	127,831
Spices	62,803	53,625	55,834
Rubber, crude	6,088	6,617	3,102
Fibers, excluding cotton	906	1,113	727
Other hort products	1,360,181	1,387,525	1,492,875
Hops, including extract	24,270	31,794	38,638
Starches, not wheat/corn	80,045	80,061	82,103
Yeasts	38,790	39,487	37,719
Misc hort products	1,217,076	1,236,183	1,334,415
Nursery and greenhouse	204,844	218,892	221,379
Beverages, excluding juice	837,950	775,718	752,164

[1] Fiscal years Oct. 1–Sept. 30.
ERS, Market and Trade Economics Division, (202) 694–5257.

Table 15-7.—Agricultural imports for consumption: Value of Top 50 countries of origin, United States, fiscal years 2017–2019 [1]

Country	2017	2018	2019
	1,000 dollars		
Mexico	24,070,256	25,657,093	27,869,944
EU27+UK	21,359,059	23,699,510	24,678,802
Canada	21,958,461	22,961,211	23,390,158
China	4,472,800	4,770,143	4,054,120
Australia	3,093,993	3,264,828	3,419,887
Brazil	3,320,430	3,380,010	3,325,414
Singapore	81,690	2,182,709	3,126,375
Indonesia	3,586,724	3,472,153	2,983,532
Chile	2,989,725	3,039,228	2,874,354
Thailand	2,387,364	2,636,682	2,826,619
Colombia	2,590,605	2,565,535	2,699,872
India	2,526,629	2,660,230	2,680,949
Peru	1,976,529	2,168,652	2,438,736
New Zealand	2,585,348	2,586,537	2,368,045
Guatemala	2,096,941	2,132,753	2,129,079
Vietnam	2,400,214	2,382,429	2,030,625
Costa Rica	1,606,185	1,638,421	1,516,039
Switzerland	1,269,705	1,318,617	1,363,222
Argentina	1,366,579	1,415,104	1,356,260
Ecuador	1,055,404	1,034,472	1,116,640
Malaysia	964,687	997,937	1,026,316
Turkey	887,777	983,489	974,822
Philippines	1,260,625	1,164,344	958,695
Honduras	817,919	737,655	814,612
Japan	650,136	696,358	764,064
Cote d'Ivoire	1,185,412	852,707	751,703
South Korea	542,453	606,149	680,557
Nicaragua	630,915	661,630	672,043
Madagascar	384,417	524,349	477,475
Dominican Republic	405,283	514,750	467,272
Taiwan	360,331	390,637	441,630
South Africa	283,631	341,398	402,431
Israel	370,139	383,441	400,688
Uruguay	339,510	302,034	338,387
Ghana	290,304	201,474	279,892
El Salvador	225,381	218,729	228,130
Morocco	156,091	192,482	210,526
Sri Lanka	190,158	198,549	189,093
Ukraine	104,397	93,634	156,736
Ethiopia	161,470	175,469	155,223
Kenya	162,929	151,624	136,561
Egypt	112,226	132,616	133,582
Jamaica	120,588	132,573	129,385
Pakistan	105,239	123,591	128,438
Tunisia	[illegible]	204,381	125,592
Paraguay	97,494	70,926	108,350
Norway	91,141	100,368	105,741
Bolivia	111,017	91,753	98,287
Hong Kong	96,243	98,278	92,744
Malawi	88,690	47,638	71,909
Other countries	1,001,399	1,153,189	1,075,340
Total U.S. Agricultural Imports [2]	119,078,941	127,510,469	130,844,896

[1] Fiscal years Oct. 1–Sept. 30. [2] Totals may not add due to rounding.
ERS, Market and Trade Economics Division, (202) 694–5257. Compiled from reports of the U.S. Department of Commerce.

Table 15-8.—European Union: Value of agricultural imports by origin, 2010–2019

Year[1]	United States	EU countries	Other countries	Total
	Million dollars			
2010	10,822	329,477	113,650	453,950
2011	12,760	389,811	138,954	541,525
2012	12,049	374,067	131,836	517,952
2013	14,768	406,306	133,729	554,802
2014	15,361	405,760	136,580	557,700
2015	14,456	353,918	122,328	490,702
2016	13,672	360,318	121,664	495,654
2017	13,757	400,005	129,610	543,372
2018	16,044	420,372	133,274	569,689
2019	10,311	427,510	84,888	522,709

[1] Data on calendar year basis. Users should use cautious interpretation on reports that include summarized reporter groupings. These groupings will only include the members that have reported data for any particular year.
ERS, Market and Trade Economics Division, (202) 694–5257. Data Source: United National Commodity Trade Statistics, United Nations Statistics Division.

Table 15-9.—Fisheries: U.S. Commercial landings and value of principal species: 2017 and 2018[1]

Species	Landings	
	2017	2018
	Thousand pounds	*Thousand pounds*
Fish:		
Cod, Atlantic	1,857	2,152
Flounder	544,866	525,070
Haddock	12,101	14,455
Halibut	26,466	21,929
Herring, sea	179,920	145,792
Jack mackerel	1,043	239
Menhaden	1,413,104	1,581,578
Ocean perch, Atlantic	11,387	9,902
Walleye (Alaska) Pollock	3,388,620	3,363,901
Salmon, Pacific	1,008,198	575,972
Tuna	54,904	51,684
Whiting (silver hake)	11,800	11,393
Shellfish:		
Clams (meats)	84,883	85,670
Crabs	274,578	289,021
Lobsters, American	132,973	146,176
Oysters (meats)	31,805	30,304
Scallops (meats)	51,733	58,382
Shrimp	283,272	289,178
	Value	
	Thousand dollars	*Thousand dollars*
Fish:		
Cod, Atlantic	4,444	4,777
Flounder	141,228	153,235
Haddock	11,947	13,354
Halibut	125,785	89,318
Herring, sea	36,396	32,605
Jack mackerel	49	27
Menhaden	125,495	161,088
Ocean perch, Atlantic	6,307	5,036
Walleye (Alaska) Pollock	419,425	456,510
Salmon, Pacific	687,770	598,067
Tuna	154,392	149,053
Whiting (silver hake)	9,009	9,630
Shellfish:		
Clams (meats)	210,755	244,107
Crabs	610,3377	644,912
Lobsters, American	552,057	624,228
Oysters (meats)	236,418	258,748
Scallops (meats)	511,945	540,583
Shrimp	530,977	496,114

[1] Landings are reported in round (live) weight for all items except univalve and bivalve mollusks such as clams, oysters, and scallops, which are reported in weight of meats (excluding the shell). Landings for Mississippi River drainage are not available.
Totals may not add due to rounding. Data do not include landings by U.S.-flag vessels at Puerto Rico or other ports outside the 50 States. Data do not include aquaculture products, except oysters and clams.
U.S. Department of Commerce, NOAA, NMFS, Fisheries Statistics Division, (301) 427–8103.

Table 15-10.—Fresh and frozen fishery products: Production and value, 2017 and 2018

Product	Production	
	2017	2018
	Thousand pounds	*Thousand pounds*
Fish fillets	795,146	745,394
Cod	72,488	62,365
Flounder	11,888	9,792
Haddock	11,233	8,068
Ocean perch, Atlantic	1,166	1,847
Rockfish	2,874	3,198
Pollock, Atlantic	9,931	789
Pollock, Alaska	455,341	441,590
Other	241,458	217,745
	Value	
	Thousand dollars	*Thousand dollars*
Fish fillets	2,146,555	2,157,359
Cod	318,348	332,436
Flounder	49,941	43,785
Haddock	52,912	42,255
Ocean perch, Atlantic	3,526	7,851
Rockfish	8,587	9,187
Pollock, Atlantic	15,898	2,759
Pollock, Alaska	582,604	608,493
Other	1,114,739	1,110,593

U.S. Department of Commerce, NOAA, NMFS, Fisheries Statistics Division, (301) 427–8103.

Table 15-11.—Canned fishery products: Production and value, 2017 and 2018

Product	Production	
	2017 [1]	2018
	Thousand pounds	*Thousand pounds*
Tuna [2]	333,913	346,407
Salmon	133,878	65,585
Clam products [3]	63,191	64,293
Crab meat and specialties	153	81
Other Shellfish	28,826	20,372
Total [4]	855,551	665,148
	Value	
	Thousand dollars	*Thousand dollars*
Tuna [2]	677,721	775,900
Salmon	309,593	185,676
Clam products [3]	106,075	107,054
Crab meat and specialties	607	314
Other Shellfish	20,480	19,992
Total [4]	1,341,712	1,219,000

[1] Revised based on additional data. [2] Flakes included with chunk. [3] "Cut out" or "drained" weight of can contents are given for whole or minced clams, and net contents for other clam products. [4] Includes Sardines (Maine), Shrimp, Oysters, and other products not shown separately.

U.S. Dept. of Commerce, NOAA, NMFS, Fisheries Statistics Division, (301) 427–8103.

Table 15-12.—Fisheries: Fishermen and craft, 1977, and catch, 2017–2018 by area

Area	1977 [1]			2017 [3]		2018 [3]	
	Fishermen	Fishing vessels	Fishing boats [2]	Total catch	Value	Total catch	Value
	1,000	*Number*	*1,000*	*Million pounds*	*Million dollars*	*Million pounds*	*Million dollars*
New England States	31.7	929	15.4	556	1,266	572	1,394
Middle Atlantic States	17.3	573	11.3	620	508	628	473
South Atlantic States	11.6	1,463	6.7	122	223	109	179
Gulf States	29.3	5,328	11.0	1,386	856	1,541	887
Pacific Coast States	54.0	7,643	15.4	7,182	2,435	6,487	2,500
Great Lakes States	1.2	217	0.5	13	17	13	18
Hawaii	2.7	101	1.3	37	116	35	119
United States	182.1	17,545	89.2	9,916	5,421	9,385	5,571

[1] Exclusive of duplication among regions. Computation of area amounts will not equal U.S. total. Mississippi River data included with total. [2] Refers to craft having capacity of less than 5 net tons. [3] Great Lakes data are one year behind the heading years. Note: Table may not add due to rounding.
U.S. Department of Commerce, NOAA, NMFS, Fisheries Statistics Division, (301) 427–8103.

Table 15-13.—Fisheries: U.S. Commercial landings of fish and shellfish, 2009–2018

Year	For human food		For industrial purposes [2]		Total	
	Quantity	Value	Quantity	Value	Quantity	Value
	Million pounds	*Million dollars*	*Million pounds*	*Million dollars*	*Million pounds*	*Million dollars*
2009	6,198	3,733	1,833	158	8,031	3,891
2010	6,526	4,356	1,705	164	8,231	4,520
2011	7,909	5,108	1,949	181	9,858	5,289
2012	7,477	4,923	2,157	180	9,634	5,103
2013	8,043	5,268	1,827	198	9,870	5,466
2014	7,828	5,256	1,658	192	9,486	5,448
2015	7,750	4,972	1,968	231	9,718	5,203
2016	7,484	5,007	2,088	305	9,572	5,312
2017	8,228	5,187	1,688	234	9,916	5,421
2018	7,500	5,322	1,885	249	9,385	5,571

[1] Live weight. [2] Meals, oil, fish solubles, homogenized condensed fish, shell products, bait, and animal food.
U.S. Department of Commerce, NOAA, NMFS Fisheries Statistics Division, (301) 427–8103.

Table 15-14.—Fisheries: Disposition of domestic catch, 2017–2018 [1]

Disposition	2017	2018
	Million pounds	*Million pounds*
Fresh and frozen	8,091	7,443
Canned	289	180
Cured	136	139
Reduced to meal, oil, etc	1,400	1,623
Total	9,916	9,385

[1] Live weight catch. In addition to whole fish, a large portion of waste derived from canning, filleting, and dressing fish and shellfish is utilized in production of fish meal and oil in each year shown.
U.S. Department of Commerce, NOAA, NMFS, Fisheries Statistics Division, (301) 427–8103.

Table 15-15.—Fishery products: Supply,[1] 2017–2018[2]

Item	2017	2018
	Million pounds	
For human food	19,805	19,478
Finfish	14,422	13,941
Shellfish[3]	5,383	5,538
For industrial use	2,461	2,625
Domestic catch	9,916	9,385
Percent of total	45	42
For human food	8,228	7,500
Finfish	7,121	6,409
Shellfish[3]	1,107	1,091
For industrial use	1,688	1,886
Imports[4]	12,350	12,718
Percent of total	55	58
For human food	11,577	11,979
Finfish	8,074	8,271
Shellfish[3]	4,276	4,447
For industrial use[5]	773	739
Total	22,266	22,103

[1] Supply totals are the domestic catch and imports without accounting for exports taken out. [2] Live weight, except percent. May not add due to rounding. [3] For univalve and bivalves mollusks (conchs, clams, oysters, scallops, etc.), the weight of meats, excluding the shell is reported. [4] Excluding imports of edible fishery products consumed in Puerto Rico; includes landings of tuna caught by foreign vessels in American Samoa. [5] Fish meal and sea herring.

U.S. Department of Commerce, NOAA, NMFS, Fisheries Statistics Division, (301) 427–8103.

Table 15-16.—Processed fishery products: Production and value, 2017–2018[1]

Item	Production		Value	
	2017	2018	2017	2018
	Thousand pounds	*Thousand pounds*	*Thousand dollars*	*Thousand dollars*
Fresh and frozen:.				
Fillets	795,146	745,394	2,146,555	2,157,359
Steaks	5,269	5,344	30,909	32,042
Fish sticks	55,245	55,087	85,085	93,248
Fish portions	100,135	73,620	177,179	139,313
Breaded shrimp	84,235	84,391	344,274	338,958
Canned products[2]	855,551	665,148	1,341,712	1,219,000
Fish and shellfish	560,321	497,056	1,116,793	1,090,983
Animal feed	[illegible]	100,092	224,919	128,017
Industrial products	(X)	(X)	679,740	753,578
Meal and scrap	568,882	630,256	379,806	418,073
Marine animal oil	112,253	154,777	108,175	114,771
Other	(X)	(X)	191,759	220,734

(X) Not applicable. [1] Includes cured fish. [2] Includes salmon eggs for baits.

U.S. Department of Commerce, NOAA, NMFS, Fisheries Statistics Division, (301) 427–8103.

Table 15-17.—Selected fishery products: Imports and exports, 2017–2018[1]

Product	Quantity	
	2017	2018
	Thousand pounds	*Thousand pounds*
Imports		
Edible	5,919,333	6,086,590
Fresh and frozen	5,001,948	5,125,531
Salmon[2]	299,253	306,437
Tuna[2]	257,944	188,924
Groundfish fillets, blocks[3]	298,908	300,639
Other fillets and steaks	1,315,789	1,413,517
Scallops (meats)	39,438	44,775
Lobster, American and spiny	111,471	108,690
Shrimp and prawn	1,460,711	1,528,745
Canned	723,205	778,726
Sardines, in oil	42,577	34,786
Sardines and herring, not in oil	43,695	43,761
Tuna	311,414	345,326
Oysters	12,164	15,250
Pickled or salted	63,082	61,538
Cod, haddock, hake, pollock, cusk	12,758	12,877
Nonedible meal and scrap	138,056	131,983
Exports		
Canned salmon	63,380	55,150
Fish oil, nonedible	139,036	140,597

Product	Value	
	2017	2018
	Thousand dollars	*Thousand dollars*
Imports		
Edible	21,519,015	22,438,476
Fresh and frozen	18,959,483	19,502,541
Salmon[2]	1,072,424	1,173,173
Tuna	653,261	618,903
Groundfish fillets, blocks[3]	720,659	808,018
Other fillets and steaks	4,747,576	5,262,319
Scallops (meats)	258,427	237,208
Lobster, American and spiny	1,039,585	1,162,162
Shrimp and prawn	6,511,108	6,197,363
Canned	1,961,002	2,349,728
Sardines, in oil	79,040	84,788
Sardines and herring, not in oil	61,283	63,318
Tuna	631,774	765,982
Oysters	34,211	43,447
Pickled or salted	110,103	110,047
Cod, haddock, hake, pollock, cusk	33,590	35,460
Nonedible meal and scrap	111,918	106,220
Exports		
Canned salmon	159,750	166,556
Fish oil, nonedible	146,279	154,218

[1] Includes Puerto Rico. [2] Excludes fillets. [3] Includes cod, cusk, haddock, hake, pollock, ocean perch, and whiting.
U.S. Dept. of Commerce, NOAA, NMFS, Fisheries Statistics Division (301) 427–8103.

Table 15-18.—Fishery products: Imports and exports, 2009–2018 [1]

Year	Imports [2]				Exports			
	Total value	Edible products		Non-edible, value	Total value	Edible products		Non-edible, value
		Quantity	Value			Quantity	Value	
	Million dollars	*Million* *pounds*	*Million* dollars	*Million* dollars	*Million* dollars	*Million* *pounds*	*Million* dollars	*Million* dollars
2009	23,554	5,161	13,124	10,430	19,636	2,546	3,980	15,656
2010	27,352	5,447	14,811	12,542	22,386	2,733	4,389	17,997
2011	30,943	5,349	16,618	14,326	26,218	3,267	5,447	20,771
2012	31,107	5,384	16,690	14,417	27,384	3,254	5,470	21,914
2013	33,156	5,415	18,006	15,150	29,113	3,324	5,584	23,529
2014	35,915	5,567	20,264	15,650	29,978	3,402	5,754	24,225
2015	34,400	5,736	18,791	15,609	28,396	3,141	5,567	22,829
2016	35,875	5,827	19,486	16,389	27,989	2,931	5,384	22,605
2017	38,372	5,920	21,520	16,853	28,973	3,200	5,730	23,243
2018	40,304	6,087	22,438	17,865	28,755	2,938	5,590	23,165

[1] Includes Puerto Rico. [2] Includes landings of tuna by foreign vessels in American Samoa.
U.S. Department of Commerce, NOAA, NMFS, Fisheries Statistics Division, (301) 427–8103.

Table 15-19.—Fish trips: Estimated number of fishing trips taken by marine recreational fishermen by subregion and year, Atlantic, Gulf, and Pacific Coasts, 2017–2018

Subregion	2017	2018
	Thousands	*Thousands*
Atlantic and Gulf:		
North Atlantic	16,751	15,103
Mid-Atlantic	46,004	39,029
South Atlantic [1]	76,870	75,100
Gulf	58,633	55,755
Total	198,258	184,987
Pacific: [2]		
Southern California	2,350	1,411
Northern California	1,054	615
Oregon	187	210
Washington	146	127
Hawaii	1,280	3,420
Alaska	545	539
Total	[illegible]	[illegible]

[1] Does not include trips from headboats (party boats) in the South Atlantic or Gulf of Mexico. [2] Pacific state estimates do not include salmon data collected by recreational surveys.
Note: Recreational estimates have been revised back through 1981 (as of November 2019). Any data previously provided (for past reports) are no longer appropriate or valid.
U.S. Department of Commerce, NOAA, NMFS, Fisheries Statistics Division, (301) 427–8103.

Table 15-20.—Fish harvested[1] by marine recreational anglers by subregion, area, and mode, Atlantic, Gulf Coasts, and Pacific Coasts, 2017–2018

Subregion	2017	2018
	Thousands	*Thousands*
Atlantic and Gulf[2]:		
North Atlantic	33,338	27,101
Mid-Atlantic	76,606	45,848
South Atlantic[2]	114,242	104,252
Gulf	167,340	145,541
Total	391,526	322,742
Pacific:[3]		
Southern California	4,426	3,905
Northern California	3,175	2,234
Oregon	646	539
Washington	421	398
Hawaii	3,012	10,360
Alaska	1,395	1,208
Total	13,075	18,644

Area	2017	2018
	Thousands	*Thousands*
Atlantic and Gulf:[2 4]		
Inland	204,628	181,527
State Territorial Sea[5]	141,141	106,204
Federal Exclusive Economic Zone[6]	37,152	28,948
Total	391,526	322,742
Pacific:[3]		
Inland	1,851	2,727
State Territorial Sea[5]	8,399	12,653
Federal Exclusive Economic Zone[6]	1,430	2,056
Total	11,680	17,436

Mode	2017	2018
	Thousands	*Thousands*
Atlantic and Gulf:[2]		
Shore	188,523	160,879
Party/charter	12,604	10,378
Private/rental	190,399	151,485
Total	391,526	322,742
Pacific:[3]		
Shore	5,678	9,740
Party/charter	3,412	3,578
Private/rental	2,590	4,118
Total	11,680	17,436

[1] "Harvested" includes dead discards and fish used for bait but does not include fish released alive; totals may not match due to rounding. [2] Does not include trips from headboats (party boats) in the South Atlantic or Gulf of Mexico. [3] Does not include recreational catch from Alaska. Pacific state estimates do not include salmon data collected by recreational surveys. [4] Includes fish harvested from an undetermined area. [5] Open Ocean extending 0 to 3 miles from shore, except West Florida (10 miles). [5] Open ocean extending to 200 miles offshore from the outer edge of the State Territorial Seas.

Note: Recreational estimates have been revised back through 1981 (as of November 2019). Any data previously provided (for past reports) are no longer appropriate or valid.

U.S. Department of Commerce, NOAA, NMFS, Fisheries Statistics Division, (301) 427–8103.

Table 15-21.—U.S. Recreational Harvest[1] by species group and year, 2017–2018[2]

Species group	2017	2018
	Thousands	*Thousands*
Atlantic Cod	229	28
Atlantic Croaker	14,308	11,997
Atlantic Mackerel	17,745	9,495
Black Drum	2,433	2,001
Black Sea Bass	7,467	4,826
Blue Runner	15,787	7,837
Conger Eels	5	3
Crevalle Jack	2,438	1,711
Cunner	116	130
Epinephelus Groupers	317	362
Florida Pompano	2,404	1,506
Freshwater Catfishes	1,968	2,220
Gray Snapper	6,590	5,771
Greater Amberjack	122	116
Gulf Flounder	452	381
King Mackerel	1,201	1,204
Kingfishes	22,626	18,472
Lane Snapper	1,524	1,289
Little Tunny/Atlantic Bonito	849	803
Moray Eels	-	-
Mycteroperca Groupers	391	397
Pigfish	1,525	1,455
Pinfishes	12,345	13,143
Pollock	606	386
Red Drum	4,350	3,909
Red Hake	158	191
Red Porgy	492	436
Red Snapper	3,107	2,864
Saltwater Catfishes	908	1,655
Sand Seatrout	10,105	5,567
Scup	13,823	14,544
Sheepshead	6,130	4,942
Silver Perch	2,355	480
Skates/Rays	204	388
Southern Flounder	1,169	1,291
Spanish Mackerel	8,147	7,211
Spot	23,037	12,831
Spotted Seatrout	11,041	9,427
Striped Bass	3,008	2,455
Striped Mullet	6,026	7,069
Summer Flounder	3,233	2,428
Tautog	2,073	1,072
Vermilion Snapper	2,314	2,702
Weakfish	296	132
White Grunt	3,634	3,551
White Perch	6,818	3,794
Winter Flounder	327	158
Yellowtail Snapper	1,548	1,695
Other Barracudas	272	325
Other Bluefish	14,166	10,436
Other Cods/Hakes	1,828	1,005
Other Dolphins	2,491	2,935
Other Drum	909	488
Other Eels	74	151
Other Flounders	840	310
Other Grunts	2,065	3,918
Other Herrings	85,085	66,612
Other Jacks	3,438	8,606
Other Mullets	23,253	21,883
Other Porgies	574	501
Other Puffers	876	897
Other Sculpins	2	8
Other Sea Basses	388	863
Other Searobins	926	759
Other Sharks	383	357
Other Snappers	435	285
Other Temperate Basses	-	1
Other Toadfishes	133	18
Other Triggerfishes/Filefishes	875	624
Other Tunas/Mackerels	1,249	1,018
Other Wrasses	231	89
Other fishes	22,682	24,328
Total[3]	391,526	322,742

- Represents zero. [1] "Harvested" includes dead discards and fish used for bait but does not include fish released alive. [2] Data do not include headboats (party boats) in the South Atlantic and the Gulf of Mexico. [3] Totals may not add due to rounding.

Note: Recreational estimates have been revised back through 1981 (as of November 2019). Any data previously provided (for past reports) are no longer appropriate or valid.

U.S. Department of Commerce, NOAA, NMFS, Fisheries Statistics Division (301) 427–8103.

Table 15-22.—Fish harvested[1] by marine recreational anglers by species group and year, Pacific coast, 2017–2018[2]

Species group	2017	2018
	Thousands	*Thousands*
Albacore	1	6
Barred Sand Bass	41	50
Barred Surfperch	451	10
Bigeye Scad	1,064	3,639
Bigeye Trevally	....	1
Bigscale Soldierfish	74	481
Black Perch	21	2
Black Rockfish	698	579
Blackspot Sergeant	11	89
Blacktail Snapper	9	57
Blue Rockfish	482	471
Bluefin Trevally	77	117
Bluestripe Snapper	79	94
Bocaccio	137	158
Brown Rockfish	123	150
Cabezon	26	22
California Corbina	16	7
California Halibut	36	46
California Sheephead	39	34
Canary Rockfish	146	125
Chilipepper Rockfish	13	9
Chub Mackerel	1,419	1,188
Conger Eels	1	....
Convict Tang	58	273
Copper Rockfish	237	195
Giant Trevally	11	39
Goldring Surgeonfish	78	230
Gopher Rockfish	114	95
Greater Amberjack	4	12
Green Jobfish	19	38
Greenspotted Rockfish	38	33
Halfmoon	13	14
Hawaiian Flagtail	94	206
Hawaiian Hogfish	8	2
Highfin Rudderfish	2	7
Island Jack	19	26
Jacksmelt	512	186
Kawakawa	8	33
Kelp Bass	99	93
Kelp Greenling	23	11
Lingcod	312	276
Mackerel Scad	108	404
Manybar Goatfish	14	57
Moray Eels	5	10
Northern Anchovy	215	212
Olive Rockfish	61	75
Opaleye	43	16
Pacific Barracuda	10	19
Pacific Bonito	96	86
Pacific Cod	20	15
Pacific Hake	-	-
Pacific Herring	67	56
Pacific Tomcod	-	-
Pile Perch	10	1
Pink Snapper	10	56
Queenfish	17	17
Quillback Rockfish	18	22
Razorfishes	44	115
Redtail Surfperch	148	-
Rock Sole	-	2
Sanddabs	259	252
Shiner Perch	15	24
Silver Surfperch	57	7
Skates/Rays	9	1
Skipjack Tuna	114	213
Smallmouth Bonefish	19	45

See footnote(s) at end of table.

Table 15-22.—Fish harvested[1] by marine recreational anglers by species group and year, Pacific coast, 2017–2018[2]—Continued

Species group	2017	2018
	Thousands	*Thousands*
Spiny Dogfish	-	-
Spotted Sand Bass	3	1
Squirrel Fishes	...	2
Starry Flounder	1	-
Striped Bass	27	30
Striped Mullet	14	72
Striped Seaperch	36	3
Surf Smelt	-	...
Unicornfishes	3	16
Wahoo	32	127
Walleye Surfperch	56	24
White Croaker	59	47
White Seaperch	6	3
Whitemouth Trevally	-	-
Whitesaddle Goatfish	2	12
Whitetip Soldierfish	...	...
Widow Rockfish	15	46
Yellowfin Tuna	82	216
Yellowstripe Goatfish	380	1,651
Yellowtail	61	15
Yellowtail Rockfish	176	180
Other Anchovies	...	-
Other Barracudas	2	14
Other Cods/Hakes	-	-
Other Damselfishes	10	28
Other Dolphins	47	216
Other Drum	59	25
Other Flounders	385	386
Other Goatfishes	25	317
Other Greenlings	-	-
Other Groupers	3	18
Other Herrings	156	108
Other Jacks	45	66
Other Mullets	21	163
Other Rockfishes	1,429	1,424
Other Sablefishes	23	26
Other Scorpionfishes	180	220
Other Sculpins	2	1
Other Sea Basses	-	-
Other Sea Chubs	26	96
Other Sharks	8	7
Other Silversides	69	82
Other Smelts	9	10
Other Snappers	9	91
Other Soldierfishes	8	279
Other Sturgeons	-	-
Other Surfperches	68	10
Other Surgeonfishes	27	201
Other Tunas/Mackerels	47 58	
Other Wrasses	26	56
Other fishes	1,471	1,488
Total[3]	13,075	18,644

- Represents zero. [1] "Harvested" includes dead discards and fish used for bait but does not include fish released alive. [2] Pacific estimates do not include salmon data collected by state recreational surveys. [3] Totals may not add exactly due to rounding.

Note: Recreational estimates have been revised back through 1981 (as of November 2019). Any data previously provided (for past reports) are no longer appropriate or valid.

U.S. Department of Commerce, NOAA, NMFS, Fisheries Statistics Division, (301) 427–8103.

Table 15-23.—Catfish water surface acres used for production and total sales - States and United States: 2018–2020

State	Acres intended for utilization during January 1-June 30					Acres taken out of production during Jul 1-Dec 31 prev. year
	Foodsize	Fingerlings	Broodfish	Currently under or scheduled for: Renovation	Currently under or scheduled for: New construction	
	Acres	*Acres*	*Acres*	*Acres*	*Acres*	*Acres*
2019						
Alabama	16,500	110	(D)	300	(D)	350
Arkansas	3,000	910	235	440	(D)	550
California	910	(D)	35	90	-	(D)
Mississippi	27,100	4,900	1,300	(D)	660	540
North Carolina	1,200	(D)	(D)	(D)	-	(D)
Texas	1,700	55	50	80	(D)	195
Other States [1]	1,220	1,010	210	4,575	120	255
United States	51,630	6,985	1,830	5,485	780	1,890
2020						
Alabama	15,600	250	25	25	115	690
Arkansas	2,700	770	(D)	(D)	-	230
California	(D)	(D)	35	35	(D)	(D)
Mississippi	26,700	4,200	1,400	1,400	(D)	700
North Carolina	(D)	(D)	(D)	(D)	(D)	(D)
Texas	1,700	(D)	35	35	-	(D)
Other States [1]	2,650	1,200	285	285	265	880
United States	49,350	6,420	1,780	1,780	380	2,500

- Represents zero. (D) Withheld to avoid disclosing data for individual operations. [1] Other States include State estimates not shown and States suppressed due to disclosure.
NASS, Livestock Branch, (202) 720–3570.

Table 15-24.—Catfish water surface acres used for production total sales - States and United States: 2018–2020

State	Water surface acres used for production during Jan 1 - July 30		Total sales	
	2019	2020	2018	2019
	Acres	*Acres*	*1,000 dollars*	*1,000 dollars*
Alabama	16,800	15,900	91,128	97,714
Arkansas	4,300	4,000	21,624	21,671
California	1,100	(D)	9,109	(D)
Mississippi	35,700	35,300	207,543	226,194
North Carolina	1,300	(D)	2,932	(D)
Texas	1,900	1,800	20,889	17,969
Other States [1]	2,220	4,245	7,176	15,600
United States	63,320	61,245	360,401	379,148

(D) Withheld to avoid disclosing data for individual operations. [1] Other States include State estimates not shown and States suppressed due to disclosure.
NASS, Livestock Branch, (202) 720–3570.

Table 15-25.—Catfish: Sales by size category, by State and United States, 2018–2019

Size category and State	Number of fish		Live weight		Sales			
					Total		Average price per pound	
	2018	2019	2018	2019	2018	2019	2018	2019
	1,000	*1,000*	*1,000 pounds*	*1,000 pounds*	*1,000 dollars*	*1,000 dollars*	*Dollars*	*Dollars*
Foodsize:								
Alabama	63,600	60,300	104,600	102,500	91,002	97,375	0.87	0.95
Arkansas	10,900	10,700	18,300	18,600	18,666	19,716	1.02	1.06
California	1,600	1,210	2,850	2,400	9,063	7,632	3.18	3.18
Mississippi	121,000	113,000	192,000	203,500	188,160	213,675	0.98	1.05
North Carolina	1,400	(D)	2,500	(D)	2,900	(D)	1.16	(D)
Texas	8,520	(D)	20,200	(D)	20,806	(D)	1.03	(D)
Other States [1]	1,780	11,235	3,151	20,990	4,409	23,650	1.40	1.13
United States	208,800	196,445	343,601	347,990	335,006	362,048	0.97	1.04
Stockers:								
Alabama	(D)	(D)	(D)	(D)	(D)	(D)	(D)	(D)
Arkansas	(D)	(D)	(D)	(D)	(D)	(D)	(D)	(D)
California	(D)	(D)	(D)	(D)	(D)	(D)	(D)	(D)
Mississippi	(D)	(D)	(D)	(D)	(D)	(D)	(D)	(D)
North Carolina	(D)	-	(D)	-	(D)	-	(D)	-
Texas	(D)	(D)	(D)	(D)	(D)	(D)	(D)	(D)
Other States [1]	65,465	22,450	6,553	2,819	7,727	5,181	1.18	1.84
United States	65,465	22,450	6,553	2,819	7,727	5,181	1.18	1.84
Fingerlings and fry:								
Alabama	(D)	310	(D)	9	(D)	68	(D)	7.60
Arkansas	12,400	(D)	472	(D)	939	(D)	1.99	(D)
California	190	(D)	5	(D)	42	(D)	8.30	(D)
Mississippi	168,000	146,000	5,950	3,850	14,340	8,971	2.41	2.33
North Carolina	(D)	(D)	(D)	(D)	(D)	(D)	(D)	(D)
Texas	(D)	(D)	(D)	(D)	(D)	(D)	(D)	(D)
Other States [1]	9,865	23,240	315	704	956	2,464	3.03	3.10
United States	190,455	169,550	6,742	4,653	16,277	11,503	2.41	2.47
Broodfish:								
Alabama	(D)	(D)	(D)	(D)	(D)	(D)	(D)	(D)
Arkansas	(D)	(D)	(D)	(D)	(D)	(D)	(D)	(D)
California	(D)	-	(D)	-	(D)	-	(D)	-
Mississippi	(D)	(D)	(D)	(D)	(D)	(D)	(D)	(D)
North Carolina	(D)	(D)	(D)	(D)	(D)	(D)	(D)	(D)
Texas	-	(D)	-	(D)	-	(D)	-	(D)
Other States [1]	410	75	1,708	296	1,391	416	0.81	1.41
United States	410	75	1,708	296	1,391	416	0.81	1.41

- Represents zero. (D) Withheld to avoid disclosing data for individual operations. [1] Other States include State estimates not shown and States suppressed due to disclosure.
NASS, Livestock Branch, (202) 720–0585.

Table 15-26.—Trout: Value of fish sold and distributed, by State (excluding eggs), and United States (including and excluding eggs), 2018–2019

State	Total value of fish sold		Total value of distributed fish	
	2018	2019	2018	2019
	1,000 dollars	*1,000 dollars*	*1,000 dollars*	*1,000 dollars*
Arkansas	-	-	3,479	2,550
California	(D)	(D)	8,278	9,434
Colorado	2,978	2,085	6,427	6,452
Georgia	(D)	(D)	1,213	(D)
Idaho	40,290	37,416	(D)	(D)
Michigan	1,558	1,636	2,565	3,658
Missouri	(D)	(D)	4,252	3,738
New York	736	714	5,553	4,760
North Carolina	8,790	7,627	1,973	1,940
Oregon	(D)	(D)	(D)	(D)
Pennsylvania	6,685	6,457	14,823	14,588
Utah	997	1,629	7,961	7,857
Virginia	1,733	1,483	1,983	2,266
Washington	(D)	(D)	(D)	19,269
West Virginia	1,005	1,116	2,663	2,916
Wisconsin	1,493	1,525	1,514	(D)
Other States [1]	35,029	33,884	65,939	56,878
United States				
Value excluding eggs	101,294	95,572	128,623	136,306
Value including eggs	111,879	105,631	(NA)	(NA)

- Represents zero. (D) Withheld to avoid disclosing data for individual operations. (NA) Not available. [1] Other States include State estimates not listed and States supressed due to disclosure.
NASS, Livestock Branch, (202) 720–3570.

Table 15-27.—Trout: Egg Sales, United States, 2014–2019

Year	Number of Eggs	Average Price per 1,000 Eggs	Total Sales [1]
	1,000	*Dollars*	*1,000 dollars*
2014	427,125	20.50	8,774
2015	431,475	20.20	8,706
2016	422,904	21.10	8,921
2017	442,145	21.00	8,844
2018	461,947	22.90	10,585
2019	441,404	22.80	10,059

[1] Due to rounding, total number of eggs multiplied by average price per 1,000 eggs may not exactly equal total sales.
NASS, Livestock Branch, (202) 720-3570.

Table 15-28.—Trout: Sales by size category, States and United States, 2018 and 2019

Size category and State	Number of fish		Live weight		Sales			
	2018	2019	Total [1]		Total [2]		Average price per pound	
			2018	2019	2018	2019	2018	2019
	1,000		*1,000 pounds*		*1,000 dollars*		*Dollars*	
12 inch or longer:								
Arkansas	-	-	-	-	-	-	-	-
California	(D)	(D)	(D)	(D)	(D)	(D)	(D)	(D)
Colorado	430	(D)	591	(D)	2,695	(D)	4.56	(D)
Georgia	(D)	(D)	(D)	(D)	(D)	(D)	(D)	(D)
Idaho	22,200	19,900	27,000	25,000	39,960	37,250	1.48	1.49
Michigan	(D)	(D)	(D)	(D)	(D)	(D)	(D)	(D)
Missouri	(D)	(D)	(D)	(D)	(D)	(D)	(D)	(D)
New York	(D)	(D)	(D)	(D)	(D)	(D)	(D)	(D)
North Carolina	3,640	(D)	4,000	(D)	7,600	(D)	1.90	(D)
Oregon	(D)	(D)	(D)	(D)	(D)	(D)	(D)	(D)
Pennsylvania	1,210	1,090	1,200	1,200	5,136	5,280	4.28	4.40
Utah	200	260	192	288	939	1,336	4.89	4.64
Virginia	460	440	512	540	1,577	1,453	3.08	2.69
Washington	(D)	(D)	(D)	(D)	(D)	(D)	(D)	(D)
West Virginia	450	400	435	410	1,005	1,074	2.31	2.62
Wisconsin	370	340	357	314	1,339	1,410	3.75	4.49
Other States [3]	6,975	9,960	13,261	16,006	31,508	38,039	2.38	2.38
United States	35,935	32,390	47,548	43,758	91,759	85,842	1.93	1.96
6 inch-12 inch:								
Arkansas	-	-	-	-	-	-	-	-
California	(D)	(D)	(D)	(D)	(D)	(D)	(D)	(D)
Colorado	(D)	(D)	(D)	(D)	(D)	(D)	(D)	(D)
Georgia	60	(D)	22	(D)	45	(D)	2.05	(D)
Idaho	(D)	(D)	(D)	(D)	(D)	(D)	(D)	(D)
Michigan	50	80	30	40	150	252	5.20	6.30
Missouri	(D)	(D)	(D)	(D)	(D)	(D)	(D)	(D)
New York	75	65	34	27	214	154	6.30	5.70
North Carolina	(D)	(D)	(D)	(D)	(D)	(D)	(D)	(D)
Oregon	(D)	(D)	(D)	(D)	(D)	(D)	(D)	(D)
Pennsylvania	580	420	339	206	1,454	1,092	4.29	5.30
Utah	(D)	(D)	(D)	(D)	(D)	(D)	(D)	(D)
Virginia	(D)	20	(D)	12	(D)	30	(D)	2.53
Washington	(D)	3,800	(D)	600	(D)	2,226	(D)	3.71
West Virginia	(D)	(D)	(D)	(D)	(D)	(D)	(D)	(D)
Wisconsin	(D)	95	(D)	26	(D)	111	(D)	4.28
Other States [3]	7,285	4,615	1,765	1,268	6,283	4,554	3.56	3.59
United States	8,050	9,095	2,190	2,179	8,152	8,419	3.72	3.86

Size category and State	Number of fish		Live weight		Sales			
	2018	2019	Total [1]		Total [2]		Average price per 1,000 fish	
			2018	2019	2018	2019	2018	2019
	1,000		*1,000 pounds*		*1,000 dollars*		*Dollars*	
1 inch-6 inch:								
Arkansas	-	-	-	-	-	-	-	-
California	(D)	(D)	(D)	(D)	(D)	(D)	(D)	(D)
Colorado	(D)	(D)	(D)	(D)	(D)	(D)	(D)	(D)
Georgia	(D)	-	(D)	-	(D)	-	(D)	-
Idaho	(D)	(D)	(D)	(D)	(D)	(D)	(D)	(D)
Michigan	(D)	(D)	(D)	(D)	(D)	(D)	(D)	(D)
Missouri	(D)	(D)	(D)	(D)	(D)	(D)	(D)	(D)
New York	(D)	(D)	(D)	(D)	(D)	(D)	(D)	(D)
North Carolina	(D)	(D)	(D)	(D)	(D)	(D)	(D)	(D)
Oregon	(D)	(D)	(D)	(D)	(D)	(D)	(D)	(D)
Pennsylvania	210	280	5	7	95	85	452	304
Utah	(D)	(D)	(D)	(D)	(D)	(D)	(D)	(D)
Virginia	(D)	-	(D)	-	(D)	-	(D)	-
Washington	(D)	(D)	(D)	(D)	(D)	(D)	(D)	(D)
West Virginia	(D)	(D)	(D)	(D)	(D)	(D)	(D)	(D)
Wisconsin	(D)	40	(D)	1	(D)	4	(D)	111
Other States [3]	6,505	5,421	149	159	1,288	1,222	198	225
United States	6,715	5,741	154	167	1,383	1,311	206	228

- Represents zero. (D) Withheld to avoid disclosing data for individual operations. [1] Due to rounding, total number of fish multiplied by the average pounds per unit may not exactly equal total live weight. [2] Due to rounding, total number or live weight multiplied by average value per unit may not exactly equal total sales. [3] Other States include State estimates not listed and States supressed due to disclosure.

NASS, Livestock Branch, (202) 720-3570.

Table 15-29.—General storages: Gross and usable cooler and freezer space, by State and United States, October 1, 2019 [1]

State	Cooler		Freezer		Total	
	Gross	Usable	Gross	Usable	Gross	Usable
	1,000 Cubic Feet					
Alabama	613	551	32,808	28,340	33,421	28,892
Alaska	(D)	(D)	(D)	(D)	(D)	(D)
Arizona	(D)	(D)	(D)	(D)	4,103	3,487
Arkansas	4,374	3,780	77,216	69,879	81,590	73,659
California	70,357	53,929	318,953	265,346	389,310	319,275
Colorado	(D)	(D)	(D)	(D)	(D)	(D)
Connecticut	(D)	(D)	(D)	(D)	(D)	(D)
Delaware	(D)	3,241	(D)	15,151	25,033	18,392
Florida	104,771	80,282	147,105	124,800	251,876	205,081
Georgia	33,301	26,860	155,753	132,150	189,054	159,010
Hawaii	-	-	-	-	-	-
Idaho	7,006	5,830	58,358	48,570	65,365	54,400
Illinois	32,521	26,740	158,329	126,798	190,849	153,538
Indiana	(D)	(D)	(D)	(D)	93,964	74,824
Iowa	12,146	9,504	58,526	49,986	70,673	59,490
Kansas	(D)	(D)	(D)	(D)	41,639	33,042
Kentucky	1,529	(D)	22,512	(D)	24,041	22,127
Louisiana	(D)	(D)	(D)	(D)	(D)	(D)
Maine	(D)	(D)	(D)	(D)	7,211	5,638
Maryland	(D)	(D)	(D)	(D)	(D)	(D)
Massachusetts	9,494	7,201	49,977	41,296	59,471	48,497
Michigan	6,912	5,632	82,258	67,135	89,170	72,767
Minnesota	22,219	14,657	73,827	59,231	96,047	73,888
Mississippi	(D)	(D)	(D)	(D)	13,556	11,386
Missouri	27,330	22,249	63,978	55,135	91,308	77,385
Montana	(D)	(D)	(D)	(D)	(D)	(D)
Nebraska	4,325	2,770	43,595	35,195	47,920	37,966
Nevada	(D)	(D)	(D)	(D)	(D)	(D)
New Hampshire	-	-	-	-	-	-
New Jersey	49,632	38,109	87,698	72,773	137,331	110,882
New Mexico	(D)	(D)	(D)	(D)	11,873	8,730
New York	19,074	16,041	42,099	37,939	61,173	53,980
North Carolina	4,453	3,376	58,511	46,693	62,964	50,069
North Dakota	(D)	(D)	(D)	(D)	10,325	7,800
Ohio	6,700	6,179	47,264	39,003	53,963	45,182
Oklahoma	716	(D)	8,824	(D)	9,540	7,330
Oregon	6,102	3,968	134,530	107,026	140,633	110,994
Pennsylvania	48,955	36,683	184,744	158,816	233,699	195,499
Rhode Island	-	-	-	-	-	-
South Carolina	(D)	(D)	(D)	(D)	26,362	17,990
South Dakota	(D)	(D)	(D)	(D)	11,627	6,279
Tennessee	(D)	(D)	(D)	(D)	60,742	52,432
Texas	65,021	52,975	177,175	144,807	242,196	197,782
Utah	12,126	10,636	32,590	26,121	44,715	36,757
Vermont	(D)	(D)	(D)	(D)	4,818	3,219
Virginia	13,079	11,442	64,545	53,597	77,624	65,039
Washington	13,085	10,914	268,557	210,979	281,642	221,893
West Virginia	(D)	(D)	(D)	(D)	(D)	(D)
Wisconsin	113,286	83,501	133,879	115,974	247,166	199,475
Wyoming	-	-	-	-	-	-
United States	758,826	583,333	2,886,664	2,384,326	3,645,495	2,967,658

- Represents zero. (D) Withheld to avoid disclosing data for individual operations. [1] Totals may not add due to rounding.
NASS, Livestock Branch, (202) 720–4751.

Table 15-30.—Refrigerated warehouses: Gross refrigerated space by type of warehouse, United States, biennially, October 2011–2019 [1] [2]

Type	2011	2013	2015	2017	2019
	1,000 Cubic Feet				
General:					
Public	3,028,243	3,076,959	3,138,463	2,834,824	2,683,640
Private and Semiprivate	931,117	978,426	1,030,460	767,331	961,851
Total	3,959,354	4,055,385	4,168,921	3,602,154	3,645,495

[1] Warehouse space is defined as all space artificially cooled to temperatures of 50 degrees F. or less, in which food commodities are normally held for 30 days or longer. [2] Totals may not add due to rounding.
NASS, Livestock Branch, (202) 720–4751.

Table 15-31.—Alaska crops: Acreage harvested, volume harvested, and value of production, 2010–2019

Year	Oats for grain [1]	Barley for grain	All hay	Potatoes [2]
	Acreage harvested			
	Acres	*Acres*	*Acres*	*Acres*
2010	800	4,200	20,000	750
2011	1,000	4,800	19,000	720
2012	900	4,300	22,000	650
2013	400	3,300	20,000	620
2014	1,000	5,100	18,000	620
2015	1,000	4,300	18,000	540
2016	1,200	4,700	22,000	530
2017	900	5,200	21,000	540
2018	(NA)	4,000	22,000	500
2019	(NA)	5,000	22,000	(NA)
	Volume harvested			
	Bushels	*Bushels*	*Tons*	*Cwt.*
2010	48,000	185,000	24,000	150,000
2011	80,000	175,000	22,000	134,000
2012	59,000	207,000	27,000	140,000
2013	15,000	110,000	15,000	130,000
2014	57,000	217,000	25,000	155,000
2015	47,000	146,000	20,000	140,000
2016	74,000	230,000	30,000	147,000
2017	66,000	239,000	25,000	120,000
2018	(NA)	172,000	29,000	140,000
2019	(NA)	190,000	29,000	(NA)
	Value of production			
	Dollars	*Dollars*	*Dollars*	*Dollars*
2010	161,000	814,000	7,320,000	3,570,000
2011	276,000	788,000	6,600,000	3,176,000
2012	212,000	1,107,000	8,505,000	3,864,000
2013	56,000	594,000	5,925,000	3,055,000
2014	211,000	1,183,000	9,625,000	3,395,000
2015	179,000	796,000	7,400,000	2,884,000
2016	274,000	1,208,000	10,200,000	3,308,000
2017	241,000	1,255,000	9,000,000	3,446,000
2018	(NA)	894,000	10,295,000	3,276,000
2019	(NA)	988,000	10,150,000	(NA)

(NA) Not available. [1] Alaska removed from the National Oats Program in 2018. [2] Alaska removed from the National Potato Program in 2019.
NASS, Crops Branch, (202) 720–2127.

Table 15-32.—Crop ranking: Major field crops, rank by production, major States, 2019

Rank	State	Corn, grain	State	Soybeans	State	All wheat
		1,000 bushels		*1,000 bushels*		*1,000 bushels*
1	IA	2,583,900	IL	532,440	KS	338,000
2	IL	1,846,200	IA	501,600	ND	320,760
3	NE	1,785,420	MN	297,880	MT	219,265
4	MN	1,254,250	NE	283,140	WA	142,735
5	IN	814,580	IN	273,360	OK	110,000
6	KS	800,660	MO	230,460	ID	98,755
7	SD	557,280	OH	209,230	CO	98,000
8	MO	463,450	KS	186,335	MN	79,800
9	WI	443,220	ND	170,100	TX	69,700
10	OH	421,480	SD	146,200	SD	66,055
	US	13,619,928	US	3,552,241	US	1,920,139

Rank	State	Winter wheat	State	Durum wheat	State	Other spring wheat
		1,000 bushels		*1,000 bushels*		*1,000 bushels*
1	KS	338,000	ND	25,500	ND	291,550
2	WA	119,000	MT	22,145	MT	102,120
3	OK	110,000	AZ	3,432	MN	79,800
4	CO	98,000	CA	2,244	ID	39,160
5	MT	95,000	ID	435	SD	26,015
6	TX	69,700		....	WA	23,735
7	ID	59,160		....		....
8	NE	55,290		....		....
9	OR	49,640		....		....
10	SD	40,040		....		....
	US	1,304,003	US	53,756	US	562,380

Rank	State	Sorghum, grain	State	Barley	State	Oats
		1,000 bushels		*1,000 bushels*		*1,000 bushels*
1	KS	204,000	ID	54,080	ND	9,890
2	TX	85,400	MT	43,660	WI	6,480
3	SD	14,000	ND	32,040	MN	6,200
4	OK	13,260	CO	7,176	SD	6,150
5	CO	12,710	WY	7,062	IA	4,002
6	NE	12,090	WA	5,880	PA	2,650
7		....	MN	3,685	NY	2,340
8		....	CA	2,838	TX	2,000
9		....	OR	2,418	ME	1,444
10		....	AZ	1,764	MI	1,425
	US	341,460	US	169,566	US	53,148

Rank	State	All cotton	State	Peanuts	State	Rice
		1,000 bales		*1,000 pounds*		*1,000 cwt.*
1	TX	6,337	GA	2,752,200	AR	84,257
2	GA	2,740	FL	589,000	CA	41,933
3	MS	1,621	AL	522,600	LA	26,408
4	AR	1,506	TX	488,000	MO	12,747
5	NC	1,040	NC	448,800	TX	11,028
6	AL	1,028	SC	235,600	MS	8,302
7	TN	960	AR	171,600		
8	MO	915	VA	111,600		
9	CA	821	MS	76,000		
10	OK	659	OK	56,000		
	US	19,913	US	5,466,487	US	184,675

Rank	State	All hay, baled	State	Alfalfa hay, baled	State	Other hay, baled
		1,000 tons		*1,000 tons*		*1,000 tons*
1	TX	9,216	MT	4,515	TX	8,640
2	MO	7,367	SD	4,465	MO	6,665
3	SD	7,003	ID	4,444	OK	5,320
4	KS	6,315	CA	4,118	TN	4,025
5	MT	6,225	NE	3,610	KY	3,960
6	NE	6,085	CO	2,701	KS	3,795
7	OK	5,935	KS	2,520	AR	2,750
8	CA	5,795	IA	2,380	SD	2,538
9	ID	5,111	AZ	2,324	NE	2,475
10	KY	4,424	MN	2,263	VA	2,420
	US	128,864	US	54,875	US	73,989

Rank	State	All tobacco	State	Dry edible beans	State	Potatoes
		1,000 pounds		*1,000 cwt.*		*1,000 cwt.*
1	NC	234,700	ND	7,691	ID	130,900
2	KY	123,390	MN	4,101	WA	104,960
3	TN	30,490	MI	3,662	WI	28,700
4	VA	30,406	NE	1,883	OR	25,311
5	GA	18,900	ID	1,067	MI	20,370
6	SC	15,770	CA	729	CO	19,666
7	PA	14,300	WA	665	ND	19,430
8		....	CO	623	MN	17,845
9		....	WY	390	CA	16,842
10		....		....	ME	16,738
	US	467,956	US	20,811	US	424,419

NASS, Crops Branch, (202) 720–2127.

Table 15-33.—U.S. crop progress: 2019 crop and 5-year average

[In percent]

Week-ending date	Winter wheat							
	Planted		Emerged		Headed		Harvested	
	2018	Avg	2018	Avg	2019	Avg	2019	Avg
2018:								
Sep 9	5	5						
Sep 16	13	14						
Sep 23	28	26						
Sep 30	43	40	14	14				
Oct 7	57	54	30	28				
Oct 14	65	67	44	41				
Oct 21	72	77	53	55				
Oct 28	78	85	63	67				
Nov 4	84	90	70	77				
Nov 11	89	94	77	83				
Nov 18	93	97	81	88				
Nov 25	95	99	86	92				
2019:								
Apr 7	....	....	....	....	3	4		
Apr 14	....	....	....	....	6	9		
Apr 21	....	....	....	....	9	18		
Apr 28	....	....	....	....	19	29		
May 5	....	....	....	....	29	41		
May 12 ...	....	....	....	....	42	54		
May 19 ...	....	....	....	....	54	66		
May 26 ...	....	....	....	....	66	76		
Jun 2	....	....	....	....	76	84		
Jun 9	....	....	....	....	83	91	4	10
Jun 16	....	....	....	....	89	95	8	20
Jun 23	....	....	....	....	94	99	15	34
Jun 30	....	....	....	....	97	100	30	48
Jul 7	....	....	....	....	....	....	47	61
Jul 14	....	....	....	....	....	....	57	71
Jul 21	....	....	....	....	....	....	69	79
Jul 28	....	....	....	....	....	....	75	86
Aug 4	....	....	....	....	....	....	82	92
Aug 11	....	....	....	....	....	....	89	96
Aug 18	....	....	....	....	....	....	93	98
Aug 25	....	....	....	....	....	....	96	99

Week-ending date	Spring wheat							
	Planted		Emerged		Headed		Harvested	
	2019	Avg	2019	Avg	2019	Avg	2019	Avg
2019:								
Apr 7	1	5						
Apr 14	2	13						
Apr 21	5	22						
Apr 28	13	33						
May 5	22	49	4	19				
May 12 ...	45	67	10	34				
May 19 ...	70	80	26	51				
May 26 ...	84	91	47	69				
Jun 2	93	96	69	84				
Jun 9	97	99	85	93				
Jun 16	....	....	95	97	2	12		
Jun 23	....	....	....	....	7	29		
Jun 30	....	....	....	....	25	52		
Jul 7	....	....	....	....	56	73		
Jul 14	....	....	....	....	78	87		
Jul 21	....	....	....	....	92	94		
Jul 28	....	....	....	....	97	98		
Aug 4	....	....	....	....	....	....	2	14
Aug 11	....	....	....	....	....	....	8	30
Aug 18	....	....	....	....	....	....	16	49
Aug 25	....	....	....	....	....	....	38	65
Sep 1	....	....	....	....	....	....	55	78
Sep 8	....	....	....	....	....	....	71	87
Sep 15	....	....	....	....	....	....	76	93
Sep 22	....	....	....	....	....	....	87	97
Sep 29	....	....	....	....	....	....	90	99
Oct 6	....	....	....	....	....	....	91	99
Oct 13	....	....	....	....	....	....	94	100
Oct 20	....	....	....	....	....	....	96	100

See footnote(s) at end of table.

Table 15-33.—U.S. crop progress: 2019 crop and 5-year average—Continued

[In percent]

Week-ending date	Rice							
	Planted		Emerged		Headed		Harvested	
	2019	Avg	2019	Avg	2019	Avg	2019	Avg
2019:								
Mar 31	12	12	2	3				
Apr 7	19	21	7	8				
Apr 14	26	35	13	15				
Apr 21	31	47	18	25				
Apr 28	38	57	27	37				
May 5	48	69	35	50				
May 12	55	82	42	63				
May 19	73	90	52	75				
May 26	84	96	63	83				
Jun 2	91	98	76	91				
Jun 9	96	99	87	96				
Jun 16	......	......	94	99				
Jun 23	......	......	97	100	5	8		
Jun 30	......	......	......	......	10	15		
Jul 7	......	......	......	......	16	22		
Jul 14	......	......	......	......	24	31		
Jul 21	......	......	......	......	31	43		
Jul 28	......	......	......	......	42	57		
Aug 4	......	......	......	......	60	73		
Aug 11	......	......	......	......	76	85	7	9
Aug 18	......	......	......	......	88	93	10	13
Aug 25	......	......	......	......	96	97	15	18
Sep 1	......	......	......	......	......	......	21	27
Sep 8	......	......	......	......	......	......	30	37
Sep 15	......	......	......	......	......	......	46	48
Sep 22	......	......	......	......	......	......	58	61
Sep 29	......	......	......	......	......	......	68	71
Oct 6	......	......	......	......	......	......	76	80
Oct 13	......	......	......	......	......	......	87	88
Oct 20	......	......	......	......	......	......	93	94
Oct 27	......	......	......	......	......	......	97	98

Week-ending date	Corn													
	Planted		Emerged		Silking		Dough		Dented		Mature		Harvested	
	2019	Avg	2019	Avg	2019	Avg	2019	Avg	2019	Avg	2019	Avg	2019	Avg
2019:														
Apr 7	2	2												
Apr 14	3	5												
Apr 21	6	12												
Apr 28	15	27	3	5										
May 5	23	46	6	13										
May 12	30	66	10	29										
May 19	49	80	19	49										
May 26	58	90	32	69										
Jun 2	67	96	46	84										
Jun 9	83	99	62	93										
Jun 16	92	100	79	97										
Jun 23	96	100	89	99										
Jun 30	......	......	94	100										
Jul 7	......	......	98	100	8	22								
Jul 14	......	......	......	......	17	42								
Jul 21	......	......	......	......	35	66	5	10						
Jul 28	......	......	......	......	58	83	13	23						
Aug 4	......	......	......	......	78	93	23	42						
Aug 11	......	......	......	......	90	97	39	61	7	16				
Aug 18	......	......	......	......	95	99	55	76	15	30				
Aug 25	......	......	......	......	......	......	71	87	27	46				
Sep 1	......	......	......	......	......	......	81	93	41	63	6	13		
Sep 8	......	......	......	......	......	......	89	97	55	77	11	24		
Sep 15	......	......	......	......	......	......	93	98	68	87	18	39	4	7
Sep 22	......	......	......	......	......	......	96	100	79	94	29	57	7	11
Sep 29	......	......	......	......	......	......	......	......	88	98	43	73	11	19
Oct 6	......	......	......	......	......	......	......	......	93	99	58	85	15	27
Oct 13	......	......	......	......	......	......	......	......	96	100	73	92	22	36
Oct 20	......	......	......	......	......	......	......	......	......	......	86	97	30	47
Oct 27	......	......	......	......	......	......	......	......	......	......	93	99	41	61
Nov 3	......	......	......	......	......	......	......	......	......	......	96	100	52	75
Nov 10	......	......	......	......	......	......	......	......	......	......	......	......	66	85
Nov 17	......	......	......	......	......	......	......	......	......	......	......	......	76	92
Nov 24	......	......	......	......	......	......	......	......	......	......	......	......	84	96
Dec 1	......	......	......	......	......	......	......	......	......	......	......	......	89	98
Dec 8	......	......	......	......	......	......	......	......	......	......	......	......	92	100

See footnote(s) at end of table.

Table 15-33.—U.S. crop progress: 2019 crop and 5-year average—Continued

[In percent]

Week-ending date	Sorghum									
	Planted		Headed		Coloring		Mature		Harvested	
	2019	Avg	2019	Avg	2019	Avg	2019	Avg	2019	Avg
2019:										
Mar 31	13	9								
Apr 7	14	14								
Apr 14	16	19								
Apr 21	17	22								
Apr 28	20	25								
May 5	22	29								
May 12	24	33								
May 19	26	38								
May 26	28	44								
Jun 2	35	53								
Jun 9	49	68	14	12						
Jun 16	69	81	15	16						
Jun 23	84	91	17	20						
Jun 30	94	96	20	23						
Jul 7	97	99	22	26	13	16				
Jul 14	...	...	24	31	14	19				
Jul 21	...	...	27	40	16	22				
Jul 28	...	...	33	50	21	25				
Aug 4	...	...	45	62	23	30				
Aug 11	...	...	61	74	26	35	19	23		
Aug 18	...	...	75	83	31	43	21	26		
Aug 25	...	...	86	90	41	52	22	30	20	20
Sep 1	...	...	92	95	52	64	24	33	21	22
Sep 8	...	...	97	98	65	74	27	37	22	24
Sep 15	...	...	...	...	79	84	34	44	24	27
Sep 22	...	...	...	...	90	90	42	53	26	31
Sep 29	...	...	...	...	95	95	54	63	30	35
Oct 6	...	...	...	...	...	...	65	73	33	40
Oct 13	...	...	...	...	...	...	81	82	40	46
Oct 20	...	...	...	...	...	...	92	89	49	53
Oct 27	...	...	...	...	...	...	96	94	65	62
Nov 3	...	...	...	...	...	...	...	...	78	72
Nov 10	...	...	...	...	...	...	...	...	88	80
Nov 17	...	...	...	...	...	...	...	...	93	87
Nov 24	...	...	...	...	...	...	...	...	97	92

Week-ending date	Soybeans											
	Planted		Emerged		Blooming		Setting Pods		Dropping Leaves		Harvested	
	2019	Avg	2019	Avg	2019	Avg	2019	Avg	2019	Avg	2019	Avg
2019:												
Apr 21	1	2										
Apr 28	3	6										
May 5	6	14										
May 12	9	29										
May 19	19	47	5	17								
May 26	29	66	11	35								
Jun 2	39	79	19	56								
Jun 9	60	88	34	73								
Jun 16	77	93	55	84								
Jun 23	85	97	71	91								
Jun 30	92	99	83	95								
Jul 7	96	99	90	98	10	32						
Jul 14	...	...	95	99	22	49						
Jul 21	...	...	...	...	40	66	7	28				
Jul 28	...	...	...	...	57	79	21	45				
Aug 4	...	...	...	...	72	87	37	63				
Aug 11	...	...	...	...	82	93	54	76				
Aug 18	...	...	...	...	90	96	68	85				
Aug 25	...	...	...	...	94	99	79	91				
Sep 1	...	...	...	...	96	100	86	96				
Sep 8	...	...	...	...	...	...	92	99				
Sep 15	...	...	...	...	...	...	95	100	15	38		
Sep 22	...	...	...	...	...	...	...	...	34	59		
Sep 29	...	...	...	...	...	...	...	...	55	76	7	20
Oct 6	...	...	...	...	...	...	...	...	72	87	14	34
Oct 13	...	...	...	...	...	...	...	...	85	93	26	49
Oct 20	...	...	...	...	...	...	...	...	94	97	46	64
Oct 27	...	...	...	...	...	...	...	...	97	99	62	78
Nov 3	...	...	...	...	...	...	...	...	...	...	75	87
Nov 10	...	...	...	...	...	...	...	...	...	...	85	92
Nov 17	...	...	...	...	...	...	...	...	...	...	91	95
Nov 24	...	...	...	...	...	...	...	...	...	...	94	97
Dec 1	...	...	...	...	...	...	...	...	...	...	96	99

See footnote(s) at end of table.

Table 15-33.—U.S. crop progress: 2019 crop and 5-year average—Continued

[In percent]

Week-ending date	Cotton, Upland									
	Planted		Squaring		Setting Bolls		Bolls Opening		Harvested	
	2019	Avg	2019	Avg	2019	Avg	2019	Avg	2019	Avg
2019:										
Mar 31	4	3								
Apr 7	6	5								
Apr 14	7	7								
Apr 21	9	9								
Apr 28	11	13								
May 5	18	19								
May 12	26	32								
May 19	44	45								
May 26	57	58								
Jun 2	71	72	8	7						
Jun 9	75	87	11	11						
Jun 16	89	94	19	18						
Jun 23	96	98	30	28	3	5				
Jun 30	...	...	37	39	7	9				
Jul 7	...	...	47	54	13	16				
Jul 14	...	...	60	69	20	25				
Jul 21	...	...	78	80	33	37				
Jul 28	...	...	86	87	45	48				
Aug 4	...	...	95	93	59	61				
Aug 11	...	...	...	...	77	76	20	10		
Aug 18	...	...	...	...	85	85	24	13		
Aug 25	...	...	...	...	90	91	28	19		
Sep 1	...	...	...	...	97	96	36	27		
Sep 8	...	...	...	...	...	...	43	37	7	6
Sep 15	...	...	...	...	...	...	54	47	9	8
Sep 22	...	...	...	...	...	...	64	57	11	11
Sep 29	...	...	...	...	...	...	77	67	16	14
Oct 6	...	...	...	...	...	...	83	75	25	20
Oct 13	...	...	...	...	...	...	87	83	32	27
Oct 20	...	...	...	...	...	...	93	89	40	35
Oct 27	...	...	...	...	...	...	95	93	46	43
Nov 3	...	...	...	...	...	...	...	...	53	51
Nov 10	...	...	...	...	...	...	...	...	62	59
Nov 17	...	...	...	...	...	...	...	...	68	66
Nov 24	...	...	...	...	...	...	...	...	78	74
Dec 1	...	...	...	...	...	...	...	...	83	81
Dec 8	...	...	...	...	...	...	...	...	89	...

Week-ending date	Barley								Oats							
	Planted		Emerged		Headed		Harvested		Planted		Emerged		Headed		Harvested	
	2019	Avg	2019	Avg	2019	Avg	2019	Avg	2019	Avg	2019	Avg	2019	Avg	2019	Avg
2019:																
Mar 31	...	...	...	...	...	...	...	...	25	25	25	23				
Apr 7	2	9	...	...	...	...	...	...	27	32	25	26				
Apr 14	8	19	...	...	...	...	...	...	30	40	26	28				
Apr 21	17	29	2	7	...	...	...	...	36	51	27	33				
Apr 28	28	41	6	15	...	...	...	...	43	61	31	41				
May 5	37	56	12	27	...	...	...	...	50	72	36	51				
May 12	59	72	25	42	...	...	...	...	62	83	43	64				
May 19	76	84	39	57	...	...	...	...	77	90	53	76				
May 26	87	93	54	74	...	...	...	...	85	96	65	86				
Jun 2	94	97	73	85	...	...	...	...	91	98	77	93	23	33		
Jun 9	97	99	86	92	...	...	...	...	96	99	87	97	28	41		
Jun 16	...	...	92	96	2	12	...	...	...	...	94	99	33	54		
Jun 23	...	...	97	99	9	30	...	...	...	...	97	100	43	68		
Jun 30	...	...	...	...	31	52	...	...	...	...	...	...	58	81		
Jul 7	...	...	...	...	55	75	...	...	...	...	...	...	74	90		
Jul 14	...	...	...	...	75	89	...	...	...	...	...	...	87	95		
Jul 21	...	...	...	...	90	95	...	...	...	...	...	...	94	98	12	22
Jul 28	...	...	...	...	96	98	...	...	...	...	...	...	97	100	21	35
Aug 4	...	...	...	...	...	...	3	18	...	...	...	...	...	...	32	49
Aug 11	...	...	...	...	...	...	15	39	...	...	...	...	...	...	48	64
Aug 18	...	...	...	...	...	...	31	59	...	...	...	...	...	...	60	78
Aug 25	...	...	...	...	...	...	54	74	...	...	...	...	...	...	75	86
Sep 1	...	...	...	...	...	...	72	83	...	...	...	...	...	...	84	91
Sep 8	...	...	...	...	...	...	82	92	...	...	...	...	...	...	89	95
Sep 15	...	...	...	...	...	...	87	96	...	...	...	...	...	...	92	97
Sep 22	...	...	...	...	...	...	92	99	...	...	...	...	...	...	96	99
Sep 29	...	...	...	...	...	...	96	100								

See footnote(s) at end of table.

Table 15-33.—U.S. crop progress: 2019 crop and 5-year average—Continued

[In percent]

Week-ending date	Sugarbeets				Sunflower			
	Planted		Harvested		Planted		Harvested	
	2019	Avg	2019	Avg	2019	Avg	2019	Avg
2019:								
Apr 7	3	3						
Apr 14	8	16						
Apr 21	14	34						
Apr 28	25	48						
May 5	31	67						
May 12	63	80						
May 19	90	89	....	....	3	12		
May 26	94	97	....	....	9	27		
Jun 2	97	100	....	....	19	44		
Jun 9	....	....	....	....	42	65		
Jun 16	....	....	....	....	68	80		
Jun 23	....	....	....	....	85	89		
Jun 30	....	....	....	....	95	95		
Sep 15	....	....	8	9	....	....		
Sep 22	....	....	11	13	....	....		
Sep 29	....	....	16	20	....	....		
Oct 6	....	....	19	40	....	....	1	5
Oct 13	....	....	30	60	....	....	5	13
Oct 20	....	....	42	73	....	....	9	27
Oct 27	....	....	58	84	....	....	17	45
Nov 3	....	....	70	91	....	....	31	62
Nov 10	....	....	96	96	....	....	44	75
Nov 17	....	....	....	....	....	....	47	83
Nov 24	....	....	....	....	....	....	56	89
Dec 1	....	....	....	....	....	....	65	94
Dec 8	....	....	....	....	....	....	73	....

Week-ending date	Peanuts					
	Planted		Pegging		Harvested	
	2019	Avg	2019	Avg	2019	Avg
2019:						
Apr 21	2	3				
Apr 28	8	8				
May 5	22	19				
May 12	40	36				
May 19	63	55				
May 26	79	72				
Jun 2	86	85				
Jun 9	91	93				
Jun 16	94	97	16	10		
Jun 23	97	99	34	24		
Jun 30	....	....	47	38		
Jul 7	....	....	58	53		
Jul 14	....	....	67	66		
Jul 21	....	....	78	77		
Jul 28	....	....	84	85		
Aug 4	....	....	92	91		
Aug 11	....	....	96	95		
Sep 15	....	....	....	....	5	5
Sep 22	....	....	....	....	14	10
Sep 29	....	....	....	....	26	19
Oct 6	....	....	....	....	41	30
Oct 13	....	....	....	....	55	42
Oct 20	....	....	....	....	67	55
Oct 27	....	....	....	....	77	67
Nov 3	....	....	....	....	84	78
Nov 10	....	....	....	....	89	85
Nov 17	....	....	....	....	93	90
Nov 24	....	....	....	....	96	94

NASS, Crops Branch, (202) 720–2127.

Appendix I

Telephone Contact List

Appreciation is expressed to the following agencies for their help in this publication. The information offices are listed to provide help to those users who require additional information about specific tables in this publication.

Agricultural Marketing Service:
USDA/AMS
Room 2619 South Bldg.
Washington, DC 20250
202–720–8998

Agricultural Research Service:
USDA/ARS
5601 Sunnyside Ave
Bldg 1, Rm 2251
Beltsville, MD 20705–5128
301–504–1636

Animal and Plant Health Inspection Service:
USDA/APHIS
4700 River Rd
Riverdale, MD 20737
301–851–4100

Center for Nutrition Policy and Promotion:
USDA/CNPP
3101 Park Center Drive
Alexandria, VA 22302
703–305–7600

Economic Research Service:
USDA/ERS
355 E Street, S.W.
Washington, DC 20024-3221
202–694–5050

Farm Credit Administration:
FCA
1501 Farm Credit Dr.
McLean, VA 22102
703–883–4056

Farm Service Agency:
USDA/FSA
Room 4078 South Bldg.
Washington, DC 20250
202–720–7163

Food and Nutrition Service:
USDA/FNS
3101 Park Center Drive, Room 914
Alexandria, VA 22302
703–305–2062

Foreign Agricultural Service:
USDA/FAS
Room 5076 South Bldg.
Washington, DC 20250
202–720–7115

Forest Service:
USDA/FS
2nd Floor Central Wing, Yates Bldg.
Washington, DC 20250
202–205–8333

National Agricultural Statistics Service:
USDA/NASS
Room 5038 South Bldg.
Washington, DC 20250
202–720–3878

National Marine Fisheries Service:
USDC/NOAA/NMFS
1315 East/West Highway,
SSMC III - Room 12405
Silver Spring, MD 20910–3282
301–427–8103

Natural Resources Conservation Service:
USDA/NRCS
Room 6121 South Bldg.
Washington, DC 20250
202–720–2182

Risk Management Agency:
USDA/RMA
Room 403
Kansas City, MO 64133-4675
816–926–1805

Rural Business-Cooperatives Service:
USDA/RECD/RBS
Room 4801 South Bldg.
Washington, DC 20250
202–720–1019

Rural Utilities Service:
USDA/RD/RUS
Stop 1510, Room 5135
1400 Independence Avenue, SW
Washington, DC 20250
202–720–9540

INDEX

www.ingramcontent.com/pod-product-compliance
Lightning Source LLC
LaVergne TN
LVHW052216200926
848481LV00001B/118